Madeleine G. Kalb is a graduate of Wellesley College and received her Ph.D. from Columbia University. A specialist on U.S.-Soviet relations, she has written for the *New York Times Magazine* and other publications. She lived in Moscow during the 1960–1962 period and since then has lived in the Washington, D.C., area with her husband, NBC News diplomatic correspondent Marvin Kalb, and their two children.

THE CONGO CABLES

THE CONGO CABLES

The Cold War in Africa — From Eisenhower to Kennedy

Madeleine G. Kalb

MACMILLAN PUBLISHING CO., INC.

New York

Macmillan Publishing Co., Inc.
866 Third Avenue, New York, N.Y. 10022
Collier Macmillan Canada, Ltd.

Library of Congress Cataloging in Publication Data

Kalb, Madeleine G.
    The Congo cables.

    Bibliography: p.
    Includes index.
    1. United States—Foreign relations—United States.
    2. Zaire—Foreign relations—Zaire.
    3. Soviet Union—Foreign relations—Zaire.
    4. Zaire—Foreign relations—Soviet Union.
    5. Zaire—History—Civil War, 1960-1965—Diplomatic history.
I. Title.
E183.8.Z34K34   967.5′103   81-20936
ISBN 0-02-560620-4   AACR2
                10   9   8   7   6   5   4   3   2   1

Printed in the United States of America

To my mother and my father

Contents

Acknowledgments

I AM GRATEFUL to the many diplomats, officials, and journalists who shared their recollections with me;

to Professor Alexander Dallin of Stanford University, and Professors Marshall D. Shulman, Alexander Erlich, Henry F. Graff, Richard N. Gardner, and John N. Hazard of Columbia University, who provided valuable guidance in the early stages of the research for this project;

to Marjorie M. Geddes and Patricia G. Pancoe, who typed and re-typed the manuscript with diligence and precision;

to Morton L. Janklow and Anne Sibbald, who welcomed the manu-script with enthusiasm;

and, finally, to my husband, Marvin, and my daughters, Deborah and Judith, whose encouragement and patience made it possible for me to persevere.

Preface

ON SEPTEMBER 19, 1960, the Central Intelligence Agency's station chief in Leopoldville, capital of the newly independent Republic of the Congo, received an unusual message from his superiors in Washington via a special top secret channel. Someone from headquarters, calling himself "Joe from Paris," would be arriving in about a week with instructions for an urgent mission. No further details were provided. The station chief was cautioned not to discuss the message with anyone.

"Joe" arrived a week later. He proved to be the CIA's top scientist, and he came equipped with a kit containing an exotic poison designed to produce a fatal disease indigenous to the area. He informed the station chief that this lethal substance was meant for Patrice Lumumba, the recently ousted pro-Soviet Prime Minister of the Congo, who was trying to return to power.

The poison, the scientist said, was somehow to be slipped into Lumumba's food—or even into his toothpaste. Poison was not the only acceptable method of disposing of Lumumba; any form of assassination would do, as long as it could not be traced back to the U.S. government. The astonished station chief pointed out that assassination was not exactly a common CIA tactic, and asked who had authorized the assignment. The scientist indicated that the order had come from "the highest authority"—from President Dwight D. Eisenhower himself.

How did the President, or top officials of the Administration acting in his name, come to be involved in this bizarre assassination plot? Was the idea as "uncommon" as the station chief assumed? Or had it become a routine procedure to be used against inconvenient Third World political figures when other means of removing them proved unsatisfactory? Was the CIA, which had been organized, like its predecessor the OSS, to combat totalitarian tyrannies, beginning to adopt the practices of its opponents? Or had it been doing so all along, on the assumption that certain unpleasant things were necessary in the real world and that as long as they were kept secret, American interests would be served rather than harmed by them?

These questions, which were discussed privately by a very small group of well-informed officials at the time, did not become a subject of public debate until 1975, when the American people, disillusioned by the Watergate scandal, demanded the entire truth about the misdeeds of their elected and appointed leaders, particularly about the abuses of the CIA. In this new atmosphere of candor, President Gerald Ford appointed a blue-ribbon panel headed by Vice President Nelson Rockefeller to investigate charges of illegal CIA activities within the United States. A few days later, while he was discussing Rockefeller's mandate with the editors of *The New York Times*, the President, who had just been briefed about the CIA's attempts to assassinate a series of foreign leaders, referred—inadvertently or deliberately—to these assassination attempts. Although he insisted that his remark be off the record, it was not long before the story was reported, and there were new demands for further investigation. Ford's hot potato was first handed to the Rockefeller Commission and then transferred to the newly formed Senate Select Committee on Intelligence Activities, under the chairmanship of Senator Frank Church, a liberal Idaho Democrat who had been one of the leading critics of the Vietnam War.

CIA Director William Colby followed the lead of the President and supplied the committee with witnesses and top secret documents. His cooperative attitude dismayed former Director Richard Helms, who had been responsible for the Agency's secret operations during most of the period under investigation, and who feared that not only his reputation but the Agency itself could be destroyed by this broadcasting of its secrets. Many of Helms's colleagues shared his dismay, and there were few regrets at CIA headquarters when Ford, who was persuaded by Rockefeller and Secretary of State Henry Kissinger that the disclosures had gone far enough, dismissed Colby in November, just before the Senate committee released its report. The report confirmed the CIA's involvement, over a period of ten years, under four Presidents—two Republicans and two Democrats—in a series of assassination attempts against such foreign leaders as Fidel Castro, Rafael Trujillo, Ngo Dinh Diem—and Patrice Lumumba.

Even before the report was released, I was intrigued by the news leaks indicating that Lumumba was one of the targets of the CIA assassination plots. In the summer of 1960, when Lumumba suddenly emerged as the most dramatic leader in Africa, I was living in Moscow, where my husband was the CBS News bureau chief, and gathering material for a study of Soviet-African relations. I was there when the Congo crisis began and Lumumba turned to the Russians for help. I witnessed their frustration and fury when he was murdered. I recalled their insistent charges that the "imperialists" were responsible for his death and their unofficial hints that the Americans were behind the whole affair.

At the time, these charges were dismissed as propaganda or described as highly exaggerated. Everyone knew that Lumumba had been killed by his Congolese enemies, who were very close to the Belgians. Everyone knew that the Americans were vastly relieved, because they felt that as long as Lumumba was on the scene and the Russians were encouraging him to stir up trouble, it would be impossible for the Congo to achieve any sort of political or economic stability. But the notion that the U.S. government was trying to remove Lumumba by putting poison in his toothpaste would have been regarded by most Americans outside the top levels of government—and thus unaware of the CIA's secret activities—as totally farfetched.

No one doubted at the time, however, that both the Americans and the Russians were playing for high stakes. The Congo was the largest and richest of the sixteen African states scheduled for independence in 1960, and both sides assumed that a pro-Moscow government there would have a major impact on the rest of the continent. When Soviet Premier Nikita Khrushchev decided to send planes, weapons, and military advisers to help Lumumba end the secession of Katanga—the Congo's most valuable province—he confirmed the worst fears of the Eisenhower Administration. The President and his advisers realized that the Soviet leader was taking an unprecedented step, one which threatened to alter the balance between the two superpowers. It was the first time the Russians had ever intervened militarily in a conflict thousands of miles from their borders. The decision was typical of Khrushchev's adventurism; and when it backfired, leading to Lumumba's dismissal as Prime Minister and the expulsion of the Soviet Embassy from Leopoldville, Khrushchev suffered a personal defeat. This defeat was all the more bitter because it took place while he was sailing across the Atlantic en route to New York where he had expected to make a triumphant appearance at the opening of the United Nations General Assembly, with all the new African leaders present.

To an American watching the story unfold from the unique vantage point of Moscow, it was clear that Khrushchev's setback in the Congo had a profound impact on his entire Africa policy, which he had launched with his customary enthusiasm in the spring of 1960. African students responded eagerly to his promises of a free education and flocked to the Soviet Union, where at first they were petted and treated as wonderful curiosities. African diplomats arrived to open new embassies, more wary than the students, but still impressed by a country which apparently had solved the overwhelming problems of economic development by harnessing the energies of its people through a highly organized social and political system. African leaders came, to be honored by Khrushchev and his colleagues at glittering Kremlin receptions, given a grand tour, and then sent home surfeited with offers of trade and aid agreements on terms more favorable than those offered by the West.

The only radical African leader of any consequence who never made the grand tour of the Soviet Union was, ironically, Lumumba, who was removed from power before his cordial relationship with Khrushchev could develop any further. His ouster, and then his death in early 1961, forced the Soviet leader to reexamine his optimistic assumptions and take a serious look at the realities of Africa. By 1962, after a series of disappointments and defeats in the Congo and elsewhere on the continent, Khrushchev was ready to give up his dreams of adventure and adopt a more cautious, realistic policy. He had searched in vain for an effective radical to take Lumumba's place; in the end he decided to settle for full diplomatic relations with a moderate Congolese Prime Minister who was openly pro-American.

The Soviet-American clash in the Congo was one of the most exciting stories of the 1960–1963 period. It had all the ingredients of a first-rate adventure novel—exotic location, dramatic plot, colorful and influential characters caught at a significant moment in their lives—set against a backdrop of crumbling empire, great-power rivalry, and a sudden surge of nationalism across an entire continent. There was intrigue, action, farce—and a double tragedy: eight months after Lumumba was murdered in Katanga, the world was shocked by the news that Dag Hammarskjold, the patient, subtle diplomat who had served for eight years as Secretary-General of the United Nations, had died in a mysterious plane crash while he was trying to negotiate an end to the Katanga secession. The Congo story was a classic cold war confrontation, with the irrepressible Khrushchev facing first Eisenhower, the symbol of Allied cooperation in World War II, and then John F. Kennedy, the representative of a new generation of leaders born in the twentieth century. It spanned a crucial period in Soviet-American relations, which was marked by a series of crises: the U-2 incident and the breakup of the Paris summit; Khrushchev's visit to the United Nations in the middle of the 1960 presidential campaign, when he was so angry about the Congo that he banged his shoe and threatened to bring down the Secretary-General and destroy the entire organization; and, after Kennedy's inauguration, the Bay of Pigs, the Berlin wall, the Soviet resumption of nuclear tests in the atmosphere, and, finally, the Cuban missile crisis.

Before I left Moscow at the end of 1962, I talked to a great many of the African diplomats and students who were living there. I collected every available scrap of published material about Africa in Soviet books, newspapers, popular magazines, and scholarly journals, as well as all the official government statements. When I returned to Washington, I interviewed dozens of people who were involved in the Congo story—American officials, foreign diplomats, UN officials, journalists, and scholars.

In 1975, with the release of the Senate Intelligence Committee report, there was new information available—startling information about the CIA's role in the story. I was eager to see if the government could be persuaded to release additional documents that would shed more light on American policy. The same post-Watergate mood of frankness that had prompted President Ford to mention the assassination plots, and encouraged CIA Director Colby to turn over to the Church committee hundreds of top secret documents from the CIA's files, had also produced the Freedom of Information (FOI) Act—a boon to scholars, a monstrous headache to bureaucrats. Their natural tendency to keep government documents secret was given added impetus by the act's failure to provide adequate funding to cover the costs of searching for the material requested or to hire additional staff to help the hard-pressed desk officers, who, on top of their regular duties, were responsible for reviewing the cables for declassification.

My first FOI requests were sent off in the autumn of 1975. The CIA, whose "family jewels" had already been spread out before the Senate committee, was highly obstructive. Appeals for additional information, even about the cables already cited in the Senate report, produced interminable delays—and in the end all the cables were withheld. The few documents that were released contained no information that could not have been found in *The New York Times*; and there were an astonishing number of completely blank pages. Compared to the CIA with its stonewall approach, the State Department, after an initial period of reluctance, proved to be a gold mine of information. This was due primarily to the cooperation of a few Foreign Service officers, who shall remain nameless, but who know they have my eternal gratitude. They managed to help me break through the Catch-22 system—a system which requires the outsider to request cables by number but refuses to provide even a general idea of what the numbers of the political cables in a given time span might be—and they came up with the first thousand cables, primarily from the Eisenhower period. These documents were declassified very slowly at first, but by 1977–1978 they were being released in a steady stream, with only about ten percent denied for security reasons.

Unfortunately, President Jimmy Carter's reorganization plan reached the FOI office at the State Department at the end of 1978, and the stream dwindled to a mere trickle. My last batch of documents, which arrived in February 1980, contained fewer than half the cables I had requested. It is, of course, impossible to tell whether this was because of the inefficiency of the new system or because of Carter's desire to pull back after the heyday of the post-Watergate revelations and put an end to "excessive" declassification. Before the system was changed, however, I had received some 2,149 documents, approximately half of them from the Eisenhower Administration and half from the Kennedy Administration.

The problem of identifying the relevant documents in the Kennedy period was made considerably easier by the helpful staff members of the John F. Kennedy Library. They are not permitted to declassify documents without the approval of the originating agency; but by working with them and using their lists of cables, I obtained a great deal of material from the State Department which otherwise might not have been available. In addition, the Kennedy Library provided over five hundred recently declassified documents from sources other than the State Department. These documents included fascinating White House papers, ranging from National Security Action Memoranda to detailed records of meetings between the President and his senior advisers, letters to and from the President, and reports to him from special envoys. They also included memos and cables from the Pentagon and the CIA and revealing interviews from the oral history collection.

In addition, I interviewed numerous people involved in the formulation and execution of U.S. policy during this period, including key officials at the State Department and the CIA, some of whom were more willing to talk about the Congo after the Senate revelations than they had been before. I have also drawn on the memoirs of major figures who played a role in the story, such as Eisenhower, Khrushchev, British Prime Minister Harold Macmillan, Ghanaian President Kwame Nkrumah, and Secretary General U Thant, as well as biographies of those participants who did not have the opportunity to write their own memoirs, such as John F. Kennedy, Adlai Stevenson, Dag Hammarskjold, Patrice Lumumba, Joseph Mobutu, and UAR President Gamal Abdel Nasser. I found extremely helpful the memoirs of three UN officials who served in the Congo: Rajeshwar Dayal, Carl von Horn, and Conor Cruise O'Brien. Also essential were the works of scholars and journalists such as Crawford Young, Catherine Hoskyns, René Lemarchand, Helen Kitchen, Colin Legum, and the staff members of the Centre de Recherche et d'Information Socio-Politiques (CRISP) in Brussels—to name but a few.

In the final analysis, however, the most valuable sources were the more than twenty-five hundred government documents—many of them originally classified "Secret" or "Top Secret"—which reveal how diplomacy really works: how the policy is made, and how it is carried out. The President receives conflicting advice from his chief advisers at a meeting of the National Security Council. How do they present their proposals? What sort of questions does he ask? How does he make his decision? How does he make sure that it is not sabotaged by the bureaucrats who disagree with it? How does the Secretary of State explain the President's decision to the Foreign Minister of an allied government who he knows will be violently opposed to it?

These documents constitute a contemporary record of the battles within the Eisenhower and Kennedy Administrations—the debates between the State Department and the Pentagon, the disputes between the U.S. Mission at the United Nations and the U.S. Embassy in Leopoldville—as American officials argued, connived, lobbied, and jockeyed for position, trying to ensure that their views came out on top. Some of these battles involved matters of high principle; others were essentially personality clashes.

The cables present a vivid portrait of three tough-minded diplomats who headed the U.S. Embassy in Leopoldville, each with a distinct personality, each ready to go out on a limb and disobey orders from Washington when he felt they would interfere with a policy that was in the national interest. There was Clare Timberlake, the first ambassador, who reacted to the initial crisis by calling for UN intervention and recommending that U.S. troops hold the fort until the United Nations could arrive, and who later ordered a unit of the U.S. Navy into Congolese waters on his own authority. Next came McMurtrie Godley, chargé d'affaires after Timberlake's recall, who ignored the cautious instructions of Secretary of State Dean Rusk and held out for two agonizing weeks, insisting that the Congolese Parliament could come up with a government that was not dominated by radicals. Finally, there was Edmund Gullion, Kennedy's choice, who fought his own stubborn guerrilla war for more than a year, trying to overcome the Administration's reluctance to let the United Nations end the Katanga secession by military means.

The cables also provide a how-to-do-it manual for every conceivable diplomatic situation: how to encourage a Third World country to replace one leader with another; how to encourage—or discourage—political assassination; how to persuade the Secretary-General, on the rare occasion when his policy runs counter to American policy, that one of his most trusted aides must be dismissed; how to catch Khrushchev off guard with a parliamentary maneuver at the Security Council in New York; how to pull strings in the steamy tropical city of Leopoldville and frustrate the plans of Russian agents about to penetrate the interior of the Congo.

An outsider reading these documents may be struck by the occasional seaminess of U.S. diplomacy; but it should be pointed out that the Russians do not have a Freedom of Information Act. Their public figures rarely hold press conferences. Their government has a complete monopoly on all information, including whatever appears in the press. There is no select committee of the Supreme Soviet authorized to look into the excesses of the KGB. Even with all these restrictions, there are indications in the published Soviet sources that whatever the Americans were doing in the way of bribing members of Parliament, recruiting government ministers, sending in clandestine shipments of arms, and persuading sympathetic UN officials to bend the rules a bit, the Russians were doing too. The only difference was that, in the case of the Congo, their secret operations were less successful than those of the United States.

Introduction

WHEN THE CONGO STORY BEGAN, in 1960, American power and self-confidence were at their height. Not only did we believe we had the best system for others to emulate—as opposed to a totalitarian system that trampled on human rights and liberties—but we were confident that we could make things happen the way we wanted them to, nearly anywhere in the world. We had the power to do so; it was merely a question of figuring out precisely which methods would work best.

The only cloud on the horizon was the growing self-confidence of the Soviet Union, which was reflected in the optimistic pronouncements of Premier Khrushchev. For six years he had followed an independent, unorthodox course, and he was proud of the results. He had not only denounced Stalin's excesses and dismantled most of the system of terror that had burdened Russia for a quarter of a century; he had also freed Soviet foreign policy from the shackles of Stalinist dogma. The late dictator had scorned the leaders of the new neutralist states as imperialist puppets. His view was similar to that of John Foster Dulles: if you're not with us, you're against us. All neutrals were immoral. Khrushchev, unlike his predecessor, understood the potential value of the former colonies. He picked up an old Leninist idea about outflanking the West by lining up the Afro-Asians on the Soviet side. Despite his quarrel with Mao Tse-tung, he included the eight hundred million Chinese for purposes of mathematics as part of the "socialist bloc," which then constituted one-third of the human race. The Afro-Asians constituted a second third. Together, they would form a potent majority in world affairs, tipping the balance of power away from the capitalist nations of the West, led by the United States.

The Soviet leader launched his drive in 1955 with a trip to neutralist India, Burma, and Afghanistan, where his offers of economic and technical aid were warmly welcomed as a counterweight to American assistance and influence. Before long he was supplying arms to Nasser and offering to finance his pet project, the Aswan Dam. By 1960 Khrushchev's campaign was in full swing, as the map of Africa, which had been colored mostly pink (British) and green (French) for the better part of a century, began to change with startling speed.

The process had started in 1957 when the Gold Coast, a small British cocoa-producing colony in West Africa, proudly proclaimed its independence and became Ghana—the first new black African state in over a hundred years. The British transferred power peacefully, after a long period of preparation, to a government headed by Kwame Nkrumah, a popular nationalist leader who had been educated in the United States and England. Ghana was the first of several British colonies scheduled to become independent in the same orderly fashion. With its Parliament and its court system, complete with judges in powdered wigs, it was held up as a fine example of the British tradition of gradual training in self-government.

The French had a somewhat different tradition. They placed little emphasis on local political institutions and made no long-range plans for independence. Instead, they produced a generation of French-speaking intellectuals and encouraged them to look to Paris not only as a cultural center but also as the focus of their political aspirations; prominent members of the African elite were invited to represent their people in the French Parliament. In the summer of 1958, however, President Charles de Gaulle abruptly changed course, in an attempt to defuse the worldwide criticism of French policy in Algeria, where the government was fighting an increasingly brutal war against nationalist forces demanding independence for their country. He went to Brazzaville, capital of the French Congo, and made a speech offering independence to all the colonies in French West and Equatorial Africa, either in association with France or on their own. Only one leader defied de Gaulle and chose total independence: Sékou Touré of Guinea, a radical nationalist trained in the labor movement of French West Africa, who was also the proud descendant of a tribal chieftain who had fought the French nearly a century before. The French colonial administrators left Guinea in a huff, taking everything portable with them. They even ripped out the telephones. Khrushchev, seeing an opportunity to obtain a foothold in black Africa, immediately stepped into the gap and offered Sékou Touré all the aid he needed.

The Belgians took still another path. They had been the masters of the Congo since the late 1870s, when the intrepid journalist and explorer Henry Morton Stanley surveyed the huge territory on behalf of King Leopold, an ambitious man whose own country was too small for his talents. The Congo Free State was officially recognized as Leopold's personal possession by the Berlin Conference of 1885, which parceled out nearly the entire African continent among the European powers. After twenty-three years of unbridled exploitation and fabulous profits, Leopold had provoked so much international criticism by his ruthless methods of collecting the Congo's rubber and ivory that he was forced to yield his private domain to the Belgian government. The sober, prudent officials at the new Colonial Ministry did away with Leopold's most glaring abuses and established a more humane system of government; but they continued to exploit the wealth of the Congo—diamonds, copper, and, later, cobalt and uranium—in close cooperation with the large companies.

Unlike the British, the Belgians trained neither legislators nor judges; unlike the French, they trained neither poets nor trade union leaders. They concentrated instead on turning out medical orderlies, mechanics, and clerks—and virtually ignored the question of higher education. At the time of independence in 1960, there were only sixteen Congolese college graduates in the entire country. The Belgian system was frankly paternalistic. Colonial officials prided themselves on their accomplishments in the fields of housing, health care, and primary education. They saw no need for experiments in self-government; they had no intention of granting independence in the foreseeable future. The Congolese, they explained, were "like children" and would need years and years of tutelage.

Since the Belgians had always considered the Congo a "model colony," they were shocked when de Gaulle's announcement across the river in Brazzaville awakened somnolent Leopoldville. The Congo's infant political parties, which had been permitted to take part in limited municipal elections in the major cities for the first time the previous year, suddenly began to talk about complete independence. The Belgians were even more shocked when riots broke out in Leopoldville in January 1959, and the angry crowds demanded immediate independence.

From then on, events in the Congo resembled a speeded-up movie. Concession followed concession. Dozens of parties sprang up around the country. In January 1960 their leaders were summoned to a round table conference in Brussels, and after a few weeks of hard bargaining, parliamentary elections were set for May and independence for June 30, 1960. Nowhere else in Africa had the decolonization process moved so swiftly. Nowhere else in Africa was the political situation so chaotic. While the British and French policies had encouraged a single nationalist party, or a two-party system, the Belgian government's lack of policy led to a proliferation of small parties, most of them based on tribe or region.

Of these regional parties the most significant was the Alliance des Bakongo (Abako), whose leader, Joseph Kasavubu, was generally regarded as the outstanding nationalist figure in the Congo. Serious, heavy-set, the product of a Catholic seminary education, Kasavubu believed strongly in the traditions of the Bakongo tribe, who lived in Leopoldville and the surrounding area. Abako had begun as a cultural organization reflecting these traditions, but it had burst into politics in 1956, when a group of nationalists in Leopoldville published a startling manifesto calling for political emancipation—within thirty years! Abako, in response, called for immediate emancipation. It quickly acquired a reputation as the most militant political group in the Congo. Abako swept Leopoldville in the urban elections of 1957, and Kasavubu used his platform as local burgomaster to call for national elections and self-government for the entire Congo. He fired the imagination of the Congolese and aroused the suspicions of the Belgians. Following the Leopoldville riots of January 1959, he was arrested, and after two months in jail he was flown to Belgium, where he spent another two months arguing for independence. He was dissatisfied with the Belgian response, and on his return he adopted an even more militant stand. By January 1960 his tactics, which included a massive civil disobedience campaign in Leopoldville Province, had proved successful. He went to the round table conference as the acknowledged leader of the Congolese delegation, the man whose stubborn demands had played a crucial part in convincing the Belgians to grant immediate independence.

The other significant regional party was the Confédération des Associations Tribales du Katanga (Conakat), formed in October 1958. It was led by Moise Tshombe, a shrewd businessman with an American missionary education and a great deal of charm. He had learned early in his political career that a strong anti-Communist stand would win him friends in the West, particularly in the United States, which he visited shortly before independence. From then on, he tended to brand his domestic opponents as Communist agents. Tshombe's tribal base was in south Katanga, the home of the Congo's greatest mineral wealth. His financial support came from Union Minière du Haut Katanga, the giant holding company that controlled the economy of the province. Its principal stockholders were in Belgium and Great Britain, and its political clout in both countries was considerable. It was Union Minière that had supplied the United States with the uranium it needed to build the atomic bomb in World War II, even though Belgium itself was occupied by the Nazis. Now it was supplying more than ten percent of the free world's copper and over sixty percent of its cobalt.

Both Kasavubu and Tshombe favored a federal system, which would give them considerable autonomy; in fact, they had both muttered about seceding from the Congo altogether. The Belgians, who were determined to keep their ex-colony in one piece, began looking around for other groups which shared their preference for a unitary state. They ended up supporting two parties with national rather than local ambitions. The first was the conservative Parti National du Progrès (PNP), which was formed in November 1959, with the support of the colonial administration. Its leaders included a large number of traditional chiefs, and its attitude, like that of Tshombe's Conakat, was openly pro-Belgian.

The other party with a nationwide organization turned out to be far more controversial. The Mouvement National Congolais (MNC) was originally founded in August 1956 by the group which published the manifesto demanding emancipation within thirty years; but it did not take an active role in politics until 1958. Two days after de Gaulle's speech in Brazzaville, the leaders of the group sent a polite but firm petition to the Belgian authorities asking them to set a date for the Congo's independence. One of the signers of this petition was a new-comer to the group, a tall, thin, intense young man named Patrice Lu-mumba. A few weeks later the MNC was formally organized as a political party, and Lumumba quickly became its leader.

Politics was his natural environment. Born in 1925 in Kasai, he had only a primary school education; but he continued to learn as his restless curiosity led him to various jobs in different parts of the country. He spent several years working as a postal clerk in Stanleyville, the capital of Orientale Province, where he joined discussion groups, edited the journal of the postal workers' union, and contributed articles to the newspapers on political subjects. In 1957, after a brief term in prison for embezzlement, he moved on to Leopoldville and a job as sales manager for a brewery. It was at that point that he met the founders of the MNC and was attracted by their commitment to a nationalism which transcended mere tribal allegiances.

Lumumba's horizons were broadened still further in December 1958, when he traveled to Accra for the first All-African People's Conference. Nkrumah encouraged his dream of an independent Congo, and the two men established a close friendship which ended only with Lumumba's death. The young Congolese leader was intrigued by the concept of Pan-Africanism. He looked forward to the day when his country could form a union with Ghana, Guinea, and other like-minded states, and liberate the entire African continent. He was also impressed by Nkrumah's domestic accomplishments and decided to follow his example by turning the MNC into a tightly disciplined party that would be prepared to run a highly centralized government after independence.

In the first few months of 1959, Lumumba's extraordinary abilities as a speaker and organizer helped extend the network of the MNC to every part of the country; but his progress was suddenly cut short in July, when most of the influential party leaders split with him over issues of organization, charging that he had become too dictatorial and was keeping too much power in his own hands. At this point many talented MNC workers left the ranks of the unitary nationalist movement and returned to their own regions to join existing parties or form new ones.

After the split Lumumba recruited new lieutenants, including an ambitious young journalist named Joseph Mobutu, and continued to organize throughout the country. In October he addressed an MNC congress in Stanleyville, his home base. The speech was followed by riots, and he was jailed by the Belgian authorities. He was not released until January 1960, when the participants at the round table conference insisted that he be allowed to attend the meeting.

Lumumba arrived in Brussels, displaying the marks of prison handcuffs, just as Kasavubu walked out over a procedural dispute. He took advantage of Kasavubu's absence to slip into his place as the unofficial leader of the Congolese delegation. Like Kasavubu, he had his badge of imprisonment to prove his anticolonialist credentials. At the same time, he was considered more tractable than Kasavubu on the question of the timing of independence. In fact, Lumumba had a talent for tailoring his views to his audiences and persuading conservatives, socialists, and Communists alike that he agreed with them and would follow their advice once he was in office. The Belgian Communist Party was only too glad to help a young radical who talked about nationalizing the economy and driving the foreign firms out of the Congo. As a start, the Party agreed to supply him with an initial printing of ten thousand political pamphlets for distribution in the campaign.

When Lumumba returned from Brussels, he began to prepare for the May elections. His success at forming alliances with various tribal groups and juggling their antagonisms to benefit the MNC—all the while denouncing tribalism—was a tribute to his skill as a political tactician and orator. At the beginning of this period, he was receiving substantial financial support from Belgian industrialists close to the government, who regarded him as a moderate counterweight to Kasavubu. But the Belgian view of Lumumba changed dramatically during the course of the campaign—so much so that by the time American journalists arrived to cover the elections, their Belgian sources were describing him as a dangerous radical. They charged that he was fomenting anti-European hatred, that he had dictatorial ambitions, and that he was being financed by the Belgian Communist Party. One of his rivals claimed to have a photostat of a check for approximately two hundred thousand dollars from the Belgian Communists which was meant to pay for twenty-four Skoda cars for the use of the MNC; he told the press that the cars were still sitting in a warehouse in Leopoldville because Lumumba was afraid to use the check. Lumumba denied all these charges, but his denials did not convince the skeptical Western reporters.

Lumumba's party did surprisingly well in the May elections. It won 35 of the 137 seats in the Assembly—more than any other party—and it was the only party to win seats in 5 of the 6 provinces. Lumumba became Prime Minister in spite of desperate last-minute attempts by the Belgians to transfer power to a more moderate politician. He appointed a broad coalition government, which included seven ministers from his own party and a number of other radicals. The forty-three-year-old Kasavubu—once feared as a firebrand, now by comparison a safe, familiar figure—was sworn in as President to preserve some sort of balance.

Like many other politicians before and since, Lumumba would discover that it was easier to win the election than to govern effectively. He had come to power as the head of the only nationwide party in the Congo, but he had made a great many enemies along the way. In each province his party's alliance with one tribal group had antagonized all the others. He had received little or no support from the two economic poles of the country, Leopoldville and Elisabethville. It was clear that if he wanted to broaden the base of his support, he would have to make some concessions to the leaders who represented powerful regional interests. His refusal to make these concessions contributed significantly to his downfall in September 1960.

Khrushchev was just as surprised as the Belgians by the political explosion in the Congo—but for him the surprise was a pleasant one. His Africa specialists had given him no indication that Lumumba was the man to watch. They were accustomed to the straightforward political arrangements in the British and French colonies, and they were completely baffled by the multiplicity of parties in the Congo. As late as May 1960, they were still describing Kasavubu as the leading nationalist figure in the Congo and paying comparatively little attention to Lumumba—even though Soviet political operatives in Western Europe had been channeling funds to Lumumba's party for some time through the Belgian Communist Party and various radical African groups. The Soviet Foreign Ministry was obviously basing its assessment on the original Belgian view, which regarded Kasavubu as a menace and Lumumba as a moderate alternative. The agents who disbursed the money were apparently receiving more accurate and up-to-date information from their Belgian Communist and African sources, who must have pointed out the increasing radicalization of Lumumba and his party.

It was not until the elections were over, and Lumumba was confirmed as Prime Minister, that the Africa specialists in Moscow caught up with the Soviet operatives abroad and started to refer to Lumumba in glowing terms as the leader of the most progressive party in the Congo. The Soviet journalists who went to the Congo ahead of time to cover the independence ceremonies confirmed this assessment; they reported that Lumumba favored a tough line toward the Belgians and a neutralist foreign policy.

Khrushchev was astonished that the Belgians were willing to transfer power to anyone as radical as Lumumba; but he concluded that they had no choice. They were simply too weak to stop the onrushing liberation movement, which had succeeded in transforming a sleepy colony into a new nation on the verge of independence within the short space of two years. The Soviet leader believed that Lumumba represented the wave of the future in Africa. All he had to do was establish good relations with the young Prime Minister, offer him whatever help he needed—and sit back and relax. He assumed that the Belgians would try to maintain their influence in the Congo, but he expected them to act indirectly, primarily through economic pressure. He certainly did not anticipate the kind of military intervention that took place a short time after independence or the kind of political intrigues that forced Lumumba out of office. He had no idea, at the end of June, of how difficult it would be to keep a democratically elected Prime Minister in power in a turbulent country thousands of miles away from Moscow.

While the Russians were approaching the Congo on the basis of an ideologically based geopolitical strategy, the Americans were approaching it in a state of blissful ignorance. They had not been paying very much attention to what was going on in the Congo—or in the rest of black Africa for that matter—beyond a vague, benign feeling that all nations should be independent and that the United States, thanks to Woodrow Wilson and Franklin D. Roosevelt, had encouraged the world to move in this direction. For the rest, they were content to leave matters to their allies, who retained the greatest economic stake in the ex-colonies. American investment in Africa, which has grown since that time, was comparatively limited. In 1957, when the State Department established a Bureau of African Affairs, there were more Foreign Service officers assigned to West Germany than there were in all of Africa.

The only Americans who were paying any attention to Africa were people like Chester Bowles and Adlai Stevenson, active in the liberal wing of the Democratic Party, who were interested in the newly independent countries not only because they cared about their welfare, but also because they realized what Khrushchev was up to in Africa and Asia. They felt that it was essential for the United States to counter his offensive by offering aid and sympathetic understanding to the new governments, even when they were highly critical of American policy. This viewpoint was composed of equal parts of hardheaded realism and of a sort of idealism that is hard to recapture these days, when many of the new states appear to be, if anything, more self-interested and cynical than the old. It was based on the notion that countries recently released from colonial bondage would have a keenly developed moral sense and that they could make a special contribution to world peace by offering disinterested advice to the great powers, who were threatening the world with nuclear destruction. This notion was shrewdly encouraged by India's Prime Minister Jawaharlal Nehru, who used it to build neutralism into a major political force over the next few years.

President Eisenhower had little use for this kind of thinking. He had not moved very far beyond John Foster Dulles's fierce view of neutrals, even though his new Secretary of State, Christian Herter, was a milder sort of diplomat. Still, they both looked askance at people like Sékou Touré, who had turned to the Russians out of choice. They were not particularly interested in the explosion of nationalism in Africa in 1960—until they perceived the threat of a Soviet takeover in the middle of the continent. At the time the Congo became independent, the U.S. government was aware of Belgian concern that Lumumba was a radical who had received financial support from the Communist bloc, that he had appointed a leftist cabinet, and that he might accept Soviet offers of economic aid. But there was no sense of urgency in Washington until two weeks after independence, when Lumumba turned to the Russians for military assistance.

The immediate reaction of CIA Director Allen Dulles was that Lumumba was "a Castro, or worse." The Cuban situation had begun to obsess the Eisenhower Administration as it would later obsess the Kennedy Administration. Fidel Castro had come to power in the final days of 1958 with widespread support, both from the Cuban people and from the Americans, who were no longer willing to prop up his corrupt predecessor, the dictator Fulgencio Batista. Castro had received a triumphant welcome in the United States in the spring of 1959; but after that he had moved steadily leftward, installing Communists in positions of power and aligning himself openly with the Soviet Union. U.S. officials felt betrayed. When another charismatic left-wing leader turned up in the heart of Africa and appealed to Moscow for military aid, they assumed they were seeing a repetition of the Cuban experience.

Eisenhower and his advisers responded in a direct, pragmatic fashion to what they regarded as a major Soviet challenge. They cooperated closely with Belgium and the other NATO allies; they supported the most conservative figures in the Congo; and they sent "Joe from Paris" to try to assassinate Lumumba. When Kennedy came into office, he dealt with the Soviet challenge in a somewhat different way. He parted company with Belgium and the other NATO allies on a number of key issues, including the Katanga secession; he cultivated the neutralists, both in the Congo and in the rest of Africa; and he made certain that Lumumba's self-proclaimed successor, the radical Antoine Gizenga, was not assassinated after he was removed from power. Kennedy's tactics were different from Eisenhower's, but his underlying goal was the same: he was determined to frustrate Khrushchev's plans and prevent a Soviet takeover in the Congo. The cry, "The Russians are coming!" was guaranteed to produce results in the White House, whether it was occupied by Dwight D. Eisenhower or John F. Kennedy.

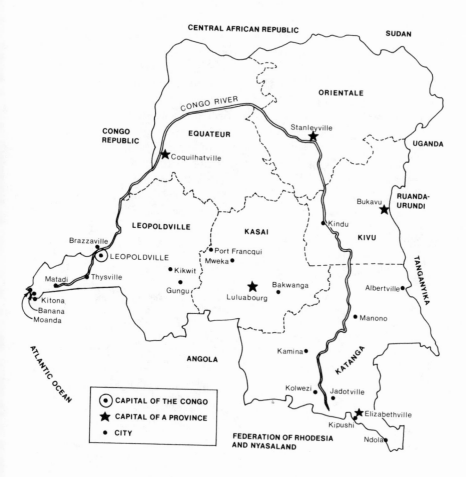

CENTRAL AFRICAN REPUBLIC

SUDAN

ORIENTALE

CONGO RIVER

CONGO
REPUBLIC

EQUATEUR

Stanleyville

UGANDA

Coquilhatville

Bukavu

RUANDA-
URUNDI

LEOPOLDVILLE

KASAI

Kindu

KIVU

Brazzaville

Port Francqui

LEOPOLDVILLE

Mweka

TANGANYIKA

Kikwit

Matadi

Thysville

Gungu

Bakwanga

Albertville

Kitona

Luluabourg

Banana

Moanda

Manono

ATLANTIC OCEAN

ANGOLA

Kamina

KATANGA

Kolwezi

Jadotville

Elizabethville

Kipushi

FEDERATION OF RHODESIA
AND NYASALAND

Ndola

CAPITAL OF THE CONGO

CAPITAL OF A PROVINCE

CITY

AFRICA IN 1960

Colony or trust territory

Independent before 1960

Independent in 1960

TUNISIA
SPANISH SAHARA
MOROCCO
ALGERIA
LIBYA
U.A.R.
SENEGAL
MAURITANIA
MALI
NIGER
CHAD
SUDAN
FRENCH SOMALILAND
PORT GUINEA
UPPER VOLTA
NIGERIA
CENTRAL AFRICAN REPUB.
ETHIOPIA
GUINEA
IVORY COAST
CAMEROON
SIERRA LEONE
GHANA
LIBERIA
DAHOMEY
TOGO
GABON
EQUATORIAL GUINEA
CONGO REPUBLIC
THE CONGO
RUANDA URUNDI
UGANDA
KENYA
SOMALIA
TANGANYIKA
ANGOLA
NORTH. RHODESIA
SOUTH. RHOD.
NYASALAND
MOZAMBIQUE
SOUTHWEST AFRICA
BOTSWANA
SOUTH AFRICA
MALAGAYSY REPUBLIC

PART ONE
The Eisenhower Policy

CHAPTER ONE

The Crisis Begins
(June 30–July 15,1960)

"This should keep bears out of the Congo caviar."

THE TROUBLE STARTED on independence day. It was June 30, 1960, and the Belgians were about to transfer sovereignty to the Republic of the Congo after seventy-five years of colonial rule. King Baudouin and Prime Minister Gaston Eyskens, accompanied by a host of distinguished officials, had flown to Leopoldville to preside over the festivities. In his opening address, the King proudly reviewed Belgium's contribution to the development of the Congo and wished the new nation success and prosperity. The President of the Congo, Joseph Kasavubu, responded in a spirit of gratitude and conciliation. It was clear that his radical period was behind him, and that now, with his goal of independence achieved, this portly, taciturn provincial politician would be willing to cooperate with the Congo's former rulers.

Suddenly the self-congratulatory mood was broken, as Patrice Lumumba, the Congo's new Prime Minister, stepped forward with a fiery denunciation of the very policy Baudouin regarded with such pride. His eyes flashing, his bearded chin thrust forward in an attitude of defiance, Lumumba accused the Belgians of bringing slavery and oppression to the Congo. He described his people's struggle for independence in terms of "tears, fire, and blood." He made no attempt to conciliate the Belgians. "Our wounds are too fresh to forget," he proclaimed.[1]

Lumumba's maiden speech was noted far beyond the borders of the Congo. The Russians were delighted by the discomfiture of the Belgian officials who had been forced to sit through his angry tirade.[2] They assumed that he was merely twisting the imperialist tail; they had no idea that his militant approach would soon involve them in a major international crisis. For the moment it seemed to them that everything was moving along smoothly in the direction Khrushchev had charted: a radical nationalist, eager to establish good relations with the

[3]

Soviet Union, was coming to power peacefully in a rich new state in the heart of the African continent.

The American reaction to Lumumba's speech was somewhat wary. The newly arrived U.S. ambassador, Clare Timberlake, a seasoned Foreign Service officer who saw the world in stark cold war terms, reported that the Belgians in Leopoldville considered it "ominous." They felt that Lumumba had "once again showed his unreliability and shiftiness."[3] They were not reassured by the fact that before the day was over Lumumba had been persuaded to offer the King a public apology.[4] They were convinced that the morning's outburst reflected his true feelings. Timberlake and his small U.S. Embassy staff were concerned about the haste of the Congo's independence arrangements and the fragility of its political balance. They hoped that the controversy about the speech would blow over and that Lumumba would realize that he needed Belgian assistance to keep his country running smoothly.

But their hopes were shattered by a sudden outburst of violence only a few days after independence. Disgruntled Congolese soldiers mutinied against their Belgian officers, touching off a series of events that would produce a major cold war confrontation between the United States and the Soviet Union.

Coping with the Mutiny

The mutiny began on the evening of July 5 in Thysville, ninety miles from the capital. Congolese soldiers locked up their Belgian officers and demanded promotions, pay increases, and the dismissal of General Emile Janssens, the commander of the twenty-five-thousand-man Force Publique. Dissatisfaction had been building up for months. Despite Belgian promises, there was not a single Congolese officer at the time of independence, and the soldiers contrasted their own dismal prospects with the new-found wealth and influence of the civilian politicians—yesterday's clerks and salesmen—who were driving around in big limousines and spending money freely.[5] Four days of independence celebrations, with extra hours on duty to put down tribal street brawls, did not help matters. The last straw came on July 4, when General Janssens, in a clumsy attempt to instill discipline, told the soldiers in Leopoldville that there would be no change in their status as a result of independence.[6]

By July 6, the unrest had spread to the capital. Angry soldiers roamed the streets and demonstrated outside the Parliament building. The Council of Ministers met in an atmosphere of panic. The ministers had no idea at first who was behind the mutiny, and a number of them had gone into hiding, fearing they would be arrested. Anicet Kashamura, the left-wing Minister of Information, suggested that they might all feel more secure if they ordered the arrest of their major opponents, who had been excluded from the government—but this suggestion was rejected. The only minister who remained comparatively calm was the pro-Belgian Albert Delvaux, who assured his colleagues that Belgium would be able to handle the situation.[7]

Lumumba quickly learned that his authority over the rebellious troops was extremely limited. When he went to the army camp and told them to obey their officers, they ignored his advice and pounded on the doors of his car. He managed to calm them down temporarily by promoting them all one rank and dismissing General Janssens,[8] but there was worse to come. On the evening of July 7 a train filled with Belgian refugees from Thysville pulled into the capital, and the horror stories about rapes and shootings by mutinous soldiers spread through the European quarter. All through the night terrified men, women, and children flocked to the river, hoping to find a place on the steamer to Brazzaville and safety. Coincidentally, Lumumba's aides arrested four Europeans outside his residence and claimed they were part of a plot to assassinate him. Congolese soldiers immediately began stopping Europeans and searching them for weapons. Other Congolese troops rushed frantically to the airport because of rumors that the Russians were invading the country.

July 8 was a day of panic and total anarchy. At 4:00 A.M. the British Embassy ordered the evacuation of nonessential personnel. At 7:00 A.M. the French Embassy followed suit. Several thousand Europeans, mostly women and children, fled to Brazzaville before the mutineers cut off their escape route. Four boats under rebel command patrolled the river, threatening to fire on anyone who tried to cross. Telephone wires were cut. The radio station stopped functioning. The U.S. Embassy's only contact with the outside world was through a walkie-talkie to the U.S. Consulate in Brazzaville. By noontime, the Embassy, where more than seventy Americans had taken refuge, was completely surrounded by mutinous troops. At one point they barged in and demanded that a photographer be handed over to them; but Ambassador Timberlake managed to stand them off.

By evening things had calmed down considerably; Lumumba had yielded to the mutineers' demands and dismissed all their Belgian officers.[9] A curfew was established and telephone communications were restored. But the mutiny could not be contained. As new trouble spots erupted, Lumumba, accompanied by Kasavubu, flew from one end of the vast country to another, trying to persuade the rebellious troops to return to their barracks. Their presence generally served to restore order for the time being; but as soon as they left the scene, violence would break out once again.

Meanwhile, as news of the refugees from Thysville began to reach their families and friends at home, there were mounting demands in the press and Parliament that the government use Belgian troops to restore order. The government, fearing that armed intervention might touch off a violent reaction in areas as yet untouched by the mutiny, was reluctant to act without a request from the Congolese. Lumumba, who had asked Belgian Ambassador Jean van den Bosch on July 6 whether the Belgians would be prepared to supply troops if the Congolese government asked them to do so,[10] still held back, refusing to issue that request.

Officials in the Belgian Foreign Office, who had never had much confidence in Lumumba, began to suspect that he was conniving with the rioters, or, at the very least, that he was reluctant to ask for Belgian help because he wanted to take advantage of the disorders to assume dictatorial powers. They worried about rumors that he was inviting a Czech military mission to run the Force Publique, and they began to speculate privately about the desirability of persuading Kasuvubu to remove him from office.[11] Lumumba, on the other hand, suspected that the Belgians were fomenting the disorders, or, at the very least, that they welcomed them as proof that his government was incompetent, so that they could return to power in the Congo in the guise of restoring order.

On July 9 the Belgian government announced that it was sending twelve hundred men to reinforce the twenty-five hundred troops already stationed at two major bases in the Congo: Kitona, near Leopoldville, and Kamina, in the southern province of Katanga. It stated that the troops would not intervene without a specific request from the Congolese government but added that it would of course be "unthinkable that Belgian soldiers . . . should stand idly by if there should be serious attacks against Europeans."[12] On July 10 the troops went into action for the first time. Eight hundred Belgian paratroopers, responding to a request from provincial president Moise Tshombe, restored order in Elisabethville, the capital of Katanga, after mutinous troops killed six Europeans. Over the next week Belgian troops would intervene in more than twenty localities throughout the Congo. Brussels issued a communiqué explaining that they were intervening only to save human lives and stressing Belgian respect for the Congo's independence.

On July 11 Kasavubu and Lumumba flew into Luluabourg, the diamond-mining capital of Kasai Province. They found the situation of the European population there so dangerous that they set aside their pride and agreed to limited intervention by Belgian troops, "provided their mission was restricted to the protection of persons and property."[13] This was the first time—and the last—that they agreed to rely on

Belgian military assistance. A few hours later they learned that Belgian forces had bombarded the port of Matadi, near Leopoldville, killing a number of Congolese,[14] and that Katanga, the richest province of the Congo, had declared its independence. The following day, as Kasavubu and Lumumba prepared to land in Elisabethville for discussions with Tshombe, the local authorities, backed by Belgian troops, refused to give them permission to land.[15]

The United States Considers Military Intervention

Kasavubu and Lumumba demanded that all Belgian troops be withdrawn immediately,[16] and cast about desperately for another source of aid. This process had in fact begun a few days earlier. On July 10 they had made an oral request for UN assistance in restoring order, through veteran diplomat Dr. Ralph Bunche, United Nations Under Secretary for Special Political Affairs, who had represented the world organization at the Congo's independence festivities and remained in Leopoldville, anticipating trouble.[17]

At the time it was not generally known that the July 10 request was initiated by U.S. Ambassador Timberlake, who acted on his own and checked with Washington afterward for approval. Timberlake believed that anarchy in the Congo would have repercussions far beyond the immediate crisis: it would play directly into the hands of the Russians by providing an opportunity for radical forces to take over and undermine Western interests in this rich and strategic part of Africa. At the same time he realized that the only action capable of preventing anarchy—intervention by Belgian troops—would also play into Soviet hands: it would antagonize the new Congolese government and give the Russians an excellent opportunity to stress their anti-imperialist solidarity with the new African states. Since it was apparent by July 9 that the Belgians had decided to intervene, even without an invitation, Timberlake concluded that the best way out of the impasse was to place the intervention under a UN umbrella. A UN commander could be sent to Leopoldville immediately to take nominal charge of the Belgian troops, who would later be replaced by other troops, from small countries. The great powers would be excluded.

"This should keep bears out of the Congo caviar," he explained to Secretary of State Herter and Under Secretary Douglas Dillon in a cable marked "Secret—Eyes Only." "I assume most Americans have not yet developed a great taste for it either."[18]

Timberlake asked Bunche how long it would take for the United Nations to "get effective forces moving" after a Security Council decision to act. Bunche replied that it could be done in "a matter of hours" but pointed out that first the United Nations would need an official request from the Congolese government. Timberlake was unable to track down Kasavubu and Lumumba until the following day, when he intercepted them at the airport. He spent an hour explaining the advantages of a UN force, which would help bring the mutinous soldiers under control and restore order.[19] At four o'clock that afternoon, Kasavubu and Lumumba met with Bunche and officially requested UN action.

Two days later, when this request had not produced immediate results, Timberlake was visited by an impatient group of Congolese cabinet ministers led by Deputy Premier Antoine Gizenga and Foreign Minister Justin Bomboko. They were an unlikely pair: Gizenga was a gloomy Marxist, who had traveled to Eastern Europe in 1959 and had come back more radical than Lumumba. Bomboko was a dapper university graduate, cheerful and lively, who enjoyed the good things of life and had no objection to profiting from his pro-Western inclinations, which were quite genuine. He had distinguished himself on July 8 by rescuing Belgian civilians from mobs of rebellious soldiers, at considerable personal risk. Gizenga and Bomboko asked the U.S. ambassador for two thousand American troops "to insure the maintenance of order in the lower Congo and Leopoldville."[20] Timberlake counseled patience, explaining first, that, the United Nations could not act so swiftly, and, second, that the U.S. government would in all likelihood refuse to send troops to the Congo on its own; the only way American troops could be sent would be under the auspices of the United Nations. He agreed to transmit the request, however, provided it be given to him in writing. Bomboko immediately went into the next room and typed out the request.

While Timberlake publicly held out little chance for a favorable response, his private reports to Washington indicated that he welcomed the request for American troops, which fit in extremely well with his own recommendations. Before Bomboko and Gizenga stopped in to see him on the morning of July 12, he had told the State Department that the situation in Leopoldville had reached a "most critical juncture." Food stocks were nearly exhausted; four thousand armed Force Publique troops might go on a rampage again at any time; and even if they did not set off a popular riot, they would be powerless to stop one. He warned:

I WOULD BE DERELICT IF I DID NOT CLEARLY INDICATE IMMINENT NEED FOR LARGE SCALE TROOP INTERVENTION WHEN (I DO NOT BELIEVE THERE IS AN IF INVOLVED) RIOTING BEGINS.

The nearest Belgian troops were fully occupied with the fighting at Matadi. French officials were ordering reinforcements to Brazzaville, to be used only if requested by the United Nations or the Congolese government. The Pentagon had announced the previous day that two companies of the U.S. Twenty-Fourth Division in West Germany had been put on alert to help evacuate refugees from the Congo if it became necessary. Timberlake suggested that if the U.S. government was prepared to "use troops on UN request" that they "airlifted immediately to Brazzaville."[21]

Once the Congolese had officially requested American troops, Timberlake could make a stronger case for U.S. intervention. Later that day he reported the situation was so critical that small numbers of French and Belgian paratroopers were standing by for emergency evacuation of Europeans. He cabled:

> I BELIEVE EVEN TOKEN FORCE OF TWO COMPANIES AMERICAN FORCES MIGHT SERVE STABILIZE SITUATION LONG ENOUGH TO PERMIT PEACEFUL ENTRY FOLLOWING FORCES. CANNOT TOO GREATLY URGE MOST IMMEDIATE DESPATCH OF THE TWO COMPANIES OF TROOPS AND WHEAT FLOUR AIRLIFT.[22]

That evening, Bomboko came back to the Embassy to see if there was any reply to his request. He showed Timberlake a message he had sent, at the ambassador's suggestion, to several African countries, asking for their support and explaining that the Congo's request for American assistance should be seen in the context of its appeal to the United Nations. This move was designed to forestall Soviet criticism of the request, which Timberlake considered inevitable. He told Bomboko that he had not had any word from Washington and repeated that he did not believe U.S. troops would be sent to the Congo except under UN auspices.[23]

At this point the summer White House in Newport announced that President Eisenhower had categorically ruled out the use of U.S. troops in the Congo under any circumstances, including participation in a UN force. The State Department denied that Timberlake had recommended the use of American troops and insisted that he had merely passed along the Congolese request. Meanwhile, the U.S. Navy announced that the aircraft carrier *Wasp*, with about fifteen light passenger planes, including helicopters, was heading for the Congo from the Caribbean on standby orders to evacuate refugees if needed.[24]

Lumumba, who was out of the capital, denounced the Gizenga-Bomboko appeal to the United States as soon as he learned about it. While his cabinet was asking for American military aid without his approval, he and Kasavubu were sending the United Nations a second request, which dramatically changed the terms of their original appeal. At first they had asked for help in restoring order; now—alarmed by exaggerated reports of the death toll at Matadi—they asked for the "urgent despatch" of UN troops to protect the Congo against an external threat. They charged that Belgian military intervention in the absence of a request from the Congolese government constituted "an act of aggression," and they accused the Belgians of masterminding the secession of Katanga.[25]

Khrushchev Takes a Stand

The Belgian intervention touched off a sharp reaction in Moscow. Premier Khrushchev had been abroad on a state visit to Austria when the first news of the mutiny broke. He had returned home on July 8, but the Congo was not at the top of his agenda. He had been under considerable pressure from his rivals in the "collective leadership" regarding a variety of domestic issues; now they were undoubtedly beginning to raise questions about his handling of foreign affairs as well.[26] His relations with his Chinese allies were becoming increasingly strained, and he was struggling to prevent an open split in the world Communist movement. His relations with the United States had taken a sharp turn for the worse in May in the wake of the U-2 incident in which a high-altitude spy plane was shot down over the Soviet Union; the Soviet leader had stormed out of the four-power summit meeting in Paris before it had a chance to begin, furious because President Eisenhower had acknowledged his responsibility for the incident but had refused to apologize. The most pressing foreign policy problem facing Khrushchev on his return to Moscow was the issue of another American reconnaissance plane, an RB-47 shot down by the Soviet Union on July 1 over what the Russians claimed was Soviet territory. The U.S. government disputed this claim; and Khrushchev did not send a protest note about the incident until July 11, which indicated a certain degree of doubt about the proper course to follow.

Up to this point events in the Congo were on the back burner. There was no reference to the mutiny in the Soviet press until July 10, when *Izvestia* mentioned it briefly.[27] But Khrushchev could not ignore the dramatic events of July 11. He had assumed that decolonization in Africa would proceed without much violence; he expected the Western powers to try to maintain their economic control over the newly independent nations and to use other indirect means of pressure to keep them in line, but this direct application of military force caught him by surprise. He could not accept the Belgian explanation that the troops had been sent reluctantly, and only to protect the lives of Belgian civilians. He felt it was much more likely that when they realized Lumumba was about to embark on a truly independent course, they decided to use force to reassert their control over the Congo. The mutiny was merely a convenient pretext. Khrushchev saw the secession of Katanga as further evidence of conspiracy: Tshombe, regarded by

Moscow as a "pro-Belgian stooge" even before independence, was attempting to deprive the struggling young Lumumba government of its most highly developed province and its major source of revenue in order to keep the area under the direct control of the giant Belgian holding company, Union Minière du Haut Katanga. The fact that Tshombe was relying openly on Belgian troops and Belgian advisers confirmed this view.

Khrushchev's instinctive distrust of Belgian motives was reinforced by reports from Soviet journalists and diplomats in Leopoldville. *Pravda* correspondent O. Orestov, for example, insisted that there was no real reason for the panic that gripped the European section of Leopoldville and caused hundreds of Belgian families to flee to Brazzaville or Brussels; it had been encouraged deliberately by "Belgian provocateurs," who were spreading false rumors to alarm the European population. He managed to retain his sympathy for the mutinous soldiers even when he became a target of their frantic search for Belgian spies. Since it was difficult for the Congolese to distinguish Russians from other Europeans, the *Pravda* correspondent found himself rounded up with the other foreigners at his hotel by Congolese soldiers, who poked rifles in their backs while their rooms were subjected to a thorough search. Before the day was over, he was released.[28]

Orestov was not the only Russian to be molested. Mirzo R. Rakhmatov, the head of the Soviet delegation at the independence ceremonies, was described at one point by the gleeful American ambassador as "roughed-up, mad and protesting."[29] Rakhmatov, a politician from Tadzhikistan who was clearly awkward in his new role of diplomat, survived several hair-raising episodes. At one point, he was summoned to the airport to find his plane impounded and the entire crew under arrest. It took hours for the Congolese minister accompanying the Soviet delegation to persuade the soldiers to release the crew. On the night of July 8, just before he left for home, Rakhmatov ventured out in the city for an evening stroll with a few friends. Suddenly they were stopped by a Congolese military patrol. "The soldiers mistook us for representatives of some foreign stock company," he wrote in his memoirs, "and for this reason they treated us at first with suspicion." But when the Soviet officials explained who they were, one of the Congolese broke into a grin and cried, "Khrushchev! Sputnik!" The Russians were released immediately, with cordial handshakes all around.[30]

On July 12 Khrushchev called a rare Moscow news conference to publicize his protest to the United States about the RB-47 incident, and he used the opportunity to blast Western policy in the Congo.[31] His remarks put the Soviet Union firmly on record in support of the Congolese government. But in this fast-moving, unprecedented situation, rhetorical support was not enough. The Soviet leader was forced to make a quick decision about a concrete course of action favored by the independent African states.

The First Security Council Meeting: July 13–14, 1960

While Khrushchev was holding his press conference in Moscow, the African delegates to the United Nations—led by Tunisian Ambassador Mongi Slim, the widely respected moderate African representative on the Security Council—were meeting in the tall glass building on the East River with Secretary-General Dag Hammarskjold, who had returned hastily from Geneva the night before to try to resolve the Congo crisis. Hammarskjold, a brilliant economist and diplomat from one of Sweden's most distinguished families, had become the United Nations' second Secretary-General in 1953, at the age of forty-seven. This slight, sandy-haired intellectual, who spent his spare time climbing mountains and corresponding with philosophers and theologians, had established a reputation as a dedicated international civil servant who was at his best in subtle, complex negotiations.

Hammarskjold had been looking forward to "Africa Year"—when sixteen new African nations were scheduled for independence—as an opportunity for the United Nations to play an expanded role in the field of economic and technical assistance. He was not expecting a major political crisis that would threaten to destroy the United Nations itself. When he received the first Congolese request for assistance, on July 10, he felt it could be handled without a formal resolution of the Security Council; but as the situation grew more complicated and violent, he changed his mind. According to Brian Urquhart, his colleague and biographer, he became deeply concerned about the possibility of great-power intervention and was convinced that only "an immediate and conspicuous military intervention by the UN" could avert this possibility.[32]

On the morning of July 13, he requested an "urgent meeting" of the Security Council to discuss the Congo situation, which posed a threat to "international peace and security."[33] By the time the Council met that evening, he and Slim were ready with a plan to send a UN force to replace the Belgian troops in the Congo—a plan designed to command the support, or at least the abstention, of all the Council members.

The first paragraph of their draft resolution called on the Belgian government to withdraw its troops from the Congo. This concession to the Afro-Asians had been made over the objections of the Western powers, who pointed out that Belgium had agreed to remove its troops willingly once the UN force had arrived and could maintain order. The second paragraph authorized the Secretary-General to provide military assistance, in consultation with the Congolese government, until the "national security forces" could "fully meet their tasks." This last point, by implication, took care of the problem of restoring order and was designed to meet Western objections.[34]

Hammarskjold knew he could count on American support. While U.S. officials were reluctant to take the lead publicly because of their fear of a Soviet veto, they were working closely with the Secretary-General behind the scenes. They agreed essentially with his approach; their primary concern was that the Tunisian draft resolution should not accuse their ally, Belgium, of aggression. Hammarskjold discussed this problem with Belgian Ambassador Walter Loridan, a courtly, soft-spoken diplomat, who assured him of Belgian cooperation. The two men agreed that the Secretary-General would not use the term "Belgian aggression" and that the Belgian government would "welcome" the UN presence in the Congo. Hammarskjold also determined that if the draft contained no charge of aggression against Belgium, the British and French would refrain from vetoing it. Although they were not enthusiastic about UN intervention, they would abstain and thus permit adoption of the resolution.

The only question mark was the Soviet Union. Hammarskjold was fairly certain that the Russians would not veto the Tunisian draft resolution. As he told the Americans, the fact that he had lined up African support ahead of time would make it "extremely difficult" for them to do so. Besides, he had spoken to Soviet Ambassador Arkady Sobolev earlier in the day, and Sobolev, a genial, gregarious diplomat, had raised no objection to the plan.[35]

Khrushchev really had very little choice. He had indicated at his press conference that he did not expect anything more of the Security Council meeting than the chance to strike a few propaganda blows. When it turned out that the Western powers were willing to permit a UN force to go to the aid of the Congolese, and that the African states were supporting this move and urging the Soviet Union to join them, he could hardly reject their appeal without undermining his reputation as a supporter of African independence.[36]

Still, the Soviet leader was not going to let the meeting go by without underscoring his differences with the Western powers on the subject of colonialism. He instructed Sobolev to read an official government statement which accused the United States and its allies of following a "dangerous policy of aggression and provocation" by joining the "Belgian plot" to "destroy the Congo's independence." It also condemned the secession of Katanga as an "illegal and criminal action, dictated by the mercenary interests of the financial and industrial magnates of the commercial powers."

U.S. Ambassador Henry Cabot Lodge, the Boston Brahmin who had been battling Soviet opponents at the United Nations since 1953, dismissed the statement as "a ponderous, long-winded bit of Communist nonsense." Sobolev then turned his attention to the carefully worded Tunisian draft resolution and introduced three amendments which would have destroyed the delicate balance created by Hammarskjold and Slim: they condemned Belgian "aggression," called for the "immediate" withdrawal of Belgian troops, and limited the UN force to African troops.[37]

All three Soviet amendments were defeated; but Sobolev refused to back down on his second demand. While he joined the United States and six other states to vote for the resolution, he insisted that the Belgian troops should be withdrawn "immediately, unconditionally, and without regard to any other provision in the resolution."[38] Lodge, on the other hand, insisted that the Belgian troops would leave only when UN troops could replace them and maintain order.

An Appeal to Moscow

While their status was being debated in New York, Belgian troops swung into action in Leopoldville for the first time. On the morning of July 13, they took over the airport, where their presence was welcomed by terrified and exhausted refugees. They then began to restore order in the European part of the city. They met with scattered resistance from Congolese soldiers. Belgian Ambassador van den Bosch sent Gizenga a note explaining that since the Congolese government had been unable to maintain order, his government had a "moral obligation" to take action to preserve lives and property. He assured Gizenga that the measure was a temporary one and promised that Belgian forces would cooperate with the UN troops once they arrived. After a stormy session of Parliament, where Kashamura accused the Belgians of "declaring war" on the Congo, Gizenga appealed to Ghana for military aid. Nkrumah responded immediately; his government was ready to send troops "either directly or through the United Nations." In the first of many warnings that would fall on increasingly deaf ears, he urged the Congolese not to seek the involvement of "powers outside the African continent."[39]

On the afternoon of July 14, Kasavubu and Lumumba flew back to Leopoldville from the provinces to find the airport controlled by Belgian troops. They expected to be arrested. Much to their surprise, they were asked to review a Belgian honor guard. They refused to do so. In the presence of a large group of Belgian paratroopers, civilian refugees, journalists, and diplomats, they engaged in a heated exchange with the Belgian commanding general about who was to blame for the bloodshed in the Congo. As the tension mounted, Lumumba spotted a familiar face in the crowd. He threw himself into the arms of John

Elliott, the Ghanaian ambassador to Moscow, and he and Kasavubu were escorted back to the city by a phalanx of Ghanaian diplomats.[40]

The confrontation at the airport was not the most dramatic event of the day, however; before they left Kindu, deep in the Congo's interior, Kasavubu and Lumumba had sent a message to Brussels announcing that they were breaking diplomatic relations with Belgium.[41] Then, in a move that set alarm bells ringing in every Western capital, they appealed to Khrushchev to follow the situation carefully and suggested that they might be forced to "ask for the intervention of the Soviet Union" if the Western camp did not "stop its aggression" against the Congo. "At the present time," they explained, "Congolese territory is occupied by Belgian troops and the lives of the President and Prime Minister are in danger."[42]

Khrushchev's reply, sent the following day, was prompt and sympathetic; but it did not commit him to any specific action. The Soviet leader pointed out that the Security Council had done a "useful thing" by adopting a resolution aimed at getting the Belgian army out of the Congo. At the same time, he warned that if the aggression continued despite the resolution, it would become necessary to take "more active measures both in the United Nations and in cooperation with other peace-loving governments."[43] What these measures might consist of was left unclear.

With this reply, as with his vote for the Security Council resolution, Khrushchev hedged his bets. He indicated a willingness to work with the African governments that were eager to utilize the United Nations; and at the same time he left the door open for further unilateral measures to aid the Lumumba government if the UN force did not accomplish what he regarded as its proper objectives.

This direct appeal to Moscow, coming immediately after the harsh Soviet statement of July 13 and the message from Kasavubu and Lumumba breaking diplomatic relations, confirmed Belgian suspicions that Lumumba was "operating under Soviet guidance." On the evening of July 14, Belgium's ambassador to NATO, Andre de Staercke, outlined his government's position at a special meeting of the North Atlantic Council in Paris. He explained that Belgian troops could not possibly be withdrawn before the United Nations was in a position to guarantee the protection of the Europeans in the Congo. If they were forced to leave, he warned, it would give the Communists a "free hand." He described Kasavubu as a "hostage of Lumumba," and referred to Kashamura, the Minister of Information, as a known Communist. The situation would be better, he remarked, if the President, the Prime Minister, and the Minister of Information all "disappeared from the scene." There was some discussion of issuing a statement on the subject of troop withdrawals, but the United States successfully opposed this move, suggesting that it might be better, for the time being, to let the Secretary-General handle the problem on his own.[44]

Secretary of State Herter took the same line the following day, when Belgian Ambassador Louis Scheyven raised the possibility that Khrushchev's threats about "further steps" might lead to "armed Soviet intervention" and urged the Secretary to warn the Russians that they would have to face the United States if they intervened in the Congo. Herter was evidently less alarmed than his visitor. He pointed out that the Russians would face a number of practical problems if they tried to intervene: it would be a "difficult and lengthy move by air," and if they tried to "move by sea" the U.S. aircraft carrier *Wasp* would be off the Congolese coast before they could get there. He assured Scheyven that he would give consideration to the matter of an American warning to Khrushchev, but he stressed that the "first responsibility" in the area now rested with the United Nations. If the United Nations failed to meet this responsibility, he added, "then perhaps we should reconsider."[45]

U.S. officials were not yet ready for a major confrontation with the Soviet Union about the Congo. They regarded Khrushchev's threats as part of a pattern of belligerent anti-Western behavior that had developed in the wake of the U-2 incident and the failure of the Paris summit: the Russians had withdrawn their delegation from the ten-nation disarmament talks in Geneva; they had shot down an American plane over international waters; and they had warned the United States that they would respond forcefully to any American attempt to intervene against the Castro regime in Cuba. American policymakers were disturbed by this pattern, but they did not yet have a clear reading of Khrushchev's intentions and they were not sure what their response should be. They were glad to see the Congo problem deposited in the lap of the Secretary-General. Ironically, both the Russians and the Americans were counting on the United Nations to deal with the Congo issue—although the two great powers were expecting somewhat different results from the UN operation, and one or the other was bound to be disappointed.

CHAPTER TWO

Testing the United Nations Option
(July 15–August 9, 1960)

"Now no one can tell me that man is irrational!"

A FEW DAYS AFTER the UN operation in the Congo got under-way, Secretary-General Dag Hammarskjold was discussing its pros-pects with one of his colleagues at the Secretariat. He drew two straight lines, which were not quite parallel; if neither one diverged from its path, they would eventually intersect. He then explained:

> "This is our policy in the Congo, and that is the policy of the Soviet Union. For the moment, our interests are nearly parallel, and the Russians will cooperate with us. But there is no doubt in my mind that we are on a col-lision course, and that eventually the two policy lines will clash. I hope we can delay that clash long enough to find a peaceful solution to the Congo's problems.

Soviet Objections to the UN Force

Khrushchev had acquiesced in the creation of a UN force for the Congo because it was the course recommended by the African states and because it seemed the best way to replace the Belgian troops, and thus to help the Lumumba government. Still, he was aware that he had taken a risk by voting to create a politico-military entity which he could not control.[1] He knew that Hammarskjold was likely to work closely with the Americans, who had brought the United Nations into the picture in the hope of strengthening their own position in the Con-go; and, as a result, he was not about to accept any of Hammarskjold's arrangements without careful scrutiny.

One of his earliest disagreements with the Secretary-General con-cerned the composition of the UN force. At the Security Council meet-ing on the night of July 13, Hammarskjold had proposed guidelines providing that troops be drawn first from African countries and then from states which were not permanent members of the Security Council (i.e., not the great powers). He did not spell out his reasoning at the meeting, but he had two purposes in mind. First, as he explained to Lodge, he wanted to make it clear to the independent African states that they had the "main responsibility" for the UN effort in the Congo; this would "stop in advance" any Soviet claims that the operation was "disguised imperialism."[2] At the same time, he wanted a free hand to send European troops as well as African ones. He realized that this was the only way to reassure the remaining Belgians, whose continued presence was essential to the "day-to-day economic and administrative life of the Congo."[3]

The Americans had already pledged their support for these guidelines, with the understanding that no Soviet bloc countries would be asked to provide troops. They were willing to make an exception for Yugoslavia, however, as long as Yugoslav troops were kept to a "reasonable number" and were not given a major command. They believed that this exception would help Hammarskjold "neutralize" the Soviet Union.[4] But the Russians, dissatisfied with these ground rules, had proposed an all-African force—presumably on the assumption that European units would be too sympathetic to the Belgian position.

After Sobolev's amendment limiting the force to African troops was defeated, the Secretary-General moved swiftly to implement the Security Council resolution according to his original guidelines. He returned to his office at 3:25 A.M., and by 6:30 A.M. on July 14 he had set in motion an unprecedented operation. The first troops arrived in Leopoldville on the evening of July 15. By July 17 the UN force, created from scratch, numbered over thirty-five hundred men, from Ethiopia, Ghana, Morocco, and Tunisia. By the end of the month there were over eleven thousand soldiers, including contingents from Hammarskjold's own neutral Sweden and from Ireland, another neutral European country. For practical reasons Hammarskjold used broader guidelines in his requests for technical and transport units, calling on countries closely linked with the United States and the Soviet Union for specialized assistance and asking the great powers themselves—the United States, the Soviet Union, and Great Britain—to provide an airlift to ferry the troops to the Congo.[5]

A few days after the first troops arrived, the Russians charged that the Secretary-General had tried to block the participation of Guinea, a radical African state.[6] This charge was emphatically denied by UN officials, who pointed out that Guinean troops were on their way to the Congo by the time Moscow brought up the issue.[7] In fact, however, Hammarskjold did try to delay the arrival of the Guinean contingent. He informed Sékou Touré that he did not need Guinean troops immediately, and firmly declined the Guinean President's offer of "political advisers," who, he confided to Lodge, would be "impossible."[8] Hammarskjold preferred to launch the UN force with troops from the more conservative African states, which had no political axe to grind in the Congo.[9]

Keeping Guinean troops out was bad enough, from the Soviet point of view; but bringing American troops in was totally unacceptable. On July 19, Soviet Foreign Minister Andrei Gromyko called the American chargé d'affaires, Edward Freers, to his office and presented him with a note stating that the reported arrival of twenty American soldiers in Leopoldville was an "impermissible act" and demanding their "immediate" withdrawal.[10] A State Department spokesman quickly responded that these were not combat troops; they were specialists who had been requested by the Secretary-General to help with the airlift of UN troops and supplies. He termed the Soviet charge a "desperate and almost frantic" effort to stir up trouble in the Congo.[11]

Soviet officials were not impressed by this argument; what the United States described as a generous contribution to the UN peacekeeping effort consistent with America's traditional policy of support for the world organization, they saw as the opening wedge of an American drive for total control of the Congo operation. They became more and more convinced that their analysis was correct as they learned of the scope of the American effort. The "twenty soldiers" whose presence led to Gromyko's protest on July 19 were, according to a U.S. Defense Department statement released the same day, actually one hundred men—fifty sent by the Army to help Ambassador Timberlake in the "operation, maintenance, and ground support of six light planes and three helicopters for use in evacuation"; and fifty sent by the Air Force to help the United Nations with "traffic control, weather service, airport operations and maintenance."[12]

The American contribution did not stop there. From the start of the operation, the bulk of UN troops were flown into the Congo by the U.S. Air Force. By July 18, four days after the adoption of the first resolution, 2,522 soldiers from Tunisia, Morocco, and Ghana had arrived on American planes.[13] By July 28 some eighty U.S. transport planes—C-130 Hercules turboprops and C-124 Globemasters—had made 211 flights to Leopoldville carrying Ghanaian, Moroccan, Tunisian, Swedish, Liberian, and Guinean troops, and twenty-six flights from Addis Ababa to Stanleyville, in the northeastern part of the Congo, carrying Ethiopian troops; and they were in the process of flying Irish troops from Ireland direct to Bukavu in the southeastern part of the Congo. Moreover, the United States was providing ten DC-3's and a number of helicopters to the UN command for internal flights.[14]

In contrast, the Russians were providing five Ilyushin-18 turboprops to transport food supplies from the Soviet Union and to ferry Ghanaian troops from Accra to Leopoldville. The Soviet press described these flights with great pride, less as a contribution to the UN effort than as a form of bilateral aid to a country under colonialist attack.[15] A *Pravda* correspondent who accompanied one of the Ilyushin flights to Rabat, Accra, and Leopoldville repeatedly stressed the difficulties involved in the Soviet airlift. While Western planes were able to fly along the coast, on a well-established route dotted by airports, he explained, the Soviet pilots were forced to take an uncharted route, over the Sahara Desert, the Atlas Mountains, and the Atlantic Ocean. Their problems did not end when they reached their destination: he charged that on one occasion the American technicians in the control tower at the Leopoldville airport turned off the power "at the most critical moment," when a Soviet pilot needed landing instructions; and he claimed that this was but one of many such incidents.[16]

These reports were intended to demonstrate the generosity and steadfastness of the Soviet effort in the face of American provocation; at the same time they demonstrated that the Russians were operating at a disadvantage and could not compete with the United States, particularly in the mounting of a complex airborne maneuver.[17] Khrushchev's awareness of this problem would play an important role in his calculations later in the summer, when he made his decision to intervene in support of Lumumba.

Soviet concern about the American role in the Congo extended well beyond technical personnel; the Russians insisted that the leaders of the UN operation—both civilian and military—took their orders from Washington. Since Hammarskjold's first special representative in the Congo, Ralph Bunche, was an American, he was automatically regarded with suspicion; and the fact that he worked closely with the U.S. ambassador in the early days of the crisis did not help to dispel that suspicion.[18]

The Soviet reaction to General Carl von Horn, the Swedish officer chosen by Hammarskjold to head the UN force, was less automatic. Von Horn was called from UN duty in Jerusalem and, after waiting impatiently for transport for several days, arrived in the Congo on July 17, two days after his first troops had landed. After he had been on the job for ten days, *Pravda*[19] and *Izvestia*[20] had reached diametrically opposed conclusions about him—a rare occurrence in Soviet journalism. Von Horn remained in the Congo until December 1960, and by that time the more critical assessment had prevailed.[21] The Russians had concluded that von Horn was hostile to their interests in the Congo.

The Soviet government also complained about the level of officials just below the top. The original staff officers who accompanied von Horn to the Congo were from Canada, Sweden, New Zealand, and Italy,[22] and they were later joined by officers from Denmark, Great Britain, and Ghana.[23] Not one of the military advisers came from Eastern Europe.

Hammarskjold tried to deal with this kind of criticism by stressing the important jobs—both military and civilian—that were held by Africans and Asians.[24] He assumed that by giving them a large role in the operation he could refute the charge that he was working too closely with the Western powers. But this did not really get to the heart of the Soviet complaint. The Russians felt that, in general, they themselves were not sufficiently well represented at the decision-making levels of the UN Secretariat, and that in the specific case of the Congo, UN officials—American, European, or Afro-Asian—were working to further Western interests and to frustrate Soviet interests.

The first problem was not a new one. Top UN officials had traditionally been reluctant to place Soviet or East European personnel in sensitive positions because it was assumed that their primary loyalty was to their country or ideology, rather than to the international body which they were supposed to serve. This distrust was carried so far that, according to Conor Cruise O'Brien—the Irish diplomat who would play a controversial role as Hammarskjold's representative in Katanga in 1961—Georgi Arkadiev, the Soviet official serving as UN Under Secretary for Political and Security Council Affairs, "did not have access to the Congo files." Instead, they were under the control of a man who was in theory Arkadiev's subordinate but who was actually Hammarskjold's eminence grise—Heinrich Wieschhoff.[25] Other UN officials recall that Arkadiev was systematically excluded from Hammarskjold's staff meetings when they dealt with sensitive subjects, such as the Congo. In the Congo itself the same principle operated; it was inconceivable that General von Horn would have chosen a Bulgarian, a Czech, a Pole, and a Yugoslav as his first four staff officers.

The Russians, conversely, were convinced that Western officials serving in the UN Secretariat were not really dedicated to some impartial international ideal, as they claimed, but were essentially representatives of their own governments. In fact, there was usually more common ground between the principles and policies of the Secretariat and the Western governments than there was between the Secretariat and the Soviet government; as a result the problem of divided loyalties was far less acute for the Western officials serving the United Nations.

During the first two months of the Congo operation, Hammarskjold and the Eisenhower Administration saw many of the issues the same way, while Khrushchev took the opposite view. The Secretary-General and the Americans agreed that Belgian interests should be considered as well as Congolese. They agreed that there should be European troops in the UN force as well as Africans. They agreed that Guinea would play a disruptive role and that its opportunities to make mischief should be limited as much as possible.

But the main area of agreement was an unstated assumption that Khrushchev could not help but regard as hostile—the assumption that all great powers were equal, but some were more equal than others. Hammarskjold did not hesitate to ask the United States for major technical assistance—in the areas of troop transport, communications, and emergency food relief—because he believed that the United States would not try to undermine his attempts to deal with the Belgians and the Congolese in a fair and impartial manner. He simply did not have that kind of confidence in the Soviet Union.

This belief in American support was not based entirely on starry-eyed faith in the world's greatest democracy; Hammarskjold also recognized that the U.S. government would back up his policies in the Congo because they were not in conflict with its own. The Secretary-General and other UN officials repeatedly stated that they were moving into the Congo to "fill the power vacuum left by the Belgians" or to "prevent various forms of outside intervention" or to "keep the cold war out of Africa." These were all ambiguous phrases that could be interpreted in a number of ways. When President Nkrumah of Ghana spoke about "keeping the cold war out of Africa," it was clear that he meant "a plague on both your houses"—East and West. When Henry Cabot Lodge used the term, he meant that the United States would do everything in its power to prevent the Russians from gaining more influence in the area—political, military, or economic. Hammarskjold tacitly took a position that was closer to Lodge's view than to Nkrumah's. Officially, he maintained a policy of opposition to all outside interference, Belgian as well as Soviet; in the process he incurred the hostility of the Belgian government as well as that of the Soviet government. The threat of increased Soviet influence in Africa was not his major concern, as it was Washington's. But he clearly believed that the United Nations could handle the situation better if the Russians did not stir up trouble—and most of his top aides shared that view.

For Bunche and General von Horn in the early days of the operation, the primary threat of interference came from the Soviet Union. Von Horn recalled in his memoirs that shortly after his arrival, Bunche spelled out the tasks facing the UN force. After listing the official duties—replacing the Belgian troops, restoring order, training the Congolese troops—he added a point which did not appear in any of Hammarskjold's reports. "Lastly," he wrote, "since Lumumba's known Communist sympathies had already resulted in appeals for Soviet help, we must be ready to prevent any unilateral interference from outside."[26] Von Horn was receptive to this idea. His attitude was uncompromisingly pro-Western and anti-Communist. He was somewhat doubtful of Congolese abilities and ready to sympathize with the Belgian plight and accept the Belgian position at face value. He shared Hammarskjold's view of Guinea's Congo policy, and as soon as the heavily armed Guinean contingent arrived, with its "six political commissars," he sent them to a remote jungle region to prevent them from interfering in the capital, where their government wanted them to be.[27] He found it perfectly natural to detail UN guards to observe the comings and goings at the Soviet and Czechoslovak Embassies later in the summer when a massive influx of personnel arrived to aid Lumumba.[28]

These UN officials did not always see eye to eye with the American government, however; on occasion, Bunche made a decision as an international civil servant which Timberlake opposed. Perhaps the most controversial and far-reaching of these decisions involved the disarming of Congolese troops by the UN force. This was an issue on which Bunche found himself in disagreement with General Henry T. Alexander, the forceful British officer who served as Ghana's defense chief and commanded the first detachment of Ghanaian troops ordered to the Congo by Nkrumah even before the UN force was set up. Upon his arrival in Leopoldville, Alexander realized it would be extremely difficult for a small international force to maintain order while unruly bands of armed soldiers were permitted to roam the streets. He proposed disarming the Force Publique—now called the Armée Nationale Congolaise (ANC)—not totally, as he later explained, but simply to have them keep their weapons in the armory "as normal armies" do when they went home at night.[29] Alexander was strongly supported in this policy by Timberlake, who was impressed by his "level-headed" approach.[30] Von Horn, who disliked Alexander and resented the fact that he had taken charge while von Horn was waiting in Jerusalem, backed him up on this issue: Alexander's proposals, he wrote, "made extremely sound sense and would have been unhesitatingly adopted in any normal army. Unfortunately," he went on, "we were not 'any army'; we were a United Nations Force in which logic, military principles—even common sense—took second place to political factors."[31] The "political factors" were represented by Ralph Bunche. Bunche, who was eager to avoid violence, agreed that disarming and retraining the ANC was a fine idea—in fact, it was precisely what the United Nations had been called in to do in the first place—but he insisted that it could be done only with the consent of the central government. After a promising beginning, Lumumba, sensitive about his powers and his country's sovereignty, refused to give that consent. Bunche refused to ignore his wishes, and the soldiers kept their remaining arms. Many Western observers felt that a unique opportunity had been missed because of Bunche's political sensitivities. Soviet observers, on the other hand, ignored Bunche's stand and continued to charge that he was ignoring the wishes of the Congolese government and helping the Americans to sabotage the Security Council resolution.

Soviet claims that Bunche and his colleagues were tools of a conspiracy directed from Washington were grossly exaggerated; but there is no doubt that their preconceptions, attitudes, and beliefs caused them to see the situation in much the same way that the American government did. If, for example, a Yugoslav general had been named commander of the force—a possibility that Lodge raised and opposed at the very start—he might have seen the role of the United Nations in quite different terms.

Lumumba's Ultimatum: Alarm at the White House

It was perhaps inevitable, given this set of circumstances, that Khrushchev would feel the deck was stacked against him and that his disagreement with Hammarskjold over the composition of the force and the nationality of its leaders would develop into a more basic dispute about the policy the force would follow. But Hammarskjold hoped to postpone this confrontation as long as possible. His diplomatic skill had served him well in many crises, and one of his major accomplishments had been the fact that he had remained firm in a number of difficult situations involving Soviet interests without irrevocably alienating the Soviet Union. At the beginning of the Congo crisis, it appeared that he might succeed again. Khrushchev had approved the basic thrust of his mandate: to secure the withdrawal of Belgian troops from the Congo. The early communications between the Soviet government and the Secretariat were correct, though not particularly cordial; and UN officials felt that they had done much to allay Soviet as well as Congolese suspicion by their rapid action in setting up the force and arranging for it to begin replacing the Belgian troops in Leopoldville.

But they had not taken into account the unique character of the Congo's Prime Minister, Patrice Lumumba. On the evening of July 17—just forty-eight hours after the arrival of the first UN troops—General Alexander returned to Leopoldville from Stanleyville with extremely disturbing news. Alexander had asked Bunche, Timberlake, and General Roger A. Gheysen, the commander of the Belgian forces in Leopoldville, to meet him at the airport, where they were joined by Foreign Minister Bomboko and the Congo's new ambassador to the United Nations, Thomas Kanza, another of the Congo's few university graduates. Alexander handed Bunche an ultimatum signed by Kasavubu and Lumumba threatening that they would ask the Soviet Union to intervene if the United Nations did not remove all Belgian troops from the Congo by midnight on July 19. They claimed that Bunche had promised that the Belgian forces would leave upon the arrival of the UN force, and they were now holding him to that promise. Bunche denied that he had made any such promise and called the demand totally unrealistic. He pointed out that the United Nations had "never been served with an ultimatum and does not accept ultimatums." Bomboko and Kanza were shocked and said they would try to get the decision reversed at a cabinet meeting as soon as Lumumba and Kasavubu returned from Stanleyville. There was no doubt that the ultimatum was the work of Lumumba. Alexander told Timberlake he felt Kasavubu was "not happy" about the "direction being taken by Lumumba" but seemed to be "weak and under [Lumumba's] thumb."[32]

This ultimatum to the United Nations had a dramatic impact on Lumumba's political position. Its immediate effect was to put additional pressure on Belgium. The Americans joined forces with Hammarskjold to persuade the Belgians to begin a "prompt and ostentatious withdrawal" of their troops as United Nations troops moved in to provide security.[33] On July 19 Secretary of State Herter urged the Belgian ambassador in Washington to announce the withdrawal before the Security Council met the following day, so that Moscow could not exploit the issue.[34] On July 20 Bunche and von Horn reached an agreement with Belgian Ambassador Van den Bosch and General Gheysen: all Belgian troops would be out of Leopoldville by July 23. Von Horn promised unofficially that he would not hesitate to call them back if he found he needed help.[35]

In this limited sense Lumumba's tactic was successful. But in a larger sense it backfired. First, it antagonized Bunche and the other UN officials, who felt they were making an unprecedented effort to help the Congolese and could not understand why that effort was not appreciated. Lumumba's criticism of the United Nations sparked a series of violent incidents directed against UN personnel; and these, in turn, persuaded high-ranking officials of the world body that the Congo's Prime Minister was perhaps the greatest single impediment to a peaceful solution of the Congo's problems.

Next, it increased the pressure on Premier Khrushchev and probably forced him to become more deeply involved in defending Lumumba's interests than he had originally intended. In a sense Khrushchev was responsible for the UN force being in the Congo; his delegate had voted for the resolution that had set it up, rather than vetoing it. If it now turned out that the force was ignoring the wishes of the Congolese government, the Soviet leader felt obliged to set things straight. His options were still limited. He could continue along the political route and hope that the threat of Soviet intervention would persuade the United Nations to carry out the Security Council mandate as Lumumba understood it. But if that approach failed, Khrushchev might have to act on Lumumba's appeals for direct Soviet aid—or lose his credibility with the radical Afro-Asians and within the Communist world.

Finally, the ultimatum alarmed American officials who had been concerned about Lumumba's interest in the Communist bloc but had tended to accept with a grain of salt Belgian descriptions of him as a Communist. The U.S. Embassy in Leopoldville had not yet written Lumumba off; it had, in fact, made it a policy to establish a friendly relationship with the young Prime Minister. Timberlake had had a cordial meeting with him on July 7, before the United Nations entered the picture; the two men had laid the groundwork for a bilateral technical aid agreement. As the crisis developed, the two U.S. Embassy officers who were in most frequent contact with Lumumba were Frank Carlucci, the second secretary, a tough, able Foreign Service officer who developed an encyclopedic knowledge of Congolese political personalities; and Lawrence Devlin, officially posted to the Embassy but generally known as the experienced and unflappable CIA station chief in Leopoldville. It was Devlin's job, Carlucci later explained, to keep an eye on the Russians—"to know what the opposition was up to"— and to report back to the CIA through channels independent of the Embassy's communications system. When the Belgian government complained to the State Department that U.S. Embassy officers had been escorting Lumumba around Leopoldville and had flown him to Stanleyville, the Department replied, "We were trying to use whatever influence we have with Lumumba to urge on him a more moderate course."[36] This approach worked on at least one occasion. During the flight to Stanleyville, Carlucci appealed for the release of over thirty Belgian civilians who were not being permitted to leave, and Lumumba, who had taken a liking to him, replied on the spur of the moment, "Je vous les donne—un cadeau!"

On July 16, the day before the ultimatum was delivered, the State Department had sent a query to its ambassadors in Leopoldville and Brussels:

WHILE REPORTS FROM BELGIAN SOURCES OF COMMUNIST PENETRATION FORCE PUBLIQUE AND GOC [GOVERNMENT OF THE CONGO] HAVE TO BE TREATED WITH SOME RESERVE, ATTITUDE LUMUMBA VIS-A-VIS USSR AND THE WEST APPEARS MATTER FOR SERIOUS CONCERN AND DEPT WOULD APPRECIATE YOUR URGENT VIEWS ON HANDLING HIM.[37]

The Leopoldville Embassy replied the following day that despite rumors concerning

COMMUNIST INFLUENCE ON LUMUMBA AND PENDING ARRANGEMENTS BLOC ASSISTANCE OF ONE KIND OR ANOTHER THUS FAR, WE CAN GET

NOTHING FIRMER THAN COMMUNIST LINE TYPE SPEECHES BY KASH-
AMURA AND GIZENGA IN PARTICULAR.[38]

At the same time, the Department informed the Portuguese ambassador, who had asked about Lumumba's pro-Communist tendencies,
that the United States

LACKED DEFINITE EVIDENCE BUT EXCHANGE CABLES KHRUSHCHEV
WOULD SEEM POINT THIS WAY AS WELL AS SOVIET FOODLIFT.[39]

Now the ultimatum, following three days after the original appeal to
Khrushchev, fueled these suspicions by providing new evidence about
Lumumba's attitude toward the Soviet Union. At the very least it
raised doubts about his stability: Timberlake reported that both General Alexander and Bunche felt Lumumba was "irrational."[40] At worst it
raised the possibility that whether he was a Communist or not, he
might invite the Russians in—a prospect which the Americans found
alarming, since their entire effort up to this point had been directed
toward preventing the Soviet Union from taking advantage of the chaotic situation in the Congo.

The U.S. Embassy in Brussels, replying to the Department's query
on July 19, after the ultimatum had been issued, took a very strong line
regarding Lumumba, recommending openly for the first time that the
United States try to remove him from office. The U.S. ambassador,
William Burden, said he believed the situation called for

URGENT MEASURES ON VARIOUS LEVELS IF EVEN REASONABLE DEGREE
STABILITY AND WESTERN ENTRÉE INTO CONGO TO BE SALVAGED FROM
PRESENT ANARCHIC SITUATION.

Lumumba, he said, had

MANEUVERED HIMSELF INTO POSITION OF OPPOSITION TO WEST,
RESISTANCE TO UNITED NATIONS AND INCREASING DEPENDENCE ON SO-
VIET UNION AND ON CONGOLESE SUPPORTERS (KASHAMURA, GIZENGA)
WHO ARE PURSUING SOVIET ENDS.

Burden went on to recommend:

ONLY PRUDENT, THEREFORE, TO PLAN ON BASIS THAT LUMUMBA GOV-
ERNMENT THREATENS OUR VITAL INTERESTS IN CONGO AND AFRICA GEN-
ERALLY. A PRINCIPAL OBJECTIVE OF OUR POLITICAL AND DIPLOMATIC
ACTION MUST THEREFORE BE TO DESTROY LUMUMBA GOVERNMENT AS
NOW CONSTITUTED, BUT AT THE SAME TIME WE MUST FIND OR DEVELOP
ANOTHER HORSE TO BACK WHICH WOULD BE ACCEPTABLE IN REST OF
AFRICA AND DEFENSIBLE AGAINST SOVIET POLITICAL ATTACK.

He then sketched a scenario for dealing with Lumumba which laid the groundwork for future U.S. policy. He recommended that United States adopt the following measures:

—persuade the Congolese and other Africans that Lumumba was the witting or unwitting instrument of Soviet intervention in central Africa, which would bring to the continent a "new and worse form of white imperialism";

—point out privately to African leaders that if Lumumba succeeded in this effort to bring the Soviet bloc into the Congo, it would cause an "inevitable clash of East and West on the African continent" and destroy their dream of a neutral Pan-African bloc;

—encourage the Congolese Parliament to repudiate Lumumba; this would eliminate his constitutional legitimacy and permit him to retain power only by an "open coup d'etat" for which he might not have the "necessary naked force, especially in Leopoldville";

—build up the provincial governments as a de facto authority, and persuade them to adopt a position of "no confidence" toward the central government; this would weaken Lumumba, and the provincial leaders could then "build back toward some central authority exclusive of Lumumba."

On the question of who was to replace Lumumba, Burden expressed the hope that "once removed from Lumumba's malignant influence," Kasavubu might well prove to be the "rallying point for more moderate and constructive elements." He pointed out that as President, Kasavubu had the constitutional tenure that Lumumba, as Prime Minister, lacked, and, weak as he was, he still appeared to be the "best bet" for the "immediate future."

Burden concluded by noting that while the U.S. Embassy in Leopoldville had the primary responsibility for dealing with the internal political situation in the Congo, the CIA in Brussels would be "reporting separately some specific suggestions."[41]

At this point there was considerable disagreement in Washington about how the Russians would respond to Lumumba's ultimatum. Lodge expected that when the Security Council met there would be a dramatic Soviet statement announcing the arrival of Soviet or Chinese troops.[42] Herter expected a Soviet resolution demanding the immediate withdrawal of all Belgian troops.[43] On July 21 the Africa specialists at the State Department assessed the ultimatum in a briefing paper for the Secretary of State, who was to appear the next day at a meeting of the National Security Council (NSC). They concluded, "At the present time the Soviet reaction to this is not known although it is safest to assume that they will make all the trouble they can." The Soviet specialists disagreed; they felt the Russians would limit their response to a massive propaganda barrage and doubted they would "send many troops—if at all." Both sets of experts agreed, however, on the following advice:

> It is recommended that you impress upon the Council the continued gravity of the situation in the Congo and the trouble that can be caused by the irresponsible Congolese request for Soviet troops. This is indicative of the lack of maturity and ability on the part of the Congolese and probably implies as well some degree of Communist influence on Prime Minister Lumumba and his immediate entourage.[44]

CIA Director Allen Dulles, relying on his own sources of information, which came through independent CIA channels from Leopoldville and Brussels, took an even harder line at the NSC meeting. According to the NSC minutes cited by the Senate Select Committee on Intelligence Activities,

> Mr. Dulles said that in Lumumba we were faced with a person who was a Castro or worse. . . . Mr. Dulles went on to describe Mr. Lumumba's background which he described as "harrowing." . . . It is safe to go on the assumption that Lumumba has been bought by the Communists; this also, however, fits with his own orientation.[45]

Meanwhile, Lumumba, who was not completely aware of the storm he had caused, returned to Leopoldville to a mixed reception. The Senate met under the leadership of Joseph Ileo—a founder of the Movement National Congolais who had broken with Lumumba in 1959—and unanimously disavowed Lumumba's ultimatum to the United Nations, rejecting any possibility of Soviet intervention. The Council of Ministers, on the other hand, backed up Lumumba's demand. Bomboko and Kanza were unable to persuade their colleagues to reverse the decision, but they managed to modify it; now the appeal was broadened to include the African and Asian states as well as the Soviet Union—thus taking some of the sting out of it.[46] On July 20 Lumumba held a press conference, at which he complained bitterly about the United Nations and insisted that the Congo had a right to ask any nation in the world for aid. He noted that Khrushchev had said he was ready to supply military assistance much more rapidly than the United Nations. He said that he would hold off on any such requests until after the Security Council had met—but he would keep his options open.[47]

The Second Security Council Meeting: July 20–22, 1960

When the meeting opened on the evening of July 20, Ambassador Kanza backed down from Lumumba's ultimatum. He stressed that his government was "not on the point of withdrawing its confidence from the United Nations and asking for the assistance of any particular country."

Soviet Deputy Foreign Minister Vassily Kuznetsov, a shrewd and experienced diplomat who had replaced Sobolev as the head of the delegation, did not refer directly to the ultimatum; but he made it clear that his government shared Lumumba's impatience about the continued presence of Belgian troops. He introduced a draft resolution providing that Belgian troops be withdrawn within three days and warned, "If aggression continues, then of course more active measures will have to be taken, both by the United Nations and by peaceloving States which are in sympathy with the Congo's cause."

Lodge responded immediately to this statement, which he regarded as a threat of Soviet military intervention. He reaffirmed American support for the United Nations, and promised, "We will do whatever may be necessary to prevent the intrusion of any military forces not requested by the United Nations." It was "regrettable," he said, that the Soviet Union was "seeking to bring the cold war to the heart of Africa."[48]

Lodge's warning was backed up the following day by Herter, who held a press conference devoted primarily to the Congo issue. He pointed out that the Soviet government had voted for the same Security Council resolution as the United States, but that "this action had hardly been completed . . . when Mr. Khrushchev was publicly assuring the leaders of the Congo that he was prepared to intervene militarily if the United Nations action did not proceed to his satisfaction." Herter described Khrushchev's statement as "recklessly irresponsible." He said he found it "hard to believe" that the Russians would consider sending troops to the Congo when the UN operation was going so well; but he added that even if Khrushchev was bluffing, his "threat to take unilateral action in the Congo, repeated again by the Soviet delegate at the Security Council last night," could only "increase tensions in the area." The United States, he said, would "continue to back with all its moral force and material resources the action of the United Nations to restore peace and order."[49]

American policymakers had taken a large step toward the Belgian position regarding the troublemaking potential of the Russians in the Congo. This, however, did not alter their strategy; on the contrary, it strengthened their original conviction that the United Nations must move quickly to replace Belgian troops, so as to preempt the Russians and make it difficult for them to claim to be the sole supporters of the newly independent state. As a result, the U.S. delegation indicated that it would be willing to accept a resolution calling on Belgium to withdraw its troops "as soon as possible."

For the second time in a week, a compromise between the Soviet and American positions was worked out by the African states, in consultation with the Secretary-General, and sponsored by Tunisia, joined this time by Ceylon.[50] It added little to the substance of the July 14 resolution, but it put additional pressure on the Belgian government by calling on it "to implement speedily" the first Security Council resolution. The word "speedily" was used rather than the Soviet "immediately" or the American "as soon as possible." Kuznetsov withdrew his own draft and voted for the Tunisian-Ceylonese draft, which was adopted unanimously; but insisted that his government expected the Secretary-General to act to ensure withdrawal "without delay—in a few days."[51]

The Soviet dispute with the Secretary-General about the pace of the Belgian withdrawal was fairly serious, but it was essentially soluble. It was clear that the Belgian troops were in fact withdrawing, and by the end of August even *Pravda* would acknowledge that Belgian troops had been removed from the entire country—with the exception of Katanga.[52]

Katanga was the heart of the problem—the issue that would ultimately destroy both Lumumba and Hammarskjold. To the Russians, it was clear that the mineral-rich secessionist province should be returned to the control of the Lumumba government as soon as possible. To the Americans and their Belgian allies, Katanga's status was a subject of spirited debate.

The U.S. government was the first to arrive at a decision. It rejected the advice of the American consul in Elisabethville, who recommended that the United States recognize Katanga's independence, and accepted the judgment of its ambassadors in Leopoldville and Brussels, who opposed the idea, partly on the merits—the rest of the Congo was not economically viable without Katanga—but primarily because of their concern about Soviet exploitation of the situation. On July 12, the day after Tshombe announced the secession, Ambassador Burden urged the State Department to take a stand immediately, warning that

ANY TEMPORIZING OUR PART AT THIS TIME WOULD PROBABLY LEAD TO ASSUMPTION BY LEOPOLDVILLE GOVERNMENT THAT WE HAVE CONNIVED WITH BELGIANS AND OTHERS TO SUPPORT OR AT LEAST ACCEPT INDEPENDENT KATANGA. THIS COULD BE MOST RAPID AND EFFECTIVE WAY TO ALIENATE EVEN OUR FRIENDS IN GOC AND THROW MAJOR PART OF CONGO INTO COMMUNISTS' ARMS.[53]

The State Department responded quickly. It announced the following day that it favored the unity of the Congo and urged the Belgian government to do the same.

Belgian Ambassador Scheyven pointed out to Herter that Katanga "might soon be the only part of the Congo which was connected with the Free World" and suggested that the United States "might wish to reconsider" its position "if the rest of the country fell under Moscow's domination."[54] Both Burden and Timberlake agreed that this possibility should be considered as a last resort. In order to keep its options open, the State Department instructed its consul in Elisabethville to assure Tshombe that the American decision not to recognize his government should not be regarded as hostility toward him, and it informed the consul confidentially that the United States might reconsider its position if other states decided to recognize Katanga; it cautioned, however, that in no circumstances would the United States "take the lead."[55]

Belgian opinion on the subject of recognition was divided. There was a natural tendency to side with Katanga's provincial president, Moise Tshombe, since his behavior offered such a contrast to that of Lumumba: he had requested Belgian aid to quell the Force Publique mutiny while Lumumba had rejected it; and he continued to issue pro-Belgian statements while Lumumba was accusing Belgium of aggression. Moreover, Katanga was the economic center of the Congo, and Belgium's major investments were located there; therefore, there was a great temptation to salvage what could be salvaged if the rest of the Congo was about to take a pro-Soviet course under Lumumba and oust all Belgian interests. On the other hand, the Belgian government was aware that recognition of Katanga would burn its "last bridge" to the central government in Leopoldville and "further undermine Belgium's few friends there." It would confirm Moscow's accusations and alienate the African countries whose troops would be responsible for protecting Belgian interests and Belgian citizens in the other five provinces of the Congo.[56] Faced with this dilemma, the Belgian government wavered for several days.

In the end the Belgians decided against formal recognition; but they backed Tshombe's de facto autonomy by keeping Belgian troops and administrators in Katanga. They had no objection to the establishment of a UN presence in Katanga if it consisted of one or two civilian representatives; but they told Hammarskjold they saw no point in sending UN troops to Katanga, since these troops had been sent to the Congo to restore order, and order had already been restored in Katanga.[57]

The Secretary-General, for his part, did not anticipate that Katanga would be much of a hurdle. He told Lodge a few days before the Security Council meeting that he hoped to "avoid the problem" until the middle of the following week, by which time he believed the United Nations would be in a "strong position" in the rest of the Congo. At that point he would send an emissary directly to Tshombe, bypassing Lumumba, to arrange for the entry of UN troops. Once the troops were established in Katanga, Tshombe's efforts to secede would most likely "lose their footing" and Tshombe would "probably make overtures" to Leopoldville "to salvage some degree of authority for himself." Hammarskjold stressed that he did not want the UN action to have the effect of "artificially bolstering Lumumba," who the Secretary-General believed was "not very strong" and probably would not last.[58]

When Hammarskjold spoke at the Security Council meeting, he described his position in somewhat different language. He explained that he believed the UN force was in principle "entitled to access to all parts of the territory in fulfillment of its duties" but said he did not favor precipitate action toward Katanga; nor did he feel that the United Nations had a mandate to intervene in what he described as an internal constitutional dispute between the central government and Katanga's secessionist leader.[59]

These views would eventually bring the Secretary-General into direct conflict with Lumumba and with the Soviet Union; but the Katanga issue did not come to a head at the Security Council meetings on July 20 and 21. It was handled obliquely in the Tunisian-Ceylonese resolution, which asked "all states" to "refrain from any action which might undermine the territorial integrity and the political independence of the Congo."[60]

The unanimous adoption of this resolution immediately eased the tension produced by Lumumba's ultimatum. The unpredictable Prime Minister announced at a press conference on July 22 that he was "extremely gratified" and said there was no longer any need for Soviet military intervention.[61]

Lumumba's Debut at the United Nations

It was at this point that two of the chief actors in the Congo drama met for the first time. The Secretary-General, who had planned to leave for Leopoldville on July 23, delayed his departure in order to confer with Lumumba, who had decided to come to New York to seek additional support for his cause. He had made this decision on the spur of the moment, picked up visas for himself and a large entourage at the U.S. Embassy, and headed for the airport, where he commandeered a plane that had just brought Ghanaian troops for the UN force.

Lumumba arrived in New York just after dawn on Sunday, July 24, after a twelve-hour flight from London. He had slept most of the way and emerged from the plane in a buoyant mood, ready to plunge into three busy days of meetings, press conferences, luncheons, and dinners. The radical young leader, who had threatened to appeal to the

Soviet Union for armed intervention just a few days before, was all smiles as he thanked the American people for their support and expressed his "sympathy and friendship" for President Eisenhower.[62] After a luncheon at the New Rochelle home of Alex Quaison-Sackey, the sophisticated chief of the Ghanaian Mission, Lumumba, accompanied by ten of the twenty Congolese officials traveling with him, drove to UN headquarters and met for two hours with the Secretary-General.

The contrast between the two men was striking: the one inexperienced, highly excitable, passionately committed to his vision of an independent Congo; the other controlled, complex, deeply devoted in a theoretical way to helping the new states of Africa solve their problems. Hammarskjold had always regarded himself as an anticolonialist; Lumumba tended to suspect anyone who did not share his view of the colonialist role in the Congo.

Despite these differences, their first meeting went smoothly. The Congolese Prime Minister emerged saying he was "very optimistic, very satisfied."[63] The following day the Secretary-General gave a luncheon in honor of Lumumba to which representatives of the eleven Security Council members and the nine African states were invited. Lumumba presented his case with such lucidity and eloquence that an astonished Hammarskjold remarked afterward to one of his colleagues, "Now no one can tell me that man is irrational!"

Lumumba and Hammarskjold met again for several hours on Monday and Tuesday, and at the end of their talks they issued a communiqué announcing agreement on a technical assistance program. It was the political issue, however, which was foremost in both men's minds. Lumumba insisted that the Belgian troops be withdrawn immediately. Hammarskjold tried to deal firmly with what he viewed as Lumumba's "unrealistic expectations" about the "timetable" of United Nations deployment and Belgian withdrawal.[64] There was an immense gap between the two men's views of the UN role in the Congo, a gap that was never really bridged during these conversations. Lumumba continued to believe that the United Nations had been sent to the Congo to act as the agent of his government in all matters relating to the Belgians and Katanga; he had no conception of the Secretary-General's role as a mediator among many diverse interests.

Still, Lumumba remained in a hopeful, cooperative mood as long as Hammarskjold was in New York. He stopped short of demanding another Security Council meeting, as he had suggested earlier he might do; instead, he announced at a press conference that he was "satisfied" with the two resolutions already adopted and that he was relying on the Secretary-General to implement them. He struck still another conciliatory note by stating that he wanted the UN force to stay in the

Congo after the Belgians left to help reorganize his country's "young army."

At this press conference he stressed the Congo's policy of "positive neutralism," balancing favorable references to the United States, Great Britain, France, and the Soviet Union. He skillfully avoided answering questions about his attitude toward Communism and his requests for aid from the Soviet Union. In fact, he was so diplomatic that reporters covering the press conference found that he was not living up to his radical image. As one journalist put it, "There was nothing in his restrained remarks . . . to suggest the impassioned leader who had been jailed for inflammatory speechmaking."[65] The reason for this transformation was simple, and Lumumba himself stated it openly: he was ready to seek aid for his struggling country from any source whatsoever.

Lumumba's debut in international politics was watched with great interest by the delegates who had been debating the Congo's fate. Western diplomats were pleased that he had apparently calmed down and was willing to cooperate with the Secretary-General; but they felt his insistence that ideology meant nothing to him did not quite ring true. Soviet diplomats were pleased by his continuing criticism of the Belgians; but they were concerned about his enthusiastic response to the Secretary-General and his decision to invite the UN force to stay and train his army. Deputy Foreign Minister Kuznetsov, who met Lumumba for the first time on July 25, was the highest-ranking Soviet official who had had an opportunity to size up the Congolese leader in person. He was evidently impressed; cooperation between Moscow and Leopoldville continued to grow.[66]

The diplomats who were most involved with Lumumba were the Ghanaians, the Guineans, and the other Africans who had shepherded the Congolese delegation around New York since its arrival the week before. They were somewhat disturbed by his erratic behavior. He might be calm and reasonable one day and temperamental the next; he would impress a group of diplomats with his reasoned analysis of the situation in his country and then be late for an important appointment or suddenly change his mind about what he wanted to say or do. On balance, however, the African diplomats were pleased with the outcome of Lumumba's three-day stay in New York. Despite his occasional lapses, he seemed to be on the right track in his dealings with the Secretary-General.

Lumumba in Washington: First Thoughts about Assassination

After their discussions were completed, Hammarskjold and Lumumba headed in opposite directions. Hammarskjold left on the evening of July 26 for Brussels, en route to Leopoldville. The following morning, Lumumba flew to Washington in a plane provided by President Eisenhower and stayed as an honored guest at Blair House.

Although CIA Director Dulles considered him more dangerous than Fidel Castro and the U.S. ambassador in Brussels was cabling detailed suggestions about how to remove him from office, top officials at the State Department had decided to invite Lumumba to Washington because they still believed it might be possible to exert a moderating influence on him. As Under Secretary of State Dillon told the Senate Intelligence Committee fifteen years later, "We hoped to see him and see what we could do to come to a better understanding with him."[67]

Dillon and Herter were relying on the assessment of Ambassador Timberlake, who had just arrived in Washington for consultations. His views were reflected in a cable sent by his deputy, Robinson McIlvaine, on July 26:

LUMUMBA IS AN OPPORTUNIST AND NOT A COMMUNIST. HIS FINAL DECISION AS TO WHICH CAMP HE WILL EVENTUALLY BELONG WILL NOT BE MADE BY HIM BUT RATHER WILL BE IMPOSED UPON HIM BY OUTSIDE FORCES.[68]

The Congolese Prime Minister did not get to see President Eisenhower, who was in Newport, but he spent a frustrating half hour with Secretary of State Herter. Lumumba asked Herter to persuade the Belgians to withdraw their troops from the Congo; Herter advised him to rely on the Secretary-General. Lumumba asked for an American plane which he and Kasavubu could use; Herter suggested he check with Bunche and see if one of the planes supplied by the United States to the United Nations could be spared. Lumumba outlined the Congo's need for technicians and money and asked for an official loan; Herter explained that the U.S. government was prepared to help but added that all men and money would have to be channeled through the United Nations.[69]

American policymakers hoped to establish the principle that all aid to the Congo must be administered on a multilateral basis, because they had concluded that this would be the most effective way to prevent a Soviet takeover in the Congo. Even if they discounted the likelihood of Soviet military intervention, they were still concerned about the threat of peaceful Soviet penetration. As John Hay Whitney, the U.S. ambassador in London, warned, a "full-fledged Soviet response to Congolese appeals for economic, financial and technical assistance" could create a situation in which the Russians, playing upon the "anti-West feeling" of the "present Congolese leadership," might hope to achieve in the near future "their initial objective" of "isolating" the Congo from the West.[70] If Herter had been able to persuade Lumumba that all aid to the Congo should be handled by the United Nations, he would have succeeded in blocking this avenue of Soviet penetration; but as it turned out, his arguments fell on deaf ears.

When a Belgian diplomat inquired the day after Herter's meeting with Lumumba about his reaction to the Congolese leader, he was told that "Lumumba had made a pretty good impression, that he appeared intelligent and that there was no evidence that he was 'crazy.' "[71] This bland official assessment apparently concealed serious doubts about the Prime Minister. Dillon, who was present at the meeting, told the Senate Intelligence Committee in 1975 that Lumumba had struck him and Herter as an "irrational, almost 'psychotic' personality," and went on to explain:

> When he was in the State Department meeting, either with me or with the Secretary in my presence . . . he would never look you in the eye. He looked up at the sky. And his words didn't ever have any relation to the particular things that we wanted to discuss. . . . You had a feeling that he was a person that was gripped by this fervor that I can only characterize as messianic. . . . He was just not a rational being.

Dillon testified that the "willingness of the United States government to work with Lumumba vanished after these meetings," and added:

> The impression that was left was . . . very bad, that this was an individual whom it was impossible to deal with. And the feelings of the Government as a result of this sharpened very considerably at that time.[72]

Lumumba, unaware of the impression he had created at the State Department, warned at a press conference that if the Belgians did not withdraw their troops, the Congolese government might ask for troops from another country, perhaps the United States. When he was asked whether he would request troops from the Soviet Union, he dodged the question, explaining that it was his government which would make such a decision, not he personally. Lumumba was increasingly annoyed when the issue of Soviet intervention was raised and kept insisting that he had no interest in ideologies or in blocs and that his country, with its policy of positive neutralism, would accept aid from anyone provided it was sincere; he did not seem to realize that he was the one who had raised the issue of Soviet intervention, first in his appeal of July 14 and again in his ultimatum of July 17.

Lumumba reportedly had no time to see the Soviet chargé d'affaires, Mikhail Smirnovsky, who called twice at Blair House,[73] but after his press conference he granted an interview to the TASS correspondent in Washington, Mikhail Sagatelyan. He told the Soviet reporter that his country was the "only great power which supported the people of the Congo in their struggle from the very outset." He expressed his gratitude "to the Soviet people and to Premier Nikita Khrushchev personally" for their "timely and essential moral support" and for the food aid they had provided.[74]

These expressions of gratitude were not limited to the Soviet Union; Lumumba tended to thank everyone he thought had helped or could help the Congo. When he left for Canada on July 29, he embarrassed Dillon by his effusive praise of the "sympathetic" American position; Dillon feared, with good reason, that this would create a disastrous impression in Belgium, where there was already a great public outcry about the cordial welcome Lumumba had received in the United States. The implication that the U.S. government was backing Lumumba's charges against Belgium would strain Belgian patience still further.

Immediately after the Congolese Prime Minister left for Canada, the State Department assured the Belgian ambassador that his departure statement was an "adroit misinterpretation" of the American position and issued a statement commending the Belgian government for its cooperation with the United Nations.[75] A few days later, in a "Secret" cable to Ambassador Burden designed to respond to Belgian criticism, Herter spelled out the U.S. attitude toward Lumumba:

US BELIEVES WEST MUST DEAL WITH LUMUMBA AS PRIME MINISTER CONGOLESE GOVERNMENT, ALTHOUGH HIS RELIABILITY OPEN TO SERIOUS QUESTION. LUMUMBA'S INTENTIONS AND SYMPATHIES UNCLEAR, AND EVIDENCE EXISTS THAT HE WILL NOT RPT NOT PROVE SATISFACTORY. US WILL THEREFORE CONTINUE SEARCH FOR MORE TRUSTWORTHY ELEMENTS IN CONGO WHO MIGHT BE SUSCEPTIBLE TO SUPPORT AS PART OF PROGRAM OF REINSURANCE AGAINST LUMUMBA.[76]

On August 1 Ambassador Timberlake was flown to the summer White House in Newport to brief President Eisenhower and the National Security Council. While government spokesmen maintained that there was no emergency, the meeting lasted nearly two hours, and the Congo was the chief topic of discussion. The group at the meeting was larger than usual; the twenty-one participants included CIA Director Allen Dulles, Acting Defense Secretary James H. Douglas, and the Chairman of the Joint Chiefs of Staff, General Nathan Twining. After hearing the arguments of the Joint Chiefs, who were concerned about the possibility that the Belgian bases at Kitona and Kamina would fall into the hands of the Soviet bloc, the NSC decided that the United States should be prepared "at any time to take appropriate military action to prevent or defeat Soviet military intervention in the Congo."[77]

Contingency planning groups were set up to carry out this decision. The military planners came up with a variety of scenarios, ranging

from the arrival of Soviet troops to the dispatch of Soviet planes carrying military equipment for Lumumba, and tried to figure out how
American forces could counter these moves. The Pentagon persuaded
the State Department that the Russians might be deterred by the appearance of a naval task force off the coast of the Congo, and a plan
was set in motion to send a "people-to-people" naval mission, called
SOLANT AMITY, on a series of visits along the West African coast; it
would include, in addition to the customary two destroyers, "two am-
phibious-type vessels with landing craft, helicopters and about 500
United States Marines."[78] Meanwhile, other planning groups, at the
CIA and the State Department, were working on the political aspects
of the situation, stepping up their efforts to remove the Lumumba
government and set up a pro-Western government in its place.

It was at about this time, according to Dillon, that the possibility of
assassinating Lumumba first came up. The idea was broached at a Pentagon meeting which he attended along with representatives of the
Defense Department, the Joint Chiefs of Staff, and the CIA. As Dillon
later recalled the discussion, "a question regarding the possibility of an
assassination attempt against Lumumba was briefly raised," only to be
"turned off by the CIA"—not for any "moral" reasons but because the
CIA people present thought either that it was "not a possible thing" or
that the group was "too large for such a sensitive discussion." While
this conference, in his opinion, "could not have served as authorization
for an actual assassination effort against Lumumba," he believed that
the CIA "could have decided they wanted to develop the capability . . .
just by knowing the concern that everyone had about Lumumba. . . .
They wouldn't have had to tell anyone about that. That is just developing their own internal capability, and then they would have to come
and get permission."[79]

Lumumba Turns to the Russians

While Lumumba was in Washington, the Secretary-General was in
Brussels, warning the leaders of the Belgian government that the danger of Soviet intervention increased each day they delayed withdrawing their troops. He assured them that he would not move UN troops
into Katanga until the way was "cleared diplomatically." By the time
he left, he felt he had made some headway.[80]

On July 28 he arrived in Leopoldville and saw for the first time the
chaotic reality that Bunche's reports could scarcely convey. The hot,
humid tropical city was seething with tension and uncertainty. Most of
the Belgians who had kept the communications and transportation system functioning had fled, and nothing worked. UN headquarters had
been moved the previous day from the makeshift arrangements at the

Stanley Hotel to a hardly less inadequate eight-story apartment building, the Royal, which the harried force commander, General von
Horn, regarded as a security nightmare. A precise and meticulous military man, von Horn was horrified by the disorganization he faced; no
one knew when troops were arriving or how they would get where
they were going or what they should do when they got there.

On this issue great friction developed between the general and the
Secretary-General's civilian representative, Ralph Bunche, who insisted that every problem must be resolved through negotiations and that
force should be used only in self-defense. Von Horn argued that young
soldiers from a Moroccan village could not be expected to read three-
page legal documents outlining their rights and responsibilities while
facing a hostile Congolese crowd wielding pangas somewhere in the
bush. But he could not convince Bunche, who was in full charge of the
operation.[81]

Bunche was equally disturbed by the unprecedented situation he
faced in the Congo. He was an extraordinarily thoughtful and conscientious diplomat, who handled every detail himself and worked every
night until the early hours of the morning. He was also America's top-
ranking black diplomat; but he was so light-skinned that the distinction
was lost on the Congolese, who tended to consider him just another
European and to treat him accordingly.

After reviewing the situation with his aides, Hammarskjold remarked to von Horn, "My God! This is the craziest operation in history! God only knows where it is going to end. All I can tell you is that I
had no other choice but to lay it on."[82] Hammarskjold then called on
Kasavubu, who gave a dinner in his honor that evening. "I am optimistic," said the Congolese President. "I see the future in colors of rose,
but the rose is not without thorns."[83]

The thorns were painfully apparent to Hammarskjold the following
day. July 29 was his fifty-fifth birthday, and he spent it in the toughest
and nastiest negotiations of his career. He met with the Council of
Ministers, headed in Lumumba's absence by Deputy Premier Gizenga, and urged them to be patient about the Katanga issue. He assured them that the United Nations regarded Katanga as part of the
Congo but explained that it would take time to negotiate the entry of
UN troops.

The Congolese were too impatient to give him that time. They demanded immediate UN action against Katanga. After two days of talks
the government gave a buffet dinner in Hammarskjold's honor. To the
astonishment of the guests, Gizenga, instead of offering a cordial toast,
read an angry prepared statement, which virtually accused the United
Nations of complicity with the Belgians.[84]

Hammarskjold was stunned by this attitude. He had found Lumumba, reputed to be an erratic firebrand, correct and cooperative during their meetings in New York; the hostile reaction of his colleagues in Leopoldville was a shock. Friends later explained that Hammarskjold, a man of "sensibility and sensitivity" who felt that he had done a great deal for the Congolese, simply could not understand their attitude during his visit—the insults, the demands, the total lack of gratitude.

By this time Lumumba was back in New York, prepared to turn to the Russians once again. He had returned empty-handed from Ottawa, where the government took the same line Herter had taken in Washington: Canada would be happy to help the Congo through the United Nations, but bilateral aid was out of the question.[85] Lumumba had cut short his visit to Canada but had found time for a thirty-five minute talk with Soviet Ambassador A.A. Aroutunian before he left.[86] As soon as he got back to New York he conferred with Kuznetsov.[87] On July 31 he sent an impatient letter to the President of the Security Council threatening that if Hammarskjold did not move faster on the Katanga issue, he would call for another meeting of the Council.[88]

It became clear that evening that Lumumba could count on Soviet support for his demands. Arkadiev, the Soviet UN Under Secretary, stopped in to see Andrew Cordier, Hammarskjold's executive assistant, and told him there were several Security Council members who wanted the Council to meet at once "to back up the Secretary-General's efforts in the Congo." Cordier, a solidly built, strong-minded American, told Arkadiev the Security Council could not possibly improve on its last unanimous resolution. He explained that a new meeting would not help the Secretary-General but would only complicate matters for him.[89]

On August 1 the Soviet government made two moves designed to bolster Lumumba's position. First, it announced the appointment of the first Soviet ambassador to Leopoldville—Mikhail D. Yakovlev, formerly the Foreign Minister of the RSFSR, the largest constituent republic of the Soviet Union.[90] Next it issued a major statement which warned, in tougher language than Moscow had used before:

> In the event of the aggression against the Congo continuing . . . the Soviet government will not hesitate to take resolute measures to rebuff the aggressors who . . . are in fact acting with the encouragement of all the colonialist powers of NATO.[91]

In addition to making this implied threat of military action, the Soviet statement promised to provide the Congo with large-scale economic assistance, including technicians—on a bilateral basis.

Cordier, who agreed with Herter that all aid to the Congo should be channeled through the United Nations,[92] believed that the Russians would be "glad to see the UN founder" in the Congo so they could move in. He told the Americans that he would raise the matter with Lumumba immediately, even though he felt it was virtually impossible to deal with him as a "rational, logical, informed person."[93]

After a two-and-one-half hour conversation with Lumumba, Cordier felt he had made some progress: the Prime Minister backed down on his latest demands and "reaffirmed his faith" in the Secretary-General and the United Nations. He even invited Cordier to visit the Congo when peace was restored.[94] But Cordier failed to convince him of the advantages of channeling all aid through the United Nations. Diallo Telli, the Guinean ambassador to the United States, who was to leave with Lumumba the following day for a tour of several key African states, told American officials that he shared Lumumba's distaste for the idea because it smacked too much of trusteeship. He said Lumumba would "almost certainly" accept a Soviet offer of bilateral aid and suggested that if the Americans wanted to "influence him favorably" toward the West, their "only chance" was to make a "bilateral aid offer" of their own before Lumumba left the United States.[95]

While Cordier was trying to bring Lumumba around in New York, Hammarskjold continued to try to break the deadlock in Leopoldville. The Secretary-General, buffeted by Gizenga's insistent demands and Lumumba's sporadic attacks, frustrated by the Belgians' refusal to state openly that they were willing to withdraw their troops from Katanga, grew more and more pessimistic. He realized that he was working against the clock. Lumumba was due back in the Congo on August 8. The Secretary-General turned to the Americans for help, warning that if the Belgians did not make a public statement promising to withdraw from Katanga, they might set off a train of events that would lead to a full-scale civil war, complete with Soviet military intervention.[96]

U.S. officials, who had been urging Hammarskjold to go slow on the Katanga issue, thought his fears were exaggerated. They considered the threat of Soviet military intervention unlikely, but they recognized the political dangers that could result from further Belgian delay. On August 1 Herter urged the Belgian government to make the statement that the Secretary-General wanted. He said he assumed that Belgium's "long-term interest" in the Congo was to "restore and maintain" the Belgian economic presence there and "deny" it to the Communists. If this was correct, then the issue of troop withdrawal was really secondary.[97]

At last the arguments of the Secretary-General, bolstered by American pressure, bore fruit: on August 2 Hammarskjold was able to announce that the UN force would begin to move into Katanga on August 6.[98] But when Bunche flew to Elisabethville to make the final arrangements, he found, to his dismay, that although the Belgian gov-

ernment had agreed to permit the entry of UN troops, Tshombe intended to use force to prevent them from landing.[99]

The August 6 arrival date had to be postponed; both Bunche and
Hammarskjold judged that the possibility of armed resistance was so
strong that a further mandate from the Security Council would be
needed before the force could move into Katanga. The Secretary-
General left quickly for New York, explaining to the American chargé
d'affaires in Leopoldville that he wanted to call a Security Council
meeting and clarify the UN mandate before Lumumba returned to
Leopoldville. Hammarskjold described the Katanga situation as "brutal" and said the Congo was "one of the most disheartening messes he
had ever encountered."[100]

Hammarskjold's judgment of the military situation in Katanga may
have been wrong; it seems likely that there would have been less resistance at that early point and fewer lives lost than there eventually
were in the series of UN military operations in Katanga during the
next two and a half years. But this is hindsight. At the time criticism of
the Secretary-General's cautious approach came primarily from the
Lumumba government and its Soviet supporters, who complained
that Bunche had been taken in by "Tshombe's bluff" and scoffed at
the idea that anyone would pay serious attention to his threat to oppose the UN force with "six hundred Katangan soldiers."[101]

The Third Security Council Meeting: August 8–9, 1960

Hammarskjold was somewhat discouraged by the fruitless week he
had spent in Leopoldville, but he was still confident that he could
come up with a satisfactory solution to the Katanga problem. In order
to strengthen his hand in dealing with Tshombe, he was planning to
ask the Security Council to state clearly that its resolutions applied to
Katanga as well as to the rest of the Congo and that Belgian troops
must be replaced by UN troops there as well as in the other five provinces. At the same time he would reassure the Western powers by
making it clear that the United Nations had no intention of handing
the province over to the Lumumba government.[102]

The Russians suspected that Hammarskjold's stand was the result of
Western pressure; but their suspicions were only partially correct.
Hammarskjold was well aware that he could not continue the Congo
operation without American support, and he knew that the Americans
and their allies would never approve of using the UN force to bring
Katanga's riches under Lumumba's control. But his cautious policy was
determined less by his awareness of Western desires than by his own
commitment to the principle that the United Nations should not intervene in the domestic affairs of a member state. While it was obvious

that the United Nations was already up to its ears in the Congo's domestic affairs, Hammarskjold refused to intervene with military force to impose a particular political settlement.

Despite his growing differences with the Soviet Union, Hammarskjold managed to avoid a collision at the Security Council meeting on August 8. Once again he persuaded the Tunisian ambassador, Mongi Slim, to introduce a draft resolution that would strike the right balance and be acceptable to the Western powers, the Russians, and the Afro-Asians. The resolution, cosponsored by Ceylon, called on the Belgian government to withdraw its troops "immediately" from the province of Katanga. It declared that the entry of the UN force into Katanga was "necessary," but at the same time it stated that the force would not "in any way intervene in or be used to influence the outcome of any internal conflict, constitutional or otherwise." Although Slim shared the Soviet view that the United Nations had the right to use force, if necessary, to enter Katanga, he acceded to Hammarskjold's wishes and made no reference to force in his resolution.[103]

The meeting proceeded smoothly, just as Hammarskjold planned. Lodge, who had just been chosen as Vice President Richard M. Nixon's running mate on the Republican ticket, was delighted with the way things were going and was not looking for any confrontations with the Russians. Kuznetsov was in no mood for a confrontation either; but he insisted on stating his own position before going along with the Tunisian compromise. He introduced a draft resolution which proposed that the Secretary-General use any means, including force, to remove the Belgian troops from Katanga and report on his progress within three days.

Hammarskjold replied that there were limits to his authority and that he could not take the military initiative under the present mandate. "I do not believe, personally," he said, "that we help the Congolese people by actions in which Africans kill Africans, or Congolese kill Congolese."[104]

Kuznetsov repeated the Soviet pledge of August 1 and reminded the Congolese and everyone else present that other help was available if the United Nations failed. In the end, however, he withdrew his own draft and voted for the Tunisian-Ceylonese resolution, which was adopted just before dawn on August 9, with nine votes in favor and France and Italy abstaining.[105]

The Russians had reason to be pleased with this resolution, which went farther than the earlier ones toward meeting their original demands. Despite his reservations about certain aspects of Hammarskjold's policy, Khrushchev could claim a degree of success for his strategy of using the United Nations to bolster the Lumumba government. It was possible that with this new resolution he might not have to make good on his pledge of unilateral Soviet military aid to Lumumba; he could limit his involvement to economic assistance and political advice.

It turned out, however, that the August 9 resolution was the last occasion on which the Soviet Union, the United States, and the Afro-Asian neutrals were able to reconcile their differences and give their support to Hammarskjold's diplomatic efforts in the Congo. The period of uneasy cooperation between the great powers was about to end. From this point on, positions would harden and divisions would grow deeper. Bitter charges and countercharges would fill the air as the Congo issue was transformed into a classic cold war confrontation.

CHAPTER THREE

Intervention and Assassination
(August 8–September 5, 1960)

W HEN LUMUMBA RETURNED to Leopoldville on the evening of August 8, he was met by demonstrators demanding his resignation. He had been in office for a little over five weeks and had spent more than two of those weeks abroad seeking support for his cause. While he was out of the country, his enemies were growing stronger. Albert Kalonji, one of his principal rivals, was about to proclaim the independence of Kasai Province. Influential members of Abako, Kasavubu's Leopold-ville-based party, had been negotiating with politicians from other provinces who were dissatisfied with Lumumba's style of leadership. Emboldened by the Katanga secession, encouraged by the Catholic hi-erarchy, and liberally financed by Belgian business interests and trade unions, this loosely knit group was preparing to overthrow Lumumba and set up a federal structure of government, with Joseph Ileo, the head of the Senate, as Prime Minister. They had mobilized trade union committees to protest Lumumba's economic policies; they had encour-aged youth groups to distribute anti-Lumumba leaflets; and they had begun to organize "shock troops" along tribal lines, recruiting anti-Lu-mumba sympathizers from the army and the police force.[1]

Lumumba moved swiftly to deal with his domestic opposition. The day after his return he declared a state of emergency and called the army back to regular duty. He forced the Belgian ambassador to leave the country— a popular measure that was cheered by the Congolese onlookers outside the Embassy who watched the Belgian flag come down. He accused the Catholic bishops and priests of paying dissident groups in an attempt to stir up trouble. He closed the Belgian press agency and arrested Gabriel Makoso, the Congolese editor of a leading Catholic newspaper, as well as a number of political figures. He tightened security in the capital and ordered his troops to stop cars and search them for weapons.[2]

Lumumba and Hammarskjold: Confrontation over Katanga

It was in this turbulent atmosphere that Lumumba learned of the Security Council's new resolution. He assumed that the United Nations was going to supply him with the military aid he needed to end the Katanga secession. He called a press conference and announced that he would soon enter Katanga with all the members of his government.[3]

Lumumba's assumption had no relation whatsoever to Hammarskjold's plans. On the evening of August 11 Hammarskjold arrived in Leopoldville prepared to accompany the first UN troops into Elisabethville the following day. He believed that this time he had neutralized all potential opposition. He had left Belgian Foreign Minister Pierre Wigny in a "very mellow" mood after promising him that if he ran into any problems in Katanga before the full complement of UN troops arrived, he would incorporate Belgian troops into the UN force as a "temporary measure." He had met with Kuznetsov, who had assured him of Soviet support for his effort. The next potential stumbling-block was Lumumba himself. Hammarskjold had tried to avoid a confrontation by explaining to the Congolese delegation in New York—Deputy Premier Gizenga, Foreign Minister Bomboko, and UN Ambassador Kanza—that he would not take any officials of the central government to Elisabethville with him. Gizenga had "swallowed hard" but had taken the news "without protest."[4] When Hammarskjold arrived in Leopoldville, he deliberately avoided seeing Lumumba, fearing that the impetuous Prime Minister would disrupt his carefully orchestrated arrangements.

Hammarskjold's most delicate diplomatic maneuvers were directed toward Tshombe, the leader of secessionist Katanga. On his first attempt to arrange the entry of UN troops, he had dealt only with the Belgian government, assuming that if Brussels agreed to a deal, Tshombe would go along. This time he made no such error. He communicated directly with Tshombe in an exchange of telegrams on August 10, and final arrangements were made on the telephone after the Secretary-General reached Leopoldville. The Katanga leader had retreated from his position of total opposition to a UN presence in Katanga and instead had set sixteen conditions for the entry of the troops— conditions designed primarily to prevent the central government from using the UN presence to reassert its control over Katanga. While

Hammarskjold officially rejected these conditions, in fact his arrangements took some of them into account. Tshombe had demanded that no Ghanaian or Guinean troops be included in the UN force in Katanga, and no such troops were sent. He also demanded that the United Nations not interfere in the dispute between the central government and Katanga. This provision was part of the August 9 Security Council resolution, so that Hammarskjold could not really be accused of yielding to Tshombe by observing it. It was clear, however, that the detailed explanation of the resolution which he issued shortly after his arrival in the Congo was a measure designed to mollify the secessionist leader.[5]

On August 12 the Secretary-General landed in Elisabethville accompanied by 240 Swedish troops wearing light-blue UN helmets. He was met by a smiling Tshombe, who insisted on referring to these troops as Hammarskjold's "bodyguard." After Tshombe succeeded in maneuvering the Secretary-General into a position in which he appeared to recognize the flag and anthem of an independent Katanga—with news photographers flashing the picture around the world—the two men proceeded to work out the details of the transfer of duties from the Belgian forces to the UN force. The following day the Swedish soldiers took over the Elisabethville airport from the Belgians, and on August 14 the Belgian commander formally transferred power to the United Nations in a colorful ceremony. Within a few days UN troops from Morocco, Ireland, Mali, and Ethiopia were moving into Katanga.

Hammarskjold regarded his visit to Elisabethville and the peaceful introduction of UN troops into Katanga as a diplomatic triumph. Not everyone agreed. Lumumba was furious. He had expected Hammarskjold to supply him with the planes he needed to transport his troops to Katanga and end the secession. Instead, Hammarskjold had ignored him and dealt directly with Tshombe—a pair of actions which Lumumba regarded as a deliberate insult. When Hammarskjold returned to Leopoldville and informed Bomboko that he wished to report to the government, Lumumba refused to see him. Over the next two days he sent Hammarskjold three angry letters accusing him of ignoring the central government and capitulating to Tshombe's demands. "You are acting as though my government . . . did not exist," he complained. In his final letter he stated point-blank: "The government and people of the Congo have lost their confidence in the Secretary-General."[6]

Hammarskjold icily rejected Lumumba's charges as "unfounded and unjustified." He announced that he was returning to New York immediately to consult with the Security Council, which would have to judge between his interpretation of the mandate and Lumumba's. He was so angry that when the Prime Minister asked him to delay his trip for a day and give the Congolese delegation a ride on his plane, he refused to wait.[7]

Most of the African leaders who had contributed troops to the UN force were deeply disturbed by Lumumba's intemperate attacks on Hammarskjold. They were afraid that he would embroil his country and all of Africa in a major conflict between the great powers. Even his old friend and mentor, Nkrumah, urged him to work with the United Nations. The only exception was Sékou Touré, who promised Lumumba that if the United Nations failed to end the Katanga secession, he would put his troops at the disposal of the Congolese government.[8]

Lumumba decided to ignore their advice. He was certain that Hammarskjold's approach was wrong, and he resented the paternalism of UN officials who believed that they knew how to deal with the Congo's problems better than he did. He regarded the well-meaning advice of his African friends as equally unrealistic. Lumumba was obsessed with the Katanga issue for a number of reasons. He was enraged by the arrogance of the Belgian industrialists, who felt they had the right to carve a puppet state out of his newly independent country; he was concerned that the loss of the Congo's richest province would lead to economic instability in the rest of the country; but, perhaps most important, he feared that the secession would prove contagious. He had come to power as an advocate of national unity in a country one-third the size of the United States with a population of thirteen and a half million divided into two hundred tribes speaking over four hundred dialects. He was afraid that if Katanga were permitted to secede, the country would soon be fragmented into dozens of antagonistic small states.

Hammarskjold's refusal to help him end the Katanga secession intensified his suspicions of the United Nations and the Western powers. He was particularly infuriated by the fact that the Secretary-General had taken only white UN troops to Elisabethville with him. He complained that Belgian paratroopers had obtained UN armbands and were masquerading as Swedish UN troops, and demanded that all white UN troops be removed from the Congo immediately.[9] The real issue, however, was much larger than a question of mistaken identity. Lumumba was convinced that all the Westerners in the Congo were racists. According to Serge Michel, a French-Algerian leftist who served as his press attaché, he was offended by articles in the European press after his trip to Washington complaining that this "sale nègre" had slept in the same bed once occupied by President de Gaulle. He remarked angrily to Michel, "They're afraid. How can you imagine that, just like that, a hat painted blue is enough to eliminate the complexes of conservative officers from Sweden or Canada or Great Britain?" Their vision of Africa, he said, was one of lion hunts, slave markets, and colonial conquests, and they sympathized with the Belgians because they had "the same past, the same history, the same taste for our riches."[10]

Eisenhower: Green Light for the CIA

The open break between Hammarskjold and Lumumba produced shock waves in Washington. From the beginning of the crisis the United States had sought to limit Soviet involvement in the Congo by interposing the United Nations between the impatient Congolese and their former colonial masters, hoping in this way to avoid a situation in which Lumumba would turn to the Soviet Union for assistance. Despite the UN presence Lumumba had become increasingly dependent on radical Communist and pro-Communist advisers.

Perhaps the most intriguing of these advisers was Mme. Andrée Blouin, a strikingly attractive woman who was the daughter of a French father and an African mother. She was described by the U.S. Embassy as "the Madame de Pompadour of Conakry" who was playing "Catherine of Congo in various high-placed bedrooms" in Leopoldville.[11] She had reportedly been trained in Moscow and had lived in various parts of West Africa, most recently in Guinea, where she had worked closely with Sékou Touré's governing party. When she arrived in the Congo, she became a close companion of Gizenga, and, under a new law which permitted foreigners to adopt Congolese citizenship after three weeks in the country, she was named chief of protocol and was thus in a position to approve all foreign nationals who wanted to do business with the Foreign Ministry. American diplomats had first noted her presence at the end of July, when she was in charge of the official dinner at which Gizenga blasted Secretary-General Hammarskjold. Robinson McIlvaine, the deputy chief of mission, reported to Washington that this was his "first opportunity to see at first hand the Communist apparatus in action." In addition to Mme. Blouin, the guests included four Soviet officials and four Guinean advisers who spent most of the evening trying to persuade their Congolese hosts not to trust the United Nations.[12]

American officials hoped that the Secretary-General's ambitious plan for a civilian operation, which he announced formally on August 11,[13] would make it possible to limit the influence of the Mme. Blouins. Hammarskjold envisaged a high-level UN adviser for each government department, plus a large staff of technicians. The State Department had already asked the Embassy in Leopoldville to list the "sensitive" jobs where a "special effort might be warranted" to attempt to place "US or other non-Communist personnel,"[14] and it

urged the members of NATO, SEATO, and CENTO to supply qualified people for these posts—especially in the areas of government administration, press and radio, economic planning, and trade. The
Department's reasoning was clearly spelled out:

TO ALLOW SOV BLOC TAKE OVER INFLUENTIAL POSITIONS CONGO GOV-
ERNMENT WOULD HAVE DISASTROUS CONSEQUENCES FREE-WORLD
CAUSE.[15]

Now, with Lumumba's repudiation of Hammarskjold, this entire
strategy was placed in jeopardy. Hammarskjold confided to the Americans that if the non-African contingents were forced to leave the Congo, he would recommend withdrawal of the entire UN force; the
world organization could not adopt a policy of "inverted racism."
Without the protection of UN military units, the civilian operation
would have to be ended as well.[16] U.S. officials had visions of their
worst-case scenario coming true. "We believe UN withdrawal from
Congo would prove calamitous," Under Secretary Dillon told Lodge.
Lumumba would "probably" turn to the Soviet Union for help, and
the conflict might well spread beyond the Congo.[17]

There was, however, another alternative—one which the U.S. government had been considering for some time and which was now
raised indirectly by Hammarskjold. Lodge informed the State Department on the evening of August 16 that the Secretary-General apparently had concluded that the "UN effort could not continue with
Lumumba in office. One or the other would have to go."[18] The idea
that the United Nations would stay and Lumumba would go became
more and more appealing to American policymakers as alarming reports continued to roll in from the Congo.

U.S. Ambassador Timberlake was aware that Lumumba's opponents
were planning to stage a coup d'état between August 15 and 20.[19] He
had kept in close touch with these leaders ever since Kalonji stopped
in to see him on July 11 to ask for funds to help overthrow the Lumumba government. Timberlake reported deadpan:

I INFORMED HIM IMPOSSIBLE GRANT SUCH REQUEST SINCE USG DOES NOT
INTERFERE IN INTERNAL AFFAIRS OF FOREIGN GOVERNMENTS.[20]

At that time, Kalonji had predicted that the Lumumba government
would fall within two months. Timberlake was eager to speed up the
timetable. On August 17 he recommended that Lumumba's opponents
be encouraged to remove him from power as soon as possible. "We
feel whiphand is Lumumba's and unless he is stopped he will very
shortly neutralize or eliminate the opposition near him," he warned
the State Department. He realized that it would not be easy to replace
Lumumba, since there was "no one with national stature" in the oppo-

sition. He was not particularly sanguine about Kasavubu as a rallying point:

WE ARE NOW SATISIFIED KASAVUBU WILL CONTINUE TO BE A POLITICAL ZERO SO LONG AS LUMUMBA IS ACTIVE; IN MY OPINION HE IS NAIVE, NOT VERY BRIGHT, LAZY, ENJOYING HIS NEW FOUND PLUSH LIVING AND CONTENT TO APPEAR OCCASIONALLY IN HIS NEW GENERAL'S UNIFORM.

He went on to note that Ileo, the leader of anti-Lumumba sentiment in the Senate, would be the "most likely successor" to Lumumba if his government were "unseated by legal means." He spoke highly of Foreign Minister Bomboko as a "moderate" who had displayed courage during the mutiny, and he described Kalonji and his allies as moderates with "considerable regional backing." All, he said, were "reasonable men who would work for constructive solutions to the problems of the Congo." He pointed out that since they had had little experience with parliamentary tactics, their opposition to Lumumba might take a more direct form; in fact, he would not be "surprised if an attempt [were] made on Lumumba's life." This would not be an unmixed blessing, he added:

WHILE LUMUMBA'S ELIMINATION WOULD REMOVE ONE PROBLEM, IT MIGHT WELL CREATE MANY MORE. GIZENGA WOULD PRESUMABLY SUCCEED HIM AND IS UNDER SAME INFLUENCE OF COMMUNIST ADVISORS. MORE COLOR WOULD BE GIVEN TO THE BELGIAN PLOT THESIS AND MORE REASON FOR MARTIAL LAW. UN WOULD ALSO BE ACCUSED AT LEAST OF NEGLIGENCE, IF NOT OF COMPLICITY.[21]

Timberlake regarded Lumumba's demand for the withdrawal of all white UN troops as part of a larger strategy. He was certain that Lumumba was deliberately encouraging the soldiers of the Force Publique to harass UN personnel and create an atmosphere of disorder in which the remaining Europeans would leave the Congo, and that he was acting under the guidance of his "anti-white, pro-Communist" Ghanaian and Guinean advisers. He explained:

THE OBJECTIVE SEEMS CLEAR. REMOVE THE BULK OF EUROPEANS AND YOU ELIMINATE EFFECTIVE WESTERN INFLUENCE. ONCE EUROPEANS HAVE GONE, NATIONALIZE THEIR PROPERTY ON SIMPLE THEORY THAT BUSINESS AND INDUSTRY MUST RUN TO KEEP CONGOLESE EMPLOYED AND IF EUROPEANS WILL NOT RUN THEM CONGOLESE GOVERNMENT MUST. FINALLY GOC WOULD INVITE COMMIE BLOC EXPERTS IN TO KEEP BUSINESS AND INDUSTRY GOING.[22]

A few hours after he sent this report, Timberlake learned that six American crewmen had been arrested and held for some time by unruly Congolese soldiers at the Leopoldville airport before they were rescued by Ghanaian UN troops. He pointed out that this was not an isolated incident; it was one more example of the serious consequences of Lumumba's policy.[23]

The following day, after a group of Canadian UN technicians who had just arrived at the airport were brutally beaten by Congolese soldiers,[24] the CIA station chief in Leopoldville, Lawrence Devlin, summed up the situation in even more alarming terms:

> EMBASSY AND STATION BELIEVE CONGO EXPERIENCING CLASSIC COMMU-
> NIST EFFORT TAKEOVER GOVERNMENT. MANY FORCES AT WORK HERE:
> SOVIETS . . . COMMUNIST PARTY, ETC. ALTHOUGH DIFFICULT DETERMINE
> MAJOR INFLUENCING FACTORS TO PREDICT OUTCOME STRUGGLE FOR
> POWER, DECISIVE PERIOD NOT FAR OFF. WHETHER OR NOT LUMUMBA AC-
> TUALLY COMMIE OR JUST PLAYING COMMIE GAME TO ASSIST HIS SOLIDI-
> FYING POWER, ANTI-WEST FORCES RAPIDLY INCREASING POWER CONGO
> AND THERE MAY BE LITTLE TIME LEFT IN WHICH TAKE ACTION AVOID
> ANOTHER CUBA.

To counter this threat, Devlin proposed an operation whose objective was "replacing Lumumba with [a] pro-Western group."[25] Bronson Tweedy, the chief of the Africa Divison of the CIA's clandestine services, replied immediately and said he was seeking State Department approval for Devlin's plan, based on "your and our belief Lumumba must be removed if possible."[26]

The same day, worried CIA and State Department officials brought the matter before President Eisenhower at a meeting of the National Security Council (NSC). According to the minutes of the meeting published in the report of the Senate Intelligence Committee, Dillon said it was essential to prevent Lumumba from forcing the United Nations out of the Congo:

> The elimination of the U.N. would be a disaster which, Secretary Dillon
> stated, we should do everything we could to prevent. If the U.N. were
> forced out, we might be faced by a situation where the Soviets intervened
> by invitation of the Congo.

Dillon said that Lumumba was "working to serve the purposes of the Soviets" and Dulles added that Lumumba was "in Soviet pay."

Eisenhower's reaction, the minutes made clear, was one of outrage:

> The President said that the possibility the U.N. would be forced out was
> simply inconceivable. We should keep the U.N. in the Congo even if we
> had to ask for European troops to do it. We should do so even if such ac-
> tion was used by the Soviets as the basis for starting a fight.

Dillon indicated that that was how the State Department saw it, but he explained that Hammarskjold and Lodge doubted the United Nations could keep its force in the Congo if the Congo put up "really determined opposition."

In response, the President stated that Mr. Lodge was wrong to this extent—we were talking of one man forcing us out of the Congo; of Lumumba supported by the Soviets. There was no indication, the President stated, that the Congolese did not want U.N. support and the maintenance of order. Secretary Dillon reiterated that this was State's feeling about the matter. The situation that would be created by a U.N. withdrawal was altogether too ghastly to contemplate.[27]

Several important points emerge from this record. First, it conveys the mood of high-level Washington in the midst of the Congo crisis and reflects the deep concern felt by all the top officials, right up to the President. He considered the possibility that the United Nations would be forced out "inconceivable" and indicated that he was willing to risk a "fight" with the Soviet Union over the issue.

Second, it suggests the absolute moral certainty with which the President and his closest advisers regarded the Congo problem. When Dillon mentioned the possibility, raised by Hammarskjold and Lodge, that the United Nations might in fact be forced to leave the Congo, the idea was dismissed out of hand. The men at the NSC meeting reacted in a manner reminiscent of John Wayne in a traditional American western. It was clear to them that the UN peacekeeping force was good for the Congolese and good for the free world, and they were determined that it would not be stopped by one hired gun in the pay of a band of rustlers—even if he was the elected Prime Minister of the Congo.

Third, it raises the central question that dominated the deliberations of the Senate committee and disturbed the American people more than fifteen years later: did the President of the United States authorize the assassination of the leader of a foreign government?

One official who was present at the meeting testified that that was his "clear impression at the time"; Robert Johnson, a member of the NSC staff from 1951 to 1962, told the committee:

At some time during that discussion, President Eisenhower said something—I can no longer remember his words—that came across to me as an order for the assassination of Lumumba who was then at the center of political conflict and controversy in the Congo. There was no discussion; the meeting simply moved on. I remember my sense of that moment quite clearly because the President's statement came as a great shock to me.

Johnson went on to say that "in thinking about the incident more recently" he had "had some doubts" about the accuracy of his impression. It was possible, he said, that what he had heard was merely an order for "political action" against Lumumba. Still, he felt, on reflection, that his initial impression was correct.[28] The minutes, Johnson explained, would not have included such an order if it had been given; either a euphemism would have been used, or the subject would have been omitted entirely.[29]

The testimony of the other participants in the meeting was less dramatic. Marion Boggs, the NSC's acting executive secretary, could not remember hearing the President say anything that "could be interpreted as favoring action by the United States to bring about the assassination of Lumumba." Dillon, after reviewing the documents, said he did not recall a "clear cut order" from Eisenhower for the assassination of Lumumba; but he did recall that everyone in the room, including the President, agreed that Lumumba was a "very difficult if not impossible person to deal with, and was dangerous to the peace and safety of the world." In that context, Dillon went on, the President may have said, "We will have to do whatever is necessary to get rid of him"; and his statement was interpreted in different ways. Although Dillon himself did not see it as an order for assassination, he explained that it was "perfectly plausible" to assume that CIA Director Dulles took it as "implicit authorization" to proceed with an assassination plan, while keeping the President out of it—"because he felt very strongly that we should not involve the President directly in things of this nature. And he was perfectly willing to take the responsibility personally."[30]

It seems fairly clear in retrospect that this was a classic situation in which a leader demands that his closest aides "do something" about a problem that is plaguing him. As King Henry II said of Thomas Becket, who had become a thorn in his side, "Will no one rid me of this man?" Although this was not a formal authorization to assassinate Becket, its essential meaning was clear; thus it was not surprising that loyal subordinates—who agreed with their leader's wish in the first place—hastened to obey his implicit command.

In this case the next recorded step was a cable sent to Devlin in Leopoldville the following day by Richard Bissell, the CIA's Deputy Director for Plans. Bissell, who was in charge of covert operations, gave the station chief a green light for his plan to replace Lumumba with a "pro-Western group": "You are authorized proceed with operation."[31]

Khrushchev: Decision on Military Intervention

While American policymakers were agonizing about the likelihood of a Soviet takeover in the Congo, Premier Khrushchev was faced with a major decision about whether he should supply military aid to Lumumba, and if so, how much. Khrushchev had committed his prestige to a UN approach; for the past month his delegates had voted with the United States for compromise resolutions sponsored by the Afro-Asian group, hoping that the United Nations would respond to Lumumba's needs and make direct Soviet military aid unnecessary. Now, after the blowup in Leopoldville, it was clear that this approach had failed. Even if Khrushchev had been willing to accept Hammarskjold's go-slow policy, Lumumba was not. He was disillusioned with the United Nations and ready to turn to the leader of the Communist bloc and cash in on the promises he had made. On August 15 Lumumba wrote to Khrushchev and specifically requested that the Soviet Union supply him with transport planes and crews, trucks, weapons, and other equipment.[32] He was determined to end the Katanga secession and end it quickly. Khrushchev now had to decide how to respond to this request—how to balance the risk of confronting the United States with the risk of losing the respect of the Third World radicals, who had become a cornerstone of his policy.

While he was deciding, he stepped up his political assistance to Lumumba. The Prime Minister had already received expert advice in drafting his letters to Hammarskjold from Andrei Fomin, the Soviet chargé d'affaires in Leopoldville,[33] who had served with the Soviet delegation at the United Nations and was familiar with its forms and rules. Fomin had arrived with the food airlift a few weeks before for what he thought would be a brief visit and found to his dismay that he was expected to stay and run the Soviet Embassy until the new ambassador arrived. On August 17 the Embassy was officially upgraded; the new ambassador, Mikhail Yakovlev, presented his credentials to President Kasavubu.[34] The same day, Lumumba announced that the Russians were supplying an Ilyushin-18 to transport his delegation to the Security Council meeting in New York.[35] Yakovlev saw the delegation off at the airport, bestowing bear hugs and compliments on the Congolese delegates.[36]

Thus far, Soviet support for Lumumba had cost little—a few flamboyant gestures, strong words at the United Nations, planeloads of food, extra hours for the advisers on the Embassy staff in Leopoldville. But now Khrushchev realized that a decisive moment had come. Lumumba was in an increasingly difficult position. Internal dissent was mounting daily. Kasai Province had seceded as well as Katanga. Lumumba had so antagonized the Secretary-General and the Western powers who were influential in the United Nations that the world organization would not help him in any way to retrieve the two secessionist provinces. There were strong indications after Lumumba's tour of the African countries that they were not willing to help either. The Soviet leader undoubtedly feared that if the rift between Lumumba and the Secretary-General on the one hand, and between Lumumba and his Congolese rivals on the other hand, grew much wider, the Western powers might well have the chance to do what the Soviet press had been warning they would do: they might take strong steps to get rid of Lumumba and his troublesome disruptions of their valuable economic system.

Khrushchev at this point had two options: he could continue his verbal support for Lumumba and hope that the Congolese leader would muddle through on his own; or he could agree to Lumumba's request and provide him with the military aid he felt he needed to reassert control over the two breakaway provinces.

The Soviet Premier was certainly well aware of the risks involved in a decision to supply Lumumba with military aid. He knew the lines of communication between the Soviet Union and the Congo were far too long to sustain any sort of military challenge to the entrenched Western powers. Even the peaceful supply flights had difficulty on the Rabat-Accra-Leopoldville route, across the Sahara; the alternative Cairo-Khartoum-Stanleyville route (which would be tried later in an attempt to supply Gizenga) was just as long and filled with diplomatic hazards.

But he must have weighed against these risks the concern that if Lumumba did not succeed in reasserting control over Katanga, his tenure as Prime Minister might be sharply limited, and Moscow might lose its best prospect in Africa; and if the Soviet Union turned down his urgent request at a time of need and he did manage to stay on as Prime Minister of a reunited Congo, he would have no reason to be grateful to Moscow for his success. If the Soviet leader was to maintain the momentum of his drive to win the friendship of the radical leaders of the Third World, he could not fail to meet this clear challenge—and opportunity.

Khrushchev concluded that it would be impossible, physically and politically, to send Soviet combat troops to the Congo, even if Lumumba seriously wanted them, which was doubtful. But he decided that limited military aid—in the form of arms, transport, and advisers—might help Lumumba through a tight spot without inviting the risk of Western military intervention and a direct confrontation with the United States.

The Soviet leader had laid the groundwork for this option from the beginning of the UN operation. Although the initial Security Council resolution had implied that all aid to the Congo was to be channeled through the United Nations, and the Secretary-General had interpreted this to mean that bilateral aid from any power was prohibited, the Soviet government had never accepted this principle and had walked a thin line between compliance and violation.

During the latter half of July and the first part of August, the Soviet Union had publicized its aid to the Congo and had implied or stated that it was being sent in response to UN requests or in accordance with UN policy. The announced aid included ten thousand tons of food, the first twenty-five tons of which arrived on the five Ilyushin-18 planes which were then used to ferry Ghanaian UN troops to the Congo, the rest sent by sea from Odessa, on the *Leninogorsk*; and one hundred trucks, accompanied by spare parts, a repair shop, and instructors, shipped from Odessa on the *Arkhangelsk* before August 6.[37] In addition, the Soviet government statement published on August 1 promised that Soviet doctors and medical supplies would soon be sent to the Congo.[38]

There were indications in these published reports of friction between the Soviet government and the United Nations about the disposition of Soviet aid once it arrived in the Congo; Soviet pilots, for example, complained that UN officials had blocked their attempts to distribute food to remote areas of the Congo by plane.[39] Despite the efforts of these officials to establish UN authority over the Soviet planes, trucks, and supplies, they remained under Soviet control.

By August 20 Khrushchev was ready to move beyond these initial measures. He ordered the dispatch of ten additional planes, complete with crews, backup crews, technicians, translators, and equipment—including weapons and ammunition for Lumumba's soldiers. He had weighed the risks and decided to embark on a bold new interventionist policy which would project Soviet power into the heart of Africa.

The Fourth Security Council Meeting: August 21–22, 1960

Meanwhile, in New York, Hammarskjold was looking forward confidently to the August 21 meeting of the Security Council, which would be taking up the Congo issue for the fourth time. "Only Lumumba," he remarked to Lodge, "would be stupid enough" to look for a showdown when the Secretary-General had all the "cards in his hand." He explained that he had published the exchange of letters so that the world could "see just what kind of man Lumumba is." He planned to let a few days elapse before the meeting so that the African and Asian delegates could be exposed to Gizenga, who would be heading the Congolese delegation. Hammarskjold described Gizenga as "evil" and "unintelligent" and predicted that he would "make a bad impression." Most of the Africans, "and especially the Asians," he said, were "fed up with Lumumba," who was a "great embarrassment to them."[40]

Hammarskjold's assessment of the Afro-Asian delegates was accurate; when Gizenga met with them he found that the only country which was not strongly opposed to Lumumba's attacks on the Secretary-General was Guinea. But the Secretary-General's contempt for Lumumba caused him to misgauge the attitude of the Soviet Union. He had met with Kuznetsov soon after his return from Leopoldville and emerged with the impression that the Russians were "fed up" with the attention which had been focused on the Congo. "Moscow," he told Lodge, "realizes that it cannot build on anyone as erratic and inept as Lumumba." He came to the erroneous conclusion that the Soviet government was interested primarily in using the Congo issue for its propaganda value in Africa.[41]

The first indication that he had misread Soviet intentions came on August 20, when Kuznetsov handed him an official government statement which backed Lumumba completely and took issue with the Secretary-General on three important points. First, it rejected his view that the Katanga secession was an "internal matter" in which the United Nations should not interfere. Second, it objected strenuously to his plans for an expanded civilian operation in the Congo. Finally, it blamed the latest airport incident on the "illegal actions" of the Canadians and pointed out that the Secretary-General's use of technicians from a NATO country was setting a precedent that could be used to justify Soviet military intervention. Citing reports that Hammarskjold was about to send "new contingents of troops from NATO countries" and rumors that Tshombe was setting up a "foreign legion" composed of "so-called NATO volunteers," the Soviet government warned: "One cannot fail to see that this may lead to a stream of real volunteers from the countries of Africa ... and also from countries situated on other continents."[42]

With this August 20 statement Khrushchev was trying to set up a legal justification for his decision to intervene in support of Lumumba. But his intention had not yet become known, and his warnings were taken for nothing more than a general hardening of the Soviet attitude on the Congo issue.

The Security Council debate itself turned out to be something of an anticlimax after all the feverish activity that preceded it. Hammarskjold completely rejected Lumumba's view that the UN force had been sent to help subdue the revolt in Katanga, and he cited chapter and verse from the Security Council resolutions to bolster his case. He then raised the issue of the increasingly serious Congolese assaults on UN personnel, which were encouraged by Lumumba's suspicious attitude. He implied that if these assaults continued, the United Nations might have to pull out of the Congo altogether.

Gizenga was not impressed by Hammarskjold's legalistic arguments or his threats. He repeated all the charges Lumumba had made and demanded that the Council send a neutral team of African and Asian observers to the Congo to ensure that the Secretary-General carried out the mandate.[43] He was backed up by Kuznetsov, who presented a draft resolution embodying his demand for a neutral observer team.[44] But Hammarskjold moved quickly to defuse the issue by offering to set up an advisory committee composed of representatives of the troop-contributing countries, who would meet with him in New York on a regular basis.[45] This was not enough to satisfy Gizenga, but it was enough to persuade the neutrals on the Council that Kuznetsov's implied rebuke of the Secretary-General should be rejected.

At the same time, the Tunisian and Ceylonese delegations were not prepared to go along with American wishes and introduce a resolution endorsing Hammarskjold's actions. Despite his admiration for Hammarskjold's accomplishment, Ambassador Slim suggested that it would be better for the Council to avoid specific action and leave the door open for the African foreign ministers, who would soon be meeting in Leopoldville, to try to persuade Lumumba to cooperate with the United Nations.[46]

Lumumba's Desperate Gamble

Lumumba's reaction to the Security Council meeting was characteristically unpredictable. On August 22, after two weeks of strong statements, threats, and demands directed at the United Nations, he issued a mild statement saying that he was "satisfied" with the Security Council's action, which, in effect, left Hammarskjold's position unchallenged and unchanged.[47] Once Lumumba realized the United Nations was not about to help him reassert control over Katanga, he lost interest in it and became preoccupied with more pressing matters—his domestic political troubles, his upcoming African conference, and his negotiations with the Russians. For the first time in many days, the Prime Minister had no time to talk to the press. He spent a good part of the day closeted with the Soviet ambassador.[48] It was probably at this meeting that Yakovlev informed him that the Soviet Union would be sending ten Ilyushin-14 planes, with crews, technicians, and weapons, to Stanleyville in the near future and would place at his disposal one hundred trucks which had just arrived at the port of Matadi in response to a UN request. Suddenly, Lumumba could see his way clear to a resolution of the Katanga question.

While he was preparing for his invasion of Katanga, he intensified his search for spies and saboteurs in Leopoldville. Life in the capital became increasingly chaotic, as Congolese soldiers arrested UN officials, European businessmen, diplomats, and journalists at random. Young demonstrators, pro- and anti-Lumumba, marched through the streets. Political meetings were broken up. Houses and businesses were ransacked. On August 23 all communications with Brazzaville, across the river, were cut off.[49]

Ambassador Timberlake was alarmed by the spreading disorders and by Lumumba's open reliance on the Russians. He told the State Department on August 24 that "arbitrary and senseless arrests" had become "common occurrences" and that the morale of the UN troops was becoming "seriously strained" because they were forced to stand by as their comrades were humiliated, beaten, and seriously wounded by "lawless and undisciplined" Congolese soldiers who had been deliberately stirred up by Lumumba. He strongly recommended that the UN force be given the authority to take over and disarm the Force Publique; only in this way, he insisted, could order be restored.

The ambassador reported that there were approximately one hundred Soviet and Czech "technicians" in the Congo with more expected shortly. He warned:

IF LUMUMBA AND HIS WIRED-IN COMMUNIST ADVISERS ARE NOT STOPPED BY A POLICY OF STRENGTH WE THINK THIS COUNTRY IS HEADED TOWARD ANOTHER CHINA BY WAY OF TECHNICIANS INSTEAD OF BAYONETS.[50]

Meanwhile, the U.S. Embassy in Brussels reported a new and disturbing development: two top Belgian Communists, Albert de Coninck and Jean Terfve, had received Congolese visas and were planning to leave for Leopoldville via Conakry in the near future. They had had "extensive contacts" in the past with Lumumba, Gizenga, Kashamura, and other radical political figures. The Embassy warned:

IF THEY AND OTHER BCP MEMBERS CAN GRADUALLY TAKE OVER FUNCTION OF ADVISING CONGOLESE LEADERS FROM PRESENT COLLECTION OF FLY-BY-NIGHTS, CARPET BAGGERS, EMBITTERED EX-CIVIL SERVANTS AND AFRICAN COMMUNISTS, RESULT COULD BE SUBSTANTIAL INCREASE IN EFFECTIVENESS AND COORDINATION COMMUNIST INFLUENCE IN CONGO GOVERNMENT.[51]

There seemed to be very little the Americans in Leopoldville could do to reverse this process. Whenever Timberlake, accompanied by his French-speaking second secretary, Frank Carlucci, went to see Kasavubu at his spacious residence overlooking Stanley Falls to try to persuade him that Lumumba was an extremely dangerous man, Kasavubu sat impassively, his eyes half-closed, listening—but would say nothing. The Americans were not sure if this was because he was not yet convinced that it was a good idea to remove Lumumba from office or because he was playing a waiting game. In either case it was a frustrating experience. As Timberlake noted in a gloomy cable to Washington, "I confess I have not yet learned secret of spurring Kasavubu to action."[52]

Devlin was not having any better luck. On August 24, the station chief reported discouraging news: anti-Lumumba leaders had approached Kasavubu with a "plan to assassinate Lumumba" but Kasavubu had refused, explaining that he was reluctant to resort to violence and that there was no other leader of "sufficient stature [to] replace Lumumba"[53]

At this point Kasavubu could not be persuaded to take action against Lumumba by the Americans or by his own Abako party stalwarts; he was persuaded, in the end, by the actions of Lumumba himself. August 24 marked the beginning of Lumumba's effort to end the secessions in Kasai and Katanga with the help of the Soviet Union.

Lumumba's first move was to demand that the United Nations turn over the Leopoldville airport to his troops and to threaten to take it by force if the United Nations refused. The United Nations had been maintaining order at the airport since the attack on the Canadians the week before. When Bunche tried to discuss the matter with Lumumba, the Prime Minister refused to see him. This rebuff, coming on top of all the violent incidents of the past few weeks, was the last straw for the Secretary-General's special representative. He felt his usefulness in the Congo had come to an end; he was more than ready to return to New York and confer there with his successor, the Indian diplomat Rajeshwar Dayal, whose appointment had been announced by Hammarskjold on August 20. "I'm a patient man," Bunche said sadly, "but my patience has worn thin."[54] UN officials managed to prevent an armed clash, but they consolidated their forces at the airport in anticipation of the "battle" that they expected would take place immediately after the African foreign ministers' conference ended.[55]

Lumumba's next move that day was to requisition five planes from Air Congo, a Sabena subsidiary, and send two hundred soldiers to Luluabourg, in Kasai. Ostensibly these troops were sent to stop the fierce tribal fighting between Luluas and Balubas; actually they were the first contingent of a force numbering nearly one thousand troops whose mission was to defeat the secessionist forces of Albert Kalonji in Kasai and then move on to end the Katanga secession.[56]

It might have been more sensible for Lumumba to wait until the Soviet planes and equipment arrived before launching this campaign. Only the day before, Gizenga had set the end of the month as a target date for the invasion of Katanga, because the Secretary-General had promised that the Belgian troops would be out by then, and Gizenga expected no resistance to the central government once the Belgians were gone.[57] But Lumumba was too impatient to wait; he was eager to make use of the Soviet trucks in Kasai, and he felt confident of success now that he knew the Soviet planes, arms, and technicians were on the way.

Besides, he was eager to show the African delegates when they assembled at the conference the next day that he was fully in control of the situation. He knew that once the military operation had started, he would be presenting them with a fait accompli, which could no longer be prevented by diplomatic pleas for moderation.

That evening, Lumumba proclaimed defiantly at a press conference, "We will settle the Katanga problem with our own forces." He hinted at the likelihood of Soviet aid in his reply to the question of a Soviet correspondent:

> Even before, and then after the proclamation of independence we enjoyed the moral support of the Soviet Union. . . . Today we are receiving not only moral but also material support. Only yesterday we received autos and tools, and before that, food. The enemies of our independence try to frighten us and have us refuse help from the Soviet Union. But we are firmly convinced this help is disinterested and humane.[58]

UN officials, listening to Lumumba and reviewing his demand for control of the airport, began to put two and two together. The next day Wieschhoff told Lodge "very confidentially" that the United Nations was "worried about arms from 'certain quarters' being imported through the airport under guise of food consignments." This, he said, might explain Lumumba's insistence about controlling the airport.[59]

Soon another piece of the puzzle fell into place. The U.S. Embassy in Athens reported that the Soviet government had asked permission for ten "Russian cargo planes carrying food to Leopoldville to overfly Greece or land for refueling" starting August 26. The Greek government replied that it was prepared to grant the Soviet request providing it had the "right to inspect and control" the cargo.[60]

The CIA Swings into Action

As these disquieting bulletins were arriving in Washington, the Special Group—a subcommittee of the National Security Council responsible for the planning of covert operations—was meeting to discuss the problem of Lumumba. Gordon Gray, special assistant to the President for national security affairs, listened with interest as Thomas Parrott of the CIA reported on the Agency's anti-Lumumba campaign. After Parrott described what was essentially a political approach—an effort to work through certain labor groups, and an attempt to arrange a vote of no confidence in Lumumba in the Congolese Senate—it became clear that this was not exactly what the Eisenhower Administration had in mind. As the minutes of the meeting stated:

> The Group agreed that the action contemplated is very much in order. Mr. Gray commented, however, that his associates had expressed extremely strong feelings on the necessity for very straightforward action in

this situation, and he wondered whether the plans as outlined were sufficient to accomplish this.

Mr. Dulles replied that he had taken the comments referred to seriously and had every intention of proceeding as vigorously as the situation permits or requires, but added that he must necessarily put himself in a position of interpreting instructions of this kind within the bounds of necessity and capability. It was finally agreed that planning for the Congo would not necessarily rule out "consideration" of any particular kind of activity which might contribute to getting rid of Lumumba.[61]

Clearly, the President was demanding more extreme action to remove Lumumba from the scene. Both Gray and Parrott told the Senate Intelligence Committee that Gray's reference to his "associates" was a euphemism for the President, which was used to preserve "plausible deniability"—that is, the ability to deny later that the President had any knowledge of the matter under discussion.[62]

Although none of the participants recalled a specific discussion of assassination, Assistant Secretary of Defense John N. Irwin II testified that the reference to "getting rid of Lumumba" was "broad enough to cover a discussion of assassination."[63] Dillon and Bissell, who were not at the meeting but were involved throughout this period in planning covert operations in the Congo, agreed with this assessment. Dillon said he thought the minutes indicated that "assassination was within bounds" and that Dulles's reference to the fact that he "had taken the comments referred to seriously" related to Eisenhower's statements at the August 18 NSC meeting. Bissell was even more specific: "The Agency had put a top priority, probably, on a range of different methods of getting rid of Lumumba in the sense of either destroying him physically, incapacitating him, or eliminating his political influence." He went on:

> When you use the language that no particular means were ruled out, that is obviously what it meant, and it meant that to everybody in the room.... You don't use language of that kind except to mean in effect, the Director is being told, get rid of the guy, and if you have to use extreme means up to and including assassination, go ahead.

Bissell testified that, "in effect," Dulles was being given a message from the President through Gray.[64]

Dulles was obviously under considerable pressure to produce results, and the news about ten Soviet planes suddenly flying to the Congo did not help matters. The next day, August 26, the CIA Director sent an emphatic cable, which he signed personally, to Devlin in Leopoldville:

> In high quarters here it is the clear-cut conclusion that if [Lumumba] continues to hold high office, the inevitable result will at best be chaos and at worst pave the way to Communist takeover of the Congo with disastrous

consequences for the prestige of the UN and for the interests of the free world generally. Consequently we concluded that his removal must be an urgent and prime objective and that under existing conditions this should be a high priority of our covert action.[65]

Dulles told the station chief that he was being given "wider authority" along the lines of the previously authorized operation—replacing Lumumba with a pro-Western group—"including even more aggressive action if it can remain covert." The Director added, "We realize that targets of opportunity may present themselves to you." He authorized an expenditure of up to $100,000 "to carry out any crash programs on which you do not have the opportunity to consult HQS." He assured Devlin that the message had been "seen and approved at competent level" in the State Department. "To the extent that Ambassador may desire to be consulted," Dulles continued, "you should seek his concurrence. If in any particular case, he does not wish to be consulted, you can act on your own authority where time does not permit referral here."[66]

Devlin was given immense leeway in dealing with the problem of Lumumba. His superiors knew that he was cool and experienced and that he was familiar enough with the Congolese political picture to make decisions on the spot without checking back for further instructions. If semilegal approaches through the Congolese Senate or anti-Lumumba labor groups did not succeed, Devlin was clearly authorized to take "more aggressive" action on his own—that is, to encourage or initiate an assassination attempt against Lumumba. The ambassador, for his part, preferred not to be consulted officially about these matters; the theory of "plausible deniability" applied at this level as well as at the presidential level.

In case there is still any doubt about what the President and his CIA Director were authorizing, it was at about this time—either just before or just after Dulles's August 26 cable—that Bissell explicitly told Tweedy to explore the idea of assassination with the CIA station in Leopoldville. As Tweedy described it:

> What Mr. Bissell was saying to me was that there was agreement, policy agreement, in Washington that Lumumba must be removed from the position of control and influence in the Congo . . . and that among the possibilities of that elimination was indeed assassination. . . . The purpose of his conversation with me was to initiate correspondence with the Station for them to explore with Headquarters the possibility of . . . assassination, or indeed any other means of removing Lumumba from power . . . to have the Station start reviewing possibilities, assets, and discussing them with Headquarters in detail in the same way we would with any operation.

Tweedy further testified that he was "sure" poison was one of the methods of assassination he discussed at that time with Bissell.[67] At about this time Bissell asked his special assistant for scientific matters, Dr. Sidney Gottlieb, to prepare biological materials and have them ready on short notice for possible use in the assassination of an unspecified African leader "in case the decision was to go ahead." Gottlieb testified that Bissell said he "had direction from the highest authority . . . for getting into that kind of operation," and Gottlieb assumed he was referring to the President. The scientist checked with the Army Chemical Corps at Fort Detrick, Maryland, for a substance that would "either kill the individual or incapacitate him so severely that he would be out of action"; he chose a material which "was supposed to produce a disease that was . . . indigenous to that area [of Africa] and that could be fatal." He then went on to describe the procedures that were followed:

> We had to get it bottled and packaged in a way that it could pass for something else and I needed to have a second material that could absolutely inactivate it in case that is what I desired to do for some contingency.

He also "prepared a packet of . . . accessory materials," including hypodermic needles, rubber gloves, and gauze masks "that would be used in the handling of this pretty dangerous material."[68]

While the CIA was taking the James Bond route, the State Department tackled the problem from another direction: it tried to prevent Soviet military aid from reaching Lumumba on the assumption that the aid would strengthen his position and make the problem of "getting rid of him" even more difficult. On August 27 the Department notified its embassies in Rome and Ankara about the Soviet request to Greece and asked them to inform their host governments and to be alert to further Soviet requests for landing rights. It also instructed Lodge to ask the Secretary-General what procedures the United Nations had established in the Congo for "inspection and control of shipments" at Leopoldville airport and other points of entry, and how the United Nations could tighten up that control "or otherwise reduce dangers inherent in this situation."[69]

Lodge's reply was not encouraging. He had asked Wieschhoff, who said there were "no formal procedures" for inspection and control of shipments to Leopoldville and other points and "no specific plans" to tighten controls. Wieschhoff's plan, Lodge reported, was to "have UN food man meet shipments with press and publicity making covert unloading as difficult as possible." Wieschhoff added that he hoped the Greeks would inspect the planes when they touched down in Athens.[70]

On August 31 the State Department sent a circular to its embassies in all the countries bordering the Mediterranean asking them to monitor any "Soviet bloc material" moving through the area. It noted that the Greek authorities had inspected the Soviet planes "but uncovered no questionable cargo."[71]

The next day the news was less reassuring. Lodge reported that the Secretary-General had confirmed the arrival of ten Ilyushin-14 transport planes in Stanleyville and that he was disturbed about their cargo. Hammarskjold, he said,

> DID NOT UNDERSTAND WHAT HAD HAPPENED TO GREEK INSPECTION; PLANES CARRIED FOOD AND SPARE PARTS FOR PLANES ALL RIGHT BUT THEY ALSO CARRIED DIS-ASSEMBLED MACHINE GUNS.

Lodge added that while the Soviet crews stationed with each plane were "theoretically civilian," the Secretary-General was "sure they were military." This, said Hammarskjold, was clearly "outside [the] rules," and he was going to protest to Kuznetsov.[72] State Department officials welcomed Hammarskjold's initiative and suggested that he try to persuade the Africans on the advisory committee to join him in exerting pressure on the Soviet government.[73]

Disaster for Khrushchev

Meanwhile, Lumumba was trying to line up the Africans on his side. He hoped that the Leopoldville conference would not only enhance his prestige in his own country but would also bolster his position in the outside world, particularly with the officials of the United Nations. The conference, however, turned out to be a great disappointment. Instead of witnessing a united people backing a popular leader, the delegates found dramatic evidence of dissension in the streets outside the conference hall.

When the heavily guarded Prime Minister arrived for the opening ceremonies on August 25, he was met by a crowd of hostile demonstrators, shouting, "Down with Lumumba!" Ignoring the demonstrators, he entered the conference hall and began to address the delegates; but his words were nearly drowned out by the rising chorus of anti-Lumumba taunts outside. Suddenly, pro-Lumumba pickets appeared, and the two groups started hurling rocks at each other. At this point the police, led by Colonel Joseph Mobutu, charged the demonstrators in an attempt to restore order. The demonstrators held their ground at first; but when the police fired their rifles into the air, threatening to shoot into the crowd, they ran for cover.[74]

The African delegates, suddenly caught up in the realities of the turbulent Congo situation, advised Lumumba to calm down, to cooperate with the United Nations, and to recognize that he had powerful enemies with whom he would have to compromise. But the rash young

Prime Minister, who regarded such a policy as "opportunism," refused to listen.

On the second day of the conference, he took time off to meet with a high-ranking Soviet official who happened to be in Leopoldville to discuss cultural exchanges—G. A. Zhukov, the chairman of the State Committee on Cultural Relations with Foreign Countries. The two men reached an agreement providing that one hundred and fifty Congolese students would be admitted to Soviet universities.[75] They probably discussed more sensitive subjects as well.

The following day, August 27, Lumumba invited a number of delegates and newsmen to accompany him to Stanleyville, his own stronghold in the northeastern part of the country. He told the press that the purpose of the trip was to "show his visitors that he and his government had political support."[76]

It turned out that another, unannounced, purpose of the trip was to make arrangements for the troops who were to join the invasion of secessionist Kasai and Katanga provinces. When Lumumba landed in Stanleyville and greeted the eight-hundred-man Congolese honor guard by saying, "I am very happy to see you in combat uniform ready to descend on Katanga,"[77] it was assumed that this was merely rhetoric. After all, six hundred miles of jungle lay between Stanleyville and Katanga. At that point few people knew that Lumumba was expecting Soviet planes to arrive in Stanleyville to ferry the Congolese soldiers to their destination.

Just before Lumumba's plane touched down in Stanleyville, ten airmen working for the United Nations—eight Americans and two Canadians—were savagely beaten by Congolese soldiers and police, and were rescued only through the bravery of an Ethiopian UN nurse.[78] The American reaction was sharp; and Timberlake described the incident as further evidence of Lumumba's instability. He reported that when Lumumba arrived in Stanleyville and saw one of the American airmen "propped up bleeding" in a jeep, he "looked, turned and walked away without a word."[79] Timberlake urged once again that the United Nations be given control of the army and police, and predicted that a "showdown" between Lumumba and the United Nations would take place in the near future. "Hope Stanleyville incident has removed any lingering trace of the fiction that we are dealing with a civilized people or a responsible government in the Congo," he wrote.[80] The Secretary-General told Western diplomats privately that he believed the incident was the result of "direct orders from Lumumba."[81] He was more convinced than ever that the crisis must soon come to a head and that "Lumumba must be broken."[82]

The delegates of all the African states except Guinea warned Lumumba at a private meeting that such incidents must cease. They followed up these warnings by adopting a resolution which stressed the importance of working in harmony with the United Nations and by sending a formal letter of appreciation to Bunche and asking him to convey their gratitude to the Secretary-General.[83] These actions constituted a major rebuke to Lumumba, who yielded to African pressure, swallowed his pride, and made a speech at the final session of the conference praising the "magnificent work of the United Nations." He could not resist pointing out, however, that the unpleasant incidents criticized by the Africans had all been the result of the UN officials' failure to consult with his government.[84]

The conference was a defeat for Khrushchev as well as for Lumumba. The Soviet leader must have realized, after the August 21 Security Council meeting, that African sentiment tended to favor Hammarskjold rather than Lumumba, but he hoped the dramatic atmosphere of Leopoldville itself would create a groundswell of sympathy for Lumumba among the African delegates.[85] The atmosphere had the opposite effect. Of all the African states present, only Guinea approved of Lumumba's controversial decision to use Soviet military aid to end the secessions in Katanga and Kasai.

African disapproval would hardly have mattered to Khrushchev if Lumumba's strategy had worked; a military victory would have consolidated his political position and vindicated Khrushchev's decision to help him. But by the time the Leopoldville conference ended, on August 31, the military outlook was extremely uncertain.

The ten Ilyushin-14 planes which had arrived in Stanleyville were being painted in the Congo's colors. Each plane had a crew of eight, including backup crews, technicians, and interpreters.[86] The planes were capable of flying several hundred Congolese troops to the battle zone at a time; but now a question arose about where the troops should be taken. At first Lumumba had hoped to have them flown directly to Katanga, but it now turned out that there were no airports where they would be permitted to land. Tshombe was in full control of the Elisabethville airport, and, on August 31, as Belgian troops officially pulled out of their base at Kamina, the site of the largest airport in Katanga, the United Nations rushed reinforcements to the base. Hammarskjold insisted that it be neutralized; he would not yield to Tshombe's demands that it be turned over to him, and he assured Lodge, who had warned him of high-level concern at the State Department and the Pentagon, that he had given strict orders not to permit any "unauthorized landings" by Soviet planes transporting Lumumba's troops to Katanga.[87]

Moreover, Lumumba found that he urgently needed troop reinforcements in Kasai, where his campaign was not going well. At the start his forces, transported by Soviet trucks and led by three Czech officers, had captured Bakwanga, Kalonji's capital, and Kalonji and his forces had fled. By August 28 one of Lumumba's units had reached a point only twenty miles from the Katanga border, and an alarmed Tshombe was rushing reinforcements to the area. But Lumumba's troops soon ran into strong resistance from the local Baluba tribesmen, and casualties were heavy on both sides.[88]

On September 3 General Victor Lundula, the commander of Lumumba's forces, flew to Kasai in a Soviet Ilyushin-14 to check on the progress of his army, now about one thousand strong.[89] His report was not encouraging. On September 5 the full fleet of ten Soviet planes began to airlift reinforcements into Kasai. On their first trip they took approximately two hundred soldiers on the five-hundred-mile journey from Stanleyville to Luluabourg, flew eighty miles to Bakwanga, the center of the fighting, and dropped them off; they then flew back to Luluabourg and on to Stanleyville to pick up more troops.[90]

These reinforcements arrived too late to save Lumumba's military campaign in Kasai, which by this time had degenerated into a massacre of over one thousand of the local Baluba population. Moreover, Lumumba's decision to use Soviet military aid in his disastrous campaign finally lit a fuse under the phlegmatic President Kasavubu. Within a few days of the arrival of the Soviet planes in the Congo, Lumumba himself would be out of power.

The Russians watched these developments with increasing dismay. For the first few days of the campaign, the Soviet press reported Lumumba's successes, without indicating in any way that Moscow had supplied him with the assistance necessary to launch his invasion.[91] Khrushchev was undoubtedly awaiting the outcome of the campaign before claiming credit for his help. But by the end of August there were no more military reports; failure was passed over in silence.

Khrushchev's decision to supply the crucial military aid to Lumumba was a gamble—and, as it turned out, a gamble that failed. A Brezhnev might not have taken the gamble. There may have been cautious voices in the Kremlin in 1960 who advised against such a risky course. But it was Khrushchev who was in control. The decision bears the stamp of his flamboyant style. He knew that the odds were against him, that the Western powers were operating from a position of strength in the Congo; but he had his reputation to maintain, and he knew that if Lumumba succeeded, it would be a personal victory for him as well. Soviet Africa policy was his invention, and he was willing to experiment and to take risks for the long-range extension of Soviet power.

CHAPTER FOUR

The Turning Point
(September 5-20, 1960)

"It's extremely difficult to break Hitlers
when the alternatives are Hindenbergs."

O_{N THE EVENING} of September 5, 1960, the ponderous, slow-moving President of the Congo, Joseph Kasavubu, drove to the Leopoldville radio station, interrupted a program devoted to English-language instruction, and announced in a brief speech that he was dismissing the Prime Minister, Patrice Lumumba, because he had "betrayed his trust," deprived "numerous citizens of their fundamental liberties," and involved the country in an "atrocious civil war." He named the president of the Senate, Joseph Ileo, to form a new government, asked the army to lay down its weapons, and called on the United Nations to maintain order and peace in the Congo.[1]

Then he returned to his residence and solemnly announced to his associates, "The President has now spoken and Lumumba will die. He may die slowly but he will eventually die."[2] Once he had made this chilling prediction, he returned to his usual state of calm, confident inactivity and left the rest of the actors in the Congo drama to deal with the consequences of his decision.

The United Nations Sides with the Moderates

Less than an hour later Lumumba was on the radio, denying Kasavubu's right to dismiss him and pointing out that Kasavubu owed his position as President to the coalition headed by Lumumba, which had been elected by the voters the previous May.[3] He returned to the radio twice more that evening, his tone increasingly angry, and accused Kasavubu of participating in a "plot mounted by Belgian and French imperialists." Kasavubu, he announced, was no longer head of state. He was a traitor who had publicly betrayed the nation.[4] Lumumba then called his Council of Ministers into urgent session. They met until dawn, and at 5:25 A.M. Lumumba issued a communiqué accusing Kasavubu of "high treason" and announcing that his functions as chief of state would be taken over by Parliament.[5]

The battle between the two rivals was now out in the open. The Americans were pleased that Kasavubu had acted at last but were far from sanguine about the outcome of the battle. Kasavubu was an unlikely hero, but, as the U.S. Embassy in Brussels had pointed out earlier in the summer, he was the best one available.

At first glance it appeared an unequal contest. Lumumba was a skilled politician, energetic and charismatic. He was backed by a majority of the Parliament, and he held the levers of control: the police and the army. In addition, he could call on fifteen Soviet transport planes to bring additional troops from Stanleyville to Leopoldville.[6]

Still, Kasavubu was not altogether without resources. Lumumba's strength lay in his persuasive tongue, Kasavubu's in his silence. While Lumumba held the world stage through the summer with his dramatic charges, his ultimatums, his wide-ranging travels, and his extraordinary negotiations with an astonished group of UN officials, Kasavubu stayed in his residence and said little. He watched Lumumba take one rash action after another. He listened patiently as American diplomats, Belgian political advisers, French officers based in Brazzaville, and members of his own Abako party urged him to move quickly to stop Lumumba before it was too late. He ignored them and bided his time. One of his aides explained his strategy this way in late August:

> We are not ready to move. . . . The time is not ripe. Lumumba is a destructive man. He is destroying the country right now. One day soon he will have destroyed it to the point where everybody will be able to see and understand what he has done. Then we shall step forward. And people will say we were right and he was wrong.[7]

Kasavubu waited until the United Nations had secured the withdrawal of the Belgian troops from the Congo, until the foreign ministers of the African countries had come to Leopoldville, seen the situation for themselves and gone home again, until, at last, the Prime Minister had made good on his promises and brought Soviet weapons and advisers to the Congo to help end the Katanga secession. He waited until opposition to Lumumba's policies had mounted to a crescendo.

By the time he was ready to move against Lumumba, he had gathered a great deal of support from the anti-Lumumba leaders within the governing coalition and outside it. These men had watched with growing concern Lumumba's deteriorating relations with the United Nations, the Western powers, and even some of the African states. They had seen what they regarded as his arrogance, suspicion, and dictatorial tendencies contribute to tension and disorder in the country.

And they were dismayed by his decision to use Soviet military aid in a disastrous military campaign.

In addition, Kasavubu knew that he could count on the allegiance of the local population in the Leopoldville area; he could always threaten a general strike which would paralyze the capital. Kasavubu's local dominance was evident the day after his radio announcement, when several hundred of his young supporters gathered to march on Lumumba's residence. They were turned back by the police, but the point of their presence was not missed by the Prime Minister.

Before acting on September 5, Kasavubu had tested the waters with the top-ranking UN official in the Congo, Andrew Cordier, executive assistant to the Secretary-General, who had arrived on September 1 to relieve the exhausted Ralph Bunche, until the new special representative, Rajeshwar Dayal, could arrive. On September 3 Kasavubu told Cordier of his intention to dismiss Lumumba and asked the United Nations to close Parliament and arrest a number of political figures. Cordier refused to do this and warned that Kasavubu's projected move against Lumumba would probably result in disorders. But while he did not encourage Kasavubu's move, he did not discourage it either. Indeed, it was no secret to Kasavubu that the UN officials in the Congo and in New York would be delighted to see Lumumba's power curtailed, since that seemed to them the only way to restore peace to the troubled country. Cordier immediately checked with Hammarskjold to ask what he should do if Kasavubu carried out his threat but received only the vaguest guidance, the gist of which was: use your own judgment.[8]

On the afternoon of September 5 Kasavubu informed Cordier that he was going to dismiss Lumumba that evening and asked once again for UN assistance. Cordier later recalled in an interview with the author that he had refused Kasavubu's request and urged Kasavubu to reconsider his decision, because he was fully aware of the problems it would pose for the United Nations. He told Kasavubu, however, that if he was determined to go ahead with his plan, he should inform UN headquarters before he acted.[9]

Kasavubu apparently believed that he had "received assurances" from Cordier that "suitable measures would be taken" by the United Nations if he dismissed Lumumba. Shortly before he was about to speak, he sent his chief Belgian adviser, A. A. J. van Bilsen, to Cordier with a copy of the speech and a letter formally requesting that the United Nations provide him with personal protection, deny the use of the radio station to Lumumba and his supporters, and prevent the Soviet planes in Stanleyville from bringing pro-Lumumba troops to Leopoldville. According to van Bilsen, Cordier indicated that he would take the necessary measures, but added, "Officially, I must be able to say that you gave me these letters one half hour from this time"[10]—in other words, after Kasavubu's broadcast.

All the top UN officials had been alerted, and they were waiting at UN headquarters for Kasavubu's announcement. General von Horn, the commander of the UN force, later described the atmosphere after the broadcast as one of "relief, almost of satisfaction."[11] Dayal, who had arrived in Leopoldville in the course of the day, did not share in this general mood; foremost in his mind was the problem of the United Nations' associating itself with a move that was not clearly constitutional.[12] His doubts as to the legality of Kasavubu's action were to play an important role in the months to come.

But Dayal was not yet in command of the UN operation. And Cordier, who was in charge, had no visible doubts. As soon as Kasavubu's speech was over, he swung into action. He conferred with von Horn about the military aspects of the situation and came to the conclusion that the United Nations should take control of the radio station and the airports and deny them to both rival factions—Kasavubu's and Lumumba's. He made this decision on the spot. There was no time to check again with Hammarskjold—and, indeed, it appeared that Hammarskjold really did not wish to be consulted about the details of Cordier's plans. Cordier later explained that he understood fully the serious consequences of the actions he was taking. Still, he felt that, given the volatile mood of the Leopoldville crowds, the sullen attitude and uncertain loyalties of the five thousand Congolese soldiers stationed in the capital, and the presence of fifteen Soviet planes transporting pro-Lumumba troops around the Congo—all factors which could easily have contributed to large-scale violence—the urgency of the situation required strong measures on the part of the United Nations. Those measures, he was convinced, prevented a civil war and saved perhaps hundreds of lives.[13]

The key factor in Cordier's analysis of the situation—a factor which he did not stress publicly at the time—was the Soviet angle. He was greatly disturbed by the inroads the Russians had made in the Congo, especially compared to the slight impact made by the United States. In a "Top Secret" cable to Hammarskjold he reported that he had met with Joseph Ileo, Kasavubu's choice for Prime Minister, the night before Kasavubu's radio speech. While Kasavubu recognized the Soviet threat, Ileo had demonstrated "astonishing naiveté" about the "game" the Russians were "playing" in the Congo, and Cordier had felt obliged to assume a "professorial role" as he tried to explain to Ileo the basic lessons of great power politics. Cordier sent an "urgent recommendation" to the U.S. government, via Hammarskjold, suggesting that it send an official to Leopoldville—"not too high level, not too junior"—who could observe the local scene, see what the Russians were up to, and make a firsthand report to Washington.[14]

Despite these private warnings, both UN officials insisted publicly that Cordier's action regarding the airports and the radio station was strictly neutral. This theoretically neutral action turned out to be the most controversial move the United Nations had made in the Congo thus far, since it had the effect of strengthening Kasavubu's position and weakening Lumumba's. Lumumba had no way of appealing to his supporters throughout the country without access to the radio; Kasavubu was soon broadcasting to his followers in the Leopoldville area on Radio Brazzaville, which his friend, President Fulbert Youlou, had placed at his disposal. Moreover, Kasavubu's most loyal troops were in Leopoldville, while Lumumba's were in Stanleyville and Luluabourg and could reach the capital only by plane. After UN forces blocked the airports at Stanleyville and Luluabourg, Soviet pilots continued to take off and land on the grassy areas surrounding the airstrips for a day or two, but they made no attempt to move Lumumbist troops to the capital. There were no exceptions to Cordier's rule. Even the Soviet plane carrying General Lundula, the commander of the Congolese army and a supporter of Lumumba, was not permitted to land in Leopoldville.

Kasavubu was pleased with Cordier's policy; the UN official had made, for his own reasons, decisions which coincided closely with the requests of the Congolese President. In a sense it was a repetition of the situation in August, when Hammarskjold took a number of steps regarding Katanga which appeared to meet the demands made by Tshombe.

Lumumba's reaction this time was even stronger. When Cordier refused to meet with him, he sent Colonel Mobutu, the army chief of staff, to UN headquarters to protest the takeover of the airports and radio station and to demand their return.[15] On September 7 Lumumba blasted Cordier's policy in a long speech to the Assembly, the lower house of Parliament, and won an important victory: the Assembly voted 60 to 19 to annul Kasavubu's dismissal of Lumumba as well as Lumumba's dismissal of Kasavubu. The following day he won a more surprising victory in the Senate, where sentiment had been strongly opposed to him. In two hours of spellbinding oratory he demonstrated his ability to turn a hostile crowd into a cheering band of supporters. The Senate swung around and supported him 41 to 2.[16] After this second stunning victory in two days, Lumumba called a press conference and announced that if the United Nations did not return control of the airports and radio station to his government immediately, he would demand that the UN force be withdrawn from the Congo.[17]

Khrushchev Blames Hammarskjold

For Soviet Premier Nikita Khrushchev, the news of Lumumba's dismissal by Kasavubu could not have come at a worse time. The Soviet leader was playing host to Guinea's radical young President, Sékou Touré, and he was scheduled to leave in a few days for New York to attend the Fifteenth Session of the General Assembly. Khrushchev had hinted in mid-August that he might head the Soviet delegation at this session and had suggested that all heads of state and government join him so that they could discuss the question of disarmament. The Western powers had dismissed his suggestion as a propaganda ploy, noting that it was the Soviet delegation which had walked out of the ten-nation disarmament talks in Geneva on July 27. Their attitude did not deter the Soviet leader. On September 1 he announced that he would definitely attend the Assembly session. The Communist leaders of Eastern Europe quickly followed suit, and a number of major neutralist Asian and African leaders decided to go to New York as well, despite Western attempts to dissuade them. This in itself was a victory for Khrushchev.

The Soviet leader, still smarting from the effects of the U-2 disaster, was determined to put the Western powers on the defensive. He saw his opportunity in the changing composition of the United Nations: sixteen newly independent African states would be admitted to the world body, creating an Afro-Asian bloc which, together with the Soviet bloc, would constitute a majority. He hoped to take advantage of this shift to form an alliance with the Third World nations and to win their support for Soviet positions on a wide range of issues. His strong anticolonialist stand was designed to appeal to these nations, and his policy in the Congo was a key element in his diplomatic campaign. If everything had gone according to plan, Khrushchev would have arrived at the General Assembly as the champion of a beleaguered new African state—a champion who had succeeded in defeating colonialist intrigues when even the Secretary-General of the United Nations had failed.[18]

The initial Soviet reaction was to discount the political harm that had been done to Lumumba and to stress the success of his counter-challenge to Kasavubu.[19] It was not until September 9, as Khrushchev left the seaport of Kaliningrad aboard the Soviet liner *Baltika* for his journey to New York, that the Soviet government issued an angry statement denouncing Cordier's actions. "There is really no limit to the overbearing colonialist attitude of Hammarskjold's representatives in the Congo," it charged.[20]

This was not the first time the Russians had charged that UN officials in the Congo were "acting in collusion" with the Belgians and the other Western powers, against the interests of the Lumumba government. But the September 9 statement represented a change in the official Soviet assessment of Hammarskjold's role. The differences of opinion between Lumumba and Khrushchev, on the one hand, and Hammarskjold, on the other, about the issue of Katanga were quite serious; but they were not important enough to cause a rupture between the Soviet leader and the Secretary-General. When Lumumba himself became the issue, however, and Khrushchev saw the Soviet position in the Congo threatened, that was quite another matter. The statement left no doubt that Khrushchev considered Hammarskjold responsible for what was going on in the Congo. During the next ten days, as Khrushchev sailed across the Atlantic accompanied by the Communist Party leaders of Bulgaria, Hungary, and Romania, the Soviet position, both in the Congo itself and at the United Nations, would deteriorate considerably, and Khrushchev's antagonism toward Hammarskjold would reach a boiling point.

Eisenhower Warns Moscow

U.S. officials realized that Kasavubu's dramatic dismissal of Lumumba was only the first step toward the elimination of Soviet influence in the Congo and that Lumumba could not be counted out just yet. Two days after Kasavubu's announcement, Timberlake sent an urgent message via CIA channels to the Secretary of State and to CIA Director Dulles: Lumumba had brought troops from Thysville to the capital and had ordered them to arrest Bomboko, the pro-American Foreign Minister, who had come to the U.S. Embassy to ask for sanctuary. The ambassador immediately asked Cordier to provide Bomboko with a safe escort to Kasavubu's residence, which was guarded by the United Nations; and while he waited for a reply, he assumed responsibility for Bomboko's safety. "I intend allow Bomboko remain temporarily Chancery and protect him if I can," he cabled Washington. "We may be visited by other prominent people who are with Kasavubu." He stressed the importance of persuading the United Nations to provide physical security for Lumumba's opponents. "UN must prevent Lumumba from locking up those opposed to him or he will regain power," he warned.[21]

CIA officials in Leopoldville backed up Timberlake's warning that the ouster of Lumumba was not irreversible. As one of them put it in a cable to Washington, "Lumumba in opposition is almost as dangerous as in office."[22] When Dulles briefed President Eisenhower and the National Security Council on September 7, he passed along this view, remarking that "Lumumba always seemed to come out on top in each of these struggles."[23]

The CIA Director expressed his continuing concern about the military equipment and personnel that Moscow was supplying to Lumumba. According to Timberlake, there were fifteen Soviet planes in the Congo, as well as some two hundred fifty Soviet technicians and eighty or more Czechs, including military advisers who might be in the field with the Congolese army.[24]

The issue of Soviet planes in the Congo was raised at the President's press conference later that day, and Eisenhower pulled out a prepared statement. "That's one question I knew I was going to get, and so I have written an answer because I want to make perfectly clear what we feel about it." The United States, he said, deplored the "unilateral action of the Soviet Union in supplying aircraft and other equipment for military purposes to the Congo, thereby aggravating an already serious situation which finds Africans killing other Africans." It would be "doubly serious," he added, if the planes were "actually being flown by Soviet military personnel" in a civil war "which has recently taken on very ugly overtones." Moscow's action, he said, "seems to be motivated entirely by the Soviet Union's political designs in Africa." Eisenhower urged the Russians to support the UN effort instead of acting on their own, and he pledged full U.S. support for the UN operation.[25]

Lumumba publicly rejected Eisenhower's arguments at a press conference the following day. He thanked the Soviet government for its help and proclaimed defiantly that the Congo would accept aid from any source that was offered "without political conditions."[26]

White House officials were so exasperated that at a meeting of the Special Group on September 8, presidential assistant Gordon Gray prodded the CIA Director, reminding him that "he hoped that Agency people in the field are fully aware of the top-level feeling in Washington that vigorous action would not be amiss."[27] The "Agency people in the field" were already hard at work on the problem. Two CIA agents had just reported that during a discussion of American aid to the new government with a prominent anti-Lumumba politician, the politician had implied that Lumumba's opponents "might physically eliminate" him.[28]

At the same time, Timberlake was still hoping to unseat Lumumba by legal means, despite his overwhelming victories in both houses of Parliament. The ambassador acknowledged that the votes were essentially a tribute to Lumumba's "masterful demagoguery" rather than the result of intimidation, but he argued that there were "quite a few Congolese leaders who could rally opinion for Kasavubu" if they could operate freely without the fear that Lumumba would arrest them. If the United Nations would guarantee their safety, it might be possible to produce a Kasavubu victory in Parliament. On the other hand, he warned:

IF THIS PRESENT CHANCE IS LOST, AND TIME IS RUNNING OUT TODAY, LUMUMBA WILL LEAVE HIS FIELD ENTIRELY BEHIND AND RAPIDLY CONSOLIDATE HIS DICTATORSHIP, WITH OR WITHOUT MORE RUSSIAN HELP.[29]

It was at this point that Timberlake received welcome reinforcements in the form of Governor W. Averell Harriman, who was on a fact-finding tour of eight African nations for Democratic presidential candidate John F. Kennedy. Harriman and his party were forced to land in Brazzaville because the Leopoldville airport was still closed. After a briefing by Timberlake, Harriman, who would be reporting to the State Department as well as to Senator Kennedy, concluded that the ambassador had a "very good grasp" of the situation.

On September 9 the two men joined forces to try to galvanize Kasavubu into action. Harriman told the Congolese President that he was surprised by Lumumba's victories in Parliament, particularly in the Senate, where anti-Lumumba sentiment was strong. He explained that these victories created the impression in the outside world that Lumumba had more support than Kasavubu and stressed that Lumumba's opponents had to have the "courage to stand up and be counted and not collapse" as they had done in the Senate. Kasavubu acknowledged that his supporters were "afraid to vote against Lumumba" because he still controlled a major portion of the army and the police. He was certain that he had made the right decision when he dismissed Lumumba, who was "surrounded by Communist advisers" and had an "evil influence" on the country; but he had no idea what he should do next.[30]

Later that day Harriman spent an hour and a half with Lumumba, who insisted that he was not a Communist and that he was "not surrounded by Russian or Communist advisers." When Harriman explained that he was playing a dangerous game by inviting direct military aid from the Soviet Union and suggested that exclusive reliance on the United Nations was a better way to protect his country's independence, Lumumba replied that he could not rely on the United Nations because Cordier was siding with Kasavubu and no longer considered him the legal Prime Minister.[31] Harriman concluded that Lumumba was not a Communist but that he was out of his depth if he believed he could use the Russians for his purposes without being used by them in turn.

Before he left the Congo Harriman had a private conversation with Soviet Ambassador Yakovlev. Although he was not an official representative of the U.S. government, he warned the Soviet diplomat that if his country kept interfering in the Congo's affairs, it might not only fail to help Lumumba, but it might antagonize the Congolese so much that they would expel the Soviet Embassy. The warning turned out to be prescient, though at the time Harriman was far from certain about the outcome of the power struggle. He was convinced, however, that the Western countries could not "stand aside and allow the Congo to be taken over by the Russians."[32]

Despite Harriman's assistance, Timberlake remained pessimistic about Kasavubu's chances. He warned the State Department once again that Lumumba would continue to gain power unless the United Nations took over the Force Publique—or unless the "opposition resorts to violence with which, as I have said before, they are more familiar. Latter now seems distinctly in the cards," he added.[33]

"How Can You Make a Revolution With Such Material?"

In the meantime State Department officials, spurred by Timberlake's warnings and by the impatient demands of the Joint Chiefs of Staff, who wanted to know why the United Nations was not moving more effectively against Lumumba and his Soviet supporters,[34] began to put pressure on Hammarskjold. They were encouraged by the fact that he essentially shared their view of the Soviet threat. They differed with him only about tactics.

Hammarskjold's "primary objective," as he explained to a member of the U.S. delegation on the night of September 5, just after Kasavubu's speech, was to "explode" the Soviet effort in the Congo. In order to accomplish this he had to approach the problem with "absolutely clean" hands. Once he had arranged for the withdrawal of all Belgian troops in Katanga, the Russians would no longer have a justification for intervention.[35] He was impatient with the Belgians, who were dragging their feet and did not seem to comprehend his strategy. The Americans did not quarrel with his basic reasoning but they kept reminding him of the dangers of a precipitous Belgian withdrawal, which might leave the rich province open to Soviet penetration. The Russians, they pointed out, would like nothing better.[36]

When it came to a choice between Kasavubu and Lumumba, Hammarskjold's preference was clear. Lumumba had done nothing but attack him and his policies for the past month, while Kasavubu was eager to cooperate with the United Nations. The day after Kasavubu's move, the Secretary-General acknowledged to a member of the U.S. delegation that "what he was trying to do was get rid of Lumumba" without "compromising" his own position or that of the United Nations through "extraconstitutional actions." He compared his approach to "gamesmanship—how to win without actually cheating." The American diplomat reported to Washington that while Hammarskjold would "recognize, deal with, and by implication strongly support Ka-savubu in his struggle with Lumumba," he still had to bear in mind the possibility that "Lumumba might win the fight." If Lumumba then de-manded the withdrawal of the UN force, Hammarskjold would have to turn to the Security Council or the General Assembly for support—and he would have to be able to "explain and justify his actions" to them.[37] He was acutely sensitive to possible Afro-Asian charges that he was siding with the Western powers against the Congo's legally elect-ed Prime Minister. Cordier's decision to take control of the airports and radio station had already led to such charges, and the Secretary-General was anxious to avoid any additional actions that could be de-scribed as interference in the Congo's internal affairs. He tried to mollify his Afro-Asian critics by telling close associates that he was "dis-mayed" by Cordier's action and by describing it privately as "regret-table."[38] These private protestations were regarded with some skepticism; after all, Hammarskjold had given Cordier carte blanche to take emergency action in the Congo,[39] and he knew Cordier's views well enough to know how he would react to this sort of opportunity.

The Americans, who approved heartily of Cordier's action, kept urg-ing the Secretary-General to take stronger measures to help Kasavubu, especially as Lumumba seemed to be reversing the tide. On Septem-ber 7, after Lumumba's initial victory in Parliament, a member of the U.S. delegation asked Hammarskjold's aide Wieschhoff why UN troops had not been used to keep the pro-Lumumba Force Publique off the streets and away from the Parliament building. Wieschhoff replied that there were limits as to how far the United Nations could "stretch its authority" without being accused of intervening improperly. Be-sides, he explained, it was difficult for the United Nations to act in sup-port of Kasavubu when he did so little on his own behalf. After his speech announcing Lumumba's dismissal he had returned to his resi-dence and calmly gone to bed. "How can you make a revolution with such material?" Wieschhoff asked in exasperation.[40]

After Lumumba's second victory in Parliament, the Americans stepped up the pressure. Ambassador James J. Wadsworth, who had re-placed Lodge at the United Nations, raised the matter directly with Hammarskjold on the evening of September 9, just before the Security Council met for the fifth time on the Congo. Hammarskjold told him that the United Nations was already providing protection for Kasa-vubu and his allies and suggested that they were not capable of taking advantage of their opportunity. "If Kasavubu had any courage at all," he said, "he could have arrested Lumumba last Monday"—that is, the night of the broadcast. The "only person in the Congo with courage and ability," he added, was Foreign Minister Bomboko. Hammarskjold said he was "still convinced he must break Lumumba," and believed he would "be able to do it." He remarked, however, that it was "extremely difficult to break Hitlers when the alternatives were Hindenbergs."[41]

Hammarskjold then led off the Security Council debate with a speech that was bound to infuriate Lumumba and his supporters. To begin with, he defended Cordier's action as an "emergency measure" taken under the UN mandate for the maintenance of law and order. "I fully endorse the action taken and I have not seen any reason to revise the decisions of my representatives," he stated. Although he stressed the UN effort to maintain strict impartiality between the rival claims of Kasavubu and Lumumba, he clearly gave the edge to Kasavubu when he noted that "according to the constitution, the President has the right to revoke the mandate of the Prime Minister." Moreover, there was no mistaking his bitterness when he reviewed Lumumba's response to his effort to place UN troops in Katanga, a response which he said had made it difficult for the United Nations to "act in consultation with" the central government, as provided in the July 14 resolution. He added:

> In the United Nations, we have rich experience of such consultations in all parts of the world. . . . So far, we have never had any difficulties which have not been easily overcome. But then when a matter had been arranged with a responsible minister, his word was honored by the government. Or, when we had helped the responsible ministers to favorable results in a negotiation, we were not accused of plotting against the government and worse. When we had, correctly, informed the Foreign Minister about our moves, we were not said to have neglected the government. We have now gathered new experiences.

Hammarskjold went on to describe the slaughter of civilians in Kasai by Lumumba's army as having the "characteristics of the crime of genocide," an apparent attempt to exterminate an ethnic group, the Baluba tribe. In such a case, he explained, the United Nations was forced to act to save human lives, despite its position of neutrality between warring political factions.[42]

When it came to the key question of outside military aid to these warring factions, Hammarskjold tried to apply the strategy he had outlined to the Americans a few days before. He deplored all outside interference, but he came down much harder on the Belgians than on the Russians. He had not received an answer to the note he had sent to Moscow on September 5 raising questions about Soviet personnel in the Congo;[43] but in the meantime he had learned about a large shipment of Belgian arms to secessionist Katanga, and he had immediately fired off a protest to Brussels.[44] At the Security Council meeting he referred directly to his complaint to the Belgian government and only indirectly to his complaint to another government, which he did not name.[45]

The following day he got his reply from Moscow. The Russians, indignant about what they considered unfair treatment of Lumumba by the United Nations, were in no mood to be lectured about their own assistance to the beleaguered nationalist leader, however indirectly. They insisted that the July 14 resolution did not "restrict the right" of the Congolese government "to request assistance from the governments of other countries" and "to receive such assistance." They maintained that "far from running counter to the Security Council resolutions," their "assistance in the form of civil aircraft and motor vehicles" was "in complete accordance" with them.[46]

The Security Council met again on September 10 and 12 but failed to resolve anything.[47] The deadlock in the Congo was symbolized by the arrival in New York of two rival delegations, one headed by Kanza, representing Lumumba, and the other led by Bomboko, representing Kasavubu. The two men, both "moderates" who had opposed Lumumba's extreme positions, had been allies during the summer. But now, while Bomboko was wholly committed to Kasavubu, Kanza believed that the Congo "needed both Kasavubu and Lumumba." He told Ambassador Wadsworth that Ileo could not win a majority in Parliament. Even if all the anti-Lumumba deputies were present, Lumumba would still control a majority. Kanza said he hoped a reconciliation could be worked out before the General Assembly met because he feared that Khrushchev would "inflame the issue and make propaganda at the expense of the Congolese people."[48] Wadsworth, after some initial uncertainty, concluded that the various reconciliation schemes being discussed in the corridors of the United Nations "were almost certain to help Lumumba,"[49] and he decided to press for a temporary adjournment, hoping that the absence of any formal UN action would help Kasavubu consolidate his position.[50]

The Power Struggle in Leopoldville

The political situation in Leopoldville was still extremely unsettled, and now another element had been added: the Secretary-General's new special representative, Rajeshwar Dayal, who had taken over from Cordier on September 8, was shifting UN policy in a direction favorable to Lumumba. Dayal was one of India's top diplomats. He had worked for the United Nations during the 1958 Lebanon crisis, and Hammarskjold had persuaded Nehru to release him from his current post as high commissioner to Pakistan for a six-month tour of duty in the Congo. Dayal had gone along with Cordier's decision to close the radio station and the airports because of a sense of professional loyalty, but he did not really approve of it; he had had his doubts about the constitutionality of Kasavubu's action from the beginning, and he felt that the threat of Lumumbist troops flying into the capital and provoking a civil war was exaggerated. He believed that Hammarskjold shared his reservations about Cordier's decision and that he was "alarmed" by the "enthusiastic" Western reaction to that decision. He was convinced that Hammarskjold was ready for a change. He thought that "since Kasavubu's move had lost its momentum," it was time for the United Nations to move toward a "position of equidistance between the opposing factions."[51] Dayal decided first to negotiate the reopening of the radio station and the airports and next to try to bring about a reconciliation between Kasavubu and Lumumba.

These views did not exactly make Dayal popular at the U.S. Embassy in Leopoldville, where Timberlake assumed that his anti-Lumumba partnership with the United Nations would continue indefinitely. At the same time, Dayal was unable to satisfy Lumumba and his foreign supporters, who wanted nothing less than a UN commitment to restore Lumumba to power. The pipe-smoking, Oxford-educated Indian diplomat became an extremely controversial figure. The Congolese found him "condescending." The Western envoys considered him a "muddle-headed neutralist." But the Secretary-General and his staff had the highest respect for his abilities and his dedication to world peace.

On September 10 Dayal paid his first visits to Lumumba and Kasavubu and was struck by the contrast between them. Lumumba was an activist, restless and energetic; he was capable of switching from one approach to another within a few minutes, even if they were totally inconsistent with each other. He began the conversation by threatening to use force against the United Nations if it did not relinquish control of the radio station. After listening to Dayal, however, he abruptly shifted gears and said he hoped they could work together "harmoniously and sincerely."[52] The following day he changed his mind again and tried to enter the radio station with a group of armed soldiers. The Ghanaian UN guards on duty disarmed his escort and refused to let him in.[53]

When Dayal called on Kasavubu, he found him "affable" but "not very communicative" about his efforts to resolve the political crisis.[54] Still, there were signs that the pressure of the Americans and other Western advisers was beginning to have some effect on the Congolese President. He sent Dayal a list of Ileo's new government[55] and formally requested the United Nations to reorganize and retrain the Force Publique and reactivate the court system.[56]

While Kasavubu issued statements from his residence, Lumumba moved restlessly around the city trying to rouse his supporters. On the morning of September 12 he was arrested and taken to Camp Leopold II, where he was confronted by a crowd of angry army officers who demanded his resignation. After a few hours he was released, and he drove directly to the radio station. Once again he was turned away by Ghanaian UN troops. With one avenue to power blocked, he swiftly turned to another. On September 13 the two houses of Parliament, meeting in joint session, voted 88 to 25 to give him "special powers." Observers who were present at this session questioned the validity of the vote, first, because many members of the opposition were absent, either as a sign of disagreement or because of their fear of arrest; second, because there were armed pro-Lumumba soldiers in the hall; and third, because the total confusion made it impossible to tell if the required quorum was present.[57] Still, Lumumba presented the result to the outside world as a victory, and Kasavubu moved quickly to prevent any more legislative triumphs for his rival. On September 14 he adjourned Parliament for a month, claiming that it had acted illegally.[58] By this time Dayal had reopened the airports to civilian traffic and negotiated the reopening of the radio station, with the understanding that all factions would be free to use it provided they were working for peace and unity rather than division and violence.[59] Lumumba immediately issued a radio appeal to the people and the army, calling on them to defend the country against the "plots and maneuvers of the imperialists" who intended to "place the Congo under an international trusteeship."[60]

The Africans Swing Behind Lumumba

Throughout this period Lumumba actively sought the support of the African states which had supplied troops to the UN force. At a press conference on September 10, he "looked straight at the ambassadors from Ghana, Liberia, Sudan, and the UAR," and said it was high time they decided whether they were on the side of the Congolese people or on the side of the "plotting imperialists."[61] The Africans were caught in an awkward situation. While most of them had reservations about the mercurial Prime Minister, they still regarded him as the legal head of the government. At the same time, their troops were being used by the United Nations to back Lumumba's opponents, the conservative political figures who were supported by the Western powers.

The Guineans were the first to realize that they could turn this awkward situation to Lumumba's advantage. On September 9 the commanding officer of Guinea's contingent recommended to his government that the troops be withdrawn from the force and placed at Lumumba's disposal unless the Secretary-General reversed his policy.[62] This suggestion was welcomed by Sékou Touré, who had just spent two days in the Soviet Union and had signed a joint communiqué with Khrushchev expressing a complete identity of views about the Congo.[63]

The other radical Africans quickly fell into line. On September 10 the Moroccan government, which had three thousand troops in the Congo, announced that it was sending a high-ranking mission to Leopoldville to report to the King on the political situation.[64] On September 12 the UAR announced that it was withdrawing its six-hundred-and-fifty-man contingent from the UN force and urged other troop-contributing countries to follow its lead.[65]

The key state was Ghana. President Nkrumah was so disturbed by Lumumba's use of Soviet military aid that he had confided to the U.S. ambassador in Accra on September 5, before Lumumba was dismissed by Kasavubu, "Maybe I shouldn't say he should be displaced, but something must be done."[66] The ambassador thought Nkrumah might welcome Kasavubu's action, but this turned out to be wishful thinking. Despite his reservations, Nkrumah's sympathies were with the Prime Minister. But he was in an embarrassing position. Since Lumumba regarded Nkrumah as his friend and source of inspiration, he was particularly incensed by the fact that Ghanaian troops had refused to admit him to the radio station on two separate occasions. Immediately after the first incident he wrote to Nkrumah to express his "indignation" and threatened to break off diplomatic relations if the troops did not let him enter the radio station.[67] Nkrumah warned Hammarskjold on September 12 that if Lumumba were not allowed to use the radio station, Ghana would be forced to withdraw its troops from the UN command and place them at Lumumba's disposal. At the same time, he urged Lumumba to calm down, compromise with his enemies, and make use of the aid the United Nations was willing to provide: above all, he counseled him not to "push the United Nations troops out until you have consolidated your position."[68]

The Secretary-General tried to head off withdrawals from the force by sending messages to Nkrumah and to other heads of state explaining that if they withdrew their troops, it would "inevitably" lead to the "open and active involvement" of the major powers.[69] His arguments, and the rapid reopening of the radio station and airports, convinced them to keep their troops in the UN force for the time being.[70]

The Great Powers: Watching and Waiting

Meanwhile, the U.S. government was observing Lumumba's progress with a growing sense of impatience and frustration. Bronson

Tweedy, a high-level CIA official in Washington, summed up the Agency's feelings in a cable to Leopoldville on September 13:

LUMUMBA TALENTS AND DYNAMISM APPEAR OVERRIDING FACTOR IN RE-ESTABLISHING HIS POSITION EACH TIME IT SEEMS HALF LOST. IN OTHER WORDS EACH TIME LUMUMBA HAS OPPORTUNITY HAVE LAST WORD HE CAN SWAY EVENTS TO HIS ADVANTAGE.[71]

The same day, Ambassador Timberlake cabled, "I wish I could shed a ray of light or hope on confused situation here." He reported plaintively:

"KASAVUBU ACTS MORE LIKE A VEGETABLE EVERY DAY WHILE LUMUMBA CONTINUES DISPLAY BRILLIANT BROKEN FIELD RUNNING. IN SPITE NUMBER OF CONSTRUCTIVE SUGGESTIONS GIVEN KASAVUBU AND ILEO, THEY SEEM INCAPABLE OF ANY ACTION EVEN WHEN THEY HAVE SITUATION LITERALLY IN HAND.[72]

Timberlake noted that while Lumumba's victory at the joint session of Parliament had "no legal validity" because it was obtained through intimidation in the absence of a quorum, this did not mean that Lumumba had not "scored again." He had a keen sense of public relations and would make the most of this second parliamentary "approval," Timberlake predicted.[73]

The Russians, on the other hand, were buoyed by Lumumba's successes and the support he was receiving from African governments critical of UN policy. Soviet Premier Khrushchev, on board the *Baltika,* was enjoying his first ocean voyage. He recalled in his memoirs that while his Soviet and East European companions succumbed to seasickness and "those who could still walk" were "moving around with a strange color and a sad expression on their faces," he would "take brisk strolls in the fresh air" on the deck. "I never missed breakfast or lunch or dinner," he proudly stated, even if there was "only one other person at the table." He was introduced for the first time to the mysteries of shuffleboard and kept informed about the latest political developments in various parts of the world. "I remember we followed particularly closely the struggle then going on in the Congo between the colonialists and the revolutionary forces fighting for independence," he recalled. "All the way across the Atlantic on our way to New York we had kept in close touch with our Foreign Ministry about the situation in the Congo, sending and receiving coded messages between our ship and Moscow.[74] The Soviet leader was undoubtedly encouraged by the news that Lumumba had been released just a few hours after he was arrested on September 12 and that he had won a vote of confidence from a joint session of Parliament the following day. On September 13, in a telephone interview with the London *Daily Express*, Khrushchev blasted the Western powers and the Secretary-General and reaffirmed Soviet support for Lumumba and the "just struggle of the Congolese people."[75]

Soviet Veto at the Security Council: September 14–17, 1960

Khruschev's position was amplified in a major speech before the Security Council on the evening of September 14 by Valerian Zorin, a hardliner who had just replaced the genial Kuznetsov as the head of the Soviet delegation. Zorin accused the Secretary-General of "acting consciously in the interests of the . . . imperialists" and demanded that he return the airports and radio station to the Lumumba government and stop interfering in the Congo's internal affairs. He also called for the removal of the UN command.[76]

The Americans were eager to counter Zorin's attack with a resolution supporting the Secretary-General and barring outside military aid to the Congo except through the United Nations. They hoped that Tunisia would take the lead as it had in the past. But Tunisian Ambassador Slim, who supported Cordier's actions and implicitly blamed the Russians for precipitating the crisis,[77] felt he could not win sufficient African support for the sort of resolution the Americans had in mind. He was afraid the Russians would veto it, and he was concerned about his ability to keep the African bloc under control once the issue was taken to the General Assembly.[78]

Hammarskjold, on the other hand, encouraged the Americans to introduce their own resolution. He agreed with Slim that the Russians would probably veto it, but, unlike Slim, he had no concern about the African group "splintering" in the Assembly. He told Wadsworth that Ghana was "back in the fold" and said that when the UAR realized this, it would come back as well. The Soviet Union would find itself "isolated."[79]

Wadsworth found this a splendid prospect. He told the State Department it would be the most effective way of "putting Khrushchev squarely on the defensive" when he arrived in New York.[80]

On the morning of September 15, Wadsworth accused the Russians of trying to establish a "Soviet satellite state in the heart of Africa" by sending military personnel and supplies to the Congo against the wishes of the United Nations. This, he charged, was a "textbook illustration of the Soviet tactic of utilizing the legitimate aspirations of nationalist movements for purposes of Soviet imperialism." He then introduced the U.S. draft resolution,[81] which was diametrically opposed to the Soviet draft.[82]

It appeared for a time that Hammarskjold had underestimated African opposition to his recent policy. One after the other, the delegates of Ghana, Guinea, the UAR, and Morocco rose to condemn Cordier's actions. But in the end Slim managed to persuade these radical Africans to look beyond their disapproval of Cordier's actions and rally around the Secretary-General.[83] On the evening of September 16, he introduced a compromise draft which was cosponsored by Ceylon and supported by the entire African bloc. He had made a few minor changes to accommodate Soviet views, but essentially his draft followed the lines of the American one.[84]

Wadsworth, who was delighted by the last-minute introduction of this Afro-Asian draft, suggested that the Security Council vote on it before it took up the American draft, since there was "little substantive difference between the two texts." Zorin asked that his draft be put to a vote first, and it quickly went down to defeat, 7 to 2 (the Soviet Union and Poland), with Tunisia and Ceylon abstaining in an effort to be conciliatory. The Council then voted on the Tunisian-Ceylonese draft: 8 in favor, 2 opposed (the Soviet Union and Poland), with France abstaining.

Zorin's negative vote constituted a veto—the first Soviet veto of a Congo resolution backed by the Afro-Asian bloc. Slim was disappointed, but Wadsworth was quietly jubilant. His strategy had turned out to be even more successful than he had originally anticipated. He could now point to a Soviet veto of an Afro-Asian draft rather than an American draft. He drew the Council's attention to the "negative policy" of the Soviet Union and proposed an emergency special session of the General Assembly to deal with the crisis. Over Zorin's protest that it was illegal to call a special session without Soviet approval, the Council voted 8 to 2, with France abstaining, to move on to a new forum.[85]

It was past 2:00 A.M. on September 17 when the Security Council adjourned and Hammarskjold sat down to write to Dayal. He was somewhat surprised by the Soviet misjudgment of the situation, by the fact that the Russians had run "a harsh cold-war strategy of the oldest type" and ended by vetoing a resolution which was supported by the Africans. "This was unexpected in view of Soviet sensitivity to African opinion," he wrote, "but this round they have proven strangely unperceptive to the currents in the regional group." The Soviet delegation, he noted, was "obviously completely unaware of the latest developments" in the Congo.[86]

Colonel Mobutu Takes Over and Expels the Russians

Hammarskjold was referring to a dramatic series of events which had taken place while the Security Council was meeting. On the evening of September 14, the relatively unknown, twenty-nine-year-old chief of staff of the Congolese army, Colonel Joseph Mobutu, had announced that he was taking power in the name of the army. He was "neutralizing" Kasavubu, Lumumba, Ileo, and all the other politicians until the end of the year; he was calling back the first generation of Congolese university students from their studies abroad and asking them to serve as nonpolitical technicians and run the country until that time. Then, in a move that warmed the hearts of the CIA officials who had been cultivating him for weeks, Mobutu ordered the Soviet and Czechoslovak Embassies to get out of the Congo within forty-eight hours.[87]

The Soviet diplomats at the United Nations could not have been "completely unaware" of Mobutu's takeover—which was the lead story in *The New York Times* on September 15[88]—but they obviously did not grasp its significance. The following day *Pravda* scoffed at Mobutu's demand for the withdrawal of the Soviet Embassy and reported that his plot had been foiled, he had been arrested, and "power was in the hands of Lumumba." The Soviet newspaper continued:

> Events have showed that Mobutu was just a soap bubble. The power of the puppet colonel did not last for twenty-four hours. . . . Mobutu is already a yesterday for the Congo. . . . It is obvious that without the support of the American, French, and Belgian colonialists Mobutu would not have been in power long enough to hold a press conference.[89]

By the time this article appeared, the "soap bubble" had consolidated his power in Leopoldville. His demands had been backed up by a formal expulsion order signed by President Kasavubu and Prime Minister Ileo and presented to the astonished Soviet and Czechoslovak ambassadors. Soviet Ambassador Yakovlev went to inform Dayal of the abrupt order and to ask for his help. He explained that he did not want Dayal to intercede with Kasavubu, either to get the order reversed or to ask for a delay; he asked only that Dayal provide UN troop protection at the Soviet Embassy and at the airport at the time of departure, so that Soviet personnel could leave with dignity.

When Dayal asked Yakovlev what was to become of the one hundred trucks the Russians had shipped to the Congo, the Soviet ambassador replied that they would be left for the United Nations. "And the planes?" Dayal inquired. "They were not a gift; we are taking them home," Yakovlev responded. After some discussion he agreed to leave the medical supplies, which the United Nations badly needed. When the crates were opened some time later, the "medical supplies" turned out to include a goodly supply of vodka—which, Dayal wrote, "proved to be a blessing to our hard-pressed Ethiopian troops in Stanleyville."[90]

On September 17 Yakovlev and his staff took off for Accra in an Ilyushin-18, with thirty-five to forty passengers. Czechoslovak Ambassador

Joseph Virius and ten of his staff left on a smaller plane, bound for Stanleyville, Khartoum, Cairo, and Prague. Soviet-bloc technicians, some of whom were scattered around the country, were also forced to leave; with the Embassy personnel, they totaled about four hundred and fifty persons. A five-man goodwill mission from the People's Republic of China had left the previous day without waiting for a formal order.[91]

On September 19 the Soviet government published a statement explaining that since the "lawful government and Parliament" of the Congo had been removed through the "intrigues of the colonialists" and the "undisguised interference of the United Nations Command," and a "puppet regime obedient to the foreigners" had been installed, the "normal functioning" of the Soviet Embassy in Leopoldville had become impossible, and the Soviet government had decided to recall its diplomats "temporarily."[92] The use of the word "temporarily" could not conceal Soviet chagrin. Not only had Khrushchev's gamble on Lumumba failed to keep him in power, it had backfired and brought about the end of the Soviet presence in the Congo—just as Harriman had warned.

At the time the decision was made to pull out the Soviet Embassy, Khrushchev was still on board the *Baltika,* three days out of New York. The trans-Atlantic crossing may have done wonders for his shuffleboard, but it did little for his Congo policy. Despite the daily exchange of messages with Moscow, he was not really on top of the situation. If he had been in the Kremlin at the time of Mobutu's demand, he might well have handled it differently. He did not have enough forces in the Congo to defeat the combined power of the United Nations and the Western countries; but he had fifteen planes and a few hundred military advisers, and these, combined with Lumumba's own forces, would certainly have been enough to put up a good bluff—at least long enough for the political situation to change once again.

This was certainly what the Americans expected him to do. They were not at all confident that they had the situation under control. They had given up on the ineffectual political alternatives to Lumumba and gambled on a young military officer, hoping that he could block the threat of a Soviet takeover; but they were not even certain that Mobutu would carry through on his demand—and if he did, they were afraid the Russians would not give up without a fight. On September 15, the day after Mobutu's speech, the State Department sent a warning cable to Leopoldville:

WE MUST FACE POSSIBILITY THAT SOVIET MERCHANT OR OTHER SHIPS MAY ARRIVE UNANNOUNCED AT MATADI CARRYING ARMS OR OTHER OBJECTIONABLE CARGO OR PASSENGERS. ASSUME UN WOULD AT LEAST BE AWARE OF ANY ACTIVITY BUT ON BASIS PAST PERFORMANCE WE CANNOT

BE SURE THEY WOULD TAKE ANY EFFECTIVE INHIBITING ACTION. SUG-
GEST THEREFORE YOU MOBILIZE RESOURCES AVAILABLE TO INSURE
PROMPT RECEIPT SIGNIFICANT INFORMATION FROM LOWER CONGO AREA
AND BE PREPARED MAKE PROMPT RECOMMENDATIONS ON APPROPRIATE
COUNTER ACTION WE MIGHT TAKE IN EVENT OF UNDESIRABLE SOV AC-
TIVITY THAT AREA.[93]

By September 16 it was clear that these fears were unwarranted.
The Russians were definitely on their way out. No one was more
pleased than Ambassador Timberlake, who saw his strategy vindicated. The threat of a Soviet takeover, which had been hanging over his
head for the past two months, was suddenly lifted. He gleefully reported to Washington that expulsion orders had been delivered to the Russian and Czech Embassies, which were busily burning documents in
their backyards; most of Lumumba's staff had been arrested, and Mobutu appeared to be in control of the army in the Leopoldville area.[94]
The "events of yesterday and today give me some hope that act one of
the Congo drama has ended," he wrote. He then added:

WHILE THE RUSSIANS WILL VOLLEY AND THUNDER WITH REDOUBLED
VIGOR IF THEIR EMBASSIES ARE, AS WE EXPECT, EVICTED TOMORROW,
THEY WILL FIND IT MUCH MORE DIFFICULT TO PEDDLE THEIR POISON IN
THE CONGO AND EVEN HARDER TO INFLUENCE GOVERNMENT AND PEO-
PLE HERE. THE TRAINED SEALS ARE RUNNING FOR COVER AND EVEN THE
LOCAL CLERKS WHO WORKED FOR LUMUMBAVITCH ARE BEING METHODI-
CALLY ARRESTED. I FEEL EVEN MORE IMPORTANT A RESULT WILL BE THE
IMPACT ON WORLD OPINION OF THE FACT THAT THIS NEW AND TROU-
BLED AFRICAN COUNTRY HAS GIVEN THE BOOT TO THE BLOB, REALIZING
THAT IT BROUGHT THEM ONLY COMPOUNDED WOE.[95]

Timberlake has always maintained that the U.S. Embassy had nothing to do with Mobutu's coup. At the same time, CIA officials have
claimed that they "discovered" Mobutu and helped him to take power, thus bringing a "measure of stability" to the new state.[96] It is clear
from the record that the U.S. Embassy and the CIA station in Leopoldville were involved in a concerted campaign to remove Lumumba
from power and that one of their chief objectives was to deprive him
of the support of the army. Mobutu's name had not figured prominent-
ly in the high-priority cable traffic between the U.S. Embassy in Leopoldville and the State Department at the end of August and the
beginning of September, when American officials were discussing the
possibility of replacing Lumumba. At that point they were concentrating on civilian political leaders, with Kasavubu the most likely alternative. Mobutu's name began to appear frequently in Timberlake's
cables only after Kasavubu dismissed Lumumba on September 5,
when it became a question of which of the two rivals would win the

loyalty of the army, and there was considerable uncertainty about which way Mobutu would jump. During the turbulent period between September 5 and 14, American officials, alarmed by Kasavubu's inability to counter Lumumba's political skill on his own, urged Mobutu to throw in his lot with Kasavubu and assured him of American support if he did so.

One of the U.S. officials who had a particularly close relationship with Mobutu was Lawrence Devlin, the CIA station chief—a man his colleagues described as "a real professional," with a good sense of humor and a love of intrigue, backstage maneuvers, and secret meetings. Throughout the summer Devlin and the other CIA operatives in the Congo were doing what their counterparts were doing in most of the other newly independent countries—checking out the various political and military figures, compiling information on their feuds and alliances, developing sources, supplying favors in exchange for information, and "keeping a number of possibilities on the string," as Ray Cline, a former deputy director of the CIA, later put it. The only thing that was unique about the Congo was the fact that the local CIA officers were under intense high-level pressure from headquarters to find a way to "get rid of" Lumumba. In their effort to build up the anti-Lumumba opposition, they reviewed all the "possibilities," and Mobutu must have looked like a fairly promising one.

They were aware of Mobutu's background: he was a former journalist who had begun his political career as an ally of Lumumba; he had gone to Belgium on a fellowship and then served as Lumumba's private secretary at the Brussels round table conference at the beginning of 1960; and he had been named chief of staff, the number two position in the army, when the Belgian officers were removed just after independence. As the summer went on, Mobutu became more and more worried about the drift of Lumumba's policy, his reliance on foreign advisers—Russian, Ghanaian, and Guinean—and his strained relations with the United Nations. He tried many times to persuade Lumumba to take a more moderate line, but his warnings fell on deaf ears. Often it would be Mobutu who would try to patch things up with the United Nations after Lumumba had made a particularly outrageous statement. One of the most notable of these occasions was the incident of August 18, when a group of Canadian UN technicians were savagely beaten by undisciplined Congolese troops. While Lumumba rejected the protests of the United Nations, Mobutu apologized for the soldiers' actions.[97] By the beginning of September he had won the respect of General von Horn, the UN commander, and the affection of General Ben Hammou Kettani, the Moroccan UN officer who had been asked by Lumumba to reorganize the Congolese army.[98]

American officials were also aware of Mobutu's conviction that the army should stay out of politics and his reluctance to choose sides between Kasavubu and Lumumba. This conviction was dramatically tested in the days after September 5. Both Kasavubu and Lumumba issued strong statements and threats about each other, but neither man had the power to enforce his decisions. Each of them sought Mobutu's support. Each of them asked him to arrest the other. Mobutu, torn by conflicting loyalties, discussed his dilemma with anyone who would listen.

On September 7 he arrived at the U.S. Embassy looking for Foreign Minister Bomboko, who had taken sanctuary there earlier in the day and then had moved on to the safety of President Kasavubu's residence. Mobutu explained that he had started the day by handing Lumumba the official order for his dismissal, at Kasavubu's request. Lumumba had "hit the ceiling" and immediately ordered him to arrest Bomboko and Albert Delvaux, the two ministers who had countersigned the order. Mobutu had tipped off Bomboko, who was an "old friend," and now had come to see if he had received the warning in time.[99]

Timberlake reported to Washington that Mobutu had expressed concern about the presence of seven Soviet technicians at Camp Leopold II; they had come with the trucks, jeeps, and planes requested by Lumumba, and while they wore civilian clothes, they were actually Soviet army officers. Despite this concern the U.S. ambassador was not sure that Mobutu was ready to break with Lumumba. He had seen Mobutu at Lumumba's residence the previous evening, when he was called in to hear Lumumba's side of the story, and he concluded that the colonel was "apparently so far successfully carrying water" on "both shoulders."[100]

The following day the State Department was encouraged by the news that Mobutu had joined Ileo and a number of other anti-Lumumba figures at Kasavubu's residence.[101] When Wadsworth passed along this information to Hammarskjold on September 9, suggesting that it might indicate important army support for Kasavubu, the Secretary-General brushed it aside with the comment, "Mobutu has no influence."[102]

This was one of Hammarskjold's most startling misjudgments of the Congolese political scene. He was undoubtedly reflecting the views of his special representative, Dayal, whose first impression of Mobutu was of a "rather diffident but patriotic man who felt powerless in the face of events that he could neither fully understand nor influence."[103] Mobutu was in the habit of stopping at UN headquarters every evening to discuss his troubles with General Kettani or with Dayal. He was becoming more and more depressed with each passing day. On September 11 he told his old friend Pierre Davister, the Belgian journalist who had been his first boss, "I've quit, but Patrice doesn't want to let me go and won't accept my resignation. Tomorrow I'll give him my resignation in writing, because I can't go on like this."[104] When he arrived at UN headquarters on September 12, he told Dayal that he was so discouraged by "political interference with the army" and by the endless demands that he arrest this or that politician, that he was ready to resign. It had been a particularly bad day; Lumumba had been arrested by Congolese soldiers and then released three hours later, and Mobutu's role in both the arrest and the release was, even in Congolese terms, rather ambiguous.[105] Dayal advised him to stay on "for the good of the country."[106] When he asked Kettani's advice, the Moroccan general urged him to "play a moderating and pacifying role."[107] This was a suggestion that fit in well with Mobutu's own professed desire to seek a reconciliation between the quarreling Congolese leaders.

Most of the other people he asked for advice, however, were strongly opposed to any sort of reconciliation between Kasavubu and Lumumba. The American diplomats and CIA operatives who counseled Mobutu were not alone in their effort to persuade him to join the anti-Lumumba camp. He listened to the officers at Camp Leopold II, where anti-Lumumba sentiment ran strong, especially among the Baluba soldiers who blamed Lumumba for the deaths of their kinsmen in Kasai. He listened to the university students, who admired Bomboko and distrusted Lumumba's flirtation with the Communists. He listened to Davister, and to the other Belgian, French, and American journalists, who regarded Lumumba as a dangerous madman. And he spent more and more time at Kasavubu's residence, listening to the President, and to his Belgian and French advisers, who had worked up an elaborate legalistic defense of Kasavubu's position. All these views had the effect of reinforcing Mobutu's own doubts about the wisdom of Lumumba's policies and strengthening his allegiance to the head of state.[108]

Meanwhile, U.S. Embassy officials were not at all sure that their message was getting through to Mobutu. On September 13 Timberlake reported that Mobutu was now in charge of the Leopoldville radio station, which the United Nations had relinquished; but he could not really judge the significance of this, since, as he noted, "It is not clear whether he is for Kasavubu or Lumumba at this point."[109]

The same day, Kasavubu, prodded by the Americans, stepped up his courtship of Mobutu and the army. He dismissed General Lundula, the commander in chief of the army, who had been responsible for releasing Lumumba the previous day, and appointed Mobutu to take his place. In addition, he summoned a group of high-ranking officers to his residence, and asked personally for their support. He invited another group the following day. On both occasions they were accompanied by Mobutu.[110]

By this time the young colonel was very close to a decision. The event which apparently tipped the balance and convinced him to act was a meeting that began on the morning of September 14 at Camp Leopold II and continued all through the afternoon. Hundreds of army officers, infuriated by the impasse between Kasavubu and Lumumba, urged Mobutu to take over the government and arrest all the politicians. Mobutu, intent on avoiding violence, took what seemed to him a more moderate approach and suggested "neutralizing" the politicians instead of hanging them.[111]

He recorded a short speech announcing his decision and scheduled it for broadcast at 8:30 that evening. He then went to UN headquarters to inform Dayal of what he had done. Dayal later recalled that he was completely "caught off guard" by Mobutu's surprise move. By the time he realized that Mobutu would be announcing what was in effect a "military coup d'état" at 8:30, it was nearly 8:15. He quickly hurried Mobutu out of UN headquarters. As he explained in his memoirs, "Had he been present with me during the broadcast, no amount of explanation would have convinced the world that the United Nations was not behind his coup."[112]

Dayal's precautions did not dispel all suspicion of UN involvement in Mobutu's takeover, particularly among Lumumba's partisans.[113] Both Dayal and Brian Urquhart, his political adviser, realized that they had a credibility problem on this issue because of an action the United Nations had taken on September 10 which had the effect of reinforcing Mobutu's position in the army. Immediately after Kasavubu's dismissal of Lumumba, General Kettani had advised Cordier that the five thousand soldiers of the Leopoldville garrison represented a threat of instability and suggested that the United Nations arrange to give them their back pay. Cordier immediately asked Hammarskjold for one million dollars, and on September 10 the troops were paid at a parade supervised by Lundula, Mobutu, and Kettani. In exchange, the soldiers stacked their arms and for the first time in many days stayed in their barracks instead of roaming the streets of the capital. According to Urquhart the payments were made with the approval of Lumumba; but critics of the UN role later claimed that it had been part of a move to undermine him and to strengthen Mobutu. Both Urquhart and Dayal insisted, in their accounts, that this was not their intention.[114]

If UN money, however inadvertently supplied, gave Mobutu his first big boost, it was the additional money supplied by the CIA and by the Western embassies in Leopoldville that kept him in business from then on, according to reliable sources. Dayal, for one, was convinced that the indecisive colonel would never have taken the plunge if he had not been assured of major outside assistance. From that time on, he explained, Mobutu always had plenty of cash to pay his soldiers, even when the Congo's treasury was empty. UN liaison officers attached to Mobutu reported that from time to time Western military attachés would visit the colonel with "bulging brief-cases containing thick brown paper packets which they obligingly deposited on his table. We could not tell what they contained," Dayal wrote, "but could not help making guesses."[115]

The most valuable service that the CIA rendered to Mobutu during this period, however, was not financial; three days after he took power, CIA agents learned that supporters of Lumumba planned to assassinate Mobutu the following morning. Major Vital Pakasa, formerly a close friend of Mobutu, was to sound a general alarm at Camp Leopold II, where Mobutu lived. As he left his residence, he was to be mowed down in the ensuing confusion. On the morning of September 18, Mobutu, forewarned by his American friends, summoned Pakasa to his residence. While they were talking, Pakasa pulled a gun. As the two men struggled, Ghanaian and Moroccan UN guards arrived, disarmed Pakasa, and placed him under arrest.[116]

This assassination attempt, foiled with American help, had a decisive impact on Mobutu's political thinking. Up to this point there had been some uncertainty about his intentions. While Timberlake found his expulsion of the Russians an extremely encouraging sign, he did not know whether the colonel would be willing to work closely with Kasavubu and Ileo, or whether he took seriously his claim that he was neutralizing all political figures.[117] The day after his dramatic takeover, Mobutu indicated that he had not turned against Lumumba completely, despite Lumumba's denunciation of him; he met amicably with Lumumba at Camp Leopold II and then later in the day ordered his police to cooperate with the UN force to rescue Lumumba from an enraged band of Baluba soldiers who wanted to kill him and had him pinned down at the Ghanaian officers' mess for seven hours.[118]

After the assassination attempt, however, his attitude changed. He listened attentively to the arguments of the CIA station chief, who warned him that there were more Soviet-backed assassination plots in the works, and urged the "arrest or other more permanent disposal of Lumumba, Gizenga, and Mulele."[119] On the afternoon of September 18 Mobutu informed U.S. Embassy officials that he was ordering the arrest of Lumumba and several of his close associates. He explained that while he "logically" could not "support Ileo immediately," his council of students—the College of Commissioners—would serve as a bridge that would transfer power to an Ileo-Kasavubu government by the end of October. Timberlake reported to Washington that Mobutu seemed "completely honest, dedicated and appalled" by the enormity of the problems facing him.[120] The following day the College of Commissioners weighed in with a strong anti-Lumumba proclamation praising Mobutu as the "man who has delivered us from Communist colonialism and Marxist-Leninist imperialism" and pledging its full support to President Kasavubu, the "sole head of state."[121]

Timberlake was so enthusiastic about these developments that the State Department, in an unintentionally ironic cable, cautioned him not to overplay his hand:

> IN PRESENT CONFUSED SITUATION MAINTENANCE OF OUR POSITION OF NON-INTERFERENCE INTERNAL CONGO AFFAIRS REMAINS IMPORTANT BUT PRESUMABLY INCREASINGLY DIFFICULT IN TERMS EMBASSY LEOPOLDVILE ACTIVITIES. IN YOUR DISCRETION YOU SHOULD, UNTIL SITUATION CLARIFIES, LIMIT YOUR OWN CONTACTS TO KASAVUBU TO WHOM YOU ARE ACCREDITED AND WHO, AS HEAD OF STATE, APPEARS TO BE ONLY CONGO GOVERNMENT ENTITY OF UNCONTESTED LEGITIMACY. HOWEVER WE WISH GIVE LEAST POSSIBLE SUBSTANCE TO SOVIET LINE THAT KASAVUBU (OR ANY OTHER CONGOLESE) IS US STOOGE. AT SAME TIME WE ANXIOUS WITHIN APPROPRIATE LIMITS TO ASSIST AND ENCOURAGE CONGOLESE TOWARD POLITICAL STABILITY AND EFFECTIVE ADMINISTRATION.... YOU SHOULD BEAR ABOVE IN MIND IN REGULATING INTENSITY, LEVEL, AND NATURE OF US OFFICIAL CONTACTS WITH CONGOLESE PERSONALITIES.[122]

Timberlake replied that while the Russians and Czechs had been falling all over Lumumba, he himself had "leaned over backwards" to be discreet in his contacts with anti-Lumumba politicians. He had seen Kasavubu on only a few occasions, but he assured the Department that American views reached the President through "appropriate channels."[123]

One of the "appropriate channels" was President Youlou of the Congo (Brazzaville), who had a major stake in the outcome of the struggle in Leopoldville. Youlou, a shrewd abbé with ties to right-wing groups in France, had told Harriman that if Lumumba and the Communists won out across the river, there would be nothing he could physically do to stop them from crossing over here to bring down his regime.[124] Timberlake met Youlou for the first time on September 18, a few days after Mobutu's coup. He noted with satisfaction that Youlou was "obviously anti-Communist" and described him as "alert, intelligent," and a "man capable of action." He was impressed by Youlou's insistence that there could be "no reconciliation between Kasavubu and Lumumba" and his conviction that "Lumumba must be permanently removed." He felt that Youlou's advice had played an "important part in bolstering Kasavubu and Ileo" and would continue to be of "great value." He suggested that the State Department find a "suitable way" of assuring

him of American support—something "more tangible" than a "letter
or statement," he added.[125]

Even more important than Youlou's advice was the fact that he
served as a conduit for clandestine Western financial support to Lumumba's opponents. Timberlake noted that Ileo had been in to see
Youlou just before his own visit and had "obtained some financial
help" from him.[126] The U.S. chargé d'affaires in Brazzaville, Alan Lukens, pointed out that Youlou's operations were "expensive" and that
"he needed more money to combat Lumumba forces." His own Assembly had provided $20,000 to cover the cost of transporting, hous-
ing, and entertaining the various Congolese politicians who were
brought to Brazzaville, as well as to pay for "minor bribes."[127] But the
opposition kept raising the stakes. Youlou told Lukens that the Ghanaians were planning to give Lumumba forty million Congolese francs
($160,000) in secret to bribe members of Parliament, and he asked for
"fast counter-action by West to prevent Lumumba takeover again."[128]

Timberlake was not unaware that Lumumba was still capable of creating a number of political problems; but he believed that these problems were manageable. First, there was the possibility that if
Lumumba failed to dislodge Mobutu, he might decide to go to Stanleyville, his original base of support in the eastern part of the Congo, and
set up a rival government there with the support of the Soviet bloc.
Timberlake reported to the State Department on September 18 that
Mobutu was "aware" of this possibility and was "determined to prevent" it from happening.[129]

Second, there was the possibility that Lumumba might succeed in
his effort to get the United Nations to fly him to New York to present
his case before the General Assembly as the head of the Congolese delegation. This was an easy one to deal with: the United Nations did not
have any planes large enough to cross the Atlantic and depended on
the United States to supply them when needed. On September 18 Lumumba asked Dayal for a plane. Hammarskjold formally passed the request on to Wadsworth but sent an informal message via Wieschhoff
expressing the hope that the United States would find it impossible to
provide transportation for Lumumba. Wadsworth was glad to comply
with Hammarskjold's informal request. He told Wieschhoff he would
report Lumumba's request to Kasavubu and ask for his opinion; once
the head of state had disapproved, the U.S. government would have a
"valid reason" for turning Lumumba down.[130]

Finally, there was the possibility that a reconciliation might be
worked out between Kasavubu and Lumumba that would undo Mobutu's coup and bring Lumumba back into the government. Even before
Mobutu's takeover the African diplomats in Leopoldville had been

shuttling back and forth between an eager Lumumba and a reluctant Kasavubu; now they redoubled their efforts and produced a document which Dayal regarded as an "excellent and entirely workable compromise."[131]

The American reaction was one of alarm. When Kanza, the head of the pro-Lumumba delegation at the United Nations, announced on September 19 that Kasavubu and Lumumba had come to terms and that Lumumba would be heading the Congolese delegation at the General Assembly, the State Department shot off a cable to Timberlake demanding that Kasavubu "publicly deny" that any such agreement had been reached.[132] The ambassador quickly replied that Kasavubu had already denied the existence of the agreement to journalists and that he intended to make a formal denial of it as well.[133] Kasavubu also denied that he had any intention of compromising with Lumumba in a phone conversation with Foreign Minister Bomboko, who was in New York heading the pro-Kasavubu delegation. He assured Bomboko that he was now "working closely" with Mobutu.

This conversation was followed by one of the most bizarre incidents to occur in the course of that bizarre summer. While he had Leopoldville on the line, Bomboko had the call switched to his own apartment at the Regina Hotel so that he could talk to his family. To his surprise, Lumumba answered the phone. Bomboko, fearing that Lumumba would recognize his voice, quickly handed the phone to an assistant, who identified herself as a member of Kanza's delegation. Lumumba, who had been appearing and disappearing in Leopoldville for the past five days and was thought to be in hiding at the Ghanaian or Guinean Embassy, explained that he was hiding in Bomboko's apartment, where no one would think of looking for him, until a Ghanaian plane arrived to take him to Accra. Bomboko immediately sent a message to Kasavubu informing him of Lumumba's whereabouts and intentions, and suggested that he be arrested.[134]

The following day Mobutu sent his troops to arrest Lumumba, but they were turned away by Ghanaian UN guards. Kasavubu protested to Nkrumah; Mobutu demanded the withdrawal of the Ghanaian troops. There was some confusion about whether the Ghanaians had acted on their own or whether their action represented UN policy. Wieschhoff assured Wadsworth that the United Nations had ordered its troops to "protect Lumumba from violence but not interfere with arrest by legal warrant." He said he had already complained to Quaison-Sackey, the chief of Ghana's UN Mission, and would complain to Nkrumah in New York.[135] Despite these assurances the Ghanaian refusal to permit the arrest of Lumumba became de facto UN policy in the following weeks—thus bearing out the prediction of the CIA station chief, who had warned his superiors on September 15, the day after Mobutu's coup, that Lumumba might well have strengthened his position by placing himself in UN custody, where his safety was ensured.[136]

CIA: *"Lumumba Must Go Permanently"*

Devlin did not share Timberlake's optimistic view of the situation. While he was pleased by Mobutu's takeover and his expulsion of the Russians, he had no confidence in the stability of the colonel's new regime. He feared that the situation could be reversed at any moment, with Lumumba returning to power and inviting the Russians back to the Congo. "Only solution is remove him from scene soonest," he concluded.[137] Up to this point the U.S. Embassy and the CIA had taken a similar approach to the problem of Lumumba: they were both trying to force him out of office and to destroy him politically. Now that he was out, their priorities were somewhat different: while Timberlake saw his dismissal as a victory for the forces of moderation and was ready to move on to the next phase, the CIA continued to view Lumumba as a major threat to the U.S. position in Africa and stepped up its efforts to destroy him in a literal, physical sense.

On September 15 Devlin reported to headquarters that he was serving as an adviser to a Congolese effort to "eliminate" Lumumba.[138] On September 17 another CIA agent met with a Congolese senator who agreed "reluctantly" that "Lumumba must go permanently." He requested a "clandestine supply" of "small arms" to equip troops who had "recently arrived" in the Leopoldville area, explaining that this would provide a "core" of armed men "willing and able" to "take direct action." It seems likely that he was referring to the squadron of troops Mobutu had brought in from Thysville immediately after his coup because he did not entirely trust the Leopoldville garrison. The CIA agent told the senator that he would explore the possibility of obtaining the arms and recommended to CIA headquarters that they should have the weapons "ready to go at nearest base pending decision that supply warranted and necessary."[139]

On September 19 Devlin received what he later described as a "most unusual" cable from headquarters. It was signed by Bissell, the Deputy Director for Plans, and Tweedy, the chief of the Africa Division, and bore the code word "PROP," which, according to the report of the Senate Intelligence Committee, "indicated extraordinary sensitivity and restricted circulation at CIA headquarters to Dulles, Bissell, Tweedy and Tweedy's Deputy." According to Tweedy's testimony, the PROP channel was "established and used exclusively for the assassination operation." The station chief testified, "I believe the message was also marked for my eyes only . . . and contained instructions that I was not to discuss the message with anyone." The cable informed him that someone from headquarters would arrive on approximately September 27 and "announce himself as 'Joe from Paris.' " It was "urgent" that the station chief see him "soonest possible after he phones." The message continued: "He will fully identify himself and explain his assignment to you." According to Devlin's testimony, the cable did not refer to any specific instructions and "did not refer to Lumumba in any way."[140]

"Joe from Paris" was actually Dr. Sidney Gottlieb, the scientist who had met with Bissell during the summer to discuss a suitable poison for the assassination of an unspecified African leader.[141] Gottlieb had made his preparations, and shortly before the cable was sent, he met with Tweedy to receive instructions for his trip to the Congo. He testified that "Tweedy and his Deputy asked him to take the toxic materials to the Congo and deliver instructions from Headquarters to the Station Officer: 'to mount an operation, if he could do it securely . . . to either seriously incapacitate or eliminate Lumumba.' " Gottlieb explained that the station officer was to be responsible for finding a "feasible means of carrying out the assassination operation," while his own role was to provide "technical support."[142]

On September 21 CIA Director Dulles briefed President Eisenhower and the National Security Council. He pointed out that the "danger of Soviet influence" was still present in the Congo and said that while Lumumba had been deposed as Prime Minister he still represented a threat, particularly in light of recent reports of an "impending reconciliation" between Lumumba and the new government. He concluded that "Mobutu appeared to be the effective power in the Congo for the moment but Lumumba was not yet disposed of and remained a grave danger as long as he was not disposed of."[143] Once again, as with the Special Group meeting of August 25, there was some disagreement among the participants at the meeting about the meaning of Dulles's statement when they reviewed the record fifteen years later for the Senate Intelligence Committee. Some said they took it to mean getting Lumumba out of the Congo, or into jail, rather than assassinating him. Others felt that it was "broad enough to cover a discussion of assassination" as one way of "disposing" of Lumumba.[144]

Dulles, for his part, had no doubt about what he meant. On September 24 he sent a personally signed cable to Leopoldville in which he stated:

WE WISH GIVE EVERY POSSIBLE SUPPORT IN ELIMINATING LUMUMBA FROM ANY POSSIBILITY RESUMING GOVERNMENTAL POSITION OR IF HE FAILS IN LEOPOLDVILLE SETTING HIMSELF IN STANLEYVILLE OR ELSE-WHERE.[145]

On September 26 "Joe from Paris" arrived in Leopoldville with his deadly kit and reported to Devlin that he had been instructed by headquarters to help him assassinate Lumumba. He assured the station chief that there was "Presidential authorization for this mission."[146]

From then on, it was a whole new ballgame. Ironically, the CIA took its first concrete step toward the assassination of Lumumba three weeks after he was removed from his post as Prime Minister, twelve days after Mobutu seized power, and nine days after the expulsion of the Soviet diplomats and technicians whose arrival in Leopoldville had caused the panic in Washington that set the assassination plot in motion in the first place.

Special Session of the General Assembly: September 17–20, 1960

While the CIA was trying to make sure that Lumumba would never be able to invite the Russians back to the Congo, American diplomats at the United Nations were trying to take advantage of the new situation created by Mobutu's ouster of the Soviet Embassy. They knew that Hammarskjold's first priority at this point was a quick vote by the special session of the General Assembly that would authorize him to raise the funds he so desperately needed. They were perfectly willing, particularly after Mobutu's takeover, to provide forty percent of the one-hundred-million-dollars total.[147] But their primary aim was to put the Russians on the defensive at the time of Khrushchev's arrival in New York and for this reason they wanted a long, drawn-out special session which would still be meeting when the regular session began on September 20.[148] Their effort to extend the session was only partially successful; the first meeting took place on the evening of September 17, and the last one came to an end a little after midnight on September 20, just in time for the regular session to start on schedule.[149]

Wadsworth opened the debate by charging that the Soviet Union had chosen to "defy the Security Council decision for which it had voted, and to strike out on its own path," sending "hundreds of so-called technicians"—who had now been expelled by the Congolese authorities—as well as aircraft and trucks to "promote strife and faction" in the Congo. Zorin defended the presence of the Soviet technicians and insisted that his government had acted in "complete accord with the letter and spirit" of the Security Council resolutions. "Everybody knows how they have been employed," he said. "They were civilian specialists sent at the request of the legitimate Government of the Congo, and they have been doing work at that Government's instructions." He then took the offensive and charged that the Americans had used the Secretary-General to force Lumumba out of office because he represented a "threat" to Western interests.

After the Soviet delegate had finished, the Secretary-General turned to the delegates with an implicit appeal for a vote of confidence. "The General Assembly," said Hammarskjold, "knows me well enough to realize that I would not wish to serve one day beyond the point at which such continued service would be ... in the best interests of the Organization."[150]

Hammarskjold did not have to wait long. On the evening of September 18 Ghanaian Ambassador Quaison-Sackey, speaking for all the African members of the United Nations and several of the Asians as well, introduced a draft resolution which reflected widespread support for the Secretary-General, even among the troop contributors who considered Cordier's actions a mistake. It followed the lines of the vetoed Tunisian-Ceylonese draft, including the provisions opposed by Zorin: it requested the Secretary-General to "continue to take vigorous action" to carry out the Security Council resolutions, appealed for voluntary contributions to a Congo fund, and called upon all states to refrain from sending arms or military personnel into the Congo except through the United Nations.[151] Quaison-Sackey made it clear that this last provision was designed to keep the cold war out of the Congo.

The following day the Afro-Asian resolution was adopted 70 to 0, with eleven abstentions—the Soviet bloc, France, and South Africa. In a surprising change of position Zorin voted for the paragraph barring all outside military aid when it was put to a separate vote.[152] Perhaps he found the earlier Soviet position too embarrassing to maintain in the face of almost unanimous African opposition; perhaps he recognized that Mobutu's ouster of all Soviet personnel had made the issue a purely theoretical one for the Russians, while it could still be used against the Belgians.

Khrushchev Arrives on the Scene

It was at this point, on September 19, that Premier Khrushchev's boat docked in a hostile New York, where the mood was very different from the cordial atmosphere of his 1959 trip. There were no smiling American officials to meet him as he disembarked in a cold driving rain—only angry pickets, the official Soviet community, a curious press corps, hundreds of New York City policemen, and a UN protocol officer.[153]

The Eisenhower Administration had made it very clear that he was not welcome in the United States. When the President was asked at a press conference on September 7 if he would meet with the Soviet leader, he replied that the chances were "very very slim," and explained that before such a meeting could be held, certain conditions would have to be met—for example, the release of the two fliers from the RB-47 reconnaissance plane shot down by the Russians over international waters. "I do not intend to debase the United Nations by being a party to a . . . battle of invective and propaganda," Eisenhower said.[154] The following day Secretary of State Herter described Khrushchev's summit proposal as "ludicrous in the extreme."[155] On September 10 the State Department announced that Khrushchev and his party would be limited to the island of Manhattan during their stay for security reasons. The Soviet government protested, calling this a hostile gesture. On September 17 the State Department asked the three television networks not to give Khrushchev any extra air time, beyond what the news warranted. The networks were glad to comply. In an era of close cooperation between the government and the press, they had already arrived at that decision on their own.

As soon as Khrushchev disembarked, he discovered that the Americans had managed to outmaneuver him not only in the Congo but also at the General Assembly. One of his chief reasons for coming to New York was to court the new African heads of state and to start building a socialist-neutralist alliance which would form a numerical majority in the Assembly. Now it seemed that the combination of a Soviet veto in the Security Council and a Soviet abstention in the General Assembly—on two major Afro-Asian initiatives dealing with the Congo crisis—had isolated him from the very people he was trying to reach.

There was little the Soviet leader could do about the situation in the Congo, which had deteriorated sharply while he was crossing the Atlantic. When he left, on September 9, Lumumba's position was not clear; Kasavubu had mounted a major challenge to his authority, but it appeared that Lumumba was holding his own in the struggle for power. His parliamentary victory on September 13 indicated that he would come out on top. It was Mobutu's move, on September 14, that tipped the balance against Lumumba; while it was not yet certain that Mobutu would retain power in the long run, it seemed clear that in the short run neither Lumumba's political future nor the Soviet position in the Congo looked very promising.

While recognizing that events in Leopoldville were beyond his control, Khrushchev must have wondered what had gone wrong in New York. Why had the Soviet bloc found itself isolated, with only France and South Africa for company, in opposition to a major Afro-Asian resolution dealing with the Congo, the key issue on which he had based his hopes for an alliance with the Africans? What could be done to remedy the situation?

As the Soviet leader pondered these questions, he was probably struck by the irony of the situation: he was now isolated from the African bloc precisely because he had gone out on a limb to support a democratically elected, independent, anticolonialist African leader— the sort of leader who, in Khrushchev's view, unquestionably should have commanded the support of his neighbors, at least the more radical among them. By the end of August, at the time of the fourth Security Council meeting and the Leopoldville conference, Khrushchev had accepted the fact that there was a fairly large gap between his own attitude toward Lumumba and that of the moderate African group, exemplified by Tunisia; but he believed that the radical states, such as Guinea, Ghana, and the UAR, were in basic agreement with his position. Their assistance to Lumumba, their criticism of Cordier's decision to close the radio station and airports, and their threats to withdraw their troops from the UN force had served to reinforce that belief. Still, when it came to a showdown, they had ended up supporting the Western position and rejecting the Soviet stand. Where had he gone wrong?

Khrushchev's first major miscalculation was apparently his decision to provide direct military aid to Lumumba. While Lumumba's Guinean advisers approved, the moderate Africans were horrified, and even the Ghanaians warned Lumumba that he was treading on dangerous ground. They feared that if Africa became involved in the cold war, it had nothing to gain and a great deal to lose. If the Russian gambit had worked and Lumumba had been successful in ending the Katanga secession, his Ghanaian supporters might have stifled their scruples; as it turned out, their warnings to Lumumba proved to be justified.

Khrushchev's second major miscalculation seems to have been his assumption that Hammarskjold's policy toward the Lumumba government was so outrageous that the Africans would feel obliged to support Moscow's strong personal attacks on the Secretary-General. It was inconceivable to Khrushchev that they could continue to express confidence in the Secretary-General and extend his mandate in the Congo.

When it came to a choice, however, between supporting, on the one hand, Lumumba, a fellow African nationalist, and Khrushchev, a powerful opponent of colonialism, or, on the other hand, Hammarskjold, the embodiment of an organization which had contributed a great deal to their pride and their development, even the radical African leaders had rejected Lumumba and Khrushchev and sided with Hammarskjold.

Ghana's President Nkrumah and the UAR's President Nasser, who made no secret of their displeasure about certain aspects of Hammarskjold's Congo policy, had their own reasons for refusing to break with him on the issue of Lumumba. Nasser could not afford to antagonize the Secretary-General because he was dependent on the United Nations peacekeeping force along the Suez Canal. Nkrumah, as the senior statesman of the newly independent black African countries, was acutely aware of the helpful role Hammarskjold was playing in the decolonization process, which was still underway.

The most reluctant supporter of the Secretary-General was Guinea's President Sékou Touré. His country's independence was only two years old, and he owed nothing to Dag Hammarskjold. He had been extremely critical of Hammarskjold's policy in the Congo from the beginning of the operation. Still, even he had yielded to the entreaties of his African colleagues and confined his criticism to unnamed "United Nations officials" and instructed his delegation to vote with the other Africans to extend Hammarskjold's mandate in the Congo.

In theory, Khrushchev had two alternatives at this point. He could change course and follow the African lead, back down from his charges against Hammarskjold, and work with the Afro-Asians in their attempt to return Lumumba to power through compromise and negotiation. Or he could continue alone on his uncompromising anticolonialist course and maintain the Soviet reputation for consistency.

He soon made it clear that he had chosen the latter course and that he had no intention of backing down on any of his charges in order to mend fences with Hammarskjold or the African delegations; on the contrary, he started with a tough Soviet policy and made it even tougher, ending with a full-scale assault on the office of the Secretary-General.

Khrushchev had made a strong pitch to establish himself as the chief defender of Afro-Asian interests in the struggle against colonialism. He was furious to find this role usurped by the Secretary-General, especially since he believed that Hammarskjold was working hand-in-glove with the Western powers against the interests of African nationalism. Moreover, he believed that Hammarskjold and his associates had deliberately thwarted Soviet ambitions in the Congo, and he held them responsible for the expulsion of the Soviet Embassy, which was an unprecedented humiliation. It was not possible for Khrushchev simply to forget all that and reestablish his former relationship with the Secretary-General.

Next, there was Khrushchev's optimistic world view, his belief that time was working in his favor. The Soviet Union had lost one vote in the General Assembly; but there would be other votes, and the Soviet position was bound to improve. Khrushchev realized that Afro-Asian support for the Secretary-General's Congo policy was not wholehearted; the doubts that emerged in the speeches of the African and Asian delegates at the Security Council and the General Assembly could ripen into total disillusionment as the situation developed, with a bit of encouragement from Moscow. The Soviet leader hoped that as the

Afro-Asians became more aware of the collaboration between the Secretary-General and the Western powers in the Congo, they would realize that the Russians had been right all along and would come over to their side, thus establishing an alliance with the Soviet Union on the basis of firm principle rather than temporary expediency.

Finally, there was the chaotic situation in the Congo. It was always possible that Lumumba might return to power, and, if he did, he would be grateful to the Russians for their unwavering support. The regime which was trying to replace Lumumba was implacably hostile to the Soviet Union, and Khrushchev saw no point in trying to work out a compromise with it. Thus he had nothing to lose in the Congo itself by maintaining a strong pro-Lumumba position and, possibly, in the long run, a great deal to gain.

CHAPTER FIVE

Khrushchev at the United Nations (September 20-October 13,1960)

"I am not making war on Mr. Hammarskjold personally."

PREMIER NIKITA KHRUSHCHEV stayed in New York for almost a month, to the despair of the U.S. government and the delight of the press corps. His salty humor, his quick changes of mood, his freewheeling conversations with reporters from the balcony of the Soviet Mission on Park Avenue, and his unprecedented interruptions and shoe pounding during speeches at the General Assembly which displeased him—all dominated the front pages and demonstrated that his recent defeats on the Congo issue were not going to cramp his style.

American officials had expected that the 70 to 0 vote at the special session of the General Assembly would put the Soviet leader on the defensive as he arrived in the United States; instead, they found that he was putting them on the defensive with his dramatic brand of personal diplomacy. Despite the Soviet setbacks in the Congo, Khrushchev seemed determined to press his original plan of enlisting the nations of Asia and Africa on his side in the global battle for power. He had invited the leaders of the world to come to New York, and more than half of them had accepted his invitation. At the opening session of the General Assembly on the afternoon of September 20, he held court as head of the Soviet delegation, greeting Prime Ministers and Foreign Ministers, congratulating the leaders of the newly independent African states, rushing over to the Cuban delegation to embrace Fidel Castro with a typical Khrushchevian bear hug.

The Eisenhower Administration, embarrassed by the deluge of controversial high-ranking visitors in the midst of a presidential campaign and sensitive to the charges of Democratic candidate John F. Kennedy that the Republicans had failed to take the initiative in the cold war struggle with the Soviet Union, abruptly reversed its strategy shortly after Khrushchev's arrival. Instead of ignoring the extraordinary gathering in New York and limiting his stay to a few hours in order to avoid any contact with the Soviet leader, as he had originally planned, the President decided to put his immense prestige on the line and meet Khrushchev's challenge head-on. He arranged a series of meetings with the major neutralist leaders to try to counteract the effect of Khrushchev's blandishments with some personal diplomacy of his own.

On September 21 the White House announced that Eisenhower would confer with Yugoslavia's President Tito and Ghana's President Nkrumah the following day, after his address to the General Assembly. He would also see the Prime Ministers of Nepal and Lebanon and preside at a luncheon for the chiefs of the Latin American delegations, to which Cuba's Premier Castro was pointedly not invited. The following week he would return to New York to meet with UAR President Nasser and Indian Prime Minister Nehru, as well as other foreign leaders.

Khrushchev's Troika Proposal

Eisenhower, who was the first head of state to address the Assembly, used the occasion to deliver a strong defense of the Secretary-General and his Congo policy. Without referring to the Soviet Union by name, he charged that Hammarskjold's effort had been "flagrantly attacked by a few nations which wish to prolong strife in the Congo for their own selfish purposes." Their criticism of the Secretary-General, he said, was "nothing less than a direct attack upon the United Nations itself." He proposed that all member states "refrain from any action to intensify or exploit the present unsettled conditions in the Congo—by sending arms or forces into that troubled area or by inciting its leaders and peoples to violence against each other." He pledged a substantial contribution to the Secretary-General's one-hundred-million-dollar Congo fund. He also promised to help finance major programs of education and technical assistance for Africa.[1]

Khrushchev listened to Eisenhower's speech in silence and described it afterwards as "conciliatory"; but this assessment did not cause him to change his own approach. He intended to outbid the American President in his appeal to the new African states by proposing immediate independence for all remaining colonies and trust territories; and he hoped to use the Congo issue to rally African and Asian support for his assault on the Secretary-General, thus turning an embarrassing defeat to his own advantage.

In his speech to the General Assembly the following day, the Soviet leader reviewed his grievances against the U.S. government, beginning with the U-2 and the RB-47 incidents, moving on to the "intrigues" and "subversion" directed against Cuba, and then blasting American policy in the Congo. With characteristic bravado he refused to admit that the Soviet Union had suffered a defeat in the Congo, scoffing at such claims as "silly." The Soviet Union, he asserted, "did not and could not sustain a defeat in the Congo because we did not and could not have any troops there, nor did we or could we interfere in the Congo's domestic affairs." The Western powers were "celebrating too soon," he said; they had won nothing but a "Pyrrhic victory." They had accused Lumumba of being a Communist, when everyone knew he was "no Communist" but a "patriot" who was trying to free his people from "colonial oppression." By forcing him out of office and replacing him with a "puppet government," they had demonstrated to the Africans that they were unwilling to permit their former colonies to become truly independent—just as the Russians had always warned.

The bombshell came later in the speech, when Khrushchev launched his controversial troika proposal. He began with the premise that, as things were presently set up, the executive machinery of the United Nations was "one-sided." The Secretary-General had been chosen by the Western powers; therefore he reflected their views. His pro-Western "bias" was "particularly glaring" in the case of the Congo, where he had "virtually adopted the position of the colonialists," despite his "formal condemnation" of them. This, Khrushchev concluded, was a "very dangerous matter." In order to remedy the situation he proposed "abolishing the post of Secretary-General" and replacing him with a troika, a three-man executive representing the world's three major blocs—Western, socialist, and neutralist. Such an arrangement would "safeguard the interests" of all states, so that there could be no repetition of the Congo experience.[2]

American officials were stunned by the vehemence and the far-reaching nature of Khrushchev's assault. Secretary of State Herter rushed to Hammarskjold's defense, characterizing the Soviet attack on the Secretary-General as a "declaration of war" on the United Nations.[3] Hammarskjold himself was not overly surprised by Khrushchev's sharp attack. He had known for more than two months that he was on a collision course with the Soviet Union. He shared the American view that the Russians were trying to establish a power base in Africa, and he believed that his attempts to apply the Security Council mandate in a fair and impartial manner would inevitably run counter to this Soviet ambition. In a cable to Dayal, he described Khrushchev's speech as the "greatest compliment so far paid" to the United Nations because it meant that the Soviet leader recognized that the world organization was now the "main obstacle to an expansion of empire into Africa." The "very venom" of Khrushchev's statements, he said, constituted a "recognition of defeat."[4]

His public response was phrased more diplomatically, but he made essentially the same point when he addressed the General Assembly on September 26, three days after Khrushchev's speech. He defended his Congo policy as wholly consistent with the mandate given him by the Security Council and the General Assembly. The UN force, he insisted, was not meant to be under the orders of the government requesting its presence, and it was specifically forbidden to become a party to any internal conflict in which that government became involved. On the larger issue Hammarskjold did not refer directly to Khrushchev's troika plan, but he made an eloquent defense of his conception of the office of Secretary-General. "This is a question not of a man but of an institution," he said. He then continued:

> Use whatever words you like, independence, impartiality, objectivity— they all describe essential aspects of what, without exception, must be the attitude of the Secretary-General. Such an attitude ... may at any stage become an obstacle for those who work for certain political aims which would be better served or more easily achieved if the Secretary-General compromised with this attitude. But if he did, how gravely he would then betray the trust of all those for whom the strict maintenance of such an attitude is their best protection in the world-wide fight for power and influence. Thus, if the office of the Secretary-General becomes a stumbling block for anyone ... because the incumbent stands by the basic principle which must guide his whole activity, and if for that reason, he comes under criticism, such criticism strikes at the very office and the concepts on which it is based. I would rather see that office break on strict adherence to the principle of independence, impartiality, and objectivity than drift on the basis of compromise.[5]

The battle lines were drawn. Hammarskjold knew that if he was to save the institution of the Secretary-General from Khrushchev's assault, he would have to take his case to the neutralist leaders gathered in New York and persuade them that he had been acting impartially, on the basis of principle, throughout the Congo crisis. He was fairly confident that he could keep most of them in his camp, as he had done up to this point. He hoped they would recognize that it was in their interest to stand up for the principle of a strong Secretary-General even if they had reservations about his Congo policy and preferred Khrushchev's strong anticolonialist stand.

Ironically, Hammarskjold's staunchest defenders in this fight—the Americans—were also his greatest liability. He complained to Dayal that their "uncalled for" support was "making it more difficult" to place his dispute with Khrushchev in the proper context.[6] It appeared to bolster the Soviet leader's claim that Hammarskjold had been following U.S. orders in the Congo. Over the next few weeks Hammarskjold tried to put some distance between himself and his enthusiastic American admirers, who insisted on describing his Congo policy in cold war terms. He did not feel that a public emphasis on the anti-Communist aspects of his Congo policy was particularly helpful at a time when he was trying to reach an understanding with a group of neutralists who did not regard the UN operation in the Congo as the unqualified success that the Americans did.

Khrushchev, recognizing Hammarskjold's vulnerability on this issue, kept hammering away at the same point wherever he went—in formal debates, at impromptu press conferences, and in private conversations with key neutralist leaders. Again and again he linked his troika proposal with Hammarskjold's Congo policy, insisting that the Secretary-General was carrying out American instructions and should no longer be trusted by the Afro-Asians.

It was characteristic of Khrushchev's unorthodox approach to diplomacy that while he attacked the Secretary-General with unprecedented ferocity on an official level, he managed to maintain a civil relationship with him on an unofficial level. The most dramatic example of this took place on October 3, when Khrushchev took the offensive once again at the General Assembly, saying:

> Everyone has heard how vigorously the imperialist countries defend Mr. Hammarskjold's position. Is it not clear then, in whose interest he interprets and executes those decisions? ... Mr. Hammarskjold has always been prejudiced in his attitude toward the socialist countries; he has always upheld the interests of the United States and the other monopoly-capitalist countries. The events in the Congo, where he played a simply deplorable role, were the last drop which filled the cup of our patience to overflowing.... We do not, and cannot, place confidence in Mr. Hammarskjold. If he himself cannot muster the courage to resign in, let us say, a chivalrous way, we shall draw the inevitable conclusions from the situation.[7]

Hammarskjold was furious and wanted to respond immediately, but General Assembly President Frederick Boland persuaded him to wait until later in the day. When his temper had cooled, Hammarskjold spoke eloquently about the importance of the Secretary-General as an institution, especially for the small states in the United Nations. "It is very easy to resign," he said. "It is not so easy to stay on. It is very easy to bow to the wish of a big power. It is another matter to resist." Then he assured the small states, "I shall remain in my post during the term of my office as a servant of the organization in the interests of all those other nations, as long as they wish me to do so."[8] Ambassador Slim led the Assembly in a standing ovation for Hammarskjold. The Soviet bloc representatives did not join in the applause. Khrushchev remained seated and pounded the table with his fist.

A few hours later, when Hammarskjold and Cordier arrived at a reception at the Soviet Mission, they were cordially welcomed by Khrushchev, who greeted the Secretary-General with a bear hug and friendly banter about his last trip to Moscow in 1959. Cordier, the man who was responsible for closing the airports and radio station in the Congo and the target of official Soviet wrath, recalled in an interview many years later that there had been some question in his and Hammarskjold's mind about whether they were really invited to the reception after the stormy confrontation at the General Assembly; but they were assured by the Soviet UN Under Secretary, Georgi Arkadiev, that they would be welcome.[9]

On October 12, the day before Khrushchev left for home, he returned once more to the Congo issue, charging that Hammarskjold had done "everything possible to benefit the colonialists."[10] The following day he repeated this charge but then added, "I am not making war on Mr. Hammarskjold personally. I have met him and we have had very pleasant conversations." In the same spirit, the Secretary-General came down from the podium to wish Khrushchev a "pleasant journey."[11]

Khrushchev's competition with Hammarskjold and the Americans for the support of the Africans and Asians produced an extraordinary concentration of summit-level diplomacy in a limited time and space. When the heads of government and foreign ministers were not attending General Assembly debates, they were crisscrossing Manhattan in official motorcades on their way to a series of luncheons, dinners, receptions, and private meetings with their opposite numbers. It was not unusual for the head of a delegation to confer with six other leaders in succession in the course of a day. Khrushchev set the pace. He was engaged in a complicated diplomatic game which left onlookers breathless and his reluctant American hosts scrambling to regain their balance.

One of his most interesting diplomatic forays took place on the evening of October 12, just before he left New York, when he gave a dinner for the heads of the delegations of the new African states— Cameroun, Chad, Dahomey, Ivory Coast, Malagasy Republic, Mali, Nigeria, Senegal, Somalia, Togo, and Upper Volta. Khrushchev realized that this was a fairly conservative group; most of them were former French colonies which had decided to maintain close ties with France. Their spokesman, Charles Okala, Foreign Minister of Cameroun, a former trust territory, was strongly opposed to Lumumba and had been outspoken in his criticism of Khrushchev's speech less than three weeks before.[12]

Still, the Soviet leader felt it was worth his while to reach out to these people in order to explain his country's position. When Okala, in a friendly toast, said that while he appreciated Soviet support for the African independence movement, he himself was no Communist, Khrushchev picked up this theme and replied in a humorous vein, assuring his listeners that, despite what the imperialists claimed, Communists didn't "eat people." He invited the Africans present to "travel to our country, look at our life for yourselves and you will see for yourselves that we are not that kind of people at all."

Then he told the story of his own life, how he started to work at the age of eight or nine, first as a shepherd, then, at fifteen, as a factory worker and miner, and how he fought for three years in the civil war. "Today," he said proudly, "I am the Chairman of the Council of Ministers of the greatest, the most powerful country in the world."

Because of his background, he explained, and the similar background of all the members of his government, he understood "the needs of the people." He spoke of the benefits Communism had brought to the Soviet people—"a short working day, good housing, the world's lowest rent, good clothes, well-fed children, free tuition, state scholarships, free medical care, pensions"—and within five years, he added, taxes would be abolished.

"We want nothing from the peoples of Africa and other continents except friendship," Khrushchev concluded. "We have everything we need—a population of 214 million, a vast territory, plenty of iron ore, coal, and oil. What don't we have? We have no cocoa, coffee, pineapples, or mangoes. Thus we can trade with you to our mutual advantage."[13]

The gist of Khrushchev's message to the African leaders he met in New York was simple and meant to be alluring: we are natural allies; we in the Soviet Union have made a revolution and developed our country without the assistance of the imperialists; we can help you to do the same. Economically, we offer an alternative to dependence on your former colonial masters; we offer trade, low-interest development loans, and technical aid in building up your industry and agriculture. Politically, we support you on the issues you consider important—the abolition of colonialism, the end of foreign bases on your territory, a nuclear-free zone in Africa. Here at the United Nations we offer you an equal voice with those of the two big power blocs. If you support the troika principle, the imperialists will no longer control the policy of the Secretariat by naming the Secretary-General and filling the top staff positions.

Although few of Khrushchev's African listeners accepted all his arguments, many of them felt that he had made a good personal impression and was an effective spokesman for his country's political and economic system. They were grateful to him for focusing world attention on the importance of the Afro-Asian bloc. They responded warmly to his call for the immediate abolition of colonialism. They had been disappointed by President Eisenhower, who promised nothing more exciting than increased aid for African education, and they found Khrushchev's approach much more appealing.

Diplomatic Blackmail: Lumumba, the Troika, and the Neutralists

If the General Assembly had been convened a month earlier, Patrice Lumumba would have been among the new African leaders who met with Khrushchev in New York. Instead, the Congo was represented by two rival delegations, one sent by Lumumba, the other by Kasavubu. While the Congo was admitted to the United Nations along with the other new African states, the question of which delegation to seat was sent to the Credentials Committee, where it was expected to remain until the political situation in Leopoldville was clarified.

The key neutralist leaders in New York—Nkrumah, Nasser, Nehru, Tito, Sukarno, and Sékou Touré—were determined to see Lumumba come out on top and they decided to use their influence to force a change in Hammarskjold's policy. They realized that he had been weakened by Khrushchev's attack and was now more dependent on their support than he had been before. They indicated to him that they would back him on the troika issue in exchange for his help in restoring Lumumba to power.

Hammarskjold was reluctant to yield to this sort of diplomatic blackmail. He had hoped originally that he could persuade the neutralists to support his stand on the troika issue on the merits, but this was turning out to be more difficult than he had anticipated. His task was complicated by the fact that each neutralist leader he met had just come from or was en route to a meeting with Khrushchev, whose arguments were often more persuasive than his own, or Eisenhower, whose attempts to help the United Nations generally tended to backfire and create additional diplomatic problems for the Secretary-General.

The first neutralist leader to speak out on the Congo issue was President Nkrumah of Ghana, who was also the most deeply involved in the Congo's affairs. He had been Lumumba's guide and mentor before the Congo achieved independence and had rushed his troops to Leopoldville in response to Lumumba's request even before the UN force could get there. He was extremely unhappy about the latest developments, particularly about the fact that Ghanaian UN troops had been put in the position of preventing Lumumba from using the Leopoldville radio station. He had threatened to withdraw his troops from the UN command but had been mollified by Hammarskjold and persuaded to lead the drive for the adoption of the resolution by the special session of the General Assembly.

Nkrumah, who had worked closely with the British since Ghana became independent in 1957, was now striking out on a nonaligned path. He had just sent a high-ranking delegation to Moscow to sign Ghana's first major trade and cultural agreement with the Soviet Union;[14] and a few days before he came to New York his government announced that the fledgling Ghanaian air force would purchase fourteen Ilyushin transport planes, which would be manned by Soviet crews.[15] At the same time, he was deeply involved in discussions with the U.S. government about aid for the massive Volta River project.

This was his first trip to the United States, and it was symbolic of his new nonaligned status that his first meetings with Eisenhower and Khrushchev took place on the same day, immediately after the President addressed the General Assembly. Eisenhower was surprised to find him optimistic about the Congo.[16] After a forty-five minute talk the two men issued a joint statement reaffirming their "loyalty to the United Nations as the only practical road on which the world can achieve peace."[17]

Nkrumah then proceeded to the Soviet Mission to confer with Khrushchev. No statement was issued, but it was apparent when they addressed the Assembly the following day that while they both supported Lumumba, they differed considerably in their attitude toward the Secretary-General. While Khrushchev denounced Hammarskjold and pressed his troika proposal, Nkrumah said it would be "entirely wrong" to blame the "mistakes" that had been made on "any senior officials of the United Nations." Nkrumah's most striking proposal was the suggestion that all non-African troops in the UN force be withdrawn and an all-African command be set up to run the operation.[18] Hammarskjold regarded this as a proposal to put the entire operation under Ghanaian control and privately described Nkrumah's speech as a "step backward."[19]

The American reaction was even stronger. Eisenhower, who did not see any distinction between the two speeches, could not understand why Nkrumah had "cut loose with a speech following the Khrushchev line" immediately after he had assured the President of his support for the United Nations.[20] Herter told newsmen the following day that Nkrumah's words showed a "very close relationship" to those of Khrushchev and concluded that the Ghanaian leader was "very definitely leaning toward the Soviet bloc." Nkrumah, in turn, was startled by this assessment. He said Herter "was, in fact, the last person from whom I would expect such a remark."[21]

Herter stuck to his position. He had told British Foreign Secretary Lord Home a few days before that he was afraid that Nkrumah was "playing the Russian game" in the Congo.[22] Home took a more philosophical view. "Nkrumah," he said, "does not want Communism in Africa. After all, he is a good old-fashioned imperialist himself." He was "trying to build up Lumumba as an ally" so that he could "take over Katanga and nationalize the copper mines" and give Ghana a share. Home pointed out that Nkrumah was "extraordinarily conceited"; it

was his "vanity that led him to think that the placing of Soviet technicians in the Congo would help him."[23] Hammarskjold had a similar
view of Nkrumah's imperialist ambitions in Africa. He believed that
the Ghanaian leader was allying himself with Sékou Touré in Guinea
and Lumumba in the Congo in order to outflank his opponents in
Togo and Nigeria and eventually create a "coastal empire stretching
from Ghana down to and including the ex–Belgian Congo with an arm
into the Bakongo part of Angola." He felt that the Russians were encouraging these ambitions for their own reasons.[24]

The Secretary-General was disturbed by Dayal's reports that Nkrumah was sending instructions directly to the Ghanaian troops in Leopoldville, independent of the UN command. On September 25 two
jeeploads of Ghanaian soldiers escorted Lumumba around the capital
for more than an hour, while he announced triumphantly that he had
reached an agreement with Kasavubu and that he would stay on as
Prime Minister. Kasavubu was furious, and the Americans backed up
his protest.[25] Hammarskjold was particularly annoyed by Nkrumah's
"freewheeling political initiatives" since the Ghanaian leader had
made such a point of criticizing UN "intervention" in the Congo's internal affairs. He assured Dayal that he would raise the matter with
Nkrumah when they met for luncheon on September 26. "I am afraid
that I will not entirely be able to hide my sarcasm," he wrote.[26]

That same day, Nkrumah met again with Khrushchev, who evidently had more of an impact on his thinking than Hammarskjold did. The
Ghanaians stepped up their assistance to Lumumba in Leopoldville,
and Nkrumah retreated to some extent from his support of Hammarskjold on the troika issue. In a speech to the UN Correspondents' Association on September 30, he proposed that the Secretary-General
appoint three deputies with enlarged functions who would represent
the three blocs in the United Nations.[27]

The next pro-Lumumba leader to hear the arguments of Khrushchev, Eisenhower, and Hammarskjold was President Nasser of the
UAR. Unlike Nkrumah, Nasser had no personal interest in the Congo;
he had been persuaded to contribute troops to the UN force by the
Secretary-General and, at his urging, had tried to convince Lumumba
to rely on the United Nations and not look elsewhere for military aid.
Like Nkrumah, he was very much disturbed by the fact that his troops
had been put in a position of acting against the man he considered the
legitimate Prime Minister of the Congo. He too had been ready to pull
out his troops, but Hammarskjold had persuaded him to reconsider—
for the time being.

On September 24, his first full day in New York, Nasser conferred
with Khrushchev at Glen Cove, the Soviet estate on Long Island. (The
State Department had responded to Soviet protests by partially lifting

the travel restrictions that had limited the Soviet party to the island of Manhattan and permitting Khrushchev to spend the weekend in the country.) Their once close relationship, dating back to the days of the original arms deal in 1955 and the Suez crisis in 1956, capped by Nasser's visit to Moscow in 1958, had been strained in recent months by Nasser's decision to ban the Communist Party in his country. Nasser's confidant and adviser, journalist Mohamed Heikal, recalled in his memoirs that when Nasser arrived at Glen Cove, Khrushchev warned, "This place is bugged and we have discovered the bugging." As a result, Heikal wrote, there were no substantive discussions at their first meeting.[28]

Two days later Nasser had his first meeting with Eisenhower. The U.S. Embassy in Cairo had reported that Nasser appeared to be "disenchanted with Lumumba,"[29] but Eisenhower found no evidence of this. The Egyptian leader did not budge from his tough official line on the Congo; he deplored the UN decision to close the airports and said it had "shaken the confidence" of the entire world. When the conversation turned to the Soviet Union, he assured Eisenhower that while he was "willing to accept Soviet aid," there was "no danger Egypt would surrender to Communist domination."[30]

After the meeting an American spokesman announced that the two men were in agreement in their opposition to Khrushchev's troika plan and stated that Nasser would make his opposition clear in his speech to the General Assembly the following day.[31] There was apparently some misunderstanding; the following day Nasser claimed that he had been misquoted. He and Eisenhower had not discussed Khrushchev's troika proposal but had talked merely of strengthening the United Nations.[32] In his speech the Egyptian leader made no reference to the troika idea. He did not attack Hammarskjold directly, but he was extremely critical of UN policy in the Congo and called for the restoration of the Lumumba government.[33]

"There is a world of difference between what is said in public and views expressed behind closed doors," Hammarskjold observed in a cable to Dayal.[34] He was referring to all the neutralist leaders, but his observation was particularly applicable to Nasser, who took a very strong pro-Lumumba line for public consumption but was much more realistic in private. Hammarskjold quoted Nasser as saying, " 'All the individual leaders in the Congo are interested in nothing but their own position and none of them stick to a promise or to a view expressed for more than two hours,' " and concluded, "My guest of honor at dinner tonight obviously has been vaccinated against Lumumbism. All he now wants is a strong government without East or West influence, irrespective of who the top man is."[35]

Of all the neutralist leaders Nasser was the most helpful to the Secretary-General behind the scenes. Heikal recalled that at one point he organized a meeting between Hammarskjold and all the nonaligned leaders at the Secretary-General's apartment. Hammarskjold was "facing a hostile audience," Heikal wrote. The African leaders felt that he had betrayed Lumumba and taken part in the conspiracy against him. Nasser defended him, saying, "I have dealt with Hammarskjold over Suez and I think the man is honest." But he told the Secretary-General:

> You are facing us with a very difficult problem. . . . You have told me that various things happened without your knowledge. You are not able to control what is going on. That is why we have to criticize you. We know you. We trust you, yet we cannot approve of what you are doing. You are asking for a mandate from us, and we are going to back you against the *troika* idea, nevertheless we feel that you are undertaking something you cannot control and we can blame nobody but you.[36]

The price implicit in Nasser's support was that Hammarskjold would alter his Congo policy to favor Lumumba.

On October 1 Nasser met again with Khrushchev at Glen Cove. They spent three hours in the garden, out of range of the bugs. When Khrushchev complained that Nasser was taking part in an anti-Communist crusade in Egypt, Nasser protested, "You are my friend and you are a Communist. Tito is my friend and he is a Communist." At this point, Khrushchev burst out, "Tito is not a Communist. He is a King!" The two men ranged over a number of issues and, according to Heikal, Nasser "came away with the impression that some of their quarrels had been settled." Still, he wrote, "the feelings between them remained cool."[37] Nasser's stubborn refusal to abandon the Secretary-General over the Congo issue was one of their major points of disagreement.

Although the views of all these leaders were important to Hammarskjold, he was most concerned about the reaction of Prime Minister Nehru. "The role of Nehru will now be decisive," he wrote to Dayal. "If he sways, the public Afro-Asian front may break with very far-reaching consequences for the Organization."[38]

The Indian leader arrived on September 26 and spent the next day conferring with everyone from Khrushchev to Eisenhower. An American spokesman announced that Nehru had told the President he opposed the troika plan and would say so in his speech to the General Assembly.[39] Once again, there seemed to have been a slight misunderstanding. Nehru actually intended to propose a compromise plan in his speech—one that would bridge the gap between Hammarskjold and Khrushchev. Hammarskjold was completely opposed to this idea and tried to explain his position when the Indian leader came to dinner on

September 30. It was a difficult evening. Nehru left most of the talking to his anti-Western Defense Minister, Krishna Menon, who was more impressed by Gromyko's statements on the Congo than by Dayal's reports. Hammarskjold's bitterness overflowed in a message to Dayal:

> Frankly, we are hardened but every time you discover again that the word of Mr. Lumumba is regarded as evidence, because he is Prime Minister, while we are suspected to serve God knows what interest and therefore to colour our picture, I wonder how we are able to achieve anything at all.[40]

In the end Nasser helped persuade Nehru that if he proposed a compromise on the troika, he would damage the Secretary-General's position.

When Nehru addressed the General Assembly on October 3, he rejected Khrushchev's troika proposal on the grounds that it would weaken the United Nations. He did point out, however, that the organization was "unbalanced"; it was too heavily weighted in favor of the European countries to the detriment of the Asian and African countries. He called for the reconvening of the Congolese Parliament—a suggestion that was regarded as favorable to Lumumba—and he picked up Lumumba's idea about sending an Afro-Asian commission to the Congo to check on the withdrawal of Belgian troops—an idea which had been dropped at the time because it was considered an insult to Hammarskjold.[41]

While the Secretary-General described Nehru's speech in a cable to Dayal as "statesmanlike," many of his colleagues felt he was disappointed. By the time the Indian leader left on October 9, his support for Hammarskjold had eroded still further. He suggested to Khrushchev and British Prime Minister Harold Macmillan that Hammarskjold appoint a group of two to five senior political advisers, each from a different geographical area, to help him deal with "difficult political problems, such as the Congo." Khrushchev said he preferred his own plan but agreed to consider the Indian leader's suggestion.[42]

The last of the pro-Lumumba group to arrive in New York was also the most radical: President Sékou Touré of Guinea. He had told Khrushchev when he was in Moscow in early September that he did not plan to attend the General Assembly session because he was on his way to China and Mongolia, but Khrushchev urged him to cut short his trip so that he could go to New York and speak out on the Congo and other anticolonialist issues. The Guinean leader took his advice. He signed a major trade and aid agreement in Moscow, stayed in China long enough to sign another one, stopped briefly at home, and then proceeded to New York in early October. Ironically, his government had signed an aid agreement with the United States a few days before his arrival, but it had received no publicity at Sékou Touré's request.[43] Apparently he feared the news that one hundred and fifty Guinean students were receiving scholarships to study in the United States would damage his radical image.

When Sékou Touré addressed the General Assembly on October 10, he seconded Nkrumah's call for three assistant secretaries-general. He blasted Hammarskjold's Congo policy and called for the immediate seating of the Lumumba delegation.[44] That evening at dinner he tried to blackmail the Secretary-General into supporting his proposal. He suggested that if Hammarskjold would not go along, he would bring "out into the open" information that he claimed to have about "bribery" and "corruption" on the part of UN officials in Leopoldville. Hammarskjold rose to the challenge. He defended his staff and said he had no hesitation about opening his dossier on the Congo operation, although he was "not particularly in favour of that kind of public diplomacy."[45]

While the flap about the alleged misuse of UN funds blew over quickly, Sékou Touré's demand for the seating of the Lumumba delegation reopened the credentials issue and led to a six-week battle between the opposing forces in the General Assembly—a battle which ultimately had a major impact on the outcome of the power struggle in Leopoldville.

Khrushchev did not stay to see the outcome of this battle. When he left for home on October 13, the Congo issue was still unresolved. The Soviet leader had made less headway on his troika proposal than he might have hoped—but enough to disturb Hammarskjold and his American supporters. Although none of the neutralist leaders, with the exception of Sékou Touré, had joined Khrushchev's repeated attacks on the Secretary-General, it was clear that the Soviet leader had struck a responsive chord both with his emphasis on the need for a larger Afro-Asian voice in the United Nations and with his criticism of the Secretary-General's policy in the Congo. He had raised doubts about Hammarskjold in many minds and forced him to consider modifying his Congo policy in order to keep the allegiance of the leading African and Asian neutralists.

Summitry, Khrushchev, and the Presidential Campaign

Khrushchev came out ahead of the Americans in the competition for Afro-Asian support on still another question—that of a summit meeting between himself and Eisenhower. Khrushchev had raised the issue indirectly when he announced he was coming to New York, but Eisenhower had repeatedly stated that he was opposed to the idea unless there were firm assurances that something positive could come of it.

The chilly atmosphere began to thaw somewhat on September 22, when Khrushchev described Eisenhower's speech as "conciliatory" and hinted that he might be receptive to an invitation to meet with the President, although he would not take the initiative in arranging such a meeting.[46] Suddenly summit talk was in the air. The greatest pressure came from a group of persistent neutralists—Tito, Nasser, Nehru, Nkrumah, and Sukarno—the same leaders who were supporting Lumumba and whose support Khrushchev was trying to win for his troika proposal.

The Administration was not quite sure how to respond to this Afro-Asian pressure. On September 23 Charles Bohlen, special assistant to Secretary Herter and former U.S. ambassador to the Soviet Union, wrote a memorandum strongly advising against a meeting "unless Moscow did something beforehand to show good faith, such as releasing the fliers from the downed reconnaissance plane." If the President were to receive Khrushchev "without some demonstrable change in attitude," he said,

> it would merely convince the Kremlin leaders and a large portion of the world that the Soviet Union was so powerful that it could behave with contempt toward the United States and at any time of its choosing return to the "spirit of Camp David." In short it would mean in the eyes of many uncommitted nations that the Soviet Union was, in fact, calling the tune in international affairs.[47]

On September 27, Nasser mentioned the possibility of a summit meeting in his speech before the General Assembly.[48] Khrushchev applauded and looked toward the U.S. delegation, as if seeking approval for the idea. Still, when he was questioned after the meeting, he would not make any commitment; he seemed to be waiting for the Americans to make the first move.

On September 29 the five neutralist leaders met at a "tea party" at the Yugoslav Mission to coordinate strategy. The following day Nehru and Sukarno formally submitted to the Assembly a five-power resolution recommending a meeting between Khrushchev and Eisenhower to reduce world tension.[49]

Eisenhower was surprised by this proposal; he had met with four of the five sponsors the previous week, and not one of them had indicated that they were considering such a move. He recalled in his memoirs, "At best it seemed totally illogical; at worst it seemed an act of effrontery." He realized that he would be placed in a "most embarrassing position" if a majority of the Assembly voted for the proposal; he would then be faced with a choice between ignoring a UN resolution and "engaging in a fruitless diplomatic duel."[50] He wrote to each of the sponsors, explaining his objections to a summit meeting, and in-

structed his delegates in New York to work for the defeat of the resolution if they were unable to persuade the sponsors to withdraw it. "The
President is not going into a meeting on his knees, which is what Khrushchev wants," remarked one U.S. official.[51]

By October 5, the neutralists had to admit defeat. Through a parliamentary maneuver the United States and its allies voted to eliminate a
key provision in the draft—the phrase referring specifically to Eisenhower and Khrushchev. Without this provision the neutralists felt the
appeal was meaningless, and they withdrew their resolution. Since the
Soviet Union and its allies abstained on the vote, the Afro-Asians tended to blame the United States for sabotaging their initiative.

Khrushchev was delighted. He had managed to create the impression that he was willing to respond to their pleas and seek peace, while
Eisenhower was the one who was raising conditions and inventing obstacles—even though his own attitude toward a summit was not much
more positive than Eisenhower's. He realized that little could come of
a meeting between himself and a lame duck President. In a spirited
discussion with a group of newsmen on September 29, he said, "I don't
want to interfere with your domestic politics. But your President cannot now make serious decisions." He added that he hoped Eisenhower's successor could "make a definite improvement in our relations."
Later that day he indicated to Macmillan that he would welcome a
summit meeting after the election of a new President.[52]

The Soviet leader inevitably became part of the American presidential campaign the moment he decided to visit the United States less
than two months before the election. The Soviet challenge was already
one of the major issues of the campaign. While Vice President Nixon
was trying to run on a platform of peace and prosperity, his Democratic challenger kept raising disturbing questions about the Eisenhower
Administration's failures in foreign policy, particularly its failure to
keep pace with Soviet missile development (the famous "missile gap"
which disappeared after the election). Nixon had chosen Henry Cabot
Lodge as his running mate largely on the strength of his reputation as
the man who had been "standing up to the Russians" at the United Nations for years. Nixon himself campaigned on the basis of his "experience" in world affairs. "I know Khrushchev," he boasted. He kept
referring to his famous debate with the Soviet leader in the kitchen of
the model home at the American exhibit in Moscow the previous summer. Kennedy, he charged, was too young and inexperienced to deal
with a challenge of this magnitude.

When Khrushchev first announced that he would be coming to the
United States, Kennedy immediately seized the initiative and said he
would meet with the Soviet leader—if the Vice-President were invited
to do so as well, and if it fit into his campaign schedule. The following

day Nixon responded with a resounding negative: he would not meet with the Soviet leader. He suggested that Kennedy's criticism of Eisenhower would play into Khrushchev's hands and that a moratorium should be placed on such criticism while the Soviet leader remained in the United States. Kennedy would have none of this. No one had any idea how long the Soviet leader intended to stay; at one point he joked about spending New Year's Eve in New York. Kennedy responded to Nixon's charges by addressing a rhetorical message to Khrushchev: "You might hear us inquiring into our lost prestige, our shaky defenses, our lack of leadership. But do not be deceived. The Democratic Party is not preaching disunity." Kennedy noted that his opponent had argued that "in a time of danger it would be hazardous to change party administrations," and retorted, "I think it would be hazardous to continue four more years of stagnation."[53]

Eisenhower's decision to meet with Tito, Nkrumah, and other world leaders resulted largely from a desire to counter such criticism from the Democrats. The day before the President spoke at the General Assembly, Nixon took the offensive and attacked Kennedy for disparaging the United States and suggesting that the U.S. government should offer concessions to the Russians that would eventually lead to "surrender." Then he carefully drew back from the implication that he had accused Kennedy of being a traitor. Kennedy is "just as strong in his opposition to Communism as I am," Nixon said reassuringly; it was just his "lack of knowledge and experience" that led him to criticize American policy as he did.[54]

Kennedy refused to be intimidated. He felt that he had a good issue, and he was backed up by knowledgeable authorities. Bohlen, who had helped formulate U.S. policy toward the Soviet Union, told *New York Times* columnist C. L. Sulzberger at this point that he thought Nixon was "prattling" when he said that the country was "doing beautifully in the international power race and that we never had it so good."[55] At the end of September, Kennedy, in a swing through upstate New York, charged that the Republican Administration and Nixon had "failed to foresee developments in the Congo and Cuba and take effective counter action before they reached the crisis stage."[56]

There was a good deal of speculation at the time about Khrushchev's preference in the election. He was asked at his famous "balcony scene" press conference on September 21, "Who would you like to see take President Eisenhower's place after this election?" Khrushchev replied:

"I do not see any point in asking the head of the Soviet Union whom he wants to see as President of the United States especially at this time in history. I don't see any difference in these two candidates or the two parties."[57]

Khrushchev's official neutrality was the result of requests from both candidates. Harriman was afraid that Khrushchev's attacks on the Eisenhower Administration would help Nixon at the polls, and he sent the Soviet Premier a message urging him to be "equally harsh toward both candidates."[58] At the same time, Lodge came to Moscow to give Khrushchev a similar message on behalf of Nixon. "We met as old friends," Khrushchev recalled in his memoirs, and added:

> In our talks he tried to convince me that relations between our countries wouldn't suffer if Nixon were in the White House. He didn't say they'd get better, just that they wouldn't get worse. He said Nixon was not really the sort of man he deliberately appeared to be at election rallies. "Mr. Khrushchev," said Lodge, "don't pay any attention to the campaign speeches. Remember they're just political statements. Once Mr. Nixon is in the White House I'm sure—I'm absolutely certain—he'll take a position of preserving and perhaps even improving our relations."

Khrushchev got the impression that this approach had been worked out in advance by Nixon and Eisenhower, so that the Soviet press "would neither attack nor praise" Nixon during the campaign. Khrushchev quoted Lodge as saying, "We don't need your endorsement of Mr. Nixon.'"[59]

Although the Soviet leader had had some of his greatest successes with his flexible new policies during the Eisenhower Administration, with its comparatively rigid foreign policy ideas, he apparently rejected the argument that he would be better off with another conservative, predictable exponent of capitalism in the White House. He said in his memoirs that he concluded he would "have more hope of improving Soviet-American relations if John Kennedy were in the White House." He went on to explain:

> We knew we couldn't count on Nixon in this regard; his aggressive attitude toward the Soviet Union, his anti-Communism, his connection with McCarthyism (he owed his career to that devil of darkness McCarthy)— all this was well known to us. In short, we had no reason to welcome the prospect of Nixon as President.[60]

Since the contest seemed to be very close, Khrushchev decided to do something to tip the balance toward Kennedy. The Eisenhower Administration had been asking for the release of the RB-47 fliers. Khrushchev realized that if he released them a few days before the election, this would give Nixon a boost, so he decided to wait until after the election. When he met Kennedy for the first time, he said jokingly, "You know, Mr. Kennedy, we voted for you." When Kennedy asked, "How?" the Soviet leader responded, "By waiting until after the election to return the pilots." According to Khrushchev, Kennedy "laughed and said, 'You're right. I admit you played a role in the election and cast your vote for me.' "[61]

Khrushchev's major impact on the election, however, was his disruptive presence through nearly half the campaign. The day after the first Kennedy-Nixon debate, there were two banner headlines across the top of *The New York Times*. The four-column lead dealt with Eisenhower's meetings with Nehru and Nasser, the troika, Khrushchev, Castro, Hammarskjold, and the Congo; the second lead, with a three-column headline, dealt with the debate.[62] A *Times* survey of three hundred voters published the previous day found that Khrushchev's visit had not changed any votes and that both Kennedy and Nixon supporters felt it had strengthened their candidate.[63] But it is clear that the diplomatic carnival in New York focused attention on American foreign policy and on the apparent failure of the Eisenhower Administration to deal with Khrushchev's challenge in Cuba, the Congo, and the other new countries of Africa—and thus strengthened Kennedy's claim that the country needed new and vigorous leadership at a time of national peril.

CHAPTER SIX

Getting Rid of Lumumba:
Fair Means or Foul
(September 26–November 25, 1960)

"I do not believe democracy can be imposed upon any people overnight any more than it can be injected by hypodermic."

W HEN SENATOR JOHN F. KENNEDY linked Cuba and the Congo in his campaign speeches and charged that they were examples of the Eisenhower Administration's failure to meet the Soviet challenge, he was touching a sensitive nerve. The President and his chief advisers had been trying to deal forcefully with both situations for some time. CIA Director Dulles had linked the two as far back as July, when he described Lumumba as "a Castro or worse." He saw them both as threats to American interests; if they were not actually Communists, they were left-wing radicals whose calls for Soviet intervention were bound to upset the balance of power in the world. Khrushchev had promised them both military aid and had proved in the case of the Congo that he was not bluffing. The CIA had responded by launching parallel assassination plots—one directed against Lumumba, the other against Castro.

By mid-August the CIA's scientists had come up with a plan to poison Castro's cigars, and by the end of the month they were working on another poison to eliminate Lumumba. Castro, only ninety miles away from the United States, was considered the more immediate threat. The CIA decided that an unorthodox approach was needed to deal with him; it went outside its own ranks and enlisted the aid of the Mafia. In September, while Castro was in New York for the General Assembly session, where he met Khrushchev for the first time, a high-ranking CIA official had a meeting at the Plaza Hotel, a few blocks away, with Robert Maheu, a former FBI agent who had worked closely with the CIA for many years, and his contact John Rosselli, a Mafia chieftain who had agreed to line up anti-Castro Cubans in Miami to assassinate the Cuban leader. Although Rosselli apparently realized that he was being hired by the CIA, the three men went through an elaborate charade, pretending that Maheu represented a group of businessmen who wanted Castro out of the way so they could recover their investments in Cuba.[1]

These approaches to the underworld took time, however; while the plot against Castro was still in its earliest stages, the plot against Lumumba, which relied on regular CIA personnel, was moving ahead much more rapidly. By the time Khrushchev made his troika speech at the United Nations, "Joe from Paris" was on his way to Leopoldville with his poison kit—and with instructions to help the local station chief assassinate Lumumba.

"Joe From Paris": The CIA Tries to Poison Lumumba

When the CIA scientist arrived in Leopoldville on September 26, he told Devlin that headquarters "wanted him to see if he could use" the poison "against Lumumba." The idea was to apply it to his food or his toothbrush—"anything he could get to his mouth." Gottlieb assured the station chief that the poison would leave "normal traces found in people that die of certain diseases." He explained that poisoning was not the only means of assassination authorized by headquarters; other methods were acceptable, provided they could "not be traced back . . . either to an American or the United States government."[2]

Devlin later told the Senate Intelligence Committee that he had an "emotional reaction of great surprise" when Gottlieb informed him about this plan. "I must have . . . pointed out that this was not a common or usual Agency tactic," he said. "Never in my training or previous work in the Agency had I ever heard any references to such methods." He asked Gottlieb who had authorized the assignment, and the scientist indicated that the orders came from the President himself.[3]

The station chief described his reaction to the assignment as unenthusiastic. He told the committee:

> I looked upon the Agency as an executive arm of the Presidency. . . . Therefore, I suppose I thought that it was an order issued in due form from an authorized authority. On the other hand, I looked at it as a kind of operation that I could do without, that I thought that probably the Agency and the U.S. government could get along without. I didn't regard Lumumba as the kind of person who was going to bring on World War III. I might have had a somewhat different attitude if I thought that one man could bring on World War III and result in the deaths of millions of people or something, but I didn't see him in that light. I saw him as a danger to the political position of the United States in Africa, but nothing more than that.[4]

Devlin had practical objections to the assassination plot as well. "I looked on it as a pretty wild scheme professionally," he explained to the committee. "I did not think that it . . . was practical professionally, certainly, in a short time, if you were going to keep the U.S. out of it. . . . I explored it, but I doubt that I ever really expected to carry it out."[5] He recalled that he had told Gottlieb he "was going to look into it and try and figure if there was a way." He added, "I believe I stressed the difficulty of trying to carry out such an operation." Gottlieb recalled Devlin as "sober" and "grim" but on the whole willing to proceed with the assignment.[6]

Devlin's cable to Washington the day after their meeting suggests that if he had doubts, he was keeping them to himself, like a good bureaucrat. He told headquarters that he and Gottlieb were on the "same wavelength," and he recommended a number of exploratory steps that could be taken to get the operation moving.[7]

At the top of his list was a proposal for infiltrating Lumumba's entourage: if headquarters approved, he would instruct one of his agents to "take refuge with Big Brother" (a reference to Lumumba). The agent would act as an "inside man to brush up details to razor edge"[8]—in other words, he would check out the situation at Lumumba's residence and see if there was any practical way of administering the poison to him. Devlin warned that the anti-Lumumba forces were "weakening" under foreign pressure and might soon agree to a reconciliation with Lumumba.[9] In view of this alarming possibility, he concluded: "Believe most rapid action consistent with security indicated. . . . Plan proceed . . . unless instructed to contrary."[10]

Three days later, after Devlin had had some time to study the situation, he reported: "No really airtight op possible with assets now available. Must choose between cancelling op or accepting calculated risks of various degrees." He urged his superiors to "authorize exploratory conversations" with the agent he had in mind to find out if he was willing to take part in the assassination operation. He said he would approach him on a "hypothetical basis," not revealing the extent of the plan, but added that if the agent was "willing" to accept the assignment, he would have to tell him about the objective of the operation. He requested a speedy reply, pointing out that it was necessary to "act immediately, if at all."[11]

Headquarters responded later that day with a cable authorizing Devlin to conduct "exploratory talks" with the agent and agreeing that he seemed the best of the possibilities available. "We will weigh very carefully your initial assessment his attitude as well as any specific approaches that may emerge," the cable continued. "Appreciate manner your approach to problem. Hope . . . for moderate haste."[12]

Despite Devlin's frequent references to the need for haste, he still had reservations about the assassination scheme, and he apparently kept stalling about putting it into effect. Over the next two months he sent a steady stream of progress reports to Washington through the top secret PROP channel, but he never got around to carrying out the operation.

The first deadline passed with Gottlieb's departure from Leopoldville on October 5. The scientist told the Senate Intelligence Committee that he had dumped the poison in the Congo River before he left because "it didn't look like on this trip he could mount the operational . . . assets to do the job." The station chief had been unable "to find a secure enough agent with the right access" to Lumumba, and Gottlieb was becoming concerned about the potency of the poison; since it was "not refrigerated and unstable," he feared that it might no longer be "reliable"—in other words, it might not be sufficiently lethal to kill Lumumba.[13]

There is a major discrepancy on this point between Gottlieb's recollection and that of Devlin, who testified that he kept the poison in his office safe until December, after Lumumba's arrest, and then dumped it in the river himself. He reported to headquarters on October 7 that Gottlieb had "left certain items of continuing usefulness" and that he planned to "continue" to try to "implement" the operation.[14] He said he had conducted an "exploratory conversation" with his agent, who seemed prepared to "take any role necessary," within the limits of security, to carry out the assignment. Devlin asked him specific questions about the layout of Lumumba's residence; he wanted to know if the agent had "access to the bathroom . . . access to the kitchen, things of that sort."[15] He was evidently not completely satisfied with the responses to these queries, and he suggested to his superiors that if they concluded the agent could not be used successfully, they should send a "qualified third country national" to carry out the assignment instead.[16]

Devlin received a reply later that day from Tweedy, who said he had just had a "good discussion" with Gottlieb. The scientist may have passed along some of Devlin's reservations. "Be assured did not expect PROP objectives be reached in short period," Tweedy wrote. He explained that he was "considering dispatching" a "third country national operative" to Leopoldville as Devlin had suggested. "If you conclude he suitable and bearing in mind heavy extra load this places on you, would expect dispatch . . . senior case officer run this op . . . under your direction," he continued.[17]

The poisoning plot was apparently sidetracked for a time—until the "senior case officer" and the "third country national" could get to Leopoldville. In the meantime, Devlin did not slacken his efforts to find some other means of disposing of Lumumba. He was convinced that it would be best to work through the Congolese. Lumumba had so many enemies who wanted to get rid of him that the U.S. government did

not have to be directly involved in his assassination. All that was needed was a little American help behind the scenes—in terms of providing
money, arms, and advice. He had recommended this course in mid-
September, just three days after Mobutu's takeover. On October 6, he
received a cable from Tweedy and Bissell informing him that his recommendation had been accepted. The CIA was planning to "provide
clandestine support to elements in armed opposition to Lumumba,"
they said. "Contemplated action includes provision arms, supplies and
perhaps some training to anti-Lumumba resistance groups." They cautioned him not to discuss these plans with any representatives of the
State Department.[18]

Nine days later this subject came up again in a cable, signed by
Tweedy, which was sent through regular CIA channels: this meant
that it could be read by "appropriate personnel" at the U.S. Embassy
in Leopoldville, including the ambassador. Tweedy raised the "possibility of covertly supplying certain Congolese leaders with funds and
military aid" and then explained that the U.S. government could not
take an active, direct role in the anti-Lumumba operation. "Only direct action we can now stand behind is to support immobilizing or arresting" Lumumba, he wrote, "desirable as more definitive action
might be. Any action taken would have to be entirely Congolese."

The same day, however, Tweedy sent a second cable through the
PROP channel, marked "Eyes Only" for Devlin, which in essence told
him to ignore the previous cable:

> YOU WILL NOTE FROM CABLE THROUGH NORMAL CHANNEL CURRENTLY
> BEING TRANSMITTED A PARA ON PROP TYPE SUGGESTIONS. YOU WILL
> PROBABLY RECEIVE MORE ALONG THESE LINES AS STUMBLING BLOC
> [LUMUMBA] REPRESENTS INCREASINGLY APPARENT. ALL STUDYING CON-
> GO SITUATION CLOSELY AND HIS DISPOSITION SPONTANEOUSLY BECOMES
> NUMBER ONE CONSIDERATION. RAISE ABOVE SO YOU NOT CONFUSED BY
> ANY APPARENT DUPLICATION. THIS CHANNEL REMAINS FOR SPECIFIC
> PURPOSE YOU DISCUSSED WITH COLLEAGUE AND ALSO REMAINS HIGHEST
> PRIORITY.

Tweedy later told the Senate Intelligence Committee that the phrase
"specific purpose" referred to the assassination plan and that the cable
was intended to reinforce the view that there could be "no solution" to
the Congo problem as long as Lumumba was "in a position of power or
influence there."[19]

In this second cable Tweedy asked Devlin once more for his reaction to the idea of sending a senior CIA officer to Leopoldville on a "direct assignment ... to concentrate entirely" on the assassination
project. "Seems to us your other commitments too heavy give necessary concentration PROP," he explained. Tweedy also passed along

the latest CIA thinking on the problem of disposing of Lumumba. He suggested the possibility of using a "commando type group" to abduct Lumumba "either via assault on house up cliff from river, or, more probably" if Lumumba were to try "another breakout into town."[20] This idea, of course, was in direct contradiction to the "leave it to the Congolese" view expressed in the first cable.

On October 17 Devlin responded positively to the offer of assistance. He reported that his agent had not been able to "penetrate" Lumumba's "entourage" and thus had not been able to provide the intelligence that was needed to carry out the assignment. He said that while he was "maintaining priority interest" in the operation, he was able to "devote only limited time" to it because of all his other commitments. "Believe early assignment senior case officer handle PROP ops excellent idea. . . . If case officer available . . . would devote as much time as possible to assisting and directing his efforts." He then added the following recommendation:

IF CASE OFFICER SENT, RECOMMEND HQS POUCH SOONEST HIGH POWERED FOREIGN MAKE RIFLE WITH TELESCOPIC SCOPE AND SILENCER. HUNTING GOOD HERE WHEN LIGHTS RIGHT. HOWEVER AS HUNTING RIFLES NOW FORBIDDEN WOULD KEEP RIFLE IN OFFICE PENDING OPENING OF HUNTING SEASON.[21]

Devlin had mentioned to Gottlieb the possibility of shooting Lumumba as an alternative to poisoning him;[22] now the idea seemed to be coming up again. Tweedy told the committee that this message "clearly referred to sending to the Congo via diplomatic pouch a weapon suited for assassinating Lumumba."[23]

Despite the station chief's attempts to compete with the ingenious suggestions of his superiors in Washington, he apparently clung to the belief that the simplest solution would be the most effective. Throughout this period he urged Lumumba's opponents to arrest him, explaining that he would continue to be a "threat" to the "stability" of the Congo until he was "removed" from the scene.[24]

The Arrest of Lumumba?

Ambassador Timberlake agreed with Devlin that Lumumba should be arrested; but he had found, over the past few weeks, that this was easier said than done. By the end of September he had lost a good deal of his initial euphoria about Mobutu's coup; he had come around to Devlin's view that Lumumba was not out of the picture by any means. His Russian sponsors might be gone, but the radical African diplomats in Leopoldville were determined to see him restored to power.

In order to counter this pro-Lumumba pressure, officials in Washington asked Timberlake to persuade Kasavubu and Mobutu to put their government on a more secure legal footing. They realized that the "tactics" of the "Mobutu coup required 'neutralizing' both Kasavubu and Lumumba," but they felt this "tactical consideration" was "no longer relevant." They suggested that Kasavubu state publicly that he considered himself as head of state to be above the factional dispute but "duly empowered to appoint a government"—that is, Mobutu's College of Commissioners. "He would thus preserve the 'apolitical' character of the Mobutu coup and yet himself continue effectively in office." It would be helpful, they added, if "key Congo leaders including Bomboko and Mobutu" could support Kasavubu's statement.[25]

The State Department was apparently confident that it could control the actions of Mobutu and the other Congolese political figures and turn them on and off at will. There would be many occasions over the next few months when Washington's arrogant certainty crashed head-on into the unpredictable Leopoldville political scene. In this case, however, actual events closely followed the American scenario.

On September 26, the day "Joe from Paris" arrived in Leopoldville, Timberlake met with Kasavubu and Ileo, who listened "avidly" to his recommendations and seemed "very anxious to carry them out." They agreed to call Mobutu immediately and encourage him to take the necessary action. Timberlake, for his part, promised to try to talk to Mobutu later in the day.[26]

Three days later Kasavubu formally swore in the College of Commissioners.[27] Mobutu issued a statement rebuking the Congolese President and reminding him that he had been "neutralized" and had no business organizing the ceremony. Timberlake, mildly exasperated by the crossed wires, remarked to the State Department that it was "hard to understand" why Mobutu felt the statement was necessary; but he added that Mario Cardoso, one of the young commissioners, had told him that it was "nothing more than an effort on the Colonel's part to show his neutrality between political factions," and that "Kasavubu knew about it before it was made." Timberlake accepted this explanation. It might sound like an "exercise in semantics," he concluded, but it is the way the "Colonel's mind works even though he is in fact working fairly closely with Kasavubu."[28]

Now that Kasavubu had set up a proper government, Timberlake encouraged him to take the next step and order the arrest of Lumumba. He knew that Ghanaian UN guards had refused to admit the soldiers who tried to arrest Lumumba the previous week, claiming that they did not have a valid arrest warrant; but this had been explained away by UN officials as a unilateral Ghanaian action which did not really reflect UN policy. Timberlake was still operating on the assumption that the United Nations would honor a properly issued warrant for Lumumba's arrest. He told Kasavubu all he had to do was to inform Dayal and ask for a UN officer to accompany the arresting party in order to notify the UN soldiers guarding Lumumba that everything was in order. If these procedures were followed, he said, Kasavubu's forces should "encounter no obstruction" from the United Nations.[29]

It turned out, of course, that Timberlake was badly mistaken. His overly optimistic assessment of the UN position was based on Hammarskjold's attitude before he began to feel the effect of Khrushchev's troika speech. The Secretary-General had originally welcomed Kasavubu's dismissal of Lumumba and described it as legal, but he did not stick to this position. Attacked by the Russians and buffeted by Afro-Asian pressure, he gradually swung around to the position that his special representative, Dayal, had been advocating from the start.

The Indian diplomat felt it would be impossible to find a solution to the Congo problem without including Lumumba. He did not have much use for Lumumba as an individual—or for Kasavubu, Ileo, Mobutu, or the commissioners, for that matter—but he believed that the United Nations should deal with them strictly on the basis of legal principles and should not condone extraconstitutional actions which were the result of Western interference in a newly independent state. For this reason he had disagreed with Cordier's line and had tried to reverse it a full two weeks before Khrushchev's speech. On a more practical level, Dayal realized, before Hammarskjold did, that they both needed the support of the pro-Lumumba neutralists, and he established his credentials with them by working actively for a reconciliation between Lumumba and Kasavubu.

Neither Hammarskjold nor Dayal went so far as to treat Lumumba as the legal Prime Minister, but at the same time they refused to accept the American view that he had lost all claim to this position after his dismissal by Kasavubu. Their idea was to keep Lumumba "in cold storage" until the politicians were ready to resolve their differences and return to a constitutional form of government.[30]

This plan came as a shock to Timberlake, who assumed that the United Nations would recognize the right of the new Congolese government to arrest Lumumba. He found, to his dismay, that a different policy was in effect: the United Nations forces protecting Lumumba at his residence would oppose his arrest under any circumstances.

The issue came to a head on October 10. For several days the commissioners had tried to persuade Dayal that they were entitled to arrest Lumumba, but he kept putting them off with one excuse after another.[31] On October 9 Lumumba had left his residence and driven through Leopoldville announcing that he was returning to power and calling on the people to rally behind him and "chase the United Nations troops out of the Congo." Ironically, he was escorted by Ghanaian and Moroccan UN troops. As he traveled from bar to bar, he was greeted by cheering crowds who fought to touch him and called him "savior."[32] Mobutu decided it was time to prevent any more of these excursions. The following day he sent his troops to Lumumba's residence with a warrant for his arrest. Once again, the Ghanaian guards barred their way. Lumumba, angered by Mobutu's move, strode out onto his balcony and shouted, "I challenge Mobutu to a duel. Let him choose his weapons and we will see who is the strongest." Mobutu responded by stationing three hundred soldiers outside Lumumba's residence and issuing an ultimatum to the United Nations: if his troops were not permitted to arrest Lumumba peacefully by 3:00 P.M. the following day, they would seize him by force.[33]

At this point Timberlake stepped into the picture. He went to see Dayal, reminded him that Bunche, Cordier, and Dayal himself had stated that the United Nations would honor a "legitimate warrant" for Lumumba's arrest, and asked if his policy on this issue had changed. Dayal replied that there was "no change" in his position; he explained that his legal adviser had told him the warrant was not valid because it had been signed by a commissioner, whose legal status was not recognized by the United Nations. He then got to the real point: he believed that Lumumba's arrest was not a "proper solution" to the Congo problem but was essentially a "trick" to assassinate Lumumba. Moreover, it would "badly split" the Afro-Asian group whose "united support" was essential if the Congo problem was ever to be solved.

Dayal asked Timberlake to use his influence with Bomboko, the head of the College of Commissioners, to persuade him to drop his demand for Lumumba's arrest and to work instead for a "peaceful solution." Timberlake argued that any solution that put Lumumba back in the government would cause more problems than it would solve. Even if he did not start out as Prime Minister, he was "quite capable" of reasserting his leadership and coming out on top. He would complicate the task of the United Nations, as he had done in the early weeks of the crisis, before Dayal arrived in Leopoldville. Dayal was unmoved by these arguments; he simply repeated his request that Timberlake use his influence with Bomboko.

Timberlake then went on to a meeting of the chiefs of the diplomatic missions called by Bomboko, who explained that Lumumba represented a "dangerous" threat to peace and order, especially after his outing of the previous day. Several of his supporters had been arrested distributing weapons and money in an effort to incite the population and restore him to power. Bomboko assured the diplomats that "no physical violence" would be used against Lumumba; he would be "judged fairly and legally and would be permitted to bring in foreign lawyers if he chose to defend himself."

Timberlake warned Bomboko that he would be making a "serious error" if he permitted the three hundred soldiers outside Lumumba's residence to storm the house in order to arrest Lumumba. This would constitute "direct defiance" of the United Nations, he explained, and would have a damaging effect on the Congo's reputation abroad. At the same time, in his report to Washington, he recommended support for Bomboko's position. "I fail to see any reasonable argument," he said, "for the continued refusal" of the United Nations to honor the "arrest warrant, which appears to be entirely legal."[34] He then added a "personal comment," which turned out to be the first salvo in an escalating campaign of criticism of Dayal:

WHILE DAYAL IS FRIEND OF 12 YEARS STANDING, A MAN OF GREAT PRIN-CIPLES AND GREAT DEVOTION TO CAUSE OF PEACE, I HAVE FEELING ... HE MAY NOT FULLY UNDERSTAND BASIS OF DIVISIONS IN AFRO-ASIAN GROUP AND HIS NATURAL DESIRE TO FIND PEACEFUL SOLUTION MAY BE CONDITIONING HIS ATTITUDE TOWARD CURRENT PROBLEM.

Timberlake concluded that Dayal would need "specific instructions" from the Secretary-General before he would alter his policy and agree to Lumumba's arrest.[35]

The Secretary-General was not about to issue these "specific instructions." He cabled Dayal:

I FIRMLY UPHOLD YOUR STAND ON LEGALLY INVALID WARRANT OF AR-REST AND ON CONTINUED UN PROTECTION OF LUMUMBA AGAINST AC-TIONS OF POLITICAL VIOLENCE SUCH AS THIS.... WILL TRY TO PUT WESTERN EAGER BEAVERS STRAIGHT ON WHERE WE STAND.[36]

When American diplomats in New York asked Wieschhoff for his reaction, he talked first about Lumumba's "parliamentary immunity" but then admitted that this was an "essentially phony" issue. The real problem, he said, was that the Secretary-General "had to be extremely careful" not to create the impression that he was "out to get Lumumba."[37]

On October 11 Dayal rejected the Congolese ultimatum. Bomboko immediately telephoned Timberlake and said he was ready to carry out the ultimatum and "to give orders to take Lumumba by force." Timberlake repeated that he would be committing the "gravest of blunders" if he did so. Bomboko said he would get in touch with Mo-butu and extend the ultimatum by twenty-four hours. Timberlake urged him "not to issue any more ultimatums" but to declare publicly that his government had decided not to take Lumumba by force in order to "avoid spilling blood."[38]

That evening Bomboko and Mobutu called Timberlake and told him their troops were "demanding orders to move in on Lumumba" and could not be restrained much longer. Timberlake pleaded with them to wait until he could "obtain some reply from Washington."

He reported to the State Department the following day that the situation was "very very serious." There were nearly one thousand Congolese soldiers surrounding Lumumba's house, which was guarded by Ghanaian, Sudanese, Moroccan, and Tunisian UN troops. "I feel that force will be used some time today unless UN permits peaceful service of warrant," he warned; if the Congolese troops managed to get inside the house, the "beneficiary on Lumumba's life insurance policy" was likely to "collect promptly." Timberlake explained that he had "worked night and day" to prevent a "violent solution." While he had been successful up to this point, he felt that he could not "hold them back much longer" unless he had some word from Washington or New York indicating that the United Nations was willing to permit them to arrest Lumumba.[39]

State Department officials realized that it would be impossible to persuade Hammarskjold to reverse himself on this issue. Instead, they came up with a compromise designed to save face for Bomboko and Mobutu and avoid a bloody clash. They suggested that the United Nations move Lumumba out of the Prime Minister's residence to some other location where it could continue to offer him protection. They then instructed Timberlake to tell Bomboko that the matter was being discussed with the Secretary-General and to warn him "not to move precipitously."[40]

On the morning of October 13, Timberlake called on Bomboko and spelled out the advantages of the new plan. He suggested that the Congolese government could continue to surround Lumumba's residence with troops and could cut off his telephone. He declared that in his opinion Lumumba's "physical isolation would mean his political death." Bomboko seemed pleased with the idea and informed Timberlake that he and his colleagues had abandoned the idea of "trying to take Lumumba by force." The ambassador concluded that the "Embassy's discreet intervention with Kasavubu, Bomboko and Mobutu" had been a "major factor" in their decision.[41] The following day Mobutu celebrated his thirtieth birthday by removing some of his troops from Lumumba's residence.[42]

As it turned out, the Americans made absolutely no headway in their effort to persuade Hammarskjold to move Lumumba out of the Prime Minister's residence. They did, however, score one small victory: Lumumba no longer went on excursions accompanied by UN troops. The crisis over his arrest essentially ended in a stalemate. Lumumba's supporters were no more satisfied than the Americans; although he was safe from arrest, he was virtually cut off from contact with the people of the city and with his political supporters. The Russians charged that he was "virtually under house arrest."[43]

The Dayal Report: Blow to U.S. Policy

Despite the best efforts of the CIA and the U.S. Embassy in Leopoldville, Lumumba was still on the scene a month after Mobutu's coup. Timberlake blamed Dayal for this state of affairs. He had repeatedly explained to the Indian diplomat why Lumumba should not be permitted to return to power, but his arguments had fallen on deaf ears. He concluded that Dayal was "playing into Lumumba's hands if not deliberately supporting him." He was particularly disturbed by Dayal's refusal to deal with the young commissioners or to protect them when they were attacked and beaten by Lumumba's supporters. Timberlake acknowledged that the commissioners' government was a temporary one, but he felt they had tried to provide the Congo with a "constructive administration." In spite of this they had been "rebuffed" by Dayal, who considered them "unimportant schoolboys."[44]

Dayal had very little use for Timberlake or his opinions. He had his own view of the tangled political situation in the Congo. While the U.S. ambassador and other critics characterized his refusal to visit any Congolese leader other than the President as "typical high-caste Indian arrogance," Dayal responded with a simple explanation: only Kasavubu, he said, was accepted by all sides as the legal head of state; for the rest, supporters of Lumumba and Mobutu were welcome in his office, but he refused to confer any degree of legitimacy on either side by visiting them.

Dayal resented the influx of Belgian technicians, many of whom were returning to the Congo at the specific request of the young commissioners, who, in turn, resented the patronizing attitude of the UN consultants assigned to help them get the government departments functioning again. By mid-October he had persuaded Hammarskjold that these Belgian technicians were interfering with the efforts of the United Nations to settle the Congo crisis. They were bolstering Mobutu's military regime in Leopoldville and encouraging Tshombe to maintain his secession in Elisabethville. Hammarskjold asked the Belgian government to withdraw Tshombe's advisers; and while he was at it, he asked Belgium to "remove all military, paramilitary, or civilian personnel" serving the Leopoldville government as well.[45]

Even before the Belgians officially asked for American support, an incredulous Ambassador Burden was cabling Washington from Brussels: "I am appalled at Hammarskjold's demand for 'withdrawal' of all Belgian personnel" in the Congo. "If taken seriously it could only restore chaos of worst days of Lumumba."[46] Timberlake's reaction was just as strong. If the Secretary-General has asked for "across the board withdrawal" of all Belgians serving in the Congo, he wrote, "I am as appalled as Ambassador Burden." Only an influx of Belgian technicians and businessmen could save the Congo's economy, he warned. If the flow were suddenly reversed, it would add to the "already huge task" facing the United Nations. He urged the State Department to oppose such a policy "to the limit."[47]

Secretary Herter, who shared Timberlake's alarm about both of these issues, decided to raise them directly with Hammarskjold. He instructed Wadsworth and Bohlen to remind the Secretary-General that he had indicated he would "support Kasavubu in his struggle with Lumumba." He understood that Hammarskjold had been under pressure from the Soviet Union and that he wanted to maintain "maximum support" among the Africans and Asians. But he warned that if Hammarskjold persisted in his present policy, it could lead to "chaos" and the "return of Lumumba to power," followed by "renewed demands" for the withdrawal of the United Nations and "massive Soviet intervention." Herter was certain this was not what Hammarskjold wanted—in fact, the Secretary-General had made it clear that he felt the United Nations could not work with Lumumba—but the Secretary did not see how, from a "practical point of view," Hammarskjold's actions could lead to anything else. Herter's memorandum concluded with an implied threat: if the Secretary-General's latest views regarding Lumumba represented a "basic change" in his approach, the United States would have to make a "fundamental reassessment" of its own position.[48]

When Hammarskjold met with Wadsworth and Bohlen on October 21, he denied that there had been "any change in his attitude" and rejected the American suggestion that he had been under "pressure" from Lumumba's supporters. He insisted that the United Nations was taking an "impartial" position toward Lumumba; it did not treat him as if he *were* Prime Minister, or as if he *were not* Prime Minister. He explained that this stand merely reflected the sentiment of the General Assembly, which had not taken a position one way or the other on the credentials question. On the issue of the Belgian technicians, Hammarskjold pointed out that as long as Tshombe could turn to Belgium for help, he would not cooperate with the central government. He observed that he had asked of Belgium only what the United States itself had asked—that all aid be channeled through the United Nations. He complained that the Belgians had been "anything but helpful in this matter."

Bohlen then restated the implied threat contained in the memorandum in even stronger terms. He warned that the Russians had "not given up hope of returning" to the Congo and insisted that the Secretary-General's "rule of impartiality" was being applied in a manner that favored Lumumba. "If Lumumba comes back into power," he said, "the U.S. government does not propose to stand idly by" and allow the Congo to become a "Communist satellite." It would have to weigh carefully the possibility of a "drastic revision" of its Congo policy.[49]

Hammarskjold and the Americans left the meeting with sharply contrasting views of what had been accomplished. The Americans reported that Bohlen's strong warnings "certainly seemed to have shaken" the Secretary-General who, they felt, would be "more receptive" in the future to American suggestions, particularly about Lumumba.[50] Hammarskjold, on the other hand, was shocked by Bohlen's statements and his manner, which he regarded as an "affront." Wieschhoff told Wadsworth a few days later that the Secretary-General had been "remarkably restrained" in the face of behavior which "they might expect from Russians but certainly not from Americans." Hammarskjold resented Washington's attempt to dictate to him. He was particularly annoyed by American criticism of Dayal. Bohlen had not referred directly to Dayal's treatment of Lumumba, but he had showed Hammarskjold press reports from Leopoldville describing the shift in UN policy. Bunche later said that Hammarskjold believed all these news stories had been "planted" by Timberlake.[51]

Relations between the United States and the United Nations grew increasingly sour over the next few weeks, as the confrontation between Dayal and Mobutu came to a climax. After the colonel failed to arrest Lumumba, he sent his soldiers into the African quarter of Leopoldville to round up Lumumba's supporters. They immediately started drinking, looting, raping, and beating up civilians. The raids and arrests continued for several days and the casualty figures mounted. On October 21, the day Hammarskjold met with Bohlen, Mobutu demanded that the United Nations give him control of the airport and the major arms depot in Leopoldville. Dayal refused. He described Mobutu's troops as "rabble."[52]

On October 24, ANC units set up roadblocks and prevented all but a handful of Congolese from attending the ceremonies marking United Nations Day—ceremonies that were boycotted by Mobutu, Kasavubu, and Bomboko.[53] Dayal was furious. He told a group of Western journalists that Mobutu was a "lousy" chief of staff; he had no "mental discipline" and was afraid of his own troops; he had asked Dayal to provide him with an apartment at UN headquarters, where he would be safe. Dayal observed that the ANC should have been disarmed in the first place, as General Alexander had suggested, but he was afraid it was too late to do anything about it now. He insisted, however, that the United Nations would "never recognize" a "military dictatorship" in the Congo. He hoped that at some point Parliament would be reconvened. In the meantime, he said, Lumumba remained the head of the legal government.[54]

Timberlake, who was appalled by Dayal's remarks, learned that Mobutu had decided to go to New York to take his case to the Secretary-General "over Dayal's head." The ambassador immediately sent an emissary to urge Mobutu not to leave at such a "critical juncture," since he might lose his hold over his troops. He asked Mobutu to wait in any case for a flight which would take him straight through to Paris; he was afraid that the colonel might be removed from the plane if it landed at Accra or Conakry. He suggested that Mobutu "blunt his attacks" on the United Nations and resume his role as a "strong silent man." At the same time, he reassured Mobutu that the United States was not "dropping" him.[55]

Mobutu decided to remain in Leopoldville, but he ignored the rest of Timberlake's advice. On October 25 his troops set up roadblocks in the European sections of the capital and began to stop and search civilians. There were rumors that he would be moving armored units to Leopoldville from their camp in Thysville, ninety miles away. UN troops were on the alert to block their path.[56]

The showdown came on October 26, when Mobutu demanded that Dayal be recalled.[57] He was immediately summoned to UN headquarters, where he was confronted by Dayal and his three top generals, who told him that the United Nations would no longer tolerate the "illegal and arbitrary acts" committed by the ANC in recent days. They strongly implied that if he did not cooperate, they would disarm his troops completely. Faced with this threat, Mobutu backed down and agreed to confine them to their barracks.[58]

The State Department was concerned about the impact of this agreement on Mobutu's position. Timberlake reported that the colonel was just about holding his own. He was quite willing to withdraw some of his troops to their barracks, and it was just as well, since the "town was crawling with them." Mobutu still had his guards stationed around Lumumba's residence and in a few other key spots. The ambassador noted that, despite Dayal's assurances to the contrary, there were persistent rumors that the United Nations intended to disarm the ANC. If that were to happen, he warned, it would be a "definite assist for Lumumba."[59]

Lumumba, confined to his residence, was following these developments closely. Despite his physical isolation, he was kept informed by a rather unconventional intelligence network. According to his close friend Kashamura, he had enlisted the aid of a group of girls, aged fourteen to twenty, "the most charming in Leopoldville," to seduce Mobutu's young commissioners and then bring the information they had gathered to the Lumumbists. The ousted Prime Minister was encouraged by Dayal's clash with Mobutu and told his supporters that he was "optimistic" about his chances of returning to power.[60]

The Russians, who were watching the confrontation from a distance, were optimistic as well. By October 24 *Pravda* was citing Western news reports that Mobutu was "on the verge of collapse" and that the restoration of Lumumba was "only a matter of time."[61] The agreement of October 26 seemed to stop this process in its tracks. The Russians were disappointed by Dayal's decision to compromise with Mobutu; but they were reluctant to criticize him personally, as they had Bunche and Cordier, because he was known to have the confidence of Nehru, a leading supporter of Lumumba. Still, they felt it was time to step up their pressure on the Secretary-General and his special representative. On October 28 Soviet Ambassador Zorin sent a letter to the President of the Security Council demanding information from Hammarskjold about the lack of progress in the implementation of the Security Council resolutions. He pointed out that the Congolese Parliament still had not been reconvened and that, instead of withdrawing from the Congo, the Belgians were returning in ever increasing numbers.[62]

Hammarskjold, bombarded by criticism from all sides, asked Dayal to submit a report spelling out the problems the United Nations was facing. Dayal concluded that Hammarskjold wanted an "outspoken report giving the unvarnished facts."[63] The report was issued on November 2. Although it was consistent with what Dayal had been saying for weeks, it was considered a diplomatic bombshell. Dayal blasted Mobutu's "arbitrary assumption" of political power and charged that he was unable to control his own troops, who, instead of maintaining order, were the source of most of the "lawlessness" in the Congo. He criticized the Belgians for their involvement in Katanga and for their interference in Leopoldville, where they were encouraging the young commissioners to disregard the advice of their UN advisers. Dayal insisted that he had followed a policy of strict impartiality between the competing political factions; it was in this context that he had refused to permit Lumumba's arrest. He concluded that in this "confused political situation," there were only two pillars of legitimacy—the chief of state and the Parliament. Together they might build a national government of reconciliation.[64]

Washington's reaction was swift and angry. American officials were afraid that Dayal's stress on the role of Parliament and on Lumumba's immunity from arrest implied that he would be brought back to power under UN auspices. The State Department immediately issued a state-ment defending Belgian motives and good faith.[65] The Belgians, stunned by the severity of Dayal's attack, were extremely grateful for American support.

The Russians, at the other end of the seesaw, were favorably im-pressed not only by the substance of the report but also by the angry American reaction to it. Dayal returned to New York for consultations the day after the report was published, and one of the people he met with was Zorin, who put him through a "two-hour grilling." Dayal found the Soviet diplomat "as dogmatic in his support of Lumumba as his opponents were in their opposition to him." Zorin told Dayal he believed he was an "honest man" but insisted that Dayal's views did not correspond to Hammarskjold's. Dayal insisted that they did. "I re-plied that if Hammarskjold did not agree with me, he would ask me to leave, and if I disagreed with him, I would myself pack up and go," he later recalled.[66]

When Zorin addressed the General Assembly a few days later, he pointed to the Dayal report as a vindication of the Soviet position. "What a difference there is between this more sober and objective evaluation of the development of the situation in the Congo and the earlier triumphant reports of the Secretary-General!" he exclaimed.[67]

Dayal had more trouble explaining his position to the Belgians. Shortly after his arrival in New York, he met with Harriman, who he felt was sympathetic to the problems the United Nations faced in the Congo. Harriman invited him to a luncheon with Belgian Ambassador Loridan and another Belgian official. Despite Harriman's efforts, the luncheon did not go well. Dayal, who may have been overly sensitive, wrote of the Belgian diplomats in his memoirs: "Both gentlemen scrutinized me closely for what seemed to me symptoms of cannibal-ism."[68] In such an atmosphere there could be no meeting of the minds on the subject of the Belgian technicians in the Congo.

Tug of War over Mobutu and the Leopoldville Government

By this time officials in Washington had concluded that they could not persuade Hammarskjold to work with Mobutu's military regime and that the best way to halt the dangerous pro-Lumumba drift of his policy would be to cover Mobutu with the fig leaf of a civilian govern-ment. Hammarskjold had not been particularly enthusiastic about the idea when Bohlen first raised it during their discussion on October 21; but when it was brought up again a week later, he agreed that it would be "most helpful" if the Americans put some "fire into Kasavubu"—if they were able to act "delicately" and not "visibly," and if they "put nothing in his pocket." He thought Ileo was the best choice for Prime

Minister; both Ileo and Bomboko were intelligent, he said, but Bomboko lacked "stability." He insisted that the new government be presented to Parliament, which would meet under UN protection. He did not insist that Lumumba "had to be" in the government, but he repeated that a "solution could not be found without taking him into account."[69]

At this point cables began flying back and forth between Washington, New York, and Leopoldville, as the State Department tried to put its plan into effect. Bohlen and his colleagues seemed to feel that Kasavubu and Mobutu would follow the American lead, and that it was just a matter of deciding who should be Prime Minister. Timberlake, while emphasizing his willingness to consider their ideas, kept trying to interject a note of caution about the realities of the Congolese political scene. Their exchange evolved into a classic confrontation between the men in the Department, who were looking at the "big picture," and the man on the scene, who was much more aware of the limitations—and the opportunities.

When the Department instructed Timberlake to suggest the idea to Kasavubu, the ambassador raised a number of objections. To begin with, he did not consider Ileo the best choice for Prime Minister; he lacked the "necessary drive and flair." He suggested that Cyrille Adoula, who had just gone to New York as head of the Congolese delegation, would be the "best possibility," even though he lacked "broad political support." Timberlake described Adoula as a "moderate and strong anti-Communist labor leader," who at one time had been a leading member of Lumumba's party but since the split in 1959 had been "bitterly opposed to Lumumba." He was "well and favorably known" to the Embassy staff, and the ambassador had encouraged him to work closely with the U.S. delegation in New York.[70] There was no need to rush into a decision, Timberlake cautioned. It would take a "great deal" of planning to convene Parliament, and it should not be attempted before the end of December, unless a firm anti-Lumumba majority emerged before then. This was highly unlikely because of Tshombe's attitude; he seemed "further away than ever" from a decision to rejoin the Congo and send his delegation to a meeting of Parliament. The "central problem," Timberlake concluded, was Lumumba:

HE WOULD HAVE TO BE ALLOWED TO PARTICIPATE IN SESSION OF PARLIAMENT AS DEPUTY. THERE IS ALWAYS DANGER THAT NO MATTER HOW FIRM OPPOSITION LINEUP LUMUMBA ORATORY PLUS THREATS CAN TURN IT INTO VICTORY FOR HIMSELF.[71]

On November 2, the day the Dayal report came out, Timberlake sent the Department a long analysis, in which he tried to explain the difficulty of applying twentieth-century political concepts to the Congo. Even the "most sympathetic observers know this country cannot govern itself in an intelligent fashion and that, left to its own devices and without outside aid, [it] could not survive as a national entity," he wrote. Much as he would like to see the establishment of a stable democratic government, he felt that the Congo was "years away" from anything more than the "façade of democracy." He added:

I DO NOT BELIEVE THERE IS ONE SINGLE CONGOLESE WHO HAS MORE THAN THEORETICAL IDEA OF EVEN THE MOST ELEMENTARY PRINCIPLES OF DEMOCRACY. THEY OBVIOUSLY CANNOT PRACTICE SOMETHING THEY DO NOT UNDERSTAND. THIS DOES NOT INSULT THE MANY WELL-INTEN-TIONED CONGOLESE BUT DOES DISCOUNT THEIR ABILITY TO PRODUCE ANYTHING RESEMBLING DEMOCRATIC GOVERNMENT UNTIL THEY HAVE BEEN TAUGHT. FURTHERMORE, I DO NOT BELIEVE DEMOCRACY CAN BE IMPOSED UPON ANY PEOPLE OVERNIGHT ANY MORE THAN IT CAN BE IN-JECTED BY HYPODERMIC.

Essentially, Timberlake was pleading with Washington to go slow and not be swept along by a UN desire for an "accelerated Parliamentary solution in the Congo." He refused to accept Dayal's view that there could be no solution without Lumumba and that it would be just as well to get the "present unpleasantness over with and let him back in." Timberlake felt that this sort of policy would "blow up" in Dayal's face. If an election were held now, he explained, Lumumba "might very well emerge" with the "stamp of Parliamentary approval," but that would hardly be a victory for democracy; it would be a "compound of cupidity (bought votes), intimidation . . . and demagogic oratory," along with a few votes from genuine supporters. "We would be back to early August politically with even more dismal prospects" for preserving the unity of the Congo, he warned.[72]

This long cable urging a go-slow approach was sent the same day as an action directive from the State Department, in which the Secretary of State personally authorized Timberlake to "take appropriate steps" along the lines indicated in the earlier cables.[73] Despite this high-level reminder, Timberlake continued to drag his feet. When the Department had heard nothing from him for three days, another reminder was sent off: "Would appreciate soonest confirmation your approach Kasavubu." If the ambassador had not yet proposed the idea of a new civilian government to the Congolese President, the Department suggested he do so before Kasavubu left for New York, where he was about to launch a major effort to get his delegation seated in the General Assembly.[74]

The Americans had not originally intended to become involved in a credentials debate at this point. Adoula and the rest of the Kasavubu delegation had been in New York for more than a week, and Wadsworth reported that they were "gaining respect and some sympathy" for their cause.[75] But they were nowhere near commanding majority support. It was the Guineans and their allies who precipitated the debate by insisting that the Assembly consider their draft, which called for the seating of the Lumumba delegation and the reconvening of Parliament.[76] There was a fair amount of resistance among the African delegations to what they regarded as Guinea's "steamroller" tactics; most of them still preferred to postpone their decision until the situation in the Congo was clarified.[77] The Belgians felt that the Western powers should take advantage of this opportunity to try to get Adoula's delegation seated and suggested that Kasavubu himself might come to New York to make sure that the effort was successful.

The Americans responded enthusiastically to this idea, since they felt a "clear-cut decision" to seat Kasavubu's delegation in New York would be the best way to strengthen his position in Leopoldville. They got very little support, however, from the rest of the NATO allies, with the exception of France. The British were "distinctly negative"; they still believed that Lumumba could not be ignored and felt that conciliation was the most sensible approach. The others said it was unwise for the Americans to press for this sort of move unless they were sure of winning. The Americans warned that if they were not willing to take a "calculated risk" while Kasavubu was in New York, his power would be eroded gradually and the Western powers would have no further opportunity to influence events in the Congo. In the end they persuaded their reluctant allies that the gamble might well succeed.[78]

Timberlake evidently did not want to distract Kasavubu at this critical moment. He explained on November 7 that he had not had time to raise the idea of a civilian government with the President before he left. Besides, he was convinced that the plan was premature. He recommended that the United States continue to work with the commissioners until there was some indication that Lumumba's opponents could come up with an alternative government. He added that the prospect of Adoula emerging as their choice for Prime Minister was improving but was still far from clear.[79]

State Department officials were obviously exasperated by Timberlake's attitude. They felt he was unaware of the larger implications of their plan. They explained that a new civilian government would have an excellent chance of winning "international approval," particularly the approval of the Secretary-General, which they considered "essential." It would also reduce the "trouble-making potential" of the Afro-Asian Conciliation Commission that was being formed—if it could be set up before the Commission arrived in the Congo.

They explained that the new government would not have to be approved by Parliament in the near future. They disregarded Timberlake's pessimistic assessment of Tshombe's position; while they understood that the presence of Tshombe's Conakat deputies was essential if there was to be an anti-Lumumba majority in Parliament, they seemed to feel that the U.S. consul in Elisabethville could persuade Tshombe to send them. They parted company with Timberlake even more decisively on the question of Lumumba's participation. "Lumumba's presence" in Parliament, they said, "would have to be accepted." The "danger" could be minimized by careful advance planning.

The officials also raised questions about Timberlake's candidate for Prime Minister and proposed one of their own. Bomboko, they said, was apparently the "ablest and most dynamic anti-Lumumbist"; he was "favorably" regarded by the African diplomats in New York, and, as head of the College of Commissioners, might be "more acceptable" to Mobutu as a "face-saver" for the dissolution of the College. As an alternative, they mentioned the possibility of reviving the Ileo government, with Mobutu continuing to "maintain his strongman role" as chief of staff or Minister of Defense.[80]

Timberlake was still not convinced. On November 15 he restated his objections to the Department's policy in even stronger terms. As far as the choice of a Prime Minister was concerned, he insisted that Adoula was "as anti-Lumumbist as the others including Bomboko." He was "energetic" and had a "better general position" among the members of Parliament. In addition, he had a good relationship with Mobutu. Timberlake cautioned against trying to pick a Congolese Prime Minister from Washington. In the "last analysis," he said, it would be Kasavubu and the other Congolese who would decide. The United States could hope to "influence" their choice but could by no means "control" it. The Embassy could work with "almost any likely combination of moderates," he explained.

Timberlake's main objection to the Department's plan, however, ran deeper than a disagreement about personalities. He believed that a change of government at this point would be harmful to American interests. He felt that it would not accomplish what the Department wanted it to accomplish: neither the Secretary-General nor the Afro-Asian states would accept it as legitimate, any more than they had accepted the Ileo government or the College of Commissioners, unless it was approved by Parliament—and that would be an extremely risky move. Moreover, the formation of a new government would weaken Mobutu, who represented the "only relatively stable counter" to Lumumba. "Mobutu is the key for the present," he wrote, "even though I could wish he were more able and less impulsive."

It was Mobutu's intention to keep the commissioners in office until December 31, and Timberlake doubted that he would be willing to consider their "dissolution" before that. Besides, he pointed out that it would take "at least until then" for the provincial leaders to get together and form an anti-Lumumba majority in Parliament. It was hard to predict what Parliament would do, he said. The Soviet bloc and the UAR had already given "large amounts" of cash for pro-Lumumba votes, and the Embassy had learned recently that they were promising two thousand dollars to each deputy who voted for Lumumba the next time around. "The stakes may go even higher," he added. "I feel there is a very real risk that Parliament will vote by pocket rather than by principle in enough numbers to support Lumumba" despite the "best efforts" of a "coalition of anti-Lumumba leaders." If the moderates failed, Mobutu and the army "might have to assert themselves again," he explained. "I would not like to see them emasculated." Timberlake, ever the realist, meant that if Lumumba's opponents failed to defeat him in Parliament, Mobutu could step in once again and restore military rule.

The ambassador made it clear that he was not in any hurry to replace the commissioners, weaken Mobutu, and take the risk of covening Parliament in order to "appease" a Conciliation Commission sent by the United Nations. Moreover, he felt that Kasavubu would be offended by any action taken in his absence. He assured the Department that he had discussed with Mobutu and Ileo the desirability of establishing a government which would eventually win parliamentary approval, but he concluded:

WE CANNOT AND SHOULD NOT TRY TO PRECIPITATE THEM INTO ACTION WHICH, IN OUR VIEW, IS HIGHLY QUESTIONABLE AT MOMENT AND WHICH THEY ARE NOT PREPARED TAKE FOR MUCH SAME REASONS.[81]

Meanwhile, the CIA Tries Again

Timberlake's apprehensions about reconvening Parliament were shared by the CIA station chief in Leopoldville. On October 26, when it looked as if Mobutu might be on his way out, Devlin reported to headquarters that if Parliament were called back into session and Lumumba's opponents failed to win a majority, the "pressures" for his return would be "almost irresistible.[82] The only sure way to avoid this was to eliminate Lumumba from the scene. Devlin's preference was to have the Congolese arrest him, but the UN guards posted around his residence made that approach close to impossible. The other alternative, of course, was assassination.

Devlin had not made much progress on the assassination plot up to this point, but he kept plugging away at it, and he kept his superiors informed of the latest developments. On October 28 he reported that one of Lumumba's Congolese opponents had told his CIA contact that he was "trying" to have Lumumba "killed" but added that this would be "most difficult" since the job would have to be done by an "African with no apparent involvement" with any "white man."[83] The following day headquarters informed Devlin that the senior case officer they had discussed earlier in the month via the top secret PROP channel would soon be arriving in Leopoldville "in furtherance this project." The station chief later testified that it was "very possible" that he regarded the assignment of an additional officer as an indication that headquarters was "dissatisfied" with his handling of the instructions relayed by Gottlieb.[84]

The senior case officer, Justin O'Donnell, had his own reservations about the idea of assassinating Lumumba. In his testimony before the Senate Intelligence Committee, he explained that in mid-October Bissell had called him in and asked him to "eliminate Lumumba." O'Donnell stated, "I told him that I would absolutely not have any part of killing Lumumba." Bissell suggested he talk to Gottlieb, who filled him in on the various "lethal means of disposing of Lumumba." One of these methods, O'Donnell recalled, "was a virus and the others included poison." O'Donnell returned to Bissell and repeated that he "would not be involved in a murder attempt."[85] He took the precaution of placing his objections on the record by making the same point to anyone at the CIA who would listen: Richard Helms, who was then Bissell's deputy and Chief of Operations in the clandestine services division; Tweedy; and his own boss, William Harvey, the head of an "extraordinarily secret unit" within the Directorate of Plans.[86]

According to Bissell's testimony, O'Donnell felt that assassination "was an inappropriate action and that the desired object would be accomplished better in other ways." O'Donnell clearly drew a distinction between assassinating Lumumba and luring him out of UN custody so that he could be turned over to the Congolese for trial and punishment. This he was willing to do. He told Bissell he would go to Leopoldville and try to "neutralize" Lumumba "as a political factor."[87] He explained to the committee, "I wanted . . . to get him out, to trick him out, if I could and then turn him over . . . to the legal authorities and let him stand trial."[88] O'Donnell said he had "no compunction" about handing Lumumba over for trial by a "jury of his peers," although he realized there was a "very, very high probability" that he would be sentenced to death for his crimes.[89] "I am not opposed to capital punishment," he stated.[90]

O'Donnell arrived in Leopoldville on November 3, the day after the Dayal report was published. Devlin was alarmed about its implications. He warned his superiors once again that if the United Nations reconvened Parliament it "would probably return Lumumba to power."[91] Devlin met with O'Donnell, who struck him as "unenthusiastic" about his assignment. Devlin assumed that the assignment was "similar" to his own, "that is, the removal or neutralization of Lumumba." He told O'Donnell there was "a virus in the safe." O'Donnell assumed, after his conversation with Gottlieb, that it was a "lethal agent," intended for use against Lumumba. "I knew it wasn't for somebody to get his polio shot up to date," he remarked. Still, he was surprised that the virus was there, since he had refused to have anything to do with an assignment involving assassination. Moreover, Gottlieb had never mentioned the fact that he himself had taken the virus to Leopoldville.[92]

Although neither Devlin nor O'Donnell remembered discussing specific assassination plans, O'Donnell did recall that they had a philosophical discussion about the morality of assassinations. "From my point of view I told him I had moral objections to it, not just qualms but objections. I didn't think it was the right thing to do," O'Donnell insisted. Asked about Devlin's views on the subject, O'Donnell replied:

> He would not have been opposed in principle to assassination in the interests of national security. . . . I know that he is a man of great moral perception and decency and honor. . . . And that it would disturb him to be engaged in something like that. But I think I would have to say that in our conversations . . . at no time would he rule it out as being a possibility.[93]

Shortly after his arrival in Leopoldville, O'Donnell started to put his plan into effect. He reported regularly to headquarters and kept the station chief informed of his activities. The first thing he did was arrange to rent an "observation post over the palace in which Lumumba was safely ensconced." Next, he made the acquaintance of a UN guard whom he hoped to recruit to help lure Lumumba out of his residence.[94] In order to conceal the American role in this operation, he planned to use a "third country national"—an agent with the code name QJ/WIN.

QJ/WIN was described in CIA testimony as a "foreign citizen with a criminal background, recruited in Europe," who had very few scruples and was "capable of doing anything"—including assassination.[95] This was apparently the task the CIA first had in mind for him when Devlin found that his local agent was unable to gain access to Lumumba and thus was unable to administer the poison. On November 2 the Leopoldville station received a cable from headquarters regarding QJ/WIN. It was so sensitive that the instructions stated: "This dispatch should be reduced to cryptic necessary notes and destroyed after the first reading." The cable informed Devlin that QJ/WIN was being sent to the Congo on a mission that "might involve a large element of personal risk." It continued:

> In view of the extreme sensitivity of the objective . . . he was not told precisely what we want him to do. . . . Instead, he was told . . . that we would like to have him spot, assess, and recommend some dependable, quick-witted persons for our use. . . . It was thought best to withhold our true, specific requirements pending the final decision to use [him].[96]

O'Donnell had another purpose in mind for QJ/WIN. As he explained it:

> What I wanted to use him for was . . . counter-espionage. . . . I had to screen the U.S. participation in this . . . by using a foreign national whom we knew, trusted, and had worked with . . . the idea was for me to use him as an alter ego.

QJ/WIN was evidently delayed en route; on November 11, and again on November 13, the CIA station in Leopoldville requested his "immediate expedition" to Leopoldville. He did not arrive in the Congo until November 21.[97]

In the meantime, there was very little activity around Lumumba's residence. Devlin reported through the PROP channel on November 14:

> Target has not left building in several weeks. House guarded day and night by Congolese and UN troops. . . . Congolese troops are there to prevent target's escape and to arrest him if he attempts. UN troops there to prevent storming of palace by Congolese. Concentric rings of defense make establishment of observation post impossible. Attempting get coverage of any movement into or out of house by Congolese. . . . Target has dismissed most of servants so entry this means seems remote.[98]

Devlin had picked up one useful bit of information, however, from an agent with access to Lumumba's supporters. The only way Lumumba would leave the residence would be if he decided to join his "political followers" in Stanleyville. A decision on a "breakout" would "probably be made shortly," and the agent would advise him as soon as it was made. "Station has several possible assets to use in event of breakout and studying several plans of action," he reported.[99]

Lumumba was not yet ready to move to Stanleyville, but events in New York, thousands of miles away, would soon have an impact on his plans.

The Credentials Debate at the General Assembly: November 8–22, 1960

On November 8 President Kasavubu, who shunned the limelight and rarely made a public appearance in his own country, addressed the General Assembly and proclaimed his sole right, as head of state, to name the Congo's delegation to the United Nations.[100] By the following day, Lumumba's supporters realized that Kasavubu's presence at the Assembly, his position as head of state, and his moderate speech might swing opinion in his favor. They switched tactics, and, in a surprise move that caught the U.S. delegation off guard, Ghana called for postponement of the debate until after the fifteen-member Conciliation Commission had gone to the Congo and submitted its report.[101] The Ghanaians were appealing for the support of all those states which were opposed to hasty action—those who had objected to Guinea's attempt to ram Lumumba's credentials through the Assembly and those who felt it was premature to approve Kasavubu's credentials. As a result, the Ghanaian move was successful; the motion carried, 48 to 30, with eighteen abstentions. The Soviet bloc, most of the African and Asian states, several Latin American states, and such European neutrals as Finland, Sweden, and Ireland voted for postponement.[102]

The Russians were triumphant. This was the first time they had found themselves part of an anticolonialist majority on the Congo question. It appeared that Khrushchev's analysis was turning out to be correct. *Pravda* concluded that the United States had "suffered a serious defeat." Kasavubu's mission had been a "disaster," and the American "maneuvers to legalize the puppet regime in the Congo" had proved "absolutely futile."[103]

The November 9 vote was indeed a major setback for the Americans, but they were not about to give up their effort to get the Kasavubu delegation seated. They were afraid this might be their last chance to get rid of Lumumba. All their other efforts up to this point had failed. The CIA had been unable to eliminate him by violent means, and the diplomats had been unable to eliminate him by political means because of the stubborn opposition of the Secretary-General. Hammarskjold had implied, however, that he would alter his policy in response to a decision of the General Assembly, and the Americans were determined to produce an anti-Lumumba majority. They plunged into an intense lobbying campaign, pressuring their allies as well as the uncommitted nations, and trying at the same time to preserve the image Kasavubu had projected as a reasonable, moderate political leader. There were minor setbacks along the way; no matter how hard they tried to coordinate their efforts with the Belgians and the Congolese, things kept going wrong.

The first potential complication was fairly easy to deal with: as soon as Lumumba learned that Kasavubu was going to New York, he tried to go as well. Ileo sent a frantic message to Adoula through Ambassador Timberlake; he was making every effort to prevent Lumumba from leaving the country, but if he succeeded in reaching New York, it was essential that he be prevented from addressing the General Assembly.[104] Lumumba found that he could not leave his residence, but Kanza, his original UN delegate, who had returned to Leopoldville, and Maurice Mpolo, another leading Lumumbist, decided to go to New York and asked the U.S. Embassy for visas. Timberlake informed them that the Commissioner of the Interior had canceled their passports.[105] Kanza and Mpolo protested to Dayal's deputy, who immediately cabled Hammarskjold: "Timberlake determined not to allow any Lumumbist to enter New York to ensure that Kasavubu has all the advantages." Hammarskjold replied that the United Nations was powerless to deal with Congolese passports. "On a strictly personal basis," he wrote, "we regret the situation facing Kanza."[106]

Kasavubu did not really need active Lumumbists in New York to undermine his diplomatic effort; his own associates were perfectly capable of doing the job themselves. Evariste Kimba, Katanga's representative in the delegation, chose this moment to deny publicly that Kasavubu spoke for the entire Congo. The Americans assumed he had been put up to this by Katanga's chief Belgian lobbyist in New York, Michel Struelens, and demanded that the Belgian government do something to muzzle him. The Belgians claimed they had no control over Struelens, but they pressured Kimba into signing an agreement with Kasavubu, and the dispute was papered over for the time being.[107]

Next, Kasavubu and Bomboko, for some inexplicable reason, rebuffed the French African delegates who were their most ardent supporters in the General Assembly. Kasavubu refused to see them the night of his arrival in New York, and Bomboko told them he did not need their help. The delegate of Dahomey was particularly offended because he had introduced the motion postponing the Congo debate for one day so that Kasavubu could arrive in time to be the first speaker. The Americans pointed out that there was no point in antagonizing him or his colleagues, and they helped persuade Kasavubu to repair some of the damage by having breakfast with the representative of Dahomey the following morning and then meeting with some of the other disgruntled French African delegates.[108]

U.S. officials had little time to spare for monitoring the activities of Kasavubu and his delegation, since their main concern was to produce a pro-Kasavubu majority in the Assembly. The first step was to get the matter through the Credentials Committee. This was not difficult, although the results were somewhat embarrassing: on November 10, the committee voted 6 to 1 to approve the credentials of Kasavubu's delegation. Costa Rica, Haiti, the Philippines, Spain, and New Zealand voted with the United States; the Soviet Union was opposed; and Morocco and the UAR, the only African members of the committee, angrily refused to participate. Both were supporters of Lumumba.[109]

The next step was to reverse the vote of November 9 in favor of adjournment, so that the credentials question could be debated on its merits. This was the difficult part. The British were still extremely reluctant to move ahead on the credentials issue, complaining as late as November 14 that the Americans were putting pressure on them to "rush into activities" without giving them a chance to "express their doubts." In the end, however, they acknowledged the "reasonableness" of Kasavubu's stand and agreed to join the Americans in approaching other delegations.[110]

Over the next few days the U.S. delegation buttonholed every delegate in sight and encouraged its allies to do the same.[111] American pressure tactics created a certain amount of resentment, especially among the moderate Africans. The Tunisians agreed that Kasavubu should be strengthened but thought the Americans were going about it in exactly the wrong way. Ambassador Slim pointed out that if the United States was "too closely identified" with any group in the Congo, it would "weaken that group," and he suggested that the Americans should play a "less prominent" role in both New York and Leopoldville.[112] U.S. pressure backfired with Nigeria, which had gained a reputation for independence and leadership in the short time it had been a member of the United Nations. Foreign Minister Jaja Wachuku, who had just become chairman of the Conciliation Commission, was not enthusiastic about Lumumba and up to this point had been opposed to sending the Commission to Leopoldville without Kasavubu's approval. But when he learned that the Americans had arranged for the credentials issue to be debated in plenary session, he complained that they were interfering in the Congo's political affairs and recommended that the Conciliation Commission leave for Leopoldville as soon as possible, whether Kasavubu was ready or not.[113]

On the eve of the vote the Americans and British concluded that they could win with a five-vote margin. The pro-Kasavubu French Africans would provide the key.[114] When the vote took place, on November 18, the United States and its allies easily defeated Ghana's call for postponement, 50 to 36, with eleven abstentions.[115] The lobbying had paid off, despite the bruised feelings.

On November 22, after four days of debate on the resolution itself, the Assembly voted to seat Kasavubu's delegation 53 to 24, with nineteen abstentions.[116] At a press conference the following day, Zorin tried to minimize the significance of the vote, claiming that the resolution could not be effective since "almost half the delegations, including the leading African and Asian states and the socialist states, did not vote for it."[117] It was true that even in defeat the Russians found themselves part of a respectable minority. It was a far cry from the 70 to 0 vote in September, when the Soviet bloc abstained and was virtually isolated. Still it was a defeat, and it was clearly a blow to Khrushchev's strategy. If the French African states had lined up with the rest of the Afro-Asian bloc instead of succumbing to "Western pressure," there would have been a majority to postpone the debate or perhaps even to seat Lumumba's delegation.

A Battle and Not a War

The outcome of the credentials debate was doubly disappointing to the Russians—first, because they had had a realistic chance of victory, and second, because in the volatile atmosphere of the Congo, a victory for Lumumba could have been a decisive step toward restoring him to power and restoring the Soviet position in the Congo. This was precisely why the Americans had worked so hard to get Kasavubu's delegation seated. They assumed that the Secretary-General would now feel obliged to shift his policy away from the views of the Afro-Asian radicals, rein in Dayal, and cooperate with Kasavubu and the moderates. But they, too, were in for a disappointment.

They found that neither Hammarskjold nor Kasavubu shared Washington's assumption that the credentials vote would bring about a new era of cooperation between the Leopoldville government and the United Nations. According to Dayal, Hammarskjold was "appalled" by the pressures the United States had exerted to get the Kasavubu delegation seated and felt that the American move had "vastly increased" the problems he faced in the Congo.[118] Kasavubu continued to regard the United Nations with suspicion. He was planning to convene a round table conference of all the Congolese leaders, including Tshombe, but he was afraid Dayal would try to "impose" a solution of his own.[119] He asked Hammarskjold to remove Dayal; Hammarskjold immediately rejected the idea. He then demanded that Hammarskjold reduce the number of UN troops in the Congo; Hammarskjold retorted that Kasavubu could not maintain order without them.[120]

As Herter noted the day after the final vote, the Americans had "won a battle and not a war."[121] They had met the challenge posed by Lumumba's supporters, strengthened Kasavubu's authority, and dealt a blow to Lumumba's claim to legitimacy. But it would be more difficult than they had anticipated to dispel the Secretary-General's suspicions and convince him to work with Kasavubu and exclude Lumumba from any future Congolese political solution.

CHAPTER SEVEN

Lumumba: A Prisoner But
Still A Menace
(November 25-December 25, 1960)

"If I die, *tant pis*, the Congo needs martyrs."

O<small>N THE NIGHT</small> of November 27, while a thunderstorm raged over Leopoldville and two hundred and fifty guests at a banquet at the presidential palace were toasting Kasavubu's triumphant return, Lumumba slipped past the double ring of UN and Congolese troops guarding his house and drove away in a dark car with a few friends, in the direction of Stanleyville, eight hundred miles to the east, where his supporters were in power.

Two days before he left, he tried to reassure his friend Kashamura on the telephone. "Don't worry about me," he said. "Don't try to stick with me on the trip. I am happy to see you leave. You will escape. As for me, if I die, *tant pis*, the Congo needs martyrs." Kashamura left for Stanleyville with one group of Lumumba's supporters on the morning of November 26, and Lumumba left with another group the next night.[1]

It was not until November 28 that anyone realized he was gone. In the morning a Moroccan guard informed his superiors at UN headquarters about the departure of a large black car, but there was some uncertainty about whether Lumumba had been one of the passengers until the afternoon, when UN troops searched the house and found it empty. Lumumba had left a letter explaining that he was going to Stanleyville for the funeral of his infant daughter, stillborn in Geneva; he had asked the United Nations to provide transportation for him but Dayal had refused. Lumumba said he intended to return after the funeral and take part in Kasavubu's round table conference. But the UN soldiers who looked through his house found that everything was gone—even the ashtrays. It did not look as if he meant to return.[2]

According to Kashamura, the General Assembly vote seating Kasavubu's delegation was the "fatal blow" that persuaded Lumumba to go.[3] He knew it would be dangerous to leave the comparative safety of

Leopoldville without the guarantee of UN protection; but when he learned of the outcome of the credentials debate, he assumed it would be equally dangerous to remain in the capital since UN troops would no longer be responsible for his safety. Dayal tried to reassure him on this point, informing him on the telephone as well as through African diplomats that, as far as UN protection at his residence was concerned, there had been no change in his status; but he failed to persuade the deposed Prime Minister. Moreover, Lumumba realized that his defeat in New York had altered his political prospects. For some time his Deputy Premier, Antoine Gizenga, and other prominent Lumumbists had been urging him to return to his home base in Orientale Province to lead a new popular movement that would sweep him back into power as the undisputed leader of the Congo. The General Assembly's decision must have persuaded him that there was no point in waiting in Leopoldville any longer. He could no longer realistically hope to be reinstated as Prime Minister by the United Nations, and his only chance of returning to power was to follow the advice of his supporters in Stanleyville.

Four Days of Suspense

The Americans were caught off guard by Lumumba's sudden departure. Although the CIA had reported the strong possibility of a "breakout" two weeks before, the exact timing of his move came as a surprise. U.S. Embassy officials were the first to tell Kasavubu and Mobutu that Lumumba had escaped. As soon as they heard the news from UN headquarters, they got word to the ambassador, who was across the river in Brazzaville with the Congolese leaders, helping President Youlou celebrate his country's independence. Mobutu immediately sent Bomboko back to Leopoldville with "instructions for setting up roadblocks."[4] The CIA was eager to help. Devlin reported to headquarters that he was "working closely" with Congolese officers "to get roads blocked and troops alerted" to cut off any "possible escape route."[5]

Just to be on the safe side, in case these efforts failed, the CIA was prepared to follow Lumumba to Stanleyville and deal with him there. O'Donnell's agent, QJ/WIN, had arrived in Leopoldville only a few days before and had barely had a chance to start working out a plan to "pierce both Congolese and U.N. guards" and "escort" Lumumba out of his residence when Lumumba left on his own. QJ/WIN had no intention of giving up his quarry so easily. On November 29 Devlin sent a cable to headquarters stating that in "view change in location target, QJ/WIN anxious to go Stanleyville and expressed desire execute plan by himself without using any apparat." Tweedy replied the next day, approving the idea; his only concern was to minimize the appearance of American involvement. "Concur QJ/WIN go to Stanleyville," he wrote. "We are prepared consider direct action by QJ/WIN but would like your reading on security factors. How close would this place [United States] to the action?"[6]

At this point the question was academic. Lumumba's exact whereabouts were unknown for four full days. There was, however, no shortage of rumors about his progress. He seemed to be taking an indirect route to Stanleyville and stopping along the way to rally his supporters. There were reports that he had arrived in Kikwit, about two hundred and fifty miles east of Leopoldville, and that the local population had clashed with pro-Mobutu troops stationed in the area. There were indications that he might proceed next to north Kasai, where his own tribe, the Batetela, would offer him refuge. There were also reports that he might be flown to Ghana or to Guinea. American officials followed these rumors with great interest[7]—and so did the Russians, who were well aware of the stakes involved.[8]

As the suspense mounted, Dayal found himself under intense pressure from both sides. Kasavubu and Bomboko demanded that he provide them with air and road transport to pursue Lumumba, but he refused to do so. At the same time, the Ghanaian troops stationed in Kasai announced that they intended to provide protection for Lumumba if he asked for it. Dayal responded to these conflicting demands by instructing all units not "to provide or transmit intelligence to either side concerning the movements or whereabouts of pursued or pursuers."[9] He was greatly alarmed by the implications of Lumumba's escape. "We are entering upon a new phase of developments which may radically change balance of forces in the country and next week or two could well be crucial," he cabled Hammarskjold. "If Lumumba manages to get to Stanleyville, the whole situation would change in a flash."[10]

Stanleyville was already in turmoil in anticipation of Lumumba's arrival, and the Ethiopian troops were having difficulty maintaining order. On November 28 hundreds of Europeans were rounded up and beaten by the pro-Lumumba authorities. The UN civilian administrator sent a frantic appeal to Leopoldville for air evacuation of approximately one thousand whites, including UN personnel.[11]

When McIlvaine, the deputy chief of mission at the U.S. Embassy, went to see Dayal to urge him to take strong action, he found him "depressed and confused." Dayal said he could not spare extra troops to go to Stanleyville, but he was sending General Iyassu Mengesha, the Ethiopian officer who had installed the troops in Stanleyville in July and then served as von Horn's chief of staff in Leopoldville. McIlvaine reported that the U.S. army attaché considered Iyassu an "able aggressive type" who could be expected to "bolster" the Ethiopian troops; the only problem was that he was still on home leave in Addis Ababa.[12]

McIlvaine warned the State Department that if Lumumba reached Stanleyville and consolidated his power there, he would try to take over the entire country. He would be "actively assisted" by the Soviet Union and the UAR and "to a lesser extent by Ghana and Guinea." McIlvaine then raised a number of questions. How would the United Nations react to the arrival of Soviet or UAR planes and volunteers? Would it prevent Mobutu's forces from entering the area to combat Lumumba? Were the Russians or the Egyptians capable of supporting a large-scale military operation in the Congo? How would the Sudan react to overflights of its territory? What would the U.S. position be?[13]

State Department officials had been considering these questions ever since Kasavubu's credentials victory, and Lumumba's sudden flight from Leopoldville only intensified their concern. They instructed Wadsworth to take up the problem with the Secretary-General. They wanted to be sure that the United Nations would be able to prevent the Russians and their allies from using the airfields in the area to "supply and assist" the Lumumbists. They also wanted a commitment from Hammarskjold that he would not "obstruct" any effort Mobutu might make to reassert his authority in Orientale Province.[14]

Wadsworth was unable to secure any commitments from the Secretary-General, who felt that American fears were exaggerated. He acknowledged that "as many as twenty states" might recognize a Lumumbist government in Stanleyville, which would be able to obtain "military equipment and possibly some planes" from abroad, but he did not seem particularly alarmed by this prospect. He thought a civil war was highly unlikely, since he doubted that Mobutu could handle the logistics of sending a force to Orientale Province, and he said that even if Mobutu could get there, he "could not match" Lumumba's three-thousand-man force. If fighting did break out, he believed the best thing the United Nations could do was to step between the two groups in order to prevent any armed conflict. Hammarskjold saw this policy of "interposition" as operating "equally in both directions." Wadsworth, on the other hand, saw it operating against the Leopoldville government alone. It was obvious to him that Hammarskjold shared Dayal's contempt for the Leopoldville leaders; he spoke constantly of "rebuking" them or "chastening" them, and he complained that they "acted like children."[15] It was clear that if Lumumba did succeed in reaching Stanleyville, the U.S. government could not count on the Secretary-General to support any further action against him.

The Arrest

By December 2 the suspense was over. The U.S. Embassy in Leopoldville reported that the ANC had captured Lumumba, as well as a
number of his supporters, in Kasai Province. Mobutu was sending a
plane to bring them back to the capital. They would be imprisoned
without trial until Alphonse Songolo and the other deputies who were
under arrest in Stanleyville were freed.[16] Songolo, formerly Lumumba's Minister of Communications, had defected in mid-October and returned to Stanleyville with several colleagues to "try to whip up
anti-Lumumba sentiment." Up to this point the United Nations had
been unable to secure their release.[17]

There are several versions of Lumumba's capture and the role
played by the United Nations. The most dramatic is that of Lumumba's
comrade Kashamura, who managed to escape to Stanleyville. According to his story, on December 1, the day before Lumumba was captured, he reached Mangai, a little town in the eastern part of
Leopoldville Province. There he addressed a large public meeting and
denounced the clergy, imperialism, Kasavubu, and Mobutu, in a
speech which lasted five hours. The local bishop notified the security
police of his whereabouts, but the police could not catch up with him
because the local population barricaded the roads and tore down the
bridges after he had passed. Toward evening Lumumba arrived at
Gungu, just south of Kikwit. There he was stopped for two hours by
primitive tribesmen, who refused to believe he was really Lumumba.
At last he persuaded them to let him continue his journey. Meanwhile,
Captain Gilbert Pongo, the security man in charge of the search, set
off in a helicopter to try to pick up Lumumba's trail once again. According to Kashamura, Timberlake persuaded Brazzaville's President
Youlou to furnish the helicopter. The following day, Lumumba
reached Kasai Province and tried to cross the Sankuru River, but the
ferrymen refused to take him across, explaining that they had orders
from the president of Leopoldville Province, Cleophas Kamitatu, to
transport no one but Lumumba. Once again he had to persuade skeptical supporters that he really was Patrice Lumumba. They had always
seen photographs of him in a suit and tie, and they said, "You are a liar.
We know Lumumba well. He always wears suits and glasses. But you?
Here you are in a sport shirt." Lumumba explained that he was simply
dressed because he was traveling, but they insisted that he was a "spy
for Kasavubu." At last, after showing them his photograph and identity
cards, he convinced them. They "fell on their knees, apologized, and
began to sing." Two of them went off to the neighboring village to
summon their friends so that they could hear the "words of the libera-

tor of their country." Lumumba held forth for a half hour on the "role of the peasantry" in an independent Congo. Suddenly the fugitives sighted Mobutu's soldiers. Kashamura said Lumumba could have made it across the river, but he refused to leave his wife and children. "When one struggles for one's country, when one loves one's people, one has to expect a tragic end," he said. He then proceeded to convert the soldiers who had come to arrest him. They were ready to go on to Stanleyville with him when Captain Pongo intervened and reminded them of their duty. In an instant they switched sides and began to beat Lumumba and his son. According to Kashamura, the Ghanaian soldiers who were present did nothing to help, and when Lumumba was taken to Port Francqui and appealed to the Tunisian, Ghanaian, and Nigerian officers there, they replied, "Your affairs do not concern us."[18]

The UN officials involved in the Congo operation told the story somewhat differently. Dayal, for example, maintained that, while "there were some scattered U.N. troops in the general area," Lumumba "did not approach them for any assistance." At the same time, he denied all claims by Kasavubu and Mobutu that the Ghanaian troops in Kasai had blocked Pongo's search. He insisted that these units had followed their orders to the letter.[19] According to General von Horn, the commander of the UN force, the Ghanaian troops in Kasai respected Dayal's hands-off order while Lumumba was still at large, but their commander requested "permission to rescue Lumumba" immediately after his arrest. "I do not know what arguments and counterarguments may have raged over the telephone to New York," he wrote, "but the end result was clear enough. We were instructed to refuse the request and issue orders to the Ghanaians not to intervene."[20]

Brian Urquhart provided an even more detailed report, which conflicted with Kashamura's in almost every particular. According to Urquhart, Lumumba arrived in Port Francqui on December 1 and "attended a lunch given in his honor by the provincial administrator." He seemed to be "on good terms" with the local ANC troops. He asked for a UN escort to accompany him to Mweka, fifty miles further east. The UN commander refused, in accordance with the directive from Leopoldville. Lumumba then drove on to Mweka, where he met with his "local supporters," made another speech, and "went to the Grand Hotel." That evening forty ANC soldiers "arrived in Mweka and accused the Ghana platoon stationed there of protecting Lumumba." The following morning a Ghanaian officer saw three cars drive up. Lumumba was taken out of one of the cars and beaten, and when the Ghanaian tried to intervene, the cars drove away.[21]

Urquhart defended in some detail the UN decision not to intervene "to hinder Lumumba's pursuers" or to take him into "protective custody." First of all, he noted, "the possibility of political assassination was not uppermost in anyone's mind in the Congo at the time of Lumumba's escape. . . . In nearly five turbulent months no political leader had been hurt, let alone killed." Furthermore, any action to prevent his arrest or to rescue him afterward would have constituted "flagrant interference" in the Congo's "internal political struggle." Finally, there was a practical obstacle: any such move would have placed the UN troops, "dispersed in small detachments all over the country . . . in a new and general military confrontation with the overwhelmingly more numerous ANC, a confrontation in which they would almost certainly have been defeated."[22]

There were probably other factors at work as well. Von Horn was relieved by Lumumba's capture. "There were mixed feelings" at UN headquarters, he recalled:

> A small minority were plainly alarmed and dismayed. But most of us felt quite rightly that there was now a genuine chance of the Congo returning to some degree of tranquility. To put it frankly, had Lumumba got to Stanleyville, the whole Congo might have gone up in flames."[23]

Lumumba was brought to Leopoldville in the late afternoon of December 2. His hands were tied behind his back. His face was bloody. His shirt was torn and soiled, his glasses were broken. He had obviously been beaten. He was taken to Mobutu's residence. Mobutu was waiting outside. One of his soldiers read a long statement, tore the paper to bits, and tried to stuff them down Lumumba's throat. He was then driven to the army prison at Binza, "thrown" to the ground, and "jumped on by howling troops." All this was witnessed and photographed by cameramen for the Associated Press, United Press, CBS, NBC, Fox Movietone, and Belga-Vox. When Ambassador Timberlake heard about the incident from NBC correspondent Irving R. Levine, he was concerned primarily about the public relations aspects of it. "While press accounts will be bad enough," he wrote, "movie recordings . . . will be gift of atomic bomb to Soviet bloc and friends." He had only a "dim hope" that the television networks and news agencies "could be prevailed upon to suppress" the film, but he suggested it anyway.[24]

The Americans may have been disturbed by the manner of Lumumba's arrest, because they feared it might damage Kasavubu's cause and therefore their own, but they were vastly relieved by the fact that he had been arrested and could no longer head a separatist government in Stanleyville. Wadsworth reported on the evening of December 2 that the Secretary-General did not believe Gizenga could "crystallize" the situation in Stanleyville without Lumumba, who was the only one with a claim to "legal" status.[25] Nevertheless, Hammarskjold did not share the sense of relief felt by the Americans or by General von Horn.

He felt that Lumumba's arrest would probably make matters worse. "We are in the middle of an extraordinarily complicated and indeed politically dangerous situation," he wrote to Dayal. "The emotional tension here around the Lumumba case is considerable and if things run wild or summary justice [is] executed, consequences may be very bad" both for the United Nations and for the Congo operation.[26]

Washington Polishes Kasavubu's Image

Hammarskjold was right. As soon as the news of Lumumba's arrest reached New York, the Soviet delegation issued a statement charging that it had been made possible by the "connivance" of the UN command and warning that the Secretary-General bore "direct responsibility for the safety and lives of the members of the lawful government."[27] This was followed by an official government statement demanding Lumumba's release, calling for an immediate meeting of the Security Council, and accusing Hammarskjold of "complicity" with the Western powers.[28]

The Russians were not alone in their view that Hammarskjold should have done more to protect Lumumba. The day after the arrest, he met with a number of African and Asian delegates to try to scotch rumors that Lumumba was going to be executed. He managed to reassure them for the moment by telling them that he had sent a strong letter to Kasavubu urging him to observe "due process" and to keep in mind Lumumba's parliamentary status and his standing with the international community.[29] But once the films of Lumumba's arrest were shown on American television, it was impossible for him to keep the Afro-Asians in line. Vigorous protests rolled in, not only from Lumumba's traditional supporters but also from such moderates as Tunisia, Senegal, and Nigeria.[30] By this time Hammarskjold had received a report from Dayal confirming that Lumumba had been "brutally manhandled" and noting that he was being confined under "inhumane conditions."[31] He immediately fired off a second letter to Kasavubu urging him to permit a Red Cross representative to check on Lumumba's physical condition.[32]

State Department officials, worried about the impact of the television film, backed up Hammarskjold's effort to persuade Kasavubu and Mobutu to treat Lumumba in a more acceptable manner. They cabled Timberlake:

WE BELIEVE THAT INHUMANE TREATMENT, PARTICULARLY THAT WHICH NUMBER OF PHOTOGRAPHERS AND NEWSREELS WERE ABLE TO RECORD, WILL CAUSE PRO-LUMUMBISTS AT UN TO REDOUBLE THEIR EFFORTS WITH GREATER CHANCE OF SUCCESS. WE URGE YOU TO TAKE WHATEVER STEPS APPROPRIATE TO ENCOURAGE MOBUTU TO HAVE HIS ARMY AVOID SUCH

TREATMENT IN FUTURE. BELIEVE SITUATION REQUIRES SOONEST PUBLIC
STATEMENT BY KASAVUBU THAT LUMUMBA WILL RECEIVE HUMANE
TREATMENT AND FAIR TRIAL.[33]

The following day, Mobutu acknowledged at a press conference that
Lumumba had been mistreated at the time of his arrest, but he denied
Dayal's claim that Lumumba was being held under "inhumane conditions."[34] Meanwhile, Timberlake had talked with one of the Belgian
doctors who had examined Lumumba at the prison in Thysville where
he was being held. The doctor assured him that Lumumba had suffered "only minor bruises and contusions" and that his "physical state"
was "very good." He was in a "separate room" in the "cleanest prison"
in the Congo—he even had a bed with a mattress, which was extremely unusual. The doctor was concerned about releasing such a report;
ironically, he feared that the Congolese soliders, who were not that
well treated themselves, would feel that Lumumba was being "pam-
pered," and there might be a "wave of resentment which would be
difficult to handle." Still Timberlake felt that the report might have to
be released in order to counter the impressions created by the films of
the arrest.[35]

The State Department suggested that Kasavubu send the Secretary-General "documentary evidence" supporting his case against
Lumumba before the Security Council meeting on December 7.[36] Kasavubu was making himself scarce, but Timberlake managed to talk to
him briefly when he received an American senatorial delegation accompanied by Edward Kennedy, the brother of the President-elect.
Bomboko assured him that the documents were on their way to New
York.[37]

The immediate problem facing officials in Washington was to improve Kasavubu's image before the Security Council meeting. At the
same time, they were working on the long-range problem of persuading him to name a government that the United Nations could "recognize and deal with." They had raised the issue again with Timberlake
immediately after Kasavubu's credentials victory. They were much
more relaxed about it than they had been before. They conceded a
number of points Timberlake had raised about the importance of not
rushing into things and not jeopardizing Mobutu's position, but they
still felt Kasavubu could take advantage of his victory to name a civilian government.[38]

In the excitement of Lumumba's escape and capture, Timberlake
had not had time to respond to this cable. He answered it on December 7, in the context of other recent cables which seemed to have been
written on the assumption that he had Kasavubu and Mobutu in his
"pocket." Timberlake tried to disabuse the State Department of this

notion. He said that while he had tried to advise the Congolese about legal safeguards for Lumumba, they rarely consulted the Embassy before making their decisions, and they tended to act impulsively. "It would be necessary to live twenty-four hours a day with the principals in this drama," he said, "to know what role they may decide to play at any given moment."

As far as the formation of a new government was concerned, Timberlake understood that the U.S. delegation was having a "very rough time in New York and that a government with more claim to legitimacy would make it easier" for them to deal with attacks from the Soviet bloc as well as with the Africans. Despite all his efforts, however, he had "not made measurable progress" in convincing Kasavubu, Mobutu, or the other moderate leaders of the desirability of going back to the Ileo government or of forming a new government. "We cannot dictate either terms or timing," he concluded.[39]

Meanwhile, in New York, pro-Lumumba pressure continued to mount. On the eve of the Security Council meeting, the UAR, Ceylon, and Yugoslavia announced that they were withdrawing their troops from the UN force, and there were indications that other supporters of Lumumba, such as Guinea, Indonesia, and Morocco, would follow suit.

The Sixth Security Council Meeting: December 7–14, 1960

The Security Council meeting, which began on December 7 and lasted for a week, was a duel between the Soviet Union, which blamed the Secretary-General for Lumumba's arrest, and Hammarskjold, who tried to defend his position in the face of Moscow's harsh criticism and the qualified but even more unwelcome criticism of the Afro-Asians. Hammarskjold argued that Lumumba had been arrested on a warrant signed or approved by the head of state, and insisted that the United Nations could not override that by force. The only thing the United Nations could do for him was to appeal for basic justice and human rights.[40]

The Russians were outraged by this hands-off attitude, and they were even more infuriated on December 9, when the Secretary-General released Dayal's report on the situation in Stanleyville. Anti-Belgian incidents and attacks on UN personnel had multiplied in the wake of Lumumba's arrest. On December 8 Lumumba's former secretary, Bernard Salumu, who had emerged as a local strong man, sent an ultimatum to Kasavubu and the United Nations threatening to arrest all the Belgians in Orientale Province and start to kill them if Lumumba was not freed within forty-eight hours. Over five hundred Europeans flocked to UN headquarters for protection. Dayal protested vigorously to the provincial authorities. He explained that the release of Lumumba was not within the jurisdiction of the United Nations and warned that the United Nations would resist any attempt to harm people under its protection.[41]

Zorin complained bitterly about the "inconsistencies" in the Secretary-General's position. If he could not stop Mobutu's "illegal bands" from holding Lumumba, Zorin argued, how could he step in to defend a group of Belgians against actions ordered by the legitimate provincial authorities in Stanleyville? How could he evacuate two thousand people from Stanleyville when he could not find a plane for "one Prime Minister"? Hammarskjold replied that if Zorin did not see the difference between saving one thousand people from being taken hostage or executed, and the "use of military initiative to liberate somebody who had been arrested, then I find it difficult to discuss, because it is then obvious that we do not speak exactly the same language."[42]

It was at about this time that ugly cartoons of Hammarskjold began to appear in the Soviet press. On December 7 he was portrayed as a skinny little man with crinkly hair and a long nose, bending solicitously over a fat, ugly colonialist with a bottle of eau-de-cologne labeled "UN," and asking, "Need some freshening up?"[43] On December 10 he appeared again, his hair formed by dollar signs, washing his bloody hands on a towel marked "Report of the Secretary-General's Representative."[44]

The Afro-Asians did not attack Hammarskjold personally, but Lumumba's arrest had definitely brought them much closer to the Soviet position. Nearly all of them agreed with Zorin that Kasavubu had acted illegally and that Lumumba must be freed; nearly all of them were highly critical of the role the United Nations had played in the arrest. The strongest position was taken, as usual, by the Guinean representative, who announced that Guinea was withdrawing from the Conciliation Commission and removing its contingent from the UN force.[45] Hammarskjold was not particularly disturbed by this prospect. He was, however, profoundly disappointed by the position taken by Foreign Minister Mahmoud Fawzi of the UAR, who, despite his personal friendship with Hammarskjold, described the UN operation as a failure and announced that his government was in "general agreement" with the Soviet draft resolution, which called for the release of Lumumba, the convening of Parliament, and the disarming of Mobutu's troops.[46] The Moroccan delegate implied that his country's troops would be withdrawn if the situation did not improve shortly;[47] he did not need to point out that these three thousand soldiers were considered the most effective in the twenty-thousand-man force. Nkrumah's representative did not speak at the meeting, but the Ghanaian leader weighed in with a letter of reproach.[48] He had been especially embarrassed by Lumumba's arrest because it was the second time in three months that his troops had been used against Lumumba's interests.

The meeting ended in deadlock in the early morning hours of December 14. The positions of the Western and the Afro-Asian powers were so far apart that they could not agree on a draft resolution. The Western powers introduced a "human rights" draft, which used the same language Hammarskjold had used in his letters to Kasavubu, declaring that prisoners everywhere in the Congo should be treated according to "recognized rules of law and order," and recommending that the Red Cross be permitted to check on their condition.[49] Zorin sardonically congratulated the Western powers for proposing that the "beatings not be so violent." Although the Western draft received the necessary seven votes, it was vetoed by the Soviet Union, joined by Poland, and Ceylon, which termed it "wholly inadequate to meet the needs of the situation." Tunisia abstained. The Soviet draft was defeated 8 to 2, with Ceylon abstaining. Zorin then proposed that the Congo issue be moved to the General Assembly, since the Security Council had been "paralyzed by the position taken by the Western powers."[50] This was a significant reversal of the situation in September, when the Americans turned to the General Assembly after being thwarted in the Security Council by a Soviet veto. At that time they assumed that the Africans and Asians would be highly critical of Soviet policy in the Congo; now, after Lumumba's arrest, the Russians were assuming that Afro-Asian sentiment had swung the other way.

New Threat from the Left: Gizenga Government in Stanleyville

On December 13, just before the meeting ended, Gizenga sent a message to Zorin, as President of the Security Council, proclaiming that he now represented the lawful government of the Congo and that Stanleyville had become its legal capital.[51] The Americans were not really surprised by this move; they had been waiting for the other shoe to drop ever since Salumu's ultimatum. While they realized that Gizenga could not command the international support that Lumumba did, and thus would pose less of a threat, they were still alarmed by the prospect of a separatist government recognized and supported by the Soviet bloc and the radical African states.

For several days the U.S. Embassy in Leopoldville had been preoccupied with the fate of the Belgian hostages in Stanleyville. While the Russians were angered by Hammarskjold's decision to offer them protection, the Americans, predictably, did not think that Dayal was doing enough to help them. Timberlake and his Western European colleagues organized a consular mission which went to Stanleyville, with Dayal's approval, to intercede with the local authorities.[52] For a time it appeared that the Western diplomats would join the other hostages; McIlvaine, the American member of the mission, was held at gunpoint for two hours by Congolese soldiers rounding up Europeans before he was freed by Ethiopian UN officers.[53] He and the other diplomats managed to win a postponement of the ultimatum—although they could not get it lifted altogether—and they returned to Leopoldville on the evening of December 13.[54] By this time Gizenga had made his announcement, and Timberlake's concern about the hostages was overshadowed by his concern about Soviet military intervention. Dayal had just told him that he was planning to withdraw the UN troops from the outlying parts of Orientale Province and concentrate them in the capital. Timberlake was afraid that this decision would play into the hands of the Russians. He warned the State Department that it would leave large parts of the "vast Congo hinterland without even token contingents" and would increase the likelihood of a take-over by pro-Lumumba forces.[55]

On December 15 *The New York Times* reported that a Soviet Ilyushin-14 plane had landed in Stanleyville with a cargo of weapons and other materiel.[56] The following day Under Secretary Dillon instructed the U.S. Embassies in Teheran, Ankara, Athens, and Rome to be alert to any Soviet requests for landing or overflight rights for planes heading toward Stanleyville and to suggest to their host governments that they apply "stringent" controls to these flights, including "careful inspection" of their cargo. He pointed out that the Greek government had established a useful precedent in September by inspecting the Soviet planes "allegedly carrying relief supplies" to Lumumba, even though their search failed to turn up the arms which were "almost certainly" part of the cargo. U.S. officials assumed that the UAR would cooperate with the Soviet Union in supplying arms to Gizenga and that the two would put considerable pressure on the Sudanese, who might yield and "accord landing or at least overflight rights" to the Soviet planes. They had discussed this problem with Sudanese President Ibrahim Abboud, and they hoped he would stand firm in the face of Soviet demands.[57]

Timberlake and his Western European colleagues felt the United Nations should be in a strong enough position in Stanleyville to inspect any incoming aircraft in order to "prevent the landing of troops, arms or supplies from outside the Congo."[58] At the same time they realized that it would be "extremely difficult" for the United Nations to "assure surveillance of all airports," since there were dozens of small airfields in Orientale Province and in Equateur Province, where the pro-Lumumba UAR contingent was stationed. Twelve of those airfields could handle DC-3s; six could handle a DC-4; and two, including Stanley-ville, could take "anything except a jet." The U.S. ambassador had gone over these technical difficulties in some detail with his British and French colleagues to see if there was any way of using radar to check on incoming aircraft. The British ambassador had recommend-ed to his government that a surveillance effort be made from Uganda, a British protectorate east of Orientale Province, while the French am-bassador suggested a parallel effort from Bangui, in the newly inde-pendent Central African Republic, north of Equateur Province.[59]

American diplomats in Leopoldville were convinced that "Commu-nist agents" were already active in Stanleyville and that their oper-ation would expand once diplomatic and technical missions from the Soviet bloc were formally accredited to the Gizenga government.[60] The CIA tried to counter the efforts of these agents by organizing an intelligence network of its own. On December 17 the Leopoldville sta-tion chief reported to headquarters that he had instructed a newly ar-rived agent, code-named WI/ROGUE, to "build cover" and "spot persons" for a "surveillance" team which would operate in Orientale Province.[61]

On paper WI/ROGUE sounded like the perfect choice for this as-signment. He was described in CIA documents as a "forger and former bank robber," a "soldier of fortune" who was "essentially stateless." He was given his assignment by two members of the Africa Division on September 19. He was then trained in "demolition, small arms, and medical immunization," and provided with "plastic surgery and a tou-pee" so that he would not be recognized. On October 27 the Africa Division recommended him to Devlin as a man who "learns quickly and carries out any assignment without regard for danger." It said further:

> He is indeed aware of the precepts of right and wrong, but if he is given an assignment which may be morally wrong in the eyes of the world, but necessary because his case officer ordered him to carry it out, then it is right, and he will dutifully undertake appropriate action for its execution without pangs of conscience. In a word, he can rationalize all actions.

He was expected to act as a "utility agent," who would "organize and conduct a surveillance team . . . intercept packages . . . blow up bridges . . . and execute other assignments requiring positive action." His ac-tivities were "not to be restricted to Leopoldville."[62]

Devlin, who later described WI/ROGUE as a "man with a rather un-savory reputation, who would try anything once, at least," testified that he used WI/ROGUE as a "general utility agent" and said he had no connection with any assassination plot. WI/ROGUE, however, seems to have had other ideas. Ironically, in his effort to recruit a team of agents to work in the Stanleyville area, he contacted QJ/WIN, not realizing that he was already working for the CIA. On December 14 he offered QJ/WIN "three hundred dollars per month" to participate in an intelligence network and be a member of an "execution squad." When QJ/WIN said he was "not interested," WI/ROGUE told him there would be "bonuses for special jobs." WI/ROGUE acknowledged that he was working for the Americans, but QJ/WIN did not reveal his own affiliation. He reported the conversation to Devlin, who complained to headquarters about WI/ROGUE's "free wheeling approach," his disregard for "security," and his failure to follow instructions. He suggested that if WI/ROGUE did not shape up, he should be recalled.[63]

Devlin told the Senate committee that he had never instructed WI/ROGUE to enlist anyone for an "execution squad." "I am sure he was never asked to go out and execute anyone," he said. "His idea of what an intelligence operative should do, I think, had been gathered by reading a few novels or something of the sort." WI/ROGUE was an "unguided missile . . . the kind of man that could get you in trouble before you knew you were in trouble."[64]

Western fears that the Russians were ready to resume their involvement in the Congo—complete with large-scale military aid—as soon as the opportunity presented itself proved to be somewhat exaggerated. The Russians were, if anything, even more confused by the new situation caused by Lumumba's arrest than the Americans were. They were out of touch with the latest political developments; for three months they had been forced to rely on secondhand reports from the pro-Lumumba Africans, from the United Nations, and from the Western press.

Premier Khrushchev clearly sympathized with Gizenga. *Pravda* immediately reported his announcement that he would assume Lumumba's duties while the Prime Minister was under arrest,[65] and *Izvestia* ran a complimentary account of the pro-Soviet atmosphere in Stanleyville by a correspondent who had been there during the summer.[66] Still, the Soviet leader found it difficult to decide what concrete steps he should take in support of the Stanleyville regime. His hesitation was reflected in his treatment of a message sent to Moscow on December 14 by Gizenga, who announced that the central government had moved to Stanleyville and warned that Mobutu was poised to invade Orientale Province. It took Khrushchev ten days to reply to this message. His response was friendly and consistent with past Soviet statements, but it made no new pledges of support. It did not specifically mention recognition of Gizenga's government, and it addressed him as Deputy Prime Minister, rather than Acting Prime Minister.[67]

In July, when Lumumba and Kasavubu had appealed for Soviet

"watchfulness," Khrushchev had responded the next day. The ten-day lapse in December suggests that he had become more wary as a result of his experience with Lumumba. He had gambled once by providing military aid to the recognized Prime Minister of the entire Congo, and the move had backfired. He was not about to leap into a similar commitment to the leader of a dissident government with power in only one province. Instead, he would study the situation and assess Gizenga's chances before he went beyond polite generalities about freedom and independence. In the meantime, he would follow the lead of Lumumba's African and Asian supporters, as he had done in July, and see if the General Assembly could do anything to restore Lumumba's position.

Deadlock at the General Assembly: December 16–20, 1960

The General Assembly debate was essentially a replay of the Security Council meeting. Yugoslavia and seven Afro-Asian powers—India, Ghana, Morocco, the UAR, Iraq, Indonesia, and Ceylon—introduced a draft resolution that differed from the Soviet position only in that its criticism of the Secretary-General was implicit rather than explicit; on the substantive issues of releasing prisoners, convening Parliament, expelling Belgian advisers, and disarming the ANC, it followed the same lines.[68] The sponsors believed that the United Nations could have taken some action to prevent Lumumba's arrest and that there were no insuperable obstacles to an activist policy that would free Lumumba and restore a constitutional government to the Congo. They could not understand how the Secretary-General could protect the Belgians in Stanleyville at the same time that he was refusing to protect Lumumba in Leopoldville.

Hammarskjold explained once again that the UN force did not have a mandate to release Lumumba. It could use force only in "self-defense," as it had done when it protected the Europeans in Stanleyville or Lumumba's residence in Leopoldville. When Lumumba left his residence, the United Nations did not even know where he was; and after he was arrested, the UN forces could have freed him only by attacking the Congolese forces—which they were not authorized to do.[69] Responding to complaints that he had been too passive, Hammarskjold suggested a number of positive steps the General Assembly could take. It could urge the convening of Parliament, the reestablishment of a civilian government, the end of foreign support for the army, and an end to the various secession movements—but it could not authorize the United Nations to carry out these measures by force, as the Afro-Asians wanted.[70]

Hammarskjold's suggestions were incorporated into an American-

British draft resolution, which also included the main points of the "human rights" resolution that had been vetoed in the Security Council.[71] There was no Soviet draft, since Zorin found the Afro-Asian draft close enough to his own position to warrant his support, and he undoubtedly thought it would have a better chance of success than anything he could propose. When the two drafts were put to a vote on December 20, neither the Western draft supporting Hammarskjold nor the Afro-Asian draft ignoring him was able to win the necessary two-thirds majority. The Afro-Asian draft was defeated 42 to 28, with 27 abstentions. The Western draft missed a two-thirds majority by only one vote: the final result was 43 to 22, with 32 abstentions. Not a single African state voted for it—not even the Congo.[72] Once again, as at the Security Council, the result was a deadlock.

The Danger of Civil War

The stalemate at the General Assembly reflected a stalemate in the Congo. The Russians found the situation extremely frustrating. Although the debate strengthened the Soviet alliance with the more radical Afro-Asian states and demonstrated a dramatic shift away from the United States, it accomplished nothing in terms of helping Lumumba. After all the talk, nothing had changed. At year's end the man Khrushchev was backing seemed to stand no chance of being released by the United Nations. The failure of the Security Council and the General Assembly to provide a new mandate meant that the Secretary-General would continue the operation as before. His interpretation of the mandate as it related to Lumumba left the Russians little room for hope. The one bright note in the picture was Stanleyville, but they were not sure how effective Gizenga would be or how much they should do to support him.

At the same time, the Americans, who were disturbed by their failure to win any African support in the General Assembly, regarded Gizenga as a major threat and were worried about the Secretary-General's attitude toward him. While they approved of Hammarskjold's handling of Lumumba's arrest, they were not sure what he might do next. They feared that his desire to prevent further withdrawals from the UN force might compel him to make concessions to the pro-Lumumba Afro-Asian group—concessions that would weaken Kasavubu and Mobutu. Hammarskjold's relations with Kasavubu were no better than before; Dayal was still on the scene; the Conciliation Commission was arriving in Leopoldville; and the Secretary-General himself would be going there in early January. There were a great many unknowns in the situation, and State Department officials were uneasy.

After the debate was over, Herter instructed Wadsworth to discuss the Stanleyville issue once more with the Secretary-General and to point out the "extremely dangerous situation" which would arise if the Gizenga regime were recognized by the Communist bloc and the "extremist Afro-Asians" and supplied by aircraft from the UAR and the Soviet Union. He suggested that it might be helpful if Hammarskjold visited Stanleyville in the course of his trip to the Congo.[73]

Wadsworth found that the Secretary-General still did not take the situation as seriously as the Americans did. He explained that he would not be able to visit Stanleyville himself but would send General Sean McKeown, the Irish officer who had just succeeded von Horn as commander of the UN force, in his place. He did not plan to stay in the Congo for more than two days "because he did not want to get too much entangled in internal problems."

At the end of the meeting the conversation came around to the subject of Lumumba. The Secretary-General referred to the story in that morning's *New York Times*, which stated that Lumumba was now having his meals at the officers' mess at the army camp in Thysville. Hammarskjold said "he would not be surprised" if he heard that Lumumba was "dining with Kasavubu again."[74] The Americans agreed. Even after Lumumba's arrest and imprisonment, they were not confident that he had been eliminated from the Congolese political scene.

CHAPTER EIGHT

The Death of Lumumba
(December 25, 1960–
January 20, 1961)

"Thanks for Patrice. If we had known he was coming
we would have baked a snake."

D URING THE LAST FEW WEEKS of the Eisenhower Administration,
American Congo policy was dominated by the fear that Lumumba
would turn the tables on his captors and return to power and that the
Russians would end up on top after all. Despite all their advantages,
Kasavubu and Mobutu seemed unable to cope with the growing mili-
tary and political strength of the Lumumbists, and U.S. officials in Leo-
poldville warned with increasing urgency that the problem of
Lumumba had to be settled once and for all.

A Losing Battle

Although Lumumba himself was still in prison, his allies in Stanleyville, led by Gizenga, managed to consolidate their control over Orientale Province and then began to move out into neighboring areas. On
Christmas Day sixty soldiers from Stanleyville arrived in Bukavu, the
capital of Kivu Province, south of Orientale, kidnapped the provincial
president and three of his ministers, as well as the pro-Mobutu commander of the army garrison, and established control over the provincial government. The garrison, nominally loyal to Mobutu, took no
action to stop them, and the local population offered no objection. The
UN troops stationed in the area did nothing to prevent the takeover.

On January 9 Lumumbist forces moved south from Kivu to link up
with the anti-Tshombe Baluba tribes of northern Katanga; some fifteen hundred soldiers, disregarding the neutral zone established by
the United Nations, captured the tin-mining town of Manono and proclaimed it the capital of a new province of North Katanga. Once again,
the UN troops in the area watched passively.

Meanwhile, other soldiers loyal to Stanleyville moved west, into the
border areas of Equateur Province, several hundred miles north of

Leopoldville, up the Congo River. Since this was an area that was manned by UN troops from the UAR, the Americans were particularly alarmed; they had been receiving unconfirmed reports about arms and military advisers from Cairo arriving in Stanleyville, and they had visions of Nasser intervening actively to aid Gizenga¬through the use of his UN contingent. There was still another center of pro-Lumumba tribal sentiment in the northern part of Kasai Province, in the central part of the country. Altogether, by mid-January, forces loyal to Lumumba controlled almost half the Congo's territory.[1]

American officials in Leopoldville were disturbed by Mobutu's inability to counter these military thrusts. They felt that Gizenga's successes were due at least in part to the assistance he was receiving from his foreign advisers, and they were eager to right the balance. In late December the Embassy and the CIA station discussed the possibility of supplying covert aid to Mobutu for a military operation against Orientale Province, but the idea never got beyond the planning stage. Officials in Washington concluded that there were too many political risks involved. Mobutu's soldiers might find themselves in conflict with UN troops, who had been ordered to prevent hostilities between the two opposing factions; and if it became known that the Western powers were supporting Mobutu in his "defiance" of the United Nations, the Communists and the radical African states could use this as an excuse for "more overt and effective outside aid to Gizenga."[2]

In the end the State Department fell back on Timberlake's report that Mobutu himself preferred a blockade of Orientale Province to direct military invasion. The ambassador advised Washington that such a blockade would be effective "barring substantial airborne assistance" from the Soviet bloc and the UAR, which he felt would be "most difficult" for them to arrange from the "standpoint of logistics." He predicted "economic collapse" in Stanleyville in "two to four weeks" and pointed out that once the population was "hungry and out of work" it would be extremely difficult for the Gizenga regime to maintain its position.[3]

While Mobutu was reluctant to invade Orientale Province itself, he was goaded into military action by the Lumumbist takeover in neighboring Kivu. He quickly planned an operation designed to oust the intruders: one hundred loyal troops would be flown to Bukavu to reassert Leopoldville's authority. The only problem was the fact that the airport serving Bukavu was across an international border, in the Belgian trust territory of Ruanda-Urundi. On December 28 Foreign Minister Bomboko explained the scheme to the Belgian ambassador in Brazzaville and asked for his government's cooperation. He implied that if the Belgians would help him with the Bukavu operation, he would be willing to negotiate a resumption of diplomatic relations.

The following day Kasavubu sent a note to the Belgian government via the French ambassador in Leopoldville officially requesting permission to use the airfield in Ruanda-Urundi.[4] The Belgians felt they had no choice but to help Mobutu; as the U.S. Embasssy in Brussels reported, "The Belgian government recognizes the probably adverse international repercussions" of their decision but "believes Belgium cannot stand by supinely and refuse to permit the Congolese Government to take every justifiable step in endeavoring to hold on to Kivu."[5]

The Belgian decision to support Mobutu's Bukavu operation turned out to be a diplomatic disaster—and a military fiasco as well. On December 30 Mobutu's soldiers were flown eastward, from Luluabourg, in Kasai, across the border to Ruanda-Urundi. There, the Belgian authorities, who insisted officially that their first notice of the move came when the soldiers actually landed, immediately took them by truck to the Congolese border—not to the nearest crossing point, twelve miles away, but to a point some ninety miles away, near Bukavu, their destination. When they arrived on New Year's Day, they were surprised to find that the Bukavu garrison was in fact hostile to Mobutu. They decided to surrender rather than fight.[6]

Mobutu's failure to retake Bukavu confirmed Timberlake's estimate of his military capabilities. On January 6 he reported there was little likelihood of success for "any extended military operation" mounted by Mobutu's army "without the help of foreign experts particularly in logistics and planning." Reminding his superiors that Mobutu was operating at a disadvantage, he noted, "We are reasonably sure that this element has been supplied to Gizenga's forces in Stanleyville while we have been understandably inhibited from marshaling suitable experts in aid of Mobutu."[7]

Bomboko, aware of these inhibitions, took his case directly to the NATO ambassadors in Paris and then went on to Brussels, where he asked the government for fifteen thousand automatic rifles, one hundred and twenty million francs per month to ensure the loyalty of the Leopoldville and Thysville garrisons, and one hundred Belgian officers to replace the Moroccan training instructors who had just been withdrawn. On January 12 the Belgians told the U.S. Embassy that they were willing to go along with this request, despite the risks involved, but would not do so without the "full support" of their allies, particularly the United States.[8] This put the ball back squarely in Washington's court. The Americans were not yet ready to endorse the idea of overt military aid to Mobutu,[9] and they continued to watch the military situation deteriorate with a growing sense of gloom.

American officials were equally discouraged by Kasavubu's failure to act on the political front. After his credentials victory at the General Assembly in November, he had failed to follow up by naming a government which would have some chance of gaining international respectability, despite the pleading of the U.S. government. When Timberlake raised the issue forcefully in mid-December, Kasavubu put him off once again, explaining, in his maddeningly patient way, that everything would be settled at a round table conference, which would bring together all the anti-Lumumba leaders, including the secessionists, Tshombe and Kalonji.[10] On January 2 Kasavubu announced that the round table conference would open on January 25. Three days later, however, Tshombe announced that he would not attend the conference if it were held in Leopoldville. Kasavubu, for his part, was unwilling to have the conference take place in Elisabethville, Tshombe's capital.

Timberlake reported, "Politically I feel we have come to another at least temporary dead end." Since the round table idea was proving to be "abortive," he felt "it might be more promising to encourage those leaders who are prepared to get together to form a cabinet which could be installed by Kasavubu against the day when Parliament might again be called." He added, in a surprising reversal of position:

WE ARE CERTAINLY OF THE OPINION THAT THIS SOLUTION WOULD BE BETTER THAN THE CONTINUANCE OF THE PRESENT GOVERNMENT OF COMMISSIONERS. IT SEEMS TO US ON THE SPOT THAT THE LATTER HAVE LOST MOMENTUM RECENTLY WITH TOO MANY OF THEM MORE INTERESTED IN HIGH LIFE THAN IN THE SERIOUS BUSINESS OF PROVIDING A GOVERNMENT.[11]

Timberlake, who had defended the commissioners against Dayal's contemptuous dismissal of them as lightweights and schoolboys, had evidently changed his mind and, after months of argument, had come to accept the State Department's view that they had to be replaced.

A few days later Timberlake noted the further erosion of Kasavubu's position: the highly respected pro-Lumumba speaker of the Assembly, Joseph Kasongo, who had indicated in mid-December that he would be willing to join a government named by Kasavubu and headed by the pro-Western Ileo—a move hailed by the Embassy as a sign of progress—was now disgusted by Kasavubu's attitude. He told an Embassy officer that "one can at least argue with Lumumba but Kasavubu is hopeless. He just sits and smiles even if you insult him." Kasavubu's inaction had persuaded Kasongo that the only solution was the release of Lumumba. Lumumba, he said, "now realizes he committed many errors and will act much more responsibly." Timberlake concluded:

KASONGO'S ATTITUDE IS A REFLECTION OF THE GROWING DISSATISFACTION WITH KASAVUBU'S FAILURE TO CONVENE PARLIAMENT OR TO TAKE OTHER POSITIVE ACTION. IN VIEW OF GIZENGA'S RECENT SUCCESS THE

PROSPECTS FOR INSTALLING A MODERATE GOVERNMENT, WHICH ABOUT
A MONTH AGO WERE REASONABLE, HAVE CONSIDERABLY DIMMED.[12]

Dayal and Hammarskjold: Caught in the Middle

Timberlake's frustration was compounded by the feeling that while
the United States was paying for a substantial part of the UN operation, the policy followed by Dayal was producing a situation diametrically opposed to American interests. The ambassador believed that
since Kasavubu had been seated by the General Assembly, the United
Nations should treat him and his Leopoldville government as the sole
legitimate authority in the Congo. Not only did Dayal persist in treating the Leopoldville group as one among several competing factions,
but in Timberlake's view he favored the Lumumbist faction whenever
possible. Timberlake objected to Dayal's passivity in the face of major
Lumumbist troop movements; he believed the United Nations should
restore order in the rebellious, unsettled provinces of Orientale and
Kivu, thus limiting the influence of the Lumumbists who had taken
power there or ousting them altogether.[13]

Dayal's priorities were totally different. To begin with, he believed
strongly in the role of the United Nations as an impartial arbiter, and
he would not consciously tailor his policy to favor one side or the other.
At the same time, he had become caught up emotionally in the situation. He had been exposed to Mobutu's erratic policies for four
months, and he reacted much as Hammarskjold had reacted to Lumumba's unreasonable demands the previous summer. Dayal had
started with a philosophical bias against Mobutu, whom he considered
an unconstitutional usurper who was preventing a return to parliamentary government. He grew more and more hostile to the colonel
and his American and British backers as Mobutu stepped up his harassment of the UN force, blocking its transport, stealing its trucks, and
molesting its personnel. These incidents had, in fact, increased after
Kasavubu was seated by the General Assembly in November. So Dayal
was not about to regard the Leopoldville regime as a bastion of order
and its opponents as automatic outlaws. Finally, his assessment of the
situation was colored by his anticolonialist views. While he saw the
main function of the United Nations as preventing civil war between
the various Congolese factions, he felt that Timberlake and British
Ambassador Ian Scott took a much more parochial view of the situation. As he wrote in his memoirs:

> My diary and telegrams to New York are full of detailed accounts of meet-
> ings with the Western envoys whose sole interest appeared to be the de-
> ployment of the entire U.N. force in rescuing European settlers and in
> guaranteeing protection to their extensive and far-flung properties....

Hardly a day passed when there was not a deputation of a dozen ambassadors asking for instant action in situations which though serious were often greatly exaggerated, and the U.N. Force Commander was hard put to it to find the troops to meet these influentially backed demands.[14]

Dayal's viewpoint was not unanimously shared by the UN military commanders in the Congo. General Iyassu, the Ethiopian officer who had just been named to command the UN troops in the Stanleyville area, told Timberlake that when he got there he would take firmer measures "to protect lives and property" than had been taken up to that point. He would also keep a "close watch" on the activities of the UAR contingent, which he suspected was trying to aid Gizenga. At one point he said he wished Gizenga could be arrested. Timberlake reported:

I FOUND IYASSU ACUTELY AWARE OF DANGER OF STANLEYVILLE SITUATION AND OF MEASURES WHICH NEED TO BE TAKEN. IF HE WERE GIVEN FREE HAND I AM SURE CHANCES OF SOLUTION WOULD BE GREATLY ENHANCED. UNFORTUNATELY HE FEELS HIMSELF RESTRICTED BY OVERLY IDEALISTIC EFFORTS OF DAYAL WHO WISHES AVOID APPEARANCE OF TAKING SIDES.[15]

Dayal was aware that Timberlake and the other Western envoys were critical of his policy, and he was extremely resentful of their attempts to undercut him. But if he did not have the wholehearted backing of all the military commanders in the Congo, he could count on the unstinting support of the Secretary-General, who arrived in Leopoldville on January 4 for a short visit. It was his first trip to the Congo since August, when he successfully introduced UN troops into Katanga without letting Lumumba take over the secessionist province. He had avoided seeing Lumumba at that time, although he was Prime Minister, because he feared unnecessary complications that would upset his arrangements. This time, the situation was even more complicated. Lumumba was in jail, and the United Nations was under fire from his supporters for its role in his arrest; at the same time there was a breakdown in the relations between the Secretary-General's representative and Lumumba's opponents.

Hammarskjold made no progress in repairing the breach between Dayal and the Leopoldville authorities. Dayal described his meeting with Kasavubu and with the commissioners as a *"dialogue des sourds"*—a dialogue of the deaf—with both sides talking past each other. The Congolese refused to listen to Hammarskjold's suggestion that all political prisoners should be released, and accused the United Nations of "fomenting trouble in the country." Dayal became so angry that he was speechless; he found that the Secretary-General was translating for him, rather than the other way around.[16]

Hammarskjold's sympathies were entirely with Dayal in this situation. He assured his special representative that they were "functioning on the same wavelength" and urged him to persevere in his difficult task. He shared Dayal's view that the Western envoys were overly concerned about the threat of renewed Soviet intervention in the Congo. At one point during his visit the British ambassador came to see him in an agitated state and showed him an intercepted cable from Gizenga to Khrushchev "allegedly appealing for help against an attack by Belgian paratroops on Kivu and Orientale Provinces." The Secretary-General told the ambassador there was "little physical possibility of any such help coming" and "suggested reference to a map of the world." He later remarked to Dayal that the "Leopoldville air had a strange effect on some people."[17]

The Casablanca Conference: African Allies for Khrushchev

Hammarskjold was correct in his assumption that Khrushchev was not prepared to send military aid to the Congo at this point. The Soviet leader was as frustrated by the situation there as the Americans were. While he was encouraged by the military successes of Gizenga's troops, he realized that Lumumba's position was becoming more precarious as his forces picked up additional strength—and his enemies grew more and more alarmed. Still, he was waiting to see what the Afro-Asians would do. While Hammarskjold was in Leopoldville, Lumumba's chief African supporters—Nasser, Nkrumah, Sékou Touré, King Mohamed of Morocco, and President Modibo Keita of Mali—were meeting in Casablanca, where they formed a bloc that quickly emerged as a radical counterweight to the pro-Kasavubu bloc of former French colonies that had been organized in Brazzaville in December.[18]

The Casablanca leaders were unable to agree on measures to assist Lumumba and Gizenga. Nasser, Sékou Touré, and Keita were ready to withdraw their troops from the UN force immediately and unconditionally and put them directly at the disposal of the Gizenga regime,[19] but Nkrumah refused to go along with this idea. He maintained that "withdrawal would only play into the hands of Lumumba's enemies."[20] When it came to sending arms and military equipment to Gizenga, Nkrumah, once again, was the dissenting voice. He argued that the logistical problems would be insurmountable.[21] He had already experienced difficulties on this score: on December 22 he had written to President Abboud of the Sudan, asking for landing rights at Khartoum for planes carrying food and medical supplies to Stanleyville.[22] His appeal was turned down; the Sudanese government, under considerable pressure from Washington and London,[23] refused to grant transit rights to anyone other than the UN force. After a long debate, which delayed the end of the meeting and the release of the final communiqué by one day,[24] the Casablanca conference decided against a public commitment to provide aid to the Stanleyville regime. Gizenga's name was not even mentioned.[25]

This did not mean, of course, that those leaders who wanted to send supplies to Gizenga could not proceed on their own. The Soviet government encouraged them to do so in its statement of January 12,[26] which contained no specific pledge of aid but implied strongly that the Soviet Union would be willing to follow the lead of the African states if they could find a way around the practical difficulties and work out a common policy of support for the Stanleyville regime.

The Seventh Security Council Meeting: January 12–14, 1961

In the meantime there was little the Russians could do to help either Lumumba or Gizenga but keep up their pressure on the Secretary-General by focusing the spotlight of international attention on the Congo. On January 7 Zorin wrote to the President of the Security Council calling for an urgent meeting to discuss the threat to the peace posed by Mobutu's abortive attack on Bukavu.[27] A meeting was scheduled for January 12.[28]

Hammarskjold was in South Africa by this time; he was planning to stop in Cairo and New Delhi on his way back to seek support for his Congo policy from Nasser and Nehru. He had already dealt with the incident by sending a sharply critical note to the Belgian government on January 1,[29] and he was extremely reluctant to cut short his trip and return to New York to discuss the latest Soviet charges about what he considered a comparatively minor episode. In the end, however, he felt he had to return. Nasser and Nehru would have to wait.[30]

Zorin opened the Security Council discussion by accusing Belgium of a "blatant violation of the international status of a United Nations trust territory." Ignoring the fact that the Secretary-General had rebuked Belgium, he charged that the operation had been carried out "with the knowledge and obvious connivance" of the UN command. He did not propose a draft resolution but urged the Council to condemn Belgian aggression and called for the withdrawal of all Belgian personnel from the Congo. He insisted that Lumumba be freed and endorsed the Congo resolution adopted by the Casablanca conference.[31]

The Americans found themselves in an embarrassing position. They realized that by aiding Mobutu the Belgian government had put itself on the wrong side of international law, but they were determined to prevent the adoption of a resolution condemning their NATO partner.[32] When a draft resolution critical of Belgium was introduced by the three Afro-Asian members of the Council, the United States abstained, along with six of its allies, thus ensuring its defeat. Only Zorin voted with the three sponsors.[33]

Just before the vote the Secretary-General rejected Zorin's accusations about his handling of the case as "groundless." The Soviet Union, he said, was trying to "drive a wedge" between the African states and the Secretariat but it would not succeed. The African delegates could judge for themselves Soviet "flattery and efforts to win them by sowing hate and distrust."[34]

The fact that Zorin and Hammarskjold were trading charges once again did not mean that the old partnership between the Secretary-General and the Americans had been revived. On the contrary, American officials still felt that Hammarskjold was yielding too much to Soviet pressure, and they were eager to exert some counterpressure of their own. The State Department instructed Wadsworth to tell the Secretary-General that if the Congo fell under "Communist domination" while the United Nations was "sharing major responsibility" for the security of the country, the impact on "US public and Congressional opinion" was likely to be "extremely damaging." For the first time, the Americans demanded that Dayal be replaced as soon as possible. They asserted that they had "no doubt" of Dayal's sympathy for the restoration of Lumumba to power and charged that his conduct of the UN operation had "contributed substantially" to the deterioration of the situation in the Congo.[35]

Hammarskjold reacted to this demand "with emotion and anger." He told Wadsworth that he was "very determined" to keep Dayal at his post. He had concluded after his visit to Leopoldville that Dayal "was being subjected to unfair and malevolent attacks," which came primarily from the Congolese but were inspired by the Western Embassies. He insisted that "he knew much more about Dayal's attitude and position than anyone else, and he regarded Dayal as completely loyal" to the United Nations.

While Wadsworth found Hammarskjold's "general attitude" to be "antagonistic" to the U.S. approach, he was "not too concerned." He could take some satisfaction in the outcome of the Security Council meeting and in the fact that Hammarskjold had finally come to accept Washington's evidence about the subversive role the UAR was playing in the Congo. He hoped that in time he might come around on the question of Dayal as well.[36]

The Death of Lumumba

None of the other U.S. officials dealing with the Congo were as complacent as Wadsworth. They had a sense that time was running out, that events were moving so quickly that the situation would soon be out of control. This sense of urgency reached a climax just one week before the Kennedy Administration took office, when it appeared for a few hours that Lumumba might be on his way back to power.

On the morning of January 13 the garrison at Thysville, the town ninety miles from Leopoldville where Lumumba was being held prisoner, mutinied, demanding higher pay. At noon Ambassador Timberlake alerted the State Department. The CIA had just informed him that Kasavubu, Mobutu, Bomboko and security chief Victor Nendaka had flown hurriedly to Thysville in an attempt to contain the mutiny before word of it reached other military units. Despite Kasavubu's desire to keep the news from spreading, the press had found out about his trip and, according to Timberlake, were "on the trail of the story."[37] Rumors that Lumumba had been freed and was on his way to Leopoldville at the head of the disaffected troops swept through the capital. Hundreds of Europeans and anti-Lumumba Congolese fled the city in near panic. The ferries to Brazzaville were filled to capacity, and after they stopped running, at sunset, a number of desperate Belgians hired motor launches and risked the dangerous after-dark crossing. By evening the nervous capital learned that Kasavubu had won back the mutinous garrison with promises of a substantial pay raise, and Lumumba was back under lock and key. He had been at liberty for a few hours, but when Kasavubu and his colleagues offered him a ministerial post in Ileo's government, he refused to have anything to do with them. He insisted he would accept liberty only as head of the legitimate government.[38] It was a brave, principled stand, but it turned out to be the most disastrous in a series of impetuous, politically foolhardy acts that led to Lumumba's destruction.

The mutiny did not come as a complete surprise to Lumumba's opponents. Kasavubu and his closest allies had had their doubts about the reliability of the Thysville garrison for some time. They were troubled by the fact that Lumumba had had Christmas dinner with the officers and by reports that he was fraternizing with the soldiers. They knew what a persuasive speaker he was, and they did not think it at all unlikely that he would turn the tables once more and lead a march on the capital.[39] Furthermore, there had been unrest for several days in Leopoldville, where the soldiers were demanding higher pay.[40] Devlin, the CIA station chief, who realized that the unrest would inevitably strengthen the Lumumbists, had warned Kasavubu and his colleagues that both the army and the police were ready to mutiny "unless drastic action" was taken to satisfy their demands.[41]

Still, even if they were not completely unexpected, the events of January 13 came as a shock to Kasavubu. Not since September 5, when he announced Lumumba's ouster, had he moved so quickly. He had managed to deal with the immediate threat in Thysville, but he knew this was only a temporary solution. He and his advisers had been discussing the question of transferring Lumumba to a more secure prison since December, but now they were convinced it was time to act.

The first and most obvious choice was Elisabethville, Tshombe's capital. There was a precedent for sending Lumumba there; back in September Tshombe had agreed to take custody of Gizenga and another ally of Lumumba who were accused of a plot against Mobutu's life. At the last minute Dayal had persuaded Mobutu to release them.[42] Kasavubu and Mobutu had sent an emissary to Tshombe several days before the mutiny to ask him to take custody of Lumumba, but they were unwilling at first to accept his terms.[43]

The next alternative was Bakwanga, capital of Kalonji's secessionist state of South Kasai, where Lumumba would be at the mercy of his worst enemies, the Baluba, who were eager to make him pay for the atrocities of the August campaign. According to one account, Kasavubu's Belgian advisers preferred Bakwanga because they considered it less controversial than Elisabethville, where the Belgian presence was much more noticeable.[44] On January 14, just one day after the mutiny, Devlin's Congolese government sources told him that the decision had been made: Lumumba would be transferred to a prison in Bakwanga.[45]

By January 16 all the arrangements were set. Before dawn on January 17, Nendaka, Fernand Kazadi, the Commissioner for Defense, and a small group of soldiers arrived in Thysville. They sent a politician named Jonas Mukamba, whom Lumumba knew and trusted, to tell him that a coup in his favor had taken place in Leopoldville and that he was to return immediately to form a new government. With some difficulty they persuaded the troops guarding Lumumba to relinquish their prisoner as well as the two companions who had been arrested with him, Maurice Mpolo and Joseph Okito. They drove about twenty-five miles to Lukala, to a small landing strip belonging to a cement company, where they were picked up by a light plane chartered from Air Brousse, a Belgian-owned airline. They then flew to Moanda, on the coast, where an Air Congo DC-4 was waiting. The locations had been chosen carefully: neither of these airstrips was manned by a UN garrison, so there was no danger that the prisoners would be snatched away. The DC-4 took off for Bakwanga with Kazadi and the prisoners aboard, but in mid-flight the pilot was ordered to take the prisoners to Elisabethville instead. No reason was given for the sudden change of plans.[46] Lumumba and his two companions were brutally beaten throughout the five-hour flight by their guards, who were Baluba tribesmen; the treatment of the prisoners was so cruel that the Belgian crew, after ineffectual protests, locked themselves in their cabin. (Ghana's President Nkrumah later commented, "I can think of a more courageous reaction, though doubtless they considered it no part of their business to interfere."[47])

When the plane landed in Elisabethville, it was immediately surrounded by jeeps, trucks, an armored vehicle, and approximately one hundred and thirty Katangan troops. There were only six Swedish UN soldiers on duty, at the opposite end of the airfield. They watched from a distance as a high-ranking official stepped out of the plane, followed by three blindfolded prisoners with their hands tied behind their backs. One had a small beard. As they stumbled off the plane, they were kicked and beaten by the Katangan soldiers—in the presence of their Belgian officers—and then thrown into a jeep and driven off, never to be seen again.[48]

There was a great deal of confusion and uncertainty about Lumumba's whereabouts over the next few weeks—until the Katanga authorities announced, first, his escape, on February 10, and then his capture and death, on February 13. Their version of Lumumba's death was accepted by no one. The subsequent UN investigation was unable to establish any definite account of his death, but the best information available suggested that he and his two companions were murdered immediately after their arrival in Katanga, on the night of January 17, by Katanga officials and Belgian mercenaries, with the personal participation or approval of Tshombe and his Interior Minister, Godefroid Munongo.[49] According to one version that made the diplomatic rounds, Munongo helped kill Lumumba and then telephoned Tshombe, who was at a dinner party. Tshombe returned from the phone looking gray.

Although Tshombe put up a fairly effective smokescreen, insisting that Lumumba was alive and well, there was no shortage of speculation about his fate or of rumors that he had already been killed. The U.S. consul in Elisabethville, William Canup, felt that international pressure on Tshombe might make it "impossible" for him to continue to hold Lumumba alive. He reported on January 18 that there was a "certain chance" that the Katanga authorities would "permit harm to him, possibly 'suicide' or other mishap."[50]

UN officials, who were sensitive to charges that they had failed to protect Lumumba from mistreatment at the Elisabethville airport, hoped against hope that this speculation would prove untrue. In fact, Hammarskjold's aide Wieschhoff told an American diplomat in New York that Lumumba was "in no great danger of losing his life" because the Congolese had "no record of killing their political leaders"; they were more apt to "indicate their displeasure by beating them (preferably by rifle butt)."[51] The UN representative in Elisabethville, Ian Berendsen, warned Tshombe the day after Lumumba's arrival that if he were harmed, it was likely to produce "severe international censure of Katanga."[52] Tshombe admitted that he had seen Lumumba and his companions shortly after their arrival and said they were in a sad state after the beatings on the plane. The following day Berendsen brought Tshombe a message from the Secretary-General urging that the prisoners be treated humanely, that they receive a fair trial, and that representatives of the Red Cross be permitted to visit them. Hammarskjold also sent a message to Kasavubu demanding that Lumumba be brought back to Leopoldville and assured a fair trial. While Tshombe continued to receive Berendsen—and to lie to him about Lumumba's condition—Kasavubu, who had demanded Dayal's recall, refused to meet with the Secretary-General's representative and ignored his communications.[53]

Meanwhile, the State Department, which was operating on the assumption that Lumumba was still alive, told Canup that if there was any truth to the press reports that Lumumba had been "severely beaten" in the presence of a white officer, he should inform Tshombe that the U.S. government deplored this sort of treatment and hoped Lumumba would be given "humane treatment" and "medical attention as necessary" and that his case would be disposed of in accordance with law.[54] When Canup raised these questions with Munongo on January 20, the Interior Minister assured him that Lumumba was "in safe keeping outside Elisabethville" and was receiving the "same treatment as any prisoner anywhere" in the world. He did not, however, indicate that Lumumba was being "well-treated" or was in "good physical condition." At the same time, Canup reported that the Katanga government had issued a denial that Lumumba had been beaten on his arrival in Elisabethville, explaining that he had "arrived with head injuries."[55]

Canup was somewhat skeptical about these assurances. He cabled Washington: "Believe impossible totally disregard persistent rumors Patrice Lumumba died shortly after arrival as result mistreatment here. Minister Interior Munongo denied rumors to me but continuing mystery of Lumumba's whereabouts obliges me to keep open mind."[56]

Fury in Moscow

The Russians, understandably, were outraged. Their reaction to the tumultuous events of the past few weeks had been the mirror image of the Americans' reaction: each Lumumbist success buoyed their hopes as it intensified American fears. While they would never admit it publicly, they must have realized that their constant attacks on Hammarskjold had produced a gradual shift in UN policy. A few more victories by Gizenga's forces, a few more defections from the still unformed Ileo government—and Lumumba would be back in power, and Khrushchev's flamboyant gamble would no longer look so foolhardy to his conservative Kremlin colleagues. Running through the elation of January, however, was the constant fear that Lumumba himself might be eliminated from the picture; and now the warnings about his safety were turning out to be fully justified.

The Soviet press had followed in unusual detail the developments of the preceding week—the mutiny in Thysville, Kasavubu's hasty trip to placate the rebellious soldiers, Lumumba's refusal to negotiate with him. Even though the mutiny was put down, *Pravda* ended its account on an upbeat note, citing a Reuters report that Lumumba's supporters in Leopoldville, backed by part of the local garrison, were preparing a large demonstration to demand that he be freed.[57] On January 16, however, there was a new note of alarm in the Soviet coverage. *Pravda* reported the rumors circulating in Leopoldville that Mobutu feared a repetition of the Thysville mutiny and wanted to see Lumumba transferred to a "safe place."[58]

On January 18 *Pravda* published a brief bulletin noting that Lumumba had been taken by plane "under strong guard" to Elisabethville, headquarters of the "Belgian puppet, Tshombe."[59] The following day, when there was more information available, the Soviet newspaper reported the brutal treatment of Lumumba and accused the U.S. government of masterminding the entire move. *Pravda* charged that Ambassador Timberlake had been responsible for Lumumba's ouster and for Mobutu's "appearance on the scene and his illegal expulsion of the diplomatic representatives of a number of socialist and African countries." It then explained that "from Eisenhower's point of view these developments in the Congo were a compensation for the American defeat in Cuba." Recently, however, Timberlake's "successes" were turning sour; Mobutu, despite all the "help he was getting from the United Nations and the United States," was proving to be a "bad strategist and an even worse politician," and the Lumumbists now controlled one-third of the country. Timberlake, worried by this turn of events, was "preparing a new blow" against the Congo's independence. "The life of Lumumba is in danger," *Pravda* warned.[60]

On January 20 Victor Mayevskii, *Pravda*'s senior foreign affairs analyst, reported that President Keita of Mali had warned that if Lumumba were not released immediately he might be killed. "According to M. Keita," he stated, "a large sum of money has reached the Congo through Paris and Brazzaville to be paid to 'hired murderers' who have been instructed to destroy Lumumba." Citing a *New York Times* report about the deteriorating military and political position of Kasa-vubu and Mobutu, Mayevskii charged that the Americans and the Belgians were "preparing to do away with" Lumumba out of desperation and fear that his fight for "freedom and independence" would be successful.[61]

The Role of the CIA

As far as the U.S. role is concerned, Mayevskii was closer to the truth than most Americans outside the government believed at the time. Documents released in the few past years have revealed that it was not for want of trying that the CIA failed to assassinate Lumumba and left the job, in the end, to the Belgians and the Katangans. A review of the evidence leaves little doubt that U.S. officials encouraged Lumumba's Congolese opponents to eliminate him at a time when it appeared that he might resume his position as Prime Minister and turn the clock back to the summer of 1960, with the Russians restored to a position of influence.

U.S. officials were disturbed not only by the military successes of the Lumumbist forces and Mobutu's failure to respond to them, by the political successes of the Lumumbists and Kasavubu's failure to respond to them, by the attitude of Dayal and Hammarskjold's failure to respond to American advice about how to deal with him; they were also alarmed by a number of new factors, which cropped up in mid-January. First, there was the unpredictable nature of the UN Conciliation Commission, which was determined to meet with all factions in the Congo, including the imprisoned Lumumba. While the Nigerian chairman, Wachuku, was critical of Dayal's policy, there were indications that the rest of the Commission would call for a resumption of Parliament or for the establishment of a broad-based government including Lumumba. Among those who were concerned about this prospect was Cordier, Hammarskjold's assistant, who felt that any new government including Lumumba would mean the end of the UN operation in the Congo.[62] Next, there was Kasavubu's plan for a round table conference, which was still scheduled to open on January 25, even though Tshombe had refused to attend; there were rumors that because of Kasavubu's political weakness, he would be forced to release Lumumba in time for him to participate in the conference.[63] Next, there were unconfirmed reports that the Casablanca powers had secretly agreed to use their troops in the UN force to support a pro-Lumumba coup d'état.[64] Finally, there was considerable uncertainty about the steadfastness of the troops in the Leopoldville area. When Devlin reported to CIA headquarters on January 12 about the unrest in the army and the police force, he stressed the political implications of a mutiny, warning that it "almost certainly would . . . bring about [Lumumba's] return to power."[65] The mutiny in Thysville the following day drove his point home.

Both the State Department and the CIA were afraid that one way or another, Lumumba would return to power—either through military action or through a reconvened Parliament or round table. On January 13 Devlin sent an alarming cable to Washington:

STATION AND EMBASSY BELIEVE PRESENT GOVERNMENT MAY FALL WITH-
IN FEW DAYS. RESULT WOULD ALMOST CERTAINLY BE CHAOS AND RE-
TURN [LUMUMBA] TO POWER.

Devlin was totally opposed to the idea of reconvening Parliament under UN supervision—an idea to which Timberlake had paid lip service, if the conditions were right, that is, once Kasavubu and Ileo had formed a government and an anti-Lumumba majority was assured. The CIA station chief found this unacceptable. He warned:

THE COMBINATION OF [LUMUMBA'S] POWERS AS DEMAGOGUE, HIS ABLE
USE OF GOON SQUADS AND PROPAGANDA AND SPIRIT OF DEFEAT WITHIN
[GOVERNMENT] COALITION WHICH WOULD INCREASE RAPIDLY UNDER
SUCH CONDITIONS WOULD ALMOST CERTAINLY INSURE [LUMUMBA] VIC-
TORY IN PARLIAMENT.

He then added:

REFUSAL TAKE DRASTIC STEPS AT THIS TIME WILL LEAD TO DEFEAT OF
[UNITED STATES] POLICY IN CONGO.[66]

What did Devlin mean by "drastic steps"? The *Senate Intelligence Committee Report* noted that neither this cable nor the one sent the previous day, warning of the likelihood of a mutiny that would put Lumumba back into power, was sent through the secret PROP channel, and that neither referred to assassination "even indirectly"[67]—but that was hardly necessary. Since Lumumba was already in the custody of the Leopoldville authorities, there was no longer any point in surrounding his residence with hired assassins armed with poisoned toothpaste; he could simply be left to the tender mercies of his enemies.

The day after the mutiny the CIA station chief was informed by his high-level Congolese sources that Lumumba was going to be transferred to a prison in Bakwanga; it did not take much imagination to figure out that his life would be in jeopardy there. As the Senate report noted: "Cables from the Station Officer demonstrated no CIA involvement in the plan to transport Lumumba to Bakwanga. But the Station Officer clearly had prior knowledge of the plan to transfer Lumumba to a state where it was probable that he would be killed."[68] Neither Devlin nor any other American official lifted a finger to prevent this transfer; no one suggested that Lumumba be brought to trial in Leopoldville or released, with the other prisoners, as Hammarskjold had recommended, to attend a round table conference or a reconvened Parliament. U.S. officials, by their silence, or their tacit encouragement, were following a policy that had been set the previous summer, when Dulles compared Lumumba to Castro, and Eisenhower agreed he was a threat to world peace: they were to get rid of Lumumba, one way or another. If murder directly ordered by the U.S. government and carried out by an assassin hired by the CIA was acceptable, then murder carried out by Lumumba's Congolese opponents, with the help of the Belgians, was not going to offend anyone's sensibilities.

At some point between January 14 and 17 a decision was made to send Lumumba to Elisabethville instead of to Bakwanga. At the time it appeared that this was a last-minute change of plans; according to one version, Lumumba's captors were afraid that the UN troops stationed at Bakwanga, who were Ghanaian, would intervene and rescue Lumumba; according to another, Kasavubu had a sudden change of heart and communicated his decision to the pilot by radio.[69] Tshombe insisted to Berendsen and to anyone else who would listen that he was completely surprised by the news of Lumumba's arrival; while the Leopoldville authorities had asked him for some time to take custody of the prisoners, he had consistently refused. More recently he had agreed to consider the idea in principle, but he had never given Kasavubu a definite answer.[70] Then, suddenly, "Lumumba was dropped into his lap, making the whole thing a fait accompli."[71]

There was some speculation, however, that Elisabethville had been the destination all along. Dayal, for example, doubted that there was a last-minute change; he cited, among other things, the preparations that had been made at the Elisabethville airport to receive the prisoners.[72] Moreover, according to the U.S. Consulate in Elisabethville, some five hundred supporters of Lumumba were rounded up and arrested between January 14 and 17[73]—which suggests some foreknowledge on Tshombe's part. Another indication that the decision to send Lumumba to Elisabethville was the result of the ongoing negotiations between Kasavubu, Mobutu, and Tshombe was the fact that on January 17, the very day that Lumumba was flown to Katanga, both sides announced that the long-delayed round table conference would take place in early February—in Elisabethville.[74] This concession may have been Kasavubu's payment to Tshombe for taking charge of his troublesome prisoner.[75]

If the plan to send Lumumba to Elisabethville instead of Bakwanga was not a last-minute decision, as seems likely, it would also seem likely that the CIA station chief in Leopoldville, with his excellent sources, would have been informed of the switch; but in his testimony before the Senate Intelligence Committee he insisted that he was not informed about it. The CIA had apparently decided, in the post-Watergate environment of 1975, that it was better to admit an intelligence failure than to admit any sort of involvement in, or knowledge of, Lumumba's murder in Katanga. While Devlin conceded that the CIA was in close contact with Congolese officials who "quite clearly knew" of the decision to send Lumumba to Katanga "because they were involved,"[76] he maintained that neither he nor Ambassador Timberlake knew anything about the change of plans. "To the best of my knowledge," he told the Senate committee, "neither the Station nor the Embassy had any input in the decision to send him to Katanga."[77] Devlin's testimony was supported by the famous cable sent to headquarters by the CIA base chief in Elisabethville on January 19, two days after Lumumba was flown to Katanga:

> THANKS FOR PATRICE. IF WE HAD KNOWN HE WAS COMING WE WOULD HAVE BAKED A SNAKE.

The base chief added that his local sources had given him "no advance word whatsoever" of Lumumba's flight to Katanga; evidently no information had leaked from Leopoldville either. In fact, he was so much in the dark about what was going on that he informed headquarters that the Congolese central government "does not plan to liquidate Lumumba"[78]—and this was written two days after Lumumba was killed.

CIA officials point to this cable as evidence that they were in no way involved in Lumumba's death. As the Senate report stated:

> Despite his perception of an urgent need to prevent Lumumba's return to power at this time, the Station Officer testified that the CIA was not involved in bringing about Lumumba's death in Katanga and that he did not have any first-hand knowledge of the circumstances of Lumumba's death.[79]

Devlin's immediate superior, Bronson Tweedy, told the committee there was no CIA involvement "whatsoever" in Lumumba's death. "The fate of Lumumba in the end was purely an African event," he said.[80] Other CIA officials took the same line.

In a technical sense that may very well be true. By establishing that they had no idea Lumumba was to be sent to Katanga, CIA officials could wash their hands of whatever happened to him after he arrived. But the larger picture remains the same. If U.S. officials had no objection to Bakwanga, one must assume that if they *had* been informed about the change of plans, they would have had no objection to Elisabethville either. The result would have been identical. Devlin recognized this clearly when he told the committee, "I think there was a general assumption, once we learned he had been sent to Katanga, that his goose was cooked, because Tshombe hated him and looked on him as a danger and a rival."[81]

Certainly American diplomats in Elisabethville did not match even the halfhearted efforts of the United Nations to save Lumumba's life. When the U.S. consul, Canup, called on Munongo on January 20 to urge humane treatment of Lumumba, he pointed out that the State Department's "interest in his welfare" stemmed from "considerations of international opinion and not from tender feelings toward him." Munongo replied that he did not care about "world opinion" and said he was "astounded" that the U.S. government would raise questions about the welfare of one prisoner when the "Communist Lumumba" was responsible for so many deaths throughout the Congo. At this point Canup thought it the better part of valor not to broach the other sensitive issue he had been instructed to raise—the recent arrival in Elisabethville of hundreds of European mercenaries.[82]

Canup had first gotten wind of Tshombe's latest plan for combatting the Lumumbist invasion of North Katanga two weeks before. Tshombe's Belgian military adviser, Major Guy Weber, explained that Tshombe had lost confidence in his own troops, who were "frequently undisciplined, given to inter-tribal disputes, and increasingly suspicious of white officers"—so much so that "several minor mutinies" had occurred. Tshombe had agreed to the "organization of an entirely white company to be recruited in Belgium, France, etc., which would serve as protection" if the African forces got out of hand. Tshombe remarked to Weber, "In these matters I trust only whites."[83] Several days later Canup reported the arrival of the first two or three hundred recruits—"Belgian paratroopers, former members of German SS and former Italian Fascist soldiers." The Katanga government had attempted to conceal the operation, but "reliable sources" informed the Consulate that the recruits were taken directly from the airport to a "nearby staging area before being sent to camps and operational units farther north."[84]

The State Department, sensitive to the impact this unsavory news would have, suggested that Canup point out to Tshombe that his recruitment of European mercenaries, coming on top of the brutal treatment of Lumumba, would "further isolate him" from even the moderate Africans and "further discredit all pro-Western moderates" in the Congo.[85] Now, after his stormy conversation with Munongo, Canup cabled Washington for further instructions. He wondered if the matter of Lumumba's treatment should be taken up with Tshombe himself and offered his opinion that such a move would be "counterproductive," and would "dissipate" the "little remaining influence" the U.S. government still had in Elisabethville. In addition, he said he believed that "any effort to convince the Katanga government not to make use of its white legion" in combating the Lumumbist forces in the north was "doomed to failure" and would "probably lead to another explosive incident" between Tshombe and the Consulate.[86]

January 20 was a Friday, Inauguration Day, and Canup did not get his reply until the following Monday, the first working day of the new Administration. It was signed by the new Secretary of State, Dean Rusk, but it revealed no change from the arm's-length attitude of the previous week. The State Department replied:

APPROACH TO MUNONGO APPEARS SUFFICIENT ACTION RE LUMUMBA AT LEAST FOR TIME BEING AND AGREE DÉMARCHE TO TSHOMBE MIGHT BE COUNTER-PRODUCTIVE.[87]

It is somewhat ironic that the first official instructions of the Kennedy Administration dealing directly with Lumumba's plight should have been so similar to the approach taken by the Eisenhower Administration, since there is some evidence to suggest that one of the reasons for the hasty disposal of Lumumba may have been concern on the part of his enemies that the new Kennedy Administration would adopt a totally new policy—one that would envisage the freeing of all political prisoners, including Lumumba, and the reconvening of Parliament. This was the policy Dayal and Hammarskjold had been advocating, a policy which the hardliners in the State Department and the CIA believed would result inevitably in Lumumba's return to power.

The first straw in the wind appeared on December 12, when a group of U.S. Senators headed by Tennessee's Albert Gore, Kennedy's replacement as chairman of the Senate Foreign Relations Committee's Subcommittee on Africa, and Frank Church of Idaho, a first-term liberal, met for two hours with Ghana's President Nkrumah after their fact-finding visit to the Congo. They were accompanied by the President-elect's youngest brother, Edward Kennedy. The Congressional delegation "urged vigorously" that all members of the Congolese Parliament should be released. Their position was in clear contrast to the position of the Eisenhower Administration, which had studiously avoided advocating the release of all the political prisoners for fear that Lumumba would again end up on top. Three days later in a major speech, Nkrumah, who had previously demanded only the release of Lumumba, broadened his demand to reflect the view of the delegation from Washington.[88] On a continent where family ties were the most important ingredients of political life, Edward Kennedy's position was read as an indication of the position his brother would take—

even though John Kennedy had taken a hard line on the Congo during the campaign.

The next indication was a conversation Ambassador Timberlake had with Dayal on December 14, a few weeks after the UN official returned from New York. Relations between the two men had reached a low point. Dayal had been telling a series of American journalists, including Stewart Alsop, Paul Hoffman of *The New York Times*, and Irving R. Levine of NBC, that it was Timberlake's fault that the Congo was on the verge of civil war. When Dayal implied that the United States was "in league with the Belgians" in a drive to "get the UN out of the Congo," Timberlake assured him that this was not the case and explained that some of the Belgian advisers in the Congo were serving a useful function. At this point Dayal remarked pointedly that he had been "reassured" by his conversations in New York with Dean Rusk, Chester Bowles, and Averell Harriman, all of whom were "satisfied that the new administration would take a firm position especially with regard to the problem presented by Belgium and Belgian technicians."[89] By the time Dayal related this conversation to Timberlake, Rusk and Bowles had been named to the two top State Department posts, and it was assumed that Harriman would be given a high-level post as well. Although Dayal was later disappointed by Rusk's attitude when he actually became Secretary of State, the impression created by the conversation in New York was more important than the subsequent reality.

Apparently Dayal's impression was widespread among UN officials in the Congo. On January 6 a U.S. Embassy official talked with Gustavo Duran, the new UN representative in Stanleyville, who was in town for Hammarskjold's visit. Duran told him that he had had a long conversation with Gizenga, whom he found "highly intelligent," and that when "Gizenga voiced anti-American sentiments," Duran "counseled patience," stating that "changes" would occur when Kennedy, Rusk, Stevenson, and Bowles took office.[90]

By the beginning of January, it was generally accepted by officials and diplomats in the Congo, even in far-off Stanleyville, that a change could be expected from the new Administration—and if it was a change that would be welcomed by Gizenga, or Dayal, it was ipso facto a change that would not be welcomed by Timberlake, Devlin, Kasavubu, Mobutu, Tshombe, or the Belgians. The Belgians, like their European neighbors, had not forgotten Kennedy's maiden foreign policy speech in the Senate, in 1957, when he advocated the independence of Algeria while America's NATO ally, France, was engaged in a long, drawn-out war against the Algerian rebels. They were uneasy about the fact that Kennedy was not part of the NATO-oriented establishment and about his deliberate emphasis on Africa, which they feared would be detrimental to the interests of the colonial powers of Europe. Given this background, they were not surprised by the reports that Kennedy would strike out on his own in the Congo—but they were worried about them.

It does not seem farfetched to suggest that much of the sense of urgency in the first few weeks of January which led to the death of Lumumba came not from the internal situation in the Congo, troubling though that may have been, but from fear of the impending change in Washington. The coincidence in dates is striking: Lumumba was flown to Katanga on January 17 and probably murdered immediately; the Kennedy Administration took office on January 20, three days later.

PART TWO
The Kennedy Policy

CHAPTER NINE

The Changing of the Guard
(January 21–March 1, 1961)

"Lumumba is apparently the best rabble rouser speaker in the Congo ...
and everybody fears that if he just is let loose a little, he will end up by
having control of everything."

A FEW DAYS AFTER John F. Kennedy was sworn in as President, the new Assistant Secretary of State for International Organization Affairs, Harlan Cleveland, found himself chairing a high-level meeting devoted to the Congo, the Kennedy Administration's first foreign policy crisis. The former editor, publisher, and academician felt considerably outranked. The other participants at the meeting were four former governors with a long history of service to their party and country: Adlai Stevenson of Illinois, twice the Democratic candidate for President and now the U.S. ambassador to the United Nations, with cabinet rank; W. Averell Harriman of New York, Roosevelt's ambassador to Moscow and London, Truman's Secretary of Commerce and his choice for the presidential nomination in 1956, now Kennedy's roving ambassador; Chester Bowles of Connecticut, Truman's ambassador to India, Kennedy's leading foreign policy adviser during the campaign, and now Under Secretary of State; and G. Mennen Williams of Michigan, a popular four-term governor who was now Assistant Secretary of State for African Affairs. Two of these men, Stevenson and Bowles, had been considered front-runners for the job of Secretary of State in the new Administration, speculation encouraged by Kennedy in the period between his nomination and election victory. One of them, Williams, was the first top diplomatic appointment announced by Kennedy, even before he chose Dean Rusk as Secretary of State. The timing of Williams's appointment was intended to demonstrate that the continent of Africa would play an important role in Kennedy's foreign policy.

Their mandate, Cleveland recalled, was to review the developments of the past six months and come up with new recommendations—quickly. They were to consider all possibilities, even the most outrageous; they were not to be bound by the precedents set by the Eisen-

[199]

hower Administration. Lumumba's opponents were correct in their assumption that Kennedy favored a new approach in the Congo, but he did not come into office with a detailed blueprint in his pocket. He was certain of only one thing: the Congo situation was so dangerous that it might explode into a full-scale civil war involving the Soviet Union and the United States unless action was taken to defuse the crisis. He ordered the State Department to devise a dynamic new policy that would eliminate the threat of a Soviet takeover and would, at the same time, emphasize America's interest in working with the new nations of Africa.

This high-level assault on the Congo problem was typical of Kennedy's activist approach to most foreign policy issues. The new President was personally involved in the formulation of American Congo policy. Over the next two years, he would issue a steady stream of questions and suggestions, prodding the State Department to take more decisive action. He would not be satisfied until the Soviet threat was removed.

It is ironic, in retrospect, that in those early days of the Kennedy Administration, when the new policymakers were willing to consider unorthodox ways of dealing with an inherited crisis, they apparently were unaware that the most intractable element of that crisis no longer existed. Patrice Lumumba, the major obstacle to a peaceful solution on terms acceptable to the United States, had been eliminated before President Kennedy took office.

Hammering Out a New Congo Policy

For ten days, a battle raged within the U.S. government about the new Congo policy. It was part of a larger foreign policy debate that had begun in December and continued through January and February, by which time the policy lines were basically set. It was a classic argument between liberals and conservatives, innovators and traditionalists.

On one side was a loose coalition that ranged from the liberal Stevenson wing of the Democratic Party to the more hardheaded Soviet specialists in the U.S. Foreign Service. It included such articulate New Frontiersmen as Chester Bowles and Harvard professors John Kenneth Galbraith and Arthur Schlesinger, Jr., who had supplied much of the foreign policy rhetoric of Kennedy's campaign. This group heartily endorsed Kennedy's contention that the country needed a change, especially in two vital foreign policy areas—relations with the emerging nations of Africa and Asia and relations with the Soviet Union—two areas which they felt were closely related.

They believed that the Eisenhower Administration had displayed too little imagination and ignored too many promising opportunities in its dealings with the new Third World nations, and they meant to rectify this. Neutrality was no longer to be considered immoral, as in the days of John Foster Dulles; controversial nonaligned leaders, such as Nasser, Nkrumah, Sukarno, and Sékou Touré, were not to be avoided; they were to be welcomed at the White House and given a sympathetic hearing and a frank explanation of American problems and policies.

These leaders were not to be wooed merely for their own sake: the American courtship of the uncommitted, particularly in Africa, was closely linked to U.S. policy toward the Soviet Union. During the campaign Kennedy had criticized Eisenhower's lack of interest in the new African states and had warned that Khrushchev's barrage of aid and propaganda was about to win them over to the Communist side in the cold war. Particularly in such places as the UAR, Ghana, and Guinea, the New Frontier approach was designed to thwart Soviet ambitions and to present radical new regimes with an alternative source of aid and support.

Africa, of course, was only one area of competition with the Soviet Union. Kennedy had pledged in his campaign speeches that he would do a better job of defending American interests against Soviet expansionism on all fronts. His cold war rhetoric, however, did not exclude the possibility of accommodation with the Soviet Union in the interests of peace. On this point he listened carefully to the arguments of a trio of highly respected Soviet specialists—two former ambassadors to Moscow, George Kennan and Charles Bohlen, and the current ambassador, Llewellyn Thompson—who were backed up by the experienced Averell Harriman. They felt that basic relations between the two great powers must be retrieved from the low point reached after the U-2 incident. New talks, perhaps a new summit meeting, might steer them back on a course that would keep the peace, at least the nuclear peace, of the world. An early meeting between Kennedy and Khrushchev might help pave the way toward agreement on Berlin, disarmament, nuclear testing, Laos, and several less important but useful symbolic issues. Thompson in particular felt that Kennedy would not really know what he was up against until he had met and talked with Khrushchev.

Another influential voice in favor of personal contact with Khrushchev was Adlai Stevenson, who was fairly sanguine about the prospects of an accommodation with the Soviet leader. "I think we will not find anyone easier to deal with than Khrushchev is," he told Kennedy a few days before the inauguration. He recommended as a first step that the President send a high-ranking emissary to Moscow (he suggested himself) to find out what Khrushchev was thinking and to learn more about his problems with the extremists in Peking and Moscow. "I think it is important to find out whether he wants to expand the cold war," Stevenson said. "Does he want an effective UN, or is he deter-

mined to destroy it? I know how he reveals himself in conversation,"
he explained, and such a mission could "determine quite a good deal,
especially if he wants to do business." Stevenson argued that it was
time for the United States to make an overture:

> I think they have been taking the initiative too long now. This would re-
> capture the world's imagination which is one of the first jobs to be done—
> and I don't think we can do it by being too cautious.[1]

On the other side of the debate were the men who believed very
much in caution, especially when it came to dealing with the Soviet
Union. They included such senior advisers as Dean Acheson, Truman's
Secretary of State and the architect of the NATO alliance, and John J.
McCloy, Kennedy's disarmament adviser and the archetype of the
"Eastern Establishment" figure—a Republican who served Republican
and Democratic Presidents alike in demanding foreign policy roles.
These men took a more skeptical view of Khrushchev's interest in accommodation and of Soviet intentions in general. They preferred to
emphasize the solidarity of the NATO alliance and deal with the Russians from a position of strength. All across the board they favored
more traditional policies; they did not believe in change for the sake of
change. They felt that Stevenson, Bowles, and Williams were overem-
phasizing the importance of the Afro-Asian countries and the United
Nations. McCloy summed up his philosophy later in the year in a tren-
chant remark:

> World opinion? I don't believe in world opinion. The only thing that mat-
> ters is power. What we have to do now is to show that we are a powerful
> nation and not spend our time trailing after the phantom of world
> opinion.[2]

McCloy and Acheson backed the policies of America's NATO allies
whenever they came into conflict with the anticolonialist views of the
Africans and their supporters among the New Frontiersmen. Their
views on this subject were shared by Paul Nitze, a brilliant foreign
policy analyst who had worked for Truman and had just been named
Assistant Secretary of Defense for International Security Affairs.

This policy debate made for a lively few months, with each side leak-
ing its point of view to the press. Speculation and analysis flourished.
After an intensive period of foreign policy review, the views of the first
group emerged as the dominant attitude of the Kennedy Administration. The new President had decided to work toward some sort of accommodation with the Soviet Union, to the extent that this was
possible, and at the same time to meet the Soviet challenge in the developing countries through greater American initiative and understanding. This liberal approach, however, was tempered by caution, in

large part as a result of Kennedy's experience with the Russians during the Congo crisis.

The President and the Secretary of State had told the officials working on the Congo not to be inhibited by past attitudes. "Take the ceiling off your imaginations," they said—but this was difficult to do. There was "almost immediate agreement on the diagnosis," one participant recalled, but it was quite another matter when it came to recommending a new policy. These were Democrats coming into office after eight years in the political wilderness. The accusatory question, "Who lost China?" was still fresh in their minds. They had no intention of starting off by recommending a course of action that would expose the Kennedy Administration to the charge, "Who lost the Congo?" While everyone agreed that the present situation was precarious, it could still be argued that the Eisenhower Administration had managed to keep a pro-Western government in power in Leopoldville and keep the pro-Communist Lumumba in jail. The new policymakers realized that there were risks involved in any significant departure from the Eisenhower policy; they certainly did not want to be blamed for turning the Congo over to the Communists. At the same time, they knew that maintaining the present course entailed risks of its own. It was a question of balancing the risks.[3]

The first to weigh in with their advice, even before Kennedy took office, were the hardliners—the State Department and Pentagon officials who did not think current U.S. policy in the Congo was tough enough. They believed that the U.S. government should continue to support Kasavubu and Mobutu, no matter how disappointing their performance had been, and that it should exert its influence to force the Secretary-General to retreat from his pro-neutralist position. They were alarmed by reports that Kennedy intended to compromise with the Secretary-General, and they leaked their views to *The New York Times* in an attempt to stiffen the spine of the new Administration. The *Times* reported on January 18 that senior career officials in Washington planned to tell the new President that the UN operation in the Congo should be subjected to a "cold, hard reappraisal." They cited the disturbing reports Timberlake had been sending to the Department for weeks: Kasavubu and Mobutu were losing ground; the Lumumbists were gaining strength; the Stanleyville regime was receiving military supplies by air from the UAR, possibly with Soviet help; Dayal was siding with the Lumumbists; Hammarskjold was under "such heavy pressure" from the Communists and the Afro-Asians that he was "unable or unwilling to correct the situation." These officials then posed two questions: "Can the United States and its allies afford to permit forces hostile to the West to take over the Congo? Assuming the answer is no, what can the United States and its allies do to reverse the trend?" The answer was clear—press for Dayal's removal. Until now, the *Times* noted, American officials were "reluctant to express their feelings" about Dayal, but now they had concluded that his usefulness in the Congo had come to an end.[4]

These hard-line views were defended at the State Department meetings by the Assistant Secretary for European Affairs, Foy Kohler, a veteran Foreign Service officer, an expert on the Soviet Union, and a staunch Achesonian; and by George McGhee, head of the Policy Planning Council, an Oklahoma oil millionaire who had served with Rusk in Truman's State Department.

They were challenged by a number of the new Kennedy appointees, among them the Assistant Secretary for African Affairs, "Soapy" Williams. He came armed with an extremely useful document—an analytical chronology reviewing developments in the Congo from the beginning of the crisis through January 20. It had been prepared by officials in his bureau as a "briefing paper for a restricted number of top Department of State officials of the new Administration." Access to it was limited because of the "highly sensitive information" it contained. The authors explained that it had not been cleared by all the interested bureaus because if it had, "the document would have reflected compromises and would have inevitably submerged some of the more contentious aspects of the situation." As it was, it described with considerable frankness some of the disagreements within the State Department, especially between the African and European bureaus, and raised a number of questions about the wisdom of American policy up to that point. The President read it with interest and later asked for an update.

The chronology, which ran seventy-three pages, single-spaced, was not written as a brief, arguing the merits of one particular policy. It set an objective and unemotional tone by developing its arguments indirectly, piling up fact after fact. Although it relied heavily on cables from Timberlake for many of these facts, it did not always go along with his conclusions. In the course of the narrative, it made several notable points. First, it was very difficult to draw a line between pro-Communist and "hyper-nationalist, anti-colonialist, Marxist thinking" in the Congo, the implication being that neither Lumumba nor Gizenga could automatically be labeled pro-Soviet. Second, the United States had decided to support the UN operation because it was the "best means of keeping out Soviet assistance and its inevitable subversive accompaniments." Third, American concern about "NATO solidarity" had prevented the U.S. government from establishing a clear position "in favor of speedy implementation of the UN resolutions," particularly regarding the withdrawal of Belgian troops and the status of Katanga. Fourth, this reluctance on the part of the United States to support the United Nations fully had led to a situation in which the Americans had become identified with the colonial powers in the minds of the African and Asian states, whose support was essential if the UN effort was to succeed. Fifth, and finally, there was a noticeable inconsistency between American opposition to Soviet aid to Lumumba or Gizenga and the American failure to object to Belgian aid to Tshombe or Lumumba's other opponents. The chronology pointed out that the U.S. government was so out of touch with African opinion that at the recent General Assembly meeting, not a single African state had voted for the draft resolution sponsored by the United States and Great Britain.[5]

As far as the most recent developments were concerned, the chronology cited the same facts that were cited by the supporters of a hard-line policy, but it interpreted them somewhat differently. It suggested that Gizenga's successes could not be explained merely by the limited military assistance he might be receiving from the Casablanca powers or the Soviet bloc, or by Dayal's partiality toward the Lumumbists; they were due far more to internal political factors and to the fact that Mobutu was extremely ineffective as a military leader. It pointed out that there was no lack of money or arms on Mobutu's side, only a lack of motivation. It noted that even Timberlake, one of Mobutu's staunchest supporters, took a dim view of the colonel's latest request for additional U.S. aid. "The problem lies in discipline and in a willingness to use what they have," he told the Department. More money, he remarked scornfully, "will not cure the disease from which Mobutu's army is suffering but will simply provide expensive aspirin tablets to reduce fevers temporarily."[6]

The chronology ended with a trial balloon—a proposal that was to become the starting point of the new U.S. policy. It suggested that the United Nations take over and neutralize all the armed forces in the Congo. This was carefully presented as a suggestion that had originated with Timberlake, who could never be accused of yielding to Communist or neutralist pressure. By January 18 Timberlake had become so discouraged about Mobutu's prospects that he retreated from his earlier demands that the United Nations disarm the Gizengist troops alone and suggested that the Department consider the idea of getting a "mandate for the UN Command to disarm all, and I mean all, military and police forces in the Congo."[7]

The authors of the chronology noted that Timberlake's suggestion was "not far removed" from a proposal made by Ghana and India at the General Assembly in December. They deliberately blurred the distinction between the two positions: Timberlake wanted to keep Lumumba in jail and Parliament suspended while the United Nations restored order to the country; Ghana and India insisted that Lumumba be released and Parliament reconvened as essential parts of an overall package that would include the removal of the army from the Congo's political life.[8]

Williams, Bowles, and the other liberals in the planning group considered Ghana and India the most responsible of Lumumba's supporters. They were aware that Ghana had not yet followed the lead of the other Casablanca states who were pulling their troops out of the UN force. They also knew that the Secretary-General had sent a special appeal to Nehru, asking him to contribute a substantial number of troops to the depleted force. They believed that the United States should be able to come up with some sort of political compromise that would permit Nkrumah to keep his troops in the force and encourage Nehru to agree to Hammarskjold's request.

Nkrumah and Nehru were obviously hoping for major policy changes from the new Administration. On January 24 Nkrumah sent an impassioned appeal to President Kennedy, urging him to intervene personally to secure the release of Lumumba and warning that if Lumumba were murdered, it would have a "most serious effect" on African-American relations. Nkrumah recalled Kennedy's first major speech advocating Algerian independence and said he hoped the President would show the "same courage and realism" in the case of the Congo.[9] Nehru told Hammarskjold that he would be willing to consider his request for troops only if the Secretary-General made a "direct approach to the Americans and the Russians" and persuaded them to agree on a "minimum common policy" designed to remove the Congo from East-West contention and encourage the formation of a broad coalition government.[10]

When Hammarskjold met with Stevenson on January 25, he suggested that a "quiet direct approach to Khrushchev on a cold war truce in the Congo" might be helpful. He felt that the Russians had "realized they could not have their way in the Congo" and that they were somewhat interested in settling the issue.[11] He spoke quite openly about the difficulty of maintaining the UN operation in the face of the threatened troop withdrawals by the Casablanca states and suggested that a "strenuous diplomatic effort" by the United States might help "stem the tide." He pointed out, however, that an American appeal to such states as Ghana and India could be effective only if the United States was willing to abandon the Congo policy of the Eisenhower Administration and use its influence "in the direction of bringing about a neutralist course inside the Congo." The Americans would have to make it clear that they were willing to look beyond Kasavubu and his allies in their search for a solution and to consider the "possibility of adjustments and constructive compromises."[12]

Stevenson endorsed the Secretary-General's Congo policy at Kennedy's first cabinet meeting, where he spoke about the importance of re-capturing the confidence of the new countries of Africa and Asia. He explained that the American position at the United Nations had dete-riorated not only because of the increase in Soviet power but also be-cause of "our own mistakes and unpopular positions"—intolerance of neutralism, support for colonialism, and a preoccupation with the cold war.[13]

By this time the liberals at the State Department had come up with a number of controversial proposals. One involved the reconvening of Parliament "under conditions which would not completely exclude the participation of ex-Premier Lumumba or his representatives." An-other involved the formation of a "broadly based government" which would incorporate all the major factions in the Congo, including rep-resentatives of Lumumba or Lumumba himself. They realized that there were risks attached to such proposals. They did not want to ad-vocate "measures which might result in a disaster," as one participant put it. But they felt that the United States had to pay a price in order to get Afro-Asian support because the entire operation would collapse without that support, and they would then be faced with the prospect of a civil war and great power intervention.

The conservatives retorted that a "broadly based government" which included *all* political factions was too high a price to pay for Afro-Asian support. They were opposed to any hasty action that would help put Lumumba back into power. They pointed out that Kasavubu had managed to get his round table conference convened in Leopold-ville on January 25, as he had planned originally; and they felt he should be given more time to organize his anti-Lumumba coalition. They suggested that he could form his own "broadly based govern-ment" with Ileo as Prime Minister and that in time he might be able to obtain an anti-Lumumba majority in Parliament, which would give the Ileo government the necessary stamp of legitimacy.

The liberals were unimpressed by this line of reasoning. They ar-gued that it was nothing more than the plan the State Department had been urging on Kasavubu since October, without noticeable success. They did not believe Kasavubu would ever agree to reconvene Parlia-ment. They understood perfectly well why he and the other anti-Lumumba politicians were opposed to the idea: all the Embassy and CIA reports indicated that even if they started out with a solid anti-Lumumba majority, Lumumba could easily swing it around in his fa-vor, if he were released from prison and permitted to take part in its deliberations. Lumumba still dominated the Congolese political scene, even from his jail cell in Katanga (where he was presumed to be). The liberals found this situation "highly embarrassing"; they did not think it was right for the United States, the world's leading democracy, to be opposed to the convening of the Congolese Parliament or the release of its leading politician and former Prime Minister. Furthermore, they agreed with Hammarskjold's view that the Congo's political problems could not be solved without his participation.[14]

While the State Department was deliberating, President Kennedy was growing impatient. Every day there were more alarming bulletins from the Congo: mounting anti-European violence in Orientale and Kivu provinces; clashes between Lumumbist troops and Mobutu's forces in Equateur Province; threats of additional troop withdrawals from the UN force; reports of clandestine arms drops to the Stanleyville regime; reports that one hundred Belgian military instructors were being sent to Leopoldville to help Mobutu; reports that more European mercenaries were arriving in Katanga to join Tshombe's heavily armed foreign legion.[15]

Kennedy was determined to do something to demonstrate American concern. He hit upon a highly symbolic gesture that did not commit the United States to any substantive policy change. He opened his first press conference, on the evening of January 25, with three announcements. The first and third dealt with major developments in America's relations with the Soviet Union—the resumption of disarmament talks in Geneva and the release of the two surviving crewmen of the RB-47 plane shot down by the Russians in July 1960. The second dealt with the Congo. The President announced that the United States had decided to "increase substantially its contribution towards relieving the famine in the Congo." It would be airlifting one thousand tons of food supplies—rice, corn, dry milk—from America's surplus stocks.[16] The first planes were on their way to the Congo the following morning.

Next, Kennedy tried his hand at rewriting the State Department's rather stilted draft reply to Nkrumah's letter, which had been sent to him for signature. It was merely an interim reply, acknowledging Nkrumah's message and promising a substantive reply as soon as the policy review was completed, but Kennedy's editing sharpened the focus of the letter and conveyed a clearer impression of urgency and concern.[17] The President was quickly acquiring a reputation for being not only his own Secretary of State but his own desk officer as well.

Meanwhile, the debate at the State Department was reaching a climax. On Saturday, January 28, Secretary of State Rusk met with Williams, Cleveland, and other members of the Congo planning group. There were still sharp divisions between the hardliners, who felt that the United States must maintain a strong pro-Western government in the Congo, and the liberals, who argued that there could be no solution without an expanded government, even at the risk of including Lumumba. The steadily deteriorating situation in the Congo tipped the balance in favor of the liberals. Cleveland's deputy, Joseph Sisco, was asked to draft a policy paper incorporating many of their recommendations. By January 31 it was ready to submit to the President. The liberals had won the debate, at least for the time being.

Sisco began his paper by summing up the situation in terms that Hammarskjold himself might have used:

> Gizenga, aided and supported directly by the UAR and indirectly by the USSR, exercises control in Orientale province; Tshombe has had increasingly to rely on open Belgian assistance to maintain himself in the Katanga; it is an open question as to whether Kasavubu can exercise the kind of leadership at the current Round Table which will result in the early establishment of cabinet government in the Congo; the increase of open Belgian activity in the Congo and the ineptness of the Kasavubu-Bomboko-Mobutu leadership has resulted in identifying United States policy increasingly with the colonialists to the detriment of our position in the Congo, in Africa, and in the world generally; and with the impending withdrawal of military contingents of Guinea, UAR, Morocco, and Indonesia, the United Nations force will be weakened thereby increasing the prospect of civil war and presaging possibly an ignominious withdrawal of the United Nations. The United Nations will have been seriously, perhaps irreparably, discredited particularly in the eyes of the Africans and Asians, and Khrushchev's recent attack against the Organization will have been given greater momentum perhaps bringing Hammarskjold's resignation.

He then described the purposes of the new policy in terms that would appeal to conservative and liberal alike. On the one hand, he stressed the importance of preventing Gizenga from turning Orientale Province into a "Communist stronghold" which could then spread its influence "to other parts of the Congo and Africa"; on the other hand, he talked about "regaining the United States position in Africa and Asia" by replacing the present "discredited" policy. He defined the U.S. objective as the "establishment and maintenance of a stable unified Congo with reasonable safeguards against a Communist takeover" and proposed a three-point program designed to accomplish this goal.

The first point recommended a "strengthened mandate" for the United Nations so that it could maintain law and order and neutralize all the principal military elements in the Congo. Specifically, it would bring under control and retrain the army and police, prevent civil strife, and deter all outside intervention and assistance. Sisco noted that the Secretary-General was prepared to take an initiative along these lines and that he would welcome U.S. support. He explained that Hammarskjold intended to try "political means in the first instance" but that if any of the Congolese forces refused to be brought under control, "the United Nations would have to use force." Sisco anticipated a hostile reaction to this plan in Leopoldville and Elisabethville, where the authorities would undoubtedly suspect that it was directed against them; he pointed out that the United States would probably be "called upon to exert great pressure on the Belgians, Tshombe, and Mobutu." At the same time, the proposal envisaged the replacement of Dayal—a gesture that was intended to mollify Kasavubu and Mobutu.

The second point was even more controversial. It recommended the formation of a "broadly based government including all principal political elements of the Congo." This was a clear victory for the liberals, who believed the United States must take certain risks—including the possible re-emergence of Lumumba as a political leader—in order to avoid a complete disaster in the Congo. This proposal was expected to cause even more of a storm in Leopoldville than the neutralization plan.

The third point called for what was essentially a UN trusteeship over the Congo. Kasavubu would request major administrative and technical assistance from the United Nations; while there would be no formal infringement of Congolese sovereignty, "the United Nations would be running the country on a *de facto* basis." It would continue to administer the government and the economy, with the help of Belgian technicians, "for a number of years," until the Congolese were trained to run the country themselves. Sisco pointed out that this arrangement, "coupled with the neutralization of all Congolese military forces," would provide an effective "safeguard against a Lumumba takeover."

By the time the paper left the State Department for the White House on February 1, there had been a dramatic change in the wording of the second proposal. Instead of a "broadly based government including all principal political elements of the Congo," the paper now spoke of "a middle-of-the-road government under Ileo as prime minister." It noted that Kasavubu had "convened a Round Table of Congolese political leaders" and recommended that he be "encouraged and assisted with a view to achieving the earliest possible agreement among the participants." Only if the round table approach failed would the U.S. government support a "broadly based government which would include representatives of all principal political elements in the Congo"—a stand now described as a "fall-back" position. Political prisoners would be freed only "after neutralization of all principal Congolese military elements was accomplished, or at least well under way, and a new broadly based Congolese Government was agreed upon." This time sequence was designed to "provide a safeguard against Lumumba assuming the position of prime minister." At the very end of the process, "Kasavubu would submit the new government to Parliament for its approval."[18]

The new wording represented a return to what officials in the African Bureau regarded as the "discredited" policy of the Eisenhower Administration. They suspected that the "fall-back" position was included merely as window dressing—a sop to the liberals—and they feared that the African and Asian states whose support the Kennedy Administration was seeking would find nothing new in an American approach that was still wedded to Kasavubu, Ileo, and the anti-Lumumba politicians attending the round table conference.[19]

Why did this change take place? Ambassador Timberlake, who was horrified by what he regarded as the naiveté of the new Administration, was summoned home for consultations, but he did not arrive in Washington until the evening of January 31, too late to have much influence on the paper. The other advocates of a hard-line policy were at the Pentagon and the CIA; but, ironically, the Pentagon had approved Sisco's original draft on January 31 with only a few minor reservations. Assistant Secretary of Defense Nitze had warned of "the danger that the proposed coalition might fall into the hands of individuals whose purposes are known to be inimical to Western interests," but he concluded, "notwithstanding the risks involved," that "a new policy along the general lines indicated should be adopted on an urgent basis."

Nitze saved his hard-line suggestions for the Pentagon's fall-back position—a detailed plan for a "vigorous unilateral course of action" which he felt should be adopted if the effort to get a new UN mandate failed. He enclosed a list of steps, "short of armed intervention," which the United States could take to undermine the Lumumbists: it could persuade neighboring countries to deny overflight or transit rights to military aircraft or materiel destined for Stanleyville; undertake "extensive covert operations to isolate and weaken" the Stanleyville regime; and use "all feasible means," including American financial aid to anti-Lumumba factions, to "discredit or eliminate pro-Lumumba or other Sino-Soviet supported elements as an effective political force."

If armed intervention should become necessary at some point, Nitze assured Cleveland that the Joint Chiefs of Staff had concluded that the United States was "capable of successful military intervention in the Congo without degrading its general war posture to an unacceptable degree." They cautioned, however, that its "capability to successfully conduct other similar type operations elsewhere in the world would depend on the extent of US commitment of forces to the Congo."[20]

Clearly, the Pentagon's fall-back position was diametrically opposed to that of the State Department. These hard-line views may have had some impact on the final version of the State Department's policy paper. According to one account, however, the decisive argument in favor of the change came from an unlikely source—Adlai Stevenson. He was, once again, reflecting the views of the Secretary-General. Stevenson's biographer, John Bartlow Martin, writes that it was Stevenson who suggested that the broad coalition become the fall-back position, "to be taken only after we had failed in efforts to use our influence with the Belgians, Kasavubu and others to establish a middle-of-the-road government under Ileo." Martin noted that on the afternoon of January 31, after a conversation with Hammarskjold, Stevenson telephoned Cleveland and told him that Hammarskjold "wanted a Kasavubu government with Ileo as Prime Minister" and that only after the Congolese army had been brought under control and the Ileo government established should the "political prisoners, including Lumumba, be released. Parliament should be called later."[21]

This would mean that for a short time the State Department had adopted a more radical position than the Secretary-General; it had gone further toward releasing Lumumba and restoring him to power in order to please the Afro-Asians than Hammarskjold himself was willing to go. The quick about-face was an interesting indication of the attitude of the new Administration—the liberal impulse, and then the cautious pulling back, on second thought, to a more conservative, traditional position.

Sisco's revised paper was presented to the first meeting of the National Security Council on February 1 by Secretary of State Rusk and approved by the President. Prodded by the impatient Kennedy, the slow-moving Department of State had produced a major new policy statement in less than two weeks. The next step was to see if it would work.

Kennedy and Stevenson: An Uneasy Partnership

Over the next ten days Kennedy Administration officials tried to sell their new Congo policy—to the Africans and Asians, to the Russians, to the NATO allies, and to the U.S. Congress. They did not plan to unveil the three-part program as official U.S. policy; they planned to discuss it privately with a number of "suitable Afro-Asians, including India, Nigeria, and Ghana," who would then take the lead, along with the Secretary-General, and promote it as their own idea—which the United States could then support.[22]

The only thing wrong with this approach was that U.S. officials had not really come to terms with the issue that was of central importance to the Afro-Asians whose support they were seeking—the question of Lumumba. The dispute within the Administration about the "broadly based government" and Lumumba's role in it had barely been resolved before the policy was approved by the President. As a result, American officials were simultaneously promoting two versions of the plan—the moderate Ileo government and the broad coalition government—depending on whom they were addressing. When President Kennedy wrote to Nkrumah to enlist his support for the U.S. plan, he never referred to Lumumba by name; but he managed to convey the impression that the United States might agree to his participation in the government by stating, "I want to assure you that I am prepared to use whatever influence I have to encourage the earliest possible establishment of a broadly based government."[23] Nkrumah might have concluded from this that what Kennedy had in mind was a government of all the factions, which would logically include Lumumba. There was no indication in Kennedy's letter that the U.S. government had redefined the phrase to mean "a middle-of-the-road government headed by Ileo," with a broad coalition government envisaged merely as a fallback position. The same deliberate ambiguity about the "broadly based government" appeared in Rusk's instructions to the U.S. ambassadors in New Delhi and Lagos, who were supposed to explain the new policy to Nehru and to Prime Minister Abubakar Tafawa Balewa.[24]

This lack of candor led to all sorts of complications and misunderstandings without producing a consensus in support of the new U.S. policy. American efforts were, of course, cut short by the announcement of Lumumba's death; but during the first ten days of February the Administration proceeded on the assumption that he was very much alive and the major political factor in the Congo.

According to the strategy worked out by the State Department, the President would make no public statements about the new policy. At his press conference on February 1, Kennedy went along with this plan. Although he cited the Congo as an area of grave concern, he gave no indication that the National Security Council had approved a new Congo policy earlier in the day. Kennedy had struck a gloomy note about the world situation in his State of the Union message on January 30, and when a reporter asked if he had "found conditions very much worse upon taking office" than he had anticipated, he replied:

> I think the situation is less satisfactory than it was last fall. . . . I'm not convinced as yet that the tide in some of the critical areas in which the United States is involved has turned in our favor. I think that anyone who reads the daily papers knows of the critical events in Laos, the Communist intervention in that area. I think they're aware of the fact that the situation in the Congo has deteriorated sharply recently, with a steady withdrawal of troops taking place by United Nations countries.

But when he was asked if the United States had come up with any new proposals to deal with the Congo situation, he edged away from a specific answer. He noted that Ambassador Timberlake had arrived home for consultations and that the Administration was considering the matter of the Congo carefully in order to decide "what useful steps might be taken which would prevent a further deterioration. I do not have anything further to say just at this time," he stated.[25]

Since the President would be remaining in the background, the task of promoting the new policy would be left primarily to Stevenson at the United Nations. Kennedy was not entirely happy about Stevenson's prominence in the field of foreign affairs. His resentment flared up in his answer to the first question of the press conference, when a reporter asked if Stevenson was "correct in his guess" a few days before that Kennedy "would be happy to meet with Khrushchev if he should come to this country for the United Nations session." Kennedy responded sharply:

> As Governor—Ambassador Stevenson said, I have not discussed the matter with him. I have no idea whether Mr. Khrushchev is coming to the United States or not. There's been no indication, either publicly or privately, that he is planning a visit to the United States, and therefore I think it would be appropriate to wait in regard to what plans we might have as far as seeing him . . . until we have some idea whether he's going to come or not.[26]

Kennedy's implied rebuke of Stevenson for his freewheeling speculation about the sensitive subject of U.S.-Soviet relations was typical of the relationship between the two men. It was somewhat uneasy from the start. The Kennedy family resented the fact that Stevenson had refused to declare himself out of the race for the nomination in the summer of 1960 and leave a clear field for Kennedy. Stevenson was disappointed by the fact that Kennedy had not asked him to be Secretary of State, and he was reluctant at first to accept the UN job until he knew who was going to be Secretary of State and whether he could work with him. His hesitation surprised and annoyed Kennedy—according to Robert Kennedy he was "absolutely furious"—and confirmed the old impression of Stevenson as a man who could not make up his mind. Stevenson's friends—his law partners, William Blair, Willard Wirtz, and Newton Minow, all of whom accepted high-ranking jobs in the Kennedy Administration, as well as George Ball, Senator Hubert Humphrey, and many others—urged Stevenson to take the job as ambassador to the United Nations. Ball echoed Kennedy's explanation that Stevenson would be too controversial as Secretary of State and told him he would strengthen the Administration at the United Nations; Wirtz said it was "only natural that Kennedy wanted to be the Number One man in his own Administration," and if Stevenson were named Secretary of State, people abroad would think Kennedy was "a little boy being guided by a senior statesman." Kennedy assured Stevenson that he would be in the mainstream of American foreign policymaking, that he would be a member of the cabinet, and that he could choose his own staff—and in the end Stevenson yielded.[27]

Once he actually got into the job, the awkwardness increased. Stevenson was seventeen years older than Kennedy, and, according to his top aide, Francis Plimpton, an establishment Republican New York lawyer who had been Stevenson's law school roommate, Stevenson was "always a little uncomfortable in taking orders from someone who he thought was not only younger but much less experienced and much less informed and wise." Plimpton recalled that Stevenson "used a good deal of self-restraint in holding back what obviously was his confidence in his own knowledge and ability to handle foreign affairs. . . . I never heard him say an unkind thing about Kennedy." The closest he ever got was to refer to him as "that young fellow down there in the White House." Still, Plimpton acknowledged that "there was a little jealousy between the two of them; there's just no doubt about it."[28]

Stevenson shared a great many ideas with Kennedy—about the importance of the developing world, disarmament, accommodation with the Soviet Union—but he was perceived by the hard-nosed realists in the White House as "soft," "idealistic," "rambling"; as a result his views sometimes were not taken too seriously. At meetings, Kennedy would grow impatient with Stevenson's philosophical discussions of long-range problems. He was far more comfortable with crisp, decisive thinkers who could come up with operational recommendations without hesitation, like his pragmatic Secretary of Defense, Robert McNamara. Stevenson complained to his friends that Kennedy was too impulsive. Kennedy's advisers, in turn, often spoke disparagingly of Stevenson—and it was often the President himself who reminded them how valuable Stevenson really was. Still, there was an underlying tension between Stevenson and the Kennedy White House, despite the assignment of presidential adviser Arthur Schlesinger, Jr., an old Stevenson supporter, as liaison, to smooth out the rough edges.

At the State Department the rough edges were smoothed out by Cleveland, who was Stevenson's choice as Assistant Secretary for International Organization Affairs, and his deputy, Sisco. They were very protective of Stevenson and very careful about his feelings; although they were theoretically working for him, they were in fact writing his instructions. The way the UN job worked out, Stevenson seldom had the time to come to Washington for cabinet meetings or State Department policy meetings, so that most issues were discussed on the telephone. From the very beginning, Stevenson would complain to old friends that he was "on the wrong end of the telephone" and that he should never have taken the job. Cleveland recalled that every time Stevenson went to a diplomatic dinner he would tell his troubles to whatever attractive woman was seated next to him; he kept threatening to resign, and eventually the news got back to Washington. Kennedy was upset by the rumors. His victory had been a close one, and Stevenson represented the liberal wing of the Democratic Party; if it deserted him he would be in political trouble. Cleveland asked Ball for advice, and Ball, who knew Stevenson well, assured him he would never resign over this sort of issue—"that's just not his style."

Both Stevenson and Kennedy were proud, sensitive men. For the first few months of the new Administration, Cleveland recalled, the President would pick up the morning paper and find "three articles about himself and three about Stevenson—and he was always surprised to find out what Stevenson was up to, at the United Nations—about the Congo, or Angola, or whatever the issue might be." After a while, Cleveland worked out a system, with Rusk's approval: each night he prepared a one-page memo on Stevenson's activities that day and sent it directly to McGeorge Bundy at the White House for the President's bedtime reading, so that when he saw the story in the paper the following day, it did not come as a surprise. This technique was helpful, but it did not entirely eliminate the tension between the two men.

Testing the Soviet Waters

Because of this underlying tension it often appeared that Stevenson was more respected and his views were more influential outside the councils of government than inside; he was acclaimed by the public, by the press, and by foreign statesmen and diplomats. While Kennedy was holding his press conference on the afternoon of February 1, and scolding Stevenson for his comments about Khrushchev, Stevenson was receiving the plaudits of the Security Council, where he was making his debut as the American representative. Even Soviet Ambassador Zorin joined the chorus of tributes. He expressed the hope that Stevenson, whom he described as an "advocate of international cooperation," could help the Security Council to be more effective than it had been in the past in reaching "mutually acceptable decisions" and perhaps even "unanimity" on important world issues.

Stevenson listened intently to the translation of Zorin's remarks and jotted down notes on a yellow scratch pad. His response was characteristically witty, diplomatic, and at the same time very much to the point. He was conciliatory: he stressed the importance of the United Nations as a forum in which such questions as disarmament could be settled, and he referred to President Kennedy's hope that the United Nations could be used to end the cold war; but at the same time he firmly supported the role of the Secretary-General and emphasized the importance of adequate financing for the United Nations—both points of contention with the Soviet Union.[29]

There had been some speculation in the press that Stevenson would present a new American Congo proposal when he addressed the Security Council, but Stevenson, like the President, referred to the Congo in only the most general way. At the same time, he informed Hammarskjold privately that "the Department's thinking was moving along more or less parallel" with his own, and that the President was about to make a final decision on the new policy.[30]

After Stevenson replied to the speeches of welcome, the Secretary-General rose to make an important statement. He told the Security Council that Kasavubu's decision to transfer Lumumba to Katanga had increased the danger of civil war in the Congo, and he asked for a new mandate empowering him to bring the army under control and take it out of politics. If the army could be neutralized and turned into a "unified, disciplined" force, he explained, this would be an important step toward national reconciliation.[31]

With this speech the Secretary-General launched the first part of the plan he had discussed with Stevenson. He made no specific reference to the other parts of the plan, but he had good reason to believe that the Americans were now committed to the "minimum common policy" suggested originally by Nehru, (i.e., they would seek an agreement with the Russians to remove the Congo from cold war contention and would support the formation of a broad coalition government which might ultimately include Lumumba). The next step was to see if the Russians were willing to cooperate.

Up to this point the Soviet government had taken a conciliatory stand toward the Kennedy Administration. Khrushchev had sent the President a warm note of congratulations on his inauguration and released the RB-47 fliers as a goodwill gesture; the Soviet leader specifically informed Ambassador Thompson that the release had been delayed to benefit Kennedy rather than Nixon.[32] The Soviet press noted with pleasure on January 24, "Moscow and Washington are talking directly to each other for the first time since the U-2 incident and the failure of last year's summit conference."[33] Khrushchev clearly wanted to start off on a fresh basis with the new President, and U.S. officials thought that this conciliatory mood might have some effect on his Congo policy.

The Soviet leader was in a difficult position. He had mounted a massive propaganda campaign on Lumumba's behalf, but it had accomplished nothing concrete, and by January 20 he was beginning to suspect that it might be too late to save Lumumba. He was having no better luck in helping Gizenga, even though he was working closely with the Cairo-based Afro-Asian Solidarity Council in its effort to get "volunteers, arms, and other material assistance" to the Stanleyville regime.[34] Khrushchev was well aware of the practical problem which

Nkrumah had raised at Casablanca—transit through the Sudan—and he used all his diplomatic charm to try to get around the obstacle. Soviet relations with the Sudan had been improving by leaps and bounds. A Sudanese trade delegation had been feted in Moscow in early January, and President Abboud had accepted an invitation to visit the Soviet Union in the near future.[35] On January 28 Khrushchev tried to put this new relationship to the test. The Soviet Red Cross and Red Crescent wrote to Abboud explaining that they wanted to send food and medical supplies to Orientale and Kivu, "in response to governmental and private requests." They had raised the money and arranged for a boat to take the supplies as far as Port Sudan and twenty trucks to carry the supplies to Stanleyville. All they needed from the Sudanese government was the right of transit. But Abboud remained firm, despite the pressure from Moscow and from Cairo. No transit would be permitted except under the auspices of the United Nations.[36]

The Soviet leader had been stymied in his attempt to establish a supply route to Stanleyville; and he was disturbed by the fact that the Gizenga regime, after its impressive gains in the first half of January, seemed to be losing the initiative in the face of new military threats from Tshombe and Mobutu. Once again, he decided to see if anything could be accomplished on the diplomatic front, which looked somewhat more promising.

It was just at this point that Stevenson, spurred by Hammarskjold's suggestion about a cold war moratorium, went to discuss the situation with Zorin on an informal, exploratory basis. He told the Soviet delegate that the United States hoped for "improved relations" and an "end to public acrimony." After a brief discussion of disarmament he raised the question of the Congo. He said that "speaking personally" he felt the new Administration would favor the "early establishment of constitutional government," prohibition of outside assistance except through the United Nations, and "full support" for the Secretary-General. Zorin replied that his government would "welcome a return to legal government, particularly by Lumumba," and insisted that "the only outside interference was coming from Belgium."

Stevenson concluded from this conversation that while Zorin seemed to want to "establish more friendly relations," he had given "no indication" of a "softening of Soviet views" on either disarmament or the Congo.[37] Zorin, on the other hand, must have found in Stevenson's remarks an encouraging indication of a new flexibility in the American position that might yet offer a chance for the return of Lumumba to power, if he was still alive, or at least a chance for the survival of the Stanleyville regime.

When Zorin addressed the Security Council on February 2, he took a tough line toward Hammarskjold and a conciliatory one toward Stevenson. He ignored Hammarskjold's neutralization proposal, and accused him of deliberately undermining the Security Council resolutions. At the same time, he indicated that his government was awaiting with considerable hope the outcome of the policy review mentioned by Kennedy and Stevenson. Despite his polite tone, Zorin yielded nothing of substance. Essentially he was asking the United States to agree to the policy the Soviet Union had advocated all along: the removal of the Belgians, the release of Lumumba, the reconvening of Parliament, and the disarming of Mobutu. After repeating these proposals, Zorin stated, "Above all, we await a reply from the new United States representative as to whether or not he is ready to accompany us along this road."[38]

Too Radical for Some, Too Cautious for Others

Stevenson and his staff launched their diplomatic offensive on February 3 with calls on nineteen delegations. They found that while the Nigerians seemed willing to take the initiative in coming up with a resolution along the lines of the American plan, most of the other Afro-Asians continued to insist that Lumumba's release must come first.[39] But this was only part of the problem. Administration officials had concentrated so hard on making their program acceptable to the Secretary-General, the key Afro-Asians, and the Soviet Union that they had neglected to some extent the probable reaction of their own allies. They soon discovered that the new plan, which was not radical enough to satisfy the Afro-Asians, was too radical for the Europeans.

The British had become accustomed to vigorous American initiatives in the Congo; only three months before, they had been less than enthusiastic about the Eisenhower Administration's determination to push Kasavubu's case through the General Assembly, and now they saw the Kennedy Administration moving rashly in the opposite direction. With their years of colonial experience in Africa, they felt themselves far more qualified to size up the situation than the Americans were, and their instinct was always to approach the Congo with caution. They were not about to antagonize the new Administration, however; Prime Minister Macmillan, who had had a warm personal relationship with Eisenhower going back to the days of World War II, was determined to establish a good relationship with his successor, who represented a new generation and was something of an unknown quantity. British reservations about the new Kennedy policy were therefore expressed in muted tones; the Foreign Office had no desire to "worry" the United States but simply wished the State Department to have the benefit of its preliminary views.

The British reported that their Embassy in Leopoldville said things were "looking up"; the "Gizenga crowd" was discouraged, Mobutu was about to take the offensive, and the round table conference seemed to be making progress, with the possibility of agreement on a new government which would include supporters of the left-wing Gizenga and Kashamura but would not include them personally. Under the circumstances the British felt the new U.S. plan would "discourage Kasavubu and encourage Gizenga." They were also concerned that part of the plan might be carried out while other parts were not; specifically, they feared the premature release of Lumumba. Still, despite their reservations, the British indicated that they would go along with the American approach.[40]

The Belgians, on the other hand, were furious—both because they had not been consulted in advance and because they felt the plan itself was naive and dangerous. They argued that the American failure to consult with a NATO ally, especially one with an overriding responsibility in the area, placed Belgium on the same plane as the neutralists and the Soviet opponents of NATO, who were all informed about the new policy at the same time. More important, they warned that Kennedy's plan would play directly into the hands of the Communists. The French took the same position.[41] Meanwhile, in Leopoldville, Mobutu, who had recently been promoted to the rank of major general, warned that the army would fight rather than allow itself to be disarmed.[42]

Administration officials were disturbed by these negative reactions. They did not like to acknowledge that they were the result of the policy changes that had been proposed; instead, they put the blame on leaks, which had inevitably led to "distortions," such as the emphasis on disarming Mobutu's troops or freeing Lumumba.[43] There is no doubt that the policy paper approved by the President did envisage the use of force by the United Nations to disarm Mobutu if necessary, as well as the release of Lumumba—but U.S. officials argued that these proposals were being taken out of context.

As a result of these leaks and rumors, there was a good deal of alarm and confusion about the new policy on Capitol Hill. On Monday, February 6, Assistant Secretary Williams went over to brief the members of the Senate Foreign Relations Committee. Timberlake accompanied him. The ambassador had been home for nearly a week, and was due to return to the Congo the following day. He had almost despaired of convincing the new policymakers that their plan was in some respects hopelessly naive when his luck turned, and he was asked to brief the President on Saturday, February 4. He explained to Kennedy that the situation could not be understood in conventional Western terms: the Congo was an extremely primitive country with no tradition of democracy; there were only sixteen university graduates in a population of fourteen million; and when you talked about constitutional procedures or a coalition government, you were talking about people who had no conception of what these things meant—not even the members of Parliament, who were influenced primarily by bribery, intimidation, and violence. Timberlake found the President receptive and many of the Senators even more so. They raised a number of tough questions and gave him an opportunity to express his reservations about the new policy.

Williams led off the briefing. He was engaging, conciliatory, and somewhat vague; it was only his third week in the job, and he was not sure of all the players. He summarized the new policy and tried to dispel a number of the misconceptions that had arisen in the past few days. On the first point—neutralization—he assured the Senators that despite all the talk in the newspapers about "disarming" the troops, what the Administration had in mind was "training missions" run by the United Nations to "give some discipline to these troops and get them responding to a proper authority." He acknowledged that disarming the troops would be a very "ticklish proposition" and insisted that the Administration thought of it "only as a last resort."

On the second point—the "broadly based government"—he followed the policy paper and stressed that the State Department's preference was "to have Kasavubu develop some kind of middle-of-the-road government." The fall-back position, which involved a "government of all the elements," was "not a hard and fast program of the Department, but one where we are seeking to gain a consensus with people in the Afro-Asian group"—specifically, Nigeria, Tunisia, Ghana, India, and Ethiopia—who would then present the policy as their own. Williams pointed out that they had run into a problem here: since Stevenson was consulting with so many delegations at the United Nations, the story had got into the newspapers, and "the more newspaper talk there is the more difficult it is to get the Afro-Asians to front for this thing, because it gets to look more and more that this was a US plan."

Williams then approached the most sensitive topic of the day. "Now, whenever we talk about an all-element government," he said, "the problem comes up of Lumumba. . . . Lumumba is apparently the best rabble rouser speaker in the Congo . . . and everybody fears that if he just is let loose a little, he will end up by having control of everything." Williams assured the Senators that "while there would eventually be a general release of political prisoners, we do not feel that Lumumba should be released until such a time as neutralization of the military forces and the government are pretty well along."

A number of Senators, particularly Frank Lausche, a conservative Democrat from Ohio who was one of Tshombe's staunchest supporters, kept pressing Williams on this point, and the more Williams tried to explain the State Department's position on the coalition government and Lumumba's connection with it, the deeper he got into the contradictions of American policy. He insisted that the Department was not encouraging the release of Lumumba but said there were a great many people who favored the idea. If Kasavubu and Mobutu failed to get their act together and the Afro-Asians stepped in to get a coalition organized, there would be considerable pressure to release Lumumba, and there was not much the United States could do to stop it. Lausche, unconvinced, referred to the experience of coalition governments in China and Poland, and said:

> I feel this is the beginning of the eventual triumph of Lumumba; the coalition government will collapse, Lumumba's forces will operate, and instead of solving the problem that we have now, you will have a worse problem . . . within a year.

After Williams finished his presentation, he turned the briefing over to Timberlake, explaining somewhat apologetically that the ambassador had been called home for consultations about the new policy but that things had moved so fast at the United Nations that "we didn't have the benefit of his advice before some of the ideas got into at least a tentative stage." Timberlake, unlike Williams, said nothing to explain or defend the new policy. When Senator Frank Church of Idaho asked him, "Are you personally in concurrence with this projected program for the Congo that has been explained here today?" Timberlake answered in a roundabout fashion that made it clear he had strong reservations about it.

Senator George Aiken, the crusty Republican from Vermont, went to the heart of the matter. He asked Timberlake if he could visualize Lumumba being represented in a coalition government and "not dominating it." Timberlake replied, "No, I cannot." Aiken then asked if it would be possible to form a coalition government that would exclude Lumumba. Timberlake explained that it would probably be possible to form a coalition that would include former supporters of Lumumba who had become disenchanted with him, but he added, "This does not remove the danger of Lumumba, because this man, like Castro, has the great gift of being able to convince people." Aiken then asked if Lumumba's participation in a coalition would lead to a greater degree of Soviet influence.

TIMBERLAKE: "Certainly. He would invite them in again right away."
AIKEN: "They would be right in there. They would approve any coalition government that Lumumba could be a part of, I am sure."
TIMBERLAKE: "It would not last as a coalition government very long; it would revert—"

AIKEN: "It would be his government in no time flat, and then the Soviet government if he comes in there now."

There was considerable interest in the question of Soviet intentions and Soviet military aid. Timberlake explained that a "trickle" of Soviet-inspired aid was reaching Stanleyville from the UAR via the Sudan, despite Sudanese assurances that this would not be permitted. He mentioned a plane that was supposed to be carrying Ping-Pong balls and other recreational supplies for the UAR United Nations contingent in Equateur and was in fact carrying "hand grenades, rifles, machine guns and ammunition" for Gizenga's forces. He pointed out that it would be difficult for the UAR to send supplies by land and said the UN force could control the airfields in Orientale Province if it had enough troops. In response to a question he said there was no evidence the Russians were looking for an opportunity to intervene militarily, but he felt it was likely that they were still trying to influence the outcome through "infiltration" or "subversion."

Committee Chairman J. William Fulbright asked Timberlake about the state of civilization in the Congo, thus giving him an opportunity to expound on one of his favorite topics; and a number of Senators asked if he really thought the UN operation was worth what it was costing the United States, which gave him a chance to discourse on another favorite topic. Timberlake was the man who had suggested bringing the United Nations into the Congo in the first place, and despite its disappointing performance, he still believed it was the best alternative available. "Even if they had five thousand troops," he said, "I would still rather see them stay and attempt to do a job under a mandate that gave them a little more elbow room" than contemplate any other solution. When he was asked about the possibility of unilateral American intervention to combat Soviet intervention, Timberlake said he was very much opposed to the idea; if the United Nations did not succeed, the United States might have to consider direct action, but that would be "a final and almost last ditch operation" which would have to be "conducted with some of our Western friends and not unilaterally."

Timberlake was far from optimistic about the outcome of the political contest in Leopoldville. "The sad fact is that there is not anybody down there really outside of Lumumba who has got the kind of energy and drive and imagination which would let him be Prime Minister in fact, not just in name," he explained. The problem with Lumumba was that he was "a destructive type" who was "sold to the Russians and would invite them back as he did once before." Considering the alternatives, Timberlake advised that the United States work with whoever emerged from Kasavubu's round table conference. There was not really any good solution; all you could hope for was "the best of what is available."

At one point in the briefing Senator Alexander Wiley, a Wisconsin Republican, asked, "Well, I suppose you could characterize that situation as a hell of a mess right now?" Timberlake summed it up succinctly: "It is the damnedest can of worms that I have ever seen."[44]

After the morning briefing on the Hill, Timberlake spent much of the rest of the day conferring with Rusk, who was in close touch with Stevenson in New York. Stevenson was finding it increasingly difficult to build a consensus around the American position. The Afro-Asian delegates were preoccupied with the question of Lumumba's release and his role in any future government. On February 7, Stevenson reported that even the Nigerians were "wobbling" toward the "immediate release of Lumumba due to pressure from home."[45]

The "Escape" of Lumumba

On February 9 Kennedy presided at the second meeting of his National Security Council. Stevenson briefed the top officials of the U.S. government on the latest developments at the United Nations, and Secretary of State Rusk and CIA Director Dulles reviewed developments in the Congo. It was at this point that the spotlight turned to Leopoldville and a series of dramatic announcements which would completely transform the Congolese political scene and alter the negotiating strategies of the United States and the Soviet Union.

Kasavubu, moving for the third time in six months with unaccustomed speed, announced that he had named a civilian government with Ileo as Prime Minister and that Mobutu's military rule was at an end. The College of Commissioners was dissolved, with thanks, and three of the young commissioners were sent back to Brussels to complete their college education. There was no public reaction from Mobutu, who was with his troops in Equateur Province, preparing for an assault against Gizenga's stronghold.[46]

The young general confided to his CIA friends that he was deeply disappointed by this turn of events; but he understood that Kasavubu was responding to pressure from the Kennedy Administration. As McIlvaine explained it, the Congolese were afraid that the United States was joining forces with the Casablanca states to impose a coalition government on them, and their fear had a "galvanizing effect" upon them.[47] What Timberlake could not accomplish with gentle persuasion, the new Administration had accomplished with threats.

On February 10 there was a second dramatic bulletin from the Congo: Lumumba's captors in Katanga announced that he and his two companions had escaped from the prison farm where they were being held. They had allegedly fled in a car after overpowering their guards.

McIlvaine reported that this story was viewed with "widespread skepticism" in Leopoldville. It was generally believed that Lumumba was dead and that the announcement of his escape was merely a "preliminary" to a further announcement that he had been "killed resisting recapture."[48] The U.S. consul in Elisabethville agreed. He noted that the announcement had been greeted with "disbelief and levity" and concluded that since none of the Katanga officials appeared "really concerned" about the escape, the story was "probably fabricated." He speculated that they had been alarmed by rumors of a U.S. plan to free Lumumba and had come up with the escape story to "cover up" the fact that he had "already been killed."[49] The CIA base chief in Elisabethville claimed to have no definite knowledge of Lumumba's whereabouts; he reported several versions of Lumumba's death that were making the rounds, but concluded: "Lumumba fate is best kept secret in Katanga."[50]

The Russians were alarmed and angry. Zorin wrote to Hammarskjold and demanded an immediate investigation.[51] He went to see Stevenson and told him that if Lumumba had been killed, the atmosphere in the Security Council would be "extremely unpleasant" and the situation in the Congo would be "uncontrollable."[52]

For three days the Katanga authorities kept up their pretense that Lumumba had escaped, and there was no hard information one way or the other. Stevenson warned the State Department that if he had been killed, many Afro-Asians would suspect that the Belgians and the French were responsible and that the American plan was a "smokescreen" to cover their operation. He felt the United States should take a "firm public position" in order to demonstrate that its plan had been "put forward in good faith" and was not part of a Western maneuver to cover up Lumumba's murder.[53] State Department officials replied that the situation was "too fluid" to try to agree on a new formula. One problem, fortunately, would be eliminated if Lumumba was dead: the United States would be able to endorse the immediate release of all political prisoners, since there would be "no one left whose release would result in instability and/or civil war."[54]

The suspense and uncertainty about Lumumba's disappearance ended on the morning of Monday, February 13, with the third dramatic bulletin from the Congo. Katanga Radio announced that Lumumba and his companions had been captured and killed by hostile villagers. Interior Minister Munongo refused to reveal the name or location of the village, but he said the inhabitants would receive a reward amounting to eight thousand dollars. Munongo proclaimed defiantly, "If people accuse us of killing Lumumba, I will reply, 'Prove it.' "[55]

President Kennedy expressed "great shock" at the news of Lumumba's death.[56] Other American officials reacted with a sense of relief. While Senator Fulbright deplored the use of violence, Senator Aiken reflected the view of many people when he pointed out that there would have been more violence if Lumumba had escaped to "Communist-controlled territory."[57]

American policymakers were faced with two major questions at this point. First, how would Lumumba's death affect their plans for the Congo, which were based on cooperation with the Afro-Asians, many of whom supported Lumumba? Second, how would the Russians react to Lumumba's death and what effect would it have on the gradually developing thaw in U.S.-Soviet relations?

Stevenson did not have to wait long for an answer to the second question. As soon as the news was broadcast on the radio, Zorin and his deputy, Platon Morozov, came storming into the U.S. Mission, accusing Stevenson, Plimpton, and the entire U.S. government of being responsible for Lumumba's murder. This was clearly an unofficial reaction; when the Soviet delegate spoke at the Security Council later that morning, he blasted the Secretary-General and the "Belgian colonialists," but he did not repeat his accusations against the United States.[58]

Stevenson had invited Zorin and his aides to lunch that day, but after the meeting a messenger arrived to tell him that they would not be coming after all.[59] This message, coming on top of Zorin's speech, persuaded Stevenson that Lumumba's death had virtually eliminated the possibility of an agreement with the Russians about the Congo. Still, the fact that Zorin had not followed up his early morning outburst with a public accusation against the United States suggested that there might be some chance of preserving the progress that had been made in other areas of Soviet-American relations.

The answer to the first question concerning the Afro-Asians' reaction was somewhat more complicated. In one sense, as the State Department had pointed out a few days before, Lumumba's death would make it easier for the United States to agree with the Afro-Asian states on a draft resolution, since the Americans would no longer have any reason to object to the release of the political prisoners. In a larger sense, of course, Lumumba's death made the process of reaching an agreement far more difficult. A wall of suspicion now existed between the Afro-Asians and the Western powers. It was hard for even the moderate Africans not to suspect that the United States had conspired in Lumumba's murder. Guinea and Mali immediately jumped to this conclusion, and while the other African states were more cautious in their public pronouncements, there was an undercurrent of wariness and hostility in their attitude toward the United States.

The top officials at the State Department assumed that the Casablanca states would join the Russians to demand the condemnation of Belgium and perhaps even the total withdrawal of the United Nations from the Congo. But Stevenson found in the course of Monday afternoon that the radical Afro-Asians were thinking along quite different lines. They had been persuaded by Hammarskjold that it was in their own interest to support a strengthened mandate for the UN force. His reasoning was simple. With Lumumba gone, their first priority was to preserve the regime of his successor, Antoine Gizenga, in Stanleyville. They were extremely worried about Mobutu's threatened invasion of Orientale Province, and they wanted the Secretary-General to block his advance, either by taking control of all forces on both sides or establishing a "neutral zone" through which his forces could not pass.[60]

Hammarskjold's anti–civil war proposal touched off another bitter dispute between the hardliners and the liberals in the U.S. government. On one side was Timberlake, who was back in Leopoldville and feisty as ever. He believed that the United States should encourage Mobutu to take advantage of Lumumba's death to reassert Leopoldville's control over Orientale Province, eliminate the Communist threat, and end at least one of the secessions that were tearing the Congo apart. He warned:

I HOPE DEPARTMENT AND USUN FULLY REALIZE SERIOUSNESS SYG [SECRETARY-GENERAL] PROPOSAL TO HALT MOBUTU'S OFFENSIVE AGAINST STANLEYVILLE.[61]

On the other side were the officials at the U.S. Mission in New York—not just Stevenson and his political appointees but the career diplomats such as Charles Yost. Yost did not have much use for Timberlake or what he regarded as Timberlake's shortsighted approach to the Congo. He argued that while all-out support for Mobutu's invasion might "eliminate the immediate Communist threat" in Stanleyville, it would strengthen the Communists in the long run. Even if the invasion did not provoke military counteraction by the Casablanca states, it would lead to the withdrawal of all the Afro-Asian troops from the UN force and thus to the breakdown of the entire operation—which was just what the Communists wanted. Given these alternatives, Yost argued that there was less danger in a compromise resolution which would give the United Nations the power to neutralize the opposing Congolese forces.[62]

"Imperialists, Take Your Bloody Hands Off the Congo!"

Contrary to everyone's expectations, Timberlake reported on February 14 that everything was calm in the Congo, even in Stanleyville, where a state of mourning had been declared.[63] For the rest of the week the Congo was the eye of a storm which raged around the world. The protests began in Moscow, where the government issued an extremely harsh statement blaming Hammarskjold, along with the Belgians and the other "colonialists," for Lumumba's murder and calling for the end of the UN operation. The Soviet government charged that the crime had been "prepared methodically, step by step," and sanctioned in the Western capitals; but it concentrated its fire on the Secretary-General, as Zorin had done at the Security Council. It accused him of conducting "from beginning to end a policy of foul betrayal of the Congolese people," and charged:

> The murder of Patrice Lumumba and his comrades in the dungeons of Katanga climaxes Hammarskjold's criminal actions. It is clear to every honest person on earth that the blood of Patrice Lumumba is on the hands of that flunkey of the colonialists and nothing can wash it off.

"His actions are a stain on the entire United Nations," the statement asserted. "He is unworthy of the high office of Secretary-General and his further tenure in that office is intolerable."[64] This was strong language even for the Russians, who had been attacking Hammarskjold with increasing ferocity for months. Now, with Lumumba gone, they saw no reason to exercise any restraint.

The Soviet government asserted that it was the "sacred duty of all freedom-loving nations" to respond to the appeal of the "legal Congolese government headed by Acting Prime Minister Antoine Gizenga" and stated that it was "prepared, together with other states friendly to the Republic of the Congo, to render all possible help and support to the Congolese people and their legal government."[65] At the same time, Khrushchev wrote to Gizenga expressing Soviet "shock and indignation" at the murder, and stating,

> You may be sure that in these grim days for the Congolese people the Soviet Union will do everything to have the criminals punished and to help the Congolese patriots in their just struggle against the colonialists.[66]

In Moscow, the statement launched a week-long propaganda campaign. The press was filled with accusations against the Belgians and their NATO allies, ugly caricatures of Hammarskjold, and stories about Lumumba—reminiscences, photographs of his family, poetry, and angry letters of protest from all over the country. Many of these letters were undoubtedly genuine. The press campaign of the preceding months had created a large reservoir of popular sympathy for Lumumba. Average Soviet citizens, who were usually not interested in foreign policy developments unless they were directly affected by them, felt close to the far-off Congolese leader. When the news of the murder broke, small groups of Muscovites gathered on the street corners to discuss the story, shaking their heads in disbelief; on the bus queues, heavy-set Russian women, bundled against the February cold, wept openly. "Such a fine young man," sighed a middle-aged peasant woman who had seen her share of tragedy during World War II. "How could they do this to him?"

On February 14 this sense of popular outrage was channeled into a "spontaneous" demonstration outside the Belgian Embassy in Moscow. It began at Friendship University, the newly opened facility for African and Asian students, which was immediately renamed Lumumba University. After a rally at which the students condemned the murder of Lumumba and demanded the "immediate resignation of Dag Hammarskjold, that imperialist toady," they marched through the snow-covered streets to the Belgian Embassy, carrying placards that read: "Shame on the Murderers of the African Hero, Patrice Lumumba!" "Down with Colonialism!" "Imperialists, Take Your Bloody Hands Off the Congo!" "Down with Hammarskjold!"[67] Western reporters witnessed crowds of about six thousand—the African students joined by Russian students and workers—assault the Belgian Embassy with rocks and ink over a period of about four hours. One reporter, Seymour Topping of *The New York Times,* was manhandled by young Africans who screamed, "You Americans are killing us!" Other American correspondents, such as Marvin Kalb of CBS News, found that they were welcomed with friendly grins when they disclosed their nationality—a response which raised some questions about the political convictions of the rioters.

The Moscow demonstration was followed by similar protests in London, Vienna, Belgrade, Warsaw, and other capitals. The UAR recognized the Gizenga government and announced that representatives of Ghana, Guinea, and the Sudan were meeting in Cairo to discuss the possibility of sending military "volunteers" as well as financial aid to Stanleyville. Nkrumah accused the United Nations of "open connivance" in Lumumba's death.[68] Sékou Touré, who was playing host to the President of the Soviet Union, Leonid Brezhnev,[69] at the time Lumumba's death was announced, sent Hammarskjold what the latter described as a "straightforward 'go to hell' message," accusing him of personal responsibility for Lumumba's murder.[70]

U.S. officials were disturbed by these developments. They concluded that Khrushchev was using Lumumba's death as a pretext to attack the Secretary-General and drive a wedge between the Afro-Asians and the West. But there was more to Khrushchev's reaction than the desire to score propaganda points—something more direct and less calculating: as with the U-2 incident, his outburst reflected anger, disappointment, and frustration with yet another example of Soviet weakness in the face of superior Western power and ability to control events. His feelings were compounded in this case by the fact that he himself had contributed to the debacle by agreeing to the resolution that sent the United Nations into the Congo in the first place. Lumumba had become the symbol of Khrushchev's new Africa policy. As long as he was alive, it was still possible that he might return to power and justify Khrushchev's controversial involvement in the Congo to his skeptical Kremlin colleagues. With Lumumba's death that opportunity vanished. Khrushchev's fury was only natural.

Still, despite his anger, Khrushchev displayed a surprising degree of self-control in one area that was very important to him: he indicated that Lumumba's death had not affected his interest in dealing with the new Kennedy Administration. The Soviet statement did not specifically blame the United States for Lumumba's murder, and the Soviet press reported Kennedy's "shock" and Stevenson's statement at the Security Council regretting Lumumba's death.[71]

In New York Stevenson was still taking a conciliatory line toward the Russians, hoping against hope that they would draw back from their condemnation of the Secretary-General. Shortly after the Soviet statement was released, he addressed a luncheon meeting at the UN Correspondents' Association. While he reaffirmed American support for Hammarskjold, he tried not to attack the Soviet Union head on; he referred in general to all critics of the United Nations as he warned that a failure in the Congo could plummet Africa into "cold war turmoil or worse" and destroy the usefulness of the United Nations. At one point he said he hoped that the "United States was on the eve of improved relations with the Soviet Union." When he was asked whether the Russians could achieve improved relations with the United States while attacking Hammarskjold, he replied with a smile that it would "take some doing."[72]

Stevenson and Kennedy Warn Against Soviet Intervention

This was the last of conciliation from the Americans for some time. Once they had studied the Soviet statement, they were convinced that Khrushchev was not seriously interested in an accommodation with the West. When the Security Council resumed its discussion on Wednesday, February 15, Stevenson switched abruptly from the line he had taken the previous day and delivered a speech that reminded the Russians of Henry Cabot Lodge. He explained that he had hoped to speak only of constructive moves but instead was faced with a Soviet statement and draft resolution which were "virtually a declaration of war on the United Nations."[73]

Just as he was asking, "Shall the United Nations survive?" an unprecedented violent pro-Lumumba demonstration erupted in the visitors' galleries. In addition to those actually present, millions of American television viewers witnessed the extraordinary sight of the decorous Security Council meeting being interrupted by hate-filled voices and swinging fists. The fifty to sixty demonstrators were mostly black Americans, members of African nationalist organizations, who reportedly obtained visitors' passes from two West African delegations, both of which immediately denied that they were involved. The demonstration was obviously well planned; one African delegate told reporters he had been approached the night before to help organize it but had refused. The Secretary-General stayed in the Council chamber until an aide, who heard the rioters shouting, "Get Hammarskjold, get Hammarskjold!" insisted that he leave. Extra security precautions were taken despite Hammarskjold's objections. According to his biographer, "He was shocked to learn that one of the UN elevator operators had heard a girl from the Ghana Mission say, after the riot . . . that she hoped the demonstrators would get to Hammarskjold and kill him." More than two dozen persons were injured, including eighteen UN guards, who were unarmed, and two press photographers.[74]

Anti-American sentiment seemed to be spreading along with support for Gizenga: the U.S. ambassador in Cairo telephoned a report that a mob had stoned the Embassy after setting the Belgian Embassy on fire,[75] while in Accra the U.S. Embassy was besieged by protesting crowds after the Ghanaian government officially recognized the Stanleyville regime.[76] Rusk conferred with British Ambassador Sir Harold Caccia about the steps they could take to help the Secretary-General if their worst fears were realized, that is, if the Russians and the radical Africans intervened militarily in support of Gizenga and the United Nations "lost control" of the situation. Rusk suggested that both powers see what "military forces, including aircraft," were available in the area. He also urged the British to work with the Americans in persuading the Sudan to "stand firm" on the transit issue and in warning the UAR and "other states likely to recognize Gizenga" that the Western powers would take a "grave view" of any intervention in support of the Stanleyville regime.[77]

Kennedy was scheduled to hold a press conference that evening, and after the riot at the Security Council, Stevenson telephoned him and recommended that he begin with a "tough statement on the Congo, warning against any unilateral intervention and strongly supporting the UN." Kennedy later told a visitor he was "pleasantly surprised" by Stevenson's call. He remarked, "Adlai's got an iron ass, and, my God, in this job, he's got the nerve of a burglar."[78]

Kennedy opened the press conference with a strong statement along the lines Stevenson had proposed. He did not mention the Soviet Union by name, but he left no doubt that he had the Russians in mind when he warned that he was "seriously concerned at what appears to be a threat of unilateral intervention" in the Congo. "I find it difficult to believe that any government is really planning to take so dangerous and irresponsible a step," Kennedy said. He continued:

> Nevertheless, I feel it important that there should be no misunderstanding of the position of the United States in such an eventuality. The United States has supported and will continue to support the United Nations presence in the Congo. . . . Only by the presence of the United Nations in the Congo can peace be kept in Africa. I would conceive it to be the duty of the United States . . . to defend the Charter of the United Nations by opposing any attempt by any government to intervene unilaterally in the Congo.

The President tried not to go beyond the statement when he was asked about the impact of the Congo crisis on Soviet-American relations, but the questioners were persistent. One reporter, noting that Khrushchev had just responded positively to Kennedy's offer to work with the Soviet Union in space exploration, asked, "Do you think this sort of pooling and cooperation . . . will still be possible under the tense conditions that developed in the UN today?" Kennedy's reply was conciliatory; he said he hoped it would be possible for the two countries to "cooperate in peaceful ventures." A second reporter asked the perennial question about a summit meeting with Khrushchev. Kennedy said there were no plans for a meeting, but he did not rule one out. Another reporter went to the heart of the problem by asking:

> Is it your view that we can proceed in serious negotiations with the Soviet Union in such areas as arms control and nuclear test ban while they continue to agitate the situation in the United Nations and in the Congo? In other words, can we conduct relations with them in compartments?

Kennedy neatly sidestepped that one by repeating his hope that all members of the United Nations would decide to operate through the world organization rather than through "unilateral intervention" outside the United Nations.[79]

Although Kennedy was careful to limit his criticism of Soviet policy to the Congo issue and to leave open other areas of compromise, his statement that the United States would oppose unilateral intervention in the Congo—with the implication that it would use force to do so if necessary—created the impression that the new Administration had turned a corner in its assessment of the Soviet threat. Up to this point the Administration had spoken softly to and about the Russians as it reexamined the old cold war attitudes. Some of the top officials, such as Stevenson and Kennedy himself, seem to have thought they could undo the errors of the Eisenhower Administration's dealings with the Russians and handle the relationship better through greater intelligence and understanding. To the proponents of this rationalist approach, Khrushchev's assault on Hammarskjold came as a shock. It struck them as irrational, particularly at a time when the Soviet leader knew the new Administration was involved in a major foreign policy review. They had hoped he would "exercise restraint" until Kennedy had charted his course. "Moscow has acted in such a way as to make the new Kennedy Administration plot its course in a far more skeptical way than it was doing before the Soviet Union's statement yesterday," wrote James Reston in an analysis that reflected the mood of the Administration. Khrushchev might succeed in bringing down the Secretary-General, "but the price in Washington may be higher than he thinks." The Administration would be studying other belligerent statements by Khrushchev, such as his January 6 speech, more carefully and "looking at its military budget, its plans for nuclear testing and disarmament talks, and its relations with the allies in the hard light of Mr. Khrushchev's latest moves," Reston concluded.[80]

Ironically, Reston's reference to Khrushchev's speech of January 6 represented a major misunderstanding of Soviet intentions on the part of the U.S. government. The speech, in which Khrushchev boasted that the Communist countries could defeat the capitalists, including the United States, without war, was intended more for the Chinese than for the Americans and constituted a defense of the "softer" Soviet line toward the West against Peking's militant hard-line approach.

American diplomats and journalists in Moscow found the Administration's surprise at the Soviet outburst somewhat naive. They had learned over the years that Khrushchev's doctrine of "peaceful coexistence" did not mean cooperation across the board; the Soviet leader really did think he could keep his relations with the United States in compartments. In Khrushchev's mind there was no contradiction between his assault on Hammarskjold and his attempt to develop cordial relations with the Kennedy Administration. Despite his genuine concern about preventing nuclear war, and his desire to deal with the Americans on such important matters as disarmament, Khrushchev would not give up his freedom to compete with the Western powers in Africa and Asia or to attack the Secretary-General as part of an anticolonialist campaign—even though such attacks ran the risk of disturbing the slowly developing thaw with Washington.

Khrushchev undoubtedly found Kennedy's response rather strong, for in his own way he had "exercised restraint." He had refrained from accusing the United States of involvement in Lumumba's murder, which he surely would have done if Eisenhower had still been in office when Lumumba's death was announced. Still, even after Stevenson's speech and Kennedy's statement, the Soviet attitude toward the United States remained mild. Khrushchev's two-track approach was dramatically illustrated by the front page of *Pravda* the following day: next to a major editorial denouncing Hammarskjold as a "butcher" and a "Judas" was the full text of Khrushchev's reply to Kennedy's cable of congratulations on the Venus satellite—the message Kennedy had referred to at his press conference.[81]

The Eighth Security Council Meeting: February 16–21, 1961

Khrushchev apparently thought his conciliatory attitude toward Kennedy would more than compensate for his attack on Hammarskjold, but he miscalculated the depth of American support for the Secretary-General. He made a similar miscalculation about the Afro-Asians. He apparently assumed that once the news of Lumumba's murder was out, the Afro-Asians would share his sense of outrage and turn on Hammarskjold. But with a few exceptions this did not turn out to be the case. Hammarskjold's well-known concern about the needs of the smaller states outweighed the doubts of most Afro-Asians about his Congo policy. When the Africans spoke at the Security Council on February 16, the only ones who denounced the Secretary-General and demanded his resignation were Guinea and Mali. Perhaps the most disappointing African speech, from Khrushchev's point of view, was that of the Sudanese delegate, who deplored the "hideous crime" but reaffirmed his government's policy that "no transit to the Congo across the territory of the Sudan—whether by air or land—is permitted except at the request of the Secretary-General."[82] In other words, not even the murder of Lumumba could persuade the Sudanese to alter their policy regarding the transshipment of supplies for the Stanleyville regime. This decision must have suggested to Khrushchev that even in the best of circumstances, African unity in the "fight against imperialism" was extremely elusive.

At the same time, the Americans were finding it difficult to persuade the Afro-Asians to come up with a draft resolution that the United States could support. Part of the problem was that two of the three Afro-Asian members of the Security Council—Ceylon and the UAR—were supporters of Gizenga. They had followed Hammarskjold's recommendations up to a point: their draft, which was introduced on Friday, February 17, authorized the UN force to prevent civil war through neutral zones and ceasefires and called for the "immediate withdrawal" of all Belgian military and political advisers, the reconvening of Parliament, the reorganization of the ANC, and an investigation of Lumumba's assassination.[83] But they refused to alter the three features that Stevenson found objectionable: first, their draft made no reference to the Secretary-General; second, it authorized the use of force to prevent civil war; and third, while it prohibited foreign military personnel—a provision directed primarily against Belgian aid to Mobutu and Tshombe—it did not prohibit the sending of arms and other military supplies—a provision directed against aid to Stanleyville.[84]

Over the weekend, while Stevenson tried to drum up support for his amendments from the Afro-Asian moderates, such as India and Nigeria, Nkrumah weighed in with his own plan, which was more radical than the Afro-Asian draft. He proposed a new all-African command, which would disarm the ANC by force if necessary, arrange for the departure of all Belgian military personnel, free the political prisoners, and convene Parliament. In order to eliminate any cold war competition, all foreign diplomatic missions were to leave the Congo at once.[85]

The U.S. ambassador to Ghana, Francis Russell, pointed out that Brezhnev had arrived in Accra two days before Nkrumah sent his plan to Hammarskjold, but he added that the Ghanaians insisted the plan was entirely their own idea. Russell talked with Nkrumah immediately after Brezhnev's departure and reported that Nkrumah was planning to come to New York for the General Assembly session in early March and wanted to be invited to Washington. The ambassador recommended that Kennedy see him and suggested that if Kennedy was interested in dispelling the "widespread feeling in Africa" that the United States was associated with Lumumba's death, he might consider accepting Nkrumah's plan as a basis for discussion. In any case a meeting with Nkrumah would be a good opportunity for the President to put into practice his ideas about improving relations with the neutralist leaders, and it might help persuade the Africans that the United States was not irrevocably tied to the European colonial powers.[86]

Stevenson was concerned about the same issue. On Sunday afternoon he told the State Department that the United States might want to "consider" the possibility of voting for the Afro-Asian resolution, even if his efforts to amend it failed, in order to avoid alienating the moderates and losing everything that had been gained by the new American policy over the past few weeks.[87]

In the end Stevenson's effort to build a moderate consensus around the U.S. position was undermined by another dramatic bulletin from the Congo. When the Security Council met on Monday morning, the Secretary-General announced that six political prisoners sent from Leopoldville to Bakwanga for safekeeping had been executed. He expressed his "revolt and shock" and said he had written a letter of protest to Kasavubu. Zorin immediately accused Hammarskjold of responsibility for these deaths and reminded the Council that he had warned a further delay would lead to more trouble.[88]

The Bakwanga murders created a new mood of urgency and made it impossible for Stevenson to persuade India or Nigeria to support any

U.S. amendments that might delay the adoption of the resolution or produce a Soviet veto. He gave in gracefully and announced that he would vote for the Afro-Asian draft, despite his reservations. He was particularly concerned about the authorization of the use of force "in the last resort"; he said he understood the phrase to mean that force would not be used unless negotiations failed.[89] The British delegate, Sir Patrick Dean, followed Stevenson's lead and voted reluctantly for the resolution, which was adopted 9 to 0, with the Soviet Union and France abstaining.[90] Dean stressed that in his view the United Nations could use force only to "prevent a clash between hostile Congolese troops." He insisted, "There can be no question of empowering the United Nations to use its forces to impose a political settlement."[91] Dean's interpretation was more restrictive than Stevenson's; this was an important distinction which would come up repeatedly in the course of the next two years.

End of the Honeymoon

The Kennedy Administration had come through its first foreign policy crisis intact, if not with flying colors. A month of new initiatives and patient diplomacy had paid off. Thanks to Stevenson's willingness to compromise and the President's ability to project a pro-African image, the United States had managed to weather the storm produced by Lumumba's murder with only a minimal loss of confidence among the Afro-Asians who were essential to the UN operation. Stevenson pointed out that if the United States wanted to keep their support, it would have to help the Secretary-General implement the new resolution promptly.

Stevenson anticipated trouble from Dayal as long as he remained in the Congo, but he anticipated even more trouble from "our friends"— Kasavubu, Tshombe, and the Belgians. He realized that the United States needed Kasavubu as the legal chief of state, but at the same time he insisted that it could "not afford" to be put in the position of defending him to the world when "his ultimate responsibility" for the "recent executions" was only too apparent. "Unless he brings indiscriminate killings to end and cooperates more closely with UN I am afraid his position—and ours—will crumble," Stevenson warned. He regarded Tshombe as the "most serious problem" and suggested that if the United States could not control him either directly or through the Belgians, it would have to be prepared to "oppose him firmly" and support the Secretary-General's efforts to make him cooperate with the United Nations. Finally, Stevenson felt the United States must persuade the Belgians to comply with the new resolution, even though he knew it would be difficult, since their attitude toward the United Nations involved a "great complex of emotional, political, and economic problems."[92]

The reactions to the resolution in Brussels, Leopoldville, and Elisabethville were uniformly negative, as Stevenson expected. The Belgians were shocked to receive a communication from the Secretary-General demanding the immediate withdrawal of military and political advisers without any reference to their replacement.[93] Tshombe called the resolution a "declaration of war against Katanga and the Congo." Ileo charged that it violated Congolese sovereignty. Both men warned that they would fight if the United Nations tried to carry it out.[94] Timberlake was livid. He called the demand for the withdrawal of Belgian political advisers "dynamite" and explained that the United Nations could not find qualified replacements for the technical and administrative personnel who would be forced to leave. He warned:

> "COMMUNISTS WILL HAVE FIELD DAY PUSHING OUT PRESENT NON-UN ADVISERS MUCH FASTER THAN THEY CAN BE REPLACED. . . . I AM VERY MUCH AFRAID THAT APPLYING ALL OF THE MEASURES APPROVED BY THE SECURITY COUNCIL WILL PUT US ON THE DEFENSIVE UNDER CONDITIONS OF ADVANTAGE TO THE SOVIETS.[95]

Kennedy and Stevenson were not unaware of the Soviet threat in the Congo; their new policy was designed to outflank the Russians by winning away their Afro-Asian supporters. While they assumed that Lumumba's death had reduced the likelihood of an immediate Communist takeover, they realized that it had not eliminated the possibility of a civil war between the pro-Western government in Leopoldville and the Gizenga regime in Stanleyville, which had now been recognized by Guinea, Morocco, Mali, Cuba, Ghana, and the UAR, as well as the Soviet bloc. Administration officials were seriously concerned about the possibility of Soviet military intervention in support of Gizenga, and they were not reassured by the belligerent anti-Hammarskjold statements that kept pouring out of Moscow.

Khrushchev, for his part, was still smarting from his humiliating defeat in the Congo. He had scored a minor victory at the Security Council, where the threat of a Soviet veto had forced the Afro-Asians to eliminate all references to the Secretary-General from their resolution; but it was a rather hollow victory, since it was perfectly obvious that Hammarskjold would continue to run the Congo operation just as he did before. The day after the resolution was adopted, Khrushchev wrote to Nehru and other neutralist leaders proposing that the Secretary-General be replaced by a troika and the UN operation by an all-African commission which would work closely with the Gizenga government—a suggestion that was clearly influenced by Brezhnev's recent conversations with Nkrumah. "To put it bluntly," Khrushchev wrote, "it was, in essence, Hammarskjold who murdered Lumumba. Whoever held the knife or gun is, after all, not the sole murderer. The chief assassin is the one who handed him the weapon."[96]

Stevenson, who was asked about the letter on February 25, spoke more frankly about his estimate of Soviet intentions in the Congo than he had done at the Security Council meetings. He said he thought Khrushchev was attacking the United Nations because it was "an obstacle to Soviet penetration of central Africa," and added that it was "a pity" that the Russians would not "give the Afro-Asian UN resolution a chance for implementation before renewing their attack on the Secretary-General and the UN itself."[97]

This blunt talk had immediate repercussions in Moscow. Ambassador Thompson returned to the Soviet capital on the evening of February 27 with a private message from Kennedy to Khrushchev expressing the hope that differences about the Congo would not develop into a "serious obstacle" to an improvement in Soviet-American relations and suggesting a late spring summit meeting in Vienna or Stockholm. Khrushchev was aware of Thompson's arrival, but he left for an agricultural conference in Sverdlovsk early the next morning without making any arrangements to receive the American envoy.[98]

Khrushchev's snub was underscored by the first ugly Soviet press attack on Kennedy's foreign policy. *Izvestia* declared that while the new leaders had been expected to clean the "Augean stables" left behind by the Eisenhower Administration, they had instead "created the impression that Washington has become accustomed to the stink of unclean stables."[99]

Two days later Stevenson escalated American criticism of Soviet Congo policy at an official New York City luncheon given in his honor. He urged the Russians not to try to replace the Belgians in the Congo. "Africa is the Balkans of today," he warned. "Any outside power seeking to manipulate its griefs and searchings and first fumbling efforts to stand alone risks bringing down on Africa and on the world the dread possibility of nuclear destruction." He warned the Soviet Union: "Stay your ambitions. Think twice about your intervention. . . . Do not sabotage the only institution which offers an alternative to imperialism."[100]

The Russians rejected Stevenson's arguments politely but sharply. *Izvestia* criticized his "cold war" approach, describing it as the essence of the "bankrupt Eisenhower-Dulles policy" and implying that better things were expected of the Kennedy Administration.[101]

Lumumba's murder had obviously had an impact on the relations between the two great powers. It marked the end of the honeymoon and the beginning of a more realistic policy on both sides. The Americans began to realize that on certain basic issues Khrushchev could not be budged by "reasonable" talk; his world view was firmly fixed, and he would defend his principles with stubborn determination. Khrushchev had also begun to understand the nature of his new adversary. He apparently misread the conciliatory attitude of the Kennedy Administration during its first few weeks and assumed that the Americans would not react so strongly to his assault on the Secretary-General. It took him a while to realize that they meant to act on the lines laid down in the Kennedy and Stevenson statements of February 15 and that they intended to counter vigorously Soviet moves against the Secretary-General and in the Congo, as well as in other parts of the world. Khrushchev's decision to leave Moscow without seeing Thompson was essentially a delayed reaction to the tough line taken by the Kennedy Administration. At the same time, the Soviet leader realized, once Thompson and his summit proposal caught up with him in Siberia, that Kennedy shared his interest in accommodation on the major issue of war and peace. Though he did not respond to Kennedy's overture for more than two months, he had already decided to move toward a summit meeting with the new American President.

CHAPTER TEN

Nonalignment, American Style
(March 1–September 1, 1961)

"Did Ambassador Timberlake notify the Department before he requested
the Admiral to turn around with his ships?"

O~N~ SUNDAY MORNING, March 5, Ambassador Timberlake put in a
call to the U.S. Navy and requested the commander of a small task
force which was off the coast of Angola and heading south toward
South Africa to reverse course and head for the Congo instead. He was
alarmed about the situation at the port of Matadi, the lifeline for all incoming supplies for the UN force, where a small contingent of Sudanese UN troops had been battling Congolese troops loyal to the
Leopoldville government since Saturday morning. The Sudanese had
been forced to withdraw from the naval base at Banana, eight miles
away, on Friday night. They were greatly outnumbered by the Congolese at Matadi. They had suffered a number of casualties, and were reportedly running out of ammunition. The United Nations had not
asked the ambassador for military help, but Timberlake had developed
the habit of taking the initiative without waiting for formal requests or
instructions. He felt the situation was urgent enough to order the ships
to Congolese waters as a precautionary measure in case they were
needed.

Moreover, Timberlake felt he had a right to call on this particular
task force, which was named SOLANT AMITY, and was composed of
five naval craft—two destroyers, two landing ships, and one tanker—
with amphibious equipment, tanks, six helicopters, five hundred marines, and seven hundred and fifty sailors. It had been set up at the beginning of August, just about the time the assassination plot against
Lumumba got under way, for the same reason: the U.S. government
was alarmed about the growing Soviet involvement in the Congo and
decided a military response to the Soviet challenge might be useful.
The ships did not appear off the coast of Africa until November, by
which time Lumumba was under house arrest and the Russians had

been gone for two months. Since that time the task force had justified its existence by paying goodwill visits to 11 ports, and by delivering emergency food supplies to the Congo and taking home the 738 Guinean soldiers who pulled out of the UN force.

When President Kennedy learned from news reports later that day that an American ambassador had ordered up a unit of the U.S. Navy, apparently on his own, he shot off a memo to Secretary of State Rusk and Secretary of Defense McNamara demanding an explanation:

> Did Ambassador Timberlake notify the Department before he requested the Admiral to turn around with his ships? Did the Admiral notify the Navy Department before he acceded to the request? If neither Department was informed before action was taken, is this because of faulty communications or because of the procedures that were followed in this case? In view of the importance that this decision has been given it seems that we should take action in the future to have an opportunity to review these decisions before they are finalized.[1]

Kennedy was a former naval officer who liked to run a tight ship of his own. He was about to hold his first meeting with an African head of state, Ghana's President Nkrumah, a prickly neutralist who was opposed to any sort of American military involvement in the Congo. Kennedy had just gone through an extremely tense period and had managed to retain the good will of the neutralists in spite of Lumumba's murder by stressing American respect for African independence and assuring the Africans that the United States, unlike the Soviet Union, had no desire to throw its weight around in the Congo. The last thing he needed at this point was an American proconsul who ordered up the fleet before the United Nations even called for assistance.

It took the President two days to get the order reversed. On March 6 State Department spokesman Lincoln White assured curious reporters that there was nothing out of the ordinary about Timberlake's request, which was merely an exercise in "foresight and caution."[2] By March 7, the day before Nkrumah's visit to Washington, White announced that the task force would not be going to the Congo after all. He repeated that Timberlake had full authority to order the ships to Congolese waters and assured reporters that the State Department stood behind both his original action and the later reversal.[3]

This incident was typical of the confusing situation in the Congo, where everyone seemed to be working at cross-purposes. It was also an indication of the complicated relationship between President Kennedy, who was following the Congo crisis on a day-to-day basis, and Ambassador Timberlake, who felt he understood the Soviet threat in Africa far better than the new Administration and often despaired of getting his views through to the President.

The Ambassador Has a Difficult Week

Timberlake's request to the U.S. Navy came at the end of a difficult week. It began on Monday, with queries from Washington about reports that three hundred Gizengist troops had taken over Luluabourg, in Kasai Province, hundreds of miles from Stanleyville, without firing a shot, and that another group of Gizengist soldiers was heading west toward Coquilhatville, the capital of Equateur Province. Meanwhile, Mobutu, who might have been expected to counter these moves, had reportedly given up his intention of leading an offensive against Gizenga's forces in Orientale Province and had "disappeared for a weeklong river journey in the company of his favorite young lady, aboard a riverboat filled with officer friends and well stocked with beer and champagne."[4]

The State Department wanted to know why Gizenga's forces were meeting no resistance, what Mobutu was up to, and whether Kasavubu and Ileo had any plans for "defensive measures."[5] Timberlake replied that there was no cause for alarm: the Gizengist offensive against Coquilhatville had not materialized and the attack on Luluabourg had "fizzled out." Some of the soldiers had withdrawn; others, who came from the area, had melted into the local population. Timberlake conceded that the appearance of Gizengist troops in various parts of the Congo had an "immediate psychological and political shock effect," but he felt it was exaggerated out of all proportion to reality.

The real danger in the situation, according to Timberlake, was not the possibility of a civil war but the likelihood of an "outbreak of fighting" between Mobutu's troops and the UN force. Both sides, he said, were "suspicious, jumpy, and near the point of spontaneous combustion."[6] Relations between the United Nations and the Leopoldville government had gone from bad to worse in the wake of the February 21 Security Council resolution, and violent attacks on UN personnel had become a daily occurrence. On February 27 Dayal protested the "bestial behavior" of the Congolese troops. Kasavubu countered with a radio broadcast calling up the army reservists and appealing to the people to mobilize against the threat of a UN takeover. Kasavubu still refused to have anything to do with Dayal and kept demanding that he be recalled.[7] Timberlake agreed that the only way to reduce the tension was to remove Dayal, but he was afraid that repeated public demands for his recall would only strengthen Hammarskjold's determination to keep him in the Congo.[8]

Timberlake had leaked his views to the American reporters stationed in Leopoldville, and the word had gotten back to Washington. The President was asked at his March 1 press conference if the U.S.

government was satisfied with UN policy in the Congo, where the "pro-Communist Gizenga government" seemed to be gaining ground, and if the United States had "made any representations" to Hammarskjold about it. Kennedy replied cautiously that the situation was uncertain, the Security Council resolution was only a week old, and the United States would continue to concern itself with its "successful implementation."

Kennedy was also asked about his Assistant Secretary for African Affairs, Soapy Williams, who had stopped in Nairobi on his eleven-nation African tour and offended his British hosts by stating that "Africa was for the Africans." Kennedy defended Williams and explained that "he was talking about all those who felt that they were Africans," whatever their color or race might be. "I do not know who else Africa should be for," the President remarked.[9]

By this time Williams had arrived in Leopoldville for a five-day visit to assure Kasavubu of American support and to persuade him to cooperate with the United Nations. Timberlake did not have much respect for Williams; he had concluded during their discussions in Washington that the former governor was hopelessly naive about the Communists and knew nothing about Africa. His experience escorting Williams around on his official calls in Leopoldville did nothing to alter that opinion. When Williams met with Kasavubu on February 28, the Congolese President adopted a conciliatory line toward the United Nations, which contrasted sharply with his inflammatory broadcast of the previous day.[10] But Kasavubu was perfectly capable of ignoring American political advice, as he had demonstrated over the past eight months. While he was telling Williams what Williams wanted to hear in Leopoldville, his Prime Minister, Ileo, was meeting with the two right-wing secessionists, Tshombe and Kalonji, in Elisabethville, and heading in the opposite direction.

All these leaders were alarmed by the adoption of the Security Council resolution; they had visions of the United Nations, led by Dayal, removing their Belgian advisers, disarming their troops, imposing a Gizengist government on them, and trying them for Lumumba's murder. They announced at the end of their meeting that they had agreed to combine their forces in a military pact, which would be directed against the double threat of "Communist tyranny and United Nations tutelage." They left open the question of the independent status of Katanga and Kasai and stated that they would hold a summit meeting on March 5 in Tananarive, capital of the Malagasy Republic. They hoped Gizenga would join them there.[11] This decision to hold a meeting of the rival Congolese leaders outside the country, on the peaceful island of Madagascar, off the East African coast, flew in the face of the Security Council resolution, which implied that the only legitimate road to a political solution was through the convening of Parliament.

On Thursday, March 2, Timberlake sent a tough cable to Washington explaining that the United States was on the threshold of a "new effort" in the Congo and urging the Administration to exercise "statesmanship" and not to be stampeded into a position that would threaten American interests in Africa. "I understand confusion among sincere and honest government leaders over what should be done in the Congo," he said, in an obvious reference to Williams. Still, it was essential for the U.S. government to recognize the complexity of the problem and to understand what the Russians and their Ghanaian and Guinean allies were up to.

They had supported Lumumba—an "irresponsible and opportunistic demagogue"—because he was prepared "consciously or unconsciously" to take the Congo into their camp, while Kasavubu and his allies were "equally determined" to look to the West for help. Now, with Lumumba gone, the Russians and their African allies had changed their tactics. They were trying to use the United Nations to reduce the Congo to "complete chaos and ruin" and create a vacuum into which they could move. Their first step was to blur the distinction between Kasavubu, who had been recognized by the General Assembly as the legal head of state, and the Gizenga regime in Stanleyville, which had been recognized by the Soviet bloc and the radical Africans but which did not have a "shred" of legality to it. If the United States did not challenge this Communist ploy by reaffirming its support for Kasavubu, the United Nations would probably end up adopting the view that it was dealing with two rival governments of equal stature.

Timberlake warned that Gizenga's supporters were pressing for a government of national conciliation because they believed it would give them an opportunity for "sabotage and subversion from within." The ambassador was not opposed to the creation of a "broadly based government," which would include important figures from Lumumba's and Gizenga's parties, but "not necessarily Gizenga himself." The important point was that such a government had to be built around Kasavubu; it could not replace him. Timberlake conceded that he was discouraged by the calibre of Kasavubu's leadership, but he pointed out that the Lumumbists were no better. The elimination of Lumumba meant that there were no strong leaders in the Congo.[12]

After spending a few days with Williams, Timberlake felt he was fighting a one-man battle against the prevailing drift of the Kennedy Administration; but he had made an impression on the President during their conversation in early February, and Bundy made sure that Kennedy got to see the text of his cable the following day, before the

President met with his top advisers about the Congo. While Kennedy could not go along with Timberlake's conviction that Ghana and Guinea were irrevocably committed to the Communist camp, he accepted the ambassador's evaluation of Dayal and ordered the State Department and Stevenson to step up their efforts to have him replaced.[13]

While the President and his advisers were discussing the Congo on the afternoon of March 3, the violence which Timberlake had predicted erupted at Banana. Prime Minister Ileo ignored the building crisis and flew to Tananarive, accompanied by Interior Minister Adoula and other members of his government. They were less interested in the battle with the United Nations than in reaching a political settlement with the other Congolese leaders. Kasavubu kept delaying his departure—less because of the Matadi crisis than because of his fear of flying to Tananarive via Elisabethville, where Lumumba had just been murdered. He finally left on Sunday afternoon, as the fighting in Matadi reached a climax, but only after Tshombe got on the phone, assured him of his safety, and pleaded with him to lend his prestige to the conference. Kasavubu disembarked from his plane in Elisabethville looking nervous and frightened; he was uncertain, despite Tshombe's assurances, about what would happen to him. Once he saw the honor guard lined up on the field, his face brightened, but it was not until he reached Tananarive that his fears were dispelled and he could relax. Most of the other leaders felt the same way.

Malagasy President Philibert Tsiranana, a jovial man who wore Truman-style flowered shirts and a large straw hat, was determined to make the meeting a success. He gave the Congolese an ideal conference site—a picturesque nineteenth-century Scottish castle built on a hillside, surrounded by gardens. The climate was agreeable, the food the best French cuisine outside Paris. In this pleasant atmosphere, far removed from the turmoil and suspicion of the Congo, the barriers of distrust began to come down. The assembled leaders waited for Gizenga, who had indicated to Dayal that he intended to come. But on March 8 Gizenga issued a statement denouncing the conference as a meeting of "traitors and puppets" and demanding the reconvening of Parliament and the recognition of his government as the sole legitimate one.[14]

The participants formally regretted Gizenga's absence, but privately were pleased that he had decided not to come to Tananarive. It made their task of reconciliation much easier. They simply followed Tshombe's lead and adopted his plan for a confederation that would scrap the existing constitution and replace it with a much looser arrangement between Leopoldville and the provinces—an arrangement particularly beneficial to Katanga. Tshombe dominated the conference by the force of his personality and his pocketbook; the other participants were aware that he was the only Congolese leader who was solvent, thanks to the Belgian mining interests in Katanga. He had offered to pay most of the costs of the military pact with Ileo and Kalonji, and he had unblocked some of the funds Katanga owed to the central government and turned them over to Ileo before the Tananarive meeting. Tshombe's hostility toward the United Nations was reflected in a message sent to Hammarskjold at the end of the conference. The participants demanded the suspension of the February 21 Security Council resolution. They contended that there was no longer any reason for the United Nations to impose a settlement on the Congo, since they had reached agreement among themselves without any foreign interference and had proved that the Congolese could manage their own affairs.[15]

Timberlake's reaction to the Tananarive conference was one of "restrained optimism." He felt that a confederation was "better adapted to tribal realities" than the present centralized government—a point he had made repeatedly since the previous summer. But he pointed out that it was necessary, in theory, for Parliament to approve any constitutional change, and he felt it would be unwise to convene Parliament and risk a showdown with Gizenga in the absence of any assurances that Leopoldville could command a majority of the votes.[16]

State Department officials, on the other hand, were less than overjoyed about Kasavubu's new alliance with Tshombe and his ultimatum to the Secretary-General. While they welcomed the fact that the Congolese leaders were trying to come to grips with the problem of national unity, they warned that there could be no true reconciliation until Gizenga was brought into the talks, and they reaffirmed U.S. support for the Security Council resolution of February 21.[17]

While the rest of the Congolese government was in Tananarive, Foreign Minister Bomboko was left to cope with the consequences of the Matadi incident. After two days of fighting, the outnumbered Sudanese contingent was disarmed and forced to withdraw. On March 6 the Sudanese government announced that it was pulling its troops out of the UN force.[18] This was extremely disturbing news for the Americans. They had counted on the Sudan to hold the line for the West by preventing Communist aid from reaching the Gizenga regime in Stanleyville. Now that the Sudanese troops had been humiliated by Mobutu's soldiers, the Soviet Union and the UAR would undoubtedly try to take advantage of President Abboud's disappointment to persuade him to change his mind about the transshipment of supplies through the Sudan.[19]

The Sudanese defeat at Matadi did have one beneficial effect, however: Bomboko apparently realized that his government had acted foolishly by antagonizing the Sudan, which had never interfered in Congolese politics. He tried to make up for it by his cordial treatment of the Sudanese diplomat, Mekki Abbas, the newly arrived temporary replacement for Dayal, who was going to New York for two weeks of consultations. The news that Dayal was leaving, even temporarily, transformed the attitude of the Congolese in Leopoldville; suddenly the negotiations about Matadi took a turn for the better, and Dayal felt he could leave Abbas in charge with a clear conscience.[20] Abbas was jovial, friendly—and African. The Congolese welcomed him with open arms. While Dayal and Hammarskjold, reading his cables in New York, felt he was too conciliatory and yielded to the Leopoldville authorities on too many questions of principle,[21] Timberlake and the other Western envoys were delighted with him and were sorry that he was available for only a temporary assignment.

A few days after Dayal arrived in New York, he had his first encounter with Stevenson. He had been looking forward to meeting this well-known champion of the United Nations and to having a serious discussion with him about the problems he was facing in the Congo. He was certain that Stevenson would be sympathetic. To his dismay and astonishment, Stevenson had absolutely no interest in hearing Dayal's views. "He seemed obsessed with the idea that I was exhausted and in need of a long vacation," Dayal recalled ruefully. "He refused to talk about anything else."

On March 20, the day *The New York Times* ran an article asserting that Hammarskjold had asked Dayal to stay on for at least another two or three months, Stevenson went to see Hammarskjold and "really laid it on the line hard," stressing that Kennedy was very much opposed to Dayal's return to the Congo. Hammarskjold conceded that Dayal's "inability to get on with the Congolese made it desirable to have him replaced," but he explained that the "under the table" pressure from the Western powers had complicated the problem of replacing him. If Hammarskjold appeared to be yielding to Western demands for his removal, it would damage the prestige of the United Nations. In addition, it would upset Nehru, who thought very highly of Dayal, at a time when he desperately needed Indian troops to bring the UN force up to full strength.[22]

Hammarskjold's problem was compounded by the fact that he had great respect for Dayal's character, intellect, and diplomatic ability. Hammarskjold himself had very much the same reaction to the "impossible" Congolese that Dayal had, and he sympathized with Dayal's difficulties in dealing with them. He was very reluctant to let his trusted collaborator go, but at the same time, he was forced to acknowledge that Dayal's only flaw was a serious one: he could not maintain a relationship with the Congolese government in Leopoldville and he had antagonized the Western powers whose diplomatic and financial support Hammarskjold needed to make the Congo operation a success. Still, he kept putting off a final decision and finding new tasks for Dayal in New York.

Although Hammarskjold kept insisting that his recall was only temporary, Dayal's original two-week absence from Leopoldville stretched on and on, and the Americans in the Congo breathed a sigh of relief. Lumumba's disappearance from the scene had eliminated the most serious threat to American interests—the possibility that the charismatic young leader would return to power and invite the Russians back to Leopoldville. Dayal's absence removed, for the time being, the new threat Timberlake had outlined in his cables—the possibility that the United Nations, because of Dayal's hostility toward Kasavubu and Mobutu, would promote a settlement favoring the Gizengists, which might result in the establishment of yet another pro-Soviet regime in Leopoldville.

Dayal's "temporary" departure opened a new period of cooperation between the United Nations, the U.S. Embassy, and the Leopoldville government, which ultimately led to the convening of Parliament and the formation of a coalition government, including Gizenga and his allies, on terms highly favorable to Leopoldville. This was not an easy process. The next few months were filled with delays and hesitations on the part of the Congolese, sudden reversals in Soviet policy, and dramatic debates within the U.S. government.

New Opportunities in Stanleyville

In the middle of March a rapprochement between Leopoldville and Stanleyville seemed an extremely unlikely prospect. The U.S. Embassy, however, had been working quietly in this direction for some time. As Timberlake explained to the President, he had nothing against a "broadly based government" including Gizengist elements as long as it was under the control of Leopoldville, and he believed that with the proper preparation this might be possible—certainly more possible than when Lumumba was alive. While Timberlake was alarmed about Gizenga's impact on the international scene, particularly in New York, he believed that Gizenga's foreign supporters tended to exaggerate his actual strength in the Congo itself, where his forces were plagued by jealousy and rivalry. As evidence, the ambassador cited a recent falling-out between Gizenga's most prominent allies: Anicet Kashamura, an extroverted Marxist, who had infuriated the Europeans in Leopoldville with his incendiary broadcasts in the summer of 1960, when he served as Lumumba's Minister of Information; and Christophe Gbenye, Lumumba's Interior Minister, and his successor as head of the MNC, unpredictable, distrusted by his colleagues, strongly anti-American, and characterized by Timberlake as a "potentially dangerous vindictive stupid racist."[23]

Gizenga had repeatedly ordered Kashamura to report to Stanleyville to face charges that he had accumulated ten million francs illegally from the sale of exit visas in Bukavu, where he was running the Kivu provincial government. When Kashamura refused to obey, Gizenga sent Gbenye and a team of paracommandos to Bukavu to bring him to Stanleyville by force. They had scarcely left Bukavu, with Kashamura in tow, when they were intercepted by a group of local soldiers, who escorted Kashamura back to Bukavu and then, on his orders, arrested Gbenye, beat him up, and took him away. Before they could dispose of him, however, they were stopped at a roadblock manned by still another group of soldiers, who took custody of Gbenye and turned him over to the United Nations.[24] A few weeks later Gizenga succeeded in getting Kashamura to Stanleyville, where he was placed under house arrest.

Timberlake believed that the United States could take advantage of these weaknesses and divisions within the Lumumbist camp to strengthen the moderates and isolate Gizenga and the other extremists. His main source of information about Stanleyville was the second secretary of the U.S. Embassy, Frank Carlucci, who made periodic trips there on consular business, protecting American nationals and reporting on the political scene. One of his chief responsibilities was to keep tabs on the members of Parliament; he had met most of the Stanleyville politicians in Leopoldville the previous summer, when they served in Parliament before Lumumba's downfall, and he kept up his contacts with them after they fled to Stanleyville. Carlucci was noted not only for his level-headed behavior in difficult situations but also for his vivid and often hilarious accounts of his experiences in Stanleyville, which bore a striking resemblance to Evelyn Waugh's satirical novel *Scoop*. He undoubtedly scored a first in diplomatic negotiations in February, when he was invited to the hotel room of Gizenga's Minister of Justice to discuss U.S. aid and found there "an attractive young Congolese lady" who grew bored with the conversation, "stepped behind a curtain, undressed and fell on the bed, covering only the bare essentials with part of her skirt." Suddenly there was a "violent pounding" on the door, and a Congolese came "bounding in, shouting that he wanted to see his wife." After a scuffle the man was "carted off by the police, probably never to be heard from again." Carlucci continued to sip his beer and talk politics with the Minister of Justice.[25]

Carlucci never knew what to expect in Stanleyville: on some occasions he was treated as an honored guest, on others as a spy. When he arrived on March 9 to check on the fate of a group of American missionaries, he found the atmosphere very different from his previous visit in mid-February, just after Lumumba's death was announced. At that time, Gizenga had charged on Stanleyville Radio that two battalions of American paratroopers were planning to invade Stanleyville the next day and that Carlucci had come "clandestinely" to prepare the way.[26] In March, however, he was given the red carpet treatment. Gizenga saw him privately for over an hour and organized a reception in his honor, which was attended by General Lundula, six key members of Gizenga's government, and two members of the provincial government. They insisted they were not Communists and appealed for U.S. understanding and aid.[27]

There were three reasons for this startling about-face. First, and most obvious, Lumumba's death had dealt a major blow to the regime. As Carlucci noted after his February visit, "Lumumba was a virtual god in Stanleyville and Gizenga was obviously riding on his coattails."[28] A few weeks later it was clear that Gizenga could not command the undivided loyalty and respect that had been given to his predecessor. Stanleyville had been Lumumba's home base; Gizenga was an outsider who was far from charismatic. While he reportedly ran the government more efficiently than Lumumba, he rarely left his house and made no attempt to build up popular support. There were as yet no open challenges to his rule, but Gbenye was maneuvering on the left, and Lundula had taken such a moderate stance that the Europeans in Stanleyville practically "worshipped" him.[29]

Second, the blockade, which had been maintained by the Leopoldville government since December, was beginning to hurt; although its effects were felt primarily by European businessmen and plantation owners, and Western predictions that it would bring down the Gizenga regime in a matter of weeks had to be extended again and again, the government was finally beginning to run out of such essential items as gasoline and money to pay its troops. Carlucci concluded that Gizenga and his ministers had put on an elaborate show of cordiality toward the United States because they were in "desperate economic straits."[30]

The third reason for the change of attitude in Stanleyville was ironic, given the American concern about Soviet involvement in the Congo. The Gizengist politicians had turned to the United States for help because they were disillusioned with the Communists, who had promised a great deal but had come through with nothing tangible. Khrushchev, who had learned from bitter experience to act cautiously in the Congo, had studied Gizenga's position carefully and had decided to maintain his rhetorical support for Gizenga but to take no concrete action until the situation was clarified. Since none of the African governments which had recognized Gizenga had sent an ambassador or diplomatic staff to Stanleyville, Khrushchev did not do so either. He relied instead on a less official form of contact. When Carlucci visited Stanleyville in mid-February, he found three Czech journalists in town (one of whom was an agent, according to UN officials) and one Polish journalist;[31] after he left, a Soviet reporter, Georgii Fedyashin, arrived to reopen a TASS bureau in the Congo for the first time since all Soviet personnel were expelled by Mobutu in September. Ten days after his first dispatch describing the gratitude of the Stanleyville officials was published in *Pravda*,[32] Fedyashin and his Polish and Czech colleagues were expelled, because their governments had given no aid to the Gizenga regime.[33]

This Soviet setback, combined with the divisions among the Lumumbists and their concern about the blockade, provided new opportunities for U.S. policy. Carlucci had suggested in February that the lifting of the blockade could be used as a "carrot" to encourage negotiations between the Leopoldville government and the moderates in Stanleyville—a tactic which would isolate Gizenga and his followers. The idea appealed to Timberlake. When Carlucci returned to Stanleyville in March, he announced that the Leopoldville authorities were willing to send a barge to Stanleyville containing such essential supplies as food, clothing, soap, and salt, as soon as they received a guarantee that Gizengist soldiers would not molest the crew.[34]

Carlucci's offer was eagerly accepted. Over the next few weeks negotiations between the two sides moved along at a brisk pace. Gizenga, who distrusted Kasavubu and considered Ileo a "nonentity," agreed to meet with Adoula and other moderate Leopoldville politicians at a little town on the Orientale-Equateur border.[35] The Ileo government announced that it was lifting the four-month-old blockade; the first river boat loaded with American flour would leave for Stanleyville in a few days.[36]

At the last minute, however, the meeting was called off, and the departure of the river boat, which was loaded and ready to leave, was postponed indefinitely. Mobutu and Kasavubu apparently had had second thoughts about the entire arrangement. Timberlake's original idea—to use the negotiations to isolate Gizenga from the Stanleyville moderates—was not working out exactly as he had planned. Instead, Gizenga's stubborn insistence on convening Parliament was wearing down the resistance of the Leopoldville moderates and attracting a number of the undecided politicians, who were "increasingly disillusioned with Ileo's vacillation." Carlucci warned that if the present

trend continued, many of the uncommitted deputies would swing behind Gizenga, but he pointed out that "the position of various deputies
can change on a moment's notice, particularly if money is involved."[37]

Khrushchev Backs Down: The General Assembly Debate, March 21–April 15, 1961

Pressures for a meeting of Parliament were building up not only in
the Congo but also in New York, where the General Assembly had
been debating the issue for several weeks. The Russians, in a dramatic
reversal of position, had shifted from their original demand that Hammarskjold be replaced and the UN Congo operation be ended within
one month, which was repeated by Foreign Minister Gromyko on
March 21,[38] to a draft resolution calling on the United Nations to organize and protect a meeting of Parliament in twenty-one days, which
was introduced by Zorin on April 7.[39]

The scaled-down Soviet demand represented a major change in
Khrushchev's thinking. He was obviously discouraged about the situation in Stanleyville. The TASS correspondent had been readmitted,
along with two other Soviet journalists, but they had less access to government officials than the Western reporters did. Khrushchev realized
that with the unpredictable Gizenga in charge, the chances of sweeping to power from a base in Orientale Province were practically non-
existent. Even more important, the Soviet leader had become aware
that the Afro-Asian states, which played a major part in his long-range
strategic calculations, favored a compromise in the Congo and were
unwilling to turn against the Secretary-General.

The first blow was Nehru's response to Khrushchev's letter of February 22: the Indian leader said he was satisfied with both the Security
Council resolution and the Secretary-General, and he backed up his
words by sending forty-seven hundred troops to the Congo. The second was the reaction of Nkrumah, who addressed the General Assembly on March 7 and then flew on to Washington and a triumphant
reception from President Kennedy, who was determined to dramatize
his new Africa policy and contrast his treatment of Nkrumah with the
cool attitude of Eisenhower and Herter the previous fall. Kennedy
overlooked the differences between the U.S. and Ghanaian positions
and applauded Nkrumah's "support for the United Nations."[40] The
Ghanaian leader had criticized the "hesitation, vacillation, inconsistency and weakness" of the UN officials in the Congo that had made Lumumba's murder possible, but he had stopped short of blaming
Hammarskjold personally and had indirectly criticized the Soviet campaign to unseat him.[41]

Khrushchev was obviously disappointed by Nkrumah's stand. His antagonism toward Hammarskjold was so strong that he instructed Gromyko and Zorin to boycott the luncheon the Secretary-General gave in Nkrumah's honor; Soviet officials explained privately to the Ghanaian delegation that no slight to Nkrumah was intended.[42] At first Khrushchev was unwilling to consider Nkrumah's suggestion that Parliament be reconvened under UN auspices, but after a few weeks of debate the Soviet leader realized that sentiment favoring such an approach was so widespread that it was no longer realistic to think in terms of removing the UN force from the Congo. He began to think instead of using it in pursuit of his own policy.

The Soviet draft was defeated, but the call for a reconvened Parliament was included in a draft sponsored by a group of moderate Afro-Asians, which included four military allies of the United States. The Americans voted for the draft, while Zorin, ironically, voted against it, because of its references to the Secretary-General and its implied approval of the constitutional changes adopted at the Tananarive conference. A separate vote on the phrase referring to the Secretary-General produced an overwhelming vote of confidence for Hammarskjold, 83 to 11, with only Guinea and Cuba joining the Soviet bloc in opposition.[43]

The Bay of Pigs: Another CIA Legacy

The Americans were relieved about the relatively harmonious conclusion of the debate, which turned out to be the last full-dress Congo debate in the General Assembly. But their relief was overshadowed by a new crisis in Soviet-American relations—involving Cuba.[44]

On the afternoon of April 15, as the General Assembly was voting on the Congo resolutions, Stevenson was at an emergency meeting of the Political Committee responding to the charges of Cuban Foreign Minister Raul Roa, who accused the United States of bombing Cuba in preparation for a long-planned invasion.

Roa's charges were not far from the truth. Early that morning eight B-26 planes piloted by anti-Castro Cubans had taken off from Nicaragua in the first stage of an American-backed effort to overthrow the Castro regime. They had bombed three Cuban airfields in an attempt to neutralize Castro's air force and prepare the way for the fourteen hundred anti-Castro exiles, trained by the CIA at camps in Guatemala, who were scheduled to land at the Bay of Pigs at dawn on April 17.

Stevenson denied that the United States was involved in any way. He maintained that the two Cuban pilots who had flown to Florida that morning were defectors from the Cuban air force who had bombed Castro's airfields before leaving Cuba. He was not aware that this was a cover story concocted by the CIA to conceal the real facts.

Stevenson repeated the assurances Kennedy had given at his press conference on April 12 in response to Cuban charges that the United States was planning an attack: there would be no intervention in Cuba by U.S. armed forces, and the United States would do everything it possibly could to make sure that no Americans participated in any actions against Cuba.

Stevenson was not completely in the dark about the operation, but he was caught off guard by its timing. He had been informed on April 8 by Schlesinger and Tracy Barnes of the CIA that an operation was planned and that the U.S. government was training a group of anti-Castro exiles and supplying them with weapons; but the briefing was vague, and Stevenson was under the impression that it was to be essentially a guerrilla raid. Plimpton later recalled, "I had the impression that we were going to send a few canoes across in the dead of night and gather up in the mountains and then, eventually, do something." He felt there was a "great lack of candor" in the briefing.[45] Although Stevenson was assured that there would be no U.S. combat troops involved, he was opposed to the idea, and he wondered if Kennedy had really thought it through and considered the consequences. He finally concluded:

> Look, I don't like this. If I were calling the shots, I wouldn't do it. But this is Kennedy's show. All I ask is three things: First, don't do anything till the Assembly adjourns. Second, nobody leaves from U.S. territory. Third, no American participation.[46]

On Monday morning, April 17, after the exile brigades landed, Bundy told Stevenson the entire story, including the use of false markings on the planes. Stevenson was extremely upset. His government had lied to him, and, as a result, he had lied to the General Assembly. Still, he went ahead and spent the next few days debating with Roa and defending the United States against Cuban charges of aggression.

The Bay of Pigs operation was plagued by miscalculations. Everything that could possibly go wrong did so: Castro's forces were not caught off guard; his air force was not knocked out and it was able to strafe the men on the beach; the underground did not rise, as the planners expected. It was clear by Tuesday that the United States was involved in a fiasco of massive proportions. Kennedy resisted the impulse to intervene with American forces to salvage the operation. He had stated publicly that U.S. forces would not intervene in Cuba, and, despite the fact that CIA pilots had participated in the bombing and CIA frogmen had been among the first fighters ashore, he was determined that there would be no overt U.S. military intervention.

This was the second time that a CIA legacy from the Eisenhower Administration had created serious problems for Kennedy. The first was the murder of Lumumba—but since his death apparently took place before Kennedy came into office, world reaction was comparatively mild. Even the Soviet government gave Kennedy the benefit of the doubt and assumed he was not responsible. As things worked out, he did not have to make any hard decisions about a man who was perceived to be a threat to American interests; all he had to do was deal with the diplomatic consequences of Lumumba's death—and he had done that with considerable skill.

The Bay of Pigs was another matter. Kennedy had inherited the plans for the attack, but it was his decision to proceed. He went ahead, despite his misgivings and those of a number of his top aides and advisers, because it seemed easier to do so than to deal with the consequences of abandoning the operation. What could Kennedy do with all those brave anti-Communist Cuban exiles who were in CIA training camps in Guatemala ready to invade Cuba and restore democracy? If they were prevented from launching their invasion, they would tell the world that Kennedy was a coward and his campaign rhetoric about freedom was meaningless. Moreover, the CIA had warned Kennedy that this was his last chance to rid the hemisphere of a dangerous threat: if he did not act immediately, Castro would have Soviet jets and Czech pilots, and it would be impossible to overthrow him. The President, bombarded by these arguments, ended up believing the overly optimistic estimates of the CIA and the Joint Chiefs of Staff. His reservations and doubts were swept away by the reassurances of the professionals.

Although Kennedy was aware that an invasion of Cuba might jeopardize the chances of an agreement with Khrushchev about other important issues, concern about the Soviet reaction does not seem to have played an important part in the Administration's calculations. On April 18 Khrushchev sent a message to Kennedy reminding him of his statement a few days before that the United States "would not participate in military activities against Cuba" and pointing out that it did not square with the fact that the men invading Cuba had been "trained, equipped, and armed" by the United States. He urged Kennedy to "put an end" to the "aggression" against Cuba and warned that a "so-called 'little war'" could easily "touch off a chain reaction in all parts of the globe." He stated:

AS FAR AS THE SOVIET UNION IS CONCERNED, THERE SHOULD BE NO MISTAKE ABOUT OUR POSITION: WE WILL RENDER THE CUBAN PEOPLE AND THEIR GOVERNMENT ALL NECESSARY HELP TO REPEL ARMED ATTACK ON CUBA. WE ARE SINCERELY INTERESTED IN A RELAXATION OF INTERNATIONAL TENSION, BUT IF OTHERS PROCEED TOWARD SHARPENING, WE WILL ANSWER THEM IN FULL MEASURE.

Kennedy and his advisers regarded this message as a tough and angry warning. Actually, considering the circumstances, Khrushchev's tone was rather conciliatory; except for his pledge to help the Cubans repel an armed attack, which was practically obligatory given his previous assurances to Castro, he appeared to be interested primarily in improving relations with the United States. He seemed to be genuinely puzzled by what he regarded as Kennedy's contradictory policies. How could there be a relaxation of tension, he asked, if, as soon as one crisis was settled, a "new conflagration" was "ignited in another area"?[47]

In his response Kennedy tried to take the offensive, knowing he had a very weak case. He repeated that the United States intended "no military intervention in Cuba" but warned that if any outside force tried to intervene militarily, the United States would protect the hemisphere against "external aggression." He hoped Khrushchev's statement did "not mean that the Soviet government, using the situation in Cuba as a pretext," was "planning to inflame other areas" of the world. "I would like to think that your government has too great a sense of responsibility to embark upon an enterprise so dangerous to general peace," he wrote. At the end of his message Kennedy struck a conciliatory note. He said he agreed with Khrushchev about the desirability of improving the international atmosphere; he specifically mentioned a "prompt ceasefire" in Laos, "cooperation with the United Nations in the Congo," and a "speedy conclusion" of a treaty banning nuclear tests.[48]

Khrushchev's reply of April 22 was angrier than his original message, although by this time the operation had ended in defeat and Kennedy had taken full responsibility for it. The Soviet leader was tired of being lectured about irresponsible actions on his part—first after Lumumba's murder, now after an American-sponsored invasion of Cuba. He scoffed at Kennedy's attempt to "justify and even to praise" the invasion as a blow for freedom, and he rejected Kennedy's assurance that the United States did "not intend to undertake military intervention in Cuba," in the light of the facts about American military involvement in the training, financing, and arming of the invasion force, and the fact that the operation was supported by American planes.[49]

As a result of the Bay of Pigs operation Khrushchev concluded that Kennedy was not only young and rash but that he was also indecisive and lacked nerve. The Soviet leader assumed that once the operation was started, the United States would go in and finish off the Castro regime as Khrushchev himself had done in Hungary in 1956. This impression of Kennedy's weakness played an important part in Khrushchev's calculations about how far he could push the United States on the question of Berlin—the most serious crisis of 1961—and it later encouraged him to place offensive missiles in Cuba, which led to the confrontation of October 1962.

The other consequences of the Bay of Pigs fiasco were less damaging than the Administration feared they would be. For a short time Kennedy's prestige dipped, and his confidence in his own judgment was shaken. But it did not take him long to bounce back and restructure his Administration so that he could get the kind of advice he needed. Stevenson, who had considered resigning because he felt his reputation would never recover, soon found that the diplomats at the United Nations had short memories; apparently lying was taken for granted, and since most of the diplomats expected the United States to follow Khrushchev's example in Hungary, they were impressed by Kennedy's determination to strike out on a new noninterventionist path.

One of the people who was most vividly struck by the Third World's failure to stay angry at the United States was Kennedy's new ambassador to Guinea, William Attwood, a journalist and former Kennedy speechwriter, who had volunteered for the job because he thought it was important to improve U.S. relations with the new nations of Africa, particularly those leaning to the left. His offer was quickly accepted by Bowles, who had foiled what he regarded as a State Department plot to staff seven new African embassies with tired career diplomats close to retirement and was filling the jobs instead with vigorous young men who were more sympathetic to the aspirations of the new African leaders. Kennedy had told Attwood to raise the issue of Lumumba's death with Sékou Touré; the President said he was very much disturbed by the Guinean charge that the United States was in some way responsible.

Attwood was crossing the Atlantic on his way to his new post when he heard about the Bay of Pigs operation.[50] His first thought was that it would be even harder to make a case for American policy in the Congo now that the Cuban invasion had demonstrated U.S. involvement in trying to get rid of another new pro-Communist regime. But when he arrived in Guinea he found the same phenomenon Stevenson had found at the United Nations: most government leaders and diplomats were so accustomed to lies and so absorbed in their own affairs that they quickly forgot the American debacle in Cuba. Even Sékou Touré, a committed revolutionary who had just received the Lenin Peace Prize, was absorbed with his own problems. While he sent Castro a strong message of support,[51] his horizons were essentially limited to Africa—and here the Kennedy Administration was moving in a direction that he favored. Stevenson had just emphasized the change in policy by voting with the Russians and the Afro-Asians, and against America's European allies, on the issue of independence for Angola, a long-somnolent Portuguese colony south of the Congo, where a violent

uprising had begun in February.[52] Attwood was also helped by the
clumsiness of the Soviet diplomats and technicians who had come to
aid the Guineans and by Kennedy's decision to send his brother-in-law
Sargent Shriver, the head of the Peace Corps, to discuss the American
aid program with Sékou Touré. The success of Kennedy's policy could
be measured by one dramatic fact: the next time the United States was
involved in a confrontation with the Soviet Union and Cuba, during
the missile crisis of October 1962, Sékou Touré refused to let Khrushchev's planes refuel at Conakry en route to Cuba.

Timberlake's Last Recommendation

The policy moves that Attwood found encouraging were not at all
popular with Timberlake, who was dismayed by the latest political
trends in Washington—and in Leopoldville as well. By mid-April Kasavubu and his allies had become disenchanted with Tshombe. They realized that the Tananarive conference had bolstered Katanga's
separatist interests at the expense of the central government. The
stage was set for a confrontation when the next summit meeting
opened on April 24 in Coquilhatville, a hot, dusty river town in Equateur Province. Once again, all the Congolese factions had been invited. Once again, Gizenga refused to attend. This time, however, he
sent a delegation of soldiers as a conciliatory gesture. Lundula had just
reached an agreement with Mobutu's negotiating team, and a ceasefire had been established along the Equateur-Orientale border.

As soon as the meeting began, Tshombe realized that the mood of
the delegates had turned against him. On April 26 he walked out and
headed for the airport, intending to fly home to Elisabethville. But before he could board his plane, he was arrested by soldiers from Leopoldville and Stanleyville who were unwilling to let him break up the
conference before unity was restored. Bomboko tried to persuade him
to return, but the Katanga leader refused to yield. He camped out at
the airport, refusing to eat or drink. After a few days he was moved to
a villa, where his status remained somewhat ambiguous. It was not until May 7 that Bomboko charged him with "high treason," including
the murder of Lumumba.[53]

Michel Struelens, Tshombe's New York lobbyist, went to see Stevenson as soon as he learned of the arrest and asked him to help persuade
the Secretary-General to get Tshombe released, but the State Department instructed Stevenson to take no action on this request until the
situation was clarified.[54] Timberlake was horrified. He thought the situation was perfectly clear, and he did not hesitate to express his views
to the Department or to the Congolese government. He did not see

any point in keeping Tshombe in Coquilhatville under lock and key when Kasavubu needed all the conservative support he could get.[55]

The ambassador pointed out that Tshombe's arrest had coincided with an alarming upsurge in Gizenga's political strength. Carlucci, who had just returned from Stanleyville, reported a steady influx of disillusioned deputies and noted that Gizenga and his supporters now believed they could win a test of strength in Parliament. "If the present drift continues," he warned, "Gizenga's fairly solid faction may well be able to defeat the disjointed Ileo-Kasavubu group which has so far failed to maintain its political fences in Parliament."

Carlucci reported that there had been a perceptible shift to the left since his last visit. The government seemed to be getting a good deal of advice via radio from Cairo and the Communist bloc. The "most dangerous" new factor in the situation was the arrival of an ambassador from Mali and a chargé d'affaires from Yugoslavia, which had contributed immeasurably to the pride and self-confidence of the Gizenga regime. When Gbenye was told that the United States planned to open a consulate in Stanleyville, he retorted, "Send an ambassador and we will give him a party like we gave the Mali ambassador." André Mandi, Gizenga's Foreign Minister, told Carlucci he was expecting four more ambassadors in the near future, including one from Ghana and one from Guinea. It was a far cry from the isolation of early April. The government was even discussing the possibility of setting up its own airline to establish direct ties with the outside world.[56]

Gizenga and his allies all insisted that they would attend a session of Parliament if their security were guaranteed by the United Nations, but Timberlake was extremely skeptical. He believed that Gizenga was stalling until the Communist bloc could find some way to "put him in the saddle" in Leopoldville. He did not think that Gizenga would risk a parliamentary solution unless he were certain of winning, and he felt this would be possible only if the "bribes" Gizenga was "prepared to use lavishly" were "translated into votes." This could be a risky operation for Gizenga, the ambassador added. "Votes can be bought both ways, as he also knows."[57]

On May 12 Kasavubu announced that Parliament would be convened in Leopoldville under UN protection immediately after the close of the Coquilhatville conference.[58] Gizenga's response to this challenge came in two stages. On May 14 he ordered the arrest of seven leading moderates in his government, including Foreign Minister Mandi, who was accused of being too pro-American.[59] Two days later he issued a strong statement condemning Kasavubu's decision to reconvene Parliament in Leopoldville as "illegal" and proclaiming that his own government had decided to convene Parliament at the UN-held base at Kamina. Only troops from Ghana, Guinea, Mali, Sudan, Togo, India, and the UAR would be permitted within a sixty-mile radius of the meeting site. Congolese soldiers would be banned, as would the press and foreign diplomats.[60]

Gizenga's counteroffer raised a number of questions in Washington.[61] First, was he genuinely concerned about the problem of security in Leopoldville? Or was it merely an excuse to put off a decision? Timberlake acknowledged that Gizenga's fear might be genuine, but he believed that essentially Gizenga was trying to leave his options open as long as possible. If he had been certain of victory, he would have leaped at Kasavubu's offer. But Kasavubu had made his move at just the right time; Gizenga was steadily building up his strength, but he was not quite ready for a showdown. Kasavubu had succeeded in calling his bluff. Since he could not afford to be put in a position of opposing the reconvening of Parliament, he had done the next best thing—proposed conditions that Kasavubu would find unacceptable in order to gain more time.

The State Department then wanted to know if Gizenga could be persuaded to back down and attend Parliament on Kasavubu's terms. Timberlake replied that there was no way of knowing until the day Parliament opened whether Gizenga would come or not. If he felt he had a chance of controlling a majority, he might attend; if not, he might agree to come and then decide at the last minute to make some excuse and stay away, along with his deputies, hoping to discredit the meeting and to persuade world opinion that the Leopoldville leaders were "bumbling incompetents" who were responsible for still another failure.

Next, what were the chances of getting a moderate government approved? Timberlake cautioned that Carlucci's figures were "highly tenuous" because of the "fickle behavior" of the deputies, but he said it was conceivable that an early meeting of Parliament could produce a moderate government, if Ileo were replaced by a more dynamic Prime Minister, such as Adoula. Gizenga's presence might make a difference. If he attended the meeting, he would "undoubtedly be able to pick up some votes among the fence sitters by the liberal use of bribes, threats to families and persuasion." If he boycotted the meeting, the moderates would have a better chance of enlisting these fence sitters on their side.

Finally, could Gizenga be "induced" to accept a ministerial post in an "otherwise moderate" government? In answering this question Timberlake openly parted company with the Administration, the United Nations, and even people within his own Embassy, such as Carlucci. The ambassador disagreed with the prevailing assumption that Gizenga's participation in the government was essential for a lasting settlement. He maintained, on the contrary, that if Kasavubu offered Gizenga a post in order to gain the "illusory advantage" of a government of "national unity," he would be compounding the country's problems instead of solving them. He believed that the Congo's first coalition government had proved a disaster because Lumumba was influenced by Communist advisers who urged him to invite the Russians in, and he did not want to see a repetition of that experience. He had always favored the establishment of a moderate government. The only obstacle in the past had been the fear that Lumumba's oratory would sway Parliament and prevent the moderates from obtaining a majority. Now, with Lumumba out of the way, it seemed possible that Kasavubu's forces could obtain a majority, and Timberlake did not see any point in asking for trouble by including Gizenga in the government, even if he did decide to attend the meeting.

Timberlake knew that his views ran counter to those of the Administration, which had been prepared in February to accept a government of national unity even if it ran the risk of including Lumumba. He had lost that round, and he believed that the new American policy had been saved from disaster only by Lumumba's death. Now, the Congo was approaching another crossroads, and he hoped that cooler heads would prevail this time around. In what turned out to be his last substantive recommendation from Leopoldville, he argued forcefully for the adoption of a "hard-line" policy: he wanted the U.S. government to encourage Kasavubu to press his advantage, convene Parliament quickly, and install a government composed exclusively of moderates.

Timberlake was aware that if Kasavubu succeeded, Gizenga would probably "try to go it alone in Stanleyville" and would claim, with Soviet and Afro-Asian support, that Parliament had been convened illegally in an "unrepresentative rump session." But he welcomed this as an opportunity to settle the question of Gizenga once and for all. He explained that if Gizenga moved back to Stanleyville, it would no longer be a question of bringing about a reconciliation with him but of "eliminating his regime" after stripping it of its "pretension of legitimacy."[62]

Timberlake's hard-line views were supported by Devlin and other officials at the CIA and the Pentagon, who were opposed to taking any risks with neutralists or pro-Communists; they believed in strengthening center-to-right forces and then worrying about threats from the left, which could be dealt with, if necessary, by military or paramilitary action. Bowles, Williams, and the other liberals at the State Department believed, on the other hand, that the best way to counter the Soviet threat was to outflank the Russians by bringing in the left-wing neutralists and giving them a stake in the system. They had advocated this approach on a continent-wide basis in Africa, and Kennedy had already moved to implement it by improving U.S. relations with Nkrumah and Sékou Touré. They were following the same line of reasoning in the Congo, where they recommended that Kasavubu offer Gizenga a "non-sensitive post" in an "otherwise moderate" government. They argued that Gizenga would represent less of a threat as part of a coalition government in Leopoldville, where he could be watched and countered by the other members of the government, than he would be in Stanleyville, heading a secessionist government backed by the Soviet Union.[63]

The disagreement between Timberlake and the State Department was resolved in an unusual manner. By the middle of May, after a great deal of soul-searching and pressure from the Western powers, Hammarskjold decided not to name a new special representative to replace Dayal. Instead, authority would be divided, with Sture Linner, a capable Swedish businessman, continuing in charge of economic and technical aid; General McKeown continuing to command the UN force; and two persuasive Africans, Robert Gardiner of Ghana and Mahmoud Khiary of Tunisia, continuing their negotiations with the various political groups. When Abbas went to Coquilhatville to pay a farewell call on Kasavubu and inform him that Dayal would be returning briefly to launch the new command arrangements, he touched off a violent reaction. Kasavubu threatened to abrogate all the agreements he had signed with the United Nations. Mobutu swore he would turn his soldiers on the UN force and threatened to assassinate Dayal. Dayal was a brave man, but he decided it would be madness to endanger the lives of the UN personnel or the success of the operation, and he resigned gracefully, after sending a message to Nehru urging him to continue his support for the Secretary-General and the Congo operation.[64]

Hammarskjold managed to extract a price for Dayal's resignation: his two chief adversaries, Timberlake and British Ambassador Scott, were pulled out of Leopoldville before their tours would normally have ended. Timberlake left on June 16, before he had completed a full year in the Congo, in the midst of the crucial negotiations to convene Parliament and set up a new government. Scott left later in the summer. There was, of course, some question about whether the Kennedy Administration was really reluctant to pay this price. Yost and the other diplomats at the U.S. Mission had made no secret of their dislike for the outspoken ambassador, whom they found narrow-minded and uncooperative, and Bowles, Williams, and the other New Frontiersmen at the State Department were not sorry to see him go. His most recent cable opposing the inclusion of Gizenga in the new government was simply the last in a series of disagreements about the direction of American Congo policy.

To replace Timberlake, Kennedy named Edmund Gullion, a Foreign Service officer who had impressed him when he visited Vietnam as a young congressman in 1951. Gullion could not be spared from his disarmament work with McCloy until the end of August, so the Embassy was left without an ambassador during this critical two-and-a-half-month period. The gap was filled by a vigorous new deputy chief of mission, McMurtrie Godley, a forceful man who would later return to the Congo as ambassador and then go on to other trouble spots, such as Laos and Lebanon.

Kennedy and Khrushchev at the Vienna Summit

The dispute between Timberlake and the State Department which led to the ambassador's removal was a continuation of the debate that had been going on since the beginning of the Kennedy Administration about the nature of the Soviet threat in the Third World and the best way of responding to it. A similar debate was going on over the question of Laos, where Soviet military involvement was far more extensive than it had been in the Congo and the American response had been correspondingly greater. The Eisenhower Administration had promoted a right-wing coup in the period between the election and Kennedy's inauguration; here again, as with the Congo and Cuba, the new Administration had to decide what to do next.

In the case of the Congo Kennedy and his advisers opted for a coalition government which ran the risk of including Lumumba, before they found that the risk no longer existed. In Cuba they decided to proceed with an operation that was bound to fail without direct American military involvement but drew back from committing American forces to the battle. In Laos the fighting—and the debate— dragged on throughout March and April. The Pentagon kept suggesting plans which would involve an increased U.S. military commitment, while the liberals kept arguing that a political solution would be preferable to getting bogged down in a land war in Asia. The only possible political solution was a coalition government headed by the former neutralist Prime Minister, Souvanna Phouma, who had been ousted by the right-wing coup—a government in which the Communists would play a major role. Even if the Administration could bring itself to contemplate another coalition in Asia—shades of China!—there was some question about whether Khrushchev would go along with the idea.

On April 1, just as the first glimmer of hope about a compromise began to appear in the Congo, Khrushchev indicated that he might consider a compromise in Laos. The Bay of Pigs fiasco helped put the Laos situation in perspective for Kennedy: if the United States would not fight to prevent Communism in Cuba, ninety miles away, how could it justify sending troops to prevent a Communist takeover in Laos, halfway around the world? His inclination to choose a political solution in Laos was strengthened on May 1, when the Russians agreed to a cease-fire.[65]

On May 18, just a month after the Bay of Pigs operation, Soviet Ambassador Mikhail Menshikov brought Kennedy a personal message from Khrushchev: it was a positive response to the letter Kennedy had sent at the end of February, when passions were running high about the Congo, suggesting a spring summit meeting. Khrushchev proposed a meeting in Vienna in early June, after Kennedy's visit to President de Gaulle, and Kennedy quickly accepted his proposal.[66]

The summit meeting was a mixed success. Khrushchev found Kennedy "more intelligent than any of the Presidents before him," particularly Eisenhower (the only other President Khrushchev had met), who had to turn to his advisers every minute for information. Kennedy "felt perfectly confident to answer questions and make points on his own," Khrushchev recalled in his memoirs. "This was to his credit, and he rose in my estimation at once." The Soviet leader was glad that Kennedy understood the importance of "peaceful co-existence" and the avoidance of war, but he was disappointed by Kennedy's refusal to accept the Soviet position on Berlin. He recalled that Kennedy seemed "deeply upset" about their failure to agree and added:

> I couldn't help feeling a bit sorry and somewhat upset myself. . . .I knew his enemies, especially aggressive politicians, would take advantage of him and tease him, saying "See? You wanted to show off your abilities by meeting Khrushchev and sweet-talking him into an agreement. We've always said the Bolsheviks don't understand the soft language of negotiations; they understand only power politics. They tricked you; they gave your nose a good pull. You got a going-over from them and now you've come back empty-handed and disgraced." That's what I imagined the President expected to hear when he got home.

Khrushchev may have anticipated a similar sort of reaction from his own "aggressive politicians" in the Kremlin. He feared that the failure to reach an agreement on Berlin had "aggravated the Cold War," which meant the "Americans would start spending more money on weapons, forcing us to do the same thing"; but he concluded that "despite our worries and disappointments, it was still worth something that we had met and exchanged opinions."[67]

It was particularly worthwhile, as Thompson had suggested in February, for Kennedy to have a chance to deal with the Soviet leader face to face. Although Thompson and Bohlen did not find anything out of the ordinary in Khrushchev's blustering performance, Kennedy was shaken by the encounter. He was well briefed on the issues, but he was not prepared for Khrushchev's violent attacks on American policy or his refusal to give an inch on any subject. Kennedy was used to the give and take of debates with his political opponents at home or the polite exchanges with the Western European leaders he had met in the past few months. Negotiating with Khrushchev was another matter entirely. Kennedy found it a new and unpleasant experience. At their last meeting, when it had become clear that there would be no progress on the key issues of Berlin and nuclear testing, Kennedy remarked, "It's going to be a cold winter." He described the meeting to columnist James Reston a few hours later as the "roughest thing in my life." He came to the conclusion that Khrushchev had threatened him about Berlin in such a hostile way because of the Bay of Pigs. Kennedy explained:

> I think he thought that anyone who was so young and inexperienced as to get into that mess could be taken, and anyone who got into it, and didn't see it through, had no guts. So he just beat hell out of me. So I've got a terrible problem. If he thinks I'm inexperienced and have no guts, until we remove those ideas we won't get anywhere with him. So we have to act.[68]

On July 25, after several weeks of debate within the Administration, Kennedy announced a partial mobilization of the reserves and an increase in the defense budget. Khrushchev responded on August 13 with the Berlin wall, which further intensified the crisis.

The only concrete accomplishment of the Vienna summit meeting was the agreement that both sides would support the neutralization of Laos. At least the danger of an immediate confrontation between the two great powers in Asia seemed to be eliminated. But Kennedy and his advisers concluded from Khrushchev's impassioned defense of his January 6 speech pledging support for "wars of national liberation" that he was not prepared to back away from all such confrontations in other parts of the world, such as the Congo. They were alarmed by the implications of his stand and felt it was all the more urgent to draw Gizenga into a coalition so that the Soviet leader would not be tempted to jump in and support a "war of national liberation" in the middle of Africa. At the same time, they realized that the agreement about Laos might provide a useful precedent. If Khrushchev was willing to accept a coalition government in Laos, he might be willing to accept one in the Congo, where the lineup of forces was somewhat similar. There were differences, of course. In Laos the Chinese were part of the equation, and the Administration assumed Khrushchev was willing to make a deal with the United States in order to keep the Chinese out or reduce their influence. The Chinese had not yet appeared in Stanleyville; for that matter there were no Soviet diplomats there either. But

Mali and Yugoslavia had already broken the ice, and the Americans were sure it would not be long before Khrushchev sent a diplomatic mission to try to restore the Soviet position in the Congo.

Bringing in the Leftists

A few days after he returned to Washington from Vienna, Kennedy asked Bundy for a briefing on all American covert activities in support of foreign political leaders and parties. On June 10 Bundy told him that a meeting had been set up and that the first item on the list was a "proposal for action in the Congo which has the support of the ambassador and our Department of State."[69] The U.S. government was about to launch a major effort to help its friends in Leopoldville emerge from a session of Parliament with their position enhanced and with Gizenga's independent power base eliminated.

Carlucci had just returned from his latest reconnaissance mission to Stanleyville, accompanied by Thomas Cassilly, who had been assigned to establish a permanent consulate if conditions improved. He reported that the atmosphere was very different from his last trip at the end of April: the mood of quiet confidence had been replaced by one of instability and tension. Gbenye had pushed Gizenga aside and become the "real power" in the government; two moderate ministers were still under arrest; and Carlucci was politely informed on his arrival that he was being expelled on the next plane and would be placed under house arrest in the meantime. The expulsion order charged that he had tried to "sow dissension" between the provincial government and Gizenga's central government. This was essentially true, but the Stanleyville authorities could produce no proof of improper activities; their only specific complaint was that Carlucci had offered scholarships to members of the provincial government without proper authorization. In fact, Carlucci had cleared the offer with Mandi, Gizenga's Foreign Minister, but Mandi was now under arrest.[70]

The Acting Foreign Minister, Arsène Dionge, was so embarrassed that he tried to deny the facts altogether. He was enlightened about the true nature of the situation by an incident reminiscent of the earlier, more chaotic days in Stanleyville. When Dionge arrived at Carlucci's apartment on June 9 with exit permits for Carlucci and Cassilly and asked if Carlucci had enjoyed his stay in Stanleyville, the American diplomat replied that he was not happy about his expulsion or his arrest. Dionge protested that "there was no formal expulsion order," whereupon Carlucci handed him a copy of the order. After studying it for a few minutes, Dionge was forced to concede that "some people might construe this as an expulsion order." He then assured Carlucci that he was not under house arrest; the soldiers outside his door were there as a "protective measure." At this point, Carlucci reported, there was a "loud knocking on the door" and two sturdy soldiers entered with "tommy guns which they proceeded to point at the Acting Foreign Minister." They said they were under orders to arrest anyone who entered the apartment. Dionge pointed out that this was "absurd"; he was the Acting Foreign Minister, and here were the exit permits he had brought. He "began to sweat and kept up a rapid line of chatter," explaining who the Americans were and trying to persuade the soldiers to leave. Their response was to point their tommy guns at Dionge and motion toward the door. After a few more tense moments, the soldiers decided to leave. Dionge "swallowed a few times and wiped his brow. It was really unfortunate, he observed, that some people did not understand the workings of diplomacy." Cassilly asked Dionge how he would describe the present situation if Carlucci was "not under house arrest." Dionge "spread out his hands, started to reply and then smiled weakly."[71]

Since Carlucci was officially forbidden to leave his apartment (although he did slip out a few times), Cassilly met with Gbenye, who seemed to be responsible for the expulsion order, and Gizenga, who left most of the talking to his colleague. Gizenga struck Cassilly as a "rather mild, almost scholarly individual with a weary smile who confined himself to soothing generalities" and appeared somewhat embarrassed by the expulsion order, which he seemed to be hearing about for the first time.[72]

It was difficult for Cassilly to get a reading on Gizenga's intentions regarding Parliament. But Chrysostome Weregemere, one of the leading moderates in Stanleyville, who was unhappy about Gbenye's treatment of Carlucci, slipped past the guards one night and had a long talk with the two American diplomats. He confided that many members of Parliament were eager for a settlement and would desert Gizenga if he refused to go to a meeting of Parliament which was protected by the United Nations. They were all genuinely concerned about their safety in Leopoldville and would prefer Kamina; but they thought Gizenga had blundered by claiming that he had the authority to convene Parliament at Kamina and to specify which UN troops should provide security. He said Gizenga had recognized his mistake and had informed Hammarskjold that he was now willing to accept another location, provided the security precautions were truly ironclad.[73]

Hammarskjold seized this opportunity and sent Gardiner to Stanleyville to wrap up the deal. After seven hours of talks Gardiner persuaded Gizenga to send a three-man delegation back to Leopoldville with him to discuss security arrangements for the meeting and, in a real sense, to test those arrangements. The delegation spent a week at UN headquarters negotiating with Adoula and other representatives of the Leopoldville government, under the guidance of a team of UN officials.

At the same time, the U.S. Embassy was pushing parallel discussions with Tshombe. On June 10 Adoula and Bomboko met with the Katanga leader, who was still under house arrest, and soon there were rumors that he would be released and given a major cabinet post in exchange for a promise to send his deputies and senators to Parliament.[74] Three days later, when Timberlake took Godley, the new deputy chief of mission, to pay his first call on Kasavubu, the Congolese President confirmed that Tshombe appeared ready to cooperate and implied that the case against him would be dropped.[75] On June 16, when Bomboko appeared at the airport with Mobutu and a number of other pro-American officials to bid farewell to Timberlake, the Foreign Minister said he had "high hopes" about Katanga returning to the fold; but he flatly denied rumors that Tshombe would be released before the end of the month. He was less enthusiastic about the negotiations with the Stanleyville delegation, but he felt a compromise would be arranged and Gizenga would probably attend the session.[76]

Later that day Mobutu made a last-ditch attempt to block an agreement with Gizenga's delegation. He announced the arrest of forty soldiers, claiming that they had been conspiring to poison or kidnap him and other Congolese leaders. A number of civilians were arrested as well, and the police set up security checks and moved against "underground organizations of Lumumbists."[77] Despite the tension in the capital, UN officials managed to reassure the Stanleyville delegates about their safety, and on June 19 the two sides reached a milestone agreement. Parliament would meet on June 26 at Lovanium University, fifteen miles outside Leopoldville.

The members would be confined to the campus, and UN troops would keep all outsiders away. Congolese troops in the Leopoldville area would stack their arms in arsenals, and the United Nations would make sure that they remained disarmed during the session. There would be no alcohol, firearms, money, valuables, or women permitted at Lovanium.[78] There was some concern among UN officials about Mobutu's willingness to accept the provision requiring the temporary disarming of his troops, but he assured them that as a "good soldier" he would accept the political decisions of his government.[79]

As soon as the agreement was announced, the U.S. government intensified its behind-the-scenes effort to ensure a favorable outcome. The first step was to reestablish the informal partnership between the U.S. Embassy and UN headquarters which had existed in the summer of 1960. With Dayal and Timberlake gone, it was fairly easy for their successors, Linner and Godley, to make a fresh start. Their relationship became so close that Godley saw most of the cable traffic to and from

Hammarskjold and on occasion even helped Linner draft a report to the Secretary-General. In fact, the State Department was concerned that he might be working so closely with Linner that he could compromise the UN official's nonpartisan reputation, but Godley assured Washington that his relations with Linner were "most discreet."[80]

The new relationship was not merely a question of personalities. It reflected the fact that the U.S. government and the Secretary-General were now committed to essentially the same policy, although for slightly different reasons. Hammarskjold was determined that the Congo would have a functioning Parliament and a moderate coalition government including Gizenga by the time the General Assembly met in September, because he knew the Communists were planning an all-out assault on him and his Congo policy, and he wanted to be in a position to counter it. As a result he was extremely receptive when Yost came to him the day after the agreement was signed and urged him to "use his influence" to make sure the Congo ended up with a "moderate government" in which the Gizengists were not given a "disproportionate influence." Yost assured the State Department that the Secretary-General was thinking along the "same lines as we are" and was "maneuvering effectively" to produce as "sound and moderate" a government as possible. Hammarskjold was optimistic about the probable outcome of the meeting; he believed Adoula would emerge as Prime Minister and Gizenga would end up with some other post.[81]

Godley was somewhat more cautious in his assessment. He described the situation as extremely fluid, with the vote count changing "from hour to hour." He was also worried about reports that Tshombe's deputies and senators would refuse to attend the meeting. He pointed out that if they did not participate, there would be virtually no chance of forming a moderate government.[82]

This particular worry vanished on June 22, when Tshombe, flanked by Ileo, Adoula, Bomboko, and Mobutu, held a press conference to announce that he had been released and would henceforth cooperate with the Leopoldville government. He promised to send his parliamentary delegation to Leopoldville but pointed out that it would be impossible for him to round them up by June 26. Tshombe did not seem the least bit chastened by his two-month detention. He blasted the United Nations just as he had always done and indicated that Mobutu was the only Leopoldville leader for whom he had any real respect.[83]

Godley was encouraged by the prospect of a Leopoldville-Elisabethville alliance. He believed that if Kasavubu and his allies moved quickly and took advantage of this new opportunity, they might succeed in forming the kind of government the Administration had in mind.[84] But he had serious doubts about their ability to move quickly or effectively. He was particularly annoyed by Ileo's stubborn refusal to step down as Prime Minister and let Adoula take over the job. He had no qualms about expressing his views to the Congolese. He told Bomboko and Mobutu that the Leopoldville leaders could achieve their objectives only by "stopping these stupid squabbles" and rallying behind the strongest man available.[85]

Godley's insistence on haste was reinforced by reports that Gizenga was picking up additional support abroad as well as at home. Two Chinese Communist journalists had just arrived in Stanleyville, and there were rumors that Chinese diplomats were expected shortly.[86] Even more disturbing was the news from the State Department, which learned on June 24 from an "excellent source" that the Russians had just offered to establish an embassy in Stanleyville.[87]

The Russians Take the Plunge

The Russians, after an initial period of uncertainty,[88] had decided to encourage Gizenga to try his fortunes in Parliament, even at the risk of going to Leopoldville. Khrushchev had concluded that Gizenga had nothing to lose by responding to Kasavubu's challenge and possibly a great deal to gain. Although the Soviet Press generally painted the Stanleyville scene in rosy hues,[89] there were occasional indications that Gizenga was weak and isolated.[90]

Khrushchev was particularly struck by Gizenga's failure to win any African support outside the Casablanca bloc. None of the other African states had followed the example of Ghana, Guinea, Mali, Morocco, or the UAR, which had recognized the Stanleyville regime in February; in fact, most of the swing states had recently moved closer to the more conservative Brazzaville group. In mid-May they had formalized their position at a twenty-nation conference held in Monrovia, the capital of Liberia, where they signed a document implicitly critical of Gizenga and his African and Soviet supporters.[91]

This attitude was brought home to Khrushchev quite vividly just two weeks later, when one of the participants in the Monrovia conference, Somali Prime Minister Abdi Rashid Ali Shermarke, arrived in Moscow for a state visit. Even after ten days of lavish Soviet hospitality, which included a generous aid agreement and several long talks with Khrushchev, Shermarke could not be budged from his position on the Congo. The final Soviet-Somali communiqué contained a noncommittal statement condemning "imperialist aggression" in the Congo without mentioning Gizenga's name.[92]

On the positive side the Russians were aware by the first week in June that Gizenga controlled at least 40 of the 137 deputies. Lumumba, in May 1960, had controlled 41 votes, and had ended up as Prime Minister. They realized that Gizenga was no Lumumba; he could not dominate Parliament by sheer force of persuasion. Still, even without Lumumba's political skill, it was conceivable that Gizenga might be able to obtain a majority by claiming to be Lumumba's legitimate heir and the only true nationalist, while accusing the Leopoldville group of collaborating with the "colonialists." At the very least he would probably emerge from Lovanium with a considerable share of power in a coalition government. The Russians, like the Americans, felt that the risk was worth taking. The situation was extremely fluid and anything could happen.

The Soviet gamble appeared to be justified by political developments in the last week of June. On June 24 Tshombe was permitted to leave Leopoldville and return home. Before he left, he signed an agreement with Ileo promising to end the Katanga secession. But no sooner had Leopoldville Radio proclaimed the news than Tshombe, safe again in Elisabethville, reneged on his promises. He bitterly attacked the Leopoldville leaders, with the exception of Mobutu, who he said was responsible for his release; he scoffed at Ileo's announcement that the secession was over; and he indicated that he might not send his deputies and senators to Parliament after all.[93]

Godley's Gamble

The Congo celebrated its first anniversary, on June 30, in a state of uncertainty about its political future. Over the next few weeks, as the negotiations leading to the convening of Parliament and the formation of a government moved toward a climax, the political balance shifted from hour to hour, and each day brought new rumors of deals, bribes, double crosses, and coups.

While Godley was urging the Congolese to proceed full steam ahead, officials in Washington were beginning to have second thoughts about the wisdom of convening Parliament immediately in the wake of Tshombe's defection. They realized that delay would damage Kasavubu's reputation abroad, but they argued that it would be far more damaging, for Kasavubu and for the United States, if Gizenga were to wind up in control of the new government.[94]

Godley disagreed with this analysis, and he maintained his position through thick and thin, despite mounting pressure from Washington. He pointed out that the United States had always recognized there were risks involved in convening Parliament, and these risks were certainly more evident in the light of Tshombe's latest move. But he insisted that the risks had to be faced. If Kasavubu did not convene Parliament in Leopoldville, Gizenga would convene it in Stanleyville, where he could easily assemble a quorum among the disillusioned dep-

uties. This would bolster his claim to be the head of the legal government and make it easier for the Communists and the Afro-Asians to
round up a majority in his favor at the United Nations.[95] Besides, Kasavubu had decided to proceed with Parliament, and once he had made
up his mind, he could be extremely stubborn. "We are currently faced
with a Bantu palaver the details of which outsiders cannot accurately
assess" and on which we can "exert little if any influence," Godley reported on July 15.[96]

The following day, UN planes brought sixty-two members of Parliament from Stanleyville to Leopoldville. They were greeted by Adoula
and then taken by helicopter to Lovanium. The group was headed by
Gbenye. There was no sign of Gizenga. Kamitatu, a political fence-sit-
ter who had gone to Stanleyville to make the final arrangements, explained that Gizenga was ill and would be coming in another day or
two. He denied speculation that Gizenga's absence was due to the advice of the Soviet delegation that had arrived in Stanleyville on July 7.
The eight-man group was headed by Leonid Podgornov, who had
served in the Soviet Embassy in Leopoldville.[97] Kamitatu maintained
that the Russians had come merely to "sound out" the situation and
would probably be leaving in a few days.[98] Although his estimate of
their travel plans turned out to be inaccurate, he was correct in insisting that they were not responsible for Gizenga's failure to show up.
The Soviet chargé spent the next two weeks urging Gizenga to go to
Lovanium to strengthen the Stanleyville team. But he had no more
luck in trying to influence "his" Congolese than the Americans did
with "theirs."[99]

By July 18 there were one hundred and sixty members of Parliament
at Lovanium. They hoped to start their formal sessions at the end of
the week, and they asked Gardiner and Khiary to stay at Lovanium to
help.[100] The Leopoldville politicians were finding it difficult to strike a
deal with the uncommitted deputies and senators; while Gbenye, as
the unquestioned head of the Stanleyville delegation, could promise
them the moon, the moderates had no single leader who could speak
for them. Ileo still refused to resign, and Adoula was in limbo. In desperation Adoula and Bomboko asked Linner and Godley to persuade
Kasavubu to force Ileo to resign so that he could name a replacement
who could unify the moderate camp.[101]

On July 19 Linner warned Kasavubu that he was about to "meddle in
internal Congolese affairs." He then proceeded to tell him that there
were times in a country's history when its great leaders must enter the
political arena, as de Gaulle had done in France, and that Kasavubu
must demonstrate his leadership by going to Lovanium and guiding
the politicians toward a satisfactory outcome—a government headed
by Adoula. Linner offered Kasavubu a helicopter so that he could go

back and forth easily, and urged him to listen to the advice of the UN officials and the Americans and to keep in "daily or even hourly contact" with him. By the end of their talk Kasavubu's initial reluctance had been overcome and he agreed to go the very next day and any other time Linner thought it necessary.[102]

After Linner reported this conversation to Hammarskjold, he received a "delightful" message, which he shared with Godley; the Secretary-General reminded Linner that the United Nations "must never meddle in internal affairs," but then he added that he "personally" would have done the same thing if he had been in Linner's shoes and "would continue to do so."[103]

On July 22 Godley reported that the two sides were "evenly balanced" and it was "virtually impossible" to predict the outcome of the meeting.[104] But on July 24 there was an alarming development: Joseph Kasongo, the former president of the Assembly and one of the leaders of the Stanleyville group, was elected to his old post by a vote of 61 to 57. Although the margin was slight, Godley feared the vote might produce a stampede to Gizenga's side. He reported that Kamitatu was leaving for Stanleyville to try to persuade Gizenga to come to Lovanium and put his team over the top.[105]

The Congolese military reacted sharply to Kasongo's victory. Devlin reported that Colonel Boboso, the commander of the Thysville garrison, who had warned that he would never accept a Gizenga government, had telephoned Lovanium three times in the course of the day. He was ready to mount a military coup to prevent Gizenga from taking power.[106] Mobutu, who had been very quiet for weeks, suddenly demanded that the United Nations give him control of the airport. Linner was afraid that if things did not work out the way Mobutu wanted, he might try to block the return of the Gizengists to Stanleyville. He told Godley he planned to remind Mobutu that he had accepted the June 19 agreement, under which the United Nations had guaranteed all members of Parliament a safe round trip. Linner was willing to ignore the fact that Mobutu's forces had already violated the agreement by failing to deposit their arms in depots, but he refused to yield on the question of the airport. Godley asked the State Department for authorization to inform Mobutu that the United States would not "support him in this blackmail." At the same time, he suggested that Linner could placate Mobutu by informing him about the latest encouraging reports from Lovanium.[107]

The pro-Gizenga tide had turned dramatically on July 25: the Senate, encouraged by Gardiner and Khiary, had elected a moderate president. Godley described the vote as a "clear victory" for the Leopoldville group and said he hoped it would offset Kasongo's victory in the lower house the previous day. To top matters off, Kamitatu returned to Leopoldville that evening—without Gizenga.[108] The excuses about illness were beginning to wear thin, and it was becoming clear that Gizenga's absence would inevitably hurt his cause.

While Godley was breathing a little more easily because of the events of July 25, top officials in Washington were still reacting with alarm to the events of the previous day. On July 26 Kennedy sent a memo to Rusk asking what the State Department was doing about the political crisis in the Congo. Bundy explained that the President was bothered by the fact that there was no ambassador in Leopoldville and wondered whether the problems there were "receiving the consideration" they deserved.[109]

Rusk sent a personal message to Godley stressing the seriousness with which he viewed the possibility that "Gizenga could emerge as Prime Minister." He pointed out that if Gizenga were elected by Parliament, the United Nations would be "under pressure" to recognize him, and the United States would be placed in an "extremely difficult position." He instructed Godley to see Kasavubu and urge him to take delaying action while he tried to bring Tshombe on board.[110] The secessionist leader had told the Americans that he would send his delegation to Lovanium if Kasavubu and the other leaders agreed to meet him at a summit conference before Parliament was convened.

Godley politely but flatly refused to carry out these instructions. It must have been something about the Leopoldville air—first Timberlake, with his hard line, and now Godley with his soft line, each envoy in conflict with a State Department that simply did not seem to grasp the realities of the situation in the Congo itself. Godley explained that Kasavubu had already opened Parliament with a speech urging the presentation of the new government "right away."[111] He felt that it was no longer realistic to expect Katangan participation; if Kasavubu agreed to a delay on the "remote chance" that Tshombe might change his mind, he would appear to be "tied to Elisabethville's apron strings." Godley admitted that the outlook was "uncertain" and that a moderate victory could not be "predicted confidently at this point," but at the same time he pointed out that the likelihood of a "decisive Gizenga victory" was equally uncertain. He argued, moreover, that "on balance" the risks of delay were greater than the risks of going ahead.[112]

Then, "at the risk of being presumptuous," he lectured Rusk on the sensitivity of the leaders of newly independent states to outside pressure, citing Sékou Touré and Sihanouk as examples, and concluded that a démarche to Kasavubu would be "counter-productive," because he would probably resent it and because it could be used effectively by his adversaries. Godley explained that American views reached Kasavubu through a number of effective channels—Linner, Khiary, Gardiner, and Mobutu's "young team" of pro-American advisers. He appreciated the "extremely unfortunate reaction at home and damage to our prestige abroad at this critical time" if Gizenga was named Prime Minister, but said he was convinced that the "wisest though perhaps most frustrating course" for the United States was to "lie low" in the Congo.[113]

The next communication from the State Department came from Deputy Under Secretary U. Alexis Johnson, who conceded that Kasavubu's speech had affected the arguments in Rusk's cable but then went on to rebuke Godley:

> SECRETARY DESIRES EMPHASIZE FOR YOUR GUIDANCE THAT GIZENGA AS PRIME MINISTER NOT ONLY QUESTION PRESTIGE ABROAD AND REACTION AT HOME BUT INVOLVES OUR MOST VITAL INTERESTS IN AFRICA AND OUR FUTURE ABILITY SUPPORT UN IN SUCH SITUATIONS. AS YOU ARE AWARE FROM PREVIOUS INSTRUCTIONS, BLOCKING GIZENGA FROM CONTROLLING GOVERNMENT IS A SPECIFIC OBJECT OF POLICY FOR WHICH YOUR FULL ATTENTION AND IMAGINATIVE EFFORT ARE REQUIRED. SECRETARY CONSIDERS YOU ARE DOING EXCELLENT JOB IN DIFFICULT CIRCUMSTANCES BUT HE WANTED TO UNDERLINE GRAVITY THIS MATTER.[114]

For the next few days it looked as if Godley's defiance of a direct order from the Secretary of State might backfire. Still, he had confidence in Carlucci's vote count and in his own judgment, and he refused to give up hope that Parliament would come up with an arrangement favorable to American interests.

On the afternoon of July 29 Tshombe arrived in Brazzaville with a few members of his government, but no members of Parliament. Kasavubu refused to go to Brazzaville to see him, and when Khiary and Gardiner crossed the river to try to persuade Tshombe to come to Leopoldville, they found him extremely evasive and negative. They concluded that he was stalling, hoping Parliament would break up without reaching agreement on a new government.[115]

The chances of this happening were very good. The Stanleyville bloc was leading in the Assembly, the moderates controlled the Senate, and Parliament had reached an impasse. The members were "fretting" under the "monastic restrictions" at Lovanium; at one point the Leopoldville group had their bags packed and were ready to leave, complaining that they "could not vote unless they saw some women." They were persuaded to stay, however, until August 1. Ironically, they did not welcome the prospect of reinforcements from Katanga; they felt they had endured the hardships of Lovanium for the past ten days, and they resented the idea that Tshombe's delegation would be arriving once victory was in sight.[116]

The crisis was finally resolved in an unexpected way. On the morning of August 1 Tshombe left Brazzaville for home without having seen Kasavubu or any of his emissaries. It was this development which finally galvanized Kasavubu, who decided that he had to do something to forestall adverse reaction to Tshombe's departure. He quickly persuaded Ileo to resign and named Adoula to succeed him. Godley anticipated a narrow victory for the moderates,[117] but he was pleasantly surprised the following day when both houses confirmed Adoula and his government with a nearly unanimous vote. Gizenga was named Deputy Prime Minister, Bomboko stayed on as Foreign Minister, and the moderates controlled most of the key ministries. The only significant exception was Gbenye at the Interior Ministry; but Godley pointed out that Gbenye was so completely lacking in personal principles or ideological convictions that he would go whichever way the wind blew strongest. He concluded that the government was "as good as we could reasonably expect" and pointed out that the moderates had given away "the absolute minimum" consistent with the reunification of the country.[118] Kasavubu and his allies agreed. On the evening of August 2 jubilant deputies and senators emerged from their two-week period of isolation in a festive mood and broke out the champagne.[119]

Kennedy's First Victory

The reaction in Washington was equally enthusiastic, but the State Department refrained from any public celebration so that Gizenga and his Soviet friends would have no grounds for complaint. Johnson commended Godley and the Embassy staff and asked him to congratulate Linner on a "job well done." He cautioned that the role of the U.N. officials must be kept "strictly" from the public.[120] Stevenson congratulated Hammarskjold, who assured him that Adoula was a "strong and good man who could handle Gbenye." The Secretary-General's optimism was tempered, however, by his view that "anything" could happen in the Congo.[121]

Rusk had waited to respond to Kennedy's July 26 memo until the situation was clarified. Now, after a hair-raising week, he was able to report to the President that U.S. policy had succeeded. Adoula, "the strongest and most attractive of the moderate Congolese leaders," had become Prime Minister, just as the State Department hoped. Rusk characterized his victory as "the second Soviet defeat in the Congo" and noted that the Soviet and Czech missions, which had just arrived in Stanleyville, had been placed in an "embarrassing position." While Gbenye, "the most powerful of Gizenga's lieutenants," had been given the "politically sensitive" post of Minister of Interior, Rusk hoped he would not hold the job for long. He explained that the inclusion of several Gizengists in the government was "less of a risk than leaving Gizenga in his Orientale redoubt," where he was a "standing invitation to Communist penetration." He assumed that Gizenga would "not be pleased" with his "politically unimportant" job as Deputy Prime Minister and that he would be tempted to remain in Stanleyville—and would be encouraged to do so by the Russians. Rusk concluded by noting that the State Department was "doing everything possible" to hasten the arrival of Ambassador Gullion, as Kennedy requested, but in the meantime he cited the "excellent" performance of the U.S. chargé in Leopoldville.[122]

Rusk's memo was included in the President's "weekend papers," as top priority reading, along with a memo from Walt W. Rostow, Bundy's deputy, who suggested in his usual enthusiastic way that if all went well and Gizenga and Tshombe joined in, "we could be witnessing the most encouraging new development since you became President." He continued, "There is optimism all over town that the Congo situation is on the way toward solution." Kennedy had his first victory over the Russians—but he couldn't crow about it openly, for fear of ruining Adoula's chances of establishing himself as a respected neutralist leader.[123]

Rusk and his advisers assumed that the Russians would urge Gizenga to remain aloof from the new government, but the Soviet reaction was not exactly what they expected. The two-week period between the arrival of Gizenga's delegation in Leopoldville and the formation of the Adoula government had been filled with tension and suspense for the Russians just as it was for the Americans. They had believed it was possible that the Gizengists might obtain a numerical majority in Parliament, particularly if Gizenga listened to their advice and went to Leopoldville to lead his team in person. But as the days went by and Gizenga continued to plead illness, they began to have serious doubts about his courage and his political ability. Furthermore, they were skeptical about whether the United States and the United Nations would actually permit a Gizenga victory even if his forces did control a majority.

Khrushchev was particularly interested in the outcome of the meeting since he was playing host to two major African leaders—one a leading radical, the other a leading moderate—who were deeply involved in the Congolese situation. President Nkrumah of Ghana, a leader of the Casablanca bloc and a mentor of Lumumba and Gizenga, had arrived on July 10 for his first visit to the Soviet Union, a two-week redcarpet tour which had the effect of drawing him closer to the Soviet bloc; President Abboud of Sudan, the man who had single-handedly blocked the transit of arms and supplies from Cairo to the blockaded Gizenga regime in Stanleyville, arrived on July 17 for ten days of banquets, receptions, and trips, which were reported in great and glowing detail by the Soviet press but which did not significantly alter Abboud's neutralist position. Both men talked at length with Khrushchev about the Congo, and Khrushchev indicated that he was prepared to be flexible. On July 25, at the end of Nkrumah's visit, the two sides issued a communiqué declaring their "unanimous support" for the legitimate government "headed today by Antoine Gizenga."[124] Two days later, as Abboud left for home, he and his Soviet hosts issued a communiqué proclaiming their support for the legitimate government chosen by Parliament—without any reference to Gizenga.[125]

By this time Khrushchev was probably disgusted with Gizenga because he refused to seize the opportunity offered to him. In any case, once the Adoula government was formed, the first indications from Moscow suggested that the Soviet leader had decided to accept Adoula's victory and try to derive some advantage from it.[126] He made no immediate move to recognize the new government, but he kept an open mind and avoided any criticism of Adoula while he waited to see what Gizenga would do.[127]

The reaction in Stanleyville was less philosophical. Cassilly reported that there was a total news blackout for several days after the Adoula government was formed. Gizenga's supporters had been confident of victory, especially after Kasongo was reelected to his old post on July 24. They responded to the news with "stunned disbelief" and demanded that the United Nations bring Gbenye and four of his companions back to Stanleyville to explain what had gone wrong. It was only after Gbenye reported to Gizenga in person on August 5 that they believed the reports from Leopoldville. Stanleyville radio did not announce the formation of the new government until the following day.

The diplomats stranded in Stanleyville were even more disappointed than Gizenga when his government announced that it no longer existed. At this point there were thirty-six diplomatic representatives in town—ten Russians, two of whom had just arrived on August 4; six Chinese, who had arrived on July 31; six Yugoslavs, four Poles, four Czechs, four from the UAR, one from Mali, and one from Ghana. The Yugoslav chargé could not understand what had happened, since he was convinced that the Gizengist forces had control of both houses of Parliament. He "ruefully congratulated the American Embassy for successfully influencing the outcome," and when Cassilly pointed out that no foreigners had been permitted in Lovanium, the Yugoslav diplomat brushed aside his protest, remarking, "We know you have influence with Mobutu, Kasavubu and the United Nations."[128]

Even after the official announcement was made, Gizenga refused to go to Leopoldville. It was clear that he was losing ground with his own supporters by remaining in Stanleyville. Gbenye flew back to Leopoldville with Cassilly on August 6 and spoke contemptuously about Gizenga's cowardice; it was generally acknowledged by then that his "illness" was diplomatic in nature.[129]

After ten more days had passed, and Gizenga persisted in his refusal to come to Leopoldville, Adoula, in a courageous act of reconciliation, went with a very small entourage to Stanleyville, where he received a warm welcome from the local population. He was greeted by Lundula at the airport and met with Gizenga at his residence. Two days later Gizenga appeared in public for the first time in five months, and, standing arm-in-arm with Adoula, announced that he recognized the Adoula government as the only legal Congolese government. Still, he gave no indication about when or if he would go to Leopoldville to take up his post as Deputy Prime Minister.[130]

Once again, the American assumption that the Russians were encouraging him to take a hard line was belied by the Soviet press coverage of Adoula's trip, which indicated that Khrushchev was leaning toward recognition of the Adoula government and was interested in moving his diplomatic mission to Leopoldville in the immediate future.[131] On August 31 Khrushchev sent a formal message of congratulations to Adoula and announced that the Soviet government was ready to "continue to maintain diplomatic relations" with the Congo.[132] He glossed over the fact that diplomatic relations between the two countries had been broken. He had made his choice between trying to prop up an ineffective though friendly secessionist regime and taking his chances with a less friendly but potentially more effective central government. He undoubtedly hoped that Soviet influence would have a greater impact in Leopoldville than in an increasingly isolated Stanleyville. Moreover, there were Lumumbists in positions of power in Leopoldville. Gizenga might have some leverage as Deputy Prime Minister if he ever decided to take up the job. Gbenye held the strategic Interior Ministry. And if all else failed, there was always the option of returning to Stanleyville and launching a Lumumbist rebellion.

By the end of August Adoula had become so effective at projecting a nonaligned image that the Americans began to be alarmed. Their strategy was succeeding all too well. They were afraid that in his effort to promote the acceptance of his government among the Afro-Asians, he might go too far and make too many concessions to the Gizengists. They were particularly worried about reports that he planned to authorize the reopening of the Communist diplomatic missions in Leopoldville. He had told U.N. officials that this would be consistent with his policy of nonalignment, and it might also spare his government the necessity of being wholly dependent on American aid. Since Assistant Secretary Williams was planning to stop in Leopoldville on his latest tour of Africa, Rusk asked him to assure Adoula that he could count on American support for his efforts to maintain a moderate, responsible government in the Congo, in the hope that this assurance would help him resist the pressure from the leftists for additional concessions.[133]

Williams was encouraged by his talk with Adoula. He found the new Prime Minister "strong and articulate" and concluded that he had a "better than even chance of coming out on top" in the struggle with Gizenga and Tshombe. "He will follow a policy of nonalignment but will probably remain cooperative with the West," Williams reported to Rusk and the President.[134] At the beginning of September Kennedy sent Ambassador Gullion off to Leopoldville with warm personal messages of support for both Adoula and Kasavubu.[135] Despite his lingering concern about the Katanga secession and his new concern about the quality of Adoula's neutralism, the President felt that the Congo was entering a hopeful new phase.

CHAPTER ELEVEN

The Death of Illusions
(September 1–November 3, 1961)

"We wanted a united Congo but not a Communist Congo."

ON SEPTEMBER 3, a month after he was elected Deputy Prime Minister by the Congolese Parliament and three days after Khrushchev sent his message of recognition to Prime Minister Adoula, Gizenga finally came out of seclusion and flew to Leopoldville to take up his new duties. He was far from enthusiastic about the trip. Adoula's mission to Stanleyville in mid-August had not dispelled his suspicions of the Leopoldville politicians, especially Kasavubu and Mobutu, whom he regarded as his sworn enemies. He had little confidence in the assurances of UN officials—even after the parliamentary meeting at Lovanium, where they had provided protection for his delegation. Only a few days before, UN officials in Stanleyville, acting at the request of the Adoula government, had impounded a plane which had been making regular trips between Stanleyville and Cairo and which constituted Gizenga's only direct link with the outside world. In retaliation, Gizenga had ordered a UN representative arrested at gunpoint, but he had agreed to release him after the Ethiopian troop commander threatened to shell his residence. Gizenga had also ordered the arrest and expulsion of Thomas Cassilly, the visiting U.S. consul, on the assumption that the Americans were behind the UN move.

Despite his lingering suspicions, Gizenga had yielded to the entreaties of his old colleague Gbeyne, now Interior Minister in Leopoldville, who had flown to Stanleyville on September 1 with the most persuasive of the UN diplomats, Mahmoud Khiary, to convince Gizenga of the importance of making the trip at this time. Both Gizenga and Adoula had been invited to Belgrade to represent the Congo at the first summit meeting of the nonaligned powers. The reluctant Gizenga stayed in the capital for only a few hours—long enough to confer with Adoula at his residence and then to accompany him to the airport, where the two men reviewed a company of Mobutu's paratroopers and then took off on a UN plane for Belgrade.[1]

Diplomatic Respectability and Nuclear Blackmail

It was an advantageous arrangement for both of them. Gizenga felt much safer leaving Stanleyville for a specific foreign destination; he was fairly certain that, with the world press waiting for him in Belgrade, Mobutu would not dare to harm him. At the same time, Adoula realized that Gizenga's presence at his side was his passport to respectability in the high-stakes world of neutralist diplomacy. It guaranteed his acceptance as Lumumba's legitimate successor by the pro-Lumumba states which had set the ground rules for invitations to Belgrade and defined who was truly nonaligned and who was not. The most important criterion was that the state in question have no formal ties to any colonial power and no foreign military bases on its territory. The Brazzaville states were ruled out from the start because of their links with France. Pro-Western Tunisia was invited only after its bloody clash with France in July over the base at Bizerte. Nigeria was not invited until the last minute and angrily rejected the invitation.[2]

Adoula had worked hard throughout the month of August, with American encouragement, to be included in this select group. As late as August 11, several days after Gizenga had indicated his acceptance of the new government, many of the leading members of Hammarskjold's Congo Advisory Committee—Ghana, Guinea, Mali, and the UAR, which had diplomatic representatives in Stanleyville, and even Ethiopia and India, which did not—urged the Secretary-General to hold off on formal recognition of the Adoula government because it was not yet clear that Gizenga had "fully accepted" it.[3] It was only after Adoula went to Stanleyville and won Gizenga's personal approval that the logjam began to break up. Sékou Touré was the first of the Casablanca group to congratulate Adoula, on August 16. Nkrumah was far more cautious; he waited until late October to recognize the new government. Nasser, Gizenga's chief source of aid and advice, had concluded by the end of August that his protégé's best chance of success lay in compromising with Adoula, joining him in Belgrade, and taking a moderate line once he got there.[4]

The twenty-four-nation conference was nearing its conclusion by the time the two Congolese leaders arrived; but the participants were eager to hear from them, and a special meeting was set up for September 5. Although they both stressed reconciliation, there was a marked difference in tone between the two speeches. One observer jokingly remarked to U Thant, who was there with the Burmese delegation, that they sounded as if they had been "drafted by NATO and the Warsaw Pact."[5]

Adoula spoke first. He reaffirmed his government's policy of nonalignment, which he credited to Lumumba; denounced colonialism, particularly in neighboring Angola; and announced his recognition of the Algerian provisional government. At the same time, he praised the United Nations, with all its faults, and pointed out that the Congo's experience had proved the usefulness of a single Secretary-General; if a three-man directorate had been in operation, he said, it would have been impossible to achieve any practical results.[6]

Gizenga's speech was much more dramatic. He won a round of applause when he referred to Lumumba as a hero and a victim of colonialist injustice, and then went on to describe himself as Lumumba's "spiritual heir" and the "guardian of his ideals." He was far more critical of the United Nations and the Belgians than Adoula had been.[7] After Gizenga spoke, Indonesian President Sukarno proposed that everyone rise for a minute of silence in memory of Lumumba. Among those who stood in tribute was Lumumba's bitter enemy, Congolese Foreign Minister Bomboko.[8]

At this point, the Congo problem, which seemed well on its way to solution, was no longer the focus of international attention. The Afro-Asian leaders gathered at Belgrade were preoccupied with the threat of war between the United States and the Soviet Union over the unresolved issue of Berlin. This threat was deliberately intensified by Khrushchev when he announced on the eve of the conference that he was about to resume nuclear testing in the atmosphere in order to perfect a 100-megaton bomb.[9] The Russians, the Americans, and the British had observed an informal moratorium on atmospheric tests since October 1958, while they tried to negotiate a comprehensive test ban in Geneva.

The Americans were astonished that Khrushchev would knowingly hand them such a propaganda victory on the eve of the Belgrade conference. Kennedy managed to hold off demands from the Pentagon and Capitol Hill that he respond immediately with atmospheric tests of his own by explaining that if he did so, he would lose a priceless opportunity to turn world opinion against Moscow. A White House statement issued on August 31 called Khrushchev's decision "primarily a form of atomic blackmail, designed to substitute terror for reason" and charged that the Russians were trying to frighten the West into making major concessions on Berlin.[10] The British suggested that Khrushchev had timed his announcement precisely for the eve of the Belgrade meeting because he shrewdly calculated that the initial resentment of the neutralists would give way to fear, which would lead to pressure on the Western powers to reach an accommodation with Moscow at any price—in order to avoid a nuclear war.

The initial neutralist reactions to Khrushchev's announcement were highly critical. The Yugoslavs were privately furious. They suspected that Khrushchev was trying to undercut his old rival Tito and that he had timed his announcement to undermine the success of the conference. Nasser rewrote his opening day speech to express his "shock" and dismay about the Soviet decision. Nehru warned that the Soviet tests had brought the world "to the brink of war." Even Nkrumah, who came to the conference direct from Sochi, on the Black Sea, where he had been vacationing and conferring with Khrushchev, called the action "a shock for me and for you, too."[11]

The Soviet journalists covering the meeting were prepared for this sort of reaction. They started out on the defensive. They even acknowledged, with unusual frankness, that Nkrumah was shocked by the Soviet decision.[12] But they soon reported that "Western attempts to turn the meeting into an anti-Soviet gathering" had failed, because the neutralist leaders had taken a realistic approach to the situation and had accepted Khrushchev's explanation of the Soviet move.[13] By the end of the conference, *Pravda* concluded that it had been a success for the Soviet Union and a "disappointment" for the United States.[14]

This assessment was essentially correct. American officials, from the President on down, were disappointed by the neutralists' failure to follow up on their initial expressions of disapproval of the Soviet action and their failure to appreciate the Western response, which was designed to keep Khrushchev on the defensive. On September 3 Kennedy and Macmillan proposed that the Soviet leader join them in refraining from any further nuclear tests in the atmosphere.[15] Khrushchev ignored their appeal and set off two more nuclear explosions. The reaction in Belgrade was muted. Khrushchev's strategy seemed to be working. The shock, rather than alienating the neutralists, had forced them to move farther to the left so that they could remain equidistant between the two great powers. Instead of condemning the Russians, they condemned nuclear testing in general and urged the Russians and Americans to negotiate. Adoula's remarks were typical: while he stated that the resumption of the tests defied the "legitimate hopes of mankind," he did not refer to the Soviet Union by name, and he called on the great powers to settle their differences peacefully.[16]

By September 5 Kennedy had become impatient. He decided to respond to Khrushchev's move in a way that would satisfy the demands at home for a stronger defense but would not give the rest of the world cause for complaint. He announced that the United States had decided to resume underground nuclear tests but would refrain from tests in the atmosphere, because of the danger of fallout. When Stevenson expressed regret over this decision, Kennedy replied, "What choice did we have? They had spit in our eye three times. We couldn't possibly sit back and do nothing at all. We had to do this." Stevenson objected, "But we were ahead in the propaganda battle." To this Kennedy responded:

> What does that mean? I don't hear of any windows broken because of the Soviet decision. The neutrals have been terrible. The Russians made two tests *after* our note calling for a ban on atmospheric testing. Maybe they couldn't have stopped the first, but they could have stopped the second. All this makes Khrushchev look pretty tough. He has had a succession of apparent victories—space, Cuba, the wall. He wants to give out the feeling that he has us on the run. The third nuclear test was a contemptuous response to our note. Anyway, the decision has been made. I'm not saying that it was the right decision. Who the hell knows? But it is the decision which has been taken.[17]

Macmillan, who had been given only one and a half hours' notice of Kennedy's decision, felt that it had "unnecessarily helped to get the Russians 'off the hook.'" He thought it was unfortunate that Kennedy had given in to domestic pressure and responded to Khrushchev's provocation. He believed the President was "still suffering from the effect of his unlucky interview with Khrushchev in Vienna. . . . For the first time in his life he met a man wholly impervious to his charm."[18]

Macmillan was right about the impact of Kennedy's decision in Belgrade: the distinction between atmospheric and underground testing was too subtle to matter in that highly charged environment. Now that the Americans had announced that they would resume testing too, the Afro-Asians felt more justified in doing what they had wanted to do all along—call on both powers to stop all tests and urge Kennedy and Khrushchev to meet and negotiate a peaceful solution to the Berlin crisis. They decided to send identical messages containing these suggestions to Moscow and Washington. Kennedy's message would be hand-delivered by Sukarno and President Keita of Mali. Khrushchev's would be brought by Nehru, whose visit to Moscow had been scheduled for months, and by Nkrumah.[19] When Kennedy heard that Nehru and Nkrumah were going to Moscow, he remarked to Stevenson, "Khrushchev certainly drew the pick of the litter."[20]

Nehru was affected more deeply by the possibility of failure than the other neutralists. He arrived in Moscow on September 6 looking frail, old, and discouraged. He felt he was the only political leader who was truly seeking the peace of the world. He had maneuvered against the radicals in Belgrade in order to tone down their strident protests against imperialism, so that the voice of neutralism would be listened to with respect in Washington; but Washington viewed the results of the conference with a feeling of disappointment and betrayal. He had condemned the Soviet tests and urged Khrushchev to reconsider, but the Soviet leader had refused to call them off. Nehru emerged from a long talk with Khrushchev on September 7 in a gloomy mood and warned, "Once again the foul winds of war are blowing."[21]

Sukarno and Keita arrived in Washington on September 12, just as the seventh Soviet explosion went off. Kennedy spoke to them very frankly about American resentment of the stand taken by the participants at Belgrade, who reacted to the Soviet tests by appealing to both leaders "to rush into a meeting." He would have preferred it if they had called on Khrushchev to halt the tests first. He explained that he could not meet with Khrushchev while the Soviet leader was threatening nuclear war over the issue of Berlin. But while there was no possibility of a summit now, the channels of diplomacy were open. Rusk and Gromyko would be meeting at the General Assembly the following week.[22]

When the Belgrade conference was over, Kennedy remarked, "Do you know who the real losers of this weekend have been? Bowles and Stevenson."[23] It was on the advice of these men, along with Galbraith and a handful of others, that Kennedy had tried to strike out on a new path with the Afro-Asians. He had started with a new Congo policy, which risked the return of Lumumba, and had then set a precedent by voting against Portugal on the Angola question. It was not easy for him to implement this policy, against the ingrained opposition of the foreign policy establishment. Even on the simple matter of sending a presidential message of greetings to the Belgrade conference, he and the White House staff had had to fight a guerrilla war against the State Department and were rescued in the nick of time by Carl Rowan, then Deputy Assistant Secretary of State for Public Affairs, who came up with a suitable draft.[24] After all this effort Kennedy was disappointed by the attitude of the participants, who still seemed to be using a double standard when they judged the actions of the United States and the Soviet Union. He knew that they would have condemned the United States without hesitation if it had been the first to resume atmospheric testing.

There was no escaping the fact that Khrushchev had violated a fundamental tenet of the neutralist faith and had come through the experience unscathed. This was a tribute to the skill of his policy toward the Afro-Asian world for the past few years. At Belgrade Khrushchev was spending the political capital he had accumulated by giving his full support to the anticolonialist drive throughout the world. Although the Congo was no longer center stage, it had already played its role. The radical Africans were particularly grateful to Khrushchev because of his commitment to the Lumumbist cause; it would have been extremely difficult for them suddenly to turn and attack the Soviet

Union over a cold war issue. Even the dreaded nuclear tests could be rationalized: as Keita explained after his friendly talk with Kennedy, the Russians were merely doing what the French had done before them—and at that time there were no anguished protests from the United States.[25] Kennedy's effort to work with the Afro-Asians was appreciated, but he was fairly new to the game. His policy could not be consistently anticolonialist, as Khrushchev's was. The Kennedy Administration had taken on Belgium and Portugal, but it had reluctantly parted company with Tunisia over the issue of Bizerte in order to protect its relationship with France.[26] Khrushchev had no such problems of competing loyalties. He emerged from the Belgrade conference confident of his standing with the neutralists, and ready to wave the anticolonialist banner at the General Assembly, which would be opening in New York on September 19.

The Death of Hammarskjold

The Secretary-General was also looking forward to the General Assembly meeting with a good deal of confidence. He believed that the Congo issue, which had clouded his relations with the Afro-Asians for more than a year, was essentially settled and that his success in convening Parliament and setting up a coalition government would mollify his Soviet and Afro-Asian critics. There was just one remaining issue to be dealt with—the Katanga secession—and he was fairly optimistic about that. He was going to Leopoldville a week before the General Assembly meeting to discuss plans for economic and technical assistance with Adoula, and he hoped that he could use the opportunity to bring Adoula and Tshombe together. He would then be able to give the Assembly a firsthand report on the progress toward reconciliation.[27]

Hammarskjold's assumption that the Congo crisis was over turned out to be tragically mistaken. On September 17 he was killed in a plane crash near Ndola, in Northern Rhodesia, while he was flying to meet Tshombe in an effort to end five days of inconclusive fighting between the UN force and Tshombe's European-led gendarmerie.

Everything was comparatively peaceful in the Congo when the Secretary-General left New York on September 12. But by the time he arrived in Leopoldville the following day, the Congo was once again the lead story all over the world. The UN force, in a surprise operation, apparently had overthrown the Tshombe regime after a brief but fierce battle. The UN representative in Elisabethville, Conor Cruise O'Brien, announced, "The secession of Katanga has ended. It now is a Congolese province run by the Central Government." He explained that the United Nations had acted under the February 21 Security Council resolution to prevent a civil war between Tshombe's regime and the Leopoldville government.[28] Two of Tshombe's top ministers had been arrested, but Tshombe himself was in hiding, and his formidable Interior Minister, Godefroid Munongo, had fled across the border to Northern Rhodesia, then a British territory.

The UN claim of victory proved to be premature. The September 13 Katanga operation which led to Hammarskjold's death was marked by extraordinary military and political confusion, and many of the participants later told conflicting stories about what went wrong. The key figure in the episode was O'Brien, a controversial Irish diplomat and writer who had served on his country's delegation at the General Assembly for several years when Hammarskjold, who was impressed by his literary essays, tapped him for the Katanga post. According to Brian Urquhart, O'Brien's successor in the job, the officials at the Irish Foreign Ministry would have told Hammarskjold that O'Brien did not have the calm diplomatic temperament to handle the touchy situation in Elisabethville—if he had asked them.[29] O'Brien himself later wrote that when Hammarskjold asked Frederick Boland, the Irish President of the General Assembly, for the names of suitable compatriots, Boland recommended O'Brien for his "originality" and another member of the delegation, with more experience in African affairs, for his "reliability." O'Brien maintained that Hammarskjold deliberately chose the less "safe" candidate. It was not merely a matter of admiring O'Brien's writing style; the Secretary-General was looking for someone of his temperament to handle the Katanga issue—someone who was considered "radical" on colonial questions and would implement the February 21 Security Council resolution fully even if the British disapproved.[30] O'Brien's critical view of British policy in the Congo was reciprocated in full measure. Sir Patrick Dean, whose reservation about the use of force[31] drew O'Brien's scorn, considered the Irish diplomat highly irresponsible. This view was shared to some degree by O'Brien's colleagues in the UN Secretariat, particularly after he published his version of the September events upon resigning from his post a few months later.[32] Still, even the officials who disagreed with his judgment and questioned his account of the events in Katanga admired his courage and persistence in an extremely difficult situation.

O'Brien arrived in Elisabethville in mid-June and spent a good part of the summer trying to carry out the February 21 resolution by persuading Tshombe's foreign military and political advisers to return home. He had a few notable successes, but the fundamental problem remained unchanged. As often as not, the mercenaries who were expelled from Elisabethville one day would turn up again a few days later, having returned via a route which the United Nations did not control.

At the beginning of August there were still about five hundred foreign military officers in Katanga.[33] The new Belgian government, with Paul-Henri Spaak as Foreign Minister, was somewhat more conciliatory toward the United Nations than its predecessor and had promised to repatriate the two hundred remaining Belgians; but the process was going very slowly because of objections from Tshombe, Munongo, and Union Minière. Spaak refused to take responsibility for the three-hundred-odd non-Belgian mercenaries—called *les affreux* because of their wild appearance and wilder behavior. They were a motley crew, recruited from South Africa, Rhodesia, England, and various countries in Western Europe. The most experienced soldiers were French officers who had fought and lost in Algeria; they regarded Katanga as an extension of that campaign—the white man's last bastion in central Africa. Most of the others were attracted by the high pay and the promise of excitement and violence. These unsavory characters swaggered through the bars of Elisabethville armed to the teeth and led Tshombe's soldiers on "pacification" missions in the rebel areas of north Katanga, burning Baluba villages and terrorizing their inhabitants.[34]

O'Brien was convinced that Tshombe could not be persuaded to dismantle his independent state and rejoin the Congo until these people were completely removed. Hammarskjold agreed. He advised Adoula to issue an order requiring the immediate departure of all foreign military advisers and mercenaries in Katanga and requesting the United Nations to carry out this order, under the February 21 resolution. Adoula issued the order on August 24.[35]

On August 28, armed with their new authority, O'Brien and his military counterpart, Indian Brigadier K. A. S. Raja, carried out a successful, peaceful operation, dubbed "Rumpunch," in the course of which they managed to round up eighty-one foreign officers for deportation. In order to lessen the risk of bloodshed, O'Brien had suggested the temporary detention of Munongo and the temporary occupation of the radio station and post office. These measures proved to be effective; Munongo, caught off guard, was unable to incite the public against the United Nations. By 11:00 A.M. Tshombe had agreed to announce on the radio that he would cooperate with the United Nations and dismiss all the foreign officers. By the middle of the afternoon the operation was over. O'Brien stopped arresting mercenaries at the request of the Belgian consul, who promised that he would arrange for the repatriation of the remaining officers.[36] The following day O'Brien wrote to his fiancée, "We're very happy here . . . and probably dangerously cocky and euphoric about our coup of Monday."[37] The Secretary-General, who, according to Urquhart, was not happy about O'Brien's decision to suspend the arrests,[38] sent his Elisabethville representative a warm message of congratulations for an "exceedingly sensitive operation carried through with skill and courage."[39]

The reaction to Rumpunch in Washington was somewhat less enthusiastic. The Americans, who publicly supported the action, privately echoed the concern of their Belgian and British allies that the United Nations might end by going too far in Katanga. On September 1 the State Department instructed Godley to inform Adoula and Linner that while the U.S. government approved of the removal of Belgian military personnel from Katanga at the "earliest possible date," it did not believe that "all peaceful means" had been exhausted. The Department hoped the United Nations would use its "new position of strength" not to "destroy" Tshombe and his entire "political framework" but rather to persuade him to cooperate with the Adoula government.[40]

There were clearly two different ways of ending the Katanga secession—through negotiations or through force. The Americans and their Western European allies favored the first course, on the assumption that it would keep Tshombe in power as Katanga's provincial president and leave the Belgian economic position intact. The Russians and the Afro-Asians favored the second course, on the assumption that Tshombe would be removed from office and Belgian economic influence would be sharply curtailed. The Americans and the British were afraid that if the United Nations used force to eliminate Tshombe and restore Leopoldville's control over Katanga, it might soon find the Leopoldville government dominated by its most extreme elements— the Gizengists, backed by the Soviet Union, which would then control the riches of Katanga. Macmillan put it succinctly in response to charges that he was supporting the Katanga secession. "We wanted a united Congo," he wrote, "but not a Communist Congo."[41]

Hammarskjold and O'Brien were caught in between these two viewpoints. While Hammarskjold argued that the Security Council resolutions did not explicitly authorize the United Nations to end the Katanga secession by force and agonized over each step his subordinates took to bring Tshombe around, O'Brien took a much more direct approach. His dealings with Tshombe and his European supporters had left him in no mood for legalistic interpretations of the mandate. He simply wanted to see the Katanga secession ended as swiftly as possible. Tshombe had the same effect on him that Mobutu had had on Dayal, and Lumumba had had on Hammarskjold himself: exasperation made all three men more impatient and less diplomatic than they might have been in a more normal situation. In the case of Katanga the difference between Hammarskjold's cautious global view and O'Brien's impatient local one led to a tragic misunderstanding.

The two-week period following Rumpunch was one of increasing tension between the United Nations and the Tshombe regime. To begin with, the Belgian consul had not lived up to his commitment to repatriate all the foreign mercenaries; while the majority of them had left by September 8, there were at least 104 mercenaries still at large. They put on civilian clothes and faded into the European population, ready for trouble. In addition, Tshombe, who had taken a somewhat conciliatory line toward the United Nations immediately after Rumpunch, was soon stirred up again by his backers at Union Minière. A disgruntled mercenary confided to O'Brien that he had been hired by Munongo to assassinate a number of UN officials including O'Brien's deputy, Michel Tombelaine. O'Brien immediately demanded that Tshombe dismiss Munongo. Tshombe refused. On September 10 Tombelaine was arrested by a Belgian officer from the Katanga Sureté, Munongo's secret police. O'Brien managed to get him released and demanded that all the Belgians serving in the Sureté be removed within three days. On September 11 Tshombe complained that O'Brien had given him an ultimatum demanding that he go to Leopoldville to meet with Adoula. O'Brien explained to the press that there was no ultimatum; he had "simply told Mr. Tshombe that this was the last time he would ask him to meet with the Leopoldville leaders." On September 12 Khiary asked Tshombe to go to Leopoldville to meet with Hammarskjold, who would be arriving the next day. Once again, Tshombe refused.[42]

Khiary had not come all the way to Elisabethville just to press this invitation on Tshombe. According to O'Brien's account, he had come with final instructions for O'Brien and Raja about an operation they had been discussing for the past week. The new operation, which was called "Morthor," was to be similar in some ways to Rumpunch but more far-reaching. O'Brien was given five warrants issued by the Leopoldville government for the arrest of Tshombe, Munongo, and three other top leaders. Tshombe was to be arrested only as a last resort; O'Brien was to persuade him to cooperate with the United Nations in "peacefully liquidating the secession of Katanga."[43] UN troops were to secure not only the post office and radio station but also the headquarters of the Sureté and the Ministry of Information, and to arrest their top European and African officials. They were to raise the flag of the central government on all public buildings and to assist a representative of that government who would be arriving from Leopoldville on a UN plane to take control of the province. In carrying out these instructions, O'Brien and Raja were to do their best to avoid clashes with Tshombe's gendarmerie. Khiary asked how long it would take to secure these objectives if the gendarmerie did resist, and Raja assured him it would take no longer than two hours. He and O'Brien assumed they could persuade Tshombe to get on the radio, as he had done on

August 28, and order his troops to cooperate with the United Nations. As Khiary left for Leopoldville, his last words to O'Brien were, "Surtout pas de demi-mesures."[44]

Morthor was launched at dawn on September 13, the day the Secretary-General was due to arrive in Leopoldville. Unlike Rumpunch, it turned out to be neither peaceful nor successful. This time, the crucial element of surprise was missing. There was unexpected resistance from the Katangan forces, led by the remaining mercenaries, and bitter fighting broke out at the radio station and the post office. The most serious error—O'Brien called it a "fatal flaw"[45]—was the failure of the UN troops to surround Tshombe's residence. When O'Brien spoke to him on the telephone at dawn, he seemed ready to cooperate; but before Tombelaine could pick him up and take him to the radio station, he had disappeared. O'Brien later learned that he had fled to the nearby home of the British consul and then gone to Rhodesia. As a result of this slip-up, the United Nations lost contact with a key figure at the most critical point in the operation.[46]

Despite his triumphant announcement that the Katanga secession was over, O'Brien realized quite early in the day that things were not going according to plan, and by mid-afternoon, when Hammarskjold touched down in Leopoldville, the UN officials there knew they had a crisis on their hands. Hammarskjold was greeted by the leaders of the new government he had helped to create—Adoula, Gizenga, Mobutu, and Bomboko—but he had very little time to enjoy the apparent harmony reigning in the capital. He stopped briefly at Adoula's residence and then sat down with Linner, Khiary, and McKeown to try to find out what was going on in Elisabethville.[47]

It is at this point that the accounts of the September 13 operation begin to diverge, and the first major controversy arises: Was the operation cleared in advance with the Secretary-General? On one side is O'Brien, who maintains that he had no reason to doubt that the plan had Hammarskjold's approval; he got his orders from Khiary, and he assumed Khiary was getting his orders from the Secretary-General, via Linner. This impression was strengthened when Khiary came to Elisabethville to give O'Brien his final instructions and emphasized that Morthor should be carried out either before Hammarskjold's arrival in the Congo or after his departure. He told O'Brien that "Hammarskjold had given authority for these operations, but it would be embarrassing for him if fighting were actually going on in Katanga while he was in Leopoldville." O'Brien recommended that the United Nations act as quickly as possible, and the operation was set up for the morning of September 13, on the assumption that it would all be over by the time the Secretary-General's plan landed.[48]

Hammarskjold's defenders, on the other hand, have maintained that he gave no orders for the September 13 operation and that he was surprised and dismayed by the reports of the fighting, which first reached him during a stopover in Accra. Cordier, for example, recalled in an interview with the author in 1971 that Hammarskjold had gone to Leopoldville in an optimistic mood to review the progress that had been made and insisted that a military operation against the Katanga regime was the farthest thing from his mind. Urquhart concluded, after reviewing in detail the complex instructions Hammarskjold had given to Linner and Khiary, that while he was aware of their recommendations for military action and had authorized them to proceed with their planning, he did not want the plans implemented until he had had a chance to study the situation himself. Urquhart explained the disparity between the Secretary-General's instructions and the actions of his subordinates as the result of the fragmented command structure established after Dayal's departure. Linner, who was nominally in charge, was not particularly forceful, while Khiary, his strong-minded deputy, shared O'Brien's views about the need for immediate action and was in a position to put those views into effect.[49] According to Dayal's account, Khiary claimed that he was acting "on Linner's authority," while Linner denied that he had given Khiary any authority. Dayal concluded that the men in the field were motivated by the hope that a "swift and sudden action would produce the desired results which would then be presented to the Secretary-General as a fait accompli"[50]—a hope which Urquhart described as "misguided."[51]

There was, in fact, ample precedent in the Congo for just this sort of initiative. The exchange of messages between New York and Leopoldville cited by Urquhart was fairly ambiguous, and it is not unreasonable to suppose that Linner and Khiary felt they would be more faithful to their chief's true intentions if they read between the lines of his instructions rather than following them to the letter. Cordier had taken this approach in September 1960 and had never been disowned by Hammarskjold; Linner had exceeded his instructions regarding Parliament as recently as July and had won Hammarskjold's praise. This kind of creative insubordination would have been fine if the September 13 operation had been successful. Since it was not, the Secretary-General and his top aides found themselves in an embarrassing position.

It was not made any easier by O'Brien's initial announcement that the United Nations had just ended the Katanga secession. This statement led to a second controversy: What was the true purpose of the September 13 operation? While O'Brien insisted that the UN troops had been ordered to arrest the leaders of the Katanga government and take over various key points in Elisabethville as part of a prearranged plan to end the secession,[52] Hammarskjold and Linner issued an official report on September 14[53] which explained that the troops had been forced to act in self-defense while trying to accomplish the more limited aim of rounding up mercenaries; in other words, Morthor was merely a continuation of Rumpunch which had unfortunately gotten out of hand. The two men continued to operate at cross-purposes for the next few days. O'Brien, who was unaware of the report at the time, continued to talk to the press about his determination to end the secession, and on September 17, after Tombelaine took the same line on Katanga radio, Hammarskjold sent a strong message rebuking them both for distorting the UN position.[54] O'Brien was puzzled by what he thought was a shift in Hammarskjold's position; he assumed that the Secretary-General had backed down because of the angry reaction of the Western powers, particularly the British.

This assumption was at the heart of the third and final controversy surrounding the September 13 operation: Was Western pressure responsible for Hammarskjold's effort to achieve a ceasefire—an effort which ended in his death? O'Brien was convinced that it played a major role in his decision to halt the operation short of victory and to sue for peace. He was totally opposed to the idea of Hammarskjold's flying to Rhodesia, Tshombe's sanctuary—a step which he regarded as close to surrender. In fact, he later compared Hammarskjold's journey to Chamberlain's trip to Munich.[55] O'Brien was not alone in his belief that Western pressure was ultimately responsible for Hammarskjold's death. Dayal, who, unlike O'Brien, retained his deep respect and admiration for the Secretary-General, described his decision to fly to Ndola as a "desperate gamble," forced upon him by the "pressure of political circumstances." Dayal felt that he had "agreed to meet on doubtful terrain to negotiate a truce, practically on Tshombe's terms," because he was "haunted by the ultimatum of the British Government and the warnings of the United States."[56]

Urquhart, on the other hand, rejected the idea that Hammarskjold was forced to abandon his principles or his good judgment because of Western pressure. He denied that there was a British ultimatum and argued that the Secretary-General was determined from the moment he arrived to stop the bloodshed as soon as possible. In other words, the British and the Americans were no more eager for a ceasefire than Hammarskjold was himself; they were "pushing on an open door."[57]

There are probably elements of truth in both viewpoints. The last five days of Hammarskjold's life were filled with tension and disappointment. He had hoped to go to the General Assembly with a solid record of achievement behind him. The formation of the Adoula government had created a consensus among the Americans, the British, the Russians, and the Afro-Asians in support of his policy for the first time since the beginning of the Congo operation. The September 13 action, which was probably intended to crown that achievement with a bloodless triumph, instead put it in jeopardy by destroying the consensus which had been built so carefully over the past six months. Hammarskjold was unwilling to blame his subordinates for this setback, but he was determined to limit the damage and get the negotiating process back on track.

His aides assured him at first that the fighting would soon be over, but as he saw it stretch into a second day, and then a third and a fourth, he realized that the UN force was facing defeat, or at best a stalemate. An Irish company had been surrounded in Jadotville, a mining center fifty miles from Elisabethville, where it had been sent at the request of the European population. The soldiers were now cut off without food or water by Katanga troops led by Europeans, and there were reports—which turned out to be false—that fifty-seven of them had been killed and ninety taken prisoner.

Hammarskjold was aware that the Katanga forces had one important military advantage—control of the skies. Their air force consisted of one Fouga Magister jet fighter, which was one more fighter than the United Nations possessed. It was able to bomb and strafe UN positions, including O'Brien's headquarters, and the UN force was powerless to prevent it. On September 15 Hammarskjold urgently requested Ethiopia to send two or three fighters to right the balance. The Ethiopians agreed, but the British stalled about granting permission for the planes to overfly Uganda en route to the Congo and tried to persuade Hammarskjold that it would be wiser to avoid aerial combat altogether. He was also turned down by the U.S. government when he requested transport planes to take additional UN troops from Leopoldville to Elisabethville.[58]

These two negative responses graphically illustrated the rift that had developed between the Secretary-General and his principal Western supporters, who were unwilling to contribute in any way to the expansion of the UN military role in Katanga. Hammarskjold knew that any action he took to satisfy them would inevitably antagonize the other members of the consensus—the Afro-Asians and the Russians. They had welcomed O'Brien's initial statement, but Hammarskjold knew they would be disappointed by his decision to break off the fighting short of total victory. Soviet support was grudging at best. *Pravda* made the point that Hammarskjold could have launched the same operation at any time during the past year if he had wanted to do so and suggested that the only reason he had acted now was that he "obviously feared sharp criticism" at the General Assembly. As the fighting continued, the Russians grew more suspicious; they insisted that the UN force was strong enough to win if it was ordered to do so. They found it "odd" that Tshombe had managed to escape, and they sus-

pected that the Americans were deeply involved in the effort to restore him to power, despite their ostensible support for the United
Nations. They concluded that the U.S. government was "changing its
tactics" and taking a more subtle approach than it had in the past.
They noted that the hardliner, Timberlake, whom *Pravda* described as
a "participant in Lumumba's murder," had been recalled and a new
ambassador with a reputation as a "moderate" had been sent to Leopoldville to take his place.[59]

Ambassador Gullion, who arrived between Rumpunch and Morthor,
took a somewhat different view of the Congo situation from that of
Timberlake; but during the September crisis he found himself working
almost as closely with the new British ambassador, Derek Riches, as
Timberlake had with his predecessor. Riches went to see Hammarskjold on the evening of September 13 to express his government's
shock about the fighting in Elisabethville. He asked the Secretary-
General to explain the discrepancy between his assurances to Dean
just before he left New York that the United Nations would not use
force to settle the Katanga problem and the statements made by
O'Brien earlier in the day. He pointed out that his government could
not continue to support the UN mission if it was embarked on a policy
of offensive military action unauthorized by the mandate. Hammarskjold responded with the line he would take in his official report the
following day. He explained that there had been no change in UN policy: the troops had been ordered to round up foreign mercenaries,
which was clearly part of their task under the February 21 resolution,
and they had used force in self-defense. He assured Riches that he
would try to arrange a ceasefire as soon as possible and asked for British cooperation.[60]

The Americans, who had warned against further use of force in Katanga after the comparatively mild Rumpunch operation, continued to
support the United Nations publicly, but in private they took a line
that was very close to the British position. On September 14 Bunche
reported to Hammarskjold that Kennedy and Rusk were "extremely
upset" by the fact that he had failed to consult with the U.S. government, which was paying most of the bills for the Congo operation.
Rusk warned that American support would "evaporate" if the Gizenga
line prevailed, and he urged the Secretary-General to bring Adoula
and Tshombe together for talks. Hammarskjold was angered by this
message. He felt that the U.S. government had made no effort to persuade Tshombe to meet Adoula halfway, and he resented the implication that he had to follow American advice because he was dependent
on American financial support.[61]

That evening, Kennedy discussed the problem with Macmillan, who
warned him that the Communists might end up controlling the valu-

able properties of Union Minière. "Unless we and the Americans act quickly and resolutely," he wrote in his diary, "we shall have undone in a week all we have done—at huge expense—in a year." He urged Kennedy to help him persuade Hammarskjold to support a federal solution in the Congo, and when Kennedy asked if he wanted Tshombe back in power, Macmillan replied, "Either Tshombe or someone else."[62] It was the principle that mattered, not the particular politician. Lord Home, the British Foreign Secretary, was in New York for the General Assembly session, and he reported to Macmillan two days later that Kennedy and Rusk were "very worried about the Congo. Their politicians, like ours, are asking what all our expenditure of energy and treasure has been for."[63]

The Anglo-American effort reached a climax on September 16, when Gullion presented Hammarskjold with a joint démarche from Kennedy, Rusk, and Home, urging him to remain in the Congo until the fighting was ended in order to demonstrate his "seriousness." Once again, Hammarskjold was somewhat annoyed by the tone of the Western message. He told Gullion he would have to "judge from day to day," but in fact he had already decided to try to meet with Tshombe to set up a ceasefire.[64] He had discussed this idea earlier in the day with Lord Lansdowne, Macmillan's special emissary, who had come to Leopoldville to impress upon the Secretary-General the depth of British concern that the UN action might inadvertently "hand the Katanga on a plate to the Gizengists" and to point out the "deplorable effect" the fighting was having on the British government and on British public opinion. He was apparently impressed by Hammarskjold's assurances that O'Brien's statements did not represent UN policy; he reported to Macmillan the following day that the September 13 action, in his opinion, was the result of "folly and inexperience rather than of malice."[65]

Hammarskjold had no trouble securing Lansdowne's approval of his letter to Tshombe proposing a meeting in Northern Rhodesia and a ceasefire. He then showed it to Adoula, who raised no objections.[66] But when he asked O'Brien to transmit it to Tshombe, the Irish diplomat strongly advised against the meeting and asked Hammarskjold, at the very least, to pick him up at Kamina and take him along to Ndola; he hoped to "dissuade him from going to Rhodesia at all."[67] Hammarskjold turned down this request, as he turned down Khiary's offer to go to Ndola in his place. He believed that he was the only one who could persuade Tshombe to come to Leopoldville to negotiate with Adoula, and he undoubtedly felt that after the events of the past few days, the presence of O'Brien or Khiary would not be particularly helpful.[68]

On the morning of September 17 Hammarskjold received a message from Tshombe accepting the idea of a meeting and a ceasefire but raising a number of unacceptable conditions. Hammarskjold immediately fired off a message rejecting the conditions, but when he learned that Tshombe had left for Ndola without receiving his message, he decided to proceed with his plan and fly to Ndola as well. He knew that he would be criticized for this decision and that the Russians and tKe Afro-Asians would charge that he was acting at the suggestion of the Western powers, but he felt it was unavoidable if the Congo conflict was ever to be resolved.[69]

On the afternoon of September 17 Lansdowne left for Ndola on a UN plane; he had offered to accompany Hammarskjold, but the Secretary-General pointed out that it would be awkward, diplomatically.[70] Lansdowne arrived in the evening, checked out the arrangements for the meeting, and left for Salisbury as planned, so that he would not be present at the Hammarskjold-Tshombe talks.

The Secretary-General left Leopoldville in the late afternoon. The plane he was using had been shot up by the Katanga jet fighter when it was leaving the Elisabethville airport the previous day, but the damage was comparatively minor, and the plane had been repaired and thoroughly checked out by UN technicians before Hammarskjold's departure. In order to escape detection and avoid the danger of another attack, Hammarskjold's plane took a long, indirect route to Ndola and maintained radio silence during most of the trip. Shortly after midnight the pilot approached the Ndola airport and announced he was descending. Then nothing more was heard. The airport officials waited for a while and then decided to go home, assuming Hammarskjold had changed his plans at the last minute for political reasons. It was not until the following afternoon that the wreckage of the plane was found, just nine miles from the airport. Hammarskjold and all his companions had been killed, with the exception of one security guard who was in critical condition and died a few days later.[71]

Because Hammarskjold's plane crashed when he was on a controversial mission in the midst of a combat zone, there were inevitably suspicions of foul play. The lone survivor reported a series of explosions just before the crash. A UN spokesman in Leopoldville said he could not rule out the possibility that the plane had been shot down or sabotaged.[72] The Soviet press quoted this statement and strongly implied that Tshombe was responsible.[73] O'Brien argued that it was not in Tshombe's interest to kill the Secretary-General; he pointed to Munongo and his diehard European mercenaries as the most likely suspects, since they had the means to sabotage the plane and they stood to gain the most from Hammarskjold's death.[74] Adoula blamed the forces of "capitalist imperialism" which controlled Katanga. He described Hammarskjold as "the victim of certain financial circles for whom a human life is worth less than a gram of copper or uranium."[75]

An investigation commission was set up to sift through the evidence and try to establish what happened, but it failed to come to any definite conclusion. It could not exclude the possibility of sabotage or attack by another plane; on the other hand, it was possible that the pilot, exhausted from the strain of the past few days and flying an unfamiliar route after dark, misjudged the altitude of the plane and crashed into a line of trees as he was on his way in for a landing. The commission's report criticized the negligence of the Rhodesian authorities; while all but one of the passengers and crew were apparently killed immediately, the lone survivor might have been saved if help had reached him sooner.[76]

Dag Hammarskjold's death was a tragic blow to the United Nations, and it was mourned throughout most of the world—but not in the Soviet Union. A Soviet spokesman immediately announced that his government would press its demand for a troika; and the Western and Afro-Asian delegations feared that it would be impossible to choose a successor to Hammarskjold and the world organization would be paralyzed. Kennedy, who had been debating the pros and cons of addressing the General Assembly for several weeks, decided that he must go to New York to reassure the delegates and the UN staff that the United States supported the United Nations and would do everything in its power to maintain the office of the Secretary-General. On the evening of September 18 he announced this decision and paid tribute to Hammarskjold's "dedication to the cause of peace." Kennedy stated, "It is tragic and ironic that his death came during a mission he was undertaking in order to bring about a ceasefire in Katanga."[77]

The Selection of a New Secretary-General

On September 19 Gromyko publicly confirmed that his government would settle for nothing less than a troika.[78] There was a hint of flexibility, however, in his private diplomacy; that same day he sent one of his top aides to see U Thant, the head of the Burmese delegation, to tell him that while the Soviet government would continue to insist on a troika, "as an interim measure it would like to have an interim Secretary-General and three undersecretaries acting collectively." He told Thant that if he became a candidate, the Soviet government would not support him unless he agreed in advance to name these three deputies and define their functions. Thant replied that his government was opposed to the troika concept in any form and that, in any case, he was "not at all interested in the post."[79]

Thant's disclaimers were not taken seriously. He quickly emerged as the leading candidate to succeed Hammarskjold. The quiet Asian diplomat had built a reputation over the years as a scrupulously honest neutralist who was fair to both sides. During the Congo debate at the General Assembly in September 1960, he had been the only delegate outside the Communist bloc to regret the expulsion of the Soviet and Czech Embassies from Leopoldville; at the same time, he had supported Hammarskjold and opposed Soviet military aid to Lumumba.[80] Hammarskjold had thought very highly of him. He had told Yost in March that he would like to name Thant as a replacement for Dayal if he could persuade him to take the job. At that time he described Thant as "mild on the outside but solid on the inside."[81] A few weeks before his death, Hammarskjold told close friends that either Thant or Tunisian Ambassador Slim would be his first choice to replace him as Secretary-General.[82]

Slim, who had just been elected President of the General Assembly, was considered too pro-Western by the Russians. He was also faced with the hostility of the French, who were still angry about the recent Bizerte incident; of the Ghanaians and Guineans, who considered him too moderate on African issues; and of the Israelis, who objected to Tunisia's refusal to recognize the state of Israel. Thant, on the other hand, was acceptable to all these countries, as well as to the Americans—although he was not their first choice. His only problem was the fact that Burma maintained close relations with Israel, and it was assumed that this would lead to objections from the Arab states. This, however, did not prove to be much of an obstacle. Ironically, the Israeli and Egyptian delegates came to see Thant the same day to urge him to announce his candidacy.[83]

Once there was unofficial agreement on a candidate, the next problem was to reconcile the Soviet and American views of his office—and this took another five weeks, as the Russians backed down, little by little, from their initial insistence on a troika. Finally, on November 3 the General Assembly, on the recommendation of the Security Council, unanimously named U Thant Acting Secretary-General, with no legal strings attached.[84]

While the selection of Thant was not exactly a triumph of Soviet diplomacy, the Russians made the best of it. An Asian had replaced a Western European as Secretary-General, and this signified a shift in power away from the Americans and their allies within the United Nations and a recognition of the important role of the newly independent countries of Asia and Africa.[85] Moreover, Khrushchev probably assumed that the new Secretary-General, aware of his predecessor's problems, would be wary of antagonizing the Soviet Union, particularly with only an eighteen-month term ahead of him. Thant's approach to the Congo question turned out to be quite different from Hammarskjold's, but ironically the Russians would find this Asian neutralist as hostile to their interests in the Congo as his Western European predecessor had been.

The Americans were more pleased with their success in defending the principle of a single Secretary-General than with the man who was going to fill the job. Stevenson established a good relationship with Thant, whom he considered "basically pro-Western,"[86] but it was never as close as his relationship with Hammarskjold. His colleagues at the U.S. Mission had little in common with this "Burmese pacifist," as Cleveland described him. It was not so much a question of his anticolonialist views, though these were strongly held; he came from a land which had achieved independence in 1948, after a century of British rule, when even the highest-ranking Burmese officials were unable to join the prestigious clubs in Rangoon, because they were "exclusively European."[87] The Americans could understand this, but they found it difficult to comprehend Thant's philosophical approach to life. He had cultivated the Buddhist virtues of tolerance, compassion, and detachment—reached through meditation—and felt it was essential to attain inner peace in order to be able to help make peace among others.[88] All this was rather foreign to the men at the U.S. Mission, who found the new Secretary-General phlegmatic and indecisive. Plimpton remarked caustically many years later that Thant was easy to get along with; he always agreed with the last person he talked to.

As far as these American diplomats were concerned, the best thing about Thant's Congo policy was that he left it almost entirely in the hands of Ralph Bunche. Bunche had been deeply involved in the operation since his eventful tour in the summer of 1960, but he had always worked under Hammarskjold's direction. Thant was much more detached about the Congo. For him, it was one problem among many. His own personal prestige was not involved in a solution. While Hammarskjold made four trips to the Congo in a little more than a year, and lost his life in an attempt to end the Katanga secession, Thant managed to preside over the ending of the secession without going to the Congo at all.

CHAPTER TWELVE

The New Frontier Strains
the Old Alliance
(November 3 –December 31, 1961)

*"If it's imperialist to try to halt fighting
before it gets out of hand, then we're imperialist."*

O N NOVEMBER 3, the day U Thant was sworn in as Acting Secretary-General, three moderate African states which had been the main-
stays of the UN operation—Ethiopia, Nigeria, and Sudan—called for an
immediate meeting of the Security Council to deal with the Katanga
situation.[1] They were convinced that the United Nations had called off
its effort to end the secession because of pressure from the Western
powers. Soviet Ambassador Zorin, who was President of the Council
for the month of November, supported their request. The Americans
and the British insisted on a delay. The two allies needed time to con-
cert their own policies, which had diverged sharply over the past six
weeks.

Switch in U.S. Strategy: Forcing Tshombe to Negotiate

The Americans had been working closely with the British to moderate UN policy ever since the August 28 roundup of mercenaries, but
their attitude changed dramatically as a result of Hammarskjold's
death. Kennedy had planned to propose a major expansion of the United Nations' peacekeeping capacity and of Hammarskjold's role as Secretary-General.[2] Now that entire plan had to be scrapped, and the
Americans felt they had to come up with a salvage operation in order
to prevent the Soviet Union from wrecking the office of the Secretary-
General altogether. Their first priority was to take a stand on the Katanga issue that would dispel the suspicions of the Afro-Asians and
bolster their support for the United Nations—support that was essential if the troika was to be defeated.

The impact of Hammarskjold's death was first seen in a new American willingness to give the United Nations important military support.
While the U.S. government had dragged its feet on supplying the

transport planes the Secretary-General requested just a few days before his death, it now agreed to send four planes immediately. They were placed at the disposal of the UN force and, for the first time, were authorized to carry troops and supplies *within* the Congo.[3]

Even more significant than this public reversal was the fact that, on September 19, before the ceasefire was signed, Kennedy privately agreed to make eight jet fighter planes available to the United Nations if no other nation was willing to do so. The Joint Chiefs of Staff, in approving this request, had recommended that the fighters be given "enough latitude to attack any hostile elements attempting to destroy the transport aircraft"; in other words, they should be authorized to "seek out and destroy either on the ground or in the air the Fouga Magister jets." They added, however, that if the President or the Secretary of State felt this was not politically advisable, then the fighters would simply play a defensive role. The President chose the more cautious position. He authorized the fighters "to support and defend" U.S. and UN transport planes which "might come under air attack" but insisted that there would be "no effort to seek out and destroy Fouga Magister jets not attacking US or UN forces without further authority from the President."[4]

The day after Kennedy approved this offer, UN officials signed a ceasefire agreement with Tshombe which left the secessionist leader in firm control of the province.[5] Adoula warned that his government refused to be bound by the ceasefire; it was ready to use its own armed forces to end the secession.[6] The Russians, who denounced the ceasefire as a "capitulation" to Tshombe and the "imperialists," applauded Adoula's stand.[7] The British, who welcomed the ceasefire, defended their effort to get the two sides together, as well as their decision to block the arrival of the Ethiopian jet fighters which Hammarskjold had requested. "If it is imperialist to try to halt fighting before it gets out of hand, then we're imperialist," remarked one British official.[8]

Kennedy and his advisers still preferred a negotiated settlement to a military solution, and they welcomed the ceasefire as an opportunity to persuade Tshombe to listen to reason; but they quickly realized that Tshombe was flushed with success and in no mood to compromise. As Under Secretary of State George Ball put it in a memorandum to the President, Tshombe felt he had won a victory over the United Nations, and as long as he believed he was "in control of the military situation," he would refuse to negotiate with Adoula. Ball insisted that the United States must destroy "Tshombe's assurance in his own military supremacy." It must build up the "fighting power" of the United Nations to a point at which Tshombe would realize he could not win. "If the UN makes a sufficient show of strength," he said, "it should not find it necessary to employ it."[9]

Ball's views were shared by Rostow, Williams, and other officials at the State Department and the White House. They hoped to enlist British support for their new approach; but when they found that the British were reluctant to contemplate the threat of force, they decided the situation was so urgent that the United States would proceed on its own to bolster the military position of the United Nations. As it turned out, the U.S. fighter planes were not needed. Four Ethiopian jet fighters arrived in Leopoldville on September 27, and they were followed within the next two weeks by five Swedish fighters and six Indian Canberra fighter bombers.

Kennedy's activist advisers were determined to end the Katanga secession in order to eliminate once and for all the danger of a Soviet takeover in Leopoldville. They were afraid that if Adoula failed to produce results, he would be replaced by extremists who would be only too happy to turn to the Russians for military assistance.[10] The British, who regarded Tshombe as the only anti-Communist bulwark in the Congo, had little use for Adoula. They felt he was hostile to Western interests and dominated by Gizenga.

Adoula's most outspoken advocate was the new U.S. ambassador in Leopoldville. Gullion argued that Adoula had demonstrated his independence of left-wing pressures by refusing to accept the credentials of the Communist and Afro-Asian diplomats who had been stationed in Stanleyville. When he learned that the Russians were back in Leopoldville looking for a forty-room building to house a large embassy,[11] Adoula quickly told the Soviet ambassador-designate that he must go home and re-apply for accreditation before he could set up his mission in Leopoldville.[12]

Gullion assured the State Department that Adoula was keeping a "sharp eye" on the "Gizenga menace" and was playing a "tricky but courageous game" in an attempt to limit his power. The results of this game had been encouraging so far; the CIA, which was helping Adoula build a "solid political base" and launch a "psychological campaign" against Gizenga, reported that Gizenga's efforts to penetrate the Sureté and the Ministry of Communications had been unsuccessful, and that he seemed to be losing ground with his former allies, such as Gbenye.[13]

On October 3, after checking with Adoula, Gullion had his first meeting with Gizenga. He found the leftist leader "courteous and collected" and "relatively sophisticated" and concluded that he would "make a good impression face-to-face if there were not something serpentine about him." Gizenga complained that the Western press had "distorted his position"; reporters were always looking for Soviet technicians in Stanleyville—but Gizenga insisted "there were none." He told Gullion that he was planning to leave for Stanleyville the next day on a brief visit and expected to be back in Leopoldville by October 7.[14]

The following day Gullion called on Kasavubu, who assured him that there was no need to worry about Gizenga. He had been riding Lumumba's coattails but had "no real popular support" of his own. Kasavubu compared him to a "leopard which presented no danger so long as its range of action" was "known and circumscribed." That was why Kasavubu and the government had approved his trip to Stanleyville.[15]

Gullion won important political support for his pro-Adoula stand in mid-October from a visiting delegation of U.S. Senators, which was headed by Albert Gore of Tennessee, the chairman of the African Affairs Subcommittee of the Foreign Relations Committee, and included two other liberal Democrats—Maurine Neuberger of Oregon, and Philip Hart of Michigan. After conferring with Adoula, they told the press they were "deeply impressed" by him and felt he was one of the ablest African leaders they had met. They had no doubt that he was capable of handling the problems posed by Gizenga and the militant left. At the same time, the Senators bolstered Gullion's credibility with Adoula by expressing their support for the United Nations and for a united Congo. Their statements helped counter the impression created by the pro-Katanga Senators, particularly Thomas Dodd of Connecticut, that the Americans really backed the secession and that the Kennedy Administration was not serious about its promise to work for the reintegration of Katanga.[16]

All of this left the Russians in a rather awkward spot. They were not particularly pleased by Adoula's entente cordiale with the U.S. Senate or by his pro-American brand of nonalignment, but they felt they had no alternative. After three months' exposure to Gizenga, they had become disillusioned with him and concluded that he was nothing more than a "third-rate theorist."[17] They had made their choice and now they would have to wait patiently until the pressure of events pushed Adoula leftward or forced him out altogether. They knew that he valued Khrushchev's letter of recognition because it helped establish his credentials at Belgrade as something more than an American puppet, and they felt that it would not be long before a Soviet Embassy was officially installed in Leopoldville, because Adoula needed it there to protect his neutralist image.[18] Meanwhile, the Soviet diplomats ignored Adoula's expulsion order and remained in the Congolese capital in an unofficial capacity, urging the government to invade Katanga and hinting that Moscow would be ready to provide substantial aid in exchange for the reestablishment of diplomatic relations.

Khrushchev himself took an extremely cautious approach to the question of Adoula when he addressed the opening meeting of the Twenty-second Congress of the Soviet Communist Party on October 17. He intended to use this occasion to demonstrate to his foreign and domestic critics the success of his new Africa policy. Among the Communist delegations from all over the world were three non-Communist but pro-Soviet delegations representing the radical governments of Ghana, Guinea, and Mali. Khrushchev's triumph would have been complete if there had been a radical Congolese delegation sitting there as well; but his plans for the Congo had been thwarted, and he had been forced to settle for second best. He was aware that the Chinese were highly critical of his decision to encourage Gizenga to join the Adoula government and that they were ready to pounce at the first sign that he had blundered and walked into a Western trap. As a result he tiptoed around the Congo issue. He noted the formation of the new Congolese government in positive terms, but he managed to restrain his enthusiasm.[19]

He was undoubtedly aware that the dispute between Adoula and Gizenga was now out in the open. Gizenga had never returned from his short visit to Stanleyville. After a few weeks there, he managed to oust the moderate pro-Western president of Orientale Province, place him under house arrest, and replace him with one of his own supporters.[20] Adoula counterattacked by persuading General Lundula, the Stanleyville military commander, to come to Leopoldville, swear allegiance to the central government, and join forces with Mobutu for an offensive against Katanga. Adoula had no illusions about this offensive ending the secession, but he recognized the political value of a warlike stance.

On November 2 Mobutu announced that his troops had crossed the Katanga border and penetrated thirty-five miles into the secessionist province.[21] Kennedy asked for a report. Ball warned that Adoula, whose patience was "nearly at an end," might turn to the Security Council and ask for a new mandate which would authorize the United Nations to join the Congolese army in a "major attack on Katanga." This was precisely what the Russians were proposing, and the idea appealed to a number of the Afro-Asian countries as well. Ball believed that a "large scale attack" would be disastrous, but he did not altogether rule out the possibility of a military solution. He pointed out that since the fighting in September, the United Nations, encouraged by the U.S. government, had improved its military position to a point of "clear superiority," and he suggested that if the Katangans were to attack again, the UN command should not settle for a "stalemate" but "should quickly demonstrate to Tshombe the futility of continued hostilities."[22]

The Ninth Security Council Meeting: November 13–24, 1961

On November 7 the top American policymakers—Rusk, Stevenson, Ball, Williams, and Cleveland—met with the newly appointed British ambassador, David Ormsby-Gore, to try to agree on a common strategy before the Security Council meeting. Ormsby-Gore, who was related by marriage to both Macmillan and Kennedy and was a contemporary and close friend of the young President, would play a major role in Kennedy's deliberations about the Congo over the next year or so, balancing the activist views of the New Frontiersmen at the State Department and the White House with traditional British advice: go slow, avoid the use of force, and consider the economic ramifications of your policy. At this meeting the ambassador pointed out that the sharp differences between Washington and London, which had been patched up to some extent after the September fighting, might be renewed if the United Nations tried to remove the mercenaries by force. Stevenson agreed that the "last thing" the United States wanted was to "resolve the issue by force of arms," but he warned that Western policy in the Congo was "on the verge of ruin"; the United Nations, he said, was "about to leave the Congo with its tail between its legs unless we can bring this Tshombe to heel."[23]

The Americans assured the British that they would oppose any resolution authorizing the United Nations to engage in military action against Tshombe or to participate in joint operations with the ANC against the Katanga secession. But beyond that, the two allies agreed to disagree. The Americans felt that the United Nations should be given the "authority to arrest and evacuate mercenaries" and other foreign advisers listed in the February 21 resolution—on the understanding that its action "should not lead to hostilities." The British refused to go that far.[24]

The Americans also wanted the United Nations to build up Adoula's military position so that he would not be tempted to turn to the Russians for help.[25] Bomboko, who had recently asked the United States for two or three fighter planes to counter the steadily growing Katangan air force, played skillfully on American fears. He pointed out that the Soviet Union and the other Communist countries were eager to reopen their missions in Leopoldville and were offering all the aid the Congo needed—including aircraft—to end the secession. The Americans realized that Bomboko might be bluffing in order to get his planes, but they also realized that the bluff might turn out to be real if the Katanga issue were not settled quickly.[26] Gullion warned Mobutu that if the Congolese government accepted the offer of Soviet planes, it would repeat "Lumumba's most fatal error and cut its own throat."[27] At the same time, the ambassador urged the State Department not to reject out of hand the Congolese request for "free world aircraft," because it would be hard for Adoula to explain to his cabinet why Tshombe could have an air force and he could not.[28] Officials at the Department were reluctant to set a precedent of bilateral military aid, which could later be used by the Russians. They felt that a Security Council resolution authorizing the United Nations to retrain the Congolese army and provide it with a small air force would satisfy Adoula without encouraging him to go too far toward a military solution.[29]

Rusk pointed out to the President on November 11 that even the limited measures advocated by the State Department might lead to renewed hostilities and criticism from the NATO allies; but he argued that the United States had to "take this calculated risk in order to avoid the much greater risk of full scale civil war," which would open the country to "Communist penetration" and leave Katanga an "economic wreck." Besides, there was reason to hope that the new approach would work without producing hostilities. Bunche and Linner had assured the United States that they would give "top priority to negotiations" and would "try to avoid provoking a fight." They would "move carefully against the mercenaries only to the extent needed to encourage Tshombe to negotiate."[30]

Along with this political recommendation, Rusk sent the President a far-reaching proposal designed to relieve the financial crisis caused by the refusal of many countries, including the Soviet bloc, France, and Belgium, to pay their share of the cost of the UN Congo operation, which was running ten million dollars each month. The United Nations was in danger of going bankrupt. The new plan, which involved raising two hundred million dollars through a special bond issue, was described as "fight now, pay later." Fifteen or twenty key states would put up the money, which would be repaid over twenty-five years at two percent interest. Ten million dollars would be needed annually to pay back the principal plus interest, and all UN members would be obliged to pay their share of this amount as part of the regular budget. The United States, Rusk explained, would probably have to put up one hundred million dollars, half the bond issue. He hoped to win the support of U.S. congressional leaders for the plan, and he hoped that Stevenson could persuade the new Secretary-General to present it to the General Assembly during his "honeymoon" period.[31]

When the Security Council met on November 13, the Ethiopian delegate demanded a strengthened mandate which would authorize the Secretary-General to evict the mercenaries by force and help the central government restore law and order in Katanga.[32] This last point was too much for the Americans and the British, and the Council was adjourned for forty-eight hours so that the Western powers and the neutralists could work out a compromise. By the time it met again, on November 15, there had been two dramatic developments—one which was damaging to Tshombe and to the pro-Western forces in Leopoldville, another which was damaging to Gizenga.

The first development was the publication of the report of the UN

Commission of Investigation, which concluded that Lumumba had probably been killed in Tshombe's presence and that "in all probability" Kasavubu and his associates had acted deliberately in sending Lumumba into the hands of his "bitterest enemies" and were therefore equally responsible for his death.[33] Kennedy was curious about the report; he asked Cleveland whether it contained the "true story or whether it was all hearsay." He was "particularly interested in any hard indications as to whether Tshombe was present at the time of the murder." He wanted an assessment of the report "from a lawyer's point of view." The State Department's legal adviser noted that the first conclusion was based on hearsay evidence that would not stand up in an American court, such as the accounts of the mercenaries, who were not particularly reliable and who gave conflicting testimony about who actually killed Lumumba. The second conclusion, about Kasavubu's responsibility, was based on even flimsier evidence and dealt with the Congolese leader's state of mind.[34] Despite the nature of the evidence, the report, which confirmed what virtually everyone assumed to be true, was generally accepted at the United Nations, and it was expected to strengthen the hand of the Russians and the Afro-Asians, who favored forceful action against Katanga.

The second development was the mutiny of seven hundred Congolese troops—theoretically under Gizenga's command—who took control of the town of Kindu, in Kivu Province, surrounding the two hundred Malayan UN troops stationed there. They arrested and severely beat thirteen Italian airmen who had flown two UN transport planes into Kindu. On November 14, after earlier attempts to free the Italians failed, Lundula and Interior Minister Gbenye flew into Kindu, accompanied by UN officials, to try to negotiate the prisoners' release. The mission was a failure; Lundula was virtually forced to flee from his own troops. Their commanding officer, Colonel Pakassa, was unable to control them and refused to cooperate with Lundula or the United Nations.[35] Meanwhile, another group of Stanleyville soldiers crossed the provincial border from Kivu into north Katanga and headed for Albertville, where they began to loot and riot.[36]

To UN officials on the scene these were not mere isolated incidents of violence but part of a dangerous new pattern. They noted that Gizenga had reportedly been in the Kindu area since November 11 and had made no effort to control his troops or to help Lundula or the United Nations win the release of the Italian airmen. They began to speculate that he had concentrated his troops there not to attack north Katanga, as he claimed, but to strengthen his own bid for power against the Leopoldville government. Adoula, who had no doubts about Gizenga's designs, asked the United Nations to neutralize his forces.[37]

The new Secretary-General was suddenly faced with a second major challenge, in the eastern Congo, before he had begun to cope with the first challenge, in Katanga. The mild Burmese pacifist took an unexpectedly strong stand. On November 15 he ordered his representatives in the Congo to take "every measure possible" to restore order in the areas affected by the mutiny.[38]

These developments were not discussed at the November 15 Security Council meeting, which was devoted to the Katanga issue. The Americans had persuaded the Afro-Asians to tone down their draft. It now authorized the Secretary-General, for the first time, to use "force, if necessary" to arrest, detain, and/or deport the mercenaries, and it declared all secessionist activities in Katanga illegal and demanded that they cease.[39] It stopped short, however, of demanding UN military action, alone or in conjunction with the Congolese army, to end the secession.

The storm broke on November 16, with the news that the Italian airmen had been murdered soon after their arrest and their bodies dismembered—thrown into the river or displayed as trophies. This atrocity shifted the focus of attention from Tshombe to Gizenga. Thant, who later described it as his "first grim experience of the Congo,"[40] instructed Linner to demand the immediate arrest of Colonel Pakassa and the punishment of those guilty of the murders. UN officials moved to seal off the Kindu area, disarm the one thousand troops there, and search for the murderers. In a radio broadcast Adoula promised that the guilty would be punished. "I am disgusted with my Congolese brothers," he declared.[41]

When the Security Council met that afternoon, Stevenson stated that the murders demonstrated the need to make the resolution apply to secessionist activity in Stanleyville as well as in Katanga. Zorin, on the other hand, was ready to support the Afro-Asian draft as it stood and claimed that Stevenson was trying to divert the Council's attention from the main problem before it by raising the Kindu issue.[42] The debate continued the following day, with Zorin pressing for an immediate vote and Stevenson securing a delay to try to win Afro-Asian support for his amendments.[43]

On November 18, Ambassador Gullion returned home to press for a tougher policy toward Tshombe and back up the officials who felt that there must be a Security Council resolution even if the Afro-Asians refused to accept the U.S. amendments.[44] But there was powerful counterpressure from the Katanga lobby, which was opposed to the resolution even with the U.S. amendments. Tshombe's great supporter, Senator Dodd, who was just about to leave for the Congo, called on the President and warned him that the task of conciliation—which they both favored—would be "gravely complicated and perhaps made impossible" if the United Nations were authorized to use force against Katanga.[45]

When the Security Council met on November 24, Stevenson's key amendment, designed to make the resolution applicable to Gizenga as well as to Tshombe, went down to defeat because it failed to get the necessary seven votes. The Soviet Union and the UAR voted against the U.S. position, while Ceylon, Liberia, and France abstained.[46]

At this point Stevenson asked for a fifteen-minute suspension of the meeting, checked with Washington, and then returned to announce that the United States would vote for the draft—with "great reluctance." Gullion and his allies had carried the day. The resolution was then adopted 9 to 0, with Britain and France abstaining. Dean, who had been reluctant to vote for the resolution with Stevenson's amendments but had agreed to do so as a gesture of solidarity, refused to support the draft in its unamended form. He warned that the wording on the mercenaries went "dangerously far" in encouraging the use of force.[47]

This was the ninth time the Security Council had met to consider the Congo crisis, and it would be the last. Since July 1960 it had adopted five resolutions. The moderate policy favored by the United States had gradually lost the support of the Afro-Asians, and, after a period of deadlock and vetoes at the end of the Eisenhower Administration, the Kennedy Administration had gone with the prevailing drift and reluctantly compromised with the Afro-Asians even when it meant yielding on matters of principle. The last two resolutions—in February and now in November—had come closer and closer to the Soviet position. With the United Nations authorized to use force to oust the mercenaries and, by implication, to end the Katanga secession, the Russians had nothing more to demand. They regarded the November 24 resolution as a victory, achieved despite Western attempts to sidetrack the debate.[48]

Battle in Katanga: Kennedy and Macmillan Part Company

The repercussions of the November 24 Security Council resolution were felt immediately in Elisabethville, where Tshombe, encouraged by the diehard European settlers and the officials at Union Minière, flatly refused to cooperate with the United Nations. The day after the resolution was adopted he called on his people to resist and kill the soldiers of the international force in any way they could; if they had no automatic rifles they could use poisoned arrows.

It was not long before this exhortation to violence produced results.

On the evening of November 28 the two top UN civilian representatives in Elisabethville, George Ivan Smith and Brian Urquhart, were seized and brutally beaten by Katangan paracommandos just as they arrived at a dinner party honoring the visiting Senator Dodd and his wife. As the prisoners were being driven away in an open truck, it was overtaken by the official car of the new U.S. consul, Lewis Hoffacker, who was escorting the Dodds to the dinner party. As Smith later told the story, "Mrs. Dodd was heard to exclaim, 'Why, if it isn't that nice Mr. Smith!' and Hoffacker was out of the car hurling 'paras' left and right and shouting 'Consul Américain!' "[49] Hoffacker managed to rescue Smith and a Belgian banker who had been arrested at the same time; but before he could go back for Urquhart, the Katangan soldiers realized what was happening and drove off. Urquhart was taken to a military camp and was not freed until the early hours of the morning, after a UN Gurkha colonel threatened to blow up the presidential palace unless he was produced immediately. Ten minutes before the tough Gurkha troops were to storm the camp, Tshombe and two of his ministers arrived and arranged for Urquhart's release. Both he and Smith suffered broken ribs and other injuries, but they felt lucky to be alive.[50]

Even after this experience Senator Dodd lost none of his admiration for Tshombe. He described him a few days later as "one of the most impressive men I have ever met and one of the most maligned men in history."[51] Dodd spent the day after the assault touring the province with Tshombe, who kept repeating his calls for armed resistance.[52] He then left for the neighboring Portuguese colony of Angola, explaining to President Kennedy that both he and Hoffacker felt that the situation in Elisabethville was "dangerously tense" and that he should not be placed in the position of having an "incident" attributed to his presence. He advised Kennedy to send personal messages to Tshombe and the UN representatives urging them to resolve the situation peacefully.[53] Godley, who was in charge of the U.S. Embassy during Gullion's absence, was opposed to the idea of the President sending any sort of direct message to Tshombe.[54] Kennedy was reluctant to antagonize Dodd any further over the Katanga issue. He thanked him for his help, explained that he himself could not intervene personally at this point, and assured him that Stevenson would "raise urgently" with Thant the question of a negotiated settlement.[55]

Dodd and Hoffacker feared that many of the UN officials in Elisabethville were no longer interested in settling the problem by peaceful means; although they had confidence in Smith and Urquhart, they felt both men had been shaken by their experience and tended to leave things up to the military, who were "trigger-happy" and wanted to "clean up" Elisabethville and round up the mercenaries in a house-to-house search, regardless of civilian casualties. Hoffacker wrote on December 1:

ALL OF US IN CONSULATE DISAPPROVE VIGOROUSLY THIS ATTITUDE AND WILL CONTINUE DO WHAT WE CAN TO EMPHASIZE ABSOLUTE NECESSITY AVOID ANY SUCH MILITARY INITIATIVE.[56]

But it was too late to avoid military action. On December 1, Thant, at his first news conference, said he was working on a plan to implement the new resolution and remove the mercenaries, by force if necessary. He blamed Tshombe for the violent incidents in Elisabethville and described him as a "very unstable man."[57] On December 3, after Katangan troops set up roadblocks, seized more UN personnel, and fired on a UN helicopter, the Secretary-General ordered his representatives in Katanga to "act vigorously to reestablish law and order."[58] The following day Katangan officials agreed to remove the roadblocks, but the next morning the United Nations found that, far from being dismantled, the roadblocks had been strengthened during the night. Thant ordered his commanders to take whatever air or ground action was necessary to restore UN freedom of movement in Elisabethville. At noon on December 5 General Raja took over from the civilian representatives. Serious fighting broke out as Gurkha troops approached the roadblock on the key road to the airport and were met with fire from the Katangan position. By late afternoon the UN forces had opened the road to the airport, but fighting had broken out in several other parts of the city, with casualties on both sides.[59]

Technically, the United Nations claimed it was acting in self-defense, responding to Katangan attacks and provocations. At the same time, there were a great many UN officials who were determined to interpret the November 24 resolution as broadly as possible and end the secession once and for all. They were glad of the opportunity to go into action.

The Kennedy Administration took much the same view. Ever since the standoff in September, the State Department advocates of a tough line toward Tshombe—Stevenson, Ball, Williams, Cleveland, and Gullion—had been urging the United Nations to build up its strength so that Tshombe would be compelled to negotiate with Adoula and end the secession, thus eliminating the threat of a Communist takeover in the Congo. If it took another round of fighting to convince Tshombe of UN military superiority, they were willing to go along with that—as long as the operation was well planned and was over so quickly that there would be no time for Tshombe's partisans in the United States and Western Europe to stir up trouble. These officials felt that peaceful efforts to get Tshombe to the negotiating table had gone as far as they could go. He had refused to listen to anyone, including the President's roving ambassador, Averell Harriman, who was the only State Department liberal with any sympathy for his position.[60] It was clear that military pressure was needed to persuade the secessionist leader to negotiate.

Thus, despite the reservations of the U.S. consul in Elisabethville, the U.S. government was actively supporting the UN military operation. Indeed, the operation would hardly have been possible without American assistance. On December 5 six American Globemaster planes began ferrying UN troop reinforcements from Leopoldville to Elisabethville, along with antiaircraft guns and armored cars, and on December 6, as the fighting went into its second day, the State Department announced that the United States would provide up to twenty-one more large transport planes, which would be used to fly additional troops from their home countries to Leopoldville, as well as within the Congo. The Defense Department reported to the President that over the next week eighteen hundred troops—Irish, Swedish, and Nigerian—would be flown to Elisabethville to join the three thousand UN troops already there and that as soon as the buildup was completed the United Nations should be able to "establish a positive military posture in Katanga."[61]

This was a sharp contrast with the situation in September, when the Kennedy Administration had turned down Hammarskjold's request for transport planes. Another major difference was the fact that Katanga's lone Fouga jet fighter no longer controlled the skies. Encouraged by the United States, the United Nations had obtained at least fifteen jet fighters of its own. Some of these were providing air cover for the American transport planes. Others, starting on December 6, attacked military targets in Elisabethville as well as in the mining towns of Jadotville and Kolwezi, producing anguished protests from the Belgians, particularly the officials of Union Minière, who feared that their installations would be damaged. The air strikes also raised questions among the general public about the propriety of the UN action; there was a strong feeling in the United States, which was even more widespread in Western Europe, that the United Nations had no business being involved in a military operation that was likely to harm innocent civilians.

Stevenson, Williams, and Gullion took up this problem with Thant on December 6. Stevenson said he wanted to be absolutely clear about UN objectives in order to respond to "public opinion pressures" in the United States and Europe. Thant assured him that his objectives were "limited": the United Nations intended to clear the roadblocks and other obstacles to free movement and, if attacked, to "retaliate with all possible means in order to defend" its positions. He had no intention of seeking the "conquest" of Katanga or of destroying its mines and factories. At the same time, Thant appealed to the Americans to help persuade the British to supply bombs for the Indian Canberra jets the United Nations was using; they had been requested six weeks before, and the British government was still stalling. "We need those bombs," Thant insisted.[62]

The Macmillan government was torn between a desire to stand by the United States, as it had done, despite minor differences, throughout the Congo crisis, and a feeling that this time the United States was going too far. The deciding vote may have been cast by Conor Cruise O'Brien, who resigned on December 1, charging that Britain and France had sabotaged the UN operation in September—a charge that was picked up by influential Commonwealth leaders, such as Nehru, whose troops were now under attack in Katanga. In order to salvage Britain's reputation with these leaders and demonstrate its willingness to support the United Nations, the Macmillan government decided on the evening of December 7 to grant Thant's request for twenty-four one-thousand-pound bombs to be carried by the Canberra planes. The offer was hedged about with restrictions: the bombs could be used only "against aircraft on the ground or airstrips and airfields."[63] Still, the government, in the words of U.S. Ambassador David Bruce, had "badly misjudged the temper of backbench opinion."[64] By the time the decision was announced the following day, there were reports of intensified fighting in Elisabethville, with a number of civilian casualties. A hospital had been hit by UN mortar fire intended for a nearby Katangan military camp.

Macmillan was caught up in a major parliamentary flap, and for a few anxious days it seemed possible that his government might fall over the Congo issue. The opposition Labour Party demanded that the bombs be supplied immediately, while the right wing of the Conservative Party demanded that the government stop supporting the UN operation altogether. Macmillan decided to hold up delivery of the bombs until the situation in Katanga was clarified, and tried to arrange for an immediate ceasefire.[65] Dean raised the idea informally with Thant, but Thant replied that Tshombe had shown no sign of being prepared to negotiate seriously with Adoula. The British hoped to win American support for a joint appeal, but the U.S. government took much the same position Thant did. Stevenson told Dean there could be no ceasefire until "Tshombe was brought to the water and drinking."[66]

President Kennedy had been closely involved in the formulation of U.S. Congo policy since Hammarskjold's death. He had authorized the large-scale American military assistance that was making the UN operation possible, but he was not happy about the rift that was developing between the United States and its closest ally. He was scheduled to meet with Macmillan in Bermuda on December 20 to discuss the resumption of atmospheric nuclear tests, and he did not want to have a major disagreement on the Congo interfere with progress on more vital matters. He spent the next ten days trying to work out a solution that would satisfy both sides—the activists in his own Administration, who felt the secession must be ended quickly, even at the risk of antagonizing the NATO allies; and the NATO allies themselves, who feared that the United Nations would destroy the Tshombe regime and with it the economic stability of Katanga.

On December 13 Kennedy and Ball conferred by trans-Atlantic telephone with Rusk, who was in Paris for the NATO Foreign Ministers' meeting. Rusk reported that the Congo was "the most pressing item of business in Paris" and that the UN operation was "considered our war." Lord Home had warned him that if the fighting spread into the "heart of Elisabethville" the British government might have to withdraw all support.[67] Ball informed Rusk that the UN offensive was set to start the following day. He stressed that as soon as the United Nations seized the "key points" in Elisabethville, there would be a ceasefire. Rusk proposed instead that there be an immediate call for a ceasefire "and then the UN might be given two or three days to get its military action over with while arrangements for the ceasefire were being worked out." Ball pointed out that it might take more than two or three days. Rusk said he hoped that "it would be done fast and that it would succeed." The President noted that while he had an understanding with the top UN people in New York, UN personnel on the scene "wished to go much further than was in our interests." He suggested that Rusk get the Western Europeans to work on Tshombe and said he would talk to Macmillan and try to straighten things out.[68]

Kennedy's phone call reassured Macmillan to some extent. The Prime Minister said he was "glad to hear from him that the Secretary of State and other members of his staff were now definitely on record as favouring reconciliation rather than conquest."[69] Still, the fact remained that while the British had formally asked the Secretary-General to seek an immediate ceasefire,[70] the U.S. government was sticking to its position that there could be no ceasefire until the United Nations had achieved its "minimum objectives."

Kennedy was also under pressure from his increasingly vocal domestic critics, whose pro-Tshombe campaign was orchestrated by the well-financed Katanga lobby. On December 13 they announced the formation of the Committee for Aid to Katanga Freedom Fighters, and listed Senate Minority Leader Everett M. Dirksen as one of its sponsors. After a telephone call from the President, Dirksen drew back a bit; he issued a statement asserting that the use of his name had been unauthorized and expressing his hope for an "early ceasefire" between

Adoula and Tshombe, whom he described as "a friend of the free world."[71]

Kennedy's most unconventional phone call that day was to his ambassador in Leopoldville. He often preferred this sort of direct contact with the man in the field because he could cut through all the intervening layers of bureaucracy and get to the heart of the problem. In this case, that meant making sure that Adoula understood the "importance of early discussions with Tshombe" and that Bunche understood that UN objectives were to be "strictly limited" and that the military operation was to be concluded as soon as Tshombe was persuaded to enter into "meaningful negotiations" with Adoula.[72]

After his conversation with the President, Gullion returned to a late night meeting with Adoula, Bunche, and Linner. At 3:00 A.M. he reported that he was "relatively satisfied" that the United Nations would "try to carry out the President's wishes."[73] He spent the next day cajoling Adoula, and by evening he had come up with a major concession: the Prime Minister had agreed to meet Tshombe at the UN base at Kitona, an hour's flight from Leopoldville. But the ambassador made it clear that they were talking about a meeting *after* the UN operation was completed; Adoula had no interest in negotiations or a ceasefire before the offensive was launched.[74] Meanwhile, at 6:00 P.M. Leopoldville time, there was no word about the offensive, which was supposed to have begun at dawn.[75]

A Diplomatic Victory?

It was at this point, on December 14, that Tshombe decided to make a dramatic move. He picked up the hints that had been scattered liberally in his direction and sent a cable to President Kennedy asking him to name a "suitable negotiator" who would arrange for talks between himself and Adoula; he also appealed for an immediate ceasefire.[76] Kennedy and his aides were jubilant. If Tshombe was sincere in his offer, it meant their strategy had worked: the limited use of force had persuaded him to come around. Katanga could be integrated peacefully, and the President's critics would have to back down and admit they had been wrong.

At 4:30 P.M. Washington time, shortly after Tshombe's message came in, the President sent a reply via Hoffacker informing Tshombe that he was "proceeding immediately" to explore the possibilities and would communicate with him again in the near future.[77] He then instructed Stevenson to ask the Secretary-General to announce a forty-eight-hour ceasefire and name Bunche as mediator. Thant agreed to name Bunche and Gardiner as mediators, but he poured cold water on the idea of a formal ceasefire, explaining that "Adoula would refuse to meet with Tshombe" under those conditions.[78] At the same time, he indicated to Stevenson that the fighting could be suspended de facto once Tshombe had demonstrated his sincerity by leaving Elisabethville for an agreed meeting place.[79]

Ball then sent Gullion and Hoffacker the text of Kennedy's substantive reply to Tshombe's appeal, which was to be delivered to the Katangan leader only after Gullion had obtained Adoula's approval. The President informed Tshombe that he had designated Gullion as his representative and that the ambassador would fly to Elisabethville in a U.S. plane to escort Tshombe to Kitona and home again, as an added guarantee of his safety. Ball told Hoffacker that in delivering this message he could "make clear privately" to Tshombe that the United Nations would be willing to observe an unofficial truce just as soon as Tshombe set off for his talks with Adoula.[80]

By the time Kennedy's message and instructions arrived in Leopoldville, at noon on December 15, the UN drive for control of Elisabethville was under way. It had begun at dawn, just one day later than planned, and already tough Gurkha troops had pushed nearly to the center of the city, against stiff Katangan resistance.[81] Bunche was greatly relieved to hear that the offensive had started. He told Gullion he had had a "very bad moment" when he thought the ceasefire talks were being launched before the military operation. He stressed that Adoula would not come to the negotiating table if a "formal ceasefire" preceded the talks, but he felt the arrangement Thant had worked out with Stevenson for a de facto ceasefire would be acceptable.[82] As it turned out, Gullion was unable to present Kennedy's proposal to Adoula because he had left for Kivu Province, a thousand miles away. Gullion sent him a telegram outlining the U.S. plan in fairly general terms and requesting an opportunity to consult with him as soon as possible.[83]

Kennedy continued to keep a close watch on the situation even after he left for Caracas, on his first state visit to Latin America. On December 16 he received an optimistic progress report from Ball. Gullion had just telephoned and explained that Adoula could not return to Leopoldville immediately because of a "grave domestic political crisis": Gizenga was trying to take over Kivu Province. Ball suspected that he might also be stalling until the United Nations had accomplished all of its military objectives in Elisabethville. Gullion reported that this process was almost completed: the city was practically surrounded and the major military camp and other key points were under UN control. There had not been many casualties on either side, but the Katangans had exaggerated the stories of civilian casualties and damage to installations "as usual." Although Gullion had not been able to show Adoula the full text of the President's message to Tshombe, he felt confident that once he saw the Prime Minister he would be able to "talk him into our proposal."[84]

At the same time, Ball reported to the President on the other Katanga front—the battle for public opinion at home. He noted that Eisenhower had issued a positive statement about Kennedy's effort to bring the two leaders together and suggested that since the statement had not received wide coverage, Kennedy might remedy that by issuing his own statement thanking Eisenhower. Ball also reported on Under Secretary McGhee's effort to bring some of the "Congressional and opinion leaders" around: Lodge and Herter had lined up with Eisenhower; Senators Richard Russell and John Stennis would raise no further objections; Nixon was critical of efforts to destroy anti-Communist forces but "gave no indication" he would "engage in public criticism"; Senators Barry Goldwater and James Eastland, who had been extremely critical, were avoiding McGhee's calls.[85]

On Sunday, December 17, Gullion sent a noon progress report directly to the President in Bogotá, his second and last stop in Latin America. Adoula was en route home from Kivu, and the latest word from Elisabethville was that Tshombe had accepted the U.S. plan without insisting on a ceasefire.[86] But nothing was ever simple or clear-cut in the Congo. At the same time that Gullion was reporting this good news, the U.S. Embassy in Brussels was relaying a message from Tshombe, who agreed to meet Adoula but demanded an immediate ceasefire.[87] Kennedy shot back a terse message to Ball:

I BELIEVE IT VITAL THAT ADOULA BE OBLIGED TO RESPOND IMMEDIATELY TO CEASEFIRE TELEGRAM. WOULD APPRECIATE A REPORT ON SITUATION THERE AS SOON AS POSSIBLE.[88]

At 4:30 P.M. Washington time Ball sent Kennedy the latest bulletins: the United Nations had "substantially achieved its limited military objectives" in Elisabethville, and "as a practical matter," de facto suspension of hostilities would probably precede Tshombe's departure for Kitona. Gullion and Bunche were waiting to see Adoula, who had just arrived, and Ball would call the President as soon as Gullion called him to report on the meeting.[89]

At 8:00 P.M. Ball reported that Gullion's talk with Adoula had been "generally satisfactory" and that the remaining problems did not seem "insuperable."[90] Adoula was under considerable pressure from the radicals in his government, who wanted him to take a hard line on Katanga, and it had taken Gullion two hours to persuade him to proceed to Kitona. Gullion reviewed the record of U.S. assistance to the Congolese government; he stressed that the President had put his prestige behind the negotiation effort and told Adoula that he could not promise continued American support if he did not go to the meeting. In the end Adoula reluctantly agreed. Gullion was ready to set off the next day "in the hope of rounding up the participants," but he warned his colleagues in Washington, "No one should regard it as absolutely certain that the meeting will take place as we plan it."[91]

On Monday, December 18, Gullion instructed Hoffacker to deliver the President's message to Tshombe and tell him the ambassador was leaving for Ndola, where he would pick him up for the trip to Kitona. Hoffacker was authorized to tell Tshombe that UN fire would be held while they were airborne and for the duration of the talks. The United Nations would not fire unless fired upon. But Gullion warned that if Tshombe's propagandists tried to take credit for a ceasefire as soon as he was airborne, Adoula would refuse to meet him and Gullion would turn the plane around and take him back home again.[92]

By 1:00 P.M. Gullion was in Ndola awaiting Tshombe's arrival. The Katangan leader turned up a short time later, accompanied by Hoffacker and the British and French consuls, but there was still considerable uncertainty as to whether he would agree to fly to Kitona with Gullion the following morning. He was still concerned about his personal security and insisted that all three consuls accompany him on the flight. Gullion said Hoffacker could go, but he discouraged the others, who, he said "would only have scared Adoula away."[93]

The three consuls worked with Tshombe all night, but it was "touch and go" until he actually boarded the plane the next morning. Once he was airborne, he relaxed and slept most of the way. The first day of meetings with Adoula was "generally social," and the atmosphere was good. On Wednesday, December 20, the two delegations got off to an early start and worked nonstop until 3:00 P.M. on a draft introduced by Adoula. Gullion and his UN colleagues kept out of the way until things "began to go badly haywire" in the late afternoon—at which point they began to mediate in earnest. Tshombe had agreed in principle to most of Adoula's points, but then he "suddenly declared he had no power to negotiate" and must consult his government. Adoula was "enraged." He had seen Tshombe use this tactic before to renege on agreements. The conference broke up into small "combinations of delegates" on balconies, in bedrooms, in the conference room, and on the grounds. The two delegations met again later in the evening to announce that they could not agree. Gullion and Bunche insisted that they must agree.[94]

Gullion had received a message from the President commending him for his "excellent work" in bringing the two men to Kitona and asking him to do his "utmost" to persuade them that the "conference must lead to agreement." The President was not demanding a detailed settlement—but he insisted that "there must not be a breakdown."[95] The ambassador did not need this urgent pep talk to convince him of the importance of a success, even if it was nothing more than a general agreement on principles with the specific differences to be ironed out later. He talked to Adoula and Tshombe separately and applied all the pressure he could. He told Tshombe he was the "loser" and would "have to accept things his heart rejected." He told Adoula he would lose his "battle for public opinion" in the United States if he allowed the conference to fail. Then the two delegations went back to work on a paper prepared by Bunche and Gullion, which was essentially a short form of Adoula's proposals "in language more palatable to Tshombe." Once again they failed to agree.

By midnight the conference seemed to be breaking up. The engines of the planes were warmed up. Adoula's delegation stalked out. Gullion ran after them to try to "salvage something," if only a final communiqué. Suddenly, Tshombe said he would be willing to consider the "short form" if he could add a point about consulting the Katangan authorities. Adoula and Bomboko resisted this idea for two hours. Finally Khiary thought up an ingenious formula: the agreement would be contained in one document and Tshombe's reservations about seeking Katangan approval would be contained in another—a separate letter from Tshombe to Bunche. "Adoula accepted this," said Gullion, "only under our extreme pressure."[96]

The eight-point agreement, which was released on December 21, was impressive: Tshombe recognized the unity of the Congo, the authority of the central government, and Kasavubu as head of state; he agreed to send his deputies and senators to Parliament and his representatives to a constitutional revision commission; he agreed to place Katangan military forces under Kasavubu's authority; and he agreed to respect the resolutions of the Security Council and the General Assembly.[97]

Ball immediately sent the news of Gullion's success to Kennedy and Rusk in Bermuda, with instructions to deliver the cable even if they were in conference with Macmillan and his delegation. He described it as the "most encouraging event" in the Congo since Adoula's government was approved by Parliament in August. The agreement, if carried out, would spell the end of the Katanga secession and justify Washington's firm support for the UN operation. "Such a complete capitulation on Tshombe's part," said Ball, "goes far beyond our expectations."[98]

Kennedy quickly sent a message of congratulations to Gullion.[99] But Macmillan and Home were more relieved than impressed by the outcome of the Kitona meeting. The agreement did not change their opinion that American military support for the UN operation was rash and ill-advised. Macmillan blamed "the incredible folly and weakness (mixed with vanity) of Adlai Stevenson" for the attack on Elisabethville and its toll in civilian lives.[100] At the height of the fighting he noted in his diary, "Yesterday an Ethiopian soldier shot a Swiss banker in Elisabethville with a bazooka. No one knows why, and no one cares. But even Swiss bankers ought to have some rights."[101] Given this attitude, it was only natural that Macmillan took credit for the ceasefire and the meeting at Kitona. He felt they were brought about by the "conciliatory influence of the British government," which had persuaded "the President and Secretary of State to exert themselves instead of leaving the direction to the Adlai Stevensons and other half-baked 'liberals.' "[102]

Gullion was disappointed but not surprised when Tshombe began to renege on the Kitona agreement as soon as he returned to Elisabethville. It was, after all, a familiar pattern. This time, Tshombe's office issued a statement charging that Gullion had written the Kitona declaration and forced Tshombe to sign it. Adoula, who had expected something of the sort, loyally denied Tshombe's accusation and pointed out that it was Tshombe himself who had initiated the conference by requesting Kennedy's good offices.[103] In characteristic fashion Tshombe did not close the door completely; he indicated that his parliamentary delegation would be arriving in Leopoldville on schedule. Nevertheless, his complaints about Gullion cast grave doubts on his intentions regarding the other provisions of the accord.

Once again there was a major disagreement between the Americans and the British about how to deal with Tshombe's recalcitrance. Macmillan had agreed before he left Bermuda to "continue exercising pressure on Tshombe,"[104] but the British idea of "pressure" was very different from the American one. State Department officials immediately came up with several detailed proposals designed to put economic pressure on Tshombe if he refused to cooperate. The basic idea was to divert Katanga's tax revenues to Leopoldville. They envisaged the UN force taking over the customs posts, controlling the roads and railroads to Angola and the Rhodesias, and collecting taxes on Katanga's exports—all without using force.[105] The British found these ideas naive and dangerous. They counseled patience. Ormsby-Gore told Rusk that Tshombe's administration might collapse if he was pushed too fast; he explained that the Africans would reach agreement in their own fashion. Rusk argued that if there was too much delay, Tshombe might conclude that secession was a viable option after all.[106]

There was considerable feeling among the New Frontiersmen at the State Department that Tshombe had no intention of living up to the Kitona agreement and that he was being encouraged to maintain the secession by Union Minière. At the end of December two high-ranking officials—Assistant Secretary Williams and Deputy Assistant Secretary Rowan—spoke out forcefully on this issue and implied that Union Minière was responsible for the exaggerated anti–United Nations horror stories that were coming out of Katanga.[107] Gullion immediately applauded their speeches as "forceful, useable, and quotable."[108] Union Minière protested sharply.[109] In an effort to soften the impact of the speeches, Under Secretary of State McGhee suggested in a television interview that neither speech reflected official State Department policy.[110] Clearly, the Katanga secession was a touchy issue for the United States and its European allies, and it was not going to disappear in a hurry.

CHAPTER THIRTEEN

The Road to Bula Bemba
(January 1–February 8, 1962)

"Gizenga alive is on balance a liability for the Russians; Gizenga dead would
become a great asset."

As THE NEW YEAR of 1962 began and President Kennedy surveyed the results of his controversial Africa policy, he had good reason to be pleased. His decision to seek an accommodation with the neutralists had inevitably produced serious friction with the NATO allies, but he felt that this could be smoothed over in time. More important was the fact that in a little less than a year in office he had managed to put the Soviet Union on the defensive virtually everywhere in Africa. The Eisenhower Administration had scored a short-term victory in the summer of 1960 by getting the Russians thrown out of the Congo; but that victory, followed by the death of Lumumba, had produced an anti-American backlash that threatened long-term harm to the U.S. position throughout the continent.

Kennedy, on the other hand, had seized the opportunity provided by Lumumba's death to project a new American image in Africa. He had upstaged the Russians by persuading the Africans that the United States had no use for right-wing puppets such as Tshombe, whose sole function was to protect European economic interests, and that it was willing to work with a broad coalition composed of genuine nationalists. Of course, it was much easier to press for a coalition government in the Congo once the principal leftist had been eliminated. Still, Kennedy and his advisers had handled the tricky Leopoldville-Stanleyville rapprochement with considerable skill, and they now felt they were well on their way to a peaceful solution of the Katanga question, which had been at the heart of the problem since the beginning of the Congo crisis. The Kitona agreement—which the Americans had rammed down the throats of Tshombe and Adoula—meant that Tshombe was formally committed to the reintegration of Katanga. It might take time to bring him around on the details, but they felt the agreement had won whatever time was necessary. For a few months, at least,

Adoula would not have to worry about Soviet or Afro-Asian pressure for a speedy military solution. The Russians had been deprived of a first-rate propaganda issue, which they had used to solidify their alliance with the radical Casablanca group.

In his attempt to chip away at that alliance, Kennedy had concentrated on two key members of the Casablanca group—the radical twins of West Africa, Nkrumah and Sékou Touré. In mid-December, after months of debate within the Administration, the President decided to take a risk and approve U.S. financing of Ghana's massive Volta Dam project. He made the decision "with some reluctance and misgiving,"[1] because Nkrumah had been drifting leftward ever since his red-carpet tour of the Soviet Union in the summer of 1961, and there was considerable opposition—especially from Attorney General Robert Kennedy—to the idea of helping an incipient left-wing dictator rather than his pro-Western opponents in neighboring African countries.[2] At the same time, the President feared that if he reneged on the original American promise to help finance the dam, he might end up like John Foster Dulles with the Aswan Dam. A refusal would surely throw Nkrumah into the arms of the Russians, while support for the project might slow his leftward drift.[3] In a letter to Nkrumah explaining his decision, Kennedy said quite frankly that it would be difficult to maintain the support of "American public opinion" for a long-term commitment of aid unless Nkrumah could assure him that Ghana would remain "genuinely independent" and that he would restore political liberties in his country, including freedom for the foreign press to report on events there.[4] Nkrumah's initial response was not all Kennedy wanted, but he felt he had made the right decision and he hoped the Ghanaian leader would eventually come around.

Ghana was still a question mark; but the news from Guinea surpassed the Kennedy Administration's wildest dreams. In mid-December Sékou Touré, recipient of the Lenin Prize, expelled the Soviet ambassador, Daniel Solod, from Conakry, charging that he had been involved in a left-wing plot against the government.[5] Anastas Mikoyan, the Kremlin's senior diplomatic trouble-shooter, was quickly dispatched to Conakry to reassure Sékou Touré and try to restore harmony between the two countries,[6] but the damage was done. The Russians tried to suggest that Solod had gone beyond his instructions and acted on his own initiative, but no African diplomat believed that a Soviet ambassador could take such an initiative on his own. They concluded that the Russians would never be satisfied with a radical nationalist, even if he agreed with them on most issues; what they really wanted was total control. They had picked a Communist replacement for Sékou Touré, and they could not resist the temptation to put their own man in power. This incident was a turning point for Guinea and a bonanza for the United States. Without waiting for instructions from Washington, Kennedy's unconventional ambassador, William Attwood, immediately offered to help Sékou Touré if he was "squeezed" by the Russians.[7] From this point on, the Guinean leader began to work more closely with the Americans, as well as with the French and the more conservative French African states. He did not give up his radical views overnight, but his shift meant that the Casablanca group would no longer function as a tight-knit bloc automatically supporting Soviet policies—and that the views of the African moderates would carry more weight in the future.

"Avoiding Any Impression of U.S. Participation"

The first pro-Western moderate to benefit from this shift in Soviet-African relations was Adoula, who was about to embark on a sensitive piece of unfinished business—the removal of Gizenga from his post as Deputy Premier. Adoula had assured Ambassador Gullion after the Kitona agreement was signed that Gizenga would be out of power by the end of the year. In fact, it took a little longer—and American officials in Washington, remembering Lumumba's Houdini-like tricks, had a few anxious moments before Gizenga was safely under lock and key.

The Kennedy Administration, buffeted by domestic political pressures, was becoming impatient. The President was about to ask Congress to approve the UN bond issue, and he wanted to present his Congo policy in the best possible light; he did not want to give any ammunition to the conservative, pro-Tshombe faction, which was opposed to any further American support for the United Nations. On January 6 Rusk told Gullion he would like to have Adoula visit the United States as soon as possible, in view of the "mounting Congressional interest" in the Congo, and suggested that this could be combined with his trip to the upcoming African summit meeting in Lagos. He cautioned, however, that Adoula "should not come" until the "Gizenga censure motion" had been passed. A clear victory over Gizenga would increase his stature in the United States and make it easier for him to respond to "questions and criticisms" from Congress and the press.[8]

Adoula was eager to cooperate. Over the past few weeks he had been lining up opposition to Gizenga in Parliament. In addition to the moderates, he had won over a large number of former Lumumbists who had personal grudges against Gizenga or were critical of his secessionist tendencies. He had also enlisted the support of General Lundula, Gizenga's former military commander. His greatest asset in this campaign was the behavior of Gizenga himself. The leftist leader had become increasingly isolated in Stanleyville. He rarely left his house or received visitors, except for an occasional envoy from the Communist bloc or one of the radical Afro-Asian countries. Even his staunchest African supporters were put off by his stubborn refusal to return to the capital and resume his post as Deputy Premier. Toward the end of December Nkrumah had sent two envoys to Stanleyville to try to persuade him to go to Leopoldville. Gizenga, who was afraid of Mobutu and his troops, refused to budge; he said he would "wait and see what happened as a result of the Kitona talks." When the envoys reported back to Nkrumah, they suggested that if Gizenga "persisted in his present attitude, the Lumumbists should be asked to select another leader."[9]

Adoula's first public move came on January 8, when Parliament adopted a resolution demanding that Gizenga return to Leopoldville within forty-eight hours to defend himself against grave charges of secessionist activities, by a vote of 66 to 10, with seven abstentions.[10] From then on, events moved quickly. On January 10 Gizenga sent a letter to Parliament refusing to go back to Leopoldville until the central government brought about the reintegration of Katanga.[11] On January 11, after an unsuccessful attempt to arrest General Lundula, he reversed his stand and agreed to return.[12]

This reversal alarmed American officials, who feared that if Gizenga returned to Leopoldville voluntarily, he might swing Parliament to his side by calling for an invasion of Katanga. They urged Adoula not to let him resume his job as Deputy Premier, warning that if he did, it would be extremely difficult for them to maintain popular support in the United States for their anti-Tshombe policy.[13]

Adoula needed no persuasion from Washington. On January 12 he arranged for a motion of censure against Gizenga to be introduced in Parliament. It was expected to be adopted overwhelmingly after the required forty-eight-hour delay.[14]

On January 13 Gizenga made one last attempt to reassert his authority in Stanleyville by military force. Fighting broke out between his troops and soldiers loyal to Lundula and the central government. Adoula immediately asked the United Nations for help. After Thant's last experience with Gizenga's troops at the time of the Kindu massacre, there was no question about his response. He ordered his forces to "exert all possible effort to restore and maintain law and order in Stanleyville and to avert civil war there." As it turned out, this assistance was not even necessary. The fighting was over quickly; the United Nations did not fire a shot. The following morning the thirty-four soldiers protecting Gizenga's home surrendered to Lundula; by evening all but fifty of the three hundred soldiers loyal to Gizenga had been disarmed by Lundula's forces, aided by the United Nations.[15]

Gizenga had gambled and lost. Just as Lumumba had decided to flee from house arrest in Leopoldville in November 1960, when he feared the United Nations had turned against him and would no longer protect him, Gizenga decided that, with the United Nations siding with his opponents and his military position hopeless, there was no longer any reason for him to remain in Stanleyville. In a final act of bravado, he sent a message to the capital, announcing that he would return with his staff on January 20 to resume his duties as Deputy Premier. He requested that his office and residence be made ready and asked for a UN plane to transport him to Leopoldville.[16]

Adoula was furious. He told Gullion on the morning of January 15 that he would not put up with Gizenga's "preposterous" demands. Gizenga was guilty of an "assault on the security of the state," and an order for his arrest would be issued in the course of the day.[17]

Later that morning Parliament met and censured Gizenga by a vote of 67 to 1, with four abstentions. The mood had turned even more strongly against him because of the fighting in Stanleyville, which had resulted in fourteen deaths. Spokesmen of all parties condemned him. His former ally, the radical Kashamura, declared, "He is no longer a nationalist."[18] The following day Adoula announced that Gizenga had been dismissed from his post as Deputy Premier—an automatic result of the parliamentary censure—and that legal proceedings against him had begun.[19]

On January 19 Gullion used the top secret ROGER CHANNEL to send an urgent bulletin to Washington: Adoula had just informed him that Gizenga would be brought to Leopoldville that very night as a prisoner. Everything had worked out perfectly so far, but now Adoula was in a "quandary" about the "ultimate disposition" of his prisoner. The penalty for rebellion was twenty years or death. Adoula was afraid that a long jail sentence would turn Gizenga into a "martyr" while the death penalty might turn him into another Lumumba. Gullion, who shared his concern, proposed a more attractive alternative: Gizenga might "disappear" and turn up in Cairo. Adoula "jumped" at this suggestion, which he said would "solve a very great problem."[20]

State Department officials suggested that if the "escape to Cairo" idea did not work out, Adoula might use Gizenga's "oft proclaimed ill health" as a pretext for getting him out of the country as a "humanitarian gesture." Another alternative might be banishment without a trial, since a public trial would only play into the hands of the Soviet bloc. They stressed:

WHATEVER DECISION ADOULA TAKES IT IS ESSENTIAL IT BE HIS AND UTMOST PRECAUTION TAKEN TO AVOID ANY IMPRESSION OF US PARTICIPATION.[21]

They felt Adoula had displayed "excellent" judgment in coping with Gizenga thus far, and they did "not want to be tagged" with the results of any decision he might make.

They insisted on only one point: they attached the "greatest importance" to "Gizenga's safety" and stressed that "his death by violence" would have the "most unfortunate repercussions."[22] They could not afford to have a repetition of the Lumumba experience; another murder of an anti-American Congolese politician would undo everything the Kennedy Adminstration had accomplished in the past year and set back American influence in Africa for years to come.

When Gizenga arrived in Leopoldville on the morning of January 20, there was considerable confusion about his status. The United Nations informed the U.S. Embassy that he was not a "prisoner" of the central government, as Adoula had told Gullion; nor was he officially under the "protective custody" of the United Nations, though if he requested UN protection it would be given to him.[23]

The confusion at the U.S. Embassy continued to mount, as Gizenga received a tumultuous welcome from his supporters at the airport and then was escorted to UN headquarters, where he stayed overnight. The following day he wrote Linner a note thanking him for his "hospitality and security" and notifying him that he was moving to the residence he had occupied when he served as Lumumba's Deputy Premier in the summer of 1960.[24] Linner notified Adoula, who promised that the central government would provide protection for him.[25] Just to be on the safe side, Linner sent a letter to Gizenga on January 23 confirming this arrangement, particularly Gizenga's request to leave UN headquarters; he pointed out that the United Nations was thereby "entirely relieved of all responsibility for ensuring your safety." The letter was hand-delivered to Gizenga's residence. Gizenga read and acknowledged it. A copy of the letter was sent to Adoula.[26]

This elaborate charade ended on the night of January 24, when the government moved Gizenga to a nearby army camp, claiming that he could be protected more easily there.[27] Gullion went to see Adoula the following morning to find out what was going on. Adoula told him that Gizenga was not under arrest but was in "protective custody." He had told security chief Nendaka that "no harm was to come to Gizenga"; at the same time, no one "who might cause trouble" would be permitted to see him. Gizenga would be held incommunicado, except for his lawyers, while a dossier was prepared against him. Gullion asked when the government planned to bring him to trial, but Adoula could not give him a definite answer. The ambassador warned of the dangers of delay and stressed that Adoula's "victory over Gizenga should not be frittered away." Adoula assured him that Gizenga "would continue to be excluded from public life and would be punished." Gullion concluded that Adoula really had "not made up his mind how to dispose of Gizenga" and that he felt "indefinite protective custody" was the safest solution for the time being. He pointed out that Adoula was "determined to adhere to legal forms as he has done up to now."[28]

Adoula's caution was clearly justified. As soon as it became known that Gizenga had been transferred to a military camp, his supporters, who had been surprisingly quiet up to this point, began to clamor for his release. On January 25 there was a pro-Gizenga demonstration outside the U.S. Embassy, which led Gullion to note that despite Gizenga's "personal unpopularity," he was, after all, Lumumba's heir and thus the symbol of "nationalist aspirations."[29] If Adoula moved too quickly, he would alienate the Lumumbists he had persuaded to join him in the nearly unanimous censure vote against Gizenga.

He was already having trouble with Gbenye, his leftist Interior Minister, who called a press conference to announce that he was not responsible for Gizenga's transfer to the army camp; in fact, he had not even been informed about it.[30] Gbenye had very little use for Gizenga, and he enjoyed his government job, but he decided to break with Adoula rather than publicly desert the Lumumbist cause.

Khrushchev in a Quandary

The Russians, who got into the act at this point, were faced with a similar dilemma. Khrushchev had more or less written Gizenga off as a potential leader after he refused to go to Leopoldville for the meeting of Parliament in the summer of 1961. He realized that power in the Congo had shifted to Adoula, and his diplomats had spent months trying to get the Soviet Embassy in Leopoldville reaccredited. Now that they had succeeded at last, Khrushchev was not about to jeopardize their position with a scathing attack on Adoula's role in the Gizenga affair. He was still smarting from his near disaster in Guinea, where the pro-Soviet Sékou Touré had come close to an irrevocable break with Moscow because of Soviet interference in his country's internal politics. He did not want to risk a repetition of that experience in the Congo. At the same time, he could not afford to desert Gizenga completely. He was aware of his symbolic value, just as Adoula and Gbenye were. As Lumumba's heir, Gizenga represented Congolese nationalism, and if Khrushchev wanted to keep his radical reputation and confound his domestic and foreign critics on the left, he could not let Gizenga languish in captivity without saying a word in his defense. The Soviet press solved this problem temporarily by blaming Gullion and the U.S. Embassy staff for Gizenga's downfall and suggesting— very indirectly—that Adoula was not sufficiently wary of American intrigues.[31]

Soviet suspicions of Gullion's "subversive activities"[32] were fully reciprocated. A Soviet medical mission had arrived in Leopoldville at the beginning of January and, much to the dismay of the U.S. Embassy, had arranged with the Minister of Health to leave for Stanleyville within twenty-four hours. Gullion assumed that its activities would not be limited to health care. Linner had assured him that the doctors would be turned over to the representatives of the World Health Organization (WHO) and sent wherever they could do no political harm; but it turned out that Linner was unable to control the WHO representatives. After an "unpleasant" session with Linner, and an equally "unpleasant" one with Adoula, who said he knew nothing about the plans, Gullion arranged for the UN aircraft assigned to the doctors to develop "technical difficulties" so it could not take them to Stanleyville. They remained in Leopoldville while the United Nations tried to find "innocuous jobs" for them. Foreign Minister Bomboko told Gullion he wanted the Soviet doctors out of the country altogether, and Gullion felt he should do his best "discreetly" to oblige him. He explained to the State Department that he had not wanted to become "directly involved," but it was obvious that the Congolese government "had to be assisted in every way" to thwart the latest Soviet plot.[33]

Khrushchev's concern about Adoula's treatment of Gizenga and his increasingly close relationship with the United States did not prevent the arrival of a second group of Soviet doctors on January 23, but it did affect Soviet press coverage of the event. When the first group arrived, the news was featured in *Pravda*.[34] This time, the TASS bureau in Leopoldville reported the arrival of the medical personnel, but the item did not appear in any Soviet newspaper. Khrushchev was trying to take a pragmatic approach to the latest crisis in the Congo, but pragmatism had its limits. There was no point in publicizing Soviet assistance to a government which had just placed its leading leftist under arrest.

By January 25 Khrushchev had come up with a two-pronged approach that would get him off the hook regarding Gizenga and yet not alienate Adoula—or so he hoped. On the semi-official level, he ordered a major propaganda offensive similar to the campaign launched the previous year to save Lumumba, complete with mass meetings, appeals, and protests around the world. It was always possible that these noisy demands for Gizenga's release might save his life, if not his job. On the official level, however, there was no mention of Gizenga. Even after he was moved to the army camp, there was no Soviet government statement, as there would have been in the old days when Lumumba was being mistreated.

Instead, Khrushchev decided to try an indirect approach: he would put pressure on Adoula by calling for an immediate meeting of the Security Council, ostensibly to discuss the Katanga issue. He instructed Zorin to send a letter to the President of the Security Council charging that the November 24 resolution had not been implemented.[35] In this letter Zorin made no reference to Gizenga's plight, but it was generally assumed that he would raise the matter at the meeting.

In order to build support for Zorin's demand, the Soviet delegation began spreading a rumor that Gizenga had already been killed. The Secretary-General knew that this was not true, but he told Stevenson that he was "very worried" about the possibility that Gizenga might be killed; this, he said, would give the Russians a genuine issue, which they did not have at present. Stevenson agreed. He pointed out that "Gizenga alive" was on balance a "liability" for the Russians, while "Gizenga dead" would become a "great asset." If the U.S. government "can take steps to keep him alive," he cabled the State Department, "we urge they be taken."[36]

The State Department asked Gullion to see Adoula as soon as possible and urge him to announce publicly that he saw "no need" for a Security Council meeting, since he would be addressing the General Assembly in the near future and developments in the Congo were "proceeding satisfactorily."[37] Adoula left for the summit meeting in Lagos before Gullion could raise the issue with him, but the ambassador sent a personal message to him in the Nigerian capital, pointing out that the Russians would probably use the meeting to criticize his policy toward Gizenga. This message was backed up by a similar message from the CIA station chief to Bomboko.[38]

Adoula's reaction was more than satisfactory. Not only did he send a message to the Secretary-General expressing his opposition to a Security Council meeting[39] and call a press conference at which he criticized the Soviet request as "an unfriendly act"[40]; he also persuaded all the other African leaders at the conference to send a message to the President of the Security Council opposing the Soviet move.[41] Of course, the Lagos conference was dominated by moderate and conservative African states; the Casablanca group and the North Africans had refused to attend since Algeria was not invited. Still, it was significant that twenty African leaders accepted Adoula's explanation that Gizenga was not under arrest—he was being "protected in a safe place" while the charges against him were investigated—as well as his assurances that Gizenga would not suffer the same fate as Lumumba. This was a major accomplishment for Adoula and a measure of the changes that had taken place in African politics in the past year.

The Prime Minister was buoyed up by the vote of confidence he had received from his fellow African leaders, and he came back from Lagos far more confident about his pro-Western course than he had been before. The change was apparent as soon as he stepped off the plane. Although the world press had been reporting for weeks that he would be going to Washington to meet with Kennedy after his speech at the United Nations, and cables were flying back and forth between the State Department and the U.S. Embassy in Leopoldville about his social schedule, Adoula himself had still not told Gullion definitely that he would visit the American capital. It was clear that he wanted to go, but he was under considerable pressure from local leftists and neutralist diplomats not to make the trip.[42] When he returned to Leopoldville on the evening of January 29 and was asked by waiting journalists about his plans, he replied, "I understand I have been invited by President Kennedy and one does not refuse the invitation of a man when one is passing by his door."[43]

Adoula was pleased with his decision, and he was "delighted" when Gullion informed him of the results of the Security Council meeting, which had gone according the American scenario.[44] Stevenson led off by stating that the Soviet government had asked for a meeting which no one, including the Congolese Prime Minister, wanted. He had assumed that in view of Adoula's position, which was endorsed by the Lagos conference, the Soviet government would withdraw its request. Since it had not done so, he moved that the Council adjourn. He was supported by the seven Western members of the Council. The Soviet Union and Romania opposed the move, and the UAR and Ghana abstained.[45]

Khrushchev had lost the first round in his attempt to save Gizenga by raising the issue at the United Nations. It was one thing for the moderate and conservative African states at Lagos to reject the Soviet demand for a meeting; it was quite another for the UAR and Ghana, two leading members of the Casablanca group, to refuse to go along with the Soviet request. Clearly, it was Adoula's opposition that was responsible. But the Soviet press, which blasted the Western powers for blocking the Security Council meeting, gave no indication that Adoula had sided with the West.[46] Khrushchev was apparently still hoping he could accomplish more in the Congo by courting Adoula than by criticizing him. Zorin insisted at the brief Council meeting that Adoula had been given a "distorted" account of the Soviet request, and he said he was sure the Congolese leader would approve if he had all the facts. He intended to raise the matter with Adoula as soon as possible after his arrival in New York.

Mr. Adoula Goes to Washington

It was exactly a year and a half since the Congo's first Prime Minister had visited the United Nations—and the contrast between the two men could not have been greater. Lumumba swept into town on a wave of controversy. He was dramatic and unpredictable. He had just issued an ultimatum to the United Nations, but he turned around and surprised Hammarskjold with his reasonable behavior. He irritated his African supporters, puzzled the Russians, and, by the time he left for home, confirmed the worst fears of the Americans, who decided that he must be eliminated. Adoula, on the other hand, was moderate, cautious, and conciliatory. He created no excitement. He ruffled no feathers. But beneath his mild exterior there was a streak of stubbornness and a surprising degree of political skill. He managed to accomplish what he wanted without antagonizing any of the parties to the dispute: the Afro-Asians, the Russians, the Belgians, the Secretary-General, or his enthusiastic sponsors—the Americans.

Even their personal lives were poles apart. Lumumba lived in a state of constant disorder and stimulation; he craved female companionship just as he craved intense political discussions that lasted until dawn. A story told by one of his American escort officers—perhaps apocryphal—recounts that when he arrived at Blair House, the official residence for visiting dignitaries, he looked around, checked the facilities, and then asked in some puzzlement, "But where are the women?" Adoula, on the other hand, was a family man, deeply attached to his wife, a former schoolteacher, who was six months pregnant. He was eager to bring her to the United States, and he was reluctant to accept the President's invitation to a "working lunch" at the White House until he was quite certain that suitable arrangements would be made for his wife and that she would be invited to a ladies' luncheon at the same time.[47]

Adoula addressed the General Assembly on the afternoon of February 2, a few hours after his arrival in New York. He reaffirmed his policy of nonalignment and his support for liberation movements in Algeria, Angola, and South Africa; he criticized Belgium—in a mild sort of way; he warned foreign corporations that they could not exploit the Congo's wealth without paying taxes to the central government; and he appealed for increased military assistance from the United Nations in order to implement the Security Council resolutions and expel all foreign mercenaries from Katanga. While he made no specific reference to Tshombe or Gizenga, he stressed that his government was resolved to "end the Katanga secession and all other attempts at diversion." He hoped this could be done through negotiations, but he implied that if reason failed, military means would have to be used.[48]

Adoula's speech was received cordially, but it was interrupted only once by a burst of applause—when he referred to Lumumba as "our national hero." Gullion, who had returned to the United States for Adoula's visit, tried to reassure the State Department about this by explaining that it was "mere ritual obeisance" of a kind "African leaders consider good form in speaking to a predominantly African congress"—which was what the General Assembly had become. He pointed out that Adoula was trying to portray himself to the Afro-Asians as an African nationalist and to demonstrate that "his recent actions favorable to the West"—the arrest of Gizenga, the criticism of the Soviet Union, the visit to Washington—did not mean he had abandoned his policy of nonalignment. Gullion predicted that Adoula would make his "main play for US opinion" after he got to Washington. Just to be certain, he reminded Adoula the day after his speech that it was essential that he make the most of his "public relations opportunities." His effort "so far was good," the ambassador said, but it "ought to be better."[49]

The Americans had no complaints, however, about Adoula's handling of the tricky Gizenga issue. As soon as he arrived in New York, he privately assured the Afro-Asian diplomats that Gizenga was in no danger.[50] The following day, the CIA station in Leopoldville reported that Gizenga had been transferred at dawn to the island of Bula Bemba, just off the coast. The only communication with the mainland was by a small boat controlled by the ANC. He had been moved from the military camp because he was receiving too many visitors and the government had intercepted a number of "compromising messages" from his supporters. The CIA noted that Adoula was "fully aware" of these plans before his departure for New York and that he had "approved" of the move.[51]

The Russians were dismayed by this development, but they refused to give up on Adoula. Zorin met with him on February 4 and nearly convinced him to ask the Security Council to adopt a resolution calling for the expulsion of the mercenaries from Katanga within eight to ten days.[52] *Pravda* published an entirely positive account of his General Assembly speech at the same time that it reported the news of Gizenga's transfer "to a new place of imprisonment."[53] The Russians seemed determined to keep the two issues separate, even though it was becoming increasingly difficult to do so. Each day that Adoula remained in the United States, Moscow's campaign to free Gizenga mounted in intensity. But while the Soviet press kept warning that the Americans were planning to murder Gizenga, brief items, totally unrelated to the coverage of Gizenga, reported Adoula's meetings with President Kennedy and other American leaders.[54] It was as if he were living on a different planet.

Soviet patience must have been strained by Adoula's visit to Washington, which was considered a great success by both sides. The Congolese leader spent the morning of February 5 at the State Department discussing the Katanga issue with a group of top officials headed by Under Secretary Ball. Adoula remarked that he had learned since he came to the United States that President Kennedy had to deal with domestic political pressures regarding Katanga just as he did. There was no further reference to the vocal, conservative Katanga lobby, but the position of the American officials reflected a keen awareness of the power of that lobby and of its insistence that there should be no further attempt to settle the Katanga question by force. Ball stressed the importance of implementing the Kitona accords and ending the secession without further bloodshed. He suggested that the first order of business was to persuade Union Minière and the other big companies in Katanga to pay their taxes—which amounted to some forty million dollars in 1961—to the central government rather than to Tshombe. Adoula replied that "this might all be very well, but there was a serious problem of time." He himself was under pressure to move faster toward reintegration. His government had already raised the issue of payment with the companies and with Tshombe, without much success, and he was afraid that Tshombe would simply delay as long as possible and use the time to consolidate his secession. He warned that if the situation were allowed to "drift along for a long time" it might eventually "lead again to the use of force."[55]

After a White House luncheon, at which Kennedy and Adoula exchanged cordial toasts, the two men spent an hour going over the same ground. Adoula confided that he had taken a "grave political risk" by going to Kitona without the approval or even the knowledge of his cabinet; he had done so because "he did not want to disappoint the President," and he knew that if he did not meet Tshombe, it would create difficulties for the United States. The two sides had begun to implement the Kitona accords, he said, but it was only a "very small beginning." Tshombe seemed to be "playing for time," in the hope of preserving Katanga's separate status. He simply could not be trusted. Even when he appeared to agree, one could never be sure of his "real intentions." Adoula assured the President that he wanted a peaceful solution, like everyone else, but he insisted again that the "time factor" could not be ignored. Kennedy wanted to know exactly how the United States could help. Adoula did not have any new suggestions; he picked up the point made by Ball that morning and asked the United States to encourage the Belgian government to exert pressure on Union Minière, so that it would stop financing Tshombe's secession.[56]

Adoula's next stop was a tea given by the Senate Foreign Relations Committee, where he fielded questions adroitly for two hours.[57] He then moved on to a press reception for "selected reporters" at Blair House and wound up the day at a dinner given by Assistant Secretary Williams. The next day he had breakfast with Williams and Secretary of Labor Arthur Goldberg; he then met with officials of the World Bank and the International Monetary Fund and was back in New York in time for a luncheon given by Secretary-General Thant. The reactions to this whirlwind visit were consistently positive. Officials and journalists alike were impressed by Adoula's earnestness, his intelligence, and his grasp of the problems facing his country.[58]

Whatever doubts Adoula expressed privately to Kennedy and the top State Department officials about Tshombe, his public attitude after his visit to Washington was definitely upbeat. On February 7, his last full day in the United States, he told the UN Correspondents' Association that he was opposed to military action against Katanga at that point; he said Tshombe should be given a chance to demonstrate his "good faith" and his willingness to reintegrate the province peacefully. After this speech, he met once again with Soviet Ambassador Zorin, but it was clear that Zorin's arguments had failed and that Adoula had decided to take the advice of his American hosts on the question of Katanga.[59]

On February 8 Adoula returned to Leopoldville, accompanied by Robert Gardiner, the Ghanaian UN official most responsible for the successful meeting of Parliament in the summer of 1961, who would now be replacing Linner as head of the UN operation in the Congo. One dramatic phase had ended, and a new one was about to begin. In the past month Adoula had managed to dispose of Gizenga—one of the two major threats to his government and his country's unity. But the most difficult challenge lay ahead. He still had to try to end the Katanga secession, while maintaining his political balance between right- and left-wing factions at home and his reputation as a neutralist abroad.

CHAPTER FOURTEEN

Kennedy: An Unexpected Success
(February 8, 1962 - May 31, 1963)

"The Congo continues, partly farce, partly tragedy."

ADOULA'S FIRST ORDER of business on his return was to tie up the remaining loose ends of the Gizenga affair. The issue had been raised in Parliament on February 7 by Gizenga's supporters, who were furious when they learned that their leader had been moved to the inaccessible, mosquito-ridden island of Bula Bemba; but Adoula was still in New York and the discussion was put off until his return. On February 12 he defended his policy toward Gizenga and won an impressive vote of confidence, 76 to 10, with one abstention.[1]

The Americans were relieved. The Russians responded with their sharpest criticism of Adoula to date. *Izvestia* charged that he had won the vote of confidence only because the "reactionaries" had used the time between the two meetings to bribe the members of Parliament.[2] After this outburst, however, the Soviet press drew back; it continued to print demands for Gizenga's release, but it rarely mentioned Adoula's responsibility for his imprisonment.

This was clearly the result of a top-level policy decision. Khrushchev, despite his concern about critics on the left, such as the Chinese, who felt that anything short of all-out support for Gizenga was a betrayal of the revolutionary cause, had evidently decided to keep the lines of communication open and try to steer Adoula leftward, away from an accommodation with Tshombe, toward a more militant policy that would end the Katanga secession by force and weaken the Western position in the Congo.

Adoula, for his part, was not averse to keeping the lines open. He was eager to dispel the impression that he had joined the American camp. A few days after the Gizenga debate, he disclosed that he had accepted an invitation to visit the Soviet Union.[3] He was well aware of the value of the "Soviet card" in his dealings with the United States. He had no faith at all in Tshombe's promises and was convinced that the only way to persuade the secessionist leader to negotiate was through the threat or the actual use of force. He knew that the Americans were reluctant to approve the use of force again and that the only way he could apply pressure to them was to raise the specter of a leftist takeover. With Gizenga out of the picture, this threat was considerably diminished, but Adoula was still in a position to imply that if patient negotiations failed to resolve the problem, he might give up on the U.S.-UN approach and try to settle the issue on his own—with help from the radical Afro-Asians and the Soviet Union.

Over the next ten months the Russians had plenty of opportunity to encourage Adoula to give up his moderate line. As it became increasingly apparent that Adoula's judgment of Tshombe was correct and that he was merely playing for time and had no intention of rejoining the Congo, the Prime Minister grew more impatient, and the pressure on him from the leftists in his government grew more intense. American officials were keenly aware of the difficulties of his position. Gullion, Williams, Bowles, and most of the other New Frontiersmen shared his views about Tshombe; Rusk, Harriman, and McGhee were more responsive to the views of the Belgians and the British, who were opposed to any further hostilities in Katanga. Throughout 1962 there was a tremendous volume of cable traffic between the State Department, the U.S. Mission at the United Nations, and the U.S. Embassies in Leopoldville, Brussels, and London about the Katanga issue. Although all the parties were theoretically committed to the reintegration of Katanga, there was no agreement on how to achieve it, and the experts kept coming up with one plan after another—without success.

Kennedy was in the thick of it, reading the latest cables, making suggestions, and demanding more information. Temperamentally, he was with the activists; but at the same time he was attuned to political realities. He had already had one bruising confrontation with Tshombe's domestic supporters, in December, and had luckily escaped without too much damage. He did not want to tangle with them again. Besides, he was influenced by the views of his good friend, the British ambassador. State Department officials later recalled that every time they persuaded the President that the United States must take a tougher line toward Tshombe, Ormsby-Gore would stop by at the White House for a drink and fill his head with British arguments against any dramatic action that might lead to hostilities. The word would come down to the State Department, and the activists would have to start all over again.

Tackling the Katanga Secession

Tshombe skillfully played on American divisions and on American reluctance to use force against his secession. Shortly after Adoula's return, Tshombe proposed a meeting at Kamina, a former Belgian base in Katanga now occupied by the United Nations. Adoula countered with an invitation to Leopoldville. Tshombe indicated that he would accept, but then he delayed for several weeks, insisting on ironclad guarantees from the United Nations that his security would be protected and he would be free to leave Leopoldville at any time. He asked the U.S. government to back up these guarantees. The Americans were unwilling to give him a formal commitment, but Hoffacker was instructed to inform Tshombe orally that the United States had full confidence in UN assurances.[4]

Tshombe had calculated correctly that a positive attitude toward talks with Adoula would appeal to the United States and diminish the pressure for strong UN action to implement the Security Council resolutions and remove the remaining mercenaries in Katanga. The Secretary-General and most of his advisers were eager to station UN troops in Kolwezi, Jadotville, and Kipushi—three key towns in the heart of the Union Minière empire, where most of the two hundred mercenaries were located—even if Tshombe refused to cooperate. The Americans, on the other hand, felt that if the troop movements were undertaken without Tshombe's agreement, they might lead to a third round of fighting, and, as Tshombe realized, this was the thing they feared most.[5]

When Gullion raised the matter with Gardiner, the UN official assured him that he had no interest in precipitating a third round. He was well acquainted, he said, with the inevitable American reaction to UN campaigns in Katanga. The first day the U.S. government approved; the second day it began to question the "wisdom" of the action; by the third day it had become a "blunder," and by the fourth day it was considered a "crime." He promised Gullion that he would undertake no action that could not be completed successfully within forty-eight hours.[6]

Gardiner believed that the best hope of progress lay in direct negotiations between Adoula and Tshombe, without the help of any outsiders, including UN officials. The talks would be purely Congolese. He would give them until June to reach agreement, and only then would he consider "more energetic" measures. Gullion felt that this sort of negotiating process would be "endless, labyrinthine, Byzantine, Bantu," and he wondered if Adoula could keep the lid on the extremists for that long.[7] Still, he had a good deal of confidence in the British-educated Gardiner and was more than willing to give him another chance to accomplish the impossible.

On March 15, with the preliminary skirmishing out of the way, Tshombe arrived in Leopoldville. Adoula, in a move designed to show him that he was not the ruler of an independent state but merely one

of six provincial presidents, had left earlier in the day for Coquilhatville to attend a meeting of the other provincial presidents. Tshombe
did not seem upset by this snub. He settled into a well-guarded apartment at UN headquarters, and the talks began three days later.

By March 24 there were rumors of an impasse. Acting Secretary of
State Ball decided it was time for a strong American initiative which
would force Tshombe to negotiate seriously by threatening to destroy
the economic basis of his secession if he failed to do so. He proposed a
controversial scheme, under which the UN force would protect officials of the central government who would be sent to Elisabethville to
collect the taxes and customs duties on exports from Katanga. Ball was
aware that this could lead to "renewed violence" in Elisabethville,
since it would "hit Tshombe where it hurts—in the pocketbook"; but
he was willing to take that risk in order to prevent Adoula from turning to the Russians. He stressed that the United Nations would have to
be prepared to follow through on its threat, for if Tshombe found it
was a bluff, it would not work. The United Nations would need American assurances of "full backing," including "airlift support," in the
event Tshombe opened hostilities.[8]

Ball's proposal ran into opposition not only from the Belgians and
the British, who felt the threat of a Communist takeover was exaggerated, and from Rusk, who was afraid it would lead to hostilities, but
also from Gardiner, who wanted to give the "palaver" between Adoula
and Tshombe a chance to succeed.[9] The UN official was discouraged—
temporarily—by a dramatic incident which took place on April 18. The
talks had recessed the previous day, by mutual consent.[10] Adoula had
left on a boat trip up the Congo River for a week or ten days of rest,
and he expected the talks to resume on his return. Tshombe had told
Gardiner that he might return home during Adoula's absence, but he
neglected to mention it to Adoula. Tshombe arrived at the airport just
before noon and boarded his plane. Suddenly the runway was blocked
by fire trucks, and the pilot was informed by the control tower that the
Congolese government had issued orders to prevent Tshombe's departure. Congolese troops appeared on the field to carry out the orders.

Gardiner and Khiary, who had guaranteed Tshombe's freedom to
leave, were determined that there would be no repetition of the
events of the previous April, when Tshombe was prevented from leaving the Coquilhatville conference and was held prisoner for several
months. They ordered four platoons of Nigerian UN troops to protect
the plane and tried to persuade the Congolese government to reverse
its decision. Gardiner was disgusted. He complained that six months
of hard work had been "cancelled by infantilism" and remarked
that "not even Tshombe" could have thought up such a "trick in
his favor."[11] Khiary told Gullion he hoped the plane would be

able to leave by nightfall, but at 8:00 P.M. it was still at the airport.

At this point Gullion, who had backed up the UN guarantees to Tshombe, got in touch with Foreign Minister Bomboko and told him it was essential that Tshombe be allowed to leave without delay. He pointed out that Adoula would not approve of the government's action, but Bomboko insisted that the cabinet had been in touch with Adoula by radio and that he supported their decision.[12] When no progress had been made by 11:00 P.M., Gullion spoke to Bomboko again and warned that the government was making a "mistake which would have most serious consequences." Bomboko blamed the United Nations for failing to inform the Congolese of Tshombe's departure plans ahead of time.[13]

At midnight the plane was still at the airport. Neither Mobutu nor Nendaka was willing to order the blockade lifted. Nendaka warned the CIA station chief that the Adoula government might fall if Tshombe were permitted to leave.[14] Gardiner, backed by the Secretary-General, firmly stood his ground. Eventually the Congolese realized that he would not yield, and their opposition simply melted away. At 3:00 A.M. the Nigerian troops moved the fire trucks blocking the runway. There was no resistance. At 4:00 A.M. Tshombe took off for Elisabethville.[15]

Gullion hoped the damage to Adoula's reputation abroad could be limited by explaining away the incident as a misunderstanding. But he knew this did not get at the underlying problem—the fact that Adoula had apparently lost faith in the ability of the United Nations to solve the Katanga problem and that he might easily be tempted to try a more radical approach.[16] The ambassador was especially disturbed by reports that Adoula had asked the UAR for military aid[17] and that he was planning to visit the Soviet Union in May.[18]

Kennedy, who was following the Congo situation closely, thought it might help matters if he sent Adoula an encouraging personal letter recalling their talks in Washington.[19] The letter was delivered by Assistant Secretary Cleveland, who found the Prime Minister in an optimistic mood. He expected Tshombe back in Leopoldville in a few days to resume the negotiations. He stressed the urgency of ending the secession but he assured Cleveland that he was not about to abandon the "line of conduct" he had traced during his visit to the United States. He remarked that people sometimes raised questions about "Communist influence" in the Congo; he could only reply that he was "not that much of a fool." Without referring to Guinea by name, he noted that some of the African countries which had "traveled that road" had now made an about face and were "working their way back." If the Congo were to move in that direction, he said, it would merely encounter its "African brothers homeward bound."[20]

If the Americans were somewhat anxious about Adoula's political tendencies during this period, the Russians were far more confused and dissatisfied.[21] Khrushchev suspected that Adoula was working closely with the Americans, even when he appeared to criticize them; but he could not be absolutely certain, and he was determined to do nothing to antagonize the Congolese Prime Minister. Whatever the provocation, he was sticking to his policy of treating Adoula with kid gloves and hoping that eventually he would come around on the Katanga issue.

The question of Gizenga was even more complicated. Hardly a day went by that the Soviet press did not publish another reminder about his imprisonment; the French Communist Party newspaper, *Humanité,* or the Afro-Asian Solidarity Council in Cairo or the Committee of African Organizations in London would protest the conditions in which he was held or would insist that a lawyer be permitted to see him. Interspersed with the protests and appeals were reports that he was being poisoned or that he had already been killed. The Russians must have been astonished when these appeals produced results: the Adoula government permitted a group of journalists, including Fedyashin, the head of the TASS news bureau, to visit Gizenga on Bula Bemba island. Fedyashin concluded that the government's claim that Gizenga had been arrested "legally" and was being treated "humanely" was false. He deplored the fact that Gizenga had lost weight in the unhealthy prison climate and that his family had been lured back from Yugoslavia and were now forbidden to visit him.[22] But the very fact that Fedyashin's report appeared in *Pravda* must have suggested to alert Soviet readers that Gizenga's situation was less desperate than Lumumba's had been; *his* captors had never permitted journalists, particularly Soviet journalists, to visit him in jail and hear his side of the story. The implication was clear: if Adoula was responsible for Gizenga's imprisonment—and the Soviet press rarely made that connection—then he could hardly be a bloodthirsty tyrant.

The Gizenga issue came to a head on May 7, when Parliament, after a brief but bitter debate, voted 64 to 22 to strip him of his parliamentary immunity, thus theoretically making it possible for the government to bring him to trial. *Pravda* blamed Bomboko and the "pressure of the reactionaries" for the outcome but made no reference to Adoula.[23] The Soviet Embassy in Leopoldville was less restrained, and the chargé d'affaires, Podgornov, ended up overplaying his hand. On the evening of May 23 Adoula telephoned Gullion to ask his advice on a number of minor matters. In the course of the conversation he remarked, "by the way," that he no longer intended to go to Moscow. He explained that the Soviet chargé had questioned his attitude toward Gizenga, and this had given him an opportunity to tell him that he was calling off his trip.[24]

On May 25, a few days after the Adoula-Tshombe talks resumed in Leopoldville, Macmillan wrote to Kennedy stressing the importance of a peaceful solution to the Katanga problem. Kennedy replied on June 1 with a clear, forceful statement of American policy. The United States and Great Britain shared the same objectives, he said, although they differed about how to achieve them. The United States favored a federal constitution for the Congo, just as the British did, with a "considerable degree of autonomy" for the provinces; but it felt, after Kitona, that any new agreement should make it impossible for Tshombe to reassert Katanga's independence. This time, the central government must have control over Katanga's tax revenues and armed forces. The United States also had a much greater sense of urgency about the situation than the British did. Kennedy warned that Adoula's position was being eroded and that if these talks failed, he would no longer be able to "follow the counsels of restraint." In order to encourage Adoula to be patient, the U.S. government had told him that it was "prepared to give full support to the UN mediatory effort even at the risk of hostilities." This assurance, he said, had had a "positive" effect on Adoula. Kennedy realized that his policy involved certain risks, but he argued that the risks of inaction were greater. His letter closed on a hopeful note: Gardiner was taking a direct hand in the Leopoldville talks, and there were indications that they would succeed.[25]

A few days later, however, Adoula told Gullion that he did not think Tshombe would sign the final joint communiqué that was supposed to wrap up the agreement. He remarked that Tshombe was making "heavy demands" on his whiskey supply and said he needed to replenish his stock in order to keep the talks going. Gullion replied, in a jocular vein, that he would be glad to help if Adoula did not think this would confirm the allegations of "American domination" that his political enemies were spreading. "Well," said Adoula, "in our tribe we have a proverb: if people think you are a sorcerer then you must act like one."

Gullion felt that Adoula's remark summed up his attitude toward the United States at that particular moment. He had never been friendlier; he was obviously encouraged by Kennedy's pledge of support for a UN military move if it became necessary. He was openly critical of the Russians and accused them of trying to intervene in his internal affairs. At the same time, there were insistent rumors that a Soviet ambassador was expected to arrive in Leopoldville in the not too distant future.[26]

By June 25, as a result of Gardiner's patient prodding, Adoula and Tshombe had reached agreement on most important issues, but there was a deadlock on the text of the final communiqué, just as Adoula had predicted. Tshombe was due to leave at dawn the next day. Adoula wanted the talks to continue until the differences were resolved, but at 2:30 A.M. Tshombe walked out. He issued his own communiqué, claiming that progress had been made. When he returned to Elisabethville, however, he proudly announced to his people, "I have signed nothing."[27]

A Search for Sanctions

On June 30, 1962, the Congo celebrated the second anniversary of its independence in the frustrating knowledge that Katanga would be celebrating the second anniversary of its "independence" a few days later. Tshombe's secession was alive and well, and no one knew what to do about it.

Although there was no visible crisis—no headlines, no violence—the activists in the Kennedy Administration had come to the conclusion that the situation could not be allowed to drift much longer. Adoula was under mounting political pressure, and if the Katanga issue was not settled quickly, he might be replaced by a pro-Soviet radical. American prestige would suffer, and the Russians would regain their foothold in the Congo. The United Nations was running short of money and would have to reduce its troop commitment by the end of the year. Time was working for Tshombe, who was stalling until the United Nations was forced to leave and hoping that the world community would eventually accept Katanga's de facto independence.

The activists were more convinced than ever that negotiations would not bring him around and that the "only realistic alternative" was a program of strong economic pressures backed by the threat of military force.[28] As soon as the Leopoldville talks ended without a final communiqué, they came up with a carrot-and-stick plan and tried to persuade the Secretary-General to adopt it as his own. The plan envisaged a fifty-fifty split of Katanga's tax and foreign exchange revenues with the central government. If Adoula accepted this proposal and Tshombe refused to do so, a series of economic sanctions would be applied, culminating in a worldwide embargo of Katanga copper.[29] It took nearly two months to convince the Secretary-General to sponsor this plan, and during that time it went through a number of changes, as the American drafters were subjected to pressures from all directions.

Their first task was to persuade the President and the Secretary of State that the United States ought to support a program of sanctions against Tshombe. The secessionist leader played into their hands on July 17, when he organized a violent demonstration by thousands of screaming women and children, who surrounded a UN roadblock in Elisabethville manned by Indian troops, taunted them, and attacked them with rocks and sticks. The Indians fought back, using tear gas and firing their rifles in the air. They finally drove the mob back with clubs. The Katanga government immediately charged that the United Nations had shot and killed two women and wounded thirteen others. Bunche denied this and said the first shots were fired by the Katanga gendarmerie; he pointed out that the authorities had television cameras ready in the hospital shortly after the incident began.[30]

The Secretary-General, who had gone to Europe to seek support for stronger economic pressures on Tshombe, was in Helsinki when he learned about the incident. He lost his customary reserve and referred to Tshombe and and his two leading ministers as "a bunch of clowns," with whom it was impossible to reach agreement.[31]

The State Department, in its strongest public criticism of Tshombe to date, issued a statement which accused him of deliberately provoking the incident and threatened him with "all possible measures" short of military action if he persisted in his secession.[32] Rusk, who was in Geneva for the disarmament talks, made no public statement about Tshombe's behavior, but he told *New York Times* columnist C. L. Sulzberger, "U Thant wasn't too wrong when he referred to Tshombe and his group as clowns. You can't write this," he said, "but we have learned there were elements in the U.S.A. who advised Tshombe that if he could get UN troops to shoot some women—this was before the hundreds of women were organized to march—it was a sure thing the UN bond issue could be blocked in Congress. This," he concluded, "is pretty dirty stuff."[33]

Tshombe's cynical maneuver had obviously backfired. When Kennedy was asked about the Congo at his press conference on July 23, he described the situation as "very, very serious" and criticized Union Minière for refusing to pay its taxes to the central government.[34] This high-level reproof was the first official U.S. criticism of Union Minière since the State Department squelched Williams and Rowan the previous December. The activists hoped it was a sign that the President was ready to support a tough new policy.

By this time Gullion was heading home for consultations. He almost missed the ferry to Brazzaville because he was waiting for Adoula to finish a handwritten letter to Kennedy. The Prime Minister said he was so discouraged that he was considering resigning and pleaded for American support.[35] Tshombe, the anti-Communist crusader, had joined forces with the Gizengists in an attempt to bring down the government. According to Bomboko, Tshombe planned to become Prime Minister with Gizenga back in his old job as Deputy Prime Minister. He had already "bought out the Senate" and was working on the Assembly. Bomboko claimed that this alliance was being "pushed by the Soviet Embassy."[36]

On the evening of July 25, after two days of intensive consultations with allied diplomats and UN officials, Gullion and Williams briefed the President. They warned him that Adoula's government was likely to fall unless the United States took strong action to prevent it and that his "successor would doubtless be from a group more prone to work with the radical Africans and sooner or later to accept an intimate association with the Soviet Bloc." They then presented two papers—the "Proposal for National Reconciliation" and the "Course of Action"—which spelled out the plan that had been discussed with the Secretary-General at the beginning of the month. As they explained it to Kennedy, the initial steps involved no risk of hostilities and were designed to show Union Minière and Tshombe that the "game of waiting and equivocating" was over. They included such measures as the Western governments' refusing to grant visas to Katangans unless they had passports issued by the central government. If these pressures did not produce results, the United Nations would move on to measures which "would realistically involve the risk of fighting." They assured the President that the United Nations would under no circumstances take a military initiative, though it would, as a last resort, interdict rail lines carrying Katanga's exports out through Angola and Rhodesia.[37]

After listening to this report, Kennedy asked for an "action plan," and the State Department stepped up its effort to get things moving. On August 3 Ball reported that the Department, working with the Belgian, British, and French Embassies, had come up with a revised version of the "Proposal" and the "Course of Action." He recommended that the President approve the two papers as official U.S. policy.

The "Proposal" called for a federal constitution; the immediate sharing of tax and foreign exchange revenues on a fifty-fifty basis; the rapid reunification of the currency; the reintegration of the armed forces; the closing of Katanga's "Foreign Office"; freedom of movement for UN personnel throughout the country, including Katanga; representation for Tshombe's party in the national government; and a general political amnesty. Ball explained that Tshombe's acceptance of the "Proposal" would mean the end of the secession.

The "Course of Action" presented Tshombe with a series of deadlines: if he did not accept the "Proposal" ten days after Adoula accepted it, the first sanctions would automatically go into effect: the Congolese government would ask all governments to boycott Katanga copper. If the voluntary boycott failed, the plan envisaged the possibility of "even more stringent measures," such as the withdrawal of Belgian technicians, the stoppage of petroleum imports, and the blockade of Katanga's exports by UN troops, who would cut off the rail lines leading out of the province. "It should be clearly recognized that this step, if carried out, would risk the outbreak of hostilities," Ball warned.

Ball was keenly aware of the domestic political repercussions of this proposal. He told Kennedy that the State Department planned to "conduct an intensified effort to enlighten public opinion and Congress" on the reasons for the program and for whatever "stringent measures" might become necessary.[38] This effort was sorely needed. Even before the President had a chance to study Ball's recommendation, Tshombe's greatest defender, Senator Dodd, who had become alarmed by Thant's statements about economic sanctions and by newspaper reports that the U.S. government was backing him up, made a two-hour speech in the Senate denouncing Administration policy and urging the withdrawal of half the UN troops in Katanga.[39]

Tshombe really needed no defenders; he was perfectly capable of taking care of his own interests. His latest gambit was to go to Geneva for "medical treatment" and let it be known that he wanted a private meeting with a high-ranking U.S. official, preferably Harriman, the only member of the Administration who had ever paid any attention to his views.[40] When Gullion learned about this overture, he exploded. Gullion and Harriman did not exactly see eye to eye on the Congo, and neither had any respect for the opinions of the other. Harriman took a somewhat British approach to the Katanga issue, stressing its economic stability and its importance to the West and discounting the theory that failure to reintegrate the province would lead inevitably to the restoration of Soviet influence in the Congo. He saw no point in undermining Tshombe, whom he considered pro-American and one of the ablest leaders in the Congo.

Gullion's only exposure to Tshombe had been at Kitona, where he had been extremely difficult to deal with. The ambassador bitterly recalled that Tshombe had not only reneged on his commitments afterward but had publicly blamed Gullion for forcing him into the talks which he himself had initiated with his appeal to Kennedy. Now Gullion felt Tshombe was up to his old tricks, trying to confuse and divide the Americans and sabotage their tough new policy. He told the State Department he hoped that "no distinguished American" would meet Tshombe without Adoula's approval and warned that any contact with him at this point would be "against our national interest."[41]

The Department, tugged in two contrary directions, let the controversy drag on for more than a week. On August 10 Ball, who was planning to be in Europe anyway, told Gullion he was going to meet with Tshombe in order to convince him that the United States was determined to carry out the new plan.[42] Gullion argued strongly against this decision. He explained that if Ball met with Tshombe before the plan was officially presented to Adoula, it would ruin any chance of Adoula's accepting it—and he said this was precisely what Tshombe had in mind.[43] By August 13 these arguments had brought the Department around. The head of the U.S. Mission in Geneva, Roger Tubby, called Tshombe in to inform him that Ball's plans had changed and he would not be coming to Geneva after all. Tshombe naturally blamed his nemesis, Gullion, and warned that a policy of sanctions against Katanga would never succeed.[44]

While Tshombe was losing a minor skirmish in Geneva, he was making strategic gains in Washington and New York, where the new plan was assuming its final form. On August 9 Yost gave Bunche the latest American version, which had been approved by the President.[45] It was supported fully by the Belgians, but only partially by the British, who still refused to participate in a boycott or other sanctions. The French refused to participate in any way.

Three important changes had been made, which tended on balance to water down the entire package. First, at the urging of the Belgians, cobalt had been added to copper on the boycott list in order to get the United States "materially involved" in the sanctions. The United States imported about 75 percent of Katanga's cobalt and almost none of its copper—while Belgium imported about 75 percent of its copper. In fact, Macmillan had noted in his diary a few days earlier that since most of the world's copper outside of Africa was "in American hands," a boycott of Katanga copper would benefit "American shareholders."[46] The addition of cobalt would remove any suspicion that the Americans hoped to profit from the discomfiture of their allies. The second change was the result of Kennedy's decision that "American participation" in the boycott would no longer be the automatic result of Tshombe's refusal to accept the "Proposal," but would instead be subject to the President's further review.[47] The third change was the deletion of the more stringent measures envisaged in the original document.

Gardiner presented the watered-down "Thant plan" to Adoula on August 19, and by August 21 he and Gullion had persuaded Adoula to accept it.[48] But when Gardiner took the proposal to Elisabethville on August 24, Tshombe was out of town. Gardiner made a brief presentation to Tshombe's top aides and returned immediately to Leopoldville.[49] Gullion described Tshombe's absence as the "willful first installment" of a new round of "delaying tactics."[50]

This was the beginning of a tense period of waiting, which was marked by an exchange of angry cables between Gullion, who wanted to end the Katanga secession at all costs, and Rusk, who was more cautious than ever. Their first disagreement concerned American military support for the United Nations if it became involved in a third round of fighting. Gardiner had just drawn up a new military contingency plan, and Gullion sent it to the State Department, explaining that it "might have to be put into effect almost immediately" if Tshombe rejected the proposal or if "irresponsible elements" in Katanga decided to open hostilities. During the first phase UN troops would clean up the Elisabethville area; during the second phase they would fan out and take over the other key towns in Katanga. Gullion explained that an American airlift was "absolutely essential" if this plan was to succeed.[51]

Rusk was shocked by Gullion's assumption that a third round was inevitable. He sent the ambassador a personal message reminding him that he was supposed to be working for the "peaceful" reintegration of Katanga. "It is not the purpose of the UN to reintegrate Katanga by military force or to wage a Carthaginian effort to destroy Tshombe," he observed. If the present attempt to bring about reintegration through "economic persuasion" did not succeed, the United States should not rush into a military solution; it should reexamine the situation and find a new way of "securing peace" in the Congo and arranging for the withdrawal of the UN force without "creating chaos" or "seriously disturbing" U.S. relations with the European allies or the Afro-Asian bloc.[52]

Gullion was dismayed by what appeared to be a drastic scaling down of the American commitment to the reintegration of Katanga. He told Rusk that if there was a major change in U.S. policy, he would appreciate a "full opportunity to consult" about it. He stressed that Gardiner was not planning to launch an offensive. All he had done was prepare a contingency plan in case the United Nations was attacked—and this was something the U.S. military had been urging him to do for some time. Gullion reminded Rusk of Kennedy's June 1 letter to Macmillan supporting the use of force by the United Nations if necessary and other similar statements by the Department. "Presumably these statements still stand even if subject to review as circumstances change," he remarked acidly. Unlike Rusk, Gullion had no objection to the idea of the United Nations reintegrating Katanga by force. He felt in retrospect that the American decision to yield to Tshombe's call for a ceasefire and stop the United Nations short of victory the previous December had been a mistake. If the United Nations had to use force this time, he said, it should not be "Carthaginian," as Rusk feared; but, at the same time, it should not be "indecisive," as it had been in the past. It should, in Gullion's words, be "sufficient to destroy Tshombe's "means of resistance," so that he could no longer renege on every agreement he signed.[53]

The second disagreement between the two men concerned the application of the pressures outlined in the "Course of Action." Three days after Gardiner took the plan to Elisabethville, Gullion reminded the State Department that it was time to warn Tshombe that if he did not accept it within ten days, he would be faced with a boycott and other unpleasant measures. He believed this was the only way to convince Tshombe that the United Nations meant business.[54]

Rusk responded sharply in an "Eyes Only" message to Gullion that the United States was not merely going through a series of formalities "in order to reach an automatic application" of the enforcement measures. The main object of the exercise was to win Tshombe's agreement to the reconciliation plan. Rusk was convinced that this could be done best by concentrating on peaceful persuasion. Besides, he felt the United States did not have any alternative, since the "key governments" involved were either unwilling or legally unable to impose economic sanctions.[55]

Gullion assured Rusk that he had not given up on a peaceful settlement; he simply felt that Tshombe would be much more likely to agree to one if the United States stuck to its original script rather than let the sanctions "slide out of sight" while it waited for Tshombe's response. If he perceived no pressures and no time limits, he would stretch the negotiation out indefinitely. Finally, Gullion argued that even if the allies backed down on the question of sanctions, the United States had a special responsibility to follow through on the Thant plan. Everyone regarded it as an American proposal; everyone knew that Adoula and Thant had accepted it only because they believed the United States was committed to the pressures which were an "integral part" of the plan. If Tshombe were to renege at any point, and none of the pressures came into play, the United States would be blamed for the collapse of the plan and would suffer a major diplomatic defeat.[56]

Meanwhile, the peaceful pressures on Tshombe were mounting. Even Senator Dodd sent him a letter, approved by the President, urging him to accept Gardiner's good offices and resolve his differences with the Leopoldville government.[57] There were indications that his response would be fairly positive, and the State Department asked UN officials in New York and Leopoldville to put it in the "most favorable light possible" and describe it as "forthcoming."[58] Gardiner greeted this request with "incredulity but good humor." He asked Gullion, "If Tshombe told us go to hell, should we call that forthcoming?"[59]

Tshombe's reply, which was no more than a qualified acceptance, came on September 3, just before the ten-day time limit ran out.[60] Gullion was encouraged by the fact that Tshombe had responded within ten days and said it showed that pressure really did work. He noted, however, that the reply was filled with reservations. Tshombe obviously contemplated "spinning out a new negotiation" on the assumption that Adoula and the United Nations would grow weaker as time went by.[61] Adoula profoundly distrusted Tshombe's intentions but agreed to cooperate if the Secretary-General regarded the reply as positive.[62] On September 5 Thant welcomed Tshombe's response as an acceptance of his plan.[63]

"The Russians Are Coming, the Russians Are Coming!"

The only negative reaction came from the Soviet government, which denounced the Thant plan as a "conspiracy hatched by the Western powers" to prevent the reintegration of the Congo.[64] This was the first official Soviet comment on the Congo situation in quite some time. The Russians had been maintaining a rather low profile there, although that was now about to change dramatically. They had been disappointed in Adoula when he canceled his visit to Moscow and resumed his negotiations with Tshombe in May, but they had assumed he would come around when the talks collapsed. Instead, he had become even more dependent on the United States. It was at that point that they began to look around for other options, and the Soviet Embassy started funneling money to the left-wing opposition parties which were trying to bring down the Adoula government.[65]

Still, despite his disillusionment with Adoula, Khrushchev was not ready to write him off completely and leave the field to the Americans. On August 9 TASS announced the appointment of Sergei S. Nemchina as Soviet ambassador to the Congo.[66] Although the Embassy had been functioning in Leopoldville since the previous September, this was the first time it would be headed by an ambassador since September 1960, when Mobutu expelled all Soviet personnel from the Congo.

Two days later, Cardoso, the Congolese chargé d'affaires in Washington, told State Department officials that he had recently had lunch with Soviet Ambassador Anatoly Dobrynin, who questioned the desirability of keeping the United Nations in the Congo any longer, since it had been unable to end the Katanga secession, and suggested that if the United States really wanted to "organize effective pressures on Katanga," it had enough influence to do so. Cardoso said he told the Soviet diplomat that the Congolese government would "stick with" the United Nations until it became "thoroughly disappointed" in it. He felt that the Russians were convinced the Congo was approaching a "crossroads," and that this was the reason for their appointment of a new envoy.[67]

The decision to send an ambassador to Leopoldville at this time could not have been an easy one for Khrushchev to make; it seems likely that the policy debates inside the Kremlin were just as heated as those at the State Department and the White House, if not more so. Some of his advisers were strongly opposed to granting Adoula any additional mark of approval while his commitment to the reintegration of Katanga was so uncertain—and while Gizenga was still in prison. They were justifiably concerned about new charges of betrayal from the Chinese and other hardliners. Others believed that the very uncertainty of the situation offered opportunities for the restoration of Soviet influence—with or without Adoula—which should be explored at the ambassadorial level.

Those who favored the appointment of an ambassador also may have pointed out that the Soviet government would be able to do more for Gizenga if it had a senior diplomat in Leopoldville to argue his case. It was certainly not coincidental that shortly after the Nemchina announcement was made, *Pravda* revived its campaign to save Gizenga, which had been rather desultory since April, when a TASS reporter was allowed to visit him in prison. Within a two-week period at the end of August, the Soviet newspaper published seven articles reporting a new wave of pro-Gizenga protests in the Soviet Union and around the world.[68] Khrushchev evidently was demonstrating to anyone who was critical of his decision that he had not forgotten Gizenga.

Adoula was somewhat receptive to these appeals for Gizenga's release. He was uncomfortable about the fact that Gizenga was still being held without trial seven months after his arrest. He was aware that on one recent occasion Gizenga had almost made his escape from Bula Bemba island and had actually embarked in a boat with the connivance of a guard who was a fellow tribesman, when other guards stepped in and prevented his departure. Adoula told Gullion he "half wished" the escape had succeeded—provided Gizenga fled the country.[69] The ambassador urged him to resist leftist pressures for Gizenga's release, stressing that it would be "disastrously received" in the United States and would make it more difficult for the U.S. government to win public support for strong action against Tshombe.[70]

Gullion and the other activists had been warning Kennedy for months that if the Katanga issue was not resolved quickly, the leftists would take over and the Russians would be back in Leopoldville in a big way. Up to this point these warnings had been taken with a grain of salt. But the arrival of a Soviet ambassador changed the picture considerably. It was, in a way, a godsend for those who favored stronger action against Tshombe. At the same time, it made it much more difficult for them to keep Adoula in line.

Ambassador Nemchina presented his credentials to President Kasavubu on September 20.[71] The Russians had come a long way since the days when they were accusing Kasavubu of Lumumba's murder; in a formal sense, they had come full circle, back to the time of the independence celebrations in 1960, when another Soviet envoy had presented his credentials to Kasavubu and eagerly launched his courtship of Lumumba. Nemchina was authorized to offer all kinds of assistance to Adoula in order to undermine his reliance on the United Nations and the West, but at the same time he was expected to cooperate with the leftist opposition which was trying to undermine the Adoula government. In other words, he was instructed to push Adoula leftward or push him out altogether.

Nemchina arrived in Leopoldville at a time of great uncertainty. Tripartite talks were beginning in Elisabethville on the implementation of the Thant plan, but they were not going smoothly. Once again, there were violent incidents involving UN and Katangan forces. Tshombe was completely unpredictable: one day he was all smiles, toasting the United Nations in champagne; the next day he was accusing the United Nations of bombarding Elisabethville and warning that he no longer had any faith in the Secretary-General. The deadlines envisaged in the plan had mostly fallen by the wayside, as Gullion had feared. The CIA was reporting a buildup of Katanga mercenaries and air power; more Fougas had arrived, and Tshombe now had between fifteen and thirty jet fighters at his disposal.[72] When Gardiner protested this buildup, Tshombe rejected his protest.[73]

On October 3 Nemchina paid a courtesy call on Gullion and expressed strong doubts that the Thant plan would ever be carried out. He was convinced that the Western powers would never apply sanctions to Tshombe. Gullion reported that the Soviet envoy was making no secret of the fact that he was advising the Congolese to get the United Nations out of their country. At a recent dinner given by Adoula, he had held a large group of Congolese cabinet ministers spellbound as he accused the United Nations of trying to "recolonialize" the Congo in partnership with the Western powers. He had already offered Adoula a substantial number of technicians to work on roads and water transport systems, but Adoula had turned the offer aside by suggesting that the Soviet diplomat discuss it with the United Nations. He had also offered military assistance if the Thant plan failed and the United Nations left the Congo. Gullion was worried. He warned the State Department that Nemchina's offensive had coincided with a "crisis" for the Thant plan, which was also a crisis for the moderate government in Leopoldville, for the United Nations presence in the Congo, and for "US policy in Africa."[74]

It also coincided with Washington's last major effort to convince Tshombe to cooperate "without directly threatening him with forceful measures." At the end of September, Under Secretary McGhee was sent to the Congo to impress upon Tshombe that the President was determined to see the Thant plan implemented. McGhee met first with Adoula and Bomboko and assured them that if the plan failed, the United States was "ready to consider severe measures." Adoula said he was under the impression that the sanctions would begin "automatical-ly" if conciliation failed. He warned that the situation in Parliament was desperate; Tshombe was pouring in money to encourage tribal op-position to the central government, and the members had become "so corrupt they expected payment for every vote." He stressed that the Thant plan was the last chance to settle the Katanga issue through "ne-gotiation and conciliation" and that if it failed, his government would have to take action of another sort. McGhee insisted that the Congo "must show that it has exhausted every possible effort for peaceful set-tlement" before any forceful measures could be considered.

At this point it became evident that the presence of the "ever-smil-ing, ever available Sergei Nemchina," as Gullion described him,[75] had strengthened Adoula's hand vis-à-vis the United States. The cautious American approach was no longer the only one available. Bomboko pointed out to McGhee that the Russians were urging the Congolese to accept Soviet aid and promising that if they did, they would "see Tshombe arrested in fifteen days."[76]

A few days later Adoula complained to Gullion that Tshombe was getting jet planes from Turkey, a NATO ally of the United States, and asked for U.S. transport planes which were "capable of carrying trucks and dropping parachutists," as well as pilots to fly them. He suggested that if the United States refused to supply the planes, he would look elsewhere. Gullion told him he was "sure he knew better" than to fol-low the example of Lumumba. He then advised the State Department that, while this was not the first time Adoula had raised the possibility of "alternate sources," his "most recent feeler" should be treated with "more seriousness." Adoula would prefer to turn to the United States, but the "new energetic Soviet ambassador" was reportedly "ready and willing to promise him quick delivery" on a "considerable number of transport aircraft." He might be "driven or tempted to flirt with limit-ed Soviet assistance" if all other means failed.[77]

McGhee went to Elisabethville and told Tshombe plainly that he must take specific steps to implement the Thant plan. He was able to win a few concessions from Tshombe, but they were not enough to break the deadlock.[78] Meanwhile, in New York, Bunche told the Americans that the Afro-Asian radicals were eager for action. Algeria, Indonesia, and possibly Morocco, Guinea, Ghana, the UAR, and Sudan were offering troops to the United Nations to help reintegrate Katan-ga, and the Soviet Union was offering to airlift these troops to the Congo.[79]

On Sunday, October 14, President Kennedy, who was returning from a five-state campaign swing, stopped in New York to confer with Stevenson, primarily about the deepening crisis in the Congo. Press secretary Salinger denied that there was any emergency and explained that the President had to come through New York anyway. Stevenson told reporters before the meeting that the subject of Cuba might come up.[80] Neither man was aware that the biggest crisis of Kennedy's Presidency was brewing there. October 14 was the day the U-2 plane flew over Cuba and came up with the famous pictures indicating that Soviet offensive missile sites were being built on the island. The Russians had been sending unusually large shipments of weapons to Cuba since early summer. By September 4 the President had become concerned, and Attorney General Robert Kennedy had raised the issue with Dobrynin. The Soviet ambassador assured him that all the weapons were purely defensive. The U-2 photographs revealed that these assurances were untrue and that in fact the Russians were in the process of constructing launching sites for medium-range ballistic missiles with nuclear warheads capable of hitting almost every major American city east of the Mississippi.

The CIA analyzed the pictures on Monday. Bundy received the information on Monday night and briefed the President the following morning. For the next two weeks no other issue existed. The top officials of the U.S. government pretended that everything was normal while they met secretly on the seventh floor of the State Department and tried to decide how to counter the Soviet move without either retreating or touching off a nuclear war. The entire range of possibilities was considered: Should the U.S. Air Force destroy the Soviet missile sites in a neat surgical strike? Should the United States invade Cuba? Should the United States offer to compromise and withdraw U.S. missiles from Turkey in exchange for the removal of Soviet missiles from Cuba? In the end the President decided to impose a naval blockade; any Soviet ships approaching Cuba would be stopped, boarded, and searched, and if they were carrying offensive missiles, they would be turned back.

Kennedy announced the plan in a nationwide television broadcast on Monday, October 22. After four days of extraordinary tension, with the two superpowers poised on the edge of nuclear war, Khrushchev sent a message which held out some hope of a peaceful solution. The following day, however, he sent a second message, which was tough and uncompromising. Robert Kennedy suggested that the President respond to the less bellicose of the two messages and give Khrushchev a way out, as Harriman had recommended earlier in the week. By Sunday, October 28, the crucial message arrived from Moscow. Khrushchev announced that work would stop on the sites and the missiles would be removed from Cuba.[81]

When they came close to a nuclear confrontation, the Soviet military men counted nosecones and realized that the Americans had overwhelming superiority. Khrushchev was aware of this before he launched his Cuban adventure, but he went ahead anyway. He did not always learn from his previous mistakes. Two years earlier he had intervened in a less threatening way in the Congo, sending planes, arms, and military advisers thousands of miles from home in an unprecedented attempt to shore up a radical Third World leader, and the United States had reacted vigorously. The result was a Soviet humiliation. What made him think that he could succeed in Cuba, ninety miles off the coast of Florida, with a challenge not measured in rifles and Ilyushin-14 planes but in missiles with nuclear warheads which posed a mortal threat to the United States?

He may have persuaded himself that his rebuff in the Congo had been administered by Eisenhower and that Kennedy would not react in the same way; he felt, after the Bay of Pigs and the Vienna summit, that Kennedy might back down under pressure. He undoubtedly hoped that the boldness of the plan would ensure its success. He thought the missiles would be in place and ready to threaten the United States before anyone knew about them. He was willing to take great risks in order to force a Berlin settlement on his terms. He had issued ultimatums, built the Berlin wall, launched a series of nuclear tests on the eve of the Belgrade conference—and none of it had worked. West Berlin was still linked with the West. By placing missiles in Cuba, he hoped to present the Americans with a fait accompli: he would offer to remove the missiles in exchange for an American retreat on the Berlin issue.

His gamble, however, had failed. He could argue that he had forced Kennedy to promise that he would never invade Cuba, and he could point to the withdrawal of American medium-range missiles from Turkey and Italy a few months later as the result of his Cuban initiative. But he had failed to achieve his main goal—a victory in Berlin—and he had been forced to back down publicly. If the Congo experience was a humiliation for Khrushchev, his retreat in the Cuban missile crisis was a disaster of a much higher order. For the daring innovator, it was the beginning of the end; within two years he would be out of power. For the Soviet military machine, it was the beginning of a determined drive for nuclear parity with the United States, and then superiority. As Deputy Foreign Minister Kuznetsov said to McCloy when they worked out the final details of the Soviet pullback, "We'll never be in that situation again!"[82]

U.S. Fighter Planes for the United Nations?

Once the Cuban missile crisis was over, Kennedy had time to turn to other pressing foreign policy issues. He found that the Congo problem was as intractable as ever and that there was a battle shaping up within his Administration about the best way to deal with it. On one side was McGhee, who recommended that the United States continue its present policy of encouraging a negotiated settlement rather than move immediately to "stronger measures of coercion against Tshombe."[83] On the other side were Gullion, Williams, Cleveland, and Bowles, now Kennedy's roving ambassador to the Third World, who had stopped in Brazzaville to see Gullion on October 26, just after McGhee left the Congo. Gullion told him that "Tshombe had handled McGhee skillfully"; since the Under Secretary had had "little experience" in dealing with Africans, he had accepted Tshombe's assurances at "face value." Bowles immediately sent the State Department a cable urging a blockade of Katanga copper exports and other strong measures to end the secession.[84]

Kennedy's first impulse after the missile crisis was to pull back and avoid any more confrontations. On October 31, three days after Khrushchev's capitulation, he met with his advisers and told them that there "could not be any consideration at this time of military action in the Congo on the part of the United Nations forces." He knew that his European allies were opposed to strong measures against Tshombe; they had offered him magnificent support at a time of great peril, and he was reluctant to go to them now and ask them to act against their better judgment. He pointed out that Spaak was facing "political difficulties" at home and was in no position to advocate sanctions against Katanga. Furthermore, India, which was supplying one-third of the troops in the UN force, was battling a Chinese invasion for which it had been left woefully unprepared by its pro-Communist Defense Minister, Krishna Menon. Kennedy was certain that even if Nehru kept his troops in the Congo, they would not be able to "engage in serious fighting" and suffer casualties, because the government and the Indian public "simply would not stand for it."

With strong measures against Tshombe effectively ruled out, the President's only option was to apply pressure to Adoula. He said the Prime Minister must understand that the United States "simply could not carry the whole burden of forcing on Tshombe the settlement that Adoula desired." He conveniently ignored the fact that Adoula desired nothing more than the settlement originally proposed by the United States with the approval of its European allies. "Our first aim," Kennedy said, "must be to get Adoula to move."[85]

After this meeting McGhee and Williams tackled Bomboko, who had come to the United States to appeal for military support. They told him that the President had just approved a Pentagon plan for the retraining of the ANC and had agreed to finance a contract with Panama Airways which would give the ANC an "internal airlift capability." But the rest of their message was negative. They explained the international factors which made it "necessary to avoid fighting in the Congo" and suggested it was up to Adoula to take the initiative in carrying out the Thant plan.

Bomboko replied that they were "preaching to the converted." Adoula would be more than happy to carry out the plan; the problem was in Katanga. "As long as Tshombe has a large armed force," he said, "you can bring forth any Plan you want and he will not negotiate seriously." The only argument that would impress him was the threat of force. If Adoula had "three fighter aircraft in Leopoldville, Tshombe would start negotiating in earnest the very next day." Bomboko appreciated the steps the President was taking, but he said that Adoula really needed a dramatic military gesture before Parliament met on November 5. He warned that if the moderate government fell now, the United States would not get a second chance. The Soviet ambassador was very active and was picking up a great deal of support.[86]

Kennedy was so exasperated by this time that he was beginning to consider the possibility of pulling out of the Congo altogether. This was the course recommended by two of his White House aides, Carl Kaysen and Ralph Dungan, who felt, according to Schlesinger, that the United States should let the Congolese settle their dispute themselves, even if it led to a military conflict, on the theory that "every nation has a right to its own War of the Roses."[87] The day after the meeting, Kaysen wrote to Rusk, who had not been present, and told him the President would like to review with him "possible alternative courses of action, including, if necessary, paths of withdrawal from the Congo." He felt the situation was reaching a decisive point and if the Congolese leaders, "especially those in Leopoldville," did not "show more movement and flexibility in dealing with the reintegration of Katanga," further American involvement would be "useless."[88] A few days later Kennedy sent an impatient note to Rusk:

> I wish you and George Ball would take a long look as to where we are in the Congo. If the UN effort is going to collapse we should work out some alternatives. We should at least be laying our groundwork.[89]

Kennedy's defeatist mood did not last long. His reluctance to get into a confrontation with anyone after the missile crisis was gradually overcome by the pressure of events and the arguments of his activist advisers, who were determined to salvage their anti-Tshombe policy. On November 6 Williams submitted a paper to Rusk, who sent it to the White House the following day with the caveat that it did not "necessarily represent his own final view of what should be done." Williams recommended that the United States strengthen the military capacity of the United Nations by providing it with two or more U.S. cargo planes to transport weapons and other equipment to Elisabethville

and by obtaining a squadron of fighter planes from a European country, or, if this was not feasible, supplying U.S. fighter planes with pilots
of another nationality.[90] After a lively discussion with Rusk, Ball,
McGhee, Williams, and Cleveland, Kennedy reluctantly approved this
recommendation. But he still wanted it made clear to Adoula that U.S.
pressure on Tshombe would be dependent on his own performance.[91]

Over the next few weeks, however, it became apparent that Adoula
was in no position to make concessions to Tshombe. His situation was
extremely precarious. On November 23 Parliament adopted two anti-
government resolutions by acclamation,[92] and there were widespread
demands for the release of Gizenga. On November 26 Bomboko
warned Rusk that the government would fall unless something dramatic was done.[93] This time the message finally got through. Kennedy
met with Spaak the following day, and they tried to save Adoula by issuing a strong statement threatening "severe economic measures"
against Tshombe if he did not implement the Thant plan within a
"very short time."[94] When Parliament met on November 28, Adoula
barely survived the vote of confidence.[95]

After this narrow escape, there could no longer be any doubt that
the situation was desperate. The only question now was the one posed
by Stevenson, who said the United Nations must either end the Katanga secession "or get out of the Congo."[96] The present policy of waiting
and hoping for Tshombe to come around was simply not working. The
choice was up to Kennedy.

The first concrete indication of his decision came at the beginning of
December. For the first time in a year U.S. Air Force Globemaster
planes started carrying military equipment from Leopoldville to Elisabethville. On December 3 the Americans announced that they would
bring in a Norwegian antiaircraft battery with three hundred and
eighty men. They would also pick up thirty-eight hundred Indonesian
troops who were coming by sea to Dar es Salaam and fly them directly
to Katanga.[97]

The underlying reason for Kennedy's decision to take a tough line
toward Tshombe was the very same reason that had motivated American policy since the very beginning of the Congo crisis in 1960—the
desire to prevent the Russians from gaining a foothold in the heart of
Africa. This threat had receded briefly after the arrest of Gizenga,
but ever since Ambassador Nemchina's arrival in Leopoldville in
mid-September, it had emerged once more as a real—and alarming
—possibility.

On December 10 the White House received a memorandum from
the head of the State Department's Bureau of Intelligence and Research, Roger Hilsman, who noted that the Russians had indicated to
Adoula and Mobutu that they would provide them with enough mili-

tary aid to end the Katanga secession within two months after the United Nations pulled out. Mobutu, he said, could easily withstand these offers, but they were also being made to "impressionable younger ANC officers" who might be more receptive to Soviet blandishments. Adoula would accept such an offer only as a "desperate last course," but, as Hilsman pointed out, he was becoming increasingly desperate, and he might be forced to accept Soviet aid in order to "disarm his critics," who complained that he was relying too heavily on the United States and the United Nations. In any case, his successors would leap at the chance.

Hilsman cautioned that the Russians had not yet made any firm offers but said this did not mean that they might not do so at any time. He felt they were weighing the pros and cons of a major involvement, keeping in mind the disaster of 1960. On the one hand, if they ended the Katanga secession when everyone else had failed, they would wind up in a position of influence in Leopoldville—they "might even hope for a return to the palmy days of Lumumba." On the other hand, it would not be easy to end the secession; they would have to send military technicians to "assume command positions at every level of the ANC," and they might not want to make that sort of commitment. Another serious inhibition would be Khrushchev's desire to avoid another cold war confrontation with the United States so soon after the missile crisis. Of course, it was always possible that the Soviet leader might try to "begin regaining the prestige lost in Cuba" by demonstrating that he could "still seize the initiative" in the Congo. Hilsman concluded that a "major unilateral involvement sufficient to end the Katanga secession" was unlikely but that the Russians could easily continue to stir up trouble for Adoula by offering limited amounts of military hardware, and possibly technicians, to the ANC, or by channeling military aid through the radical Afro-Asian states, which were eager to help end the secession.[98]

CIA analysts came to a similar conclusion: they felt that the Russians, remembering 1960, would be wary about a major commitment but that this would not stop them from offering arms and advisers, and perhaps even a few pilots, to the extremist government which would undoubtedly replace Adoula if the United Nations pulled out without settling the Katanga issue. This would not pose an immediate threat to American interests, but the long-term effect would be extremely harmful. Once the Russians were firmly established in the Congo, they would turn it into "a base from which revolution and instability" would flow into the surrounding colonial areas. The first area to feel the effect of this change would be Angola, where the Russians had been "seeking a means to assist the rebels" for some time. (Adoula had set up a training base for the Angolan rebels in August, but he was working with the pro-Western Holden Roberto, while the Russians were supporting the left-wing party headed by Agostinho Neto—the group that ultimately triumphed in 1975.) The Congo could also be used as a base by "dissident and revolutionary elements from the Rhodesias, South Africa and other neighboring territories," thus greatly increasing the "danger of white-black confrontations" in much of southern Africa. The CIA concluded that the only limitation on the Russians would be their judgment as to how much "sheer instability and terrorism" they could promote before the Americans felt obliged to intervene.[99]

Officials at the Pentagon were equally concerned about Soviet offers of military aid. On December 7 Assistant Secretary of Defense Nitze asked the Joint Chiefs of Staff if they felt the United States should offer military support to the United Nations and the Congolese government "to counter the possibility of Soviet intervention," and if so, what sort of support should be offered. They replied on December 11, and Nitze's deputy, William Bundy, immediately passed on their memorandum to Under Secretary Ball, who had been asked by the President to gather recommendations about what should be done to end the crisis. The Joint Chiefs recommended that the United States begin by strengthening its existing airlift and other logistical support to the United Nations and, at the same time, step up military assistance to the Congolese government. As a last resort, if it was "required to prevent the collapse" of the central government, they recommended that the President offer the United Nations a "US military package consisting of one Composite Air Strike Unit with necessary support elements" and, "if necessary," promise to furnish "any additional forces required to tip the balance of power decisively in favor of the UN forces in the Congo." The objective would be to "destroy or neutralize" Katanga's "air capability" and to "provide immediate political support" for the central government. The Joint Chiefs stressed that a "direct commitment of US forces" should be made only if it was determined "at the highest level" that a "collapse" of the government was "imminent."[100]

The policy the Pentagon was recommending went beyond the measure Kennedy had approved on November 7—the offer of fighter planes, without American pilots—but it was not entirely without precedent. The Pentagon had made a similar recommendation in September 1961, after Hammarskjold's death. At that time the President was prepared to offer the United Nations fighter planes with pilots who were authorized to respond to attacks from Tshombe's air force, if the United Nations was unable to obtain them elsewhere; but as it turned out, the American planes were not needed. This time the proposal became the center of a major controversy, which was partially resolved on December 14, when the President met with his top advisers to review his Congo options.

When Kaysen gave Kennedy the papers Ball had collected, he pointed out that they were "remarkable for their unanimity in thinking that something strong needs to be done."[101] But while the President's advisers all agreed that something must be done, there was still a wide range of opinion about precisely what that something should be. The argument about the fighter planes—or, more precisely, about the timing of the offer to the United Nations—was symptomatic of the entire debate.

At one end of the spectrum was Williams, who not only supported the idea of offering fighter planes to the United Nations immediately, but also wanted to give two fighters to the Congolese government. He felt that it was essential to "neutralize" the Katangan air force and that the United Nations should now be permitted to retaliate for Katangan bombing by "destroying on the ground, as well as in the air, Katangan aircraft capable of military use."[102] Williams was backed up by Bowles, who recommended that if Tshombe did not sign an acceptable agreement within one week, the United Nations should launch a series of "immediate military operations" which would include "UN bombing of Katangan white mercenary ground forces and airplanes" and a blockade on the ground to "cut off the export of Katangan copper" through Angola and Northern Rhodesia.[103] Stevenson, "after some hesitation," lined up with Williams and Bowles.[104]

Even McGhee, at the other end of the spectrum, recommended that the U.S. government offer a fighter unit to the United Nations. He saw this offer, however, as the Joint Chiefs did, as part of a contingency plan that would be put into effect only if the United States decided, after two weeks, that "practical progress" was stalled, and after consultations with congressional leaders, the United Nations, and the British and Belgian governments. McGhee was reluctant to push ahead on the military front, especially since the events of the past few days had given him hope of a "major breakthrough" on the negotiating front.[105]

Pressures had converged on Tshombe from three directions: Adoula had declared an embargo on Katanga's copper and cobalt;[106] Gardiner had told Tshombe that the United Nations was moving into the next phase of the Thant plan and warned him that if the United Nations were attacked in the course of applying these sanctions, it would respond in legitimate self-defense;[107] and, finally, Spaak had called Tshombe a "rebel" and said Belgium would back the United Nations if it proceeded with economic measures and they led to hostilities.[108] Tshombe, who always knew when to yield just enough to divide his adversaries, responded by announcing that he would accept a proposal worked out by Spaak and McGhee whereby Union Minière would pay its taxes directly to the Leopoldville government.[109]

At the White House meeting McGhee recommended that the United States persuade Adoula to resume negotiations on the basis of Tshombe's latest offer. Only if these talks failed to produce results would he be prepared to move on to stronger measures, and even then he envisioned a "graduated scale of pressures" which bore little resemblance to Bowles's prescription for an all-out assault on the Katangan forces.[110]

Cleveland, who produced the most influential memo of the day, took a position which was much closer to Williams's than to McGhee's. He was skeptical about Tshombe's latest offer. He had come to the conclusion that Adoula was right about Tshombe: he would never reintegrate unless he was "forced" to do so. Cleveland wanted the President to place an American fighter unit in the Congo in order to demonstrate that he was determined to see Katanga reintegrated and was ready to back his determination "with the full weight of US power." With this recommendation Cleveland was essentially returning to the strategy Ball had advocated in the fall of 1961. He was suggesting an American military buildup under a "UN umbrella" in order to avoid the use of force to reintegrate Katanga. "The idea is not that the US or the UN would take a military initiative to destroy Tshombe's government," he explained. Instead, the United Nations would create a situation in which negotiations would be "the only rational choice left to him." But he warned, as Ball had on other occasions, "A democracy cannot bluff unless it means it."[111]

Kennedy and his advisers regarded Tshombe's obstinacy as the major stumbling block; but they also believed it was impossible for Adoula to take the necessary steps toward reconciliation because of the opposition of a "largely irresponsible Parliament." Williams reported that "Mobutu and other elements of the Adoula group" were seeking the "active support" of the United States for a military coup that would remove Adoula and dismiss Parliament. Williams was completely opposed to the idea,[112] but the other officials felt it had a certain appeal. Cleveland was opposed to a coup that would remove Adoula himself, but he felt the United States should convince Adoula to dismiss Parliament and "govern with backing of a pro-Western group headed by Mobutu." He argued that while Adoula was "not an ideal choice," he was "the best individual available to hold the reins of government in Leopoldville, and, even with Parliament dismissed, he would enjoy the virtue of having taken office legitimately."[113] Bowles agreed; he said the United States should tell Adoula it would back him in a "move to disband Parliament and govern directly for the duration of the emergency" in exchange for a pledge that he would "oppose Soviet intervention."[114]

While Kennedy did not make any final decisions at this meeting, he clearly took one more step in the direction of the activists. He asked Stevenson to sound out the Secretary-General and see if he would accept American fighter planes. At first Thant said he could not accept the planes without Security Council approval, and he was sure the Russians would never agree. But when Stevenson returned with Cleveland the following day, he found the Secretary-General in a more receptive mood. He was "fairly confident" that the United Nations could settle the Katanga problem by the end of February without American fighter planes; he would soon have eighteen planes from Sweden, Italy, and the Philippines, and this would be enough to immobilize Tshombe's forces. But if the matter was not resolved by March, he might accept an American military unit.

The Americans pointed out that the steps Thant was planning to take between now and March—blocking the railroads leading to Rhodesia and Angola to enforce the copper and cobalt embargo—would undoubtedly lead to fighting. Thant conceded that there would be "at least one substantial fight with the Katanga gendarmerie," but he hoped one would be enough to demonstrate UN superiority. The Americans argued that it would "obviously be preferable if Tshombe could be induced by an overwhelming show of strength in the air to get on with the reconciliation plan without the need for any messy fighting on the ground." In the end, Thant agreed to accept the American offer only after he had come up with a formula that would make it easier for him to handle Soviet objections. The request for U.S. fighter planes would come from Adoula rather than from the Secretary-General himself. Thant promised to help Adoula draft the request.[115]

On December 17 Stevenson and Cleveland took Thant's proposal back to the President and argued strongly in favor of proceeding as soon as possible. Even Kaysen, who was still doubtful about the idea, acknowledged that the two alternatives were certainly no better. If the United States continued on its present path and gave the United Nations limited logistical support, the Secretary-General's plans would lead to fighting in Katanga which would involve Europeans and "have serious domestic political repercussions, especially with Congress in session." On the other hand, withdrawal by the United States and the United Nations would involve a loss of prestige and might require renewed American intervention in a year or so to counter Soviet involvement.[116]

Faced with these alternatives the President took the classic way out:

he announced that he was sending an eight-man military mission to Leopoldville, headed by General Louis W. Truman, to study the needs of the United Nations.[117] This had the advantage of being a step that could be taken immediately, without waiting for Thant and Adoula to agree on the phrasing of a request. It was less of a commitment than the dispatch of a fighter squadron, but it would serve the same purpose, or so the Americans hoped: it would put the fear of God in Tshombe and bolster Adoula and the United Nations. It was not really necessary for the mission to go to the Congo to see what the United Nations needed; Truman called on the Secretary-General before he left and came out with a list which included transport planes, jeeps, helicopters, and pontoon bridges. Thant said he had already arranged for twenty fighter planes, and when reporters asked Yost if the United States would be supplying any, the American diplomat said it was unlikely.[118]

American officials were not surprised when Zorin attacked the Truman mission and warned of serious consequences.[119] The reaction in the Congo, however, was not exactly what they expected. Tshombe was not cowed. He accused the United States of trying to destroy him and encouraged students to assault the U.S. Consulate in Elisabethville. Even more disturbing was the reaction in Leopoldville, where the general arrived on December 21. The leftist opposition charged that the Truman mission was a "threat to Congolese sovereignty." Parliament, stirred up by anti-American fervor, voted unanimously to demand that Adoula free Gizenga within forty-eight hours.[120] Truman decided to cut his visit short and maintain a low profile for the rest of his stay so as not to embarrass Adoula any further.[121]

Meanwhile, Kennedy, who was meeting with Macmillan in Nassau to discuss NATO defense matters, tried to win his support for strong action against Tshombe. He told the British leader that Adoula's position was "becoming steadily worse, almost desperate" and that if he "failed altogether the way would be open for the Russians to return with all their sinister influence." Macmillan recalled in his memoirs:

> At the end, we were driven to accept the position that, without early and firm agreement, there must be a military operation to overcome Tshombe's resistance and to give strength to Adoula at the centre.[122]

The Third Round

This was the state of affairs when, on Christmas Eve, fighting flared up in Elisabethville. A UN helicopter was shot down by Katangan forces, and several soldiers were wounded. The next day the Katangans continued to fire on UN positions. Tshombe blamed the United

Nations and General Truman and charged that they were planning to launch a lightning war against Katanga and arrest him. The following day UN officials escorted Tshombe to a point from which he could observe the firing, and he acknowledged that it was coming from the Katangan positions. He ordered a ceasefire, but his order was ignored.[123]

On December 28 the situation changed dramatically. After four days of trying to get the Katangans to stop firing, the UN commander in Elisabethville, General Prem Chand of India, persuaded the Secretary-General to let him take the offensive and order his troops to remove the roadblocks the Katangans had set up, by force if necessary. The long-awaited third round of fighting between the UN force and the Katangan gendarmerie had begun at last. After all the planning and debating, it was touched off not by a deliberate, carefully calibrated UN effort to collect taxes or enforce the embargo but by the spontaneous actions of Katangan soldiers who did not even seem to be under Tshombe's control. Still, Gardiner's contingency plans for the operation—which was code-named "Grand Slam"—came in handy. UN forces quickly captured the gendarmerie headquarters in Elisabethville and began to establish their control over the city, with comparatively few casualties.[124]

By this time, General Truman had returned home and reported to Rusk and the Joint Chiefs of Staff, and there were newspaper reports that the United States was going to start a big airlift of military equipment in three weeks to demonstrate its support for the United Nations, although there would be no American troops or combat planes involved.[125] These reports gave the United Nations a psychological boost; but the way things were going, it did not look as if the additional military assistance would be necessary. Operation Grand Slam was nothing like the second round in December 1961. Although Tshombe went to Rhodesia and vowed to fight on indefinitely, his troops offered very little resistance. The United Nations quickly neutralized the Katangan air force with a strike on the Kolwezi airfield and began to move out from Elisabethville. Their objective was to "establish complete freedom of movement" for the United Nations "in the whole of Katanga."[126]

The U.S. government reacted to these developments just as it had reacted at the time of the first round in September 1961: it gave the United Nations public support and encouragement, but in private it urged the Secretary-General to pull back before his forces went too far. Schlesinger recalled that "things were tense" at the White House for several days after Christmas.[127] On December 29 Kaysen reported to Kennedy in Palm Beach that Rusk and Stevenson had talked to Bunche on the telephone and that he had assured them that UN military plans were limited and that the Secretary-General was prepared to make a public statement to that effect. Stevenson was going to New York to tell him that the Americans could "understand a certain amount of confusion and contradiction, given the fast-moving situation on the ground," but that their commitment to the operation was "so large, and so crucial to its success or failure" that they must be kept "fully and currently informed" about "probable military developments."[128]

By the time Stevenson arrived in New York on December 30, UN forces had taken over Kipushi, on the Rhodesian border, twenty-five miles outside Elisabethville. Once again there was practically no resistance. Gardiner was jubilant. "We are not going to make the mistake this time of stopping short," he announced at a news conference. "This is going to be as decisive as we can make it."[129] Stevenson asked Bunche for an explanation, and Bunche said the UN forces had not been authorized to move into Kipushi. He assured Stevenson no further moves were contemplated for the time being but explained that if the Secretary-General made no progress with Tshombe in the next two weeks, the United Nations would march on Jadotville and Kolwezi. He repeated that the UN command was under orders not to undertake any more military moves without approval from New York.[130]

On December 31 Thant issued a statement which the Americans found satisfactory. He stressed that the United Nations was not interested in a "military victory" and was not out to "wage war against anyone." He pledged that Tshombe would not be harmed if he returned to Elisabethville but insisted that he had no status except as a provincial leader. He gave Tshombe two weeks to take all the required steps toward reintegration.[131]

By this time Tshombe had moved his headquarters to the Union Minière facilities in Jadotville. He began the new year with an old trick: he called for a ceasefire and the start of new negotiations. One Western diplomat in Elisabethville was quoted as saying, "He is trying to get himself another Kitona. I just hope he doesn't get away with it."[132]

Kaysen reported Tshombe's latest offer to the President and noted that Adoula had dismissed Parliament and made a speech which held out the possibility of reconciliation with Tshombe. He also noted that UN troops were on the road to Jadotville but had been held up by a destroyed bridge fifteen miles outside of town. He told Kennedy that Adoula, Gardiner, and Gullion were pushing for a "complete military victory" and that Rusk and Ball thought Cleveland ought to go to Leopoldville immediately to persuade them that this would not be wise and to convince them of the need for "political negotiations."[133]

The following day Kaysen told the President that Thant objected to a visit by Cleveland at this time. He refused to negotiate with Tshombe but he assured the Americans that the UN troops were under orders to go no farther.[134]

Kennedy's top advisers were caught in an awkward situation. They were supplying major military assistance to the United Nations, but they were so concerned about the possibility of another split with their allies that they opposed any further use of that assistance by the UN force—even though they realized that the present situation would lead to a stalemate. Kaysen expected that Tshombe would soon be "well dug in at Jadotville and Kolwezi with no intention of giving himself up," but he felt that strong diplomatic pressure on all the parties might resolve the situation without any more fighting.[135] Thomas L. Hughes, in the State Department's Bureau of Intelligence and Research, was less sanguine about the possibilities of diplomacy. He pointed out that Tshombe had two options, neither of which looked very promising for American interests: he could return to Elisabethville and engage in endless negotiations, hoping to outwait the United Nations as he had done before; or he could organize his eighteen-thousand-man army with the help of the two hundred to five hundred mercenaries and establish a redoubt in the Union Minière heartland around Jadotville and Kolwezi. If he controlled both these rich centers, he could hold out indefinitely by exporting minerals and importing arms and food supplies on the railroad line to Angola. If, on the other hand, the UN forces took either Jadotville or Kolwezi, his position would be reduced to "little more than a guerrilla stronghold," which would be a nuisance rather than a threat. The only problem with this approach, Hughes explained, was that "an attack on Jadotville or Kolwezi might involve heavy fighting," and Union Minière installations might be damaged.[136]

On January 2, while the Americans were pondering these alternatives, the UN troops outside Jadotville, who had either ignored or had never received the Secretary-General's orders, resolved a major part of the problem. They seized an unexpected opportunity and stormed across the ruined bridge without any casualties. The Katangan troops on the other side of the Lufira River fled. The road to Jadotville was open, and the UN soldiers proceeded to take over the city. There was no military resistance, but unfortunately two Belgian women were killed by mistake at a UN roadblock.[137] This incident marred what was in every other way a remarkable accomplishment by the UN troops. Thant, with his strong religious views on avoiding violence, later recalled that he had heeded Western warnings that if the troops proceeded to Jadotville there would be serious fighting; ironically, if his orders had reached the troops in time and they had waited, there would have been much more resistance and loss of life. As it was, they caught the Katangans by surprise.[138] Thant issued a statement explaining that there had been a breakdown in communications and then commended the troops for a brilliant military action.[139]

The capture of Jadotville was the turning point in Operation Grand Slam, but there was still a great deal of uncertainty about Tshombe's intentions for nearly three weeks. Would he capitulate? Would he encourage his remaining forces to fight? Would he order the destruction of the plants in Kolwezi rather than give up Katanga's independence? Would he retreat to the bush and launch guerrilla warfare? Any of these courses was possible, and Tshombe, typically, kept everyone hanging in midair as he tried every trick he knew to evade the defeat which the Secretary-General alone regarded as inevitable. After his experience with Jadotville, Thant did not listen to the advice of the Western powers. He refused to make any further concessions to Tshombe. He refused to negotiate. He just sat tight and waited for the secessionist leader to recognize reality and give up.

While Tshombe moved from Kolwezi to Elisabethville to Ndola and back to Kolwezi again, changing his terms with his location, the United Nations calmly installed officials of the central government in Elisabethville to take control of the province. The Americans continued to pour military supplies into Katanga, including bridging equipment to repair the bridges to Kolwezi, which had been destroyed by the retreating Katangan forces. The British concentrated their efforts on persuading Tshombe to cooperate with the United Nations. At one point, Adoula became so angry about their dealings with the secessionist leader that he decided to sever diplomatic relations with Great Britain. Macmillan wrote in his diary:

> Congo continues, partly farce, partly tragedy. Tshombe has gone off again to N. Rhodesia, but is ready to return for a final negotiation. The great Union Minière installations are mined, and the vital dams may be destroyed at any moment. The only man who has any restraining influence is the British Consul at Elisabethville. Characteristically, Adoula ... has ordered him out of the country.[140]

The Americans managed to restrain Adoula, and his patience was rewarded. On January 15 Tshombe—realizing that his position was hopeless—announced that he was renouncing his secession. He agreed to implement the Thant plan and grant the UN troops complete freedom of movement throughout the province. The Secretary-General welcomed his statement, and Kasavubu and Adoula confirmed that they would proclaim an amnesty for Tshombe and the members of his government.[141] On January 17 Tshombe met with representatives of the United Nations in Elisabethville and signed a document promising to arrange for the peaceful entry of UN troops into Kolwezi, his last remaining stronghold.[142]

Even after this development doubts remained as to whether Tshombe would keep his word or whether he would find a way out at the last minute. But on January 21, to the surprise of everyone but the Secretary-General, the United Nations peacefully occupied Kolwezi. Tshombe bade a sentimental farewell to his troops and told them to cooperate with the United Nations.[143] After two and a half years of drama, confrontation, and intrigue, the Katanga secession was over.

A Word of Thanks

There was general rejoicing in Washington at the outcome, especially since the reintegration of Katanga had been accomplished with virtually no damage to the mining installations which produced Katanga's fabulous wealth. Best of all, Kennedy had outfoxed the Russians once again. The issue they had counted on for two and a half years to rally radical African support both inside and outside the Congo had suddenly vanished. This triumph, coming less than three months after the victory in the Cuban missile crisis, justified Kennedy's flexible new Africa policy as well as his handling of the crucially important American relationship with the Soviet Union.

The end of the Katanga secession did not mean that all the Congo's problems were settled. Adoula's political opponents continued to snipe at him and demand the release of Gizenga. The potentially rich economy was still in disastrous shape—outside Katanga. The army was still overpaid and underdisciplined, but its support was essential to keep the pro-Western Adoula government in power. Kennedy and his advisers turned their attention to helping Mobutu retrain and strengthen the army, so that it would be able to maintain order when the UN force left the Congo.[144]

On May 19 Mobutu arrived in the United States for a two-week visit as a guest of the Department of the Army. On May 31 he called on President Kennedy at the White House. He told Kennedy that the Secretary-General had given up the idea of retraining his army but explained that the Belgians were willing to take over most of the task, if the United States would supply the equipment. He assured Kennedy that if he had sufficient aid and technicians, he could maintain order after the departure of the UN force. He said that after his tour of U.S. military installations, he was eager to send a number of Congolese students to the United States for training, and he wanted to arrange six weeks of parachute training for himself and ten paracommando officers at Fort Benning and at the Special Warfare School at Fort Bragg.

Kennedy said he would be "delighted" if the general felt he could be out of the country for that long. Mobutu assured him that he had assistants whom he could trust.

Kennedy had been thoroughly briefed on Mobutu's role in defeating Lumumba and throwing out the Russians in 1960. He knew that the success of American policy in the Congo—past and future—rested largely on the shoulders of this thirty-two-year-old officer. As he invited his guest to move out into the rose garden for pictures, he said, "General, if it hadn't been for you, the whole thing would have collapsed and the Communists would have taken over." Mobutu modestly replied, "I do what I am able to do."[145]

Conclusion

PRESIDENT KENNEDY's friendly exchange with General Mobutu in the White House rose garden in the spring of 1963 symbolized the success of America's Congo policy over the preceding three years. At the same time, it foreshadowed the dilemma facing the U.S. government to this day: How does a democracy cope with a foreign policy success that falls considerably short of perfection?

When the President complimented Mobutu on his role in preventing a Soviet takeover in the Congo, he had no doubt that the general had helped the United States score an impressive victory in its cold war competition with the Soviet Union. All the goals that had been set by two Administrations had been achieved: the radicals were out of power, a moderate government and an elected Parliament were functioning in Leopoldville, and the Katanga secession had been ended with comparatively little loss of life or property. Now, more than twenty years after the crisis began, the Congo is still in pro-Western hands. In order to appreciate the significance of this achievement one has only to compare it with the outcome of the two other major Third World conflicts that dominated the foreign policy of the Eisenhower and Kennedy Administrations—Cuba and Indochina.

The Cuban crisis was, at first, the most traumatic for the United States. It was a shock to find that the friendly island ninety miles from Florida which had always been part of the American sphere of influence had suddenly become the first Communist country in the Western Hemisphere. Neither Eisenhower nor Kennedy was able to reverse the situation and reassert American control. Despite all the assassination attempts by the CIA and the Mafia, despite the Bay of Pigs and the Cuban missile crisis, Fidel Castro is still in power; Soviet combat troops are still maneuvering on Cuban soil; Soviet submarines are still calling at Cuban naval bases; and the United States, bound by Ken-

[373]

nedy's 1962 agreement with Khrushchev, is virtually powerless to do anything about it.

By the time Kennedy was murdered in November 1963, it was clear that the compromise agreement he had sponsored in Laos was not going to halt the pro-Communist guerrilla insurgency that was sweeping through Indochina. Today, all three states of Indochina are ruled by harsh Communist regimes, despite a ten-year American military effort that was at once too brutal to win the support of the American people and too ineffectual to prevent a Communist victory. The Vietnam War was even more traumatic for the United States than the Cuban experience. It not only tore the country apart as long as it lasted, with half the population objecting to the fact that we were fighting dirty—bombing defenseless people who could not bomb us back—while the other half objected to the fact that we were fighting with one hand tied behind our back, constrained by moral and political considerations, unable to use the full weight of American power to defeat the enemy. It also left a damaging legacy: it undermined our confidence in our ability to conduct a strong, principled foreign policy anywhere in the world.

Of these three trouble spots of the early 1960s, the Congo is the only place where U.S. policy could be described as a lasting success in cold war terms, and that success has rested largely on the efforts of one right-wing general. Mobutu—the man *Pravda* described as a "soap bubble" who could not last for more than a few hours—has run the Congo, directly or indirectly, for the past two decades. Every American President since Eisenhower's time has worked closely with him, some more enthusiastically than others.

From the beginning there have been two conflicting points of view about how the United States should deal with Mobutu. Those who take the traditional hard-line approach argue that nothing is perfect in this world and that the pro-Western Mobutu, with all his faults, is an important asset in the continuing global struggle with the Soviet Union. Those who take a more liberal approach argue, first, on moral grounds, that it is simply not right for the U.S. government to be supporting a military dictator who violates democratic principles, no matter how anti-Communist he may be; and, second, on practical grounds, that such support is bound to be counterproductive, because sooner or later oppressive rulers are overthrown, and if they have been closely identified with the United States there will be a violent anti-American backlash and the people will turn to the Communists or the radical left, thus bringing about precisely the situation the original policy was designed to prevent.

The first viewpoint was more characteristic of the Eisenhower Administration, though it was not limited to Republicans—or to conservatives. Harriman, who took a liberal line on most foreign policy issues, was just as pleased as Eisenhower when the Russians were thrown out of the Congo in September 1960. He would have been happier if the constitutionally elected President of the Congo had made the move on his own, but since Kasavubu turned out to be too weak to act on his own, Harriman had no strong objections to Mobutu's decision to set aside the politicians for a time and tackle the problem of Soviet intervention in his own way.

The argument that raged between Ambassador Timberlake and the State Department in the autumn of 1960 about the comparative merits of supporting Mobutu's College of Commissioners and replacing it with a civilian government was essentially a clash between these two approaches. The ambassador was convinced that only a military strongman could defend Western interests successfully at that point, while Bohlen and others in Washington argued that U.S. policy could not succeed unless it took into account the views of the Secretary-General, who was demanding a return to legality.

The hard-line approach was clearly triumphant when Lumumba was arrested by Mobutu in December 1960 and held without trial. No one in the Eisenhower Administration seemed particularly disturbed that his rights were being violated. And in January 1961, when Lumumba was sent to Katanga, where he was sure to be killed, the reaction in high circles in Washington was one of relief. This was hardly surprising; after all, the CIA had been trying to get rid of Lumumba for nearly six months, on orders from the President. Eisenhower and his top advisers had ignored the fact that Lumumba was the legally elected Prime Minister of the Congo and thought of him only as a threat to U.S. interests: as long as he remained on the scene, there would always be the possibility of a Soviet takeover. Now, at last, that threat had been removed, thanks to Mobutu and his friends.

The mood in Washington shifted significantly once Kennedy took office. The new President believed that the best way to counter the Soviet challenge in Africa was to win the respect of the neutralist leaders and to work closely with them, and he listened carefully to the advice of Stevenson, Bowles, Williams, and the other New Frontiersmen, who insisted that he must begin by adopting a new policy in the Congo. They felt that instead of relying on the right-wing anti-Communist forces which were riding roughshod over the Congo's brand new political institutions, the United States should use those institutions to create a coalition government which would have broad popular support at home and legitimacy abroad—even if it ran the risk of including Lumumba.

Kennedy agreed with this approach—up to a point. He realized that it would be extremely risky to convene Parliament and bring in the leftists without adequate preparation, and he did his best to minimize the risks. He began by instructing the U.S. Embassy in Leopoldville to come up with a moderate pro-American neutralist with impeccable Afro-Asian credentials to head the new government. He then encouraged the Embassy to use every trick in the book to make sure that he and his allies came out on top.

The formation of the Adoula government in the summer of 1961 was a dazzling triumph for the new Kennedy policy. Premier Khrushchev, who considered the cultivation of African neutralists his own special preserve, recognized the new government with the expectation that he would be able to persuade Adoula to move to the left. He assumed that, at the very least, the radical African leaders would work with him to prevent the new Congolese Prime Minister from moving too far to the right. He was dismayed to find that Kennedy had outmaneuvered him; he had wooed the African radicals and effectively neutralized them as far as the Congo was concerned. In the end Adoula was able to oust and imprison the pro-Soviet Gizenga and then settle the Katanga issue on Western terms, without disturbing his relations with the radical African states. At that point Khrushchev felt he had no choice but to accept defeat gracefully.

Could Kennedy's liberal policy have worked as well if Lumumba had still been in the picture—if Eisenhower's hard-line policy had not forced him out of office and contributed to his death? It would, of course, have been much more difficult. Even with the indecisive Gizenga in charge of the leftists, it was touch-and-go for the U.S. Embassy officials who were trying to put together a coalition government that would keep leftist influence to a minimum. With Lumumba present, it might have been impossible.

In terms of the Congolese political situation, Kennedy's task was made easier by the fact that Lumumba had been eliminated even before the new Administration took office. But in a broader sense Lumumba's murder had made his task more difficult. Most Africans tended to blame the United States for Lumumba's death, even if it was not directly responsible, and Kennedy had to break down a wall of suspicion before he could begin to put U.S. relations with Africa on a new footing. In any case the Kennedy Administration did not want any more martyrs in the Congo. When Gizenga was removed from power in early 1962, American officials insisted that no harm come to him. This decision was based as much on pragmatic considerations as on moral ones. Another assassination of a prominent leftist would not serve the purposes of American diplomacy in Africa.

By the end of 1962 Kennedy and his advisers were aware that even with an honest, principled, moderate Prime Minister in office, it was difficult to run a parliamentary democracy in a country where there was no democratic tradition and no sense of national unity and where the deputies and senators expected to be paid for each vote. As one cynical observer put it, Parliament was nothing but "tribes and bribes." Despite the successful ending of the Katanga secession in January 1963, Adoula's domestic troubles continued to mount. At the end of September Kasavubu dissolved Parliament. Several leading members of the opposition fled to Brazzaville, where a leftist coup had ousted the conservative Youlou regime a few weeks before. Encouraged by the Communist bloc embassies, they began to call for a general strike in Leopoldville and the overthrow of the Adoula government.

In October, while Adoula was on a visit to the United States, Mobutu helped a group of tough anti-Communist cabinet ministers take over de facto control of the government. When the Prime Minister returned, they presented him with a decree establishing martial law and naming an emergency committee of three to administer it. Adoula remained Prime Minister in name, but he no longer had any influence over major government decisions. This was the sort of move Kennedy's advisers had discussed in December, before the Katanga secession was ended. It was made now over the strong objections of Ambassador Gullion, who conceded that the new group would be pro-American but complained that it would also be "obscurantist, arbitrary, primitive, totalitarian, willful, and irresponsible."

Mobutu and his right-wing committee were eager to throw out all the Communist bloc diplomats, but Gullion warned them not to take such drastic action. It was fine, he said, to cut down on the size of the Communist embassies, but not to throw them out entirely. Such a move would destroy Adoula's nonaligned image and damage America's reputation in Africa. The State Department suggested that whatever measures Mobutu was considering, he should be able to justify them by pointing to specific violations of Congolese law—and he should keep the United States out of it.

Administration officials were still discussing the matter when President Kennedy was assassinated on November 22, 1963. The previous day, despite Gullion's warnings, Adoula had announced that he was breaking relations with the Soviet government and expelling the Soviet Embassy. Mobutu and his right-wing friends had found the necessary pretext. They had arrested two Soviet diplomats, carrying official documents, on the ferry to Brazzaville. As Gullion recalled the incident, the Congolese police, who had no respect for the sanctity of the diplomatic pouch, tore it open and seized the documents inside. One of the Soviet diplomats tried to swallow the papers. The enraged Congolese threatened to throw him into the river to be eaten by the crocodiles. Just at that moment, he was rescued—by the chief British intelligence agent in the Congo. In the end, European blood had proved thicker than ideology. Adoula charged that the documents proved that the Soviet Embassy was plotting to overthrow his government with the help of the radicals in Brazzaville. Despite Ambassador Nemchina's protests, the Soviet Embassy staff was forced to leave Leopoldville for the second time in a little more than two years. Once again the Russians charged that Mobutu was to blame.

Kennedy's policy of working with the Afro-Asian neutralists to outflank the Communists did not survive his death. President Lyndon B. Johnson's attitude toward Africa was much more like Eisenhower's. He was not particularly interested in the Congo, and he intervened there, in November 1964, only when he felt he had no other choice; but when he did decide to intervene, he did not spend much time worrying about the Afro-Asian reaction. He took strong, direct action in support of the right-wing, anti-Communist forces who were then running the Leopoldville government.

Adoula, his position weakened by the leftist agitators in Brazzaville and by a rural rebellion in the areas still loyal to Gizenga, had resigned on July 9, 1964, just nine days after the UN force pulled out of the Congo. President Kasavubu had then astonished everyone, with the possible exception of McMurtrie Godley, who was back in Leopoldville as U.S. ambassador, by naming Tshombe as Prime Minister. Tshombe, who had spent much of the time since the end of the Katanga secession in self-imposed exile in Europe, proceeded to strike up an excellent relationship with the U.S. ambassador, who was willing to forgive him for the trouble he had caused in the summer of 1961 by refusing to send his parliamentary delegation to Leopoldville to counter the leftists. As one member of the Embassy staff explained it, "They were both dynamic, energetic men who knew what they wanted and how to go about getting it." Although he was accepted by the Americans, Tshombe was treated as a pariah by the other African leaders, who still blamed him for Lumumba's death. In an attempt to appease them, he released Gizenga, who had been in prison for more than two years; but the Africans still refused to have anything to do with him.

Meanwhile, the leftist rebellion was picking up steam. In August the rebels took Stanleyville, proclaimed a People's Republic, and instituted a reign of terror. At least twenty thousand Congolese were executed. Many of the victims were educated or semieducated people who had worked for the government or held other posts of responsibility. Others simply belonged to the wrong tribe. Tshombe, unable to defeat the rebels with Mobutu's poorly trained ANC troops, fell back on a familiar device: he called in his Katanga gendarmes and hired more than four hundred white mercenaries, mostly from Rhodesia and South Africa, to lead them. The Johnson Administration was not eager to be associated openly with the mercenary operation, but it quietly supplied

Tshombe with all the transport and combat planes he needed; and the CIA helped him find Cuban exile pilots to fly them.

By November the Stanleyville rebels had seized more than sixteen hundred foreign hostages—including four CIA agents and one American diplomat—and were threatening to kill them. The CIA considered a rescue operation of its own to get the five American officials out, but Helms, who was then Deputy Director for Plans, argued that it would be impractical and added that the United States could not rescue its own officials without making an effort to rescue all the other hostages—missionaries, businessmen, diplomats, men, women, and children. The situation was becoming increasingly desperate. African-sponsored negotiations with the rebels in Nairobi were getting nowhere. At last President Johnson was persuaded to intervene by Under Secretary of State Harriman and Belgian Foreign Minister Spaak.

On November 24 U.S. planes dropped six hundred Belgian paratroopers into Stanleyville. Most of the hostages were rescued, but at least thirty were massacred by the rebels before the paratroopers could get to them; over the next few days, another fifty were found murdered. The Belgian troops left almost immediately, but the ANC and the mercenaries moved into the city and executed more than two thousand suspected rebels—many of whom were just as innocent as the people executed by the leftists. The African states refused to accept Johnson's explanation that the operation had been undertaken for purely humanitarian reasons. They called a meeting of the Security Council and accused the Western powers of reverting to colonialist methods in order to help Tshombe end the rebellion. Kennedy might well have handled the situation differently.

In October 1965, after fifteen turbulent months in office, Tshombe was dismissed by Kasavubu. A few weeks later, Kasavubu himself was deposed by Mobutu in a bloodless coup. The young general, weary of all the squabbling politicians, and assured of American support, came out from behind the scenes and named himself President for a five-year term. He has been President ever since.

Johnson, who was preoccupied with the Vietnam War, did not really object when Mobutu banned all the Congo's political parties in April 1967. Nixon was delighted to work with the anti-Communist general. The years of his Presidency—1969 to 1974—coincided with the period of Mobutu's greatest diplomatic prominence and his country's greatest economic prosperity. But then in 1974 everything started falling apart—for Mobutu as well as for Nixon. Some of Mobutu's problems were the result of his policies; others were caused primarily by developments outside his borders.

The first problem was an excess of Africanization. When Mobutu took over in 1965, he was eager to shed his earlier image as a CIA puppet and to establish himself as an authentic African nationalist. He began with symbolic gestures: he renamed the principal cities, changing Leopoldville to Kinshasa, Stanleyville to Kisangani, and Elisabethville to Lubumbashi. In 1971 he changed the country's name to Zaire. The following year he moved on to more controversial ground; he changed his own name to Mobutu Sese Seko and warned that any Catholic priest who was caught baptizing a Zairian child with a European name would face a five-year jail sentence. He capped these reforms with a decree that Christmas was to be celebrated on June 24. Mobutu's campaign was a direct challenge to the Catholic Church, and he followed it up with another challenge that had more serious repercussions. He nationalized all the schools, claiming that they were a hotbed of foreign influence. The Church had had a near monopoly on education, particularly in the rural areas, and Mobutu soon found that the entire educational system was collapsing because there were not enough trained teachers to replace the missionaries he had removed from their posts. In the end he changed his mind and asked them to come back, but it was hard to repair the damage that had been done.

The same pattern was repeated in the economic sphere, with equally damaging results. Mobutu's initial move, a few months after he took power, appeared extremely bold: he nationalized Union Minière, seizing assets worth eight hundred million dollars. This led to anguished protests in Belgium, but the matter was settled amicably. Western technicians continued to run the Katanga mines, and big Western investors continued to receive a warm welcome from Mobutu and an excellent return on their investments. Mobutu ran into trouble, however, when he moved beyond the symbolic to the substantive. In 1973 he decided to nationalize all the small foreign-owned businesses and plantations in the country and hand them over to his political supporters. The Greek, Belgian, and Portuguese planters and traders who had kept the rural economy going were replaced by inexperienced Africans, who soon went bankrupt. Mobutu, alarmed by the collapse of both the production and the distribution systems, eventually asked the foreign businessmen to return; but most of them were unwilling to run the risk of losing their businesses a second time.

Then, on top of the dislocations caused by the Zairianization program, came a disastrous drop in the world price of copper—Zaire's chief earner of foreign exchange—which fell more than fifty percent in the course of 1974. This blow, coupled with the 1974 rise in the price of such essential imports as oil and grain, helped to turn a country with a stable and prosperous economy into what one expert recently described as an international basket case, suffering from uncontrolled inflation, huge government deficits, and an enormous external debt. The Western banks which had poured loans into Zaire before 1974 and had encouraged Mobutu to build glamorous projects that were not really necessary now found that Zaire was unable to repay the loans on schedule. The banks were forced to reschedule the debt, and the Western governments were forced to step in with additional loans to help stave off the threat of default, which would have set a dangerous precedent for other Third World borrowers. All the reform measures that had been tried in the early 1960s were revived; in 1978 the International Monetary Fund sent a team of experts to Zaire to run the central bank, to institute controls over foreign exchange earnings, and to try to bring some order out of the chaos. They found that the single most important factor inhibiting a rational economic policy was the massive corruption of the ruling class, which continues to divert an enormous proportion—perhaps forty percent—of the government's revenues into its own bank accounts.

The third problem facing Mobutu in 1974 was the sudden revival of Soviet interest in Africa. This was the first time in more than a decade that the cold war had affected his interests in any significant way. In the early 1970s, with his Western flank secure, he had tried to win the favor of the more radical African leaders by shifting his foreign policy to the left. He began with the Middle East. Although he had won his paratrooper's wings in Israel in 1963 and had maintained a close relationship with Israel ever since, he switched signals in October 1973 and abruptly broke relations with Israel two days before the Arabs launched the Yom Kippur war. He also reached out selectively to the Communist world—with a trip to China in 1973—but only after Nixon had broken the ice. In July 1974 he announced that Chinese military instructors would be coming to Zaire to train the Angolan insurgents based there in guerrilla warfare.

Mao Tse-tung's decision to cooperate with Mobutu was a complete reversal of his previous policy; in the past he had always backed the most radical factions in the Congo and criticized the Russians for working with the pro-Western central government. But he was obviously less interested in ideological consistency than in lining up allies in his battle with the Soviet Union, as his startling new relationship with the United States demonstrated. There was only one thing that mattered in this situation: Mobutu was still strongly anti-Soviet and so was the faction he was backing in Angola.

Ever since 1962 Mobutu had provided sanctuary and training facilities for the FNLA (Frente de Libertação Nacional de Angola), the party led by Holden Roberto and backed by the United States, while the Russians and the Cubans were supporting the MPLA (Movimento Popular de Libertação de Angola), headed by Agostinho Neto. Now, as the result of the April revolution in Portugal, the four-hundred-year-old Portuguese colonial empire in southern Africa was coming to an end. With the approach of independence the rivalry between Roberto and Neto escalated into open civil war.

In August Mobutu, alarmed by the increase in Soviet and Cuban military support for Neto, sent his Foreign Minister to Washington to warn the Americans and to ask for help. He arrived just as Nixon was resigning and Gerald Ford was being sworn in as President. Despite the confusion, he managed to spend an hour outlining the problem to Secretary of State Kissinger, who assured him that he would try to build up the anti-Soviet forces in Angola.

Kissinger encouraged Ford to provide support for Roberto's group, and in January 1975 the Forty Committee authorized three hundred thousand dollars for covert political action. But when CIA Director William Colby proposed a much larger program of covert military aid for Roberto and for a third group headed by Jonas Savimbi, who was also receiving support from South Africa, he touched off a major debate within the Administration. By mid-summer, the hardliners had prevailed. Nathaniel Davis, a respected Foreign Service officer who had just been sworn in as Assistant Secretary of State for African Affairs, resigned quietly after Kissinger overruled his recommendation that the United States seek a peaceful resolution of the crisis through diplomatic measures. Ironically, the hard-line approach to Angola triumphed at the same time that the Ford Administration was taking a classically liberal approach to the revolutionary situation in Portugal itself. Instead of supporting a comeback by the right-wing generals, the United States skillfully encouraged the emergence of a moderate, left-of-center government headed by the country's leading socialist, Mario Soares. This aberration in Kissinger's policy was due largely to the advice of the U.S. ambassador in Lisbon, Frank Carlucci, who had been instrumental in setting up a similar coalition government in Leopoldville in the summer of 1961.

As part of its campaign to defeat the pro-Soviet forces in Angola, the U.S. government encouraged Mobutu to commit his troops to battle on Roberto's side. As it turned out, they were no match for the highly disciplined Cuban troops supporting the MPLA, who were armed with sophisticated Soviet weapons. In January 1976 the Zairian soldiers returned home after an ignominious defeat. By this time the U.S. Congress had voted to cut off any further covert aid to Angola, and resistance to the MPLA quickly collapsed. Kissinger, Colby, and the other hardliners in the Ford Administration condemned the liberals in Congress for refusing to stand up to the Russians and described Angola as the first casualty of the post-Vietnam syndrome—the reluctance to use force to protect American interests. The liberals responded that in the long run U.S. interests in Africa would not be served by lining up with South Africa in opposition to the vast majority of African states.

Mobutu's Angolan intervention came back to haunt him in 1977 and again in 1978, when Katanga, now called Shaba Province, was invaded by a band of armed Katangan separatists (some of them Tshombe's original gendarmes, now middle-aged), who had been trained in Angola by the Cubans and the victorious MPLA. They did little harm in 1977, but in 1978 they occupied Kolwezi, the heart of Mobutu's mining empire, and killed hundreds of people—both the European technicians who ran the mines and the Africans who helped them. The Zairian forces were powerless to stop the invaders, and it took a combined force of Belgian and French paratroopers with U.S. logistical support to drive them out and restore order.

The Carter Administration, which had come into office with the intention of avoiding cold war politics in Africa and had played down the significance of the Cuban military presence in Angola, paid little attention to the 1977 incursion. It sharply reversed its policy, however, in the spring of 1978, primarily because of the massive Soviet-Cuban intervention in the border war between Somalia and Ethiopia. Administration officials reluctantly concluded that even if they did not want to pursue the cold war in Africa, the Russians seemed to be playing by different rules. They immediately charged that the Soviet Union and Cuba were directly responsible for the Shaba invasion; but, characteristically, they backed down when they found there was very little solid evidence to support these charges. Besides, they were somewhat embarrassed to find themselves so closely associated with Mobutu, who had never been their favorite African leader.

UN Ambassador Andrew Young and his allies at the State Department had started out in 1977 with some of the same crusading spirit that motivated Assistant Secretary "Soapy" Williams in 1961 when he went to Nairobi and declared that "Africa was for the Africans"—a statement which shocked the British colonial establishment in Kenya. He and the other New Frontiersmen went on to shock the traditionalists in the U.S. foreign policy establishment by reaching out to Nkrumah and Sékou Touré, whom the traditionalists regarded as the next thing to Communists. In a similar way Young and his allies set out to overturn the conservative Africa policy of the Nixon and Ford Administrations. They were determined to forge strong links with such states as Nigeria, Tanzania, and Zambia, which favored majority rule in Rhodesia and South Africa. There was no room in their plans for right-wing figures like Mobutu. While previous Administrations, both Democratic and Republican, had accepted him as a pro-Western ally and virtually ignored the fact that he was running a military dictatorship, the Carter Administration, with its new human rights policy, took an entirely different line. It began by deliberately "distancing itself" from the Zairian leader, on the assumption that his regime was so corrupt and so inefficient that it was only a matter of time before it fell and that a successor regime would be less likely to be violently anti-American if the United States made it clear that it had broken all ties with Mobutu.

This approach ran into considerable opposition from the State Department professionals, who found it naive and overly idealistic. They were well aware of the nature of Mobutu's regime, but they felt the Carter Administration was applying a double standard and condemning abuses in pro-Western Zaire that it was overlooking in the more radical African countries it had singled out for favorable attention. They insisted that Mobutu was no Idi Amin; repression in Zaire, they said, was not planned from the top; it was haphazard, the result of corruption and incompetence in the security forces. They also questioned the assumption that Mobutu's departure would automatically lead to an improvement in the lives of the Zairian people. They warned, on the contrary, that his removal would lead, at best, to a redistribution of the spoils within the same corrupt system or, at worst, to civil war, economic collapse, and the possibility of a left-wing government that might join forces with the Soviet Union.

The second Shaba invasion, and the subsequent events in Iran and Afghanistan, raised questions about Carter's original approach, so that even some of his advisers who had come into office with the intention of "cutting Mobutu loose" began to have second thoughts and to listen more attentively to the arguments of the State Department professionals. Like the liberals in the early days of the Kennedy Administration, they did not want to wake up one day and find themselves answering the question, "Who lost Zaire?" Zaire is huge; it is rich; and it is right in the middle of Africa, with nine other states on its borders. For nearly twenty years the United States had followed a policy of keeping the Russians out and keeping Zaire in the Western orbit. After 1978, the Carter Administration was no longer eager to tamper with that policy—but it was never comfortable with the idea of Mobutu as an ally.

"If we pull away we sort of leave things to fate," one official explained in 1979. "If we work with Mobutu and use our influence to change the system, well, you get your hands dirty in the process." Since the first alternative was now considered too risky, given renewed Soviet interest in Africa, the Carter Administration felt it had no choice but to follow the second alternative, distasteful as it might be. It would support Mobutu—reluctantly and at arm's length—while continuing to press for reforms, particularly in the area of human rights.

This approach was more acceptable to the State Department professionals, who conceded that Mobutu might well be strengthened by reforms that would win back a degree of popular support. Their only fear was that if he were pushed too far in the direction of drastic reforms, he might undermine his own position and, as one official put it, "end up cutting his own throat."

The new approach, however, did not satisfy Mobutu's critics, who felt the Carter Administration had betrayed its commitment to change and was instead propping up a corrupt dictatorship. The most influential of these critics, Congressman Stephen Solarz of New York, who served until 1981 as chairman of the African Affairs Subcommittee of the House Foreign Affairs Committee, did his best to block or sharply limit U.S. military aid to Zaire in an effort to "force Mobutu to reform." He acknowledged that the Carter Administration's requests were quite small—only one-fourth of the forty million dollars provided in 1976—but he argued that a cut would demonstrate American disapproval of Mobutu's methods and disassociate the United States from him in the eyes of the Zairian people.

Mobutu's reluctant defenders at the State Department replied that the United States had been so intimately associated with Mobutu ever since 1960, when the CIA helped him take power, that it was unrealistic to think that it could disassociate itself from him. Moreover, they argued that U.S. military aid had great psychological value for Mobutu and thus could be used as positive leverage to persuade him to make the necessary reforms. As Walter Cutler, the U.S. ambassador in Zaire from 1975 to 1979, remarked, "You can't have a carrot-and-stick policy if there isn't any carrot."

The Carter policy was successful, up to a point. Mobutu felt obliged to introduce a number of political reforms—which turned out to be more form than substance—and he permitted his opponents a degree of freedom to criticize the government and its abuses. Diplomats stationed in Kinshasa in 1979 and 1980 found the arbitrary arrests and torture of prisoners, which had been on the increase for several years, according to Amnesty International, were beginning to decline somewhat due to pressure from Washington. Educated Zairians were aware that the U.S. ambassador was authorized by his government to step in and speak on behalf of political prisoners.

There could be no better measure of Mobutu's sensitivity to the political atmosphere in Washington than the fact that in January 1981, thirteen members of Zaire's legislative council who were particularly vocal critics of the government were suddenly arrested and then sent into internal exile. While officials in the Reagan Administration profess to see no connection between this development and the inauguration of a conservative American President, and explain that they are continuing to press for human rights in Zaire through "quiet diplomacy," there is no doubt that the U.S. policy shift in 1981 was just as dramatic as the one in 1977, when Carter came into office determined to do something about an embarrassing ally.

President Ronald Reagan approaches the question of Mobutu from a totally different vantage point. He is not embarrassed about having Mobutu as an ally. On the contrary, he is relieved to find an experienced, dependable anti-Communist leader in charge of this key African country.

Unlike the Carter Administration, which regarded southern Africa as a test of America's moral commitment to the principle of majority rule, the Reagan Administration tends to see the region in stark geopolitical terms. It considers the strategic minerals of the "spine of Africa"—which runs from Shaba Province south to the mines around Johannesburg—vital to the economy and defense of the West. A few months before he became Secretary of State, Alexander Haig testified before the House Mines and Mining Subcommittee as president of United Technologies Corporation, the nation's third largest defense contractor and a major user of cobalt, which is a key component of the high-quality steel used in jet engines, artillery shells, and armor plate. Haig described the Soviet Union's efforts to extend its influence in Africa as the beginning round of a "resource war" aimed at the United States and its industrial allies.

In this strategic scenario, Zaire plays a central role. It is the world's largest exporter of industrial diamonds and supplies between 60 and 70 percent of the world's cobalt and 5 to 7 percent of its copper. The United States, which has no domestic source of cobalt, is Zaire's best customer, just as it was in the early 1960s.

Equally significant is Zaire's strategic location, just north of the portion of the continent that will pose the most stubborn problems for American diplomacy in the next few years. While the Reagan Administration is less interested in pressing for racial justice in southern Africa than in building an anti-Soviet partnership with the Pretoria government, it is still somewhat committed to working for peaceful change, if only to avoid a violent upheaval that would provide new opportunities for the Soviet Union to intervene. It would be exceedingly difficult, officials say, to make any progress toward getting the Cubans out of Angola, settling the Namibia question, keeping Zimbabwe at a safe distance from Soviet blandishments, and, eventually, moving toward racial harmony in South Africa, if Zaire were in turmoil. As a result, there is no desire to push Mobutu out, or to force him to make reforms that might jeopardize his position. "You won't hear the word 'reform' used by this Administration," one State Department official said. " 'Restructuring,' perhaps. Not 'reform.' "

In fact, the Reagan Administration is making a conscious effort to reverse the policy of its predecessor and to reward those Third World countries that support the United States at the United Nations and in other international forums. Administration officials tell a story about Mobutu, who found it hard to get through to the top Carter people on his last trip to the United States. At last, he remarked to a member of the American UN delegation who agreed to see him, "I have studied the policy of your government. You seem to favor Nigeria, Tanzania, and Zambia. I have decided that I will vote the way they do in the United Nations. Then perhaps you will pay attention to me too."

On his next visit to Washington, in December 1981, Mobutu had no complaints about the attention he was getting from the top Reagan people. While his trip was billed as a private "working visit," the Administration literally rolled out the red carpet for him. He not only met with Secretary of State Haig and Defense Secretary Caspar Weinberger, he was also received by the President at the White House. Haig praised his "wisdom" and "statesmanship." Reagan praised his contributions to peace, both in Chad, where he is contributing two thousands troops to the all-African peacekeeping force that is replacing the Libyans, and in Namibia. Reagan told him that the United States was ready to help Zaire achieve its development and security goals "while recognizing that those goals required some difficult decisions," particularly in the area of "improved management."

Officials of the Reagan Administration have no illusions about Mobutu. They know that he runs a one-party dictatorship; that he and his friends have grown fabulously rich—his personal fortune is estimated at more than three billion dollars—while his country has grown poorer and is now on the verge of bankruptcy. They realize that the gap between the wealthy elite and the general population grows wider each year; that real wages have fallen steadily since independence, with the exception of the period from 1968 to 1971, and now stand at 10 percent of the 1960 level; that thousands of children die each year of malnutrition in what should be one of the richest countries of Africa. They also realize that this deterioration is due primarily to the corruption which begins at the top of the society and extends to every corner of Zairian life. The army officers pocket the pay of their soldiers, and the soldiers, in turn, extort money from the people. Nothing can be accomplished without bribery. The corruption is so blatant and so all-pervasive that Mobutu himself has felt obliged to denounce it from time to time as "le mal zairois"; but no one takes his criticism seriously since it is generally understood that corruption is an essential part of his system of government. He keeps the peace by dipping in the government's coffers to pay off not only his supporters but potential rivals and troublemakers as well.

Administration officials acknowledge all this; but they take a fairly philosophical view of it. They insist that in this respect Zaire is not very different from the other countries in Africa, whether they are ruled by right-wing or left-wing regimes. The important distinction is that Mobutu is pro-American—and they intend to demonstrate their support for him across the board.

The most obvious change will be increased U.S. military aid for Zaire. The fiscal 1981 request was approximately the same as in previous years, but during Mobutu's visit Administration officials announced that the request for fiscal 1982 will be boosted 50 percent, to a total of fifteen million dollars. In addition the Administration is proposing the renewal of Economic Support Fund (ESF) aid, the most flexible sort of assistance, which can be used by the recipient government for anything—from grain to military trucks—with no strings attached. This sort of aid has not been supplied to Zaire since 1975.

Even more important than bilateral aid will be the attitude of the U.S. government in such institutions as the World Bank and the International Monetary Fund, where it will use its considerable influence to ensure favorable treatment of Zaire's debts. Assistant Secretary of State for African Affairs Chester Crocker sees an encouraging trend in Zaire toward more responsible behavior regarding the economy. A number of top officials in Kinshasa have apparently realized that the world financial community is exasperated and that if they want to avoid total bankruptcy they will have to tighten their belts, adopt austerity measures such as devaluation of the currency, and—most important—cut down on the massive corruption that siphons funds out of the central bank and the customs bureau in order to keep the patronage system functioning smoothly.

Mobutu's critics contend that even if he agreed to make these changes, it would be too late. They feel he has forfeited the support of his people through years of oppression and neglect. They point to the closing of the university in 1980 and the arrest of thousands of unemployed youths in the capital in 1981 as evidence of his increasingly shaky position.

Reagan Administration officials dismiss these warnings. They maintain that Mobutu is no more unpopular than the rulers of dozens of African states where the elites are corrupt and prosperous and the people are hungry. Their assessment is backed up to a certain extent by the professional diplomats, who note that Mobutu has been on the ropes before, especially in 1978, after the second Shaba invasion. They feel he is capable of flexibility if he believes it to be in his own interest. They point to the visit of Pope John Paul II in the spring of 1980 as evidence of his capacity to rally support from unexpected sources. After years of feuding with the Catholic Church, which is bitterly critical of his methods, Mobutu decided that his position would be strengthened by an apparent rapprochement, and he managed to arrange things so that the Pope made Kinshasa the first stop on his trip to Africa. The day before the Pope's arrival, Mobutu wed his common-law wife in an elaborate Catholic ceremony conducted in the French language by Zaire's Cardinal Joseph Malula.

The diplomats also point out that there is very little organized opposition to Mobutu, particularly from leftist forces. There is no serious Marxist sentiment outside the universities. The former Lumumbists have either come home and made their peace with Mobutu or are in exile in Europe, where they continue to plot ineffectually against the regime. Mme. Blouin, the radical firebrand of 1960, is writing her memoirs in Paris and helping the Sheraton chain open a hotel in Ouagadougou. The last time Gizenga was in the news was in 1975, when a leftist guerrilla band operating near Lake Tanganyika abducted four Stanford University students from a research station in Tanzania, and Gizenga, who had been living in Paris and Moscow, was involved in the negotiations for their release. If the exile groups had any real popular support within the country, they had ample opportunity to demonstrate it in 1978, during the second Shaba invasion, but there were no anti-government uprisings anywhere else in Zaire.

While the Reagan Administration is sanguine about Mobutu's future, it is obliged to consider the measures it would take if his position were suddenly placed in jeopardy. Until 1981, Mobutu could count on the French to step in and protect him from any sort of threat, from an invasion to a palace coup. Since the election of President François Mitterand, he no longer has that certainty. Even if the French military mission remains in Zaire, there is no guarantee that it would intervene to save Mobutu's job. The Belgians, always sensitive about charges of interference in Zaire, would be reluctant to act. That leaves the United States.

If there were another invasion of mineral-rich Shaba Province and the French refused to supply troops as they did in 1978, would the United States fill the gap? "I wouldn't rule it out," said one high-ranking official. After all, the United States has a major stake in a united Zaire. If it had not been for American pressure during the 1960–1963 period, Katanga might have been an independent country, and the repercussions would have been felt from one end of the continent to the other. Zaire is a "strategically important swing state" in a vital area, he explained. If it were to "unravel," it would be a serious blow to Western interests, and the United States could not be expected to sit back and "send Coca-Cola, as Carter did in 1977."

If Mobutu were threatened by a palace coup that had no connection with Shaba Province, the Reagan Administration would be less likely to intervene directly—even though it prefers Mobutu to any other pro-Western military man in sight. If, on the other hand, there were a leftist attempt to take over in Kinshasa, with evidence of outside involvement—for example, Cuban or Libyan—the Administration would seriously consider using military means to preserve the status quo. It has made no secret of its disapproval of Castro and his involvement in Africa or of its distaste for Quaddafi and his terrorist tactics. In fact, there have been reports that the CIA is actively involved in plotting the assassination of Quaddafi.

After two decades, American policy in the Third World has apparently come full circle. The Reagan Administration, which found the policy of its predecessor excessively moralistic and unworldly, seems determined to return to the "good old days" when American power was unquestioned and the CIA was riding high. It is encouraging the removal of many of the Congressional restrictions on the CIA's covert operations in foreign countries, restrictions that were instituted as a result of the investigation conducted in 1975 by the Senate Intelligence Committee, which revealed the assassination plots against Lumumba and other foreign leaders. At the same time, it is eagerly supporting right-wing political figures wherever they can be found. It is almost as if the clock has been turned back to 1960, when Ambassador Timberlake argued that, whatever Mobutu's faults, he was anti-Soviet and pro-American and thus should have Washington's full support.

But the United States is in a very different position today. To begin with, the buoyant optimism that characterized American policy in those days is gone—a casualty of the Vietnam War, Watergate, and the revelations of other abuses of power, such as the CIA assassination plots, which left many Americans without much confidence in their country's ability to use its influence in constructive ways. American self-confidence was further undermined by the downfall of such staunch anti-Communist bulwarks as Haile Selassie of Ethiopia and the Shah of Iran, who were overthrown, despite massive U.S. support, by domestic forces whose potential was not recognized in Washington, and replaced by fiercely anti-American regimes.

Finally, there has been a major shift in the military balance between the two superpowers. When Khrushchev plunged into the Congo to help Lumumba in the summer of 1960, he knew he was taking a risk, since he could not sustain a military challenge to the Western powers. He had no naval capacity to speak of, and he did not have the airlift capability to transport and supply forces thousands of miles from home. When Mobutu, backed by the United States, called his bluff in September, 1960, the Soviet leader was forced to back down.

Today, however, the military equation has been dramatically altered. The Russians, spurred by their humiliation in the Cuban missile crisis, have, at a minimum, caught up with the United States in terms of both conventional and strategic weapons. In 1975, they took advantage of this radical change in the balance of power to determine the outcome of another African civil war. They transported eleven thousand Cuban troops and two hundred million dollars' worth of arms and supplies to Angola by sea and air in the space of a few months, thereby ensuring the victory of the MPLA. This move happened to coincide with political developments in the United States which inhibited the American response; but even if Congress had not cut off the funds, the result might have been the same. U.S. officials felt that no matter how high they raised the stakes, the Russians would go higher.

In 1977–1978 the Russians intervened more massively in Ethiopia, sending planes, tanks, artillery, Soviet generals, and sixteen thousand Cuban troops to help repel a Somali invasion. The U.S. government essentially watched from the sidelines.

At the end of 1979 the Russians stunned the world with another impressive logistical feat: they airlifted more than twenty-five thousand troops into Afghanistan in three days. Within a few weeks their forces in and around Afghanistan numbered close to one hundred thousand. The United States blustered and threatened but was unable to do anything about it. It is now clear that the Soviet Union has the capability to deliver military aid and personnel nearly anywhere in the world, just as the United States could in the early 1960s.

As a result of this shift in the strategic balance, the United States can no longer call the shots in the Third World. Neither of the approaches which have characterized American policy in Zaire in the past can in itself be the basis of a successful policy in the complicated new world of the 1980s. It is too simplistic to deal with Zaire as the Carter Administration did, treating Mobutu as a pariah on moral grounds and ignoring the larger strategic picture in Africa. It is equally simplistic to focus so narrowly on Mobutu's anti-Soviet stance, as the Reagan Administration does, that it ignores the explosive internal discontent that may soon erupt—as it did in Iran and Ethiopia—and destroy the position that seven American Administrations have built in Zaire.

At this point, the Reagan Administration could accomplish more with a realistic, subtle approach that combines what is best in both policies. It could assure Mobutu that the United States appreciates his pro-Western stance as well as his accomplishment in keeping the country in one piece; at the same time, it could tell him plainly that it insists on significant reforms—not merely the economic "restructuring" that will satisfy the World Bank, but fundamental political reforms that will broaden the base of his government and provide a mechanism for the gradual, orderly transfer of power. It could suggest that he follow the example of Senegal's poet-statesman Leopold Senghor, who recently transferred power peacefully to a younger man he had trained for twenty years.

The officials who know Mobutu best feel that it is unrealistic to expect him to accept this sort of advice. Whenever they warn him that he may go the way of Haile Selassie or the Shah, he laughs and explains that he knows more about his own people than any U.S. official could possibly know; he has ruled them his own way for many years, and will continue to do so. He has shown no readiness to train a successor; on the contrary, he has indicated that he resents any suggestions along those lines. In 1977, the Foreign Minister, Ngunza Karl-i-bond, a talented diplomat who represents the best of the new generation, was mentioned in the Western press as a possible successor to Mobutu. He was in the middle of medical treatment in the Netherlands when an urgent summons came from Kinshasa: the President wanted him to return immediately to carry out a diplomatic mission of great importance. As soon as he got home, he was arrested and sent to jail on a trumped-up treason charge. The Shaba invasion had just taken place, and Ngunza came from a prominent Shaba family. Although he was sentenced to death, he was released in 1979, as a result of U.S. pressure. Despite his torture and mistreatment in prison, he agreed to return to his post as Foreign Minister, and then was named Prime Minister, with responsibility for negotiations with the International Monetary Fund. Early in 1981, however, he quit and went off to Europe for "personal reasons." Soon after his arrival he denounced Mobutu and his corrupt system and challenged him to restore democratic government in Zaire. In September 1981 he came to Washington and testified before the House Foreign Affairs Subcommittee on Africa. He noted that arrests and tortures were on the increase and that popular dissatisfaction was mounting and warned that Zaire was ripe for a third Shaba invasion or a revolt in the capital. He urged the United States to end its support for Mobutu, pointing out that his policies, rather than promoting stability, were endangering American interests. Ngunza's views excited more interest on Capitol Hill than in the White House. When Mobutu came to Washington a few months later, he refused to respond to Ngunza's charges; he merely referred to him as an ingrate and a traitor.

Mobutu is only fifty-one years old and, although he has begun to look weary and slightly paunchy, he feels strong enough to govern forever. He is no longer the indecisive young colonel who turned to the U.S. Embassy for advice in 1960. He has been Zaire's supreme ruler for sixteen years, and his ego has developed along with his fortune. He appears in public as a majestic tribal leader, wearing his leopard-skin cap and carrying his elaborately carved stick, the symbols of African chieftancy. His cult rivals that of Mao Tse-tung; he too has published his thoughts, but his book is green. He has thrown out two American ambassadors as well as two Soviet ones—and in 1975 he accused the CIA of trying to overturn his government. He is obviously not an easy man to deal with. Still, the Reagan Administration, which could not be suspected of trying to turn the country over to a group of leftists, ought to try to persuade him to change his course, if it is interested in keeping Zaire and its minerals in the Western orbit for the long run.

Instead of settling for "business as usual" and falling into the old pattern of pouring money into a deteriorating dictatorship, the Administration should try to use its influence in a more constructive way. It should make it clear to Mobutu that if he refuses to move toward a broadly based government, it will, reluctantly, begin to look elsewhere. It can start by broadening its contacts with the other political figures in Kinshasa, both to put pressure on Mobutu and to ease the way for cooperation with any regime that might follow him. Even if he weathers this rough period, his days in power are inevitably numbered. When he is replaced, by either a military or a civilian government, the Americans should not be taken by surprise. They should be part of the process from the beginning.

There is an influential U.S. Embassy in Kinshasa as well as an active American business community; they have a great many contacts with the old-line politicians as well as the young Western-educated elite. One of the most useful channels of communication is an American businessman named Maurice Tempelsman, who has worked closely with Mobutu for many years. Tempelsman, the son of a diamond and metals trader who established the family firm in West Africa more than thirty years ago, is the head of one of the world's largest mineral consortiums. He is described by diplomatic sources as a pure nineteenth-century entrepreneur with a taste for politics. He was a supporter of Kennedy in 1960 and of Nixon in 1972, and he has been an occasional escort of Jacqueline Kennedy Onassis, who reportedly enjoys his yacht and his collection of antiques. To complete the circle, his firm's Kinshasa representative is none other than Lawrence Devlin, the CIA station chief who helped Mobutu get his start in 1960 and has kept in close touch ever since. Tempelsman indignantly denies suggestions that he has any connections with the CIA; he explains that he hired Devlin simply because of his access to Mobutu—an explanation that makes a certain amount of sense in a country where connections are everything.

The Reagan Administration should be able to use contacts like these to open lines of communications to alternative centers of power. It should not lock itself into a position where it is afraid of offending Mobutu by dealing with his potential rivals. The United States can no longer take for granted Mobutu's political longevity; and, by the same token, Mobutu should no longer be able to take for granted America's unwavering support. Anti-Communism alone is not enough.

A determined U.S. government should not find it impossible, through active and imaginative diplomacy, to encourage a government in Zaire that would not only protect America's strategic and economic interests but would also be willing to relieve the misery of the Zairian people—a government that would be welcomed in Zaire and would enhance America's reputation throughout Africa.

Notes

State Department cables are cited in an abbreviated form in the footnotes that follow.

For example, Leopoldville 128, 7/17/60 refers to: U.S. Embassy in Leopoldville Cable No. 128 to the State Department, July 17, 1960.

Elisabethville 420, 1/20/61 refers to: U.S. Consulate in Elisabethville Cable No. 420 to the State Department, January 20, 1961.

USUN 1137, 10/26/60 refers to: U.S. Mission at the United Nations Cable No. 1137 to the State Department, October 26, 1960.

SD 192 to Brussels, 7/19/60 refers to: State Department Cable No. 192 to the U.S. Embassy in Brussels, July 19, 1960.

Cables designated TOSEC were sent from the State Department to the Secretary of State when he was traveling.

Cables designated SECTO were sent by the traveling Secretary of State to the Department.

Cables designated TOPOL were sent to the political officer dealing with NATO affairs in the U.S. Embassy in Paris.

Cables designated POLTO were sent by the political officer to the Department.

Depcirtel refers to a State Department Circular cable sent either to all U.S. Embassies or to those with a particular interest in the subject.

"Despatch" refers to a longer report sent by diplomatic pouch rather than by cable.

The following abbreviations also have been used:

> GAOR: *General Assembly Official Records*
> SCOR: *Security Council Official Records*
> NYT: *The New York Times*

United Nations documents are cited as follows:

S/4381 refers to a Security Council document;

A/4557 refers to a General Assembly document.

Preface

For more information about the manner in which the American public learned about the assassination attempts against foreign leaders, see Daniel Schorr, *Clearing the Air* (Boston: Houghton Mifflin 1977), pp. 137–152. Schorr, who had heard about President Ford's remarks to the editors of *The New York Times,* raised the question with CIA Director Colby. Colby denied that there had been any assassination attempts in the United States. The obvious conclusion, said Schorr, was that there *had* been attempts abroad. See also David Wise, *The American Police State* (New York: Random House, 1976) pp. 210–225.

For the results of the investigation conducted by the Senate Committee under the chairmanship of Senator Frank Church, see *Alleged Assassination Plots Involving Foreign Leaders,* An Interim Report of the Select Committee to Study Governmental Operations with respect to Intelligence Activities, United States Senate (Washington, D.C.: U.S. Government Printing Office), 1975. This report is referred to hereafter as *Senate Intelligence Committee Report.*

For more information about the CIA and the men who ran it during the period under study, see Ray S. Cline, *Secrets, Spies, and Scholars: Blueprint of the Essential CIA* (Washington: Acropolis Books Ltd., 1976); William E. Colby, *Honorable Men: My Life in the CIA* (New York: Simon and Schuster, 1978); Miles Copland, *Without Cloak or Dagger* (New York: Simon and Schuster, 1974); Allen Dulles, *The Craft of Intelligence* (New

York: Harper & Row, 1963); Victor Marchetti and John D. Marks, *The CIA and the Cult of Intelligence* (New York: Alfred A. Knopf, 1974); Leonard Mosley, *Dulles: A Biography of Eleanor, Allen, and John Foster Dulles and Their Family Network* (New York: The Dial Press/James Wade, 1978); Thomas Powers, *The Man Who Kept the Secrets: Richard Helms and the CIA* (New York: Alfred A. Knopf, 1979); and Vernon A. Walters, *Silent Missions,* (New York: Doubleday, 1978).

Chapter One

1. For the full text of Lumumba's speech, see J. Gerard-Libois and Benoit Verhaegen, *Congo 1960,* 2 vols. (Brussels: Centre de Recherche et d'Information Socio-Politique, 1961), 1: 323–25; King Baudouin's speech, 1:318–20; and President Kasavubu's speech, I: 320–22.

Lumumba's Information Minister, Anicet Kashamura, in his book, *De Lumumba aux colonels* (Paris: Buchet/Chastel, 1966), pp. 73–83, suggests that Lumumba was influenced by Guinean advisers, who urged him to "inflict a last-minute humiliation" on the King, as Guinean President Sékou Touré did with French President Charles de Gaulle in 1958.

2. "Liberation from Slavery," *Pravda,* 7/2/60.

3. Leopoldville 14, 7/6/60.

4. Ibid. For more detail, see Gerard-Libois and Verhaegen, *Congo 1960,* 1: 325–26; Catherine Hoskyns, *The Congo Since Independence* (London: Oxford University Press, 1965), p. 86; and Colin Legum, "Foreword" to Patrice Lumumba, *Congo, My Country* (New York: Praeger, 1962, 1966), p. xiv.

5. For the text of a protest by the soldiers published in one of the political party newspapers, see Gerard-Libois and Verhaegen, *Congo 1960,* 1: 353–54. It is translated into English by Helen Kitchen, "The Linchpin Gives Way: Revolt of the Force Publique," in the collection of articles from *Africa Report* which she edited, *Footnotes to the Congo Story* (New York: Walker, 1967), pp. 19–20; originally published in August 1960.

6. There was considerable controversy about the origins of the mutiny. The Soviet government charged that it was the result of a deliberate Belgian plot to reimpose colonial rule, while Premier Gaston Eyskens of Belgium implied that it was the result of a Communist conspiracy. See *NYT,* 7/15/60, for reaction in the Belgian Parliament along these lines. Missionaries in the Congo who agreed with this point of view cited the fact that the mutiny broke out simultaneously in many parts of the huge country as proof that it must have been planned. Brookings analyst Ernest Lefever took a more guarded view in *Crisis in the Congo: A United Nations Force in Action* (Washington: The Brookings Institution, 1965), p. 11; he wrote, "The mutiny was probably encouraged by Communist bloc agents who had infiltrated the country."

Most Western scholars, however, discount the conspiracy theory. See, for example, Hoskyns, *The Congo Since Independence,* pp. 87–104; and Colin Legum, *Congo Disaster* (Baltimore: Penguin Books, 1961), p. 117. The latter wrote, "The pattern of revolt was by no means consistent. It had no single head, no obvious goal. The only consistency was the widespread demand for the replacement of their Belgian officers." René Lemarchand, *Political Awakening in the Belgian Congo* (Berkeley: University of California Press, 1964), p. 222, cited as a contributing factor the "climate of chronic unrest in which the electoral campaign was conducted, and which made it necessary for the Belgian authorities to keep the Force Publique on constant duty to restore order in the more troubled parts of the Congo."

One of the most balanced and thorough documentary accounts of the mutiny and the Belgian response can be found in Gerard-Libois and Verhaegen, *Congo 1960,* 1: 371–

460; and 2: 469–517; they reconstructed the period of July 4–15 in great detail with the help of press reports, government documents, both Belgian and Congolese, and eyewitness accounts.

7. Kashamura, *De Lumumba aux colonels,* pp. 96–97.

8. See Gerard-Libois and Verhaegen, *Congo 1960,* 1: 375, 377, 405–7, for the texts of these decisions and related documents.

9. Leopoldville 31, 32, 33, 7/8/60; Paris 116, 118, 129, 7/8/60; Brussels 58, 7/9/60; *NYT,* 7/9/60.

10. Brussels 39, 7/6/60.

11. Brussels 43, 7/7/60.

12. Brussels 59, 7/9/60.

13. For the text of the agreement, see Gerard-Libois and Verhaegen, *Congo 1960,* 1: 446–47.

14. A number of Western scholars regarded the Belgian action at Matadi as particularly unfortunate and unnecessary. See, for example, Crawford Young, *Politics in the Congo: Decolonization and Independence* (Princeton: Princeton University Press, 1965), pp. 317–19; and Hoskyns, *The Congo Since Independence,* pp. 98–100. Legum, while sympathizing with the decision to protect Belgian civilians by sending Belgian paratroopers, wrote, in *Congo Disaster,* p. 110: "That the Belgian motives were misunderstood is not surprising." He added (p. 17) that the "mutiny was comparatively restricted up to the time the Belgian paratroopers arrived," and concluded that "there is not the least doubt that their intervention caused the mutiny to take the turn it did."

15. For the text of Katanga's declaration, see Gerard-Libois and Verhaegen, *Congo 1960,* 2: 718–19.

16. For the text of this demand, see ibid., 1: 450–51.

17. See Brian Urquhart, *Hammarskjold* (New York: Knopf, 1972), pp. 388–89, on the Secretary-General's reasoning about the length of Bunche's stay. *NYT,* 7/5/60, reported that he was planning to stay until mid-August.

18. Brussels 88, forwarded from Leopoldville, 7/10/60.

19. Brussels 90, forwarded from Leopoldville, 7/10/60.

20. Leopoldville 54, 7/12/60.

21. Leopoldville 50, 7/12/60.

22. Leopoldville 58, 7/12/60.

23. Leopoldville 59, 7/12/60.

24. *NYT,* 7/13/60.

25. For the text of this telegram, see SCOR, Fifteenth Year, Supplement for July, August, and September 1960: S/4382.

26. For a stimulating discussion of the shifts in power around Premier Khrushchev during this key month of July 1960, see Michel Tatu, *Power in the Kremlin from Khrushchev to Kosygin* (New York: Viking, 1970), pp. 110–14.

27. "Stormy Events in Congo," *Izvestia,* 7/10/60.

28. O. Orestov, "Can't Frighten Congolese People," *Pravda,* 7/12/60. For more detail, see Orestov and L. Volodin, *Trudnye Dni Kongo* [*Hard Days for the Congo*] (Moscow: Gospolitizdat, 1961), pp. 68–76.

29. Brussels 84, forwarded from Leopoldville, 7/10/60.

30. M. Rakhmatov, *Afrika idet k svobode* [*Africa Goes Toward Freedom*] (Moscow: Gospolitizdat, 1961), pp. 69–73. On another occasion Rakhmatov had to rescue two members of the Soviet delegation arrested by Congolese soldiers who had mistaken them for Belgian paratroopers. He seemed relieved when his delegation was able to leave the Congo on July 9, 1960.

31. *Pravda,* 7/13/60.

32. Urquhart, *Hammarskjold,* p. 396.

33. S/4381; letter of the Secretary-General to the President of the Security Council, July 13, 1961. This was the first use of Article 99 of the UN Charter, which permits the Secretary-General to bring an urgent problem before the Security Council even before the issue is raised by a member state. It was not used again until 1979, when American diplomats at the U.S. embassy in Teheran were taken hostage by the Khomeini regime.

34. S/4383.

35. According to U.S. Ambassador Henry Cabot Lodge, as reported in USUN 73, 7/14/60.

36. For more detail, see the analysis of Helmut Sonnenfeldt, "The Soviet Union and China: Where They Stood in 1960," in Kitchen, *Footnotes to the Congo Story*, pp. 28–29.

37. S/4386.

38. SCOR, 873rd Meeting, July 13–14, 1960.

39. Accra 49, 7/13/60. See also the account of Kwame Nkrumah, *Challenge of the Congo* (New York: International Publishers, 1967), pp. 20–21.

40. Gerard-Libois and Verhaegen, *Congo 1960,* 2: 491–93.

41. Ibid.: 554.

42. *Pravda,* 7/16/60. See also *NYT,* 7/16/60.

43. *Pravda,* 7/16/60.

44. Paris POLTO 120, 7/15/60.

45. Memorandum of Conversation between Secretary of State Christian Herter and Ambassador Louis Scheyven of Belgium, July 15, 1960.

Chapter Two

1. For an interesting analysis of the Soviet attitude toward the United Nations during this period, see Alexander Dallin, *The Soviet Union at the United Nations* (New York: Praeger, 1962), especially pp. 115–213, on "Khrushchev and the United Nations."

Useful Soviet works are S. A. Krasil'shchikova, *OON i natsional'no-osvoboditel'noe dvizhenie* [*The UN and the National Liberation Movement*] (Moscow: Izdatel'stvo "Mezhdunarodnye Otnosheniia," 1964), particularly pp. 94–119 on the Congo; V. Ushakov, *Sovetskii Soiuz i OON* [*The Soviet Union and the UN*], (Moscow: Gospolitizdat, 1962); and G. I. Tunkin, "The United Nations Organization: 1945–1965," *Sovetskoe Gosudarstvo i Pravo,* No. 10 (1965) pp. 58–68. It is significant that *Pravda's* first account of the Security Council debate (K. Ivanov, "Colonialists—Get out of Congo," *Pravda,* 7/15/60) reported the adoption of a resolution calling for the withdrawal of Belgian troops, but made no reference whatsoever to the creation of a UN force.

2. USUN 121, 7/18/60.

3. Urquhart, *Hammarskjold,* p. 402.

4. SD 33 to USUN, 7/13/60.

5. Hammarskjold's official reasoning was spelled out in detail in his first report on the implementation of the Security Council resolution of July 14 (S/4387); see S/4389 for the original report, submitted on July 18, 1960, and Addenda 2, 3, 4, and 6, for later information on the composition and deployment of the UN troops through July 31, 1960.

6. Soviet Deputy Foreign Minister Vassily Kuznetsov raised the issue of the Guinean troops at the Security Council meeting on July 20–21 (SCOR, 877th Meeting).

On July 21, *Izvestia* implied that Hammarskjold did not want Guinean troops in the force because he found them too independent; the Soviet newspaper stressed that they were led by their own African commanding officer, and this may have been a critical reference to the Ghanaian contingent, which was led by a British officer, General Henry T. Alexander. (Observer, "Dangerous Game over Congo," *Izvestia,* 7/21/60).

7. The Secretary-General's first report (S/4389) noted that Guinea's offer of troops

was one of the first to be accepted; and Urquhart, *Hammarskjold,* p. 399, maintained that the Secretary-General from the very beginning "had in mind Guinea, Mali, Morocco, and Tunisia, all French-speaking countries, as the first governments to provide troops," in addition to Ghana.

8. USUN 121, 7/18/60. Lodge added that while Hammarskjold's message to Sékou Touré explaining that "he did not need Guinean troops since he already had as many as he could handle now" was "still being processed," he received a "formal Guinean offer of 2 battalions. However, he ordered his original reply to be sent as if formal offer had not come to his attention in time."

9. For more detail on Hammarskjold's thinking on this issue, see Joseph Kraft, "The Untold Story of the UN's Congo Army," *Harper's Magazine,* November 1960, pp. 75–84.

As of July 26, UN official figures (S/4389/Add. 4) reported 8,396 UN troops: 1,160 from Ethiopia, 2,340 from Ghana, 741 from Guinea, 1,220 from Morocco, 225 from Liberia, 2,087 from Tunisia, and 623 from Sweden.

Pravda reported on July 27 a total of 7,000 troops from Ghana, Guinea, Tunisia, Morocco, Ethiopia, Liberia, Sweden, and other countries. (Ivanov, "Savages Live in West").

10. "Withdraw American Military Group from Congo," *Pravda,* 7/20/60. See also UN document S/4398.

11. *NYT,* 7/20/60.

12. Ibid.

13. S/4400, a letter from Ambassador Lodge to the Secretary-General, July 20, 1960, described the scope of the effort.

14. *NYT,* 7/29/60. A few British, Egyptian, and Ethiopian planes were involved in the airlift as well.

15. "USSR Help to Republic of Congo," *Pravda,* 7/20/60. There were a few exceptions: for example, *Pravda* noted on July 21 that the Secretary-General had thanked Soviet delegate Sobolev for his country's aid to the Congo; and on July 23, *Pravda* noted that the Secretary-General had asked the Soviet Union to supply trucks for the use of the UN force.

16. K. Nepomnyashchii, "Thanks to Soviet Fliers," *Pravda,* 7/31/60. His articles included: "Help to People of Congo," *Pravda,* 7/21/60; "Africa Will Always be Grateful to Soviet Union," *Pravda,* 7/23/60; "Support of Moscow Gives Us Courage," *Pravda,* 7/25/60; and an article written with Orestov, "We Believe in Strength of Congolese People," *Pravda,* 7/26/60.

17. For a more detailed analysis, see the article by Seymour Topping in *NYT,* 7/22/60.

18. In its first statement on the Congo situation, on July 13, the Soviet government charged that Timberlake was "interfering in the Congo's internal affairs" and "using the presence of Bunche to work out plans to broaden the intervention of the Western powers in the Congo under the United Nations flag." *Pravda,* 7/14/60.

19. *Pravda* linked him with Bunche and complained that they were treating the Belgian soldiers as members of the UN force. Ivanov, "Savages Live in West," *Pravda,* 7/27/60.

20. *Izvestia* described von Horn as a "conscientious" soldier who "stuck to his guns" by insisting that the force move into Katanga despite Belgian opposition. K. Smirnov, "Insolent Refusal," *Izvestia,* 7/27/60.

21. Smirnov, "Poison Fruit," *Izvestia,* 11/15/60.

22. Carl von Horn, *Soldiering for Peace* (New York: McKay, 1966), pp. 141–42.

23. *NYT,* 7/29/60.

24. Hammarskjold pointed out at the Security Council meeting on August 8, 1960 (SCOR, 885th Meeting) that his military adviser for the Congo was Indian General Indar Jit Rikhye; the Ghanaian contingent in Leopoldville was led by Brigadier Joe Michel; the

Ethiopian contingent in Stanleyville by Brigadier General Iyassu Mengesha; and the Moroccans by General Ben Hammou Kettani. In his view this guaranteed a sufficient Afro-Asian role.

25. Conor Cruise O'Brien, *To Katanga and Back: A UN Case History* (New York: Universal Library, Grosset Dunlap, 1966), p. 57. O'Brien did not find Soviet resentment of this arrangement particularly "incomprehensible or irrational"; he found that African and Asian advisers agreed with the American ones that Communism must be kept out of Africa, and he pointed out that no one was representing Soviet interests in the Secretary-General's inner councils.

On the other hand, UN officials recalled that one Soviet citizen filled a fairly important post in the Congo operation for a time but was under so much pressure from his home government that he asked to be recalled to UN headquarters in New York; he found it impossible to serve as an impartial international civil servant in the highly charged atmosphere of Leopoldville.

26. Von Horn, *Soldiering for Peace*, p. 153. Urquhart, *Hammarskjold*, p. 402, in his list of the duties of the UN force, was less explicit about this task. He wrote, "To put it briefly, the UN operation was to fill a vacuum that would probably otherwise be filled by the conflicting forces and influences of East and West, and by a variety of racial, economic, ideological, political, and tribal conflicts as well."

27. Von Horn, *Soldiering for Peace*, pp. 168–69, p. 214. Despite his distrust of the Guinean contingent, von Horn was not anti-African, as the Soviet press claimed. He respected efficiency, and when he found it in the officers under his command—Ghanaian, Ethiopian, Moroccan, Tunisian, or Sudanese—he was full of praise for them and the men they led. Still, he credited their European training for most of their effectiveness, unpopular though his views were among UN diplomats. "Who," he asked," "in the hothouse atmosphere of New York, was going to be brave enough to admit the truth—that our success in saving thousands of lives had rested exclusively on Western military discipline, training, technique, and know-how or on those same qualities the new national units had inherited from the old colonial armies?" (p. 238).

28. Ibid., p. 186. According to American and Belgian diplomats stationed in the Congo, the Czech consulate, which had been in operation since 1948, was the major center of Communist bloc intelligence in the area; a highly experienced Czech agent picked up information which he forwarded to his Soviet colleagues and was the conduit for distributing Soviet bloc funds to Congolese political figures.

29. Henry T. Alexander, *African Tightrope: My Two Years as Nkrumah's Chief of Staff* (New York: Praeger, 1965), p. 38.

30. Leopoldville 106, 7/15/60.

31. Von Horn, *Soldiering for Peace*, pp. 158–59.

32. Leopoldville 133, 139, and 141, 7/17/60.

33. SD 76 to USUN 7/18/60; and USUN 124, 7/18/60.

34. State Department Memorandum of Conversation between the Secretary of State, Camille Gutt, Minister of State of Belgium, and Ambassador Louis Scheyven, July 19, 1960. See also State Department Memorandum from Assistant Secretary Francis O. Wilcox to the Secretary of State, July 19, 1960; and SD 192 to Brussels, 7/19/60.

35. Brussels 273, 7/20/60; SD 92 to USUN, 7/20/60.

See also von Horn, *Soldiering for Peace*, pp. 156–57, 167, for his dealings with General Gheysen, whom he regarded as "capable" and "forceful."

36. SD 182 to Brussels, 7/18/60.

37. SD 122 to Leopoldville; SD 147 to Brussels, 7/16/60.

38. Leopoldville 128, 7/17/60.

39. SD 25 to Lisbon, 7/16/60.

40. Leopoldville 133, 7/17/60.

41. Brussels 258, 7/19/60.

42. USUN 124, 7/18/60.

43. SD 76 to USUN, 7/18/60.

44. Memorandum from James K. Penfield of the Bureau of African Affairs to the Secretary of State, July 20, 1960.

45. *Senate Intelligence Committee Report*, p. 57.

46. For the text of this appeal, see Gerard-Libois and Verhaegen, *Congo 1960*, 2: 610–11.

47. Leopoldville 178, 7/20/60.

48. SCOR, 877th Meeting, July 20–21, 1960.

49. *NYT*, 7/22/60.

50. S/4405.

51. SCOR, 879th Meeting, July 21–22, 1960.

52. Orestov, "Struggle in Congo Continues," *Pravda*, 8/31/60.

53. Brussels 123, 7/12/60. See also Brussels 243, 7/18/60. The recommendation of the U.S. consul in Elisabethville is reported in the *Analytical Chronology of the Congo Crisis*, prepared on January 25, 1961, by the Bureau of African Affairs of the State Department as a briefing paper for top officials of the new Administration, p. 10; for Ambassador Timberlake's views, see Leopoldville 125 and 130, 7/17/60.

54. Memorandum of Conversation between the Secretary of State and Ambassador Scheyven, July 15, 1960; see also SD 137 to Brussels, 7/15/60.

55. SD 17 to Elisabethville, 7/15/60.

56. Brussels 207, 7/16/60.

57. SD 192 to Brussels, 7/19/60.

58. USUN 121, 7/18/60.

59. SCOR, 877th Meeting, July 20–21, 1960.

60. S/4405.

61. *NYT*, 7/23/60.

62. *NYT*, 7/25/60.

63. Ibid.

64. Urquhart, *Hammarskjold*, p. 407.

65. *NYT*, 7/26/60.

66. *Pravda* reported on July 27, 1960, that Kuznetsov and Lumumba had met; ("Establish Peace and Quiet in Congo").

67. *Senate Intelligence Committee Report*, p. 53.

68. Leopoldville 259, 7/26/60.

69. Memorandum of Conversation between the Secretary of State and Prime Minister Lumumba, July 27, 1960.

70. London 411, 7/22/60.

71. Memorandum of Conversation between C. Vaughn Ferguson of the Bureau of African Affairs and Jean de Bassompierre, Counselor of the Belgian Embassy, July 28, 1960.

72. *Senate Intelligence Committee Report*, p. 53.

73. *NYT*, 7/30/60.

74. "Position of USSR Meets Wishes of Congolese People," *Pravda*, 7/30/60. An interesting sidelight was thrown on this interview by Owen Roberts, the State Department's escort officer for Lumumba, who reported that the Soviet correspondent handed Lumumba "three written questions. Lumumba withdrew and wrote out answers. The whole exchange lasted less than five minutes. Lumumba was very rushed, very pressed for time and there was little conversational exchange. . . . Considering the circumstances

it seems that TASS may have elaborated on the material received." Roberts's report was included in a memorandum from James K. Penfield of the Bureau of African Affairs to the Acting Secretary of State on August 1, 1960.

75. *NYT,* 7/30,31/60; and SD 296 to Brussels, 7/29/60.

76. SD 317 to Brussels, 8/1/60.

77. *Analytical Chronology,* pp. 29–30; see also *NYT,* 8/2/60.

78. *Analytical Chronology,* p. 32.

79. *Senate Intelligence Committee Report,* pp. 53–54.

80. Leopoldville 279, 7/28/60; USUN 270, 7/30/60.

81. Von Horn, *Soldiering for Peace,* p. 173.

82. Ibid., p. 180.

83. *NYT,* 7/29/60.

84. *NYT,* 7/31 and 8/1/60. See also Urquhart, *Hammarskjold,* pp. 411–12; and Leopoldville 295 and 296, 7/31/60, describe the dinner.

85. Ottawa 96, 8/5/60, reported that the "Canadians found Lumumba articulate and clever in speeches and press conferences, highly reticent in interviews with Government officials, arrogant and autocratic in treatment of associates as well as Canadian cabinet officers and officials, and apparently quite unscrupulous."

86. *NYT,* 7/31/60.

87. USUN 271, 8/1/60.

88. S/4414.

89. USUN 271, 8/1/60.

90. *NYT,* 8/2/60.

91. "Statement of Soviet Government," *Pravda,* 8/1/60. S/4416.

92. USUN 270, 7/30/60; Cordier said this was the only way "to control what goes into Congo and what is done there."

93. USUN 271 and 274, 8/1/60.

94. USUN 280, 8/1/60.

95. SD 113 to Accra, 8/1/60.

96. USUN 271 and 274, 8/1/60.

97. SD 317 to Brussels, 8/1/60.

98. *NYT,* 8/3/60. See also S/4417, the second report of the Secretary-General on the implementation of the two Security Council resolutions; Hammarskjold told the Congolese cabinet on August 2, "The United Nations has surely done the impossible, and its efforts have been crowned with success."

99. S/4417 includes the texts of the Secretary-General's communications with Tshombe and his instructions to Bunche, as well as Bunche's conclusions after his trip. See also Urquhart, *Hammarskjold,* pp. 417–20.

100. Leopoldville 343, 8/5/60.

101. I. Aleksandrov, "Situation in the Congo," *Pravda,* 8/6/60. See also "Statement of Soviet Government," *Pravda,* 8/6/60; S/4418; and Orestov, "Failure of Hammarskjold's Mission," *Pravda,* 8/7/60.

102. USUN 326, 8/5/60.

103. S/4424.

104. SCOR, 885th Meeting, August 8, 1960.

105. SCOR, 886th Meeting, August 8–9, 1960.

Chapter Three

1. Leopoldville 357 and 359, 8/8/60; Brussels Despatch 139, 8/11/60.

2. For the texts of the measures concerning the imposition of martial law, control of

the press, limitations on meetings, and the like, see Gerard-Libois and Verhaegen, *Congo 1960*, 2: 699–703. See also *NYT*, 8/10,12/60.

3. Lumumba sent a cable of gratitude to the Security Council, in which he stated: "My concern is to see that peace and order are restored immediately throughout the entire country. I am awaiting the arrival of the Secretary-General to determine together with him all the measures to be taken to implement the decisions of the Security Council." See S/4417/Add. 3, Ann. Urquhart, *Hammarskjold*, pp. 424–25, pointed out that Hammarskjold left New York before receiving Lumumba's message.

4. USUN 377, 8/10/60. Lodge noted, in USUN 357, 8/9/60, that when he met with the Congolese delegation during the dinner recess on August 8, he found them quite conciliatory.

5. For the exchange of telegrams between Hammarskjold and Tshombe on August 10, see S/4417/Add. 4. For Hammarskjold's interpretation of paragraph 4 of the August 9 Security Council resolution, issued on August 12, see S/4417/Add. 6.

6. S/4417/Add. 7 includes Hammarskjold's letter to Bomboko of August 14 as well as the three letters from Lumumba to Hammarskjold and three replies from Hammarskjold, all sent on August 14 and 15, 1960.

7. Ibid. For a variety of views on this dispute, see Urquhart, *Hammarskjold*, pp. 424–28, for the account of Hammarskjold's colleague and biographer; Serge Michel, *Uhuru Lumumba* (Paris: René Julliard, 1962), pp. 113–16, for the account of Lumumba's press attache; Nkrumah, *Challenge of the Congo*, pp. 23–27, for the reaction of the Ghanaian President; Pierre Davister, *Katanga, Enjeu du Monde* (Brussels: Editions Europe-Afrique, 1960), pp. 146–56, for the view of a journalist sympathetic to Tshombe's cause; Hoskyns, *The Congo Since Independence*, pp. 158–80, for the view of a scholar who believed Hammarskjold did not grasp the extent of Belgian military involvement in the Katanga secession at the time; and Legum, *Congo Disaster*, pp. 125–39, for the view of a journalist who believed that Hammarskjold should have taken representatives of the central government to Elisabethville with him.

8. S/4417/Add. 1/Rev. 1 provides the exchange of telegrams on this subject between Sékou Touré and Hammarskjold, August 6 and 7, 1960.

9. For the text of this demand, see Gerard-Libois and Verhaegen, *Congo 1960*, 2: 619.

10. Michel, *Uhuru Lumumba*, pp. 110–11.

11. Leopoldville Despatch 37, 9/2/60. See also Conakry 67, 8/8/60; the U.S. ambassador noted that the Guinean ambassador to Washington, Diallo Telli, would be going to Leopoldville with Lumumba and remarked, "I cannot envisage him or any other Guinean playing a helpful role in Congo from US viewpoint."

12. Leopoldville 296, 7/31/60; see also Geneva 46, 8/18/60.

13. S/4417/Add. 5.

14. SD 371 to Leopoldville, 8/4/60.

15. SD Circular 238, 8/10/60.

16. USUN 415, 8/15/60.

17. SD 228 to USUN, 8/16/60.

18. USUN 428, 8/16/60.

19. Leopoldville 359, 8/8/60.

20. Leopoldville 41, 7/11/60.

21. Leopoldville 432, 8/17/60.

22. Leopoldville 433, 8/17/60.

23. Leopoldville 438, 8/17/60.

24. See S/4417/Add. 8 for the Secretary-General's report on this incident, which includes his protest to the Congolese government; it also includes protests by Hammarskjold and Bunche about an incident the previous day when the Congolese guards at

Lumumba's residence arrested and threatened to kill two UN officials who were trying to deliver a letter from Bunche to the Prime Minister. See also *NYT,* 8/20/60.

25. *Senate Intelligence Committee Report,* p. 14; the pseudonym "Victor Hedgman" was used in the report to refer to Devlin.

26. Ibid., p. 15.

27. Ibid., p. 58.

28. Ibid., pp. 55–56.

29. Ibid., p. 59.

30. Ibid., pp. 58–59. The reprrt (pp. 59–60) listed four possible explanations:

1. There was an explicit order from the President for Lumumba's assassination which was omitted from the record;
2. There was an implicit order to this effect to Dulles;
3. There was no such order at all and Dulles misunderstood;
4. The president authorized "contingency planning," that is, the CIA was expected to explore the feasibility of action and a decision would be made later on.

For an interesting discussion of the role of the President in authorizing assassination attempts, see Thomas Powers, *The Man Who Kept the Secrets: Richard Helms and the CIA,* esp. pp. 119–58.

31. *Senate Intelligence Committee Report,* p. 15.

32. Leopoldville 848, 9/29/60. The text of Lumumba's letter to Khrushchev was released to the press along with correspondence between Lumumba and Nkrumah by Mario Cardoso, Commissioner general for education in the government which followed Lumumba's; the documents were allegedly found in a briefcase belonging to Lumumba. The Nkrumah letters were acknowledged by Nkrumah to be genuine; it seems reasonable to suppose that the letter to Khrushchev was as well. It seems characteristic of Lumumba that while he was writing his angry letters to the Secretary-General, he also dashed off a specific request to the only country which had supported him consistently on the Katanga issue.

33. *NYT,* 8/20/60.

34. *Pravda,* 8/19/60.

35. *NYT,* 8/18/60.

36. Leopoldville 445, 8/18/60.

37. See "USSR Help to Republic of Congo," *Pravda,* 7/20/60; the articles by Nepomnyashchii, the *Pravda* correspondent who accompanied the aid to Leopoldville cited above, Chap. 2, fn. 16; a TASS report, "Soviet Autotransport for UN Force in Congo," 7/23/60; a TASS report from Odessa, "Course—to Congolese Port of Matadi," 8/6/60; and photographs on 8/7/60.

38. "Statement of Soviet Government," *Pravda,* 8/1/60.

39. Nepomnyashchii, "New Maneuvers, Old Aims," *Pravda,* 7/24/60.

40. USUN 434, 8/17/60.

41. Ibid.

42. "Statement of Soviet Government on Question of Situation in Congo Republic," *Pravda,* 8/21/60. S/4450.

43. SCOR, 887th Meeting, August 21, 1960.

44. SCOR, 888th Meeting, August 21, 1960.

45. Ibid.

46. USUN 456, 8/19/60.

47. *NYT,* 8/23/60.

48. Ibid.

49. *NYT,* 8/23,24/60. For the texts of Lumumba's accusations against his political opponents, the Catholic Church, Lovanium University, and so forth, see Gerard-Libois and Verhaegen, *Congo 1960,* 2: 690–97.

50. Leopoldville 496, 8/24/60.

51. Brussels 498, 8/19/60.

52. Leopoldville 455, 8/19/60.

53. *Senate Intelligence Committee Report*, p. 15.

54. *NYT*, 8/30/60; see also Urquhart, *Hammarskjold*, p. 435.

55. USUN 507, 8/25/60.

56. *NYT*, 8/25/60.

57. *NYT*, 8/24/60.

58. "Thanks for Disinterested Help," *Pravda*, 8/26/60.

59. USUN 507, 8/25/60.

60. Athens 469, 8/25/60.

61. *Senate Intelligence Committee Report*, p. 60.

62. Ibid. See also pp. 12–13 for a discussion of "plausible deniability."

63. Ibid., pp. 60–61.

64. Ibid., p. 61. According to Dillon, the meeting did not give the CIA the authority to assassinate Lumumba, but it certainly gave the Agency the "authority to plan." It would then check back "at least with the senior people in the State Department or the Defense Department" before proceeding, he explained; there would, of course, be no record of this.

65. Ibid., p. 15.

66. Ibid., p. 16. Bissell described Dulles's August 26 cable as a circumlocutious means of indicating that the President wanted Lumumba killed. Tweedy, Devlin's immediate superior, described the cable as the "most authoritative statement" on the "policy consensus" in Washington about the need for the removal of Lumumba by any means, including assassination.

67. Ibid., p. 20.

68. Ibid., p. 21. The pseudonym "Joseph Scheider" was used in the report to refer to Gottlieb.

69. SD 283 to USUN, 8/27/60.

70. USUN 524, 8/27/60.

71. SD Circular 326, 8/31/60.

72. USUN 566, 9/1/60.

73. SD 316 to USUN 9/3/60.

74. *NYT*, 8/26/60.

75. Orestov, "Ties Broadening between USSR and Congo," *Pravda*, 8/28/60.

76. *NYT*, 8/28/60.

77. Ibid.

78. *NYT*, 8/28, 29, 30/60; von Horn, *Soldiering for Peace*, p. 204.

79. Leopoldville 553, 8/30/60.

80. Leopoldville 545, 8/29/60.

81. USUN 526, 8/27/60.

82. USUN 517, 8/26/60.

83. *NYT*, 8/31/60; for a critical view of Lumumba by Ghana's leading Congo expert, see Alex Quaison-Sackey, *Africa Unbound: Reflections of an African Statesman* (New York: Praeger, 1963), pp. 86–87.

84. *NYT*, 9/1/60.

85. For the text of Khrushchev's message to the conference, see "Sympathy of Soviet People on Side of African Peoples," *Pravda*, 8/26/60.

86. USUN 560 and 566, 9/1/60.

87. USUN 548, 9/1/60; for detail on the meeting between high-ranking Pentagon officials and State Department officials on August 31, see *Analytical Chronology*, p. 30.

88. *NYT*, 8/28, 29 and 9/3, 4/60.

89. *NYT,* 9/4/60.

90. *NYT,* 9/6/60.

91. "Situation in Congo," *Pravda,* 9/28/60; "Arrival of Lumumba in Stanleyville," *Pravda,* 8/29/60; "Situation in Congo," *Pravda,* 8/30/60; Orestov, "Struggle in Congo Continues," *Pravda,* 8/31/60.

Chapter Four

1. For the text of Kasavubu's announcement, see Gerard-Libois and Verhaegen, *Congo 1960,* 2: 818–19.

2. Brussels Despatch 287, 9/23/60.

3. For the text of Lumumba's statement, see Gerard-Libois and Verhaegen, *Congo 1960,* 2: 820.

4. Ibid., 820–21.

5. Ibid., 823–24.

6. By September 5, the generally accepted figure for Soviet transport planes in the Congo was fifteen; see, for example, Urquhart, *Hammarskjold,* p. 445; and Leopoldville 623, 9/6/60. Newspaper reports varied. On September 3 and 4, *The New York Times* referred to fifteen Ilyushin-14 planes arriving in Stanleyville; on September 4, in another article, there were "at least ten"; on September 6, there were ten; on September 8, there were fifteen again. Some of the confusion may have arisen from the fact that in addition to the ten Ilyushin-14's reported by the United Nations (see above Chap. 3, fn. 72), there were the larger transport planes, the Ilyushin-18's, which had been used to bring food and Ghanaian troops to the Congo. In addition, the Russians had given Lumumba his own plane, with a Soviet crew. On September 18, after the Russians and Czechs were expelled, *The New York Times* reported that seventeen Soviet planes and two Czech planes which had been loaned to Lumumba were leaving the Congo.

7. *NYT,* 9/11/60.

8. According to Urquhart, *Hammarskjold,* p. 441, the Secretary-General first told Cordier that "even hypothetical discussion of later possibilities and our action in situation which may arise would place us in a most exposed position." He then added, "If you have to go ahead . . . time may be more important than our comments. . . . At any time you may face the situation of complete disintegration of authority . . . which in my view would entitle you to great freedom of action in protection of law and order." Later the same day he was more precise: "Prior to any change in political situation your line to Kasavubu is only possible one: We maintain law and order under UN rules, not being a tool for anyone."

9. Ibid., p. 440.

10. Brussels Despatch 287, 9/23/60. See also the versions of Urquhart, *Hammarskjold,* p. 442, and Rajeshwar Dayal, *Mission for Hammarskjold: The Congo Crisis* (Princeton, N.J.: Princeton University Press, 1976), pp. 32–33.

11. Von Horn, *Soldiering for Peace,* pp. 208–10, maintained that "never for a moment had there been any political bias" in Cordier's response to the crisis.

12. Dayal, *Mission for Hammarskjold,* pp. 31–32. Although he arrived on September 5, as the crisis began, he did not take over from Cordier until September 8.

13. Interview with the author, 1971. Cordier was clearly influenced as well by his assessment of Lumumba, whom he described as "volatile" and "aggressive," the kind of politician who divided people rather than united them, and whose only notion of how to create unity in the Congo was by violent means. See S/4531, Dayal's first progress report to the Secretary-General, for an official explanation of Cordier's reasoning.

14. USUN 586, 9/5/60.

15. Urquhart, *Hammarskjold,* p. 447.

16. For the text of Lumumba's speech in the Assembly and a summary of the debate in the Senate, see Gerard-Libois and Verhaegen, *Congo 1960,* 2: 828–50. See also the detailed account in Leopoldville Despatch 51, 9/16/60.

17. *NYT,* 9/9/60. See S/4486, a telegram sent to the United Nations by Lumumba on September 8, in which he charged that the crisis in the Congo was the "result of the UN authorities' interference in the Congo's domestic problems."

18. For insight into Khrushchev's plans, see *Khrushchev Remembers: The Last Testament,* trans. and ed. Strobe Talbott (Boston: Little, Brown, 1974), pp. 462–63.

19. See, for example, "New Plot Against Congo," *Pravda,* 9/7/60; and "Tense Situation in Congo," *Pravda,* 9/8/60.

20. "Soviet Government Statement on Situation in Congo," *Pravda,* 9/10/60.

21. Leopoldville (no number), 9/7/60.

22. *Senate Intelligence Committee Report,* p. 17.

23. Ibid., p. 62.

24. Leopoldville 623, 9/6/60.

25. *NYT,* 9/8/60.

26. Leopoldville 656, 9/9/60. See also *NYT,* 9/9/60.

27. *Senate Intelligence Committee Report,* p. 62.

28. Ibid., p. 17.

29. Leopoldville 652, 9/8/60.

30. Leopoldville 659, 9/9/60.

31. Leopoldville 665, 9/10/60.

32. Fifth Message from Harriman to Kennedy, from London, September 13, 1960; see also *NYT,* 9/13/60. Interview with the author, 1971.

33. Leopoldville 662, 9/9/60.

34. See the memorandum sent on September 8, 1960, by Assistant Secretary of State for African Affairs Joseph Satterthwaite to Under Secretary Livingston Merchant recommending points that should be made to the Joint Chiefs in answer to their demands.

35. USUN 586, 9/5/60.

36. USUN 605, 9/7/60. See also USUN 586, 9/5/60, and SD 316 to USUN, 9/3/60.

37. USUN 605, 9/7/60.

38. Dayal, *Mission for Hammarskjold,* p. 38; Urquhart, *Hammarskjold,* p. 446.

39. Urquhart, *Hammarskjold,* p. 444, cited what Hammarskjold called an "irresponsible observation" in his instructions to Cordier. He wrote, "In such a situation responsible people on the spot might commit themselves to what the Secretary-General could not justify doing himself—taking the risk of being disowned when it no longer mattered."

40. USUN 602, 9/7/60.

41. USUN 631, 9/10/60.

42. SCOR, 896th Meeting, September 9–10, 1960. For the text of the Secretary-General's report to the Council, see S/4482.

43. S/4503.

44. S/4482/Add. 1.

45. SCOR, 896th Meeting, September 9–10, 1960.

46. S/4503. See also *Pravda,* 9/11/60.

47. SCOR, 897th Meeting, September 10, 1960; and 898th Meeting, September 12, 1960.

48. USUN 681, 9/13/60.

49. USUN 662, 9/12/60.

50. SCOR, 898th Meeting, September 12, 1960.

51. Dayal, *Mission for Hammarskjold,* pp. 42, 47; he wrote, p. 56, that Hammar-

skjold's statement regarding Kasavubu's "legal right to remove the prime minister" was "not in keeping" with his "habitual sense of prudence."

52. Ibid., pp. 53–55.

53. See Dayal's September 11 report about this incident, S/4505.

54. Dayal, *Mission for Hammarskjold*, p. 57.

55. S/4502.

56. S/4500/Add. 1.

57. SCOR, 920th Meeting, December 13, 1960; the Secretary-General noted the report of the Moroccan representative in Leopoldville and other eyewitnesses "that in the Hall of the Chamber of Deputies there were some scores of the ANC—then loyal to Mr. Lumumba—during the debate and the voting. They were fully armed with rifles and sub-machine guns." See also *NYT*, 9/14/60; and Gerard-Libois and Verhaegen, *Congo 1960*, 2: 861–62.

58. For the text of his order, see Gerard-Libois and Verhaegen, *Congo 1960*, 2: 863.

59. Dayal, *Mission for Hammarskjold*, p. 60.

60. Gerard-Libois and Verhaegen, *Congo 1960*, 2: 858.

61. *NYT*, 9/11/60.

62. *NYT*, 9/10/60.

63. *Pravda*, 9/9/60. Sékou Touré was enroute to Mongolia and China.

64. *NYT*, 9/11/60.

65. *NYT*, 9/13/60. At this point an economic mission from the UAR was winding up a three-week stay in the Soviet Union with the conclusion of a major trade agreement, a Kremlin reception, a meeting with Khrushchev, and heavy press coverage.

66. Accra 321, 9/6/60.

67. For more detail, see Nkrumah, *Challenge of the Congo*, 38–41, 47–54. The Ghanaian ambassador in Leopoldville, Andrew Djin, a strong supporter of Lumumba, tried to recoup when Lumumba was arrested the following day by arranging his release; but he ran into the firm opposition of Brigadier Steve Otu, who refused to act without UN orders. A battle raged between Djin, who stressed the importance of the "political factors," and the Ghanaian officers, who insisted that their primary loyalty was to the United Nations.

68. Nkrumah, *Challenge of the Congo*, pp. 42–46.

69. Urquhart, *Hammarskjold*, pp. 453–54.

70. It was not until January 1961 that Morocco, Guinea, and the UAR actually withdrew their troops.

71. *Senate Intelligence Committee Report*, p. 17.

72. Leopoldville 709, 9/13/60.

73. Leopoldville 711, 9/13/60; and 718, 9/14/60.

74. *Khrushchev Remembers*, pp. 463–65, 482.

75. T. Kolesnichenko, "Stop Provocations of Colonialists in Congo," *Pravda*, 9/15/60.

76. SCOR, 901st Meeting, September 14–15, 1960.

77. Ibid.

78. USUN 679 and 680, 9/13/60. See also SD 360 and 363 to USUN 9/12/60.

79. USUN 694, 9/15/60.

80. USUN 708, 9/15/60.

81. SCOR, 902nd Meeting, 9/15/60. The U.S. draft resolution was S/4516.

82. The Soviet draft resolution was S/4519.

83. USUN, 711, and 713, 9/15/60. For the statements of Ghana, Guinea, and the UAR, see SCOR, 905th Meeting, September 16, 1960; for the statement of Morocco, see SCOR, 906th Meeting, September 16–17, 1960.

84. S/4523.

85. SCOR, 906th Meeting, September 16–17, 1960.

86. Dayal, *Mission for Hammarskjold*, p. 83.

87. For the text of Mobutu's statement, see Gerard-Libois and Verhaegen, *Congo 1960*, 2: 869.

88. *NYT*, 9/15/60. Although *The Times* ran the news as its lead story, it did not even mention the most startling development—Mobutu's demand for the expulsion of all Soviet and Czech personnel. In fact, in his report the following day, the *Times* correspondent in Leopoldville suggested that this demand, like so many others in the Congo, was not really serious and had already been forgotten. There were a good many conflicting stories coming out of Leopoldville, and it was only natural for the Russians to believe the ones most favorable to Lumumba, even if they turned out to be the most inaccurate.

89. Kolesnichenko, "Still One More Plot, Still One More Failure," *Pravda*, 9/16/60.

There were no reports at the time from the Soviet journalists stationed in Leopoldville, but the following year, two Soviet journalists from *Pravda* and *Komsomol'skaia Pravda*, Volodin and Orestov, who worked in the Congo during the summer of 1960, published an account of their experiences: *Trudnye Dni Kongo*. They recalled, pp. 140–44, that when they were summoned to a late-evening press conference to be given by a Colonel Mobutu, they had no idea who he was; but when he arrived, they remembered having seen him at diplomatic receptions, where he would chat with foreign journalists about his own newspaper experience. He had been "reserved" with reporters from the Soviet bloc and "poured out his song like a nightingale" to Western reporters, they wrote.

90. Dayal, *Mission for Hammarskjold*, pp. 75–76.

91. *NYT*, 9/18/60.

92. "Statement of Soviet Government on Temporary Recall of USSR Embassy Staff from Congo," *Pravda*, 9/19/60.

93. SD 795 to Leopoldville, 9/15/60.

94. Leopoldville 735, 9/16/60. Timberlake added a sarcastic note: "Kashamura just came in to ask for help to get back to his native Kivu. Was told how sorry we were not to be able to help him." Anicet Kashamura, Lumumba's Minister of Information, was one of the most radical of his allies and would be the last politician in Leopoldville that the U.S. Embassy would want to help.

95. Leopoldville 736, 9/16/60.

96. One of the earliest accounts of CIA involvement with Mobutu was by Andrew Tully, *CIA: The Inside Story* (New York: Morrow., 1962), pp. 219–29. Tully concluded that "the CIA came up with the right man at the right time and thereby started to bring a measure of stability to the new state." "It seems safe to say," he wrote, "that Mobutu was 'discovered' by the CIA."

In recent years this relationship has been acknowledged by former high-ranking CIA officials, such as Richard Bissell, Richard Helms, and Ray Cline.

97. S/4449. See Urquhart, *Hammarskjold*, p. 432. See also the sympathetic biography of Mobutu by Francis Monheim, *Mobutu, l'homme seul* (Brussels: Editions Actuelles, 1962), pp. 109–16, for a description of the estrangement between Mobutu and Lumumba that developed after independence.

98. Dayal, *Mission for Hammarskjold*, p. 69, wrote that Kettani "regarded Mobutu almost like his own son"; von Horn, *Soldiering for Peace.*, p. 211, described Mobutu as "virtually the only Congolese officer who was capable of exerting any real guiding influence over the ANC."

99. Leopoldville 642, 9/7/60. Delvaux was arrested but managed to escape, and turned up at the Parliament for the debate at which Lumumba's position was restored.

100. Ibid. See also *NYT*, 9/16/60, which reported that Mobutu had expelled the Soviet "technicians" who were at the army camp.

101. SD 332 to USUN, 9/8/60.

102. USUN 631, 9/10/60.

103. Dayal, *Mission for Hammarskjold*, p. 62.

104. Gerard-Libois and Verhaegen, *Congo 1960*, 2: 865.

105. Dayal, *Mission for Hammarskjold*, p. 59, wrote that Lumumba was arrested "apparently" on the orders of Mobutu; on p. 63, he stated that Mobutu told him "he had not wished to arrest" Lumumba and "had allowed him to be released." Gerard-Libois and Verhaegen, *Congo 1960*, 2: 856, stated that Mobutu's role in the arrest had not been established, despite Dayal's report that he had ordered the arrest.

106. Dayal, *Mission for Hammarskjold*, p. 62; Urquhart, *Hammarskjold*, pp. 450–51.

107. Gerard-Libois and Verhaegen, *Congo 1960*, 2: 865.

108. There were also persistent rumors, especially among his opponents, that Mobutu listened to his old friends at the Sureté, or police, with whom he had had a long-term arrangement; see, for example, Cleophas Kamitatu, *La Grande Mystification du Congo-Kinshasa* (Brussels: Complexe, 1971), pp. 13–14; Kamitatu was president of Leopoldville Province at the time.

109. Leopoldville 709, 9/13/60.

110. *NYT*, 9/15, 16/60.

111. For more detail, see Gerard-Libois and Verhaegen, *Congo 1960*, 2: 865; Monheim, *Mobutu*, pp. 131–32; von Horn, *Soldiering for Peace*, pp. 212–13, who wrote, "Mobutu had been alarmed at some of their suggestions; since it was plain a revolution of some sort was inevitable, he had decided to take the plunge while there was still a chance of keeping it under reasonable control."

112. Dayal, *Mission for Hammarskjold*, p. 64; Urquhart's account, *Hammarskjold*, p. 451, varied slightly; he wrote that Dayal and his staff "asked Mobutu, who happened to be at United Nations headquarters when his message announcing the takeover was broadcast, to leave at once."

113. Even objective scholars such as Hoskyns, *The Congo Since Independence*, pp. 215–16, doubted that Mobutu's move was a surprise to the officials at UN headquarters; she concluded that General Kettani and other officials knew about it well in advance and welcomed it. On the other hand, Monheim, *Mobutu*, p. 133, wrote that when Mobutu stopped at UN headquarters before the broadcast to inform Kettani, the Moroccan officer "did not disapprove formally . . . but reproached Mobutu for having made his decision without consulting him."

114. Urquhart, *Hammarskjold*, p. 447; Dayal, *Mission for Hammarskjold*, p. 65; Hoskyns, *The Congo Since Independence*, p. 213, on the other hand, wrote, "It was apparently agreed that Mobutu should be allowed to claim the credit for this payment, in the hope that it would help to build up his authority and increase the hold which he had on his men." See also the account in *NYT*, 9/11/60.

115. Dayal, *Mission for Hammarskjold*, p. 66.

116. For more detail, see *NYT*, 9/19/60; see also the *Senate Intelligence Committee Report*, p. 18.

117. Leopoldville 726, 9/15/60; Timberlake wrote, "Ileo also confirmed our suspicions that Mobutu had not consulted him or Kasavubu about last night's dramatic announcement." Leopoldville 731, 9/16/60; Timberlake wrote, "We do not yet know how much if any liaison there has been between Kasavubu, Ileo, and Mobutu."

118. For a dramatic account of the UN rescue of Lumumba, see Dayal, *Mission for Hammarskjold*, pp. 69–74. See also *NYT*, 9/16/60.

119. *Senate Intelligence Committee Report*, p. 18. Pierre Mulele was Lumumba's Minister of Education and a leader of the PSA party; he was a radical who later led a major rebellion against the Leopoldville government.

120. Leopoldville 746, 9/18/60.

121. For the text of the statement, see Gerard-Libois and Verhaegen, *Congo 1960,* 2: 871–72.

122. SD 846 to Leopoldville, 9/20/60.

123. Leopoldville 803, 9/23/60.

124. Brazzaville Despatch 24, 9/24/60.

125. Leopoldville 768, 9/21/60.

126. Ibid.

127. Brazzaville Despatch 24, 9/24/60, and 83, 9/26/60.

128. Brazzaville 86, 9/29/60. The currency exchange is approximate. According to Young, *Politics in the Congo,* p. 355, the official exchange rate was 65 Congolese francs to the dollar in November, 1960, which would mean $615,384 at the official rate; but the figure of 250 francs to the dollar, the black market rate unti mid-1962, was considered a more realistic figure.

129. Leopoldville 746, 9/18/60.

130. USUN 735, 9/18/60; see also USUN 736, 737, and 741, 9/18/60.

131. Dayal, *Mission for Hammarskjold,* pp. 85–89; for the text of the agreement, see Gerard-Libois and Verhaegen, *Congo 1960,* 2: 866–68.

132. SD 835 to Leopoldville, 9/19/60.

133. Leopoldville 763 and 770, 9/20/60.

134. USUN 755, 9/20/60.

135. USUN 770, 9/22/60.

136. *Senate Intelligence Committee Report,* p. 17.

137. Ibid.

138. Ibid.

139. Ibid., pp. 17–18. For more detail on the troops Mobutu brought to Leopoldville, see *NYT,* 9/16/60, and Dayal, *Mission for Hammarskjold,* p. 70.

140. *Senate Intelligence Committee Report,* pp. 22–23.

141. Ibid., p. 23.

142. Ibid., pp. 21–22.

143. Ibid., p. 62.

144. Ibid., pp. 63–64.

145. Ibid., p. 24, 62–63.

146. Ibid., p. 24, 63.

147. SD 396 to USUN, 9/15/60.

148. SD 401 to USUN, 9/16/60; and 424, 9/17/60.

149. GAOR, 858th–863rd Plenary Meetings, 4th Emergency Special Session, September 17, 18, 19, 1960.

150. GAOR, 858th Plenary Meeting, September 17, 1960.

151. GAOR, 859th Plenary Meeting, September 18, 1960. A/L.292.

152. GAOR, 863rd Plenary Meeting, September 19–20, 1960. A/1474 (E.S. IV). The vote on paragraph 6 was 80 to 0, with South Africa abstaining.

153. For more detail on Khrushchev's arrival, see *Khrushchev Remembers,* pp. 465–67.

154. *NYT,* 9/8/60.

155. *NYT,* 9/9/60.

Chapter Five

1. GAOR, 868th Plenary Meeting, September 22, 1960. For more detail on Eisenhower's view of this General Assembly session, see his memoirs, Dwight D. Eisenhower, *Waging Peace: The White House Years, A Personal Account 1956–1961* (New York: Doubleday, 1965), pp. 576–89.

2. GAOR, 869th Plenary Meeting, September 23, 1960. For more detail on Khrushchev's view of the meeting, see *Khrushchev Remembers*, pp. 467–86.

3. *NYT,* September 25, 1960.

4. Dayal, *Mission for Hammarskjold,* p. 93.

5. GAOR, 871st Plenary Meeting, September 26, 1960.

6. Dayal, *Mission for Hammarskjold,* p. 93.

7. GAOR, 882nd Plenary Meeting, October 3, 1960.

8. GAOR, 883rd Plenary Meeting, October 3, 1960. For more detail on Hammarskjold's reaction, see Urquhart, *Hammarskjold,* pp. 462–65.

9. The Soviet press noted Hammarskjold's presence among the guests; see "Stay of N.S. Khrushchev in New York," *Pravda,* 10/6/60.

10. GAOR, 902nd Plenary Meeting, October 12, 1960.

11. GAOR, 904th Plenary Meeting, October 13, 1960. See also Urquhart, *Hammarskjold,* pp. 466–67.

12. *NYT,* 9/25/60.

13. "In Honor of Delegations of New United Nations Members," *Pravda,* 10/14/60. Nigeria, Mali, and Senegal had been admitted since the opening of the General Assembly on September 20, when thirteen new African states were admitted; this brought the number up to sixteen.

14. "USSR-Ghana Cooperation," *Izvestia,* 8/29/60.

15. *NYT,* 9/16/60.

16. Eisenhower, *Waging Peace,* p. 583.

17. *NYT,* 9/23/60.

18. GAOR, 869th Plenary Meeting, September 23, 1960.

19. Dayal, *Mission for Hammarskjold,* p. 93.

20. Eisenhower, *Waging Peace,* p. 583.

21. *NYT,* 9/25/60.

22. State Department Memorandum of Conversation between Secretary of State Herter and British Foreign Secretary Lord Home, September 18, 1960.

23. C. L. Sulzberger, *The Last of the Giants* (New York: Macmillan, 1970), p. 690. For Prime Minister Harold Macmillan's views, see his memoirs, *Pointing the Way: 1959–1961* (New York: Harper & Row, 1972), pp. 273–74. Macmillan, who had not yet left for New York when Khrushchev and Nkrumah spoke, wrote in his diary, "Unfortunately, Dr. Nkrumah (Ghana) played into [Khrushchev's] hands with a demagogic speech about Africa. However, Dr. Nkrumah has the sense to support U.N. and the Secretary-General. . . . Khrushchev's line won (at least emotionally and temporarily) great support from the Afro-Asians. We must not under-rate his power with them if he can work them up and excite them. Dr. Nkrumah is a case in point. He wavers all the time between common sense and emotionalism. I fear that his speech must have been arranged to tune in with what Mr. Khrushchev wanted."

24. Dayal, *Mission for Hammarskjold,* pp. 102–3.

25. For the text of Kasavubu's protest, see Leopoldville 810, 9/25/60. See also Leopoldville 820, 9/26/60; and the account in *NYT,* 9/26/60.

26. Dayal, *Mission for Hammarskjold,* pp. 103–4.

27. Urquhart, *Hammarskjold,* p. 462.

28. Mohamed Heikal, *The Cairo Documents* (New York: Doubleday, 1973), p. 151.

29. Cairo 698, 9/24/60.

30. Eisenhower, *Waging Peace,* p. 585.

31. *NYT,* 9/27/60.

32. *NYT,* 9/28/60.

33. GAOR, 873rd Plenary Meeting, September 27, 1960.

34. Dayal, *Mission for Hammarskjold,* p. 100.

35. Ibid., pp. 98, 104.

36. Heikal, *The Cairo Documents,* pp. 183–84.

37. Ibid., pp. 151–52.

38. Dayal, *Mission for Hammarskjold,* p. 100.

39. *NYT,* 9/27/60.

40. Dayal, *Mission for Hammarskjold,* pp. 98–99.

41. GAOR, 882nd Plenary Meeting, October 3, 1960.

42. *NYT,* 10/11/60.

43. *NYT,* 10/31/60.

44. GAOR, 896th Plenary Meeting, October 10, 1960.

45. Dayal, *Mission for Hammarskjold,* pp. 101–2.

46. *NYT,* 9/23/60.

47. Charles E. Bohlen, *Witness to History, 1929–1969* (New York: Norton, 1973), p. 472.

48. GAOR, 873rd Plenary Meeting, September 27, 1960.

49. GAOR, 880th Plenary Meeting, September 30, 1960. A/4522.

50. Eisenhower, *Waging Peace,* pp. 586–88.

51. *NYT,* 10/1/60.

52. *NYT,* 9/30/60.

53. *NYT,* 9/18/60.

54. *NYT,* 9/22/60.

55. Sulzberger, *The Last of the Giants,* p. 688.

56. *NYT,* 9/29/60.

57. *NYT,* 9/22/60.

58. Arthur M. Schlesinger, Jr., *A Thousand Days: John F. Kennedy in the White House* (Boston: Houghton Mifflin, 1965), p. 150. Later, after Kennedy was elected, Khrushchev sent a message to Harriman, pointing out that he had followed his advice and remained neutral and suggesting that now a new Soviet-American relationship could be initiated.

59. *Khrushchev Remembers,* pp. 489–90.

60. Ibid., p. 489.

61. Ibid., pp. 490–91.

62. *NYT,* 9/27/60.

63. *NYT,* 9/26/60.

Chapter Six

1. *Senate Intelligence Committee Report,* pp. 75–76.

2. Ibid., pp. 24–25. The problem of not tracing the assassination attempt back to the U.S. government was raised even before Gottlieb got to Leopoldville. Tweedy had cabled the station chief on September 22: "You and colleague understand we cannot read over your shoulder as you plan and assess opportunities. Our primary concern must be concealment [American] role, unless outstanding opportunity emerges which makes calculated risk first class bet. Ready entertain any serious proposals you make based our high regard both your professional judgments." He also noted that he was considering a third-country national "who might fill bill." (pp. 23–24)

3. Ibid., pp. 25–26. See also p. 68; the station chief testified, "I thought the policy decision had been made in the White House, not in the Agency, and that the Agency had been selected as the Executive agent, if you will, to carry out a political decision."

He did not believe the President had chosen the "means of assassination," he explained. "I doubt that I thought the President had said, you use this system. But my understanding is the President had made a decision that an act should take place, but then put that into the hands of the Agency to carry out his decision."

4. Ibid., p. 70.

5. Ibid., pp. 28–29.

6. Ibid., p. 25.

7. Ibid.

8. Ibid., p. 27.

9. Ibid., p. 25.

10. Ibid., p. 27.

11. Ibid., p. 28.

12. Ibid.

13. Ibid., pp. 29–30, 30n.

14. Ibid., p. 29.

15. Ibid., p. 28.

16. Ibid., p. 29.

17. Ibid.

18. Ibid., pp. 18, 18n.

19. Ibid., p. 31.

20. Ibid., pp. 31–32.

21. Ibid., p. 32.

22. Ibid., p. 25.

23. Ibid., p. 32.

24. Ibid., p. 42n.

25. SD 886 to Leopoldville, 9/23/60.

26. Leopoldville 824, 9/26/60.

27. For the text of Kasavubu's statement, see Gerard-Libois and Verhaegen, *Congo 1960*, 2: 874–75.

28. Leopoldville 867, 9/30/60.

29. Leopoldville 824, 9/26/60.

30. Dayal, *Mission for Hammarskjold*, p. 104.

31. Leopoldville 949, 10/11/60.

32. *NYT*, 10/10/60.

33. *NYT*, 10/11/60.

34. Leopoldville 949, 10/11/60.

35. Leopoldville 950, 10/11/60.

36. Dayal, *Mission for Hammarskjold*, p. 134.

37. USUN 967, 10/12/60.

38. Leopoldville 952, 10/11/60.

39. Leopoldville 962, 10/12/60.

40. SD 654 to USUN, 10/12/60.

41. Leopoldville 974, 10/13/60. See A/4560/Add. 4 for Bomboko's protest to the United Nations, with details of the charges against Lumumba.

42. *NYT*, 10/15/60.

43. A/4547, letter of October 21, 1960, from the Soviet delegation to the President of the General Assembly.

44. Leopoldville 1006, 10/19/60.

45. A/4557/B.1. See also B.2, 3, and 4, for further exchanges. For more detail, see Gerard-Libois and Verhaegen, *Congo 1960*, 2: 945–47; and Dayal, *Mission for Hammarskjold*, pp. 105–7 and 136–40.

46. Brussels 816, 10/18/60.

47. Leopoldville 1015, 10/20/60. See also USUN 550, 9/1/60, when Hammarskjold assured Lodge that he was "fully agreed on maintenance large number of Belgians" as technicians in the Congo.

48. SD 716 to USUN 10/19/60. See also USUN 1095, 10/22/60.

49. USUN 1096, 10/22/60.

50. Ibid.

51. USUN 1137, 10/26/60.

52. For more information about this period, see Gerard-Libois and Verhaegen, *Congo 1960*, 2: 928–29; Dayal's report, A/4557. See also Leopoldville 1021, 10/21/60.

53. *NYT*, 10/25/60.

54. Leopoldville 1037, 10/24/60.

55. Leopoldville 1029, 10/24/60.

56. *NYT*, 10/26/60.

57. Gerard-Libois and Verhaegen, *Congo 1960*, 2: 903.

58. *NYT*, 10/27, 28/60.

59. Leopoldville 1062, 10/27/60.

60. Kashamura, *De Lumumba aux colonels*, pp. 158–59.

61. V. Vasiliev, "Congolese People Reject Puppets," *Pravda*, 10/24/60.

62. A/4555. "Colonialists Must Be Expelled," *Pravda*, 10/31/60.

63. Dayal, *Mission for Hammarskjold*, pp. 110–11.

64. A/4557. Von Horn, *Soldiering for Peace*, p. 230, wrote, "I do not know whether Dag approved Dayal's report. I have a feeling he may have felt it unfortunate and mistimed." On the other hand, Urquhart, *Hammarskjold*, p. 475, wrote that Dayal had Hammarskjold's full backing for the report as well as for the policy of refusing "to recognize the legitimacy of the Mobutu regime or to permit the army to arrest Lumumba."

65. For the text of the statement, see *NYT*, 11/5/60. For the Belgian reaction, see S/4585.

66. Dayal, *Mission for Hammarskjold*, pp. 114–15.

67. GAOR, 912th Plenary Meeting, November 8, 1960.

68. Dayal, *Mission for Hammarskjold*, p. 114.

69. USUN 1188, 10/29/60.

70. Leopoldville 1017, 10/20/60.

71. Leopoldville 1078, 11/1/60.

72. Leopoldville 1082, 11/2/60.

73. SD 1274 to Leopoldville, 11/2/60.

74. SD 1303 to Leopoldville, 11/5/60.

75. USUN 1237, 11/1/60.

76. A/L.319, Rev. 2, October 28, 1960.

77. USUN 1246, 11/2/60.

78. USUN 1189, 10/29/60; 1292, 11/4/60; and 1318, 11/8/60.

79. Leopoldville 1129, 11/7/60.

80. SD 1372 to Leopoldville, 11/12/60.

81. Leopoldville 1181, 11/15/60.

82. *Senate Intelligence Committee Report*, p. 18.

83. Ibid., p. 18*n*.

84. Ibid., p. 41.

85. Ibid., p. 38. The pseudonym "Michael Mulroney" was used to refer to O'Donnell.

86. Ibid., pp. 39–40.

87. Ibid., p. 39.

88. Ibid., p. 42.

89. Ibid., p. 39.
90. Ibid., p. 42.
91. Ibid., p. 18*n.*
92. Ibid., pp. 41–42.
93. Ibid., p. 42.
94. Ibid., p. 43.
95. Ibid.
96. Ibid.
97. Ibid.
98. Ibid., p. 33.
99. Ibid., p. 48.
100. GAOR, 912th Plenary Meeting, November 8, 1960.
101. GAOR, 913th Plenary Meeting, November 9, 1960.
102. For more detail, see below, fn. 115.
103. Kolesnichenko and Yasnev, "Colonialist Cards Trumped," *Pravda,* 11/11/60.
104. Leopoldville 1127, 11/7/60.
105. Leopoldville 1140, 11/8/60.
106. Dayal, *Mission for Hammarskjold,* p. 117.
107. SD 886 to Brussels, 11/9/60; Brussels 935, 11/10/60; USUN 1357, 11/11/60; and 1379, 11/12/60.
108. USUN 1343, 11/10/60.
109. A/4578.
110. USUN 1392, 11/14/60.
111. USUN 1423, 11/16/60; and 1434, 11/17/60.
112. USUN 1423, 11/16/60.
113. USUN 1405, 11/15/60; 1421, 1426, 11/16/60; and 1435, 11/17/60.
114. USUN 1434, 11/17/60.
115. GAOR, 917th Plenary Meeting, November 18, 1960.

Of the forty-eight states which had voted for the Ghanaian move for adjournment on November 9, thirty-six remained: the ten members of the Soviet bloc, plus Cuba; the eight Afro-Asian sponsors of the pro-Lumumba resolution (Ghana, Guinea, Morocco, Mali, UAR, India, Indonesia, and Ceylon); four Arab countries (Iraq, Saudi Arabia, Libya, and Yemen); three nonaligned Asian countries (Afghanistan, Burma, and Nepal); five Afro-Asian members of the Conciliation Commission, who felt this was the best way to maintain their impartiality (Malaya, Nigeria, Ethiopia, Sudan, and Tunisia); three European neutrals who shared this view (Ireland, Sweden, and Finland); Togo, a newly admitted former French trust territory; and Mexico, which was striking out on a new course as a member of the Third World. All these delegations had resisted American lobbying.

The U.S. campaign for votes did sway Pakistan, Liberia, and Somalia, members of the Conciliation Commission, who shifted from favoring adjournment to abstaining; the same was true for Cambodia, Jordan, Lebanon, and Upper Volta. The Americans also persuaded five states (Chile, El Salvador, Peru, Senegal, and Chad) to switch from favoring adjournment to opposing it; and they picked up sixteen votes opposing adjournment from states which had abstained or been absent the first time around; in some cases, such as Norway, the switch was the result of intense pressure.

116. GAOR, 924th Plenary Meeting, November 22, 1960.
117. "West Encourages Lawlessness," *Pravda,* 11/25/60.
118. Dayal, *Mission for Hammarskjold,* pp. 120, 140–41.
119. USUN 1526, 11/25/60.
120. USUN 1527, 11/25/60.
121. SD 971 to USUN 11/23/60.

Chapter Seven

1. Kashamura, *De Lumumba aux colonels*, p. 165.
2. For more detail, see Leopoldville Despatch 177, 12/2/60; A/4614, Dayal's report, December 5, 1960; Dayal, *Mission for Hammarskjold*, pp. 142–143; Urquhart, *Hammarskjold*, p. 479; von Horn, *Soldiering for Peace*, pp. 247–48.
3. Kashamura, *De Lumumba aux colonels*, p. 163. See also Hoskyns, *The Congo Since Independence*, pp. 266–67.
4. Leopoldville 1299, 11/28/60.
5. *Senate Intelligence Committee Report*, p. 48. Devlin told the committee (pp. 48–49) that "there was no Agency involvement in any way" in Lumumba's departure from UN custody and that he had no advance knowledge of Lumumba's plan. He said he consulted with Congolese officers about the possible routes Lumumba might take to Stanleyville but he was not of "major assistance" in tracking him down. O'Donnell also testified that Lumumba "escaped by his own devices and was not tricked by the CIA."
6. *Ibid.*, p. 44. The committee concluded that "despite the suggestive language of the cables at the end of November about the prospect of 'direct action' by QJ/WIN and an indication in the Inspector General's Report that QJ/WIN may have been recruited initially for an assassination mission there is no clear evidence that QJ/WIN was actually involved in any assassination plan or attempt. The Inspector General's Report may have accurately reported a plan for the use of QJ/WIN which predated Mulroney's refusal to accept the assassination assignment from Bissell. But there is no evidence from which to conclude that QJ/WIN was actually used for such an operation." (The pseudonym "Mulroney" was used to refer to O'Donnell.)
7. See, for example, Leopoldville 1314, 11/30/60; Accra 639, 11/30/60; Brussels 1024, 11/30/60; SD 308 to Conakry, 11/30/60.
8. "Situation in Congo," *Pravda*, 11/30/60. See also "Situation in Congo," *Pravda*, 12/1/60; and "Situation in Congo," *Pravda*, 12/2/60.
9. Dayal, *Mission for Hammarskjold*, p. 144, explained, "We thus hoped to keep clear of any charge of illegal interference in the Congo's internal affairs while keeping in reserve the possibility of intervention for the express purpose of preventing danger to Lumumba's life." See also von Horn, *Soldiering for Peace*, p. 248.
10. Dayal, *Mission for Hammarskjold*, pp. 142–43.
11. Leopoldville 1305, 11/29/60.
12. Leopoldville 1312, 11/30/60.
13. Leopoldville 1318, 12/1/60.
14. SD 1016 to USUN, 11/30/60.
15. USUN 1592, 12/2/60.
16. Leopoldville 1324, 12/2/60.
17. Leopoldville 1021, 10/21/60.
18. Kashamura, *De Lumumba aux colonels*, pp. 167–71.
19. Dayal, *Mission to Hammarskjold*, p. 145.
20. Von Horn, *Soldiering for Peace*, p. 248.
21. Urquhart, *Hammarskjold*, pp. 480–81.
22. Ibid., pp. 481–82.
23. Von Horn, *Soldiering for Peace*, p. 248.
24. Leopoldville 1329, 12/3/60. See also *NYT*, 12/3,4/60.
25. USUN 1615, 12/2/60.
26. Dayal, *Mission for Hammarskjold*, p. 146.
27. A/4612, December 2, 1960.
28. A/4618, December 6, 1960; published in *Pravda*, 12/7/60.

29. USUN 1619, 12/3/60. For the text of the letter, see A/4614, Ann. I, December 3, 1960.

30. USUN 1639, 12/6/60.

31. A/4614, December 5, 1960.

32. A/4614, Ann. 2, December 5, 1960.

33. SD 1534 to Leopoldville, 12/5/60.

34. *NYT,* 12/7/60.

35. Leopoldville 1340, 12/6/60.

36. SD 1542 to Leopoldville, 12/6/60.

37. Leopoldville 1353, 12/7/60; and 1356, 12/8/60.

38. SD 1510 to Leopoldville, 11/25/60.

39. Leopoldville 1351, 12/7/60.

40. SCOR, 913th Meeting, December 7, 1960.

41. S/4590, December 9, 1960.

42. SCOR, 920th Meeting, December 13, 1960.

43. "Freedom to Patrice Lumumba," *Pravda,* 12/7/60.

44. *Pravda,* 12/10/60.

45. SCOR, 919th Meeting, December 12, 1960.

46. SCOR, 916th Meeting, December 9–10, 1960. The Soviet resolution was S/4579.

47. SCOR, 917th Meeting, December 10, 1960.

48. S/4669. See also Nkrumah, *Challenge of the Congo,* pp. 94–98.

49. S/4578.

50. SCOR, 920th Meeting, December 13, 1960.

51. *NYT,* 12/14/60.

52. Leopoldville 1365, 12/9/60.

53. *NYT,* 12/15/60.

54. Leopoldville 1374, 12/12/60; and 1378, 12/13/60.

55. Leopoldville 1378, 12/13/60. See also Dayal, *Mission for Hammarskjold,* p. 159.

56. *NYT,* 12/15/60.

57. SD 1587 to Lepoldville, 12/16/60.

58. Leopoldville 1393, 12/15/60.

59. Leopoldville 1398, 12/16/60.

60. *NYT,* 12/15/60.

61. *Senate Intelligence Committee Report,* p. 46.

62. Ibid., pp. 45–46.

63. Ibid., pp. 46–47.

64. Ibid., pp. 47–48. The station chief noted that messages concerning WI/ROGUE were sent through routine channels; if he had been involved "in an actual assassination plan," messages would have been transmitted through the PROP channel. (p. 47)

65. "Statement of A. Gizenga," *Pravda,* 12/14/60.

66. N. Khokhlov, "Stanleyville," *Izvestia,* 12/17/60.

67. "Help and Support to People of Republic of Congo," *Pravda,* 12/25/60.

68. A/L.331.

69. GAOR, 950th Plenary Meeting, December 16, 1960.

70. GAOR, 953rd Plenary Meeting, December 17, 1960.

71. A/L.332.

72. GAOR, 958th Plenary Meeting, December 20, 1960.

73. SD 1200 to USUN, 12/22/60.

74. USUN 1846, 12/27/60. See also USUN 1840, 12/23/60.

Chapter Eight

1. For more information on this period, see *NYT,* 12/26/60, on the takeover of Bukavu; 1/10, 11, 12, 13/61, on the offensive into north Katanga; 12/27,30/60, on reports of UAR and Soviet bloc aid to Stanleyville.

2. SD 1627 to Leopoldville, cited in *Analytical Chronology,* p. 58.

3. Leopoldville 1429, 12/24/60; and Leopoldville 1436, 12/27/60.

4. Gerard-Libois and Verhaegen, *Congo 1960,* 2: 1017–18.

5. Brussels 1203, 12/29/60, cited in *Analytical Chronology,* p. 60.

6. For more information on this incident, see UN document S/4606, part IV, Dayal's report to the Secretary-General; *NYT,* 1/2/61; Dayal, *Mission for Hammarskjold,* pp. 161–63; Hoskyns, *The Congo Since Independence,* pp. 304–5.

7. Leopoldville 1484, 1/6/61, cited in *Analytical Chronology,* p. 71.

8. Brussels 1293, 1/12/61. According to *Analytical Chronology,* p. 71, when Bomboko went to Paris in search of military aid, the Foreign Minister, Couve de Murville, "pointed out that the French Government had always taken the position that sovereign states are entitled to aid the Congo directly and did not have to confine themselves to the UN channel."

9. SD 1329 to Brussels, 1/19/61. State Department officials told Belgian Ambassador Scheyven that the "political risks" of such a program were "unacceptable."

10. Leopoldville 1375, 12/12/60.

11. Leopoldville 1483, 1/6/61.

12. Leopoldville 1508, 1/11/61.

13. Leopoldville 1483, 1/6/61; see S/4630, Kasavubu's letter to Dayal of January 7, protesting the UN failure to act to prevent the Bukavu kidnappings, and Dayal's reply of January 14.

14. Dayal, *Mission for Hammarskjold,* p. 177.

15. Leopoldville 1432, 12/26/60. See also Leopoldville 1436, 12/27/60; Timberlake arranged a meeting between Iyassu and Bomboko to discuss the possibility of "opening negotiations" with the "provincial authorities in Stanleyville."

16. Dayal, *Mission for Hammarskjold,* p. 171.

17. Ibid., pp. 171–72.

18. For the text of the Casablanca Charter adopted at the conference, see Colin Legum, *Pan-Africanism: A Short Political Guide* (New York: Praeger, 1962), pp. 187–88. For positive and massive Soviet press comment about the Casablanca conference, see "Conference of Leaders of African States," *Pravda,* 1/5/61, which noted the arrival of the delegates, including Lumumba's representative, André Mandi, Secretary of State for Foreign Affairs; "Africa Forges Unity," *Pravda,* 1/8/61, on the Congo resolution; and "For a Free Africa!" *Pravda,* 1/10/61, reporting the adoption of the Casablanca Charter.

19. *NYT,* 1/5, 6/61.

20. Nkrumah, *Challenge of the Congo,* pp. 109–11. For the text of the Brazzaville Declaration, adopted on December 19, 1960; see ibid., pp. 176–82. Nkrumah urged the other leaders to keep their troops in the Congo as a sort of holding operation for Lumumba until an African High Command could be formed to replace the United Nations command. Although he was unable to persuade them to reconsider their decision, he did win one concession: the Congo resolution adopted at Casablanca did not oblige all the signatories to withdraw their troops immediately. Each participant was free to follow his own timetable depending on what action the Secretary-General took.

21. Legum, *Pan-Africanism,* p. 51.

22. Nkrumah, *Challenge of the Congo,* pp. 116–17.

23. For example, London 2602, 12/16/60, reported a conversation between the

British ambassador to the Sudan and President Abboud in which Abboud assured the ambassador that there was "no truth" to reports that Egyptian aid would reach Stanleyville through the Sudan.

24. *NYT,* 1/7/61.

25. Legum, *Pan-Africanism,* p. 192.

26. *Pravda,* 1/12/61.

27. S/4616.

28. *NYT,* 1/10/61.

29. S/4604, Part V; see also S/4604, Part II, a note from the Secretary-General to Belgium on December 30 warning of the possibility of the Congolese maneuver and expressing the hope that the Belgian government would not violate international law by cooperating with Mobutu.

30. USUN 1908, 1/10/61, noted that several of Hammarskjold's colleagues had urged him not to let "Russian harassment" prevent him from carrying through his important visits to Cairo and New Delhi, but that Hammarskjold had nearly made up his mind to return at that point. According to Urquhart, *Hammarskjold,* p. 499, he at first refused to cut short the trip.

31. SCOR, 924th Meeting, January 12, 1961.

32. SD 1256 to USUN, 1/9/61.

33. S/4625.

34. SCOR, 927th Meeting, January 14, 1961.

35. SD 1273 to USUN 1/12/61. The Department made the same point in a cable to Leopoldville 1651, 1/11/61) and to Elisabethville (322, 1/11/61), asking the ambassador and consul to inform Dayal and Ian Berendsen, the UN representative in Elisabethville, that the United States viewed the Lumumbist penetration "with great alarm."

36. USUN 1930, 1/14/61.

37. Leopoldville 1518, 1/13/61.

38. *NYT,* 1/14/61; see also S/4688, Dayal's report to the Secretary-General, February 12, 1961; Dayal, *Mission for Hammarskjold,* p. 190; Urquhart, *Hammarskjold,* pp. 500–1. The details vary slightly.

39. *NYT,* 1/1/61.

40. *Senate Intelligence Committee Report,* p. 49; Leopoldville 1518, 1/13/61; *NYT,*1/11,12/61, reported serious unrest in the army garrison and provincial police force in Leopoldville. There were threats of mutiny unless pay demands were met; and rifles disappeared from the police armory.

41. *Senate Intelligence Committee Report,* p. 49.

42. Dayal, *Mission for Hammarskjold,* p. 86; see also Elisabethville 138, 9/27/60.

43. Leopoldville Despatch 295, 2/7/61. *The New York Times* reported on January 10, 1961, that Mobutu's aide, Major Jacques Puati, had been sent to Elisabethville the previous day to try to work out an agreement on various issues.

44. Dayal, *Mission for Hammarskjold,* p. 192.

45. *Senate Intelligence Committee Report,* pp. 49–50.

46. There have been a number of accounts of Lumumba's transfer, with varying details. See, for example, Leopoldville Despatch 295, 2/7/61; Dayal, *Mission for Hammarskjold,* pp. 195–96; Urquhart, *Hammarskjold,* p. 501; Hoskyns, *The Congo Since Independence,* pp. 306–7.

See also S/4976, "Report of the Commission of Investigation established under the terms of General Assembly resolution 1601 (XV) of 15 April 1961."

47. Nkrumah, *Challenge of the Congo,* p. 119.

48. S/4688, Dayal's report to the Secretary-General, February 12, 1961. See *NYT,* 1/19/61. For more detail, see Dayal, *Mission for Hammarskjold,* pp. 191–92, and Urquhart, *Hammarskjold,* p. 501.

49. S/4976.
50. Elisabethville 412, 1/18/61.
51. USUN 1964, 1/19/61.
52. Elisabethville 412, 1/18/61
53. S/4637, Part I, the Secretary-General's message to Kasavubu on January 19, 1961; Part II, the Secretary-General's message to Tshombe on January 19, 1961; Part III, a second message from the Secretary-General to Kasavubu, January 20, 1961. See also Dayal, *Mission for Hammarskjold,* pp. 192–93; Urquhart, *Hammarskjold,* pp. 501–2.
54. SD 343 to Elisabethville, 1/18/61.
55. Elisabethville 421, 1/20/61.
56. Elisabethville 420, 1/20/61.
57. "Events in Congo," *Pravda,* 1/14/61; "Congo: Tension Mounts," *Pravda,* 1/15/61.
58. "Puppets Alarmed," *Pravda,* 1/16/61.
59. "Lumumba Transferred to Elisabethville," *Pravda,* 1/18/61.
60. "Congolese Won't Bow Heads," *Pravda,* 1/19/61.
61. V. Mayevskii, "Stay Hand of Butchers," *Pravda,* 1/20/61.
62. USUN 1908, 1/10/61.
63. *NYT,* 1/15/61.
64. SD 1273 to USUN, 1/12/61.
65. *Senate Intelligence Committee Report,* p. 49.
66. Ibid.
67. Ibid.
68. Ibid., p. 50.
69. Leopoldville Despatch 295, 2/7/61.
70. S/4688, Dayal's report to the Secretary-General, February 12, 1961; see Nkrumah, *Challenge of the Congo,* pp. 119–28, for Tshombe's revised version of the events of January 1961, as told to a Belgian journalist three years later.
71. Leopoldville Despatch 295, 2/7/61.
72. Dayal, *Mission for Hammarskjold,* p. 192.
73. Elisabethville 411, 1/17/61; Elisabethville 415, 1/19/61, noted, "Lumumba's arrival provides plausible explanation for recent wave of arrests in Elisabethville."
74. Elisabethville 415, 1/19/61, noted, "It appears likely Lumumba brought here by agreement between Tshombe and Kasavubu negotiated through Commandant Puati sent here by Mobutu. This agreement may foreshadow further accords between two governments on military and political subjects." See also *NYT,* 1/18/61.
75. On the other hand, Dayal, *Mission for Hammarskjold,* p. 190, suggested that Kasavubu and the commissioners apparently hoped that "with the common enemy in his hands, Tshombe would be more receptive to Leopoldville's approaches for a military alliance and political understanding."
76. *Senate Intelligence Committee Report,* p. 51.
77. Ibid., p. 50n.
78. Ibid., p. 51.
79. Ibid., p. 50.
80. Ibid., p. 51n.
81. Ibid., p. 50n.
82. Elisabethville 421, 1/20/61.
83. Elisabethville 361, 1/5/61, cited in *Analytical Chronology,* pp. 71–72.
84. Elisabethville 406, 1/17/61.
85. SD 343 to Elisabethville, 1/18/61. In fact, the news appeared in *The New York Times* on January 24, 1961, and in *Pravda* the day after that.
86. Elisabethville 421, 1/20/61.

87. SD 354 to Elisabethville, 1/23/61.

88. Accra 687, 12/15/60.

89. Leopoldville 1384 and 1389, 12/14/60.

90. Leopoldville 1482, 1/6/61.

Chapter Nine

1. John Bartlow Martin, *Adlai Stevenson and the World*, (New York: Doubleday & Company, 1977), p. 571.

2. Quoted in Schlesinger, *A Thousand Days: John F. Kennedy in the White House*, pp. 481–82.

3. For more detail on this debate, see the *Supplement to the Analytical Chronology* prepared by the Bureau of African Affairs of the State Department, March 9, 1961, p. 2.

4. *NYT*, 1/18/61.

5. *Analytical Chronology*.

6. Leopoldville 1558, 1/18/61, cited in *Analytical Chronology*, p. 73.

7. Ibid.

8. *Analytical Chronology*, p. 73.

9. Accra 825, 1/24/61; and 839, 1/25/61. Nkrumah also wrote to Stevenson, an old friend; see Nkrumah, *Challenge of the Congo*, pp. 146–51.

10. USUN 2010, 1/26/61.

11. Martin, *Adlai Stevenson*, pp. 599–600. See also USUN 2009 and 2011, 1/26/61.

12. USUN 2009, 1/26/61.

13. Martin, *Adlai Stevenson*, p. 600.

14. For more detail, see *Supplement*, pp. 1–2, and *NYT*, 1/30/61.

15. *NYT*, 1/21,24, 25/61.

16. John F. Kennedy News Conference of January 25, 1961, in *Public Papers of the Presidents, 1961* (Washington, D.C.: Office of the Federal Register, 1962), pp. 8–17.

17. The letter as revised was sent as SD 787 to Accra, 1/29/61.

18. Memorandum for the President on Suggested New Policy on the Congo, February 1, 1961.

19. *Supplement*, p. 3.

20. Letter of January 31, 1961, from Assistant Secretary of Defense for International Security Affairs Paul H. Nitze to Assistant Secretary of State for International Organization Affairs Harlan Cleveland, enclosing the memorandum "Recommended Courses of Action in the Event Proposed Strengthened UN Mandate Is Not Accepted."

21. Martin, *Adlai Stevenson*, pp. 601–2.

22. "Memorandum for the President on Suggested New Policy on the Congo," February 1, 1961.

23. SD 802 to Accra, 2/2/61.

24. SD 2069 to New Delhi, 2/2/61; SD 712 to Lagos, 2/2/61; Depcirtel No. 1153, 2/2/61.

Rusk explained, in an FYI aside to the ambassadors in New Delhi and Lagos, "We are exercising our influence with Belgians and Kasavubu with view to securing early establishment of middle-of-the-road government." The words "under Prime Minister Ileo" were crossed out in this cable, but they appeared in the Depcirtel sent to the other Afro-Asian capitals. This information was not to be passed along to Nehru or Balewa or any of the other Afro-Asian leaders.

25. John F. Kennedy News Conference of February 1, 1961, in *Public Papers of the Presidents, 1961*, pp. 30–40.

26. Ibid.

27. For more detail on this period, see Martin, *Adlai Stevenson,* pp. 551–65; Schlesinger, *A Thousand Days,* pp. 138–41.

28. Francis Plimpton, Interview by Dennis J. O'Brien, October 21, 1969, pp. 4–5, John F. Kennedy Library Oral History Program; and interview with the author, August 1978.

29. SCOR, 928th Meeting, February 1, 1961.

30. Martin, *Adlai Stevenson,* pp. 602–3.

31. SCOR, 928th Meeting, February 1, 1961.

32. Schlesinger, *A Thousand Days,* p. 302; see above, Chap. 5, fn. 61.

33. S. Vishnevskii, P. Kapyrin, N. Prozhogin, "Review of World Affairs," *Pravda,* 1/24/61.

34. For Khrushchev's message to the Cairo meeting of the Council, see "Cause of Congo Is Cause of All Honest People on Earth," *Pravda,* 1/22/61; for coverage of the Soviet proposal for "effective practical aid" to Gizenga and the resolution adopted by the conference, see I. Beliaiev, "Down with Colonialism, Freedom to Congolese People," *Pravda,* 1/23/61; and "Finish with Colonialism Forever," *Pravda,* 1/24/61.

35. V. Yuliakov, "On Path of Independent Development," *Pravda,* 1/2/61; "Reception At Sudanese Embassy," *Pravda,* 1/4/61; *Pravda,* 1/10/61, reported the signature of the trade agreement between the Sudan and the Soviet Union; "Important Event in Political Life of Sudan," *Pravda,* 1/18/61, reported Sudanese reaction to the invitation to Abboud.

36. "For People of Congo," *Pravda,* 1/30/61, includes the text of the Soviet message; for the Sudanese response, see S/4674, a letter to the Secretary-General dated February 6, 1961.

37. Martin, *Adlai Stevenson,* p. 601.

38. SCOR, 930th Meeting, February 2, 1961.

39. USUN 2098, 2/3/61.

40. SD 3802 to London, 2/2/61.

41. Brussels USIS Despatch 740, 2/8/61, reviewed press reaction; see also *NYT,* 2/7/61; and Paris POLTO 1081, 2/9/61, reporting the negative reactions at the meeting of the North Atlantic Council.

42. Leopoldville 1676, 2/4/61; *NYT,* 2/4/61.

43. *Supplement,* pp. 3–4, pointed out that "the failure to keep good security on our new policy during the one or two critical days when we should have presented it to key neutrals and allies had the result that we were soon forced to explain what it was that we did *not* mean."

44. U.S. Senate Committee on Foreign Relations, Briefing on the Situation in the Congo, February 6, 1961.

45. USUN 2123, 2/7/61.

46. *NYT,* 2/10/61.

47. Leopoldville 1705, 2/9/61.

48. Leopoldville 1710, 2/10/61.

49. Elisabethville 507, 2/11/61.

50. *Senate Intelligence Committee Report,* p. 51.

51. S/4683.

52. Martin, *Adlai Stevenson,* pp. 606–7.

53. USUN 2178 and 2179, 2/11/61.

54. SD 1458 to USUN 2/11/61.

55. *NYT,* 2/14/61.

56. Ibid.

57. Ibid.

58. SCOR, 933rd Meeting, February 13, 1961.

59. Martin, *Adlai Stevenson,* p. 609.

60. USUN 2196, 2/13/61.

61. Leopoldville 1736, 2/14/61.

62. USUN 2193, 2/13/61; see also Yost's memorandum of February 17, 1961, cited in *Supplement,* p. 6, analyzing Soviet intentions.

63. Leopoldville 1729, 2/14/61.

64. S/4704. "Soviet Government Statement in Connection with Murder of Patrice Lumumba," *Pravda,* 2/15/61.

65. Ibid.

66. "To His Excellency Mr. Antoine Gizenga, Acting Prime Minister of the Congo," *Pravda,* 2/15/61.

67. "Sea of Wrath," *Pravda,* 2/15/61.

68. *NYT,* 2/15/61.

69. Khrushchev had been invited to Africa and Brezhnev's trip was regarded as a sort of dry run. He ran into one nasty incident en route to Morocco when his plane was fired at by a French military plane over international waters; Moscow launched a strong protest.

70. Martin, *Adlai Stevenson,* p. 610.

71. "Statement of White House Representative," *Pravda,* 2/14/61. There was one ironic note in the Soviet coverage: *Pravda* reported that press secretary Pierre Salinger had refused to answer questions about reports that the Administration had begun to look more favorably on the possibility of Lumumba's participation in the Congolese government just before his death was announced. This was the first and only time that the Soviet press referred to this possibility, and it was mentioned only when all hope of such an arrangement was gone.

72. *NYT,* 2/15/61.

73. SCOR, 934th Meeting, February 15, 1961.

74. For more detail, see *NYT,* 2/16/61; and Urquhart, *Hammarskjold,* pp. 506–7.

75. SD 1598 to Cairo, 2/15/61.

76. *NYT,* 2/16/61.

77. SD 3946 to London, 2/15/61.

78. Martin, *Adlai Stevenson,* p. 611.

79. John F. Kennedy News Conference of February 15, 1961, *Public Papers of the Presidents, 1961,* pp. 91–99.

80. *NYT,* 2/16/61.

81. "Wrath of Peoples," and "Message to President Kennedy," *Pravda,* 2/16/61.

82. SCOR, 937th Meeting, February 16, 1961.

83. S/4722.

84. USUN 2220 and 2215, 2/15/61.

85. Accra 977, 2/18/61. See also Nkrumah, *Challenge of the Congo,* pp. 134–38.

86. Accra 981, 2/18/61; and 982, 983, 2/19/61.

87. USUN 2237, 2/19/61; and 2245, 2/20/61.

88. SCOR, 940th Meeting, February 20, 1961.

89. SCOR, 941st Meeting, February 20, 1961.

90. S/4741.

91. SCOR, 942nd Meeting, February 20–21, 1961. The three Afro-Asian members of the Security Council introduced a second draft (S/4733) condemning "unlawful arrests, deportations and assassinations of political leaders in Leopoldville, Elisabethville, and Kasai." Stevenson insisted that Stanleyville be added to the list. He produced reports from the Secretary-General indicating that a number of anti-Lumumba political figures

had just been murdered in Stanleyville. There reports were unofficial and unconfirmed, but within a few days it turned out that the information was correct: fifteen political prisoners, including Songolo, had been executed. Zorin vetoed Stevenson's amendment; he was joined by Ceylon and the UAR. Stevenson refused to vote for the draft without his amendment, and it failed to win the necessary seven votes.

92. USUN 2264, 2/22/61.

93. See S/4752, Ann. I and II, Hammarskjold's note of February 22, 1961, to the Belgian government and the Belgian reply of February 27, 1961; see also Brussels 1554, 2/24/61.

94. *NYT,* 2/22, 23/61.

95. Leopoldville 1784, 2/22/61.

96. *Pravda,* 2/26/61.

97. *NYT,* 2/27/61.

98. SD 1403 to Moscow, 2/27/61. See also *NYT,* 3/1/61; and Schlesinger, *A Thousand Days,* p. 305.

99. "World in Past Month," *Izvestia,* 3/1/61.

100. *NYT,* 3/3/61.

101. Observer, "In Spirit of Cold War," *Izvestia,* 3/9/61.

Chapter Ten

1. National Security Action Memorandum No. 26, March 5, 1961. Kennedy's staff investigated the incident and confirmed his initial impression that "a decision with serious foreign policy implications was made by persons at the field level without any prior consultation with Washington."

See also *Analytical Chronology,* p. 32, for more detail on the task force; S/4761, Dayal's report on the incident, March 8, 1961; and Dayal, *Mission for Hammarskjold,* pp. 224–26.

2. *NYT,* 3/7/61.

3. *NYT,* 3/8/61.

4. *NYT,* 2/26/61. For more information about these military movements, see S/4750 and Add. 1–7, Dayal's reports, February 25–March 7, 1961.

5. SD 1909 and 1910 to Leopoldville, 2/27/61.

6. Leopoldville 1813, 2/28/61; and 1820, 3/1/61.

7. *NYT,* 2/28/61; Dayal, *Mission for Hammarskjold,* pp. 218–22. See also S/4753, Dayal's report, February 27, 1961, on attacks on UN personnel; S/4757 and Add. 1, Dayal's report, March 2, 1961, on attempts to protect refugees; S/4758 and Add. 1–6, Hammarskjold's report to the Security Council, March 3, 1961, on the growing tension between the UN force and the Leopoldville government over Dayal and other issues.

8. Leopoldville 1820, 3/1/61.

9. John F. Kennedy News Conference of March 1, 1961, in *Public Papers of the Presidents, 1961,* pp. 135–43.

10. *NYT,* 3/1/61.

11. Elisabethville 576, 3/1/61.

12. Leopoldville 1835, 3/2/61.

13. Bromley Smith memorandum to McGeorge Bundy, March 3, 1961; Lucius Battle memorandum to Bundy, March 7, 1961. In order to keep on top of the situation, Kennedy asked to see the Congo chronology prepared by the Africa Bureau at the end of January once again, and he requested an update of the report that would bring it up to the present time. This update was sent to the President on March 11, 1961.

14. Cairo 1521, 3/9/61. See also Leopoldville 1847, 3/4/61, and 1856, 3/6/61; Tananarive 208 and 210, 3/7/61, on Gizenga's plans.

15. Tananarive 226 and 227, 3/10/61; and 232, 3/11/61. See also *NYT*, 3/11, 11, 13 13/61. For the text of the resolutions and a full account of the meeting, see Verhaegen, *Congo 1961* (Brussels: Centre de Recherche et d'Information Socio-Politique, 1962), pp. 27–49.

16. Leopoldville 2026, 3/16/61.

17. *NYT*, 3/15/61.

18. *NYT*, 3/7/61.

19. SD 1645 to USUN, 3/8/61.

20. Dayal, *Mission for Hammarskjold*, p. 235.

21. Ibid, pp. 246–51.

22. Memorandum from Assistant Secretary of State Harlan Cleveland to the Acting Secretary of State, March 29, 1961.

23. Leopoldville 1894, 3/12/61.

24. Leopoldville 1762, 2/18/61. See also S/4745, Dayal's report on this incident.

25. Leopoldville Despatch 326, 2/24/61.

26. Leopoldville Despatch 324, 2/24/61.

27. Leopoldville 1894, 3/12/61; and Despatch 354, 3/13/61.

28. Leopoldville Despatch 324, 2/24/61.

29. Leopoldville 1894, 3/12/61.

30. Leopoldville Despatch 357, 3/14/61.

31. Leopoldville Despatch 324, 2/24/61.

32. "Stanleyville Welcomes Statement of Soviet Government," *Pravda*, 2/18/61.

33. *NYT*, 3/1/61.

34. Leopoldville 1877, 3/8/61.

35. Leopoldville 2138, 4/5/61; and 2152, 4/7/61.

36. *NYT*, 4/8/61.

37. Leopoldville Despatch 408, 4/11/61.

38. GAOR, 965th Plenary Meeting, March 21, 1961.

39. A/L. 341 introduced at the 980th Plenary Meeting, April 7, 1961.

40. Joint Statement of President Kennedy and President Nkrumah, March 8, 1961, in *Public Papers of the Presidents, 1961,* p. 161.

41. GAOR, 961st Plenary Meeting, March 7, 1961.

42. *NYT*, 3/7/61. For the Soviet report of Nkrumah's speech, see "Curb Colonialists and Their Mercenaries," *Pravda*, 3/9/61.

43. A/L. 340. GAOR, 985th Plenary Meeting, April 15, 1961. For Zorin's view, see GAOR, 980th Plenary Meeting, April 7, 1961. See also "Congo Question and Maneuvers of Colonialists," *Pravda*, 4/8/61; and "Africa Will Be Independent," *Pravda*, 4/9/61, for Soviet criticism of the draft resolution.

44. For more background on this crisis, see Martin, *Adlai Stevenson*, pp. 622–36; Schlesinger, *A Thousand Days*, pp. 215–97; Chester Bowles, *Promises to Keep: My Years in Public Life, 1941–1969* (New York: Harper & Row, 1971), pp. 326–32; Theodore C. Sorensen, *Kennedy* (New York: Harper & Row, 1965), pp. 294–309; Powers, *The Man Who Kept the Secrets*, pp. 105–18; Peter Wyden, *Bay of Pigs: The Untold Story* (New York: Simon and Schuster, 1979).

45. Plimpton, Interview, Kennedy Library Oral History Program, pp. 10–13.

46. Martin, *Adlai Stevenson*, p. 624; see also Schlesinger, *A Thousand Days*, p. 271.

47. Moscow 2550, 4/18/61.

48. Message to Chairman Khrushchev Concerning the Meaning of Events in Cuba, April 18, 1961, in *Public Papers of the Presidents, 1961,* pp. 363–64.

49. Moscow 2561, 4/22/61.

50. William Attwood, *The Reds and the Blacks* (New York: Harper & Row, 1967), p. 27.

51. Schlesinger, *A Thousand Days,* p. 568.

52. For more detail on Stevenson's position, see Martin, *Adlai Stevenson,* pp. 616–18, 631.

53. *NYT,* 5/8, 10/61. For more detail on the arrest of Tshombe, see Verhaegen, *Congo 1961,* pp. 250–68, including reports by Interior Minister Adoula and one of Tshombe's European advisers.

54. USUN 2995, 4/26/61; SD 2138 to USUN, 4/27/61.

55. Leopoldville 2269, 4/28/61.

56. Leopoldville 2274, 5/1/61; and Despatch 434, 5/2/61. According to Verhaegen, *Congo 1961,* p. 186, Ambassador Diakite of Mali arrived on April 4, followed by Pavlovic, the Yugoslav chargé, on April 18. Gizenga had already sent a number of diplomatic representatives abroad: to Poland on March 2, to Cairo and Peking on March 17.

57. Leopoldville 2269, 4/28/61.

58. Leopoldville 2324, 5/13/61.

59. Leopoldville 2330, 5/15/61; and 2336, 5/16/61.

60. S/4811.

61. SD 2202 to Leopoldville, 5/19/61.

62. Leopoldville 2345, 5/19/61, and 2363 and Despatch 468, 5/24/61.

63. SD 2249 to Leopoldville, 6/5/61.

64. Dayal, *Mission for Hammarskjold,* pp. 258–64; Urquhart, *Hammarskjold,* pp. 517–18.

65. On the Laos crisis, see Schlesinger, *A Thousand Days,* pp. 320–42; Bowles, *Promises to Keep,* pp. 334–41; Macmillan, *Pointing the Way,* pp. 329–38, 344–347.

66. Schlesinger, *A Thousand Days,* p. 343; *NYT,* 5/19/61.

67. *Khrushchev Remembers,* p. 499. For more detail on the summit meeting and the Berlin issue, see pp. 487–509. Heikal, *The Cairo Documents,* p. 211, said Khrushchev told Nasser, "Kennedy came into that meeting like a peacock and he left like a drowned sparrow."

68. David Halberstam, *The Best and the Brightest* (New York: Random House, 1969), p. 76. On the American view of the summit meeting, see Schlesinger, *A Thousand Days,* pp. 358–74; Bohlen, *Witness to History,* pp. 480–86; Sulzberger, *The Last of the Giants,* pp. 757–65; see also Macmillan, *Pointing the Way,* pp. 356–358.

69. Memorandum from McGeorge Bundy to the President, June 10, 1961.

70. Leopoldville 2436, 6/9/61, and 2444, 6/10/61.

71. Leopoldville Despatch 487, 6/12/61.

72. Leopoldville Despatches 488 and 489, 6/12/61.

73. Leopoldville Despatch 490, 6/12/61.

74. *NYT,* 6/12/61.

75. Leopoldville 2472, 6/13/61.

76. Leopoldville 2492, 6/16/61.

77. *NYT,* 6/17/61.

78. For the text of the agreement and the statements made by the heads of the Leopoldville and Stanleyville delegations, see S/4841, Ann. I, II, and III.

79. Leopoldville 2511, 6/20/61, and 2552, 6/24/61.

80. Leopoldville 2550, 6/26/61; SD 2374 to Leopoldville, 6/28/61; Leopoldville 6, 7/1/61.

81. SD 2480 to USUN, 6/20/61; and USUN 3392, 6/22/61.

82. Leopoldville 2518, 6/21/61.

83. Leopoldville 2531, 6/22/61; *NYT,* 6/23/61.

84. Leopoldville 2550, 6/26/61.

85. Leopoldville 2551, 2552, 6/24/61.

86. Leopoldville Airgram G-355, 6/22/61.

87. SD 2507 to USUN, 6/24/61.

88. As late as June 7, *Pravda* was describing Kasavubu's plan to convene Parliament in Leopoldville as a "farce" and assuring its readers that Gizenga would never go along with it; see "New Plot Against Congo," *Pravda*, 6/7/61. But by June 23, the Soviet newspaper was presenting the agreement as a triumph for Gizenga, and predicting that his forces would sweep to victory in Parliament; see "Parliament Will Be Convened," *Pravda*, 6/23/61.

89. See, for example, 3 articles by T. Kolesnichenko, "Forward Stanleyville," *Pravda*, 4/12/61; "Second Life of P. Lumumba," *Pravda*, 4/26/61; and "Light of Stanleyville," *Pravda*, 5/4/61.

90. For example, N. Khokhlov, "Living Heart of Lumumba," *Izvestia*, 6/17/61, noted that there were only two foreign diplomats accredited to Stanleyville: the ambassador of Mali and the chargé d'affaires of Yugoslavia.

91. For the text of the Monrovia resolutions, see Legum, *Pan-Africanism*, pp. 198–201; for more detail on the conference, see pp. 52–55. The Congo was not invited because the sponsors wanted to avoid a confrontation with the Casablanca states about which regime should be recognized—Leopoldville or Stanleyville. The Casablanca powers refused to attend because the Algerian provisional government was not invited.

92. "Soviet-Somali Communiqué," *Izvestia*, 6/2/61. See also coverage in the Soviet press from May 24 to June 3, especially on Khrushchev's welcome of Shermarke at the airport, "May Friendship and Cooperation Between Soviet and Somali Peoples Grow Stronger," *Pravda*, 5/25/61; "Khrushchev Receives Prime Minister Shermarke," *Pravda*, 5/26/61, reporting their talks and speeches at a Kremlin luncheon; "For Peace and Friendship," *Pravda*, 6/1/61, an account of a Somali reception on May 31 at which Mikoyan spoke; "In Honor of Guests from Republic of Somalia," *Pravda*, 6/2/61, about the June 1 Kremlin reception.

93. *NYT,* 6/26, 27/61. For the text of Tshombe's agreement with the Leopoldville government, see S/4841/Add. 2. See also Verhaegen, *Congo 1961,* pp. 277–84, for more detail on the agreement and on Tshombe's press conference in Elisabethville.

94. SD 2374 to Leopoldville, 6/29/61.

95. Leopoldville 6, 7/1/61.

96. Leopoldville 111, 7/15/61.

97. SD 42 to USUN, 7/11/61; USUN 76, 7/12/61; Leopoldville 106, 7/14/61; and 171, 7/22/61.

98. Leopoldville 114 and 124, 7/17/61.

99. The Soviet press, which ignored the presence of the diplomatic mission in Stanleyville, reported the departure of the members of Parliament in some detail, and seemed to approve of the idea that they had gone to the meeting, which was still described as a triumph of Gizenga's policy. *Pravda* noted that Gizenga himself had remained in Stanleyville for reasons of health and made no further reference to his continued absence. See "Unity is Chief Thing," *Pravda*, 7/16/61; Mayevskii, "Congolese Stand for Genuine Independence and Unity of Country," *Pravda*, 7/18/61.

100. Leopoldville 125 and 130, 7/18/61.

101. Leopoldville 133, 7/19/61.

102. Leopoldville 142, 7/20/61.

103. Leopoldville 152, 7/21/61.

104. Leopoldville 169, 7/22/61.

105. Leopoldville 178, 7/24/61; and 189, 7/25/61.

106. Leopoldville 197, 7/26/61.

107. Leopoldville 196, 7/26/61.

108. Leopoldville 197 and 204, 7/26/61. The decisive factor in the Leopoldville victory seemed to have been a report, widely disseminated at Lovanium by Khiary, that Gizenga had sent a message to the president of Kivu Province instructing him to execute three high-ranking provincial officials. Linner had intercepted the message and warned Gizenga that he would hold him responsible if the instructions were carried out. Gizenga quickly denied that he had ever given such orders and sent Lundula to Bukavu to release the officials in question, but Linner deliberately neglected to publicize his denial.

109. Memorandum from President Kennedy to Secretary of State Rusk, July 26, 1961.

110. SD 127 to Leopoldville, 7/26/61.

111. Leopoldville 210, 212, and 214, 7/27/61.

112. Leopoldville 219, 7/28/61.

113. Leopoldville 220, 7/28/61.

114. SD 146 to Leopoldville, 7/29/61.

115. Leopoldville 239, 7/30/61; and 242, 7/31/61.

116. Leopoldville 234, 7/29/61.

117. Leopoldville 252, 253, and 254, 8/1/61.

118. Leopoldville 281, 8/3/61.

119. *NYT*, 8/3/61.

120. SD 168 to Leopoldville, 8/3/61.

121. USUN 350, 8/4/61.

122. Memorandum from Secretary of State Rusk to President Kennedy, August 3, 1961.

123. Memorandum from Walt Rostow to President Kennedy, August 4, 1961.

124. "Joint Soviet-Ghanaian Communiqué," *Pravda*, 7/26/61. See also coverage of Nkrumah's visit beginning in *Pravda* on July 10, especially "Sincere Cordiality," *Pravda*, 7/12/61, the report of the July 11 Kremlin luncheon with speeches by Khrushchev and Nkrumah.

125. "Joint Soviet-Sudanese Communiqué," *Pravda*, 7/28/61. This was similar to the communiqué issued at the end of the visit of the Somali Prime Minister in June. See also coverage of Abboud's visit, beginning July 17, especially "Soviet-Sudanese Cooperation Grows Stronger," *Pravda*, 7/19/61, on the Kremlin luncheon given by Brezhnev, with speeches; "Dinner given by N. S. Khrushchev in honor of I. Abboud," *Pravda*, 7/23/61.

126. On August 3, the day after the Adoula government was approved by Parliament, *Pravda* published Gizenga's telegram of July 31, thanking Khrushchev for his anniversary message. The very next day it reported the formation of the Adoula government in straightforward fashion, without editorial comment; but a degree of approval was suggested by the fact that it quoted Adoula's statement that his government would "try to restore peace and order in the Congo, unify the army, and carry out a foreign policy of positive neutralism." ("In Congo Parliament," *Pravda*, 8/4/61)

127. If the Russians had wanted to object to Adoula, there were sufficient grounds in his political biography, starting with the fact that he had broken with Lumumba in a party split in 1959 and ending with the fact that he had served as Ileo's Interior Minister since February. It was in this capacity that he had been mentioned, only once, by the Soviet press, as one of the group of "puppets" named by Kasavubu to replace the "legitimate government"; see "Government of People and 'Government' of Puppets," *Pravda*, 2/10/61.

128. Leopoldville Despatch 57, 8/9/61.

129. Ibid.

130. *NYT*, 8/18,19/61. For the text of their statements and Adoula's press conference on his return to Leopoldville, see Verhaegen, *Congo 1961*, pp. 495–98.

131. "Congolese People Will Not Turn Back From Path," *Pravda*, 8/20/61, reported

that Gizenga had invited the foreign diplomats to Stanleyville to meet Adoula, thanked them for their support of his government, and told them that Parliament had decided the Adoula government was its legal successor. There was a note of caution, however, in this coverage: the Soviet newspaper reported Gizenga's statement that, while he had agreed to join the Adoula government, if it did anything wrong, he would report it to the people and fight for a new government which would be faithful to Lumumba's policies.

132. *Pravda*, 9/1/61.

133. USUN 511, 8/22/61; SD 305 to Leopoldville, 8/26/61.

134. Report by Assistant Secretary of State Williams on his trip to Africa, sent by Secretary Rusk to President Kennedy, September 9, 1961.

135. Letters from President Kennedy to President Kasavubu and Prime Minister Adoula, September 1, 1961.

Chapter Eleven

1. *NYT*, 9/4/61. See also Leopoldville Despatch 83, 9/5/61, the report of Cassilly, who stressed the erosion of Gizenga's position in Stanleyville after the meeting of Parliament.

2. For more detail, see Legum, *Pan-Africanism*, pp. 59–61.

3. USUN 422, 8/11/61. See also USUN 413, 8/11/61, for Adoula's letter to the Secretary-General requesting UN recognition.

4. *NYT*, 9/6/61.

5. U Thant, *View from the UN* (New York: Doubleday & Co., 1978), p. 129.

6. For the text of Adoula's speech, see Verhaegen, *Congo 1961*, pp. 435–37.

7. For the text of Gizenga's speech, see ibid., pp. 437–39.

8. *NYT*, 9/6/61.

9. For the text of Khrushchev's announcement of the tests, see *NYT*, 9/1/61. See also "To Chairman of Conference of Non-aligned States," *Pravda*, 9/2/61.

10. *NYT*, 9/1/61.

11. *NYT*, 9/1, 2, 3, 4/61.

12. Mayevskii and Tarasov, "Decide Most Important Questions," *Pravda*, 9/3/61.

13. N. Karev, "Main Thing—Fight Against Imperialism," *Izvestia*, 9/4/61.

14. Mayevskii, "Self-exposure of Colonialists," *Pravda*, 9/9/61.

15. *NYT*, 9/4/61.

16. Verhaegen, *Congo 1961*, pp. 435–37.

17. Martin, *Adlai Stevenson*, p. 661. Also cited in Schlesinger, *A Thousand Days*, pp. 482–83.

18. Macmillan, *Pointing the Way*, pp. 396–97.

19. Nehru did not particularly want Nkrumah to join him, since they had found themselves on opposite sides of most of the issues debated at the conference. For more detail, see *NYT*, 9/5, 6, 7/61.

20. Martin, *Adlai Stevenson*, p. 661; also cited by Schlesinger, *A Thousand Days*, p. 521.

21. *NYT*, 9/8/61.

22. *NYT*, 9/13, 14/61.

23. Martin, *Adlai Stevenson*, p. 662; also cited by Schlesinger, *A Thousand Days*, p. 520.

24. Schlesinger, *A Thousand Days*, pp. 518–19.

25. *NYT*, 9/16/61.

26. See Martin, *Adlai Stevenson*, p. 658, on Stevenson's disagreement with the State Department on the Bizerte issue; he lost the battle and the United States abstained on the General Assembly resolution favored by Tunisia on August 25. See also Urquhart, *Hammarskjold*, pp. 532–41, who noted that the United States turned down Hammarskjold's request to bring home three Tunisian battalions in the Congo urgently requested by Tunisian President Habib Bourguiba.

27. Urquhart, *Hammarskjold*, p. 565.

28. *NYT*, 9/14/61.

29. Urquhart, *Hammarskjold*, pp. 548–49. According to Urquhart, O'Brien was Hammarskjold's second choice and was called in at the last minute when the first appointment fell through.

30. Conor Cruise O'Brien, *To Katanga and Back:* pp. 43–45.

31. See above, Chap. 9, p. 236

32. See *The Observer*, 12/10, 17/61. O'Brien was certainly the most vivid and talented writer to serve the United Nations in the Congo. His account of his experiences, *To Katanga and Back*, conveys the extraordinary mood of this period better than any dispassionate UN report could do—although other participants in the events he described have warned that it occasionally borders on fiction. O'Brien's play "Murderous Angels," an acknowledged piece of fiction in which he could give free rein to his imagination and invent dialogue for the principal characters, cuts to the heart of the controversy between Hammarskjold and Lumumba—at least on a psychological plane—even though many of the facts were altered for dramatic emphasis.

33. Urquhart, *Hammarskjold*, p. 554.

34. For more detail, see O'Brien, *To Katanga and Back*, pp. 123–38, 178–84, 195–203; and Urquhart, *Hammarskjold*, pp. 552–54. See also the memoirs of Belgian Foreign Minister Paul-Henri Spaak, *Combats Inachevés* (Brussels: Fayard, 1969), vol. 2, pp. 243–46.

35. For the text of the order, see O'Brien, *To Katanga and Back*, pp. 345–46.

36. Ibid., pp. 216–18.

37. Ibid., p. 219.

38. Urquhart, *Hammarskjold*, p. 556.

39. O'Brien, *To Katanga and Back*, p. 219.

40. SD 341 to Leopoldville, 9/1/61.

41. Macmillan, *Pointing the Way*, p. 444.

42. For more detail on this period, see O'Brien, *To Katanga and Back*, pp. 219–46; Hoskyns, *The Congo Since Independence*, pp. 384–435; and *NYT*, 9/1, 2, 8, 12, 13/61.

43. O'Brien, *To Katanga and Back*, p. 249.

44. Ibid., p. 246.

45. Ibid., p. 252.

46. Ibid., pp. 253–58.

47. Urquhart, *Hammarskjold*, p. 571.

48. O'Brien, *To Katanga and Back*, p. 251.

49. Urquhart, *Hammarskjold*, pp. 566–70.

50. Dayal, *Mission for Hammarskjold*, pp. 268–69.

51. Urquhart, *Hammarskjold*, p. 566.

52. O'Brien, *To Katanga and Back*, pp. 263–66, explained his reasoning. He maintained that Morthor had been designed to end the Katanga secession, under the provision of the February 21 resolution authorizing the United Nations to use force if necessary to prevent civil war, and he saw no harm in saying so. He disregarded the fact that Hammarskjold had always insisted that the United Nations was not authorized to end the Katanga secession by force, as well as the fact that Hammarskjold had always objected to the idea of the United Nations arresting Congolese political figures at the

request of the Leopoldville government. He had refused to permit this in Lumumba's case, and he was equally unwilling to go along in the case of Tshombe.

53. S/4940.

54. Urquhart, *Hammarskjold,* pp. 582–83, and O'Brien, *To Katanga and Back,* p. 266. Later, when O'Brien saw the report, he was even more disappointed by Hammarskjold's decision to "conceal the reality of what had happened" and to present the world with an "official version" which O'Brien considered "false." (pp. 264–65) He said it made "what had been an active intervention by the United Nations look like a defensive action." O'Brien argued that if Hammarskjold disapproved of the action he could have disavowed it, O'Brien, Linner, and Khiary; or he could have backed them up completely and explained that it was the job of the United Nations to cooperate with the central government to end the secession; but he chose a middle path and gave a false version of the operation, trying to disguise the purpose of the mission.

55. O'Brien, *To Katanga and Back,* p. 286.

56. Dayal, *Mission for Hammarskjold,* p. 281, said Hammarskjold was "forced into humbling his high office and risking his personal reputation and indeed his life" by the requirements of great power diplomacy.

57. Urquhart, *Hammarskjold,* p. 580.

58. Ibid., p. 577.

59. Kolesnichenko, "Congo Struggles and Colonialists Maneuver," *Pravda,* 9/15/61. See also "Events in Katanga," *Sovetskaia Rossiia,* 9/16/61, and "Imperialists Behind Tshombe," *Trud,* 9/17/61.

60. Urquhart, *Hammarskjold,* p. 572; Dayal, *Mission for Hammarskjold,* pp. 269–70.

61. Urquhart, *Hammarskjold,* p. 575.

62. Macmillan, *Pointing the Way,* p. 442.

63. Ibid.

64. Dayal, *Mission for Hammarskjold,* p. 273.

65. Macmillan, *Pointing the Way,* p. 443. Lansdowne's visit was the source of great controversy. Urquhart felt Lansdowne's influence was exaggerated after Hammarskjold's death. He denied rumors that Lansdowne presented Hammarskjold an ultimatum demanding that he stop the fighting or give up British support. He said (p. 578) Lansdowne was "restrained and courteous," but his mission was resented by the UN staff and the Congolese government, who felt British "interference" was bound to help Tshombe. Hammarskjold, according to Urquhart, considered the talk a matter of "courtesy and information" and an "additional source of irritation"—but nothing more. Dayal (p. 273) on the other hand, credited the rumors and wrote that there could be "no doubt that the conversation between the two men was tough, and for Hammarskjold, extremely unpleasant." He described Hammarskjold as "anxious and preoccupied" after the meeting.

66. Dayal, *Mission for Hammarskjold,* p. 273.

67. O'Brien, *To Katanga and Back,* p. 285.

68. Urquhart, *Hammarskjold,* p. 585. Urquhart argued (p. 581n) that while O'Brien described Hammarskjold's decision to meet Tshombe as a "virtual surrender," it was actually "a firm and realistic attempt to get the UN, and especially O'Brien and the UN Katanga command, out of an impossible situation into which they had fallen through military and other forms of incompetence."

69. Dayal, *Mission for Hammarskjold,* p. 274. Hammarskjold wrote to Bunche, "I am certain that just as every paper believes that I went to Leopoldville for the Katanga problem, every paper will take for granted, if and when the approach to Tshombe is made known, that this is result of 'constructive proposals' made by Lansdowne for Western powers."

70. Ibid., p. 276.

71. For the official UN account, see S/4940/Add. 5, "Special Report on the Fatal Flight of the Secretary-General's Aircraft," submitted on September 19, 1961. See also Urquhart, *Hammarskjold,* pp. 585–89. See also Arthur L. Gavshon, *The Mysterious Death of Dag Hammarskjold* (New York: Walker, 1962), which detailed the political infighting and misunderstandings preceding the flight and the bad judgment of Rhodesian officials following the disappearance of the plane.

72. *NYT,* 9/19/61.

73. "Death of Dag Hammarskjold," *Izvestia,* 9/19/61.

74. O'Brien, *To Katanga and Back,* pp. 286–88.

75. *NYT,* 9/21/61. See also S/4940/Add. 5, Ann., a press release issued by Adoula on September 18 charging that Hammarskjold had "fallen victim to the shameless intrigues of the great financial powers of the West."

76. S/4940/Add. 5.

77. *NYT,* 9/19/61.

78. *NYT,* 9/20/61.

79. Thant, *View from the UN,* pp. 6–7.

80. GAOR, 862nd Plenary Meeting, September 19, 1960.

81. USUN 2418, 3/9/61.

82. Urquhart, *Hammarskjold,* p. 565*n.*

83. Thant, *View from the UN,* pp. 9–10.

84. See S/4972 for the Security Council decision to select Thant, and A/Res/1640 (XVI) for the General Assembly's confirmation of the choice.

85. Ushakov, *The Soviet Union and the UN,* p. 22, claimed that Thant's selection weakened "the position of the colonialists in the United Nations."

86. Martin, *Adlai Stevenson,* p. 665.

87. Thant, *View from the UN,* pp. 36–38.

88. Ibid., pp. 20–23.

Chapter Twelve

1. S/4973.

2. *NYT,* 9/19/61.

3. *NYT,* 9/22/61.

4. National Security Action Memorandum No. 97, September 19, 1961. It stated, "In the President's view it is of high importance that US fighter aircraft be understood to intervene only in defense of beleaguered U.N. forces. He is not prepared to authorize their use at this time in offensive activities against Katangan forces."

5. S/4940/Add. 6 and 7.

6. *NYT,* 9/23/61.

7. "On Tshombe's Conditions," *Trud,* 9/22/61; "Maneuvers Against Unity of Congo," *Komsomol'skaia Pravda,* 9/23/61; "Shots Still Heard," *Komsomol'skaia Pravda,* 9/27/61.

8. *NYT,* 9/21/61.

9. Memorandum from Under Secretary Ball for the President, "US Policy Toward the Congo-Katanga Problem," September 23, 1961.

10. Ibid.; and Memorandum from W. W. Rostow to the President, September 24, 1961; and Memorandum from G. Mennen Williams for the President, "Situation in the Congo and Present US Actions," September 25, 1961.

11. *NYT,* 9/21/61.

12. Memorandum from Williams to the President, September 25, 1961. Adoula gave the same answer to the representatives of Czechoslovakia and the UAR, and he asked

the newly arrived East German envoy to leave the Congo immediately. See *NYT*, 9/30/61, and Leopoldville 884, 10/2/61. When Gullion congratulated Adoula on this move and asked if there had been any offers of aid from the Communist bloc, Adoula replied that the East Germans had presented a project which he had rejected, and that the Yugoslavs had offered a two-million-dollar loan which he would probably reject because he felt there were strings attached to it.

13. Leopoldville 850, 9/27/61. See also SD 515 to Leopoldville, 9/27/61, and Leopoldville 884, 10/2/61.

14. Leopoldville 896, 10/3/61.

15. Leopoldville 917, 10/5/61.

16. *NYT*, 10/13/61.

17. According to Leopoldville 974, 10/13/61. Alexander Dallin, "The Soviet Union: Political Activity," in Zbigniew Brzezinski (ed.), *Africa and the Communist World* (Stanford: Stanford University Press, 1963), p. 33, quoted an East European source who described Gizenga as " 'of all our African friends . . . the real pygmy.' "

18. The Soviet press was not openly critical of Adoula's delays but indicated its displeasure indirectly. It did not report Adoula's demand that the Soviet Union go through a new accreditation process; instead, it criticized Bomboko and the Congolese Foreign Ministry for trying to prevent the "consolidation of the Congo's relations with several friendly nations" and pointed out that there was considerable opposition to this course in the Congolese Parliament. See, for example, "Shots Still Heard," *Komsomol'skaia Pravda*, 9/27/61.

19. *Pravda*, 10/18/61. Khrushchev said, "After long and painful trials, a government was created in the Congo which delcared itself to be the successor to the government of Patrice Lumumba. The Soviet government is ready to provide help to the Congolese people in resolving the difficult problems facing them in the struggle to liquidate the consequences of colonialist oppression."

20. *NYT*, 10/26/61. See also Leopoldville Airgram A-86, 9/5/61, which reported that Jean Manzikala, the provincial president, had come to Leopoldville in early September, when Gizenga was in Belgrade, and had warned the government that he would be able to stay in power and get rid of the "troublemakers" only if Gizenga were kept away from Stanleyville.

21. *NYT*, 11/3/61. See S/4940/Add. 12 and 13 for more detail.

22. Memorandum from Under Secretary Ball to the President, November 2, 1961.

23. Martin, *Adlai Stevenson*, p. 672.

24. SD 1188 to USUN, 11/9/61.

25. Ibid. See also two Memoranda from Secretary Rusk to the President, "Next Steps in the Congo," and "Congo Policy," November 11, 1961.

26. SD 794 to Leopoldville, 11/11/61.

27. Leopoldville 1180, 11/11/61.

28. Ibid.

29. SD 806 to Leopoldville, 11/14/61.

30. Memoranda from Secretary Rusk to the President, November 11, 1961; and SD 797 to Leopoldville, 11/11/61.

31. Memorandum from Secretary Rusk to the President, "Financing United Nations Peace and Security Operations," 11/11/61.

32. SCOR, 973rd Meeting, November 13, 1961.

33. S/4976.

34. Memorandum from Assistant Secretary Cleveland to the President, November 28, 1960.

35. *NYT*, 11/15/61. For more detail, see S/4940/Add. 13.

36. O'Brien, *To Katanga and Back*, pp. 310–12.

37. Leopoldville 1211, 11/15/61.

38. *NYT,* 11/16/61.

39. S/4985.

40. Thant, *View from the UN,* p. 135.

41. *NYT,* 11/17/61.

42. SCOR, 975th Meeting, November 16, 1961.

43. SCOR, 976th Meeting, November 17, 1961.

44. *NYT,* 11/20/61.

45. Letter from Senator Thomas Dodd to the President, November 21, 1961. See also State Department Memorandum for Bundy, November 17, 1961, "Talking Paper for the President in Connection with Sen. Dodd's Call at the White House."

46. For the text of the U.S. amendments, see S/4989 and S/4989/Rev. 2.

47. SCOR, 982nd Meeting, November 24, 1961. S/5002

48. Kolesnichenko, "Who Votes Against?" *Pravda,* 11/29/61.

49. O'Brien, *To Katanga and Back,* p. 325. O'Brien included the account of the incident told by his fiancée, Irish Foreign Service officer Maire MacEntee, who accompanied Smith and Urquhart to a cocktail party at the Hoffackers in honor of the Dodds earlier in the evening and then was present as the Katangan soldiers kidnapped the two officials, after she tried in vain to calm the angry soldiers; she described Hoffacker as "a thin, rather lightly-built young man" who was very brave.

50. *NYT,* 12/1/61.

51. *NYT,* 12/8/61.

52. Elisabethville 678, 12/1/61.

53. Elisabethville 674, 11/30/61.

54. Leopoldville 1350, 12/1/61.

55. SD (no number) to Luanda, 12/1/61.

56. Elisabethville 683, 12/1/61.

57. *NYT,* 12/2/61.

58. *NYT,* 12/4/61.

59. *NYT,* 12/5, 6/61.

60. Memorandum from Assistant Secretary Williams to Under Secretary Ball, December 6, 1961, "Current Situation in the Congo." He noted that Hoffacker had "worked incessantly to prevent the current outbreak of hostilities by facilitating meetings between UN and Katanga officials and by urging each to restrain their respective forces" but had failed to bring Tshombe around.

61. Memorandum, "UN Military Situation in Katanga and Department of Defense Views," included with Memorandum from Secretary Rusk to the President, December 9, 1961. See also *NYT,* 12/6, 7/61.

62. USUN 1995, 12/6/61.

63. Macmillan, *Pointing the Way,* p. 449.

64. London 2304, 12/13/61.

65. Macmillan, *Pointing the Way,* pp. 449–50.

66. SD 35 TOSEC in Paris, 12/12/61; and SD 3192 to London, 12/11/61.

67. Paris 9 SECTO, 12/11/61.

68. Memorandum of Conversation between Secretary Rusk, Under Secretary Ball, and the President, December 13, 1961.

69. Macmillan, *Pointing the Way,* p. 451.

70. For the text of the appeal, see *NYT,* 12/14/61.

71. *NYT,* 12/15/61.

72. SD 1017 to Leopoldville, 12/13/61.

73. Leopoldville 1489, 12/14/61.

74. Leopoldville 1505, 12/14/61.

75. Leopoldville 1503, 12/14/61.
76. SD 461 to Elisabethville, 12/14/61.
77. Ibid.
78. Martin, *Adlai Stevenson,* p. 683.
79. Leopoldville 1517, 12/15/61.
80. SD 1028 to Leopoldville, 12/14/61.
81. *NYT,* 12/16/61.
82. Leopoldville 1515 and 1517, 12/15/61.
83. Leopoldville 1547, 12/17/61, contained the text of this message.
84. SD 706 to Caracas, 12/16/61; Eyes Only for the President from the Acting Secretary.
85. SD 708 to Caracas, 12/16/61; Eyes Only for the President from the Acting Secretary.
86. Leopoldville 1553, 12/17/61.
87. Brussels 1089, 12/17/61.
88. White House to SD 171515Z, 12/17/61; from the President to Ball.
89. SD 502 to Bogotá, 12/17/61; for the President from Ball.
90. SD 503 to Bogotá, 12/17/61; for the President from Ball.
91. Leopoldville 1560, 12/18/61.
92. Leopoldville 1559, 12/18/61.
93. Leopoldville 1622, 12/21/61.
94. Ibid.
95. SD 1064 to Leopoldville, 12/19/61.
96. Leopoldville 1622, 12/21/61.
97. Leopoldville 1610, 12/21/61.
98. SD 16 TOSEC in Bermuda, 12/21/61.
99. SD (no number) to Leopoldville, 12/21/61.
100. Macmillan, *Pointing the Way,* p. 451.
101. Ibid., p. 456.
102. Ibid. pp. 456–57. See also the next volume of Macmillan's memoirs, *At the End of the Day: 1961–1963* (New York: Harper & Row, 1973), p. 146. See also SD 1160 to Leopoldville, 12/28/61, for more detail on the Bermuda talks. See also Joint Statement Following Discussions in Bermuda with Prime Minister Macmillan, December 22, 1961, in *Public Papers of the Presidents, 1961,* pp. 817–18. This joint statement reflected the British position. Instead of following Ball's suggestion that the two leaders apply pressure on Tshombe by applauding the "agreement to reintegrate the Katanga under the national government of the Congo" and paying tribute to the United Nations, Kennedy and Macmillan made no reference to the "reintegration" of Katanga and no reference to the United Nations. They "noted with satisfaction" the "useful meeting" at Kitona and expressed their "strong hope that further progress would be made through the efforts of both parties"—thus placing Adoula and Tshombe on the same plane. They also stressed the "importance of avoiding any renewal of armed action while genuine efforts at consultation are going forward"—a phrase that could be regarded as a slap at the United Nations.
103. Leopoldville 1625, 1626, and 1630, 12/22/61; 1646, 12/24/61; and 1661, 12/26/61.
104. SD 3375 to London, 12/21/61.
105. SD (no number) to West Palm Beach for the President, 12/23/61; see also SD 1098 and 1108 to Leopoldville, 12/22/61.
106. SD 3505 to London, 12/29/61; see also SD 3489 to London, 12/28/61.
107. *NYT,* 12/28/61.
108. Leopoldville 1706, 12/30/61.

109. Brussels 1189, 12/31/61; *NYT,* 12/29/61.
110. SD 1662 to Brussels, 1/2/62.

Chapter Thirteen

1. For more detail, see SD 939 to Accra, 12/14/61, which contained the President's instructions to the ambassador and to his special negotiator, Clarence Randall, for their meeting with Nkrumah.

2. Arthur M. Schlesinger, Jr., *Robert Kennedy and His Times* (Boston: Houghton Mifflin, 1978), pp. 560–61.

3. The debate on the dam, with the various alternatives, was summed up in a State Department paper, "The Volta River Project," prepared for the National Security Council meeting, December 5, 1961.

4. SD 939 to Accra, 12/14/61.

5. For more detail, see Attwood, *The Reds and the Blacks,* pp. 60–64.

6. Ibid., pp. 65–66. See also the Soviet press coverage of Mikoyan's trip, which did not mention the actual reason behind it; for example, "Mikoyan Will Visit Republic of Guinea," *Pravda,* 12/28/61; "Departure of Mikoyan for Republic of Guinea," *Pravda,* 1/5/62; "Mikoyan in Conakry," *Izvestia,* 1/6/62; "Soviet Exhibit in Conakry," *Pravda,* 1/8/62; "May Friendship Between Peoples of USSR and Guinea Be Strengthened," *Pravda,* 1/9/62. The last article included speeches by Mikoyan and Sékou Touré, and the differences were evident, although they were not spelled out.

7. Attwood, *The Reds and the Blacks,* p. 63.

8. SD 1222 to Leopoldville, 1/6/62.

9. Nkrumah, *Challenge of the Congo,* p. 179. See also Verhaegen, *Congo 1961,* pp. 565–80, on Gizenga's deteriorating position in December.

10. S/5053/Add. 1. See also *NYT,* 1/9/62; and Verhaegen, *Congo 1961,* pp. 581–88.

11. S/5053/Add. 1.

12. *NYT,* 1/12/62.

13. SD 1252 to Leopoldville, 1/12/62.

14. S/5053/Add. 1. See also *NYT,* 1/13/62.

15. S/5053/Add. 1. See also *NYT,* 1/15/62.

16. S/5053/Add. 1/Ann. IV.

17. Leopoldville 1817, 1/15/62.

18. *NYT,* 1/16/62.

19. *NYT,* 1/17/62.

20. Leopoldville 1867, 1/19/62.

21. SD 1297 to Leopoldville, 1/21/62.

22. SD 1294 to Leopoldville, 1/19/62.

23. Leopoldville 1871, 1/20/62. See also S/5053/Add. 3/Ann. II and III.

24. S/5053/Add. 2.

25. S/5053/Add. 3 and S/5053/Add. 3/Ann. IV.

26. S/5053/Add. 3 and S/5053/Add. 3/Ann. V.

27. S/5053/Add. 3.

28. Leopoldville 1896, 1/25/62.

29. Leopoldville 1909, 1/25/62.

30. Ibid. See also S/5053/Add. 3.

31. "Life of Gizenga in Danger," *Pravda,* 1/24/62. See also Volodin, "Stop Crime!" *Pravda,* 1/25/62.

32. L. Koryavin, "Cardsharping," *Izvestia,* 1/24/62.

33. Leopoldville 1870, 1/19/62.

34. "Soviet Gift to Congo," *Pravda*, 1/6/62.

35. S/5064. The letter appeared in *Pravda*, 1/28/62, in the midst of protests about Gizenga; the context was clear.

36. USUN 2556, 1/25/62.

37. SD 1326 to Leopoldville, 1/26/62.

38. Leopoldville 1922, 1/27/62.

39. S/5066.

40. *NYT*, 1/29/62.

41. S/5069. See also *NYT*, 1/30/62.

42. Leopoldville 1942, 1/29/62.

43. Leopoldville 1947, 1/30/62.

44. Leopoldville 1961, 1/30/62.

45. SCOR, 989th Meeting, January 30, 1962.

46. "West Broke Up Security Council Meeting," *Pravda*, 1/31/62; "On Colonialists' Instructions," *Pravda*, 2/1/62.

47. Leopoldville 1942, 1/29/62; and 1961, 1/30/62.

48. GAOR, 1103rd Plenary Meeting, February 2, 1962.

49. USUN 2649, 2/4/62.

50. *NYT*, 2/3/62.

51. Leopoldville 1997, 2/3/62.

52. *NYT*, 2/8/62.

53. "Speech of Congolese Prime Minister at UN General Assembly," *Pravda*, 2/4/62; "Gizenga Moved to New Place of Imprisonment," *Pravda*, 2/4/62.

54. For example, V. Borisov, "Plot of Robbers," *Literatura i Zhizn'*, 2/4/62; "Freedom for Patriot of Congo," *Pravda*, 2/5/62; "Congolese Reaction Is Impudent," *Pravda*, 2/6/62; and, at the same time, "Adoula's Meetings in Washington," *Trud*, 2/6/62; "Talks of Adoula and J. Kennedy," *Izvestia*, 2/7/62.

55. Memorandum of Conversation between Prime Minister Adoula, Under Secretary Ball, et al., February 5, 1962.

56. Memorandum of Conversation between Prime Minister Adoula, President Kennedy, Secretary Rusk, et al., February 5, 1962.

57. *NYT*, 2/6/62.

58. SD 1395 to Leopoldville, 2/7/62.

59. *NYT*, 2/8/62.

Chapter Fourteen

1. For more detail, see S/5053/Add. 8B.

2. "Persecution of Gizenga Continues," *Izvestia*, 2/14/62.

3. *NYT*, 2/19/62.

4. SD 601 to Elisabethville, 3/1/62.

5. USUN 2797, 2/16/62; and SD 2133 to USUN, 2/17/62.

6. Leopoldville 2140, 2/22/62.

7. Ibid.

8. SD 2467 to USUN, 3/24/62.

9. Leopoldville 2450, 3/28/62; USUN 3231, 3/30/62. For Rusk's reaction, see SD 1676 to Leopoldville, 3/30/62.

10. S/5053/Add. 10, Ann. 1–10 describe the negotiations in detail.

11. Leopoldville 2626, 4/18/62.

12. Leopoldville 2622, 4/18/62.

13. Leopoldville 2626, 4/18/62.

14. Leopoldville 2620, 4/18/62.

15. Leopoldville 2637, 4/19/62. See also *NYT*, 4/19, 20/62.

16. Leopoldville 2621, 4/18/62.

17. USUN 3525, 4/25/62.

18. SD 1801 to Leopoldville, 4/20/62.

19. White House Memorandum from Bromley Smith to Ralph Dungan, April 24, 1962.

20. Leopoldville 2726, 4/29/62.

21. See, for example, Khokhlov, "Striking Leopoldville," *Izvestia,* 4/4/62. Khokhlov, a veteran Soviet journalist who had just spent a month in Leopoldville, summed up the problem in these words: "The situation in the Congo has become so complicated that it is practically impossible to give direct simple answers to many questions." This was an astonishing admission from the Soviet press, which generally had very clear guidelines about who was a hero and who was a villain.

22. Fedyashin, "Meeting with Gizenga," *Pravda,* 4/23/62.

23. "They Betray Fighter for Congolese Independence to Colonialists," *Pravda,* 5/17/62.

24. Leopoldville 2917, 5/24/62.

25. SD 6425 to London, 6/1/62.

26. Leopoldville 2990 and 2991, 6/4/62.

27. See S/5053/Add. 10, Ann. 28–46, on the talks. See also *NYT,* 6/27/62, on the breakdown in the talks. See also Leopoldville 3142 and 3145, 6/25/62; and 3147 6/26/62.

28. USUN 56, 7/6/62.

29. SD 3346 to USUN, 6/27/62; and SD 6 to Brussels, 7/2/62.

30. *NYT,* 7/18/62. See also USUN 158, 7/17/62.

31. *NYT,* 7/21/62.

32. *NYT,* 7/19/62. Elisabethville 115, 7/17/62, cited a CIA report that the demonstration was planned in advance by the Katanga government.

33. Sulzberger, *The Last of the Giants,* p. 909.

34. John F. Kennedy News Conference of July 23, 1962, in *Public Papers of the Presidents, 1962* (Washington, D.C.: Office of the Federal Register, 1963), p. 572.

35. Leopoldville 189, 7/21/62. For the text of the letter, see SD 51 TOSEC to Geneva, July 24, 1962; the letter was sent to Rusk there.

36. Bomboko conferred with top U.S. officials in New York and Washington; see USUN 22, 7/3/62, for his meeting with Yost; and SD 40 and 41 to Leopoldville, 7/7/62, for his meeting with Rusk, Ball, and McGhee.

37. Record of Understanding of the Meeting with the President, July 25, on the Congo. For the text of the "Proposal" and the "Course of Action," see Memorandum from Williams to McGhee, "Discussion with the Belgian, British and French Embassies on Congo," July 24, 1962, Tabs A and B.

38. Memorandum for the President from Ball, "Proposed Action on the Congo," August 2, 1962, which included the revised texts of the "Proposal" and the "Course of Action" as well as the draft of a National Security Action Memorandum for the President to approve.

39. *NYT,* 8/4/62.

40. Geneva 148, 8/7/62.

41. Leopoldville 330, 8/8/62; 338 and 340, 8/9/62; and 342 and 345, 8/10/62.

42. SD 235 to Leopoldville, 8/10/62; Eyes Only from Ball to Gullion.

43. Leopoldville 365 and 374, 8/11/62; Eyes Only from Gullion to Ball.

44. Geneva 181, 8/13/62.

45. *NYT,* 8/10/62. For more detail on the changes in the draft, see SD 310 to USUN, 8/9/62.

46. Macmillan, *At the End of the Day,* p. 282.

47. Memorandum from William H. Brubeck, Executive Secretary, State Department, for McGeorge Bundy, "Current Status of Proposed Action on the Congo," August 11, 1962, which included the new texts of the two papers.

48. S/5053/Add. 13, Ann. III. See also Leopoldville 430, 8/21/62.

49. S/5053/Add. 13, Ann. II. See also Elisabethville 322, 8/24/62.

50. Leopoldville 462, 8/25/62.

51. Leopoldville 412 and 413, 8/18/62; and 415, 8/19/62.

52. SD 293 to Leopoldville, 8/19/62.

53. Leopoldville 480, 8/28/62.

54. Leopoldville 471, 8/27/62.

55. SD 351 to Leopoldville, 8/27/62; Eyes Only from Rusk to Gullion.

56. Leopoldville 522, 8/31/62; Eyes Only from Gullion to Rusk.

57. SD 335 to Leopoldville, 8/24/62.

58. SD 522 to USUN, 8/31/62.

59. Leopoldville 525, 9/1/62.

60. S/5053/Add. 13, Ann. IV.

61. Leopoldville 536 and 547, 9/4/62.

62. Leopoldville 552, 9/5/62.

63. USUN 675, 9/5/62.

64. "Reply of Soviet Government to Appeal of UN Secretary-General U Thant to United Nations Members on Congo Question," *Pravda,* 9/7/62.

65. See, for example, *Pravda*'s coverage of the July 16 debate in Parliament, "Crisis of Confidence," 7/18/62; for the first time since Gizenga's arrest, *Pravda* stressed the views of Adoula's opponents, who charged that "instead of following a policy of positive neutralism, as it promised, the government has oriented itself toward the Western countries, especially the United States." "Concession to Separatists in Congo," *Pravda,* 7/31/62, denounced Adoula's plan for a federal constitution as a Western-inspired concession to Tshombe.

66. *NYT,* 8/11/62.

67. SD 243 to Leopoldville, 8/11/62.

68. "Life of Gizenga is in Danger," *Pravda,* 8/19/62; "Save Life of Antoine Gizenga," *Pravda,* 8/21/62; Freedom to Antoine Gizenga," *Pravda,* 8/22/62; "Africa Demands: Freedom for Antoine Gizenga," *Pravda,* 8/24/62; "Freedom to Antoine Gizenga," *Pravda,* 8/25/62; "Freedom to Antoine Gizenga," *Pravda,* 8/27/62; "Against Illegal Arrest of Gizenga," *Pravda,* 8/31/62.

69. Leopoldville 439, 8/23/62.

70. Leopoldville 475, 8/27/62; and 512, 8/30/62.

71. *Pravda,* 9/21/62.

72. CIA Current Intelligence Memorandum, "Katangan Air Force," September 29, 1962.

73. Elisabethville 521, 9/29/62.

74. Leopoldville 808, 10/3/62.

75. Leopoldville 832, 10/7/62.

76. Leopoldville 816, 10/4/62.

77. Leopoldville 829, 10/6/62.

78. On the McGhee mission, see Elisabethville 541 and 545, 10/4/62; 553, 10/6/62; 556, 10/7/62; 578, 10/10/62; 587, 10/11/62; and Leopoldville 837 and 845, 10/8/62; 893, 10/12/62; 915, 916, and 917, 10/15/62; 930, 931, 935, 936, and 942, 10/17/62; 944, 949, 952, and 955, 10/18/62.

79. USUN 1133, 10/9/62.

80. *NYT,* 10/15/62.

81. On the Cuban missile crisis, see Elie Abel, *The Missile Crisis,* (Philadelphia: J. B. Lippincott, 1966); Schlesinger, *A Thousand Days,* pp. 794–841, and *Robert Kennedy and His Times,* pp. 499–532; Sorensen, *Kennedy,* pp. 667–718; Martin, *Adlai Stevenson,* pp. 719–37; *Khrushchev Remembers,* pp. 509–14; and Robert Kennedy, *Thirteen Days: A Memoir of the Cuban Missile Crisis* (New York: W.W. Norton) 1969.

82. For more detail on the subsequent negotiations between McCloy, Stevenson, and Kuznetsov, see Martin, *Adlai Stevenson,* pp. 737–40.

83. Memorandum from McGhee for the President, "Mission to the Congo," October 22, 1962.

84. Bowles, *Promises to Keep,* pp. 423–25.

85. Memorandum for the Record by Carl Kaysen, "Meeting with the President on the Congo, Wednesday, October 31, 4 pm."

86. Memorandum of Conversation between McGhee, Williams, and Foreign Minister Bomboko, October 31, 1962.

87. Quoted in Schlesinger, *A Thousand Days,* p. 577.

88. Memorandum for the Secretary of State from Carl Kaysen, November 1, 1962.

89. Memorandum from the President to Secretary Rusk, November 5, 1962.

90. "Proposed Contingency Plan for the Congo," November 6, 1962.

91. Memorandum from Kaysen to Brubeck, "Congo Review," November 7, 1962.

92. *NYT,* 11/24/62.

93. *NYT,* 11/27/62.

94. *NYT,* 11/28/62.

95. *NYT,* 11/29/62.

96. Martin, *Adlai Stevenson,* p. 749.

97. *NYT,* 12/4/62

98. Memorandum from Roger Hilsman to the Secretary of State, "Possible Soviet Military Assistance to the Congo," December 7, 1962. See also Hilsman's account of the period in *To Move a Nation* (New York: Doubleday, 1967), pp. 263–67.

99. CIA, Office of National Estimates Memorandum, "Certain Consequences of the Withdrawal of UN Forces from the Congo," December 11, 1962.

100. Memorandum from Assistant Secretary of Defense William Bundy to Under Secretary of State Ball, December 11, 1962, enclosing a Memorandum from the Joint Chiefs of Staff to the Secretary of Defense, "Congo Developments," December 11, 1962.

101. Top Secret Memorandum from Kaysen to McGeorge Bundy, December 13, 1962.

102. Memorandum from Williams, "Proposed Next Steps in Congo," December 12, 1962.

103. Bowles, *Promises to Keep,* p. 427.

104. Ibid.; and Martin, *Adlai Stevenson,* p. 750.

105. Memorandum from McGhee for the President, "Recommended Course of Action on the Congo," December 13, 1962. Cleveland and Sisco concurred.

106. Letter from Prime Minister Adoula to President Kennedy, December 11, 1962.

107. Leopoldville 1389, 12/12/62. See also *NYT,* 12/11, 12/62.

108. *NYT,* 12/13/62.

109. Elisabethville 913, 12/13/62.

110. Memorandum from McGhee for the President, December 13, 1962.

111. Memorandum for the President from Cleveland and Sisco, "New Policy on the Congo," December 13, 1962.

112. Memorandum from Williams to Rusk, "Policy Alternatives in the Congo," December 10, 1962.

113. Memorandum for the President from Cleveland and Sisco, December 13, 1962.
114. Bowles, *Promises to Keep*, p. 426.
115. Memorandum from Cleveland to Ball, "Report of Conversation with Secretary-General U Thant on the Congo," December 16, 1962.
116. Memorandum from Kaysen to the President, "Congo Issues," December 17, 1962.
117. *NYT*, 12/19/62.
118. *NYT*, 12/20, 21/62.
119. *NYT*, 12/22/62.
120. *NYT*, 12/21, 22/62.
121. *NYT*, 12/27/62.
122. Macmillan, *At the End of the Day*, p. 283.
123. *NYT*, 12/26, 28, 29/62.
124. *NYT*, 12/29/62; see also Thant, *View from the UN*, p. 142.
125. *NYT*, 12/29/62.
126. Thant, *View from the UN*, p. 142.
127. Schlesinger, *A Thousand Days*, p. 578.
128. Message from Kaysen to the President, December 30, 1962.
129. *NYT*, 12/31/62.
130. Martin, *Adlai Stevenson*, p. 751.
131. *NYT*, 1/2/63.
132. Ibid.
133. Message from Kaysen to the President, January 1, 1963.
134. Message from Kaysen to the President, January 2, 1963.
135. Memorandum from Kaysen to Ball, January 2, 1963.
136. Memorandum from Thomas L. Hughes to Williams, January 2, 1963.
137. *NYT*, 1/3, 4/63.
138. Thant, *View from the UN*, pp. 143–45.
139. *NYT*, 1/4/63.
140. Macmillan, *At the End of the Day*, p. 284. See also *NYT*, 1/11, 12/63.
141. *NYT*, 1/16/63.
142. *NYT*, 1/18/63.
143. *NYT*, 1/22/63.
144. For more detail, see Memorandum from Brubeck to Bundy, "Current Status of ANC Retraining," May 7, 1963.
145. Memorandum of Conversation between President Kennedy and General Mobutu, Commander in Chief of the Congolese National Army, May 31, 1963.

Conclusion

For more information on the events of October, 1963, see Leopoldville 925, 10/25/63; Memorandum from Benjamin H. Read to McGeorge Bundy, October 25, 1963; SD 499 to Leopoldville, 10/28/63; Memorandum from William H. Brubeck to McGeorge Bundy, October 29, 1963; and a CIA Current Intelligence Memorandum, "The Situation in the Congo," October 29, 1963.

On the 1964 rebellion and President Johnson's response, see Luciano Ferraresi, *Storia politica del Congo, (Zaire) dall' independenza alla rivoluzione di Mulele* (Milano: Edizioni Jaca Book, 1973), pp. 153–159; Philip Geyelin, *Lyndon B. Johnson and the World* (New York: Praeger, 1966), pp. 118–119; Blaine Littell, *South of the Moon: On Stanley's Trail through the Dark Continent* (New York: Harper & Row, 1966); Thomas Powers, *The Man Who Kept the Secrets*, pp. 122–123; Paul-Henri Spaak, *Combats inachevés*, pp.

271–293; Benoit Verhaegen, *Rebellions au Congo,* (Brussels: CRISP, 1967); Crawford Young, "The Congo Rebellion," *Africa Report,* vol. 10, no. 4, April, 1965, pp. 6–11.

On the period after Mobutu's assumption of power in 1965 and the policies of the Nixon, Ford, Carter, and Reagan Administrations, see William E. Colby, "Intelligence, Secrecy and Security in a Free Society," *International Security,* vol. 1, no. 2, Fall, 1976, pp. 3–14; Chester A. Crocker, "South Africa: Strategy for Change," *Foreign Affairs,* vol. 59, no. 2, Winter 1980–1981, pp. 323–51; Leon Dash, two series in *The Washington Post,* December 30, 1979, to January 1, 1980, and November 8, 9, 1981; Nathaniel Davis, "The Angola Decision of 1975: A Personal Memoir," *Foreign Affairs,* vol. 57, no. 1, Fall 1978, pp. 109–24; Jorge I. Dominguez, "Cuban Foreign Policy," *Foreign Affairs,* vol. 57, no. 1, Fall 1978, pp. 83–108; Russell Warren Howe, "A Refreshing Pragmatism: The Carter Strategy in Africa," *The New Leader,* vol. 60, no. 19, September 26, 1977, pp. 5–8; David Ottaway, "Africa: U.S. Policy Eclipse," *Foreign Affairs,* vol. 58, no. 3, 1979, pp. 637–58; John Stockwell, *In Search of Enemies: A CIA Story,* (New York: W. W. Norton & Co., 1978); Jennifer Seymour Whitaker (ed.), *Africa and the United States; Vital Interests,* A Council on Foreign Relations Book (New York: New York University Press, 1978), particularly Whitaker, "Introduction," pp. 1–19, and Robert Legvold, "The Soviet Union's Strategic Stake in Africa," pp. 153–186; Crawford Young, "Zaire: The Unending Crisis," *Foreign Affairs,* vol. 57, no. 1, Fall 1978, pp. 169–85.

Bibliography

The most important sources for this study are the cables from U.S. Embassies and Consulates in Leopoldville, Elisabethville, Brussels, London, Paris, and other capitals to the State Department, and from the State Department to these Embassies and Consulates. Other important State Department documents include memoranda of conversations between the Secretary of State or other U.S. officials with foreign officials; memoranda from State Department officials to the Secretary of State; the *Analytical Chronology of the Congo Crisis* prepared on January 25, 1961, by the Bureau of African Affairs as a briefing paper for the incoming Kennedy Administration; and the *Supplement* to the *Analytical Chronology,* prepared on March 9, 1961.

Another key document is the report of the Senate committee investigating the CIA: *Alleged Assassination Plots Involving Foreign Leaders,* An Interim Report of the Select Committee To Study Governmental Operations With Respect to Intelligence Activities, United States Senate, Washington: U.S. Government Printing Office, 1975.

A colorful glimpse of the decision-making process is provided by the U.S. Senate Committee on Foreign Relations, *Briefing on the Situation in the Congo,* February 6, 1961.

Public Papers of the Presidents, Washington, D.C.: Office of the Federal Register, provides an annual compilation of press conferences, speeches, and joint statements with foreign leaders.

White House documents obtained through the John F. Kennedy Library include: National Security Action Memoranda, prepared for the President's approval at meetings of the National Security Council (NSC); summaries of NSC meetings; memoranda and briefing papers for the President from the NSC staff, the State Department, the Defense Department, and the Central Intelligence Agency; proposed drafts of speeches and letters to foreign leaders; and detailed records of White House meetings at which the President discussed the Congo issue with his top advisers.

Informal insights were provided by the interviews in the Oral History Collection of the Kennedy Library.

United Nations Documents

Security Council, *Official Records,* the meetings dealing with the Congo in July, August, September, and December, 1960; January, February, and November, 1961; and January, 1962: 873, 877–879, 884–886, 887–888, 896–906, 912–920, 924–927, 928, 930, 931–932, 933–942, 973–979, 982, and 989th Meetings.

General Assembly, *Official Records,* the meetings dealing with the Congo in September, November, and December 1960; March and April, 1961; and February, 1962: 858–863, 869, 912, 913, 914–920, 949–953, 955–958, 965–987, and 1103rd Plenary Sessions.

The four reports made by Secretary-General Dag Hammarskjold during the summer of 1960: S/4389, July 19, 1960; S/4417, August 6, 1960; S/4475, August 30, 1960; and S/4482, September 7, 1960.

The controversial report of the Secretary-General's special representative in the Congo, Rajeshwar Dayal, November 2, 1960: A/4557.

The inconclusive report about Lumumba's death by the Commission of Investigation established under the terms of General Assembly resolution 1601 (XV) of 15 April 1961: S/4976.

Other statements, reports, and messages are drawn from the Supplements to the Security Council records for 1960, 1961, and 1962, and from the Annexes to the General Assembly records for the Fifteenth Session, 1960–1961.

Books and Articles

Abel, Elie, *The Missile Crisis.* Philadelphia: J. B. Lippincott, 1966.

Alexander, Henry T., *African Tightrope: My Two Years as Nkrumah's Chief of Staff.* New York: Praeger, 1965.

Artigue, Pierre, *Qui Sont les Leaders Congolais?* Brussels: Editions Europe-Afrique, 1961.

Attwood, William, *The Reds and the Blacks: A Personal Adventure.* New York: Harper & Row, 1967.

Ball, George W., "American Policy in the Congo," in *Footnotes to the Congo Story,* edited by Helen Kitchen, New York: Walker and Co., 1967, pp. 61–68.

Bohlen, Charles E., *Witness to History 1929–1969.* New York: W. W. Norton & Co., 1973.

Bowles, Chester, "Great Challenge to the UN—Africa," *The New York Times Magazine,* August 21, 1960.

Bowles, Chester, *Promises to Keep: My Years in Public Life, 1941–1969.* New York: Harper & Row, 1971.

Brzezinski, Zbigniew, ed., *Africa and the Communist World.* Stanford: Stanford University Press, for the Hoover Institution on War, Revolution, and Peace, 1963. Includes essays by Alexander Dallin, Alexander Erlich, and Richard Lowenthal.

Bustin, Edouard, "The Congo," in *Five African States: Responses to Diversity,* edited by Gwendolen M. Carter, Ithaca: Cornell University Press, 1963, pp. 9–159.

Carter, Gwendolen, *Independence for Africa.* New York: Praeger, 1962.

Cleveland, Harlan, "The UN in the Congo: Three Questions," in *Footnotes to the Congo Story,* edited by Helen Kitchen, New York: Walker and Co., 1967, pp. 69–70.

Cline, Ray S., *Secrets, Spies, and Scholars: Blueprint of the Essential CIA.* Washington: Acropolis Books, 1976.

Colby, William E., *Honorable Men: My Life in the CIA.* New York: Simon and Schuster, 1978.

Colby, William E., "Intelligence, Secrecy and Security in a Free Society," *International Security*, vol. 1, no. 2, Fall, 1976, pp. 3–14.

Coleman, James S., and Belmont Brice, "The Role of the Military in Sub-Saharan Africa," in *The Role of the Military in Underdeveloped Countries*, edited by John J. Johnson, Princeton, N.J.: Princeton University Press, 1962, pp. 359–405.

Copland, Miles, *Without Cloak or Dagger*, New York: Simon and Schuster, 1974.

Cornevin, Robert, *Histoire du Congo-Léo*. Paris: Editions Berger-Levrault, 1963.

Crocker, Chester A., "South Africa: Strategy for Change," *Foreign Affairs*, vol. 59, no. 2, Winter 1980–81, pp. 323–351.

Dallin, Alexander, *The Soviet Union at the United Nations*. New York: Praeger, 1962.

Davis, Nathaniel, "The Angola Decision of 1975: A Personal Memoir," *Foreign Affairs*, vol. 57, no. 1, Fall 1978, pp. 109–124.

Davister, Pierre, *Katanga, Enjeu du Monde*. Brussels: Editions Europe-Afrique, 1960.

Davister, Pierre, and Philippe Toussaint, *Croisettes et Casques Bleus*. Brussels: Editions Actuelles, 1962.

Dayal, Rajeshwar, *Mission for Hammarskjold: The Congo Crisis*. Princeton, N.J.: Princeton University Press, 1976.

Dominguez, Jorge I. "Cuban Foreign Policy," *Foreign Affairs*, vol. 57, no. 1, Fall 1978, pp. 83–108.

Dulles, Allen, *The Craft of Intelligence*. New York: Harper & Row, 1963.

Eisenhower, Dwight D., *Waging Peace: The White House Years, A Personal Account 1956–1961*. New York: Doubleday & Co., 1965.

Fainsod, Merle, "Krushchevism in Retrospect," *Problems of Communism*, no. 1 (1965), pp. 1–10.

Ferraresi, Luciano, *Storia politica del Congo, (Zaire) dall'independenza alla rivoluzione di Mulele*. Milano: Edizioni Jaca Book, 1973.

Gavshon, Arthur L., *The Mysterious Death of Dag Hammarskjold*. New York: Walker and Co., 1962.

Gerard-Libois, J., and Benoit Verhaegen, *Congo 1960* (2 vol.). Brussels: Centre de Recherche et d'Information Socio-Politique, 1961.

Geyelin, Philip, *Lyndon B. Johnson and the World*. New York: Praeger, 1966.

Good, Robert C., "Four African Views of the Congo Crisis," in *Footnotes to the Congo Story*, edited by Helen Kitchen, New York: Walker and Co., 1967, pp. 45–57.

Griffith, William E., *The Sino-Soviet Rift*. Cambridge, Mass.: The M.I.T. Press, 1964.

Gunther, John, *Inside Africa*. New York: Harper & Row, 1955.

Hamrell, Sven, and Carl Gosta Widstrand, eds., *The Soviet Bloc, China, and Africa*. Uppsala: The Scandinavian Institute of African Studies, 1964. Includes papers by Colin Legum, David Morison, Walter Laqueur, Franz Ansprenger, and Richard Lowenthal.

Heikal, Mohamed, *The Cairo Documents.* New York: Doubleday & Co., 1973.

Hilsman, Roger, *To Move a Nation: The Politics of Foreign Policy in the Administration of John F. Kennedy.* Garden City, N.J.: Doubleday, 1967.

Hodgkin, Thomas, *African Political Parties: An Introductory Guide.* Harmondsworth: Penguin Books, 1961.

Hoskyns, Catherine, *The Congo Since Independence.* London: Oxford University Press, 1965.

Houart, Pierre, *Les Evénements du Congo.* Brussels: Centre de Documentation Internationale, 1961.

Hovet, Thomas, Jr., *Africa in the United Nations.* Evanston, Ill.: Northwestern University Press, 1965.

Howe, Russell Warren, "A Refreshing Pragmatism: The Carter Strategy in Africa," *The New Leader,* vol. 60, no. 19, September 26, 1977, pp. 5–8.

Kalb, Madeleine, and Marvin Kalb, "How Mr. Kennedy Looks to the Russians," *The Reporter,* no. 10 (1960), pp. 33–34.

Kalb, Madeleine, and Marvin Kalb, "Russia and/or China in Africa," *The Reporter,* no. 6 (1960), pp. 28–29.

Kalb, Marvin, "Russia's own 'Peace Corps' for Africa," *The Reporter,* no. 8 (1961), pp. 36–37.

Kamitatu, Cleophas, *La Grande Mystification du Congo-Kinshasa,* Brussels: Complexe, 1971.

Kanza, Thomas R., *Congo 196?.* Brussels: Editions Remarques Congolaises, 1961.

Kashamura, Anicet, *De Lumumba aux colonels,* Paris: Buchet/Chastel, 1966.

Kennedy, Robert F., *Thirteen Days: A Memoir of the Cuban Missile Crisis.* New York: W. W. Norton & Co., 1969.

Kitchen, Helen, ed., *Footnotes to the Congo Story.* New York: Walker and Co., 1967.

Kraft, Joseph, "The Untold Story of the UN's Congo Army," *Harper's Magazine,* November, 1960, 75–84.

Labedz, Leopold, "Introduction," *Survey,* no. 43 (1962), pp. 3–9. The issue, devoted to "Nationalism, Communism, and the Uncommitted Nations," contains articles by Curt Gasteyger, Franz Ansprenger, and John Kautsky.

Laqueur, Walter, "Communism and Nationalism in Tropical Africa," in *Africa: A Foreign Affairs Reader,* edited by Philip W. Quigg, New York: Praeger, for the Council on Foreign Relations, 1964, pp. 184–195.

Lefever, Ernest, *Crisis in the Congo: A United Nations Force in Action.* Washington, D.C.: The Brookings Institution, 1965.

Lefever, Ernest, *Uncertain Mandate.* Baltimore: Johns Hopkins Press, 1967.

Legum, Colin, *Africa: A Handbook to the Continent.* New York: Praeger, 1962.

——— *Congo Disaster.* Baltimore: Penguin Books, 1961.

——— *Pan-Africanism: A Short Political Guide.* New York: Praeger, 1962.

——— "Peking's Strategic Priorities in Africa," in *Footnotes to the Congo Story*, edited by Helen Kitchen, New York: Walker and Co., pp. 103–109.

Legvold, Robert, *Soviet Policy in West Africa*. Cambridge, Mass.: Harvard University Press, 1970.

Legvold, Robert, "The Soviet Union's Strategic Stake in Africa," in *Africa and the United States: Vital Interests*, edited by Jennifer Seymour Whitaker, New York: A Council on Foreign Relations Book, New York University Press, 1978, pp. 153–186.

Lemarchand, René, "Patrice Lumumba in Perspective," in *Footnotes to the Congo Story*, edited by Helen Kitchen, New York: Walker and Co., pp. 35–43.

Lemarchand, René, *Political Awakening in the Belgian Congo*. Berkeley and Los Angeles: University of California Press, 1964.

Lewis, William H., "Sub-Saharan Africa," in *Communism and Revolution: The Strategic Uses of Political Violence*, edited by Cyril E. Black and Thomas P. Thornton, Princeton, N.J.: Princeton University Press, 1964, pp. 367–390.

Littell, Blaine, *South of the Moon: On Stanley's Trail through the Dark Continent*. New York: Harper & Row, 1966.

London, Kurt, ed., *New Nations in a Divided World: the International Relations of the Afro-Asian States*. New York: Praeger, for the Institute for Sino-Soviet Studies, George Washington University, 1963. Includes papers by Jane Degras, Walter Laqueur, and Sergius Yakobson.

Lumumba, Patrice, *Congo My Country*, edited and with a Biographical Introduction by Colin Legum. New York: Praeger, 1962.

Macmillan, Harold, *At the End of the Day: 1961–1963*. New York: Harper & Row, 1973.

Macmillan, Harold, *Pointing the Way: 1959–1961*. New York: Harper & Row, 1972.

Marchetti, Victor, and John D. Marks, *The CIA and the Cult of Intelligence*. New York: Knopf, 1974.

Martin, John Bartlow, *Adlai Stevenson and the World*. New York: Doubleday & Co., 1977.

Mendiaux, Edouard, *Moscou, Accra, et le Congo*. Brussels: Charles Dessart, 1960.

Merlier, Michel, *Le Congo de la colonization belge à l'indépendance*. Paris: Francois Maspero, 1962.

Merriam, Alan P., *Congo: Background of Conflict*. Evanston, Ill.: Northwestern University Press, 1961.

Michel, Serge, *Uhuru Lumumba*. Paris: René Julliard, 1962.

Monheim, Francis, *Mobutu, l'homme seul*. Brussels: Editions Actuelles, 1962.

Morison, David, *The U.S.S.R. and Africa*. London: Oxford University Press, Institute of Race Relations and the Central Asian Research Centre, 1964.

Mosely, Philip E., "Soviet Policy in the Developing Countries," *Foreign Affairs*, no. 1 (1964), pp. 87–98.

Mosley, Leonard, *Dulles: A Biography of Eleanor, Allen, and John Foster Dul-*

les and Their Family Network. New York: The Dial Press/James Wade, 1978.

Nixon, Richard M., *The Emergence of Africa.* Washington: Public Services Division, Department of State, 1957.

Nkrumah, Kwame, *Challenge of the Congo.* New York: International Publishers, 1967.

O'Brien, Conor Cruise, *Murderous Angels.* Boston: Little, Brown and Company, 1968.

O'Brien, Conor Cruise, *To Katanga and Back: A UN Case History.* New York: The Universal Library, Grosset and Dunlap, 1966.

Okumu, Washington, *Lumumba's Congo: Roots of Conflict.* New York: Ivan Obolensky, Inc., 1963.

Oliver, Roland, and J. D. Fage, *A Short History of Africa.* Baltimore: Penguin African Library, 2nd Edition, 1966.

Ottaway, David, "Africa: U.S. Policy Eclipse," *Foreign Affairs,* vol. 58, no. 3, 1979, pp. 637–658.

Powers, Thomas, *The Man Who Kept the Secrets: Richard Helms and the CIA.* New York: Knopf, 1979.

Quaison-Sackey, Alex, *Africa Unbound: Reflections of an African Statesman.* New York: Praeger, 1963.

Ryckmans, Pierre, "Belgian 'Colonialism,' " in *Africa: A Foreign Affairs Reader,* edited by Philip Quigg, New York: Praeger, 1964.

Sampson, Anthony, *Common Sense about Africa.* London: Gollancz, Ltd., 1960.

Schatten, Fritz, "Africa: Nationalism and Communism," *Survey,* no. 42 (1962), pp. 148–159.

Schlesinger, Arthur M., Jr., *A Thousand Days: John F. Kennedy in the White House.* Boston: Houghton Mifflin Co., 1965.

Schlesinger, Arthur M., Jr., *Robert Kennedy and His Times.* Boston: Houghton Mifflin Co., 1978.

Schorr, Daniel, *Clearing the Air.* Boston: Houghton Mifflin Co., 1977.

Segal, Ronald, *African Profiles.* Baltimore: Penguin African Library, 1962.

Slade, Ruth, *The Belgian Congo.* London: Institute of Race Relations, 1960.

Sonnenfeldt, Helmut, "The Soviet Union and China: Where They Stood in 1960," in *Footnotes to the Congo Story,* edited by Helen Kitchen, New York: Walker and Co., 1967, pp. 28–29.

Sorensen, Theodore C., *Kennedy.* New York: Harper & Row, 1965.

Spaak, Paul-Henri, *Combats Inachevés.* Brussels: Fayard, Les Grandes Etudes Contemporaines, 1969.

Spiro, Herbert J., *Politics in Africa: Prospects South of the Sahara.* Englewood Cliffs, N.J.: Prentice-Hall, Inc., 1962.

Spiro, Herbert J., ed., *Africa: The Primacy of Politics.* New York: Random House, 1966. Includes papers by Edouard Bustin and Thomas Hovet.

Stevenson, Adlai E., *Looking Outward: Years of Crisis at the United Nations,* edited, with commentary by Robert L. and Selma Schiffer, Preface by President John F. Kennedy. New York: Harper & Row, 1961.

Stockwell, John, *In Search of Enemies: A CIA Story.* New York: W. W. Norton & Co., 1978.

Sulzberger, C. L., *The Last of the Giants.* New York: The Macmillan Company, 1970.

Tatu, Michel, *Power in the Kremlin: From Khrushchev to Kosygin.* New York: The Viking Press, 1967.

Thant, U, *View from the UN.* New York: Doubleday & Co., 1978.

Thornton, Thomas P., "Communist Attitudes Toward Asia, Africa, and Latin America," in *Communism and Revolution: The Strategic Uses of Political Violence,* edited by Cyril E. Black, and Thomas P. Thornton, Princeton, N.J.: Princeton University Press, 1964, pp. 245–269.

Tully, Andrew, *CIA: The Inside Story.* New York: Wm. Morrow & Co., 1962.

Ulam, Adam B., *Expansion and Coexistence: The History of Soviet Foreign Policy 1917–1967.* New York: Praeger, 1968.

Urquhart, Brian, *Hammarskjold.* New York: Knopf, 1972.

Van Bilsen, A. A. J., *L'Indépendance du Congo.* Brussels: Casterman, 1962.

Van Reyn, Paul, *Le Congo Politique: les partis et les élections.* Brussels: Editions Europe-Afrique, 1960.

Verhaegen, Benoit, *Congo 1961.* Brussels: Centre de Recherche et d'Information Socio-Politique, 1962.

von Horn, Carl, *Soldiering for Peace.* New York: David McKay Co., 1966.

Wallerstein, Immanuel, *Africa: The Politics of Independence.* New York: Random House, 1961.

—— *Africa: The Politics of Unity.* New York: Random House, 1967.

—— "Behind the Congo Crisis," *The New Leader,* no. 38 (1961), pp. 3–4.

—— "Congo Confederation," *The New Leader,* no. 13 (1961), pp. 3–5.

—— "Lumumbism without Lumumba," *The New Leader,* no. 31 (1961), pp. 15–17.

—— "A Program for Africa," *The New Leader,* no. 5 (1961), pp. 12–14.

—— "What Next in the Congo," *The New Leader,* no. 10 (1961), pp. 3–5.

Walters, Vernon A., *Silent Missions.* New York: Doubleday & Co., 1978.

Waugh, Evelyn, *Black Mischief.* Harmondsworth: Penguin Books, 1961.

Wauters, Arthur, ed., *Le Monde Communiste et la Crise du Congo Belge.* Brussels: Editions de l'Institut de Sociologie Solvay, 1961.

Weiss, Herbert, "Introduction" to *Congo 1965: Political Documents of a Developing Nation,* Princeton, N.J.: Princeton University Press, 1967, pp. vii–xvii.

Whitaker, Jennifer Seymour, ed., *Africa and the United States: Vital Interests,*

A Council on Foreign Relations Book. New York: New York University Press, 1978.

Wigny, Pierre, *A Ten-Year Plan for the Economic and Social Development of the Belgian Congo.* New York: Belgian Government Information Center, 1950.

Williams, G. Mennen, *Africa for the Africans.* Grand Rapids, Mich.: William B. Eerdmans Publishing Co., 1969.

Wise, David, *The American Police State.* New York: Random House, 1976.

Wyden, Peter, *Bay of Pigs: The Untold Story,* New York: Simon and Schuster, 1979.

Young, Crawford, "The Congo Rebellion," *Africa Report,* vol. 10, no. 4, April, 1965, pp. 6–11.

────── *Politics in the Congo: Decolonization and Independence.* Princeton, N.J.: Princeton University Press, 1965.

────── "Zaire: The Unending Crisis," *Foreign Affairs,* vol. 57, no. 1, Fall 1978, pp. 169–185.

The New York Times provided excellent coverage of the Congo during the 1960–1963 period. Particularly valuable were the reports of Henry Tanner, Paul Hoffman, David Halberstam, and Lloyd Garrison, who were stationed in the Congo for long periods of time; A. M. Rosenthal, who visited the Congo in the turbulent autumn of 1960; Benjamin Welles, who covered the Tananarive conference in March, 1961; and Seymour Topping, who reported the Soviet role from Moscow.

Soviet Documents

Khrushchev, Nikita S., *For Victory in Peaceful Competition with Capitalism,* New York: E.P. Dutton & Co., Inc., 1960. A collection of speeches and statements by the Soviet Premier.

──────*Zakliuchitel'noe Slovo na XXII S'ezde KPSS* [Concluding Speech at the 22nd Congress of the CPSU], October 27, 1961. Moscow: Gospolitizdat, 1961.

────── "Za novye pobedy mirovogo kommunisticheskogo dvizheniia" [For new victories for the world communist movement], *Kommunist,* no. 1 (1961), pp. 3–37. Khrushchev's speech of January 6, 1961.

──────*Khrushchev Remembers,* with an Introduction, Commentary and Notes by Edward Crankshaw. Translated and Edited by Strobe Talbott. Boston: Little, Brown and Company, 1970.

──────*Khrushchev Remembers: The Last Testament.* With a Foreword by Edward Crankshaw and an Introduction by Jerrold Schecter. Translated and Edited by Strobe Talbott. Boston: Little, Brown and Company, 1974.

Programma Kommunisticheskoi Partii Sovetskogo Soiuza [Program of the Communist Party of the Soviet Union], Moscow: Gospolitizdat, 1961.

Soiuz Zhurnalistov SSSR, *Patris Lumumba: Pravda o chudovishchnom Prestu-*

plenii kolonizatorov [Patrice Lumumba: The truth about the monstrous crime of the colonialists], Moscow: Izdanie Soiuza Zhurnalistov SSSR, 1961. A collection of documents dealing with Lumumba, including messages from Khrushchev and other leaders.

Sovetskii Soiuz—iskrennii drug narodov Afriki [The Soviet Union is a sincere friend of the peoples of Africa]. Moscow: Gospolitizdat, 1961. A compilation of Soviet and (friendly) foreign press reports dealing with President Brezhnev's visit to Africa in February, 1961.

SSSR i Strany Afriki 1946–1962 gg: Dokumenty i Materialy [The USSR and the Countries of Africa 1946–1962: Documents and Materials]. Moscow: Gosudarstvennoe Izdatel'stvo Politicheskoi Literatury, 1963. A collection of official statements, messages, and United Nations speeches published by the Soviet Foreign Ministry.

Soviet Newspapers

The most complete and authoritative source for official and semi-official Soviet comment on the Congo during the 1960–1963 period was the Communist Party newspaper *Pravda*. Among the important documents published by *Pravda* were the various statements by the Soviet government protesting the situation in the Congo, which appeared on July 14, 1960, August 1, 1960, August 21, 1960, September 10, 1960, September 19, 1960, December 7, 1960, January 12, 1961, and February 15, 1961; the text of Khrushchev's press conference of July 12, 1960, at which he made his first comments about the "imperialist plot" against the Congo's independence; the text of Khrushchev's major speech at the General Assembly on September 23, 1960, in which he first proposed the troika scheme and the removal of Hammarskjold as a result of the Congo crisis; and the various messages exchanged by Khrushchev and/or Brezhnev with Lumumba, Kasavubu, Gizenga, Adoula, and non-Congolese African leaders concerned about the Congo.

Many of these documents also appeared in the Soviet government newspaper *Izvestia*, which was run by Khrushchev's son-in-law, Alexei Adzhubei. As a rule, coverage of the Congo in these two newspapers and in the other daily papers reflected a single Soviet line. On occasion, however, one could detect a faint reflection of the policy debates in the Kremlin about such delicate issues as aid to Gizenga in Stanleyville or recognition of the Adoula government.

A great many of the stories about the Congo were second-hand reports filed by TASS correspondents in New York, London, Paris, Cairo, or Belgrade. First-hand reporting was directly related to Soviet fortunes in the Congo. In the summer of 1960, when Lumumba was in power, *Pravda, Izvestia, Komsomol'skaia Pravda*, and TASS had correspondents in Leopoldville. After Mobutu ousted all Soviet personnel in September, 1960, Soviet reporters covered Congolese events from such listening points as Accra and Conakry. G. Fedyashin established a TASS bureau in Stanleyville in February 1961 and, after a brief expulsion by Gizenga, remained there until after the formation of the Adoula government, when he moved his operation to Leopoldville. Other Soviet journalists visited Stanleyville in April, May, and June 1961. After the TASS bureau was set up in Leopoldville in September 1961, other journalists went to the capital on brief trips. These reports from the field were backed up by analyses written in Moscow; the most striking were by *Pravda*'s senior analyst V. Mayevskii, an outspoken foe of imperialism with a gift for invective.

Soviet Books

Afrika 1961–1965 gg. [Africa from 1961 to 1965]. Moscow: Izdatel'stvo "Nauka," Akad. Nauk SSSR, Institut Afriki, 1967.

Avakov, R., *Na istoricheskom pereput'e* [At a historic crossroads]. Moscow: Gospolitizdat, 1962.

Datlin, S., *Afrika sbrasyvaet tsepi* [Africa throws off her chains]. Moscow: Gospolitizdat, 1960.

Fokeev, G. V., *Vneshniaia politika stran Afriki* [Foreign policy of the countries of Africa]. Moscow: Izdatel'stvo "Mezhdunarodnye Otnosheniia," 1968.

Fetov, V., *Amerikanskii imperializm v Afrike* [American imperialism in Africa]. Moscow: Gospolitizdat, 1962.

Goncharev, L. V., and I. P. Iastrebova, eds. *Novye formy kolonializma* [New forms of colonialism]. Moscow: Izdatel'stvo Vostochnoi Literatury, Akad. Nauk SSSR, Institut Afriki, 1963.

Iur'ev, Iu. N., *Expansiia SShA v Kongo* [United States expansion in the Congo]. Moscow: Izdatel'stvo "Mezhdunarodnye Otnosheniia," 1966.

Khokhlov, N., *Tragediia Kongo* [Tragedy of the Congo]. Moscow: Gospolitizdat, 1961.

Kletskii, L. R., *Chernaia Afrika obretaet svobodu* [Black Africa wins freedom]. Leningrad: Obshchestvo po Rasprostraneniiu Politicheskikh i Nauchnykh Znanii RSFSR, 1961.

Krasil'shchikova, S. A., *OON i natsional'no-osvoboditel'noe dvizhenie* [The UN and the national liberation movement]. Moscow: Izdatel'stvo "Mezhdunarodnye Otnosheniia," 1964.

Martynov, V. A., *Zagovor protiv Kongo* [Plot against the Congo]. Moscow: Izdatel'stvo Vostochnoi Literatury, Akad. Nauk SSSR, Institut Afriki, 1960.

Modrzhinskaia, E. D., *Ideologiia sovremennogo kolonializma* [Ideology of contemporary colonialism]. Moscow: Izdatel'stvo Vostochnoi Literatury, 1961.

Nikhamin, V. P., *Mezhdunarodnye problemy sovremennoi Afriki* [International problems of contemporary Africa]. Moscow: Izdatel'stvo VPSh i AON pri TsK KPSS, 1960.

Ol'derogge, D. A., and I. I. Potekhin, *Narody Afriki* [Peoples of Africa]. Moscow: Izdatel'stvo Akad. Nauk SSSR, 1954.

Oleinikov, I. N., *Kongo*. Moscow: Gosudarstvennoe Izdatel'stvo Geograficheskoi Literatury, 1959.

Orestov, O., and Volodin, L., *Trudnye Dni Kongo* [Hard days for the Congo]. Moscow: Gospolitizdat, 1961.

Potekhin, I. I., *Afrika smotrit v budushchee* [Africa looks ahead]. Moscow: Izdatel'stvo Vostochnoi Literatury, 1960.

Potekhin, I. I., ed., *Afrika 1956–1961* [Africa from 1956 to 1961]. Moscow: Izdatel'stvo Vostochnoi Literatury, Akad. Nauk SSSR, Institut Afriki, 1961.

Rakhmatov, M., *Afrika idet k svobode* [Africa goes toward freedom]. Moscow: Gospolitizdat, 1961.

Semenov, M., *Ubiitsa s Ist-river* [Murderer from the East River]. Moscow: Gospolitizdat, 1961.

Ushakov, V., *Sovetskii Soiuz i OON.* [The Soviet Union and the UN]. Moscow: Gospolitizdat, 1962.

Vol'skii, D., *Patris Lumumba—geroi Afriki* [Patrice Lumumba—hero of Africa]. Moscow: Gospolitizdat, 1961.

Zusmanovich, A. Z., *Imperialisticheskii razdel basseina Kongo* [Imperialist division of the Congo Basin]. Moscow: Izdatel'stvo Vostochnoi Liberatury, Akad. Nauk SSSR, Institut Afriki, 1962.

Soviet Periodicals and Articles

Articles dealing specifically with the Congo generally appeared in the popular magazines, such as *Novoe Vremia* [New Times] and *Sovremennyi Vostok* [Contemporary East], which became, beginning in March 1961, *Aziia i Afrika Segodnia* [Asia and Africa Today]. Articles on broader subjects related to the Congo, such as Western policy in Africa or the development of socialism in Africa, appeared in such journals as:

Kommunist

Mezhdunarodnaia Zhizn' [International Affairs] (Moscow)

Mirovaia Ekonomika i Mezhdunarodnye Otnosheniia [World Economy and International Relations]

Narody Azii i Afriki [Peoples of Asia and Africa] (called *Problemy Vostokovedeniia* [Problems of Oriental Studies] in 1959–1960)

Sovetskoe Gosudarstvo i Pravo [Soviet State and Law]

World Marxist Review.

INDEX

Index

457